D1484066

The American Immigration Collection

The German Element in the United States

ALBERT BERNHARDT FAUST

Volume I

Arno Press and The New York Times

NEW YORK 1969

325.243
F26g
Vol. 1

Copyright © 1969 by Arno Press, Inc.

All rights reserved

Library of Congress Catalog Card No. 69-18773

Manufactured in the United States of America

THE GERMAN ELEMENT
IN THE
UNITED STATES

FEB 18 '70

HUNT LIBRARY
CARNEGIE-MELLON UNIVERSITY

THE OLD MARKET SQUARE, GERMANTOWN, PENNSYLVANIA

THE GERMAN ELEMENT
IN THE
UNITED STATES

WITH SPECIAL REFERENCE TO ITS
POLITICAL, MORAL, SOCIAL, AND
EDUCATIONAL INFLUENCE

BY

ALBERT BERNHARDT FAUST

IN TWO VOLUMES
VOL. I

NEW YORK
THE STEUBEN SOCIETY OF AMERICA
1927

COPYRIGHT, 1909, BY ALBERT BERNHARDT FAUST

·ALL RIGHTS RESERVED

———

"COPYRIGHT, 1927, BY THE STEUBEN SOCIETY OF AMERICA"

ALL RIGHTS RESERVED

PRINTED AND BOUND IN THE U. S. A.

KINGSPORT PRESS, KINGSPORT, TENNESSEE

INTRODUCTORY STATEMENT

At the suggestion of Dr. Walther Wever, German Consul-General at Chicago, Mrs. Catherine Seipp of that city offered in March, 1904, cash prizes for the three best monographs upon the subject indicated by the title of this book. Competing works were submitted under assumed names on or before March 22, 1907, to the Germanic Department of the University of Chicago. The prize judges were Professors Hanno Deiler of Tulane, Frederick J. Turner of Wisconsin, and Karl Detlev Jessen of Bryn Mawr.

In this contest Professor Faust was awarded the first prize of $3000.

STARR WILLARD CUTTING.
THE UNIVERSITY OF CHICAGO.

In July, 1911, the Prussian Academy of Sciences in Berlin awarded to the work by Professor A. B. Faust, entitled THE GERMAN ELEMENT IN THE UNITED STATES (Boston, 1909), the LOUBAT PRIZE. By the will of the donor this distinction has been conferred every five years, alternately upon a work of investigation in American history and American archæology published during the preceding interval.

THE PUBLISHERS.

PREFACE

DURING the available hours of more than the last ten years, the writer had been studying and collecting materials on the German element in the United States, entertaining a vague hope of some day embodying the results of his labors in some useful form. The prominence of the Germans as a formative element of the American people, their continuous participation in the labors of peace and the burdens of war, suggested the need of a record of the essential facts in their history, from the earliest period of their settlements in this country to the present time. Such an historical survey has never existed in the English language, nor has one been attempted in German since the publications of Löher (*Geschichte und Zustände der Deutschen in Amerika*, 1847) and Eickhoff (*In der neuen Heimath*, 1884). The question whether the time had come for the preparation of such a work, scholars commonly decided in the negative, in view of the large amount of investigation still necessary, before a complete history of the Germans in this country can be written. This attitude of cautious reserve, however, will not encourage research as much as can be hoped from an exposition of the rich stores of information already at hand. A mere hoarding of materials, without an intelligent use of them, destroys opportunity, and leaves a responsibility undischarged.

In the past few years an increasing interest in the formative elements of the population of the United States has become manifest. The subject has been admitted into lecture courses at our universities, and has been given space in the pages of our popular magazines. Moreover the subject of foreign immigration, involving the question of restriction or discrimination, has become one of the great problems of the present day. The serious consideration, therefore, of any one of the leading foreign immigrations to this country assumes a present and practical value.

The call for a comprehensive essay on the German element in the United States, by the founders of the Conrad Seipp Memorial Prizes, furnished an opportunity and incentive for the elaboration and completion of the writer's work. The prescribed title, reproduced verbatim on the foregoing title-page, presented a twofold problem ; first, an outline of the history of the Germans in the United States, and secondly, a discussion of their political, moral, social, and educational influence. The first part, contained in Volume I, tells the story of the German settlers in the thirteen colonies before the Revolutionary War, continues the narrative through the nineteenth century, and calls attention to their leading traits, their activities in peace and war, their coöperation in the building of the nation. Their record is a noble one, and should animate their descendants with the will to keep sacred such names as Weiser, Post, Herkimer, Ludwig, Treutlen, Helm, Bowman, Münch, Follen, Sutro, Sutter, Röbling, and a host of others, while Mühlenberg, Steuben, Kalb, Lieber, and Schurz should convey to them the inspiration of lasting achievement.

The second part, the discussion of German influences, contained in Volume II, seemed possible only after an historical basis had been laid, such as has been attempted in Volume I. The method followed was that of summing up instances in order to establish principles. For example, in the chapter on industrial development, illustrations are furnished, proving that in all branches requiring technical training, German influence has been predominant; under the head of politics, German independent voting receives illustration ; in the department of agriculture, the principle is maintained, that the German farmer not only applied his native skill and industry, but whenever necessary adapted himself to new conditions, using and inventing agricultural machinery, or becoming a rice-grower in the South, a big farmer in the West.

The obstructions in the path of a final solution of the questions proposed in the second part are even more serious than in the historical outline. The economic history of the United States has not been written, though steps are now being taken toward an ultimate accomplishment of that gigantic task. The volumes on manufactures in the Census Reports occasionally furnish a few meagre details, but the history of none of our great American industries has been made available. Each chapter, therefore, has furnished an entirely new field for investigation, and difficulties of a different kind. The plan of questioning experts, or representatives of a particular industry, has frequently been resorted to by the writer, as, e. g., in the departments of viticulture, lithography, and the manufacture of agricultural machinery. The writer has thus frequently gained information not accessible in books. Because of these peculiar difficulties, the second part of the work is necessarily more tentative than the first, possessing the faults of pioneer work, yet for that very reason the more fascinating to the writer, and, it is believed, the more suggestive to the reader.

Because of the necessity of restricting within moderate bounds the mass of materials belonging to this subject, a

consideration of the Dutch element has been excluded from
these pages, except in the statistical estimate of the number of persons of German blood in the United States, contained in the first chapter of the second Volume. The
Dutch are Germans of purer blood than the people inhabiting some of the eastern provinces of the German Empire,
and their history in the United States is frequently insep-
arable from that of the other German stocks. Nevertheless they frequently formed separate colonies, as in New
York State, and their history is important enough to
warrant a separate treatment.

Because of their racial distinctness, persons of Jewish
blood, born in Germany, have not been regularly considered in this work. An exception has been made where they
contributed toward bringing over from Germany various
elements of cultural, educational, or technical value. When
unmistakably derived from the German Fatherland, their
work in the arts and sciences, in education, and technical
industry, should be considered a part of the present investigation as clearly as the writings of the poet Heine are to
be included in the history of German literature. The number of Jewish immigrants coming from Germany has commonly been overestimated. During the only period in which
an accurate record has been kept, i. e., since 1898, it was
found that the German Jews numbered only one and one
half per cent of the total immigration from the German
Empire (1898–1904). In the German Empire the Jews
number only one per cent of the total population. During
periods of social persecution in the eighteenth and early
nineteenth centuries their percentage of immigration was
probably higher, but undoubtedly the average was never
above two per cent of the German immigration to the
United States.

The attempt has been made to exclude matter which could not be established with certainty. When, for instance, the German ancestry of an important individual was in doubt, his name was omitted in this record. Overstatement has perhaps been more carefully avoided than undervaluation. In the choice of examples, particularly in the second Volume, the writer was forced to use those concerning which he had accurate information, and also to discriminate in favor of those that served best as illustrations. A large number of names were thus omitted, which might well have found a place, many no doubt more worthy than those employed. The materials collected should therefore be looked upon as illustrative, not exhaustive.

The writer gratefully acknowledges courtesies extended to him by Dr. jur. Walther Wever, Consul-General of the German Empire at Chicago (1900–1908), and by Professor Starr Willard Cutting of the University of Chicago, particu larly in the matter of launching the book after the prize award had been made. Though the delay may have tried their patience, the writer's wish, to be allowed to subject the manuscript to a thorough revision before publication, was honored by them and the publishers. The writer desires to express his thanks to Professor Oscar Kuhns, author of " The German and Swiss Settlements of Colonial Pennsylvania," for the loan of valuable books; to George M. Dutcher, Professor of History in Wesleyan University, Middletown, Connecticut, who read in manuscript most of the chapters of the first Volume, and made a large number of important corrections and suggestions; to Professor B. J. Vos, of the University of Indiana, and to Professor Lane Cooper, of Cornell University, who carefully read the first draft of many of the early chapters.

A special debt is due to Walter F. Willcox, Professor

of Political Economy and Statistics, Cornell University, for his continued interest in the work during its progress, and for his criticism and direction in the chapter attempting an estimate of the number of persons of German blood in the population of the United States (Volume II, Chapter I). Acknowledgment is hereby made of aid received from the Carnegie Institution of Washington, in the collection of data for several chapters in this book. The coöperation of many other helpers is gratefully remembered ; in most cases it is acknowledged on the particular page where their valued assistance was made use of ; some others who have aided in the laborious mechanical tasks of book-making, have preferred to remain unnamed. Communications are solicited from readers who have corrections to suggest or information to impart.

A. B. F.

CORNELL UNIVERSITY,
ITHACA, N. Y., April 20, 1909.

AUTHOR'S PREFACE TO THE NEW EDITION

THE present new edition of the GERMAN ELEMENT IN THE UNITED STATES is a complete revision of the three foregoing issues of the book. The original edition was published by Houghton Mifflin Company, in two volumes, Boston, 1909. In 1911 an inexpensive popular edition was prepared by the same publishers for the Current Literature Publishing Company (New York) from the original plates, but omitting the illustrations and colored maps. In the following year appeared the German edition, with revisions, additions and certain adaptations for German readers, also in two volumes, entitled: DAS DEUTSCHTUM IN DEN VEREINIGTEN STAATEN; Band I: *In seiner Bedeutung für die amerikanische Kultur;* Band II: *In seiner geschichtlichen Entwickelung.* Druck und Verlag von B. G. Teubner in Leipzig, 1912.

Both the American and German editions met a most gratifying reception at home and in Germany, where in 1911 the Prussian Academy of Sciences in Berlin honored the original edition with the award of the Loubat Prize. Twenty years after the preparation of the first draft, the book has now received the promise of a new life on the initiative of the Steuben Society of America, who desire to make the historical materials contained therein once more accessible to their members, students of American history and general readers.

In carrying out the project of a new edition, the author has made a large number of revisions in the original plates, and in order still further to bring the new edition up to date, he has added an APPENDIX, the purpose of which is to record, chapter after chapter, the results of more recent investigations or to suggest new lines of research. Most of this material is of a date previous to 1917, the year which closes abruptly a definite period in the history of the Germans in the United States. The succeeding ten years of war and reconstruction are too near to admit of treatment that would now seem unbiased, and therefore no attempt has been made in this direction, but the collection of material for the benefit of the future historian is very much to be recommended.

The present new edition combines both volumes of the original American edition in one book, unabridged and including all the original illustrations and maps. A Special INDEX has been provided for the new material, which with the GENERAL INDEX (ii, pp. 565–605), chapter headings and tables of contents will serve as pathfinders in the mass of material.

My thanks are due to the faithful coöperation of the Book Committee of the Steuben Society in launching this new edition.

ALBERT BERNHARDT FAUST

ITHACA, N.Y.
August 1, 1927

FOREWORD

PUBLISHERS OF THE NEW EDITION

OUR citizens of German origin as a racial group have frequently been criticized for what seemed a lack of interest in public affairs. While the same criticism perhaps holds in regard to all elements in this country whose native language is not English, still the fault is recognized to exist by Americans of German descent as well, and as one that in the past has often been detrimental to their own and their country's best interests. The correction of this attitude of indifference constituted one of the reasons for the foundation of *The Steuben Society of America*,[1] and gave the Society a distinctly educational purpose. In fact the name of General Steuben was adopted by the Society because in his educational activity as the great drill-master of the American forces during the Revolution as much as in his life, character and career, he symbolized the virtues characteristic of the German race and exemplified the highest type of citizenship and public service.

A feature of the educational work of the Steuben Society is the study of American history and of the contributions made by the German element in the foundation and upbuilding of the American nation. Recognizing that justifiable race-pride is an attribute of genuine patriotism, the Steuben Society decided upon the revival of Profes-

---

[1] A brief historical sketch of *The Steuben Society of America*, its aims and purposes, are given in the *Appendix* of this edition.

sor Faust's *The German Element in the United States*, which during the war period was no longer printed, but which, ever since its first publication in 1909 has been acknowledged in this country and abroad to be the authoritative work on the subject.

The National Council of *The Steuben Society of America* therefore appointed a special committee, named the "Faust Book Committee," who obtained the author's consent to the preparation of a new edition and who purchased the plates and copyright from the original publishers, and who now offer this comprehensive historical record in a convenient one volume form to the members of the Society and to the general reader.

NATIONAL COUNCIL OF
THE STEUBEN SOCIETY OF AMERICA

Headquarters:
405 Lexington Ave., New York City.

CONTENTS

CHAPTER I

CHAPTER II

CHAPTER III

CONTENTS

CHAPTER IV

CHAPTER V

THE GERMANS IN PENNSYLVANIA

CHAPTER VI

THE EARLY GERMANS OF NEW JERSEY AND OF MARYLAND

CONTENTS

CHAPTER VII

THE GERMANS IN VIRGINIA

CHAPTER VIII

THE GERMANS IN NORTH AND SOUTH CAROLINA DURING THE EIGHTEENTH CENTURY

CHAPTER IX

GERMAN SETTLEMENTS BEFORE THE REVOLUTION IN GEORGIA AND IN NEW ENGLAND

CHAPTER X

The Location of the German Settlers before 1775 ; Their Defense of the Frontier ; and an Estimate of their Numbers

CHAPTER XI

The Germans as Patriots and Soldiers, during the War of the Revolution, 1775–1783

CHAPTER XII

The Winning of the West

I. The German Settlers in Kentucky and Tennessee

CHAPTER XIV

THE WINNING OF THE WEST

III. (A) THE ADVANCE OF THE FRONTIER LINE TO THE MISSISSIPPI
AND MISSOURI RIVERS

CHAPTER XV

THE WINNING OF THE WEST

IV. THE NORTHWEST, THE SOUTHWEST, AND THE FAR WEST

CHAPTER XVI

The German Element in the Wars of the United States during the Nineteenth Century

CONTENTS

CHAPTER XVII

A SUMMARY VIEW OF THE GERMAN IMMIGRATIONS OF THE NINETEENTH
CENTURY ; THEIR LOCATION, DISTRIBUTION, AND GENERAL CHARACTER

ILLUSTRATIONS

ILLUSTRATIONS

xxvii

PART I

AN HISTORICAL OUTLINE

THE GERMAN IMMIGRATIONS TO THE UNITED STATES;
THEIR ARRIVAL, LOCATION, PROGRESS OF THEIR
SETTLEMENTS; THEIR PART IN THE WARS
OF THE UNITED STATES, AND IN
THE WINNING OF THE WEST

THE GERMAN ELEMENT IN THE UNITED STATES

CHAPTER I

THE EARLIEST GERMANS IN THE ANGLO-AMERICAN COLONIES

Introductory — Cosmographers : Behaim, Mercator, Waldseemüller, etc. —
First German in America : Tyrker in Leif Ericson's expedition to Wine-
land (eleventh century) — Germans in earliest settlements, Port Royal
(1562), Jamestown (1607) — Peter Minuit, purchaser and governor of
Manhattan Island (1626) ; founder of New Sweden (1638) — Jacob
Leisler, governor of New York, defender of the people's cause, his martyr-
dom (1691), and services to the colonies — Explorers, etc. : Lederer
Hiens, Peter Fabian.

In the great struggle for the possession of the North
American continent, it has been well said, the Latin nations sent officers without an army, the English, both officers and an army, the Germans, an army without officers.
The Latin nations, with distinguished leaders such as Cor-
tez, Pizarro, De Soto, Champlain, Marquette, and La Salle,
whether in quest of gold or of the fountain of youth, engaged in great voyages of discovery or grand schemes of
empire. The English, with a clearer view of the future,
knew that an empire could not be established otherwise
than by colonization. Selecting the zone best adapted to
the needs of the Teutonic stock, they invited other

branches of the same racial group to cooperate in the building of an empire. The Germans, not united in one nation at home, poured streams of people into the English territory. Without organization, compelled by the need of subsistence, or conditions intolerable at home, they appeared on the threshold of a new country, as in the days of Marius and Sulla, desiring land, not conquest. Their ancient kinsmen had beaten against the barriers of the Roman Empire until they had shattered them, and then rejuvenated all of Italy, Spain, and Gaul. Similarly in modern times a migration by the same stock took place to the land of promise called America, the very name conveying to the Teutonic mind a peculiar fascination, a romantic charm, later enhanced by the halo of freedom. This *Völkerwanderung* was not accompanied by the glory of war or the glamour of fame, but went on in quiet, incessantly and irresistibly, for more than two centuries, until to-day more than a quarter of the population of the United States is of German blood.

The great waves of German immigration making their way to the American colonies did not appear until the eighteenth century. Advance movements had heralded the way, the first permanent settlement by Germans having been made at Germantown, Pennsylvania, during the last quarter of the seventeenth century. Long before this there appeared sporadic cases of German settlers, explorers, adventurers, and prominent individuals, serving under national flags, — any but German, — some of them at the very beginnings of the colonization of the United States. Their history will be the subject of the present chapter.

A conspicuous example of prominent service under a foreign king is that of Martin Behaim. He served the king of Portugal, but was a native of Nuremberg, born in 1459, of an old patrician family of that city. Fiction has been active about his great name, using misinterpretations of Portuguese documents, or even spurious records, to maintain that Behaim saw Pernambuco and the coast of Brazil almost a decade before the first voyage of Columbus, and that he gave to Magellan information needed to urge him on to his voyage around South America. But even when deprived of this distinction, Behaim remains one of the most eminent men of his age, in the first rank among cosmographers and navigators of his time. He was a friend of Columbus, whom he probably met in Lisbon between 1480 and 1484. He was likewise acquainted with Magellan. During the period named he was in the employ of the king of Portugal, and, being appointed on a commission for the improvement of navigation, he became one of the inventors of the astrolabe. In the capacity of cosmographer, he accompanied the expedition of Diogo Cão, in 1484, to the west coast of Africa. After a voyage of discovery lasting nineteen months, he settled on the island of Fayal, one of the Azores, where he married the daughter of the stadtholder of the Flemish colony established there. In 1491–92 he visited Nuremberg, his native city, for the settlement of an estate. While there he fashioned a globe representing the earth as it was known to the foremost savants of that day. On leaving he presented this globe to his native city, and it is still preserved there as the most interesting relic of the cosmographic art antecedent to the discovery of America. The globe does not prove that Behaim was acquainted with the coast of Brazil, and his influence, therefore, upon the voyages of Columbus and Magellan could have been only such as to strengthen them in their theories and ambitions, not to direct them. Before returning to Fayal, Behaim was twice captured by pirates at sea, but his release was effected through friends and his distinguished reputation. He resided at Fayal until 1506, when he was again in Lisbon, where he died the same year.

The Germans were not prominent as a seafaring people at the period of the discovery of America. The glory of the Hanseatic League had departed. Their location in the heart of Europe, with but a narrow strip of seacoast at the north, put them at a disadvantage in comparison with the English, French, Dutch, Spaniards, and Portuguese. But while they were not conspicuous as leaders in the great voyages of discovery, their scholarly instincts put them in the front rank as cosmographers and cartographers. The instance of Behaim, constructor of the Nuremberg globe and one of the inventors of the astrolabe, has just been given. Even greater is the name of Mercator (1512–94), the inventor of the Mercator system of projection, which, taking account of the curvature of the earth's surface, is an indispensable aid in nautical map-drawing. Mercator was born in Flanders (Rupelmonde, Belgium), and was of German descent, his name before Latinization being Gerhard Kremer. On commission of Charles V, he manufactured a terrestrial and a celestial globe, which are said to have been superior to any made before that time. His principal work was his atlas (first edition, Duisburg, 1594), printed from copper plates prepared by his own hand. A number of other German names appear prominently among cartographers, earlier than Mercator, such as Schöner (globes, 1515 and 1520), Reisch (map, 1513), and the Low German Ruysch (Ptolemy of 1508, with newly discovered lands indicated). The "Globus Mundi" was published at Strassburg in 1509,

MARTIN BEHAIM

showing an early use of the name " America " in the accompanying text.[1]

More important still is the fact that a German cosmographer was the first to suggest in a printed book that the name " America " be used to designate the New World. It was Martin Waldseemüller,[2] born at Freiburg about 1480. In 1507 he published his " Cosmographiae Introductio," in which an account is furnished of all the voyages of Vespucius, and the suggestion of the name " America " appears, in the following words : —

But now that these parts have been more widely explored and another fourth part has been discovered by Americus Vesputius (as will appear in what follows), I do not see why any one may justly forbid it to be named after Americus, its discoverer, a man of sagacious mind, Amerige, that is the land of Americus, or America, since both Europe and Asia derived their names from women.[3]

The credit, therefore, of first advocating in print the use of the name " America," and also of diffusing widely, by means of charts and globes, the knowledge of the newly discovered countries, belongs to German cosmographers.

The first German to land in the New World arrived be-

[1] Justin Winsor, *Narrative and Critical History of America*, vol. ii, pp. 171, 172.

[2] The name is spelt also Waltzemüller, and Walzemüller. A map accompanying this book has recently been discovered by Professor Fischer in Wollegg Castle, Würtemberg. It had long been looked for, and its existence sometimes disputed. Cf. *American Historical Review*, vol. x, pp. 150–154: "The oldest map with the name America of the year 1507, and the Carta Marina of the year 1516 by M. Waldseemüller (Ilacomilus)." Edited by Joseph Fischer and Fr. R. von Wieser. London, 1903. Cf. also E. G. Bourne, "The Naming of America," *Am. Hist. Rev.* vol. x, pp. 49, 50.

[3] A copy of the first edition, of 1507, of Waldseemüller's *Cosmographiae Introductio* is contained in the library of Cornell University (A. D. White collection).

fore the discovery of Columbus. He was a member of
Leif Ericson's expedition to Wineland. It is no longer a
matter of doubt that the Icelanders were the first Europeans to sight the North Atlantic coast, and attempt a colony somewhere between Labrador and New England. The
proof is furnished by Norse sagas, by traditions and documents of various kinds, that taken together make as good
evidence as we have of many accepted historical events,
such, for instance, as the early settlement of Jamestown.
The location of the settlement by the seafarers of Iceland
will probably remain forever unknown, beyond the limits
already mentioned ; the time, also a matter of doubt, has
been reckoned as in the eleventh century.[1] The German
in Leif's expedition was named Tyrker, and seems to have
been a faithful king's man of the type so frequently
found in German epic poetry. His discovery of the grape
is characteristic, and forebodes coming events. The Norse
saga gives the following account :[2] —

It was discovered one evening that one of their company was
missing, and this proved to be Tyrker, the German. Leif was
sorely troubled by this, for Tyrker had lived with Leif and his
father for a long time, and had been very devoted to Leif, when
he was a child. Leif severely reprimanded his companions, and
prepared to go in search for him, taking twelve men with him.
They had proceeded but a short distance from the house, when
they were met by Tyrker, whom they received most cordially.
Leif observed at once that his foster-father was in lively spirits.
. . . Leif addressed him, and asked : " Wherefore art thou so be-
lated, foster-father mine, and astray from the others ? " In the
beginning Tyrker spoke for some time in German, rolling his
eyes and grinning, and they could not understand him ; but after

[1] A. M. Reeves, *The Finding of Wineland the Good*, p. 98. London : 1890.
Cf. also J. Fischer, *The Discoveries of the Norsemen in America*, translated
by B. H. Soulsby, St. Louis: 1903, pp. 1–19.

[2] Reeves, pp. 66–67.

a time he addressed them in the Northern tongue : " I did not go much farther (than you), and yet I have something of novelty to relate. I have found vines and grapes." " Is this indeed true, foster-father ? " said Leif. " Of a certainty it is true," quoth he, " for I was born where there is no lack of either grapes or vines." They slept the night through, and on the morrow Leif said to his shipmates : " We will now divide our labors, and each day will either gather grapes or cut vines and fell trees, so as to obtain a cargo of these for my ship." . . . A cargo sufficient for the ship was cut, and when the spring came, they made their ship ready, and sailed away ; and from its products Leif gave the land a name, and called it Wineland.

The Germans, though not present in large numbers, were nevertheless well-nigh ubiquitous during the period of new settlements.[1] At Port Royal, in South Carolina, which was settled in 1562 by a band of Huguenots under Jean Ribault, there seem to have been some Alsatian and Hessian Protestants[2] at the very beginning. The settlement was destroyed by the Spaniard Menendez in 1566.

There were several Germans among the first settlers at Jamestown in 1607, as may be seen by the lists of names, which Captain John Smith records, of the original settlers of the earliest English colony of America.[3] There are also numerous direct references to the " Dutch " settlers, whom we need not suppose to have been natives of Holland, particularly since one is referred to as a Switzar

---

[1] This is also true of Spanish America. See the publications of the Alldeutscher Verband, in the series " Kampf um das Deutschtum," e. g., Wintzer, *Die Deutschen im tropischen Amerika;* Unold, *Das Deutschtum in Chile;* Sellin, *Brasilien, und die La Plata-Staaten.*

[2] *Handbuch des Deutschtums im Auslande,* Statistische Uebersicht v. F. H. Henoch, hrg. v. Allgemeinen deutschen Schulverein, p. 113. Berlin, 1904.

[3] *The True Travels,* vol. i, pp. 153, 172, 173, Reprint, Richmond, Va., 1819 (of the London edition, 1629). See also *The General History of Virginia,* vol. ii, pp. 45–56, for German names such as Unger, Keffer, etc.; for the Switzar, William Volday, *The True Travels,* vol. i, p. 231.

(Swiss). The references to this element among the settlers
are not of an enviable sort, the writer frequently stigma-
tizing them with the epithet " damned " Dutch. On re-
viewing their history as told by the vainglorious captain,
it appears that the epithet, though frankly sincere, is
rather a comment on the Dutchman's independence and
love of liberty than an evidence of any serious defect of
character. The " Dutchmen " were artisans, carpenters
mainly, whose services were valuable in the colony. At
one time three " Dutchmen " and two Englishmen were employed to construct a house for King Powhatan. The purpose of the building of the house was apparently to get the
king into the power of Captain Smith, and this treacherous
plot seems to have been revealed to the king by the
" Dutchmen." Themselves suffering under the tyranny of
the idlers of the colony, they felt in sympathy with the
red men, who were beyond any doubt treated cruelly by
the settlers of Jamestown. The " Dutchmen " chose to
remain with the Indians, preferring [1] their friendship to
that of the " gentlemen " of Jamestown. All efforts to
bring them back were unavailing. One of them was caught

---

[1] *True Travels*, vol. i, p. 208. " For the Dutchmen finding his (King
Powhatan's) plentie, and knowing our want, and perceiving his preparations
to surprise us, little thinking we could escape both him and famine; (to ob-
taine his favour) revealed to him so much as they knew of our estates and
projects and how to prevent them. One of them being of so great a spirit,
judgement and resolution, and a hireling that was certaine of his wages for
his labour, and ever well used both he and his countrymen ; that the President knew not whom better to trust ; and not knowing any fitter for that
employment had sent him as a spy to discover Powhatan's intent, then little
doubting his honestie, nor could ever be certaine of his villany till neare
halfe a yeare after." It must be remembered that as much treachery existed,
from Captain Smith's point of view, among the English settlers as among
the foreign. Between the feuds and desperate conditions prevailing at
Jamestown on the one hand, and the kindly treatment of the appreciative
savages on the other, the Dutchmen probably chose wisely, not feeling any
national pride in the English settlement.

COSMOGRAPHIAE

Capadociam/ Pamphiliam/ Lidiã/ Ciliciã/ Arme
nias maiorem & minorem. Colchiden/Hircaniam
Hiberiam/ Albaniam:& præterea multas quas sin
gillatim enumerare longa mora esset. Ita dicta ab ei
us nominis regina.

    Nunc vero & heę partes sunt latius lustratæ/ &
alia quarta pars per Americũ Vesputium(vt in se
quentibus audietur)inuenta est:quã non video cur
quis iure vetet ab Americo inuentore sagacis inge
nij viro Amerigen quasi Americi terram/siue Ame
ricam dicendam:cum & Europa & Asia a mulieri
bus sua sortita sint nomina.Eius situ & gentis mo
res ex bis binis Americi nauigationibus quę sequũ
tur liquide intelligi datur.

*Ame
rico*

RVDIMENTA

quę oppositũ vel contra denotat.Atꝗ in sexto cli
mate Antarcticũ versus/ & pars extrema Affricæ
nuper reperta & Zamziber/laua minor/ & Seula
insulę/ & quarta orbis pars(quam quia Americus
inuenit Amerigen/ quasi Americi terrã/siue Ame
cam nuncupare licet)sitæ sunt. De quibus Australi
bus climatibus hæc Pomponij Mellę Geographi
verba intelligenda sunt/ vbi ait. Zone habitabiles
paria agunt anni tempora/verum non pariter. An
tichthones alteram/nos alteram incolimus.Illius si

*Ame
rige
Pōpo:
Mel'ę*

FIRST APPEARANCE OF WORD "AMERICA"

From Waldseemüller's Introductio Cosmographiæ

later and " went by the heels." They were felt to be a
serious menace to the colony of Jamestown, whether justly
so or not, it is difficult to ascertain.

Clearly the situation at Jamestown was not of the best
for laborers. They had to do all the work for the drones.
Captain John Smith himself agrees in the following statement to the authorities at home : " When you send againe
I entreat you rather send but thirty Carpenters, husband-
men, gardiners, fisher men, blacksmiths, masons, and dig-
gers up of trees' roots, well provided, then a thousand of
such as we have ; for except wee be able both to lodge them
and feed them, the most will consume with want of necessaries before they can be made good for anything."[1] The
following throws light upon the treatment the " Dutch "-
men received : " As for the hiring of the Poles and Dutchmen," says Captain Smith, " to make Pitch, Tar, Glasse,
Milles and Sope ashes, when the country is replenished
with people and necessaries, would have done well, but to
send them and seventy more without victualls to work, was
not so well advised nor considered of as it should have
beene."[2] Again he comments on the character of the settlers as follows : " Adventurers that never did know what
a day's work was, except the Dutchmen and Poles and some
dozen other. For all the rest were poore Gentlemen,
Tradesmen, Serving-men, libertines, and such like, ten
times more fit to spoyle a Commonwealth, than either to
begin one or but help to maintaine one."[3]

There were Germans in the Dutch settlement of New
Netherland, and among them, two who were second to
none in moulding the destinies of the colony. The one
was the first governor of New Netherland, Peter Minuit,

---

[1] *True Travels*, vol. i, p. 202.
[2] *Ibid.*, vol. i, p. 193.   [3] *Ibid.*, vol. i, p. 241.

and the other the first governor of New York to represent the popular party, Jacob Leisler.

Little is known of Peter Minuit (Minnewit) before he appeared in America as director of the colony of New Netherland. All sources agree that he was born in Wesel on the Rhine, and was a Protestant. He arrived in New Amsterdam in May, 1626, with almost absolute power over the colony. Where his predecessors had been unsuccessful he built the foundation for the greatest metropolis on the American continent. It was he who bought from the Indians the Island of Manhattan (22,000 acres) for sixty Dutch guilders, or about twenty-four dollars in gold. Having obtained a secure title to the land, he next erected the first stone fort, at the Battery, and called it Fort Amsterdam. This kept the Indians in check and increased the number of settlers about the fort. The colonists soon became as busy and enterprising as their transatlantic kinsmen in the Low Countries. The Dutch West India Company supplied cattle and horses and land for the asking, while the crops raised were sufficient for the support of the colonists. Their most profitable occupation was the fur trade with the Indians. The Dutch at New Amsterdam became the rivals and superiors of the Pilgrim Fathers as fur traders. Their exportation of furs, that in 1624 had reached the sum of 25,000 guilders, in 1628, when the colony numbered 270 souls, rose to 56,000, and in 1631 to 130,000 guilders. The population steadily increased in the intervening years. Several ships arrived annually with settlers who were brought over by the company at twelve and one half cents per day for passage and board and on their arrival received as much land as they could cultivate. As early as 1631 the shipbuilders of New Amsterdam, under Minuit's administration, built the *New*

Netherland, estimated differently at six to eight hundred tons burden, and armed with thirty guns, one of the largest ships afloat[1] at that time, and an object of envy for the mother country.[2]

Minuit cultivated amicable relations with the New England colonies, but insisted upon his territorial rights. In 1629 the Dutch West India Company established the patroon system, which was destined to have an unfavorable effect on the development of the colony. Patroons were originally members of the West India Company, who assumed semi-feudal rights over large tracts, nominally bestowed on them on condition that they would plant a colony of fifty persons on the land within four years. They became manor lords carrying on colonization as a private affair. This unfortunate system aroused a great deal of opposition, and Minuit was made the scapegoat, though he had never favored the patroons beyond obeying the commands of the company. Minuit was recalled in August, 1631, and departed in 1632, leaving the colony in a most prosperous condition. After having tried in vain to get justice in Holland, he determined to offer his services to the king of Sweden.

Gustavus Adolphus is known as a mighty war lord and defender of the Protestant faith, but little is commonly heard of his far-reaching plans of colonial development. William Usselinx, a native of Antwerp, was the first to suggest to Gustavus Adolphus the enormous possibilities of colonial expansion. Not favored at home, the genius of Usselinx was given a sphere of activity under the ambitious ruler of Sweden. The Swedish South Company was

[1] Cf. Fiske, *The Dutch and Quaker Colonies,* vol. i, p. 124.
[2] *The Royal George,* 1200 tons, was built for the East India Company at Blackwall (London) about 1640.

founded in 1626–27 for trade and colonization west of the
Straits of Gibraltar, and extensive privileges were to be
given the company for twelve years. The king himself
signed for 400,000 Swedish talers. The German cities of
Stralsund and Stettin desired to become members, so also
the Duke of Pomerania, and much was hoped for from
the rich city of Danzig. Livland, with its German population, wished to subscribe 150,000 talers, and Emden,
eager to expand its commerce, was anxious to obtain a
seat and voice among the directors of the company. But
the death of Gustavus Adolphus wrecked these ambitious
plans. The chancellor, Oxenstierna, kept Usselinx in charge
until the latter seems to have given up hope. His place as
leader of the company was then taken by Minuit, who
arrived in Stockholm not earlier than 1636 and quickly
gained the confidence of the great statesman. Minuit
directed Swedish colonial ambitions toward an attainable
goal by turning the attention of the chancellor to the
country between Virginia and New Netherland, the land
that, some years after, William Penn received as a grant
from the English crown. It included the present states of
Delaware and Pennsylvania, and parts of New Jersey and
Maryland, territory that in the next century became the
most fertile soil for the expansion of the Germanic race.
Distinct advantages which Minuit possessed were, first,
his exceptional experience and keen insight, and secondly,
the prestige that Sweden had recently won on the battlefields of Europe.

Toward the end of the year 1637, with a warship and
transport bearing fifty immigrants well provisioned, he left
for the New World, arriving in Delaware Bay in April,
1638, and successfully kept the English in Virginia and
the Dutch at New York from interfering with his schemes

GERARD MERCATOR

of colonization. By means of a bold front and wise direction he kept his stand securely, knowing minutely the weaknesses of his neighbors on either hand. He built Fort Christina in honor of the Swedish queen, about two miles from the confluence of the Minquaskill and the Delaware, very near the present city of Wilmington. No one understood the fur trade better than Minuit, and even in his first year he drew 30,000 guilders of trade away from New Netherland. Colonists swarmed to the banks of the Delaware, New Sweden claiming the territory on its banks. By 1640 the colony had received many new accessions, some from Holland. It is not unreasonable to suppose that a number of Germans were among the settlers of New Sweden, since the German cities of the Baltic had shown such an active interest in the beginnings of the Swedish West India Company. Minuit died at his post in 1641, and was buried at Fort Christina. No one dared attack the colony during his lifetime. Its independence was retained fourteen years longer,[1] until in 1655 it became part of New Netherland under the energetic governor, Stuyvesant.

About fifty years later, in the early history of New York, there lived another German leader of men, Jacob Leisler, the second German governor of New York and first representative of the popular party, for whose cause he suffered martyrdom. He was born in Frankfort-on-the-Main, and arrived in New York in 1660, as a soldier in the service of the Dutch West India Company. He acquired wealth through trade with the Indians, and by

[1] John Printz, Governor of New Sweden from 1642 to 1653, according to trustworthy authority was a German nobleman (Johann Printz von Buchau) and had been a commander under Gustavus Adolphus in the Thirty Years' War. Seidensticker, *Bilder aus der deutsch-pennsylvanischen Geschichte*, p. 3 (*Geschichtsblätter*, vol. ii). New York: Steiger, 1886.

HUNT LIBRARY
CARNEGIE-MELLON UNIVERSITY

marriage became connected with the Dutch aristocracy of
New York. Instead of becoming a manor lord and proprietor, then the great goal of provincial ambition, Leisler
devoted himself to trade and business, to the full extent
of his extraordinary energy. He soon became one of the
wealthiest citizens of New York, his estate being valued
at 15,000 guilders, and only six citizens being richer than
himself. One of the three barks owned in New York in
1684 belonged to him, and in the year before he had
been appointed a member of the Admiralty Court by
Governor Dongan. He was capable of humanitarian
ventures, as when, in 1689, he bought a piece of land,
the present site of New Rochelle in Westchester County,
for the Huguenots who had landed in New York. An
evidence of wealth also was the ransom of five hundred
pounds, paid when he was captured by the pirates of
Tunis in 1678.[1]

But Leisler was as public-spirited as he was wealthy.
He gave little attention to party strife and to the in-
trigues by which leading families gained influence with the
governor, but whenever an occasion of moment arrived,
Jacob Leisler was the man that impressed the people with
his exceptional integrity, liberality, and firmness. When,
in 1675, Governor Andros fined a number of burghers
because of their opposition to " Popery," Leisler refused
to pay, preferring imprisonment to the renunciation of
his principles. At another time, when a poor Huguenot
family landed in New York and were to be sold as redemptioners, he instantly paid down the sum demanded
for their transportation, thus delivering the refugees from
years of servitude.

Conditions in New York favored the development of

[1] Cf. Kapp, p. 39.

a popular party in opposition to aristocratic rule. King James II had combined the colonies of New England, New York, and New Jersey under the governorship of Andros, an action which displeased the Dutch greatly, for they felt a danger of being overshadowed by the neighboring Puritan colony. While Governor Andros was in New England, he left New York in charge of Francis Nicholson, as lieutenant-governor. On February 5, 1689, a Dutch sea-captain brought him the first news of the landing of William of Orange in England, but Nicholson threatened the messenger with severe punishment, if he allowed the news to spread. But a week later the merchant and ship-owner, Jacob Leisler, received the news independently and made it public. The propitious moment had not yet arrived, however, for a revolt of the people against their oppressors. They lacked a leader. The man who could help was not a demagogue and would not act unless forced by circumstances. That man was Jacob Leisler, whose German birth secured for him the sympathy of the Dutch population, and whose public life was noted for public spirit, energy, and liberality. He was recognized as a good soldier, and, though connected with the aristocracy by marriage, remained a man of the people, alive to their interests, nearer to them in habits and culture or the lack of it, and admired by them for his plain honesty that never stooped to selfish ends, a practice so common among the aristocrats. All too great was his love of duty, his disinterested assent to the wishes of others, and, as later events proved, too keen his sense of responsibility in his high position.

Nicholson's unpopularity and that of the ruling class grew from week to week and from day to day, and the slightest shock was sufficient to kindle the spark of revolt.

An accidental remark of Nicholson's, " I would rather see
the city on fire than take the impudence of such fellows
as you," addressed to an insubordinate lieutenant, gave
rise to the alarming rumor that the governor was about
to set the city on fire. The flame of revolution blazed
up instantly, and spread without let or hindrance. The
mob was united in the desire to capture the fort, the
key to the city, with their oldest captain to march at their
head. " To Leisler, to Leisler's house," was the cry, — but
Leisler refused to assume the leadership. Lieutenant Stoll
of the Leisler Company, with quick decision, led them
on to the fort. Nicholson and Bayard, colonel of militia,
offered no resistance, submitting to the inevitable.

On the next day Leisler, in a public address, declared,
for himself and his party, the intention to hold the fort
for King William, at the same time entreating the citizens
to aid him in this purpose. The masses were yet unde-
cided, they still feared the lieutenant-governor, when a
false rumor spread that there were three ships in the bay
with commands of the new king. Upon this, the entire
militia company, about four hundred men with their
officers, declared themselves for Leisler, the cause of the
Protestant religion and the Prince of Orange, until they
should receive commands from the latter, their king. All
those that had wavered now joined Leisler. Nicholson
fled from the country, and his counselors escaped or concealed themselves from the wrath of the people.

The city was now without a government. Thereupon
by popular vote a committee of safety was elected, consisting of the most prominent burghers of the citizen's
party, who, on June 8, 1689, appointed Leisler commander-
in-chief of the fort and of the city, until the arrival of
the new governor from England. When the news arrived

of the coronation of William and Mary, Leisler at once made preparations for a solemn ceremony of homage, and notified the provincial and municipal officials to take part. When these refused to join in rendering homage, the ceremony took place in New York and Albany without them. Leisler in consequence dismissed the magistrate of the city, and the committee organized new elections for the vacant places of burgomaster and aldermen. The aristocrats naturally did not secure an office, and in August, 1689, the committee of safety appointed Leisler supreme commander of the province. Leisler made a complete report to King William of all that had been done, assuring him of his loyalty, his zeal for the Protestant cause, and begging for speedy instructions. Even Leisler's enemies never doubted the sincerity of this petition, and could find fault only with its English. Lieutenant Stoll was sent to England with this petition, handed it to the king in person in November, 1689, but met with no success, for Nicholson, who had arrived earlier, had poisoned the king's ear in regard to the popular party in New York, declaring that its actions had arisen from hostility to the English Church rather than from zeal for the new dynasty. Thus the reward that Leisler merited at royal hands for the successful issue of the revolution, was lost.[1] Neighbors at home, on the other hand, recognized the loyal and honest efforts of the popular governor, and sent their best wishes for the progress of the revolution, but the dethroned aristocrats spared no efforts in provoking dissension and discord. The name of Leisler was dragged through the mire. He was branded as a tyrant, usurper, demagogue, even as a Papist and Jacobite, by the very

[1] Cf. *Documents relating to the Colonial History of the State of N. Y.*, vol. iii, pp. 608 f. (Brodhead).

persons who had proved their disloyalty to the new dynasty.

One illegal act, and one only, was committed by Leisler,[1] namely, that he did not publish a certain clause of the king's address that recommended retaining all old officials with the exception of Papists. Leisler can be justified, however, on the ground that he could not have carried the revolution through successfully if the aristocrats had remained in office. The new popular principle could not be represented by them.

An unfortunate move also was his attempt to force Albany to recognize his government. Bayard had fled thither and succeeded in winning to his side influential citizens such as the Schuylers, Bleeckers, Van Rensselaers, Cuylers, and others. Leisler was provoked by the order of Bayard, issued to the militia companies that had been under his command in New York, forbidding them to obey Leisler. The latter answered this order by sending an armed company under the command of his son-in-law, Jacob Milborne, to take possession of the fort at Albany and defend the cause of the Protestant king "against Indians and other hostile attacks." The soldiers were not admitted into the city, and as Milborne was too weak to risk a battle, he was compelled to withdraw. This false step gave the fugitive aristocrats a chance to file complaints at the English court against the government of Leisler, falsely accusing him of rebellion against the English dynasty.

Not long after these events, in the beginning of December, 1689, a royal messenger arrived in Boston with a letter addressed to Francis Nicholson, "or in his absence to such as for the time being take care for Preserving the

---

[1] F. Kapp, *Geschichte der Deutschen im Staate New York*, p. 44. New York: Steiger, 1867.

Peace and administering the Lawes in our said Province of New York in America."[1] The enemies of Leisler attempted to get possession of this letter, i. e., to become its recipients while in New York, and thereby obtain authority. Bayard and Philipse, representing a part of the old government, secretly went to New York for this purpose, but, the ruling party also hearing of the letter, the messenger was taken at once to the fort, where Leisler was in command. The letter empowered the man to whom it was directed to assume command as lieutenant-governor and appoint a council to assist him in the direction of affairs. Accordingly Leisler, on December 11, 1689, assumed the title of lieutenant-governor and named a council of nine persons representing the various trades of the province. This royal message put aside any remaining scruples as to the justice of Leisler's assumption of authority, and the political affairs of the colony soon assumed an orderly and peaceful aspect.

An effort was made to capture Leisler on the streets of New York, but, the attempt proving unsuccessful, the ringleaders, Bayard, Van Cortlandt, Nicolls, and others were themselves captured and thrown into prison for high treason against His Majesty's officers. Bayard and Nicolls were captured while attempting to escape, and the sentence of death was pronounced against them. They humbly sued for mercy and Leisler relented. In the course of events they caused Leisler's ruin. Had Leisler employed the thorough methods of the revolutionary dictator, he would have destroyed his enemies while they were in his power, and thereby forever ended their opportunities for doing harm. This act of grace on the part of Leisler, while it elevates him as a man, was undoubtedly a political mistake.

[1] *Documents rel. Colonial History*, vol. iii, p. 606.

Hardly had he become master over his enemies within, before the lieutenant-governor had to meet a more terrible foe without, the French and Indians, commanded by the brave and energetic Frontenac. At the beginning of January, 1690, the French governor had planned an attack on New York by way of the Mohawk Valley and Albany. The event which stands out in lurid colors is the massacre at Schenectady. The fort was surprised, burned, and plundered, and the occupants slain or taken prisoners. This terrible misfortune had no ill effect, however, on the political fortunes of Leisler, for when he now sent troops in the defense of Albany, the city willingly opened its gates and recognized Leisler's authority. He made the city secure against hostile attacks and sent a division of 140 men fifty miles beyond to guard against surprise. The enemies of the lieutenant-governor fled to New England.

Leisler proved himself equal to the emergency. He saw that coöperative action on the part of the colonies was essential to resist the formidable foe. Accordingly, in the beginning of April, 1690, he invited the governors of Massachusetts, Plymouth, East and West Jersey, Pennsylvania, Maryland, and Virginia to a common council at New York.[1] New York, Massachusetts, Plymouth, New Jersey, and Maryland were represented in this plan of defense. The Carolinas were in their infancy, and Virginia was too remote. The meeting of this congress at New York on the first of May, 1690, was a memorable event in American history. It was the first congress of American colonies, the first of a series, that by process of evolution was to culminate in the Continental Congress.[2] The congress decided that Massachusetts should send 160 men, Connecticut 135, Plymouth 60, New York 400, and Maryland

---

[1] Cf. Kapp, p. 48.   [2] Cf. Fiske, ii, 182–184.

100, in an expedition for the conquering of Canada, while Massachusetts was also to equip a fleet for the taking of Quebec. At the same time the Mohawk Indians promised an auxiliary force of 1800 warriors to attack the French. It was the first attempt at united action on the part of the colonies, without the aid of the mother country. The great plan, however, was not destined to succeed, largely owing to the jealousies and misunderstandings among the leaders. The expedition at sea met a similar fate. Though arriving at Quebec, the fleet delayed its attack, and was forced to retreat with great loss. Contrary winds and storms on the return made its destruction almost complete, though the New York contingent were fortunate enough to reach home with their ships.

Leisler had won the distinction of equipping the first warship that went out from New York, he had added three ships to the fleet, and contributed energetically in every department. He had instituted the pursuit of six French ships that had dared to approach New York Harbor, had had them brought to New York, condemned, and sold as prizes, a stroke which remained the only fortunate event in a chain of disasters. However, as a result of the expensive operations against Canada, all of the colonies had incurred debts, and great disappointment reigned, particularly when taxation had to be resorted to. Naturally, Leisler's enemies attempted to make a scapegoat of him, and the lieutenant-governor's position grew more and more difficult, his enemies increasing in numbers day by day.

The end of the year 1690 had come, and the home government, refusing to recognize Leisler's services to the crown and colony, appointed a new governor for New York, Colonel Henry Sloughter. The latter had set out with several ships and a respectable number of troops, but, to make confusion worse confounded, a storm separating him from the rest of the ships, the second in command, Major Richard Ingoldsby, arrived in New York before the governor. Leisler's enemies were busy winning the favor of the new arrival, and the demand was made of Leisler to surrender the fort at once. This Leisler refused to do until confronted with the documents giving Ingoldsby authority. But the papers were on board the absent ship, and Ingoldsby, being discredited, felt his honor as an English officer insulted. He issued a proclamation, in which all those that should oppose him were declared rebels, and all good people were summoned to his assistance. Leisler, a few days after, February 3, 1691, protested in the name of the king and queen against all the acts of Ingoldsby, holding him accountable for all acts of violence and bloodshed that might ensue, declaring at the same time his readiness to give up the fort to the new governor, Colonel Sloughter, immediately upon his arrival. Each party seemed to be waiting for the other to risk a blow, but as time went on, it was apparent that Ingoldsby was receiving more adherents and Leisler as constantly losing friends. Ingoldsby next attacked, and took two blockhouses with their garrisons, located north of Wall Street. Leisler was now confined to the fort, and, as before, refused to give it up. Such was the condition of affairs until the arrival of Governor Sloughter, March 19, 1691. Both parties eagerly awaited the new governor as a deliverer from the unfortunate entanglement. But Sloughter was a man of no clear vision or strength of character, and even his friends could find little to say in his behalf. Upon his arrival he became the dupe of the aristocratic party, who boarded his ship to inform him of

the condition of affairs. There Sloughter appointed his
council. Immediately upon arriving, at ten o'clock in the
evening, he demanded the keys of the fort, but Leisler
wished first an understanding as to the terms of surrender,
and guarantees for his security, perhaps distrustful because
the messenger whom the new governor had sent was
Ingoldsby. Sloughter demanded immediate and uncondi-
tional surrender, placed Leisler's messenger under arrest,
and on the 20th of March took possession of the fort. He
took Bayard and Nicolls out of prison, while Leisler and
eight friends of the council had to take their places in the
same dungeon.

The condemnation of Leisler aroused general horror.
Such severity none had expected. A sham trial was instituted, in which Sloughter appointed Leisler's personal
enemies as his judges, viz. : Bayard, Nicolls, Philipse, and
Van Cortlandt, together with four Englishmen who had
just arrived. Leisler was charged with rebellion, confisca-
tion of property, and the illegal levying of taxes. The
other councilors were set free, but the enemies of Leisler
were determined to be revenged upon him. Apparently
Governor Sloughter hesitated to sign a death-warrant, a
spark of justice glimmering within him. A tradition is
handed down that the aristocrats steeped the governor in
wine and procured his signature while His Excellency was
intoxicated. Leisler, previously convicted of high treason,
was accordingly condemned to suffer death, together with
his son-in-law, Milborne. The accused had felt so sure of
the justice of their cause that, like Egmont and Horn,
they refused to defend themselves against the charge of
treason. The sentence occasioned resentment and horror
in all parts of the colony, and many of the followers of
Leisler fled into neighboring provinces, fearing similar

charges against themselves. A popular uprising was imminent in New York City. Leisler's enemies, fearing that he might still be set free, now insisted upon the fruits of their victory, the immediate execution of their victims. The urgent entreaties of Leisler's friends for delay, just as in the case of Egmont, only hastened the execution. The scaffold was erected not far from the location of the present Tombs, on the corner of Pearl and Centre streets. The day, May 16, 1691, was wet and cold, and chilled the spectators to the bone. Leisler made an address to the people, in which he resigned himself to his fate with Christian humility. His dying request to his friends was that they should forget all injury done to himself and Milborne, and honor his wish, that their ashes might destroy all vestiges of discord and dissension. His son-in-law, Milborne, called out to his enemy, Livingstone, "You are guilty of my death and I shall accuse you before the eternal judgment seat"; and to the sheriff, who asked him if he would not bless the king and queen, he said, "Why, I die for them and for the Protestant religion, in which I was born and brought up."

The blunder of this execution became apparent in England after the son of Leisler brought the case into the English courts. The case being given over to the colonial ministry, the latter declared that the deceased had been executed justly, but begged for restitution to the family of their property and position, which was granted in 1692. With this Leisler's son was not satisfied; he desired not grace but justice, and after several years more of contention in behalf of his father's memory, the English Parliament reversed the attainder against Leisler and Milborne, justified Leisler's actions in every particular, and restored to his heirs the properties confiscated by the crown (1695).

In New York, the two parties, the popular and aristocratic, continued to exist, and after the governorship of Sloughter, of Ingoldsby, and of Fletcher had ended, the popular party once more gained the ascendancy under the Earl of Bellomont, who, when governor, allowed the remains of Leisler and Milborne to be taken from their burial-place under the gallows, to the cemetery of the Dutch Church (in the present Exchange Place).[1] This removal, in 1698, was an occasion of much solemnity, fifteen hundred persons taking part. Prominent contemporaries in other colonies regarded the execution of Leisler as eminently unjust, Increase Mather, for instance, declaring that Leisler was " barbarously murdered."

There are two reasons why the career of Leisler stands out conspicuously in American history : first and foremost, because he was the man who called together the first congress of American colonies; secondly, because he was the first representative of the popular party against the aristocratic element, of plebeian against patrician, or of Democrat against Tory. Had Leisler's dreams been realized, had he received due support from William III, hailed as their national hero by the Dutch of New Amsterdam, then Leisler would have gone down in history as the first great representative of popular government in New York.[2] His administration might have been signalized as a long stride advancing toward popular government in the colonies. In view of these facts, this man's personality, in spite of his crudeness and stubbornness bordering on fanaticism, is worthy of the highest respect, being conspicuous for qualities since then always highly valued in public life, and repeatedly honored by the popular vote, viz.: unquestioned honesty and integrity, unflinching firmness and

[1] Kapp, p. 56.   [2] Cf. Fiske, vol. ii, p. 192.

energy. Experience as a soldier and uncommon success in the administration of affairs were likewise elements contributing to the confidence the people felt in him as a public man.

Some of Leisler's descendants were also prominent in American history. Hester, one of his daughters, married the Dutchman Rynders, while her sister, Mary, widow of Milborne, became the wife of the brilliant young Huguenot, Abraham Gouverneur. Mary's son, Nicholas Gouverneur, married Hester's daughter, Gertrude Rynders, and a son of this marriage, Isaac Gouverneur, was the grandfather of Gouverneur Morris, one of the ablest members of the convention that framed the constitution of the United States. "This eminent statesman was thus lineally descended from Jacob Leisler through two of his daughters." [1]

Dwelling with the Dutch settlers of New Amsterdam, there was undoubtedly quite a sprinkling of Germans. A good example is that of Dr. Hans Kierstede, who came from Magdeburg in 1638 with Director Kieft. He was the first practicing physician and surgeon in that colony. He married Sarah Roeloffse, daughter of Roeloff and Anneke Janse, the owner of the Annetje Jans farm on Manhattan Island.[2]

Among the German settlers of the seventeenth century Minuit and Leisler have represented the type of the soldier and statesman, while the "Dutch" in the Jamestown colony represented the humbler class of artisans or laborers. A third class of pioneers also had German representatives,

[1] Fiske, vol. ii, p. 187.

[2] Cf. Schoonmaker, *The History of Kingston, N. Y.*, p. 482. 1888. Also Ruth Putnam, " Annetje Jans Farm," in *Historic New York*, vol. i, p. 132, etc. Putnam, 1897.

namely, the explorers and discoverers. Of the latter there was John Lederer. He was sent on three different expeditions by Sir William Berkeley, governor of the colony of Virginia, to explore the land south and west of the James River during the years 1669–70. From his map as well as from his journal we gather that he passed through North Carolina and proceeded as far into South Carolina as the Santee River. There were no whites then living in South Carolina, and only two colonies existing in North Carolina, on the Albemarle Sound and Cape Fear River. Lederer wrote his journal in Latin. Sir William Talbot, governor of Maryland, who translated the journal into English, speaks highly of the author's literary attainments. He had at first been unfavorably biased by evil stories concerning Lederer, yet found him, as he says, "a modest, ingenious person and a pretty scholar," and Lederer vindicated himself " with so convincing reason and circumstance that removed all unfavorable impressions."

The fact is, that Lederer had not been well received by the person that sent him, the governor of Virginia, owing to prejudices created against him by the English companions that set out with him on his journey. They forsook him and turned back. In his journal Lederer declares that he had a private commission from the governor of Virginia to proceed, though the rest of the party should abandon him, and he therefore went on with one Susquehanna Indian, reaching the Santee River at $33\frac{1}{3}°$ north latitude. His former companions returned to Virginia, and, not expecting that Lederer would ever come back, they excused themselves by false reports concerning him.

The three journeys which Lederer made, according to his journal, were first, from the head of the York River due west to the Appalachian Mountains; secondly, from the Falls of the James River, west and southwest into the Carolinas; thirdly, from the Falls of the Rappahannock, west to the mountains. No doubt can attach to the fact of these early western explorations, and they unquestionably had a good effect. The tide of immigration, to be sure, did not begin to flow until 1680, but the direction had been indicated.

The first German in Texas was a Würtemberger by the name of Hiens (Heinz, Hans).[1] He was a member of the expedition of La Salle in 1687, that vainly sought for the delta of the Mississippi, with a fatal result for the leader. After the murder of La Salle, the party under the rule of Duhaut ranged aimlessly among the Indians for a while, and fell in with some deserters of La Salle's former expedition, now living among the savages. One of these conspired with Hiens, and they avenged the murder of La Salle by killing Duhaut and Liotot.[2] Hiens, perhaps fearing revenge, left the expedition, parting amicably.

Another explorer, the earliest of the three, was Peter Fabian, a Swiss German, member of the expedition sent out in 1663 by the English Carolina Company to explore the Carolinas. The report of the expedition was probably written by Fabian, the scientific man of the party, as the distances are recorded by the standard of the German mile. The report appeared in 1665 in London, signed by Anthony Long, William Hilton, and Peter Fabian. It was embodied in the earliest history of Carolina by John Lawson, London, 1709.[3] In the latter work mention is made of another Swiss German explorer, Francis Louis Mitschel

---

[1] Cf. *Der deutsche Pionier*, vol. vi, pp. 69–70. Cincinnati, 1869–87, 18 vols. The statement is there made on the authority of Louis Hennepin.

[2] Justin Winsor, *Narrative and Critical History of America*, vol. iv, p. 238.

[3] Cf. *Der deutsche Pionier*, vol. x (1878), p. 188.

(for Michel), described as sent by his home canton, Bern, to select a suitable tract for a Swiss settlement, and as having, during several years of exploration, discovered large areas among the mountain ranges lying toward the headwaters of the large rivers and bays of Virginia, Maryland, and Pennsylvania, all uninhabited save by a few savages.[1]

The foregoing chapter attempted to show that, while the Germans living in an inland country were not seafarers or discoverers, their scholarly bent made them leading cosmographers during the period of American exploration. German settlers appeared even in the earliest colonies on American soil, such as Port Royal, Jamestown, and New Amsterdam. The purchaser and first governor of Manhattan Island, Peter Minuit, who was also the founder of New Sweden, and Jacob Leisler, martyr to the cause of popular government in New York, were Germans.[2] Lederer, Hiens, and Fabian were prominent as early explorers in the southern and southwestern zone of English colonization in the seventeenth century.

---

[1] *Der deutsche Pionier*, vol. x, p. 189. Quotation from Lawson (1709). For Michel see also below, Chapter VIII, p. 213.

[2] See *Appendix*.

CHAPTER II

William Penn in Germany — The Pietists of Frankfort-on-the-Main —
Francis Daniel Pastorius, his early life and arrival at Philadelphia —
The Concord, the *Mayflower* of the Germans — Landing, October 6, 1683
— Founding of Germantown, Pennsylvania — Industries and Customs
— Pastorius as patriarch and scholar — Protest against slavery — The
Mystics, Kelpius and his followers.

THE first German settlement, properly so-called because
of its permanence and individuality, began near the close
of the seventeenth century. It was a colony of religious
refugees, mainly from the Palatinate, who settled at Germantown, Pennsylvania, in 1683. The name of William
Penn is intimately associated with its beginnings. William Penn, clinging to his faith in spite of imprisonment
and persecution, was enthused with missionary zeal. He
made two journeys into Holland and Germany, in 1671
and 1677, to spread Quaker doctrines on the continent
of Europe. Only three denominations were recognized
along the Rhine and in Germany, namely, the Catholic, the Lutheran, and the Reformed. All other forms
of worship were outlawed, and their votaries placed in
the same class with heretics and atheists. Such were the
Mennonites, of whom considerable numbers existed
in Western Germany and Switzerland, the Schwenkfelders and the Quakers. George Fox, the founder of the
Society of Friends, had sent messengers of the new doctrine to the Netherlands and Germany as early as 1655,

and when William Penn made his journeys, a small Quaker community was still in existence at Kriegsheim (or Krisheim), near Worms, in the Palatinate. In Germany, the Quakers were most successful among the Mennonites, especially in the cities of Lübeck, Emden, Hamburg, Crefeld, and in the Palatinate, so also in the Schleswig-Holstein cities, Altona and Friedrichstadt, and in Danzig, then under Polish rule. All these sectarians suffered much from the rulers of the German principalities, each of whom had the right, by the treaty of Westphalia, to establish in his land whatever confession he pleased, and to exclude all others. Even the Pietists, who were but Protestants with a greater degree of inwardness in their religious life, were denounced by the orthodox churches as dangerous innovators. The Mystics, who in the latter part of the seventeenth century reappeared in various forms, were likened unto madmen.

The existence of these various sects, and, in particular, the Pietists in Germany, had prepared the ground for the sowing of such principles as those of Penn, for indeed a great degree of similarity existed between the doctrines of the Pietist and Quaker. A higher valuation of emotion and spirituality, as opposed to rationalism and dogma, characterized both of them; a life led in imitation of the Saviour, a communing with his spirit, a religion of the heart, supplanted the outward ritualism of an established church.

The second journey of William Penn, in 1677, was noteworthy in history, disproportionately to the number of conversions to the Society of Friends. Although Penn was received with open arms in the Pietistic circle at Frankfort-on-the-Main, was listened to with reverence and admiration by devoted hearers in the Rhine country, and could count among his disciples some German women of very high social standing, still his greatest success, unknown to him, was of another kind. William Penn's journey was destined to begin an epoch of political and social, far more than religious movement, for it stirred those waves of immigration that threatened to depopulate southwestern Germany and overrun the new country that William Penn was about to open up for colonization on the banks of the Delaware. Those German sectarians who had most appreciated his simple yet eloquent sermons gave the first impetus to the new movement. The German and Dutch Mennonites in Crefeld and Kriegsheim had representatives in the first shipload that went to Penn's land.

The English government owed Admiral Penn, father of William Penn, the sum of sixteen thousand pounds sterling, for services and the advances he had made. Instead of payment of the debt, the son and heir accepted the grant of a large stretch of country north of Maryland, which was named Pennsylvania. This included the land that Peter Minuit had selected for New Sweden, wisely considering it best adapted to Germanic immigration. The royal charter was issued to Penn March 4, 1681, shortly after which there appeared in London a brief description of the new province: "Some account of the Province of Pennsylvania in America," wherein the favorable location, fertile soil, wealth in game and fish, as well as other circumstances advantageous to immigrants, were duly set forth. A translation of this book [1] appeared in the same year in Amsterdam.

[1] The title was *Eine Nachricht wegen der Landschaft Pennsylvania in Amerika, welche jüngstens unter dem groszen Siegel in England an William Penn. u. s. w. übergeben worden.* Nebenst beigefügtem ehemaligem Schreiben

The same persons who were intimate with Penn on his
journey to Germany, in 1677, became acquainted with
this book, and at once began a correspondence with his
agent, Benjamin Furley. They formed a company and
bought a large tract of land in Pennsylvania for the purpose of immigration. In 1682 a young lawyer, Francis
Daniel Pastorius, returning from extensive travels, visited
Frankfort-on-the-Main. There he became intimate with
the noted Pietistic circle, including Dr. Spener, Dr.
Schütz, the notary Fenda, Jacob Van de Walle, Maximilian Lersner, Eleonore von Merlau, and Maria Juliana
Bauer. While with them he frequently heard mention of
the name of William Penn, and also saw letters of Benjamin Furley and the printed account of Penn's province.
They soon disclosed the secret of their purchase of fifteen
thousand acres in that remote district, and the purpose of
some of their number to migrate thither with their families. " This begat," says Pastorius, " a desire in my soul
to continue in their society and with them to lead a quiet,
godly, and honest life in a howling wilderness." [1] These
were the beginnings of the Frankfort Company, that later
extended its purchases to twenty-five thousand acres, a
share of five thousand acres costing one hundred pounds.
The members of the company were originally Dr. Schütz,
Jacob Van de Walle, Kaspar Merian, Wilhelm Ueberfeldt,
Daniel Behagel, all of Frankfort, besides Georg Strausz,
Johann Laurentz, and Abraham Hasevoet. There were
several changes of membership in course of time. [2] Though

des oberwähnten William Penn. In Amsterdam gedruckt bei Christoph
Conraden, 1681. The same book was also printed in Frankfort as part of
the larger work : *Diarium Europaeum*.

[1] Cf. *German American Annals*, vol. v, no. 5, p. 288 ; M. D. Learned, *The
Life of Franz Daniel Pastorius, Founder of Germantown.*

[2] The names of Merian, Strausz, Laurentz, Ueberfeldt, and Hasevoet

all were very enthusiastic about the plan of immigration, none of the members ever came to America with the exception of Pastorius, who soon was appointed agent of the company in America.

The first actual immigrants were Mennonites from Crefeld, some of whom had become converts to Quakerism through the preaching of William Penn, while most of the others joined the Society of Friends in America. There were thirteen heads of families, the greater part interrelated by blood or marriage ties.[1] Pastorius, acting as the agent of the Frankfort Company, first visited Kriegsheim and looked after matters necessary for the long journey,[2] with the leaders, Peter Schumacher, Gerhard Hendricks, and others, after which he descended the Rhine to Crefeld. He took ship in advance of the others, and landed in Philadelphia on the 20th of August, 1683.

Six weeks later, Benjamin Furley had arranged at Rotterdam for the transportation of the first shipload of Germans. The *Mayflower* of the German immigrants to America was the good ship *Concord*, appropriately named,

dropped out, their shares being bought by Pastorius, Eleonore von Merlau (who had now become the wife of the theologian Petersen), Balthasar Jawert, and Johann Kembler of Lübeck, and Dr. Gerhard of Maastricht (syndic of Bremen), Johann Lebrün and Thomas Wylich of Wesel. A number of these were acquainted with William Penn.

[1] The names of the thirteen heads of families were as follows : Dirck, Abraham, and Hermann Op den Gräff, Lenert Arets, Tüners Kunders, Reinert Tisen, Wilhelm Strepers, Jan Lensen, Peter Keurlis, Jan Simens, Johann Bleikers, Abraham Tünes, and Jan Lücken.

The Crefelders had bought land of William Penn independently, to the extent of 18,000 acres : Jacob Telner 5000, Jan Strepers 5000, Dirck Sipman 5000, Govert Remke 1000, Jacob Isaac Van Bebber 1000, Lenert Arets 1000. Sipman and Remke did not emigrate; Arets in 1683, Telner, who had previously been in America, 1684, Van Bebber, 1687, Jan Strepers, 1691.

[2] The immigrants from Kriegsheim (Krisheim) arrived in Pennsylvania later ; the first to arrive, in 1685, were Peter and Isaac Schumacher and Gerhard Hendricks.

being the bearer of a devoutly religious and peaceful company to the City of Brotherly Love, within the territory of the Holy Experiment. Captain Jeffreys commanded the *Concord*, a well-built and roomy vessel of the West Indian service. Five pounds, one-half fare for children under twelve, was the rate for which they were carried over. They left Gravesend July 24, 1683, and arrived in Philadelphia after a moderately long but safe journey, *on October 6, 1683,* the date celebrated by all Germans in America as the beginning of their history in the United States.

Pastorius, who had sailed six weeks before from Deal, England, was accompanied by a handful of immigrants, men and women of the serving class, some of whom later became property holders in Germantown.[1] On board ship Pastorius met one who immediately became his fast friend, the Welsh physician, Thomas Lloyd, scholar of Jesus College, Oxford.[2] With him he conversed in Latin, a characteristic accomplishment of the scholars of that day, Lloyd not being able to speak German, nor Pastorius to converse in English at that time.

In the City of Brotherly Love, William Penn received the German pioneer with loving kindness. Another close friend was Penn's secretary, Lehenmann. "The governor often summons me to dine with him" (Penn), wrote Pastorius subsequently. "As I was recently absent from home a week, he came himself to visit me and bade me dine with him twice every week, and declared to his coun-

---

[1] Their names were: James Schumacher, Georg Wertmüller, Isaac Dilbeck, his wife and two boys (Abraham and Jacob), Thomas Gasper, Conrad Bacher (alias Rutter), and an English maid, Frances Simpson. The ship was called *America,* Captain Wasey. Cf. Seidensticker, *Bilder aus der deutsch-pennsylvanischen Geschichte,* p. 38.

[2] Later, president of the Provincial Council; died in 1694.

sellors that he loved me and the High Germans very much and wished them to do so likewise." The city of Philadelphia had been laid out but two years before and consisted then of a few poorly built houses. " The rest," Pastorius remarked, " was woods and brushwood, in which I lost my way several times in an area no greater than that between the river bank and the house of my friend, William Hudson. A striking impression this made upon me, coming from London, Paris, Amsterdam, and Ghent."

After the *Concord* arrived, the first problem was to select a location for the German colonists. They had purchased the right of occupying in all forty-three thousand acres,[1] and asked for a site on a navigable river, as their contract demanded. But since Penn was not willing to carry out the latter condition,[2] they finally found available a tract about six miles above Philadelphia, which is at present in the twenty-second ward of the city and bears still the original name of Germantown.[3] Pastorius recorded in his " Grund und Lagerbuch " that " the hardships and trials of the early settlers were great, only equalled by their Christian endurance and indefatigable industry, so that Germantown in the early days could well be called ' Armentown,'[4] 'the city of the poor.'" Of his temporary dwelling Pastorius tells us it was thirty feet long and fifteen broad, and the windows, because of the lack of glass, were of paper soaked with oil; but over the house-door was writ-

---

[1] Including 25,000 acres purchased by the Frankfort Company, and 18,000 by the Crefelders.

[2] For a detailed account of Penn's position, cf. *German American Annals*, vol. v, no. 6, pp. 334–341.

[3] The date for the laying-out of the township was October 24, 1683.

[4] Germantown was probably pronounced Jarmantown, when Armentown, "the town of the poor," would rhyme with it.

ten a symbol of the good cheer within: "Parva domus sed amica bonis, procul este prophani."[1]

The first settlers were mostly weavers from Crefeld. Their industry soon led to the opening of a store in Philadelphia, for the sale of their wares. Many had also been accustomed to growing the vine, and when they saw the wild grape, they grew hopeful of establishing vineyards. The people of Germantown raised flax with great success, for Pastorius tells us that the prosperity of the young city was largely due to flax-spinning and weaving. There came many accessions from Crefeld, Mühlheim, and Kriegsheim, such colonists as Captain John Smith would have welcomed in Jamestown, mostly tradesmen, weavers, tailors, shoemakers, locksmiths, and carpenters, who along with their trades also applied themselves to cultivating the soil. As early as November, 1684, there was a sale at the Philadelphia store, over which Pastorius was overseer, in the interests of the Frankfort Company. Small were the beginnings, to be sure, the sales of the first year amounting to only ten dollars, for the times were hard, and the new immigrants were generally supplied with clothes enough to last them for several years. But soon the reputation of the well-woven goods of Germantown spread far and wide, and there was a large demand for them, coming from the outside, resulting in increased industrial activity.[2]

[1] Pastorius himself translates the motto into German : —

> Klein ist mein Haus,
> Doch Gute sieht es gern,
> Wer gottlos ist, der bleibe fern.

"Whereat the Governor, Penn, when he visited it, enjoyed a hearty laugh and encouraged me to continue building."

[2] William Bradford, 1692, printed a poem by Richard Frame, "A Short Description of Pennsylvania," in which occur the lines : —

> The German Town of which I spoke before,
> Which is at least in length one mile and more,

BEGINNING OF PROTEST

END OF PROTEST WITH SIGNATURES

FACSIMILE OF PROTEST (1688) AGAINST "THE BUYING AND KEEPING OF NEGROES"

Germantown has the honor of establishing the first paper mill in the colonies. Wilhelm Ruttinghausen (Rittenhouse) of Arnheim, Holland, with his two sons, Claus and Gerhard, settled on a brook running into the Wissahickon, and there built a paper mill in 1690. The art of making paper was a family possession, their ancestors having already distinguished themselves therein at home. The paper was of excellent quality and the business, later in Claus Ruttinghausen's charge, expanded to an extraordinary degree.

In a few years the number of inhabitants in Germantown had increased to such an extent that additions were made to the town. Krisheim (Kriegsheim) with 884 acres, Sommerhausen with 900, Crefeld with 1166 were added to the 2750 acres of Germantown. All these places were on the same road, Germantown being the southernmost, nearest to Philadelphia, while Crefeld was beyond Chestnut Hill, in the present Montgomery County. In Germantown, the road, sixty feet broad, ran through the middle of the straggling city and was bordered by peach trees. Each dwelling had a vegetable and flower garden of three acres attached to it. A cross-street, forty feet in width, cut the principal street at right angles and at the crossing there was an open market-place. The fields lay north and south of the city. In a remarkably short time the stillness of the primeval forest was broken by the droning noise of mill-wheels, the whirring of the weaver's shuttle, and the merry shouts of blue-eyed children. The forests were replaced by orchards, vineyards, and vegetable gardens dotted with flowers and beehives. Pastorius himself, like

Where live High German people and Low Dutch,
Whose trade in weaving Linnin cloth is much:
There grows the flax. . . .
                              Seidensticker, p. 50.

many a "Latin farmer" of the later periods, seeing the busy tradesmen and agriculturists about him, regretted the uselessness of book-learning, declaring mournfully, "never have metaphysics and Aristotelian logic made of a savage a Christian, far less earned a loaf of bread."

Germantown was incorporated as a town on August 12, 1689. The first burgomaster was Pastorius, and he served in the same capacity in 1692, 1696, and 1697. At other times he was generally city clerk, or scrivener, for which office his skillful and accurate pen well qualified him. Other burgomasters were Dirck Op den Graeff, Arnold Cassel, Reinert Tisen, Daniel Falckner. A public office was felt to be a burden in the idyllic days of Germantown, though the terms of office were not long. A Mennonite might, because of his religion, be excused from holding office, but otherwise a citizen was fined three pounds on refusal to accept an election.[1] Pastorius wrote in 1703 to William Penn, complaining of the difficulty of getting his people to serve as public officers, and expressing the hope that the arrival of new immigrants might relieve the situation. Fines and importations becoming necessary to secure office-holders, seems an embarrassment almost inconceivable to later generations of men, yet this historical fact emphasizes a trait often exhibited by the Germans in the United States.[2]

Just as Germantown in its early period was not troubled with office-seekers, so criminals were rare within its hallowed precincts. Sessions of court took place every six weeks, and frequently they were adjourned because there

[1] December 1, 1694, Paul Wulff was elected clerk, but declining without good cause, he was fined three pounds by the General Court. Cf. *German American Annals*, N. S., vol. vi, no. 1, p. 10.

[2] Cf. Part II, Chapter IV, "Political Influence of the German Element in the United States."

was nothing to do. Routine business, sales, purchases, contracts, etc., were but rarely interrupted by punishments, fines at the worst, for the neglect of fences, concerning which Germantown citizens were very particular (an example of speedy Americanization, since they had no fences at home), or for allowing cattle to stray, or for an occasional case of drunkenness. The records, by accident perhaps, tell us that beer was brewed in the early days of Germantown. Peter Keurlis, in May, 1695, was summoned before court, because he had, on an inn-keeper's license, kept a saloon. He was the same that had been granted the privilege of selling a quantity of beer brewed for a fair that had not been held.[1] It is interesting to note that the law-makers of Germantown restricted the sale of intoxicants, limiting the same purchaser during a half-day to a quarter of a pint of rum or a quart of beer. It must not be supposed, however, that Germantown was the scene of frequent intoxication. In half a dozen years hardly a single case of drunkenness was recorded, though every detail seems to have been put down, as for instance, when Müller was imprisoned for wishing to smoke one hundred pipes of tobacco in one day as the result of a wager, or when Caspar Karsten called the policeman a rogue.[2]

In the year 1693 Pastorius and Peter Schumacher were commissioned to procure stocks for the public punishment of offenders. Very little use seems to have been made of them. Again, in the minutes of 1697, we read that Arndt Klincken gave his old house for use as a prison. No more convincing proof, however, of the Arcadian conditions of this early German settlement could be cited than the min-

---

[1] This happened in November, 1695. Peter Keurlis was, in all probability, the first beer-brewer in the American colonies.

[2] See Seidensticker, chap. viii, "Aus der Gerichtsstube," *Bilder aus der deutsch-pennsylvanischen Geschichte*, pp. 59–62.

ute : "All crimes that have been committed previous to this date are to be forgiven, but whatever evil happens henceforward shall be punished." [1]

A court seal being found desirable, Pastorius was commissioned to prepare the design. He selected a clover leaf on the three leaves of which were sketched respectively a vine, a flax blossom, and a weaver's shuttle, with the motto : " Vinum, Linum et Textrinum." [2] Annual fairs were held in 1701 or before, and semi-annual fairs in 1702, 1704, and continuously thereafter in the spring and autumn. [3]

Pastorius had frequently desired to lay down the cares of public office, and when the Frankfort Company in time relieved him, the result was not altogether favorable to the company's interests. It was in January, 1700, when Daniel Falckner, Johann Kelpius, and Johann Jawert were appointed agents of the company with full power. Kelpius, hermit and mystic, was not concerned with the affairs of this world. Falckner was a mischiefmaker, and Jawert, the only happy choice among the three, was an honest man imposed upon. [4] In October, 1701, Falckner

---

[1] Minutes of the year 1697. See Seidensticker, *supra*, chap. vii, p. 55. "Alle Strafen, welche gefallen sein in vorige Zeit, sollen alle vergeben sein, aber was nun fortan vorfällt, soll exekutirt werden."

[2] Pastorius translates this, " Der Wein, der Lein und der Webeschrein," in order to denote, as he declared, that in Germantown the principal occupations were : viniculture, flax-growing, and textile industries. Another translation has been made by Seidensticker, to the effect that agriculture, manufactures, and the merry enjoyment of life were in Germantown and have been for two centuries thereafter, in the United States, the characteristic modes of activity of the German immigrants.

[3] Perhaps the county fair which has come down to us is a survival of the Pennsylvania German " Jahrmarkt."

[4] Sachse, *German Sectarians of Pennsylvania*, gives a very sympathetic account of Daniel Falckner, who is generally, perhaps, not given entire justice. His service to Germantown was to stir it up out of its ruts, and to the Frankfort Company to insist on the measuring of the remaining 22,025

and Jawert, as agents, energetically pressed the claim for the land to which the Frankfort Company was entitled by the terms of the original purchase. This tract of twenty-two thousand and twenty-five acres, when assigned, was located in the northwestern part of Montgomery County, New Hanover Township, on the Manatawny River, which flows into the Schuylkill at Pottstown. It became known as Falckner's Swamp, and later was sold to Johann Heinrich Sprögel, at a ridiculously low figure. The sale was concluded by Falckner, who, it seems, owed [1] Sprögel some money, while Jawert was duped, or kept uninformed. Jawert complained that he had not been consulted in this somewhat obscure transaction.

A panic was caused by the adventurer Sprögel, in 1708, when he attempted to dispossess a great many of the Germantown settlers of their lands, claiming that he owned the only correct title by virtue of his purchase of the Frankfort Company's rights. The settlers appealed to Pastorius, who was always the deliverer in time of trouble, and Pastorius hastened to Philadelphia. He found that "all of the lawyers of the city were feed," which meant that all four of the lawyers residing in Philadelphia had been engaged in behalf of Sprögel's side of the case. Pastorius, not affluent enough to import an advocate from New York, consulted his friend, James Logan, and with

acres, which, however, he lost again for the company, through sale. Daniel Falckner's later career was a useful one, as pioneer and minister in New Jersey and New York. He had also been the founder of the first Lutheran church in Falckner's Swamp district (Manatawny). Daniel must not be confounded with Justus Falckner, ordained in the Swedish Lutheran church at Wicacoa, and beloved minister in New York and along the Hudson, 1703–23. His brother Daniel then served his parish for a short time, until Pastor Berkenmeyer came.

[1] Cf. "The Case of the Frankfort Company's Business briefly stated" (by Pastorius), *German American Annals*, vol. v, no. 6, pp. 353 ff.

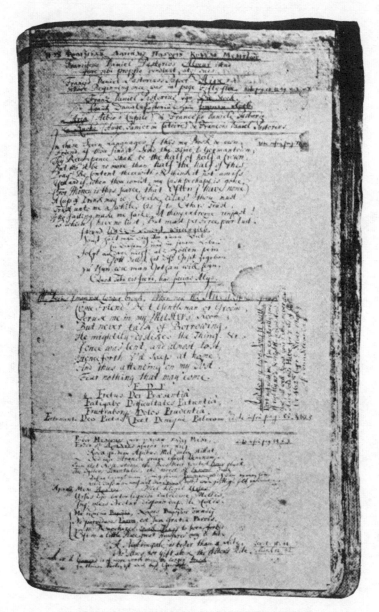

FACSIMILE OF TITLE-PAGE OF PASTORIUS' BEEHIVE

the straightforward testimony of Jawert, the injustice of ·the plot was exposed and the difficulties removed. While the settlers of Germantown retained their rights to their property, Sprögel remained in possession of Falckner's Swamp, which was by no means what the name implies, but good land, constituting, as above stated, the remaining portion of the Frankfort Company's land, about seven eighths of the twenty-five thousand acres originally purchased from William Penn.

Germantown maintained its independent government until 1707. In that year George Lowther, the queen's attorney, summarily dismissed the town's court and the newly elected officers. There were mild protests, but no serious regrets, since the citizens of Germantown were thereby relieved of at least one tax, having previously, in spite of their complaints, been required to pay a three-fold tax, viz.: for the province, for the county Philadelphia, and for their own municipality. When the old accounts were closed, the treasury of Germantown still owed Pastorius two pounds fourteen shillings, and, judging by the carefully kept books of Pastorius, that debt was never paid. This is an illustration among many of the unselfishness with which Pastorius did his work. He was in every respect a public-spirited man, the " Bradford " of Germantown, and it is well to pause a moment for closer acquaintance with this interesting man.[1]

Franz Daniel Pastorius was born in Sommerhausen, in 1651, the son of a jurist of prominence. He studied at the Universities of Altdorf, Strassburg, Basel, and Jena. Besides his special training in law and theology he was

[1] Seidensticker, *Bilder aus der deutsch-pennsylvanischen Geschichte*, iv, xi, u. xii, Abschnitt. An exhaustive treatment of Pastorius' life and work, by Professor M. D. Learned, has appeared in *German American Annals*, vols. v and vi.

a polylinguist, and probably no man among his contemporaries in America was his equal, certainly not his superior,· in classical culture and encyclopædic learning. He was remarkable as a statistician, noting every fact of knowledge or experience with characteristic accuracy and neatness, an evidence of which is his scrap-book called the " Bee-Hive," still preserved and treasured by his descendants.[1] Of his other works the best known is his description of Pennsylvania, a collection of his letters and reports, sent to his father, Melchior Adam Pastorius, and by him collected in book form and published in 1700.[2]

But better than his learning, that if chronicled at the present day might smack of pedantry (if not put us to shame), was his exemplary character. He was the mainstay of the colony, the chief cause of its initial success. The prosperity of Germantown was his life-work, excluding ever the thought of personal gain, or the feverish appetite for land speculation. He served the colony as burgomaster and town clerk, and at all times as notary, his handwriting being visible in all public and private documents, for which he exacted fees lamentably small. Nevertheless he was self-respecting, and while not wealthy, was able at his death, in 1719, to leave his widow and

---

[1] Exact title : *Francis Daniel Pastorius, His Hive, Beestock (Bienenstock), Melliotrophium, Alvear or Rusca Apum;* begun A. D. 1696. Most of the matter is written in English, for Pastorius had gained a mastery of the language. Historical, literary, geographical, didactic, sententious, and epigrammatic articles and notes to the number of 5000 are loosely strung together. Verses (doggerel, more strictly speaking), in English, Latin, German, French, Dutch, Italian, vary the monotony of this queer hive of pedantic learning. A facsimile of one of the pages is reproduced in *Americana Germanica*, vol. i, part 4, and copious extracts are published in vols. i and ii.

[2] *Umständige Geographische Beschreibung der zu allerletzt Erfundene Provintz Pennsylvania an denen End-Gräntzen Americae in der West-Welt gelegen.* Frankfurt und Leipzig, 1700.

two sons a respectable property. Besides being a public officer in Germantown, and a member of the assembly (which with the provincial council was the legislative power of the colonial government) in 1687 and 1691, he was the leader in educational matters.

In 1698 he was called to the Quaker School in Philadelphia, which he served until 1700. Two years after, when a school was established in Germantown, Pastorius became its head. The latter, a coeducational institution, was supported by a fixed rate, four to sixpence a week as the scholar's fee, while several citizens besides made voluntary contributions. A night school was established for such as labored during the day or were too far advanced in years for the day school.

However distinct and valuable were the material contributions, such as its agriculture, its paper manufacture, its weaving and milling industries, the German settlement in colonial Pennsylvania was still more remarkable for another feature, — a monument built more enduring than brass, erected for the cause of humanity, that will make Germantown forever memorable in the annals of the people of the United States. This was Germantown's protest against negro slavery, made in the year 1688, the first formal action ever taken against the barter in human flesh within the boundaries of the United States.[1] The system of negro slavery was repulsive to the German settlers from the very start, and they were shocked to find that the Quakers remained indifferent toward this criminal abuse. They failed to understand how the Quakers could harmonize slavery with their religion,

---

[1] E. Bettle, in his *Notices of Negro Slavery in America:* "To this body of humble, unpretending and almost unnoticed philanthropists belongs the honor of having been the first association who ever remonstrated against Negro slavery." Quoted by Seidensticker, *supra*, p. 67.

and hoping to awaken them from their stupor, the German settlers appealed to the Quakers' sense of honor, their pride and vaunted humanity. The protest had its origin in a gathering of Germans who met on the 18th of April, 1688, in Germantown. A document, still preserved, was drawn up, in the handwriting of Pastorius, and signed by Garret Hendericks, Franz Daniel Pastorius, Dirck Op den Graeff, and Abraham Op den Graeff. Addressed to the monthly meeting of the Quakers, about to take place in Richard Worrell's house, Lower Dublin, its design was to bring the matter of slavery before that gathering for debate and action. The monthly gathering of the 30th of April deemed the matter of such importance that they could not pretend to take action upon it. They referred it to the quarterly meeting, as the content of the protest " was quite in accord with the truth." The quarterly meeting, held in June, acted similarly, considering the case too important for their action and appointing a committee to lay the protest before the annual meeting, the highest tribunal of the Quakers. The annual meeting occurred in the same year, when " the document protesting against the buying and keeping of negro slaves, received from several German Friends," was acknowledged, but it was voted not fitting for the association to pass definite judgment upon the matter, since it stood in intimate relation with other affairs. The whole matter was laid on the table for the nonce, a diplomatic evasion. Seventeen years later the Quakers did make resolutions against the slave trade, and in 1770 the Friends were advised never to appoint slaveholders as overseers. The German Quakers may be considered the radical wing of the Quakers at that early period, on the question of abolition.

The settlement of Germantown remained a German city.

William Penn had preached there in the German language in 1683, and in 1793 President Washington attended a German service in the Reformed church, the epidemic of yellow fever in Philadelphia compelling him to remove his residence for a time to Germantown. The city became ever more prominent as the base for distribution of German immigration to the counties of Montgomery, Berks, Lebanon, York, Bucks, Lehigh, and Northampton. It long remained the centre of German culture, whence books and German newspapers were distributed to German counties and settlements. The printing-press of Christopher Sauer, that remained in operation for a period of forty years, will be mentioned later.[1] The industrial activities and the semi-annual fairs of Germantown, the latter planned for both business and pleasure, served as models for other settlements. Such was Germantown in the eighteenth century. In the nineteenth, the rural charm of the location began to attract the wealthy citizens of Philadelphia. The original aspect of the place was lost, and even the names of the pioneers, as Lücken, Schumacher, Jansen, Kunders, survive only in an English disguise, as Lukens, Shoemaker, Johnson, Conrads, many of the present inhabitants knowing naught of their German origin.

In concluding this chapter on the Germantown settlement, a serious omission would be the failure to note the arrival of a group of men, who were noted as Mystics. Their leader was Johann Kelpius; others were Köster, Falckner, Seelig, and Matthai. They believed in bodily translation to realms beyond at the moment of death, conditioned on their keeping firmly attached to their faith. Bearing the conviction that the world was coming to a

[1] See Chapter v, pp. 143-146.

speedy end, their purpose was to await the Judgment Day in the wilderness of North America, where they might, during their last years, be in closer communion with the Divine Spirit. Magister Johann Jacob Zimmermann was the real founder of this chapter of Mystics. One of the best mathematicians and astronomers of Europe, he died at Rotterdam on the eve of embarkation for America, in 1693. According to Zimmermann's calculations the millennium was to come in the autumn of the year 1694, an event he had also expected to await in America.

This group of Mystics, tarrying at Germantown, lost two of their number, one of them marrying the daughter of Zimmermann, content to build a terrestrial home among the peace-loving Germantown settlers. The others remained faithful to the higher call, following Kelpius (1694), who selected a tract for settlement known as the Ridge, then supposed to be the highest point of vacant land in the neighborhood of Germantown, a part of a range of hills drained by the flow of the Wissahickon. A small natural cave was found among the rocks of the hillside and near it gurgled a spring. Kelpius enlarged the cave and made it habitable and was wont to retire within it for prayer and contemplation. The popular name that the mystical brotherhood received was "The Woman in the Wilderness," [1] though the members themselves never acknowledged this name. One of the members, Köster, paid considerable attention to the religious life of the Germantown Germans and their English neighbors, and in Philadelphia became involved in the Keithian controversy,[2] which was then agitating the Quakers through-

[1] "Das Weib in der Wüste." — Revelation, xii, 14.
[2] The Quakers petitioned Pastorius to banish the Mystics from the colony.

out the province. The sequel was a disagreement between
Kelpius and Köster, and the withdrawal of the latter
from the Ridge for the purpose of founding a new
brotherhood. A few members of the original community
and some Keithians joined him in the attempt to form
a new religious society, that they located a short distance
north of Germantown, but the movement was not crowned
with success, and the defection of Köster is nowhere
dignified with mention in the writings of Kelpius, Seelig,
or Falckner.

It must not be supposed that the hermit on the Wissahickon and his mystical brotherhood were given exclusively to idle contemplation. Kelpius was a teacher of
children, Seelig a binder of books, and all the rest supported themselves by gardening or some other form of
employment, most frequently by giving instruction. One
of their most curious functions was the satisfaction of
the popular craving for supernatural aid. It was characteristic of the age and of the peasantry to appeal to
the stars and other mysterious agencies for favorable
influence. The horoscope was firmly believed in, even by
intelligent persons, and the Mystic chapter, from their
weird astronomical tower on the Wissahickon, cast horo-
scopes not only at nativities of human beings, but also at
the laying of cornerstones of important edifices.[1] Before
planting or sowing, the advice of the Mystics was deemed

He said he would refer the matter to the proprietor (Penn), who was soon
to come, and admonished patience. He wrote the following lines : —

> Die Fehler meiner Brüder
> Sind mir zwar ganz zuwider
> Doch wegen eines Worts
> Ihr Zeugniss zu vernichten
> Und freventlich zu richten
> Find ich nicht meines Orts.

[1] Such as the Swedish Lutheran church at Wicacoa.

of value, and at other times their divining-rod was called
into service to incline toward hidden springs or indicate
the presence of precious metals under the surface of the
earth.[1] A number of astrological instruments, with which
the brotherhood was provided, ultimately passed into the
possession of the Philosophical Society of Pennsylvania.
Another interesting superstition was their faith in talismans (*Anhängsel*). The latter consisted commonly of
small pieces of parchment or paper, or sometimes of thin
stone or metal, on which were written some magic symbols,
consecrated with occult ceremonies, at moments when the
planets were supposed to be of particular power.[2] The
talisman was supposed to be effectual in securing personal
safety, bodily and spiritual, against accidents and evil
spirits, or to be possessed of magnetic power, or virtue to
heal wounds and diseases. Mystic healing powers were
attributed also to the saintlike Kelpius, who, after the
brotherhood became better known, was visited by many
sectarians of Pennsylvania. Abel Noble, the leader of the
Sabbatarians, frequently visited the brotherhood in their
tabernacle in the forest, and conferences took place also
with the Swedish pastors, Rudman and Aurén. An effort
was made by Kelpius to combine the numerous sects under
one church roof, in a united Christianity, but it was without success. Conrad Matthai was prominent in this attempt.
The Moravian Zinzendorf, nearly half a century later, tried
again to realize that glorious dream, but was likewise
unsuccessful.

[1] Sachse, in his youth, was shown a bed of iron ore, not far from Germantown, which was said to have been located by one of the divining-rods.
See Sachse, *The German Pietists of Provincial Pennsylvania*, part I.

[2] One of the *Anhängsel* most in demand was prepared at midnight on St.
John's Eve and buried for a time where the Sonnenwend fire had been.
This special one was supposed to protect against all evil spirits. Sachse,
The German Pietists, part I.

JOHANN KELPIUS

Kelpius lived until 1708 or 1709, an interesting account of his dying day coming down to us through an attendant, named Geissler. Kelpius suffered from the widespread disease so well called the white plague, and his consumptive frame wasted away slowly. He pleaded with his Lord for a transfiguration, such as was granted Enoch and Elias, but upon the third day of his prayers he said resignedly to his faithful famulus: " My beloved Daniel, I am not to attain that to which I aspired. I have received my answer: it is, that dust I am, and to dust I am to return. It is ordained that I shall die like all other children of Adam." With that the hermit handed Geissler [1] a box which he told him to cast into the river. Geissler, thinking that the box might contain objects of value, hid it away, but on his return, Kelpius told him that he had not obeyed his behest. Frightened by such clairvoyance, Geissler took the box and threw it into the river, when it flashed and thundered (*geblitzet und gedonnert*). Returning to Kelpius, the master thanked him. This is an instance of the faith which people reposed in the occult powers of the mystic brotherhood.

The logical successor of the hermits on the Wissahickon was the Ephrata Community on the banks of the Cocalico,[2] Lancaster County. A branch of this new society flourished in Germantown and vicinity, and a massive stone building was erected in 1738 on the Wissahickon, a short distance from the spot where the original tabernacle stood. The location is within the confines of Fairmount Park, where an interesting history is hidden behind such park signs as

---

[1] Geissler, when an old man, reported these incidents to Mühlenberg, in 1742. See *Hallesche Nachrichten*, pp. 1265–1266. Reprint (Philadelphia), vol. ii, p. 640.

[2] For an account of the Ephrata cloister, and its founder, Conrad Beissel, see Chapter v, pp. 114–115.

" Hermit Glen," " Hermit Bridge," " Hermit Lane," suggesting, alas, to but few of the thousands of daily visitors, the memory of the ancient hermit of the Wissahickon.

With the settlement of Germantown in 1683 and its increasing prosperity, the Germans had gained, by the end of the seventeenth century, a permanent foothold on American soil. Located close to Philadelphia, the leading port of entry, and founded just in advance of the larger migrations of the eighteenth century, Germantown served as a base for the distribution of the German people over the area most favorable, through climatic and natural conditions, for the increase of their race. They fully availed themselves of this splendid opportunity, as will be told in succeeding chapters.

CHAPTER III

INCREASE IN GERMAN IMMIGRATION IN THE EIGHTEENTH CENTURY, AND ITS CAUSES

Conditions in the Palatinate and in the southwestern German countries — Causes for emigration — Immigrant hunting — Newlanders and their methods — The redemptionist system ; advantages and evils — Crowding, extortion, shipwrecks — The Deutsche Gesellschaft of Philadelphia improves conditions.

In the first decades of the eighteenth century there rose a great tide of German immigration. Its volume presents a strange contrast to the sparseness of German settlements in the seventeenth century, the period that has just been passed in review. The change was produced by historical causes, operating as mighty forces. Destructive wars, religious persecution, relentless oppression by petty tyrants, rendered existence unendurable at home, while favorable reports from earlier settlers beyond the Atlantic, more plentiful means of transportation, and an innate desire for adventure (the German *Wanderlust*), made irresistible the attraction of the foreign shore. The area which furnished the largest number of immigrants was the southwestern part of Germany, the Palatinate, Würtemberg, Baden, and Switzerland, perhaps in that very order. Sometimes all of the causes just mentioned united to compel an exodus from a particular district, as in the case of the Palatinate, while in Switzerland, with a nominally freer government, religious persecution was the main cause of emigration. The emigrations from the Palatinate[1] for a time surpassed in

[1] The geographical borders of the Palatinate at that time exceeded the present limits of the Rhenish Palatinate, which is to-day a part of Bavaria.

extent those from all other parts of Germany, so much so that in England and America emigrants from Germany were commonly called Palatines, and curiously enough we meet in an historical document the phrase, " a Palatine from Holsteyn."

In order to understand more clearly the situation as it existed in the Rhine country and in the southwestern part of Germany at the beginning of the eighteenth century, it will be necessary to get a closer view [1] of each of the main causes of discontent, viz., the wars, the religious persecutions, and the tyranny of small rulers.

The most destructive of all the wars that devastated Germany was the Thirty Years' War, 1618–48, than which none more terrible is known to history. It is an accepted fact that in its material development Germany was set back two hundred years. Throughout Germany seventy-five per cent of the inhabitants were killed, and the property loss was far greater. Statistics are furnished by Freytag for the county of Henneberg,[2] showing that in the course of the war seventy-five per cent of the inhabitants, sixty-

---

It extended from the Neckar Valley, downstream on both sides of the Rhine as far as Oppenheim, Alzei, and Bacharach, and from the Bergstrasse (the old Roman road running along the Odenwald from Darmstadt to Heidelberg) on the east, to the Hardt Mountains on the west. Mannheim, Heidelberg, Worms, Alzei were within its borders. Its area was about 340 German square miles, a little less than the area of the present state of Massachusetts, and the number of inhabitants about 500,000.

[1] Cf. the following : Dändliker, *Geschichte der Schweiz ;* Freytag, " Aus dem Jahrhundert des groszen Krieges," vol. iii of *Bilder aus der deutschen Vergangenheit ;* Häusser, *Geschichte der Rheinischen Pfalz.*

For brief accounts see : Kapp, F., *Geschichte der Deutschen im Staate New York* (N. Y. 1867), pp. 58–145. Reprinted in *Geschichtsblätter* (edited by Carl Schurz), vol. i, New York, 1884 ; Kuhns, *German and Swiss Settlements of Pennsylvania*, chap. i.

[2] Within the present borders partly of Saxe-Weimar, Prussia, and the Saxon Principalities, i. e., in Central Germany. For statistics, see Freytag, pp. 234 ff.

six per cent of the houses, eighty-five per cent of the horses, and over eighty-two per cent of the cattle were destroyed. He also proves that the number of houses and inhabitants in this locality did not again reach the ante-bellum number, until 1849, i. e., two hundred years later.

The southwestern part of Germany fared no better, the Palatinate worst of all, being repeatedly visited by the contending armies. The ruler of the Palatinate at the beginning of the war was the unfortunate Frederick V, the Winter King, who, after accepting the leadership of the Protestant cause, was badly defeated in Bohemia. The war was carried into his own country, when General Tilly, in 1622, laid waste that fair and prosperous land. Ten years later Gustavus Adolphus expelled the Imperialists from the Palatinate, but after the battle of Nördlingen, the troops of Sweden and Bernhard of Saxe-Weimar, far from acting as friends and allies, gave to the country, as a contemporary expressed it, "the Last Ointment." In 1635 came the Spaniards under Gallas, who exceeded even the Imperialists and Swedes in brutality and spoliation, leaving behind them only " glowing iron and millstones." As elsewhere, terrible tortures [1] were inflicted to obtain information concerning hidden treasures, and death was but a mercy, saving from torments and dreaded exile.

The Palatinate was again ravaged by the French and Bavarians in 1639, and the first good crop thereafter, that of 1641, was also destroyed. In 1644 and 1645 the old

---

[1] For a graphic description of the methods employed by the troopers of the Thirty Years' War, cf. the German contemporary novel of the seventeenth century, Grimmelshausen's *Simplicissimus*. One of the most diabolical of the tortures employed was that of putting salt on the soles of a peasant landlord and getting a goat to lick off the salt. The agonized laughter of the victim furnished amusement for the brutal bystanders, who liberated him only upon his disclosing the hiding-places of the last precious pieces of his property.

foes overran and robbed, with their traditional savagery. In the last years of the war neither friend nor foe any longer entered the Palatinate, the melancholy fact staring them in the face that there was no longer anything to steal, — the most fertile area of Germany having become a desert.

The moral degradation following in the wake of such devastation was even worse than the loss of life and property. Friend could not be distinguished from foe, and men would wrest from their starving neighbors a crust of bread. It has been recorded that not even human flesh was sacred, that the gallows and churchyards were put under guard to protect them against theft by desperate, famine-stricken people. Incredible as it may seem, in some instances even murder and cannibalism were resorted to. The neighborhood of the city of Worms, once a centre of European civilization, a free imperial city, at times the residence of emperors, now afforded cover for a group of beggars, who fell upon passers-by and devoured their bodies for sustenance. The destruction of fields and property had another disastrous effect, disposing the surviving tillers of the soil to become camp-followers, as the easiest way of procuring a living. Self-reliant toil was thus given another inducement to idleness and consequent demoralization.

A ray of hope lightened the Palatinate, when, immediately after the war, the Elector Karl Ludwig ascended the throne. He was the son of the ill-starred Winter King, a sensible, duty-loving, and economical ruler, whose character had been formed in the school of adversity. While in exile in London, he had witnessed the death of Charles I, his uncle, on the scaffold. Returning to the Palatinate, instead of a land of plenty, he found a barren waste. A dis-

aster of such magnitude could not be repaired within a
short time, but Karl Ludwig contributed more than one
man's share to the social and material betterment of his
native land. Still, even within his lifetime, there began a
new series of misfortunes. In 1674 Louis XIV sent Tu-
renne into the Palatinate, to burn and plunder. In some
districts the inhabitants dared not cultivate their fields for
the succeeding three years. The knightly challenge of the
helpless elector for a duel with Louis XIV was not accepted. The pillaging continued, and the elector was even
forced to pay tribute. In 1680 the French despot invaded
the Palatinate in time of peace. It was the year of Karl
Ludwig's death, and his successors could and would do nothing to lessen the sufferings of the people. The most
cruel invasion of all was that which Louis XIV made in
1688, again without declaration of war, and on an absurd
claim to the territory by inheritance through Elizabeth, the
late elector's daughter, who had married the Duke of Orleans, brother of the French king. The beautiful castle of
Heidelberg and the city of Mannheim were burned in the
severe winter of 1688–89. The Palatinate was to be made
and kept a desert in order not to serve as a granary for the
enemies of France. The beautiful cities of Speyer and
Worms presently shared the fate of Heidelberg and Mannheim. These cities, through centuries famed for their prosperity, now harbored a pauper population. Even less consideration was shown the people in smaller towns and in
the innumerable villages. The greed and cruelty of the
French troops surpassed even the record of the "Landsknechte" of the Thirty Years' War. When nearly five
hundred thousand Palatines were driven from devastated
fields and burning houses, no humanitarian hand was
raised to render assistance. Exile was followed by famine,

famine by pestilence, and all the finer impulses of the human heart were extinguished in the gross wretchedness of brutalizing despair.

A remarkable fact in the history of the Palatinate is, that during the brief intervals of peace, between successive invasions in the seventeenth century (and they by no means discontinued at its close), the country showed most wonderful recuperative power. Whenever a period of ten years of peace was vouchsafed, the country prospered to such an enormous degree, that it again became an alluring bait for warlike neighbors. The fertility of the soil, the industry and agricultural skill of the population, "a nation of farmers through thirty generations," invariably transformed again the desert into a garden. The invading armies in the Thirty Years' War and those of Louis XIV frequently took advantage of this ability to recover, allowing the country just time enough to grow new crops again, before reinvasion. On one occasion a French army, after having robbed a district of everything it possessed, returned seeds to the farmers, so that they might prepare another harvest for the soldiers. The farmers by and by refused to turn the sod and raise crops for others to reap.

Under the electors of the Palatinate, succeeding Karl Ludwig, another cause for popular dissatisfaction was added. Karl Ludwig, though himself a Catholic, had been tolerant in matters of religion. His successors were fanatics, or ruled entirely under the influence of Jesuit advisers. The persecution of Protestants, the Lutheran and Reformed, was carried on systematically, their church property being confiscated to a very large extent, and the worshipers in many cases expelled from the country. This was done even in contravention of treaties or agreements, and caused reprisals in the Protestant countries, taken against the Catholic inhabitants. A cessation of terrorism was thus frequently brought about, at least officially. The law of the stronger, however, continued in force, and denominations other than Lutheran or Reformed, such as Huguenots, Waldenses, Mennonites, Quakers, *et al.*, had no rights which the government was bound to respect.

The third cause for emigration which already existed in the seventeenth, but became far more compelling in the eighteenth century, was the tyranny of the princes of small domains. Germany was broken up into hundreds of practically independent principalities, whose rulers generally imitated the example of Louis XIV. They impoverished the people through heavy taxation, levied to support an extravagant court, that hunted, feasted, and reveled, until bankruptcy or revolution put an end to their riotous living. The peasant classes were the principal sufferers, and long-suffering they were indeed, throughout western Europe, until their day dawned, near the close of the eighteenth century, with the French Revolution. In the mean time the " Landesväter " (or, as they have been dubbed, " Landesverräter ") thumbscrewed their faithful subjects, until they were reduced to serfdom or beggary. Conditions were no better in Würtemberg, Baden, or any part of the southwestern German territory. Not only did the princes tyrannously disregard the economic welfare of their subjects, but several of them added religious persecution to the other inflictions. All the more did the persecuted hold fast to their religion, whatever sect they belonged to, being all that was left them, a treasure that could not be attacked by dust or rust, or the lust of princes. The history of the period is replete with instances of heroism displayed in the cause of religion, the various sectarians proving equal devotion to their particular faith. A fond hope for betterment of their earthly condition rose in their hearts with the good reports from the American colonists under English[1] rule, a hope made more vivid by the eloquence of serious men such as William Penn, — a hope that suddenly seemed capable of realization, when what appeared to the Palatines as a direct invitation from Queen Anne of England came for them to settle in her transatlantic colonies. The wretchedness of their present condition, the impossibility of future improvement seeming never so evident as now, turned sentiment into resolution, and what might be likened to a tidal wave of immigration formed quickly and swept from the Rhine to the shores of England, thence to turn impulsively and with compelling force toward the promised land. The story of this first great exodus, the Palatine immigration to the colony of New York, will be the subject of the succeeding chapter.

The principal causes of the great German immigration in the eighteenth century were found to have been religious persecutions, the tyranny of autocrats, destructive wars, failure of crops and famine, economic bankruptcy. The flames of immigration once having a good start, a gale soon arose, which fanned them into a conflagration beyond control. There were then as there are now, in our own day, various artificial aids operating toward the increase or steady continuance of immigration. Such were, firstly, more frequent opportunities of transportation, prepared by profit-seeking ship-owners or ship-companies, and secondly, more abundant information or communication supplied gratuitously by the selfish interests of ad-

---

[1] On the Continent Prussia, since the time of the Great Elector, had stood for religious tolerance, and had invited the persecuted sectarians to settle in her territory.

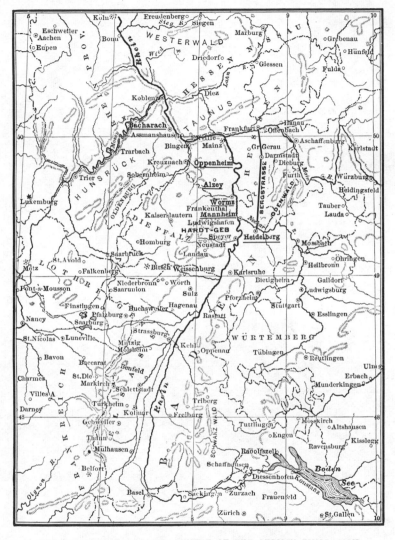

THE PALATINATE. AND THE CENTRE OF THE GERMAN EMIGRATION

DISTRICT IN THE EIGHTEENTH CENTURY

vertising agents and land speculators. The perils of the immigrant by land and sea furnish a theme that cannot be exhausted within the limits of the present chapter, but a brief survey may fittingly precede the historical outline of the German settlements in the eighteenth century, may serve to increase our admiration of the courage and heroism of the early immigrants, and remind us also that neither cleverness nor gullibility was born within our own generation.

The immigrant agents were either employed by ship companies in Holland or England, or in many cases acted on their own initiative. They were commonly called "newlanders" (*Neuländer*), and frequently had been failures as colonists in America, or at all events found immigrant-hunting a more profitable occupation. "They receive," says Mittelberger,[1] "from their merchants in Rotterdam or Amsterdam for every person of ten years and over, three florins or a ducat; whereas the merchants in Philadelphia, sixty, seventy, or eighty florins for such a person, in proportion as said person has incurred more or less debts during the voyage." The newlanders not only obtained a commission from the so-called merchants or shipowners, but had many opportunities of extracting money from the immigrants, whom they pretended to serve as friends or patrons. In their dress they affected the appearance of wealth begotten in America, wearing pocket watches with heavy gold chains as a sample of the gold to

---

[1] Gottlieb Mittelberger's *Journey to Pennsylvania* in the year 1750 and return to Germany in 1754, showing not only a description of the country according to its present condition, but also a detailed account of the sad and unfortunate circumstances of most of the Germans that have immigrated or are immigrating to that country. Translated from the German by C. T. Eben, Philadelphia, 1898. See p. 38. The German original was published in Stuttgart, 1756.

be found lying in the streets of the new country. Stories of rapid advancement in wealth or station constantly issued from their mouths, — " The maid had become a lady, the peasant a nobleman, the artisan a baron, the officers of the government held their places by the will of the people." The newlanders carried about with them letters from acquaintances, perhaps from some one of the same village, now settled in America, prosperous and anxious that his friends should share his happiness. Such letters were often forged by the skillful hand of the newlander who could " imitate all characters, marks and tokens so admirably that even he whose handwriting they had imitated, must acknowledge it to be their own. By means of such practices they deceived even people who are not credulous." [1]

Quantities of descriptive pamphlets and advertisements were circulated, revealing brilliant prospects for settlers in Pennsylvania, Carolina, and elsewhere,[2] some of them of so seductive a nature that governments found it necessary on their part to circulate literature with a view to counteracting the dangerous influence. An instance of a prohibition against newlanders was that reported by Christoph Sauer in his newspaper in 1751 : " The Elector Palatine has issued a command that no newlanders are to be tolerated in the whole of the Palatinate; that if captured they should be thrown into prison." [3] In spite of such mandates the newlanders succeeded in accomplishing their purposes by the most effective of their methods,

[1] Mittelberger, p. 42.

[2] For attempts to get German settlers to New England, see Chapter IX, pp. 254 ff.

[3] Cf. also Kapp, *Die Deutschen im Staate New York* (1867). Dokumentarischer Anhang, pp. 385–397. (5) " Kaiser Joseph's Auswanderungs-Verbot " ; (6) " Formulär eines holländischen Seelen Verkäufers Lockzettels" ; (7) " Dienstvertrag eines Auswanderers."

house to house visitation, performed in secret, under the disguise of fellow countrymen returning from America.[1] Watchful for an opportunity to make a favorable impression, they would expatiate, in the appropriate local dialect, upon the glorious opportunities waiting in America, in comparison with the restrictions and abuses at home, and then, if possible, speedily arrange a plan of exit by way of the Rhine and the Netherlands.

A good example of the literature used to excite in the common people the desire for immigration is the little book written in the interests of South Carolina, and extensively circulated throughout Switzerland and the Palatinate, entitled: "Der Nunmehro in der neuen Welt vergnügt und ohne Heim-Wehe lebende Schweitzer. Oder: Kurtze und eigentliche Beschreibung Des gegenwärtigen Zustandes der königlichen Englischen Provinz Carolina, aus den neulich angekommenen Briefen der Alldorten sich befindenden Schweitzeren zusammen getragen, von J. K. L.; Bern. Getruckt bey Johannes Bondeli," 1734. The booklet pretends to give the impressions recorded in letters of Swiss settlers located in South Carolina, notably those in Purysburg. The pleasures of house and home on large acreage are emphasized. The land literally flows with milk and honey — the cows roaming about on perfect pasturage all the year round, and honey being found abundantly in hollow trees. Wild turkeys are found in flocks of five hundred, geese, — that some of the farmers possess in flocks to the number of two hundred, — furnish choice feather beds. As for game, the

---

[1] Cf. H. A. Rattermann in *Der deutsche Pionier*, vols. xiv, xv, and xvi, in connection with his articles, "Geschichte des deutschen Elements im Staate Maine," where he furnishes a very full account of the work and wiles of several immigrant agents, with reprints of advertisements, etc.

bisons put their heads through the windows of the log
cabins waiting to be shot; the wolves are by no means as
large as the European, and can be tamed. The taste of
venison in Carolina far surpasses anything in Europe, the
bears are smaller and frequently seen herding with the
swine. The alligator (*Allegatter*) has no terrors, it is diminutive in comparison with the crocodile of the Old
World, and the Indians and negroes use its tail for food.
The danger of overpopulation, which is the main cause for
emigration in Switzerland, can never exist in Carolina,
with its length of three hundred and seventy hours[1] and
breadth of more than one thousand hours. An appendix
follows, consisting of letters from Swiss colonists located
inland, furnishing positive proof that the Switzer in Carolina is happy and lives without the dreaded homesickness,
that preys upon the Swiss when in a foreign country.

The book seems to have been so seductive in its effect,
that it called forth a reply, written perhaps under the
auspices of the Town Council of Bern, who, on March 17,
1735, gave directions for the distribution of the following
counterblast, entitled: " Neue Nachricht alter und neuer
Merkwürdigkeiten, enthaltend ein vertrautes Gespräch und
sichere Briefe von der Landschaft Carolina und übrigen
Englischen Pflanzstädten in Amerika, zufinden zu Zürich,
Bern, Basel, Schaffhausen, und St. Gallen in den Bericht-
häusern gegen Ende des Jahres Siebzehn hundert vier und
dreissig." The latter also was calculated to reach the very
heart of the immigrant. In the form of a dialogue between
a likely young fellow of twenty-five and the schoolmaster,
the whole subject of immigration to Carolina is discussed,

---

[1] An hour is about three English miles. The distances as stated are of
course overestimated ; it was not known how far the land extended westward.

in the hypercritical manner of a Mittelberger. Pictured in lurid coloring appear the dangers of the passage, the mortality on shipboard, the slavery awaiting colonists on the other side, hopelessly duped by dishonest ship captains and newlanders. Any number of irksome tribulations are emphasized, such as breaking your plow far out in the Carolina wilderness, when there is no smith within a hundred miles to repair it, or the impossibility of obtaining seed in sowing time or a spade when you want to dig, and the "plentiful" game running over the crops and ruining them, when the outraged farmer cannot buy a gun to shoot down the intruding beasts. If the harvest be rich a sickle is surely lacking, and the farmer has to pull the grain out with his hands. Such aggravating little troubles, so skillfully designed to terrify the Swiss peasant, are represented as depriving the settler of every comfort in life. Lastly the argument is made, "If Carolina be fair, Switzerland is fairer, who might gainsay that?" In conclusion follows an appeal to the patriotism of the Swiss, who is called on to decide — though he has never been in America — which of the two countries is the more beautiful. His national pride being thus appealed to, the answer cannot be in doubt for a moment.[1] This reply, so shrewdly conceived and bearing governmental sanction, undoubtedly had for a time a strong counteracting influence upon literary propagandism. However, immigration went on, regardless of literature pro and con, as if impelled by elemental forces, uncontrolled by sentiment, but governed by natural laws.

---

[1] The two above-named pamphlets are described in detail, with extracts, by Ludwig Hirzel, in a series of articles, entitled "Nach Amerika aus dem Anfang des achtzehnten Jahrhunderts." *Sonntagsblatt des Bunds*, Bern, November 8, 15, 22, 29, and December 6, 13, 20, 1896.

A system was established very early in American colonial history, by which an immigrant could get to the promised land, though not in possession of the means to pay for his passage. He would agree to serve from three to seven years in the colonies until the price of his transportation was paid off to the shipmaster who had advanced it. At the end of his term he was released, given a suit of clothes, sometimes money or land, and awarded all the rights of a free citizen. Hence the term redemptioners (because redeemed) was applied to this class of immigrants, who were also known as " indented servants." At first the system seemed humane and liberal, yielding the poor ultimately the same opportunities as the well-to-do. It had been advocated by Furley, the agent of William Penn, and had been in vogue in Virginia since the first decade of that colony's existence.[1] The system began to be applied extensively to German immigration about 1728. Mühlenberg describes the arrival of a ship in Philadelphia in the following manner :[2] —

" Before the ship is allowed to cast anchor in the harbor, the immigrants are all examined, as to whether any contagious disease be among them. The next step is to bring all the new arrivals in a procession before the city hall and there compel them to take the oath of allegiance to the king of Great Britain. After that they are brought back to the ship. Those that have paid their passage are released, the others are advertised in the newspapers for sale. The ship becomes the market. The buyers make their choice and bargain with the immigrants for a certain number of years and days, depending upon the price demanded

[1] The redemptionist system was also in existence among the French of the West Indies, and among the French and Spanish in Louisiana; " Les engagés " was the name for indented servants. Cf. Hanno Deiler, *Zur Geschichte der Deutschen am unteren Mississippi. Das Redemptionsystem im Staate Louisiana.* New Orleans, 1902.

[2] *Hallesche Nachrichten*, vol. ii, 998, note. Reprint, vol. ii, pp. 460–461.

by the ship captain or other 'merchant' who made the outlay for transportation, etc. Colonial governments recognize the written contract, which is then made binding for the redemptioner. The young unmarried people of both sexes are very quickly sold, and their fortunes are either good or bad, according to the character of the buyer. Old married people, widows, and the feeble, are a drug on the market, but if they have sound children, then their transportation charges are added to those of the children, and the latter must serve the longer. This does not save families from being separated in the various towns or even provinces. Again, the healthiest are taken first, and the sick are frequently detained beyond the period of recovery, when a release would frequently have saved them ! "

Not only tillers of the soil and artisans became serfs for their passage money, students and schoolmasters also were often sold in this labor market. The Reverend Mr. Kunze naïvely writes, that he had entertained the thought, if ever he became the owner of twenty pounds, of buying the first German student who would land at Philadelphia, put him into his garret, and there with his help begin a Latin school,[1] which he was sure would quickly pay off the outlay. People of rank, who had lost their money, fared no better than the low-born peasant. There was Frederick Helfenstein,[2] probably a lineal descendant of Count Helfenstein and the Emperor Maximilian, who was compelled to sell himself as a redemptioner in Georgia. Mittelberger tells us of a noble lady, who, with her two

---

[1] *Hallesche Nachrichten*, p. 1377. Reprint, vol. ii, pp. 709–710. The following advertisement appeared in *Pennsylvanischer Staatsbote*, January 18, 1774: "Deutsche Leute. — Es sind noch 50–60 deutsche Leute welche neulich von Deutschland hier angekommen sind, vorhanden, so bei der Wittwe Kreiderin im goldenen Schwan logiren. Darunter sind zwei Schulmeister, Handwerksleute, Bauren, auch artige Kinder, sowohl Knaben als Mädchen. Sie möchten für ihre Fracht dienen."

[2] Strobel, *History of the Salzburgers*, p. 117.

half-grown daughters and a young son, in 1753, was compelled to serve, having lost her thousand rix-talers given for safe-keeping to a newlander, who proved to be an embezzler. John Wesley speaks of John Reinier of Switzerland, who " while provided with money, books and drugs " was robbed by the captain and forced to sell himself for seven years. Advertisements were found in the newspapers that did not tactfully distinguish between redemptioner and slave. For example : —

"To be sold — A likely Servant Woman having three years and a half to serve. She is a good spinner." ("Pennsylvania Gazette," June, 1742.) "To be sold — A Dutch apprentice lad, who has five years and three months to serve ; he has been brought up to the tailor's business. Can work well." ("Pennsylvanischer Staatsbote," 14 December, 1773.) [1]

The profits in the transportation of redemptioners were greater than in that of passengers who paid their way. The latter were therefore made the victims of extortions, from the very beginning of their journey, namely, the passage down the Rhine. The number of toll stations [2] was legion, and on passing from one principality to another all the baggage had to be reëxamined, a duty never done with a view to expedition, but regulated by the convenience of the customs officials. Fees were demanded with such frequency by agents of all kinds, that the unhappy

[1] Cf. Eickhoff, *In der neuen Heimat*, p. 145.

[2] As late as 1804, Dr. Fried. Hermann (of Lübeck), who investigated the transportation facilities of German immigrants, reported on the trip from Heilbronn (on the Neckar) to Rotterdam as follows : " Diese Reise dauert blos von Heilbronn aus 4 bis 6 Wochen, weil die Rheinschiffe bis an die holländische Gränze nicht weniger als 36 Zollstätten zu passieren haben, und bei jeder derselben visitiert werden, ein Geschäft wobei die Zollbeamten m r auf ihre Bequemlichkeit als auf die schnelle Abfertigung der Schiffe ücksicht nehmen." Hermann, *Die Deutschen in Nordamerika*, 1806, p. 14. E rlier conditions were much worse. Cf. Mittelberger, *supra*, p. 18.

Redemptioners.

THERE still remain on board the ship Aurora, from Amsterdam, about 18 passengers, amongst whom are,

Servant girls, gardeners, butchers, masons, sugar bakers, bread bakers, 1 shoemaker, 2 silver smith, 1 leather dresser, 1 tobacconist, 1 pastry cook, and some a little acquainted with waiting on families, as well as farming and tending horses, &c. They are all in good health. Any person desirous of being accommodated in the above branches will please speedily to apply to
Captain JOHN BOWLES,
in the stream, off Fell's-Point:
Who offers for Sale,
80 Iron-bound Water Casks
1 chest elegant Fowling Pieces, single and double barrelled
15,000 Dutch Brick, and
Sundry ships Provisions.
July 14.   d3t-e94t

ADVERTISEMENT OF REDEMPTIONERS ON SALE

This Indenture MADE the *Thirtieth* Day of *May*
in the Year of our Lord one thousand, seven hundred and *eighty four* BETWEEN *Alexr Beard of Broughshane in the County of Antrim Taylor by Consent of his Father* of the one Part, and *John Duhey of Cullybackey in the said Country —— Gentleman* of the other Part, WITNESSETH, that the said *Alexandr Beard* doth hereby covenant, promise and grant, to and with the said *John Duhey —— his ——* Executors, Administrators and Assigns, from the Day of the Date hereof until the first and next Arrival at *Philadelphia ——* in America, and after for and during the Term of *three ——* Years to serve in such Service and Employment as the said *John Duhey ——* or *his* Assigns shall there employ *him* according to the Custom of the Country in the like Kind. In Consideration whereof the said *John Duhey ——* doth hereby covenant and grant to and with the said *Alexr Beard* to pay for *his* Passage, and to find allow *him* Meat, Drink, Apparel and Lodging, with other Necessaries, during the said Term; and at the End of the said Term to pay unto *him* the usual Allowance, according to the Custom of the Country in the like Kind. IN WITNESS whereof the Parties above-mentioned to these Indentures have interchangeably put their Hands and Seals, the Day and Year first above written.

Signed, Sealed, and Delivered,
in the Presence of

Peter Dutton

John Weir

Alexr Beard

John Duhey

FACSIMILE OF AN INDENTURE

immigrant had little left by the time he got to the Netherlands. His possessions, though carefully enshrined in
heavy oaken boxes fastened with good iron bolts, were
not secure against the cupidity of newlander or sea-captain. If boxes, trunks, and bales were numerous, they
were as likely as not to be left behind, or loaded into another vessel. The latter mode of disposing of the baggage
of immigrants became one of the greatest abuses of
transatlantic transportation. Well-to-do immigrants, who
had put into their trunks linen or clothing necessary for
their journey, or perhaps even their food and cooking
utensils, were deprived of these necessities and comforts
during the whole voyage. Often having placed all their
earthly possessions, including money, in their chests, they
never saw them again, and were compelled on arrival to
sell themselves as redemptioners in preference to becoming
paupers. Another tyrannical measure was that of holding
the entire body of immigrants on a ship responsible for
the total transportation charges. The well-to-do would
have to pay for those who could not, or be themselves
sold as redemptioners. This arrangement protected the
captain against loss, in case a large number of redemptioners died on the way, and also gave him an excuse for
extortions. The Germans of Philadelphia attempted to
legislate against these abuses, beginning in 1750, but for
a long time were unsuccessful, because of the presence
in high places of influential grafters heavily interested in
the profits of immigrant transportation.

While the immigration increased, strangely enough the
expense of a sea-passage rose from six or ten, to fourteen
or seventeen louis d'or [1] (according to Mühlenberg), thus

[1] The present money equivalent of the louis d'or is about $4.50. Its pur-
chasing power at that time was far greater than this sum.

forcing more people into the redemptionist class. With over-speculation came the crowding of large bodies of immigrants into vessels too small for their numbers. Their baggage was then quite generally put into another vessel or lost altogether. The mortality on board increased terribly. Sauer, in his newspaper in 1749, announced " that in that year over two thousand had died during transportation, mostly because they were not treated like human beings, being packed closely together, so that the sick breathed another's breath, and that from all the uncleanness and stench and failure of food, diseases arose like scurvy, dysentery, smallpox, and other contagious sicknesses." It was the rule in that day that the immigrant should furnish his own food supplies, but when his baggage was not received on board, the provision made for him was of course not ample. Starvation, and death from thirst, were of common occurrence on the long sea-trips consuming many months. Shipwrecks were frequent, and the danger ever present of being captured by hostile fleets or pirates. Heinrich Keppele, the first president of the German Society of Pennsylvania,[1] arrived in America

---

[1] Mittelberger claims that a large number of the shipwrecks were not reported in Germany, " for fear that it might deter the people from emigrating, and induce them to stay at home." (See p. 36.) Among the many shipwrecks that he tells of, the following is characteristic : "The following fatal voyage, where all the passengers were Germans, has probably not become known in Germany at all. In the year 1752 a ship arrived at Philadelphia, which was fully six months at sea from Holland to Philadelphia. The ship had weathered many storms throughout the winter, and could not reach the land; finally another ship came to the assistance of the half-wrecked and starved vessel. Of about 340 souls this ship brought 21 persons to Philadelphia, who stated that they had not only spent fully six months at sea, and had been driven to the coast of Ireland, but that most of the passengers had died of starvation, that they had lost their masts and sails, captain and mates, and that the rest would never have reached the land if God had not sent another ship to their aid, which brought them to land."

in 1738, and wrote in his diary, that of the 312½ passengers (a child was counted as one half), 250 died, not including those that died after landing. Sauer reports the loss of 160 people on one ship, 150 on another, and only 13 survivors on a third; in 1745 a ship was destined for Philadelphia with 400 German passengers, of whom only 50 survived. Mittelberger says: "Children from one to seven years rarely survived the voyage; and many a time parents are compelled to see their children die of hunger, thirst, or sickness, and then see them cast into the water. Few women in confinement escape with their lives; many a mother is cast into the water with her child." The main cause for the enormous mortality was the packing together[1] of immigrants much as negro slaves were later huddled together by African slave-traders.

The conditions were probably no worse for the German immigrants than for those of other nationalities. The Germans of Philadelphia, however, after repeated agitation, succeeded in improving somewhat existing conditions for German immigrants. They formed in December, 1764, the "Deutsche Gesellschaft von Pennsylvanien," the first of those charitable German organizations in the seacoast cities of America, that were founded to extend a helping hand to the immigrants of their own nationality. A law was drafted and put through the Pennsylvania legislature by the influential Germans of this society, rendering impossible the tyrannies and extortions before practiced by sea-captains and immigration agents, particularly in regard to the abuses already mentioned,

---

[1] Packed like herring and sold as slaves, says Pastor Kunze, *Hallesche Nachrichten*, p. 1377. Reprint, vol. ii, p. 709. Under date of May 16, 1773, he says: "Last week I heard of a ship bearing 1500 Germans, of whom 1100 died at sea."

the separation of immigrants from their baggage, over-
crowding, and holding a shipload responsible for the
profits of the captain. The society likewise established
the immigrant's right of appeal to American courts of
justice, in case of unjust treatment. A more effective law,
"an act for regulating the importation of German and
other passengers," was passed by the Pennsylvania legislature in 1818.

The sale of redemptioners was not abolished until 1820.
With its many evils the system had also had good effects.
Undoubtedly the rapid increase of the population of
Pennsylvania was due to the redemptionist system, which
allowed tens of thousands of immigrants to come to America, who would not have been able to do so for lack of
means. The period of service frequently became a training school. The Swedish traveler Kalm said : [1] "Many of
the Germans who come hither bring money enough with
them to pay their passage, but rather suffer themselves to
be sold, with a view that during their servitude they may
get some knowledge of the language and qualities of the
country and the like, that they may be better able to consider what they shall do, when they have got their liberty."
Stories are found in German-American literature, of redemptioners,[2] who concealed within a bundle of old rags
their precious coins, for which, as soon as their period of
service had closed, they bought land near the possessions
of their masters, and during the course of years, advancing in means through their industry and thrift, became ultimately the owners of the estates of their former masters.

[1] Peter Kalm, *Travels in North America*, vol. i, p. 304, 2d edition, London,
1772.

[2] Cf. Sealsfield, *Morton oder die grosse Tour*, I Teil, Kap. i, pp. 64 f.;
Kürnberger, *Der Amerikamüde*; O. Ruppius, *Der Pedlar, Roman aus dem
Amerikanischen Leben*, and *Das Vermächtnis des Pedlars*.

CHAPTER IV

THE FIRST EXODUS, THE PALATINE IMMIGRATION TO
NEW YORK

Kocherthal and his followers — Founding of Newburgh-on-the-Hudson, 1709
— The exodus of 1710; arrival in London; separation into various
groups, transportation to Ireland, South Carolina, etc. — The main group
goes with Governor Hunter to New York — Hunter's plan and its failure
— The fortunes and migrations of the Palatines in New York; East and
West Camp, Schoharie, the Mohawk, Tulpehocken, etc. — John Peter
Zenger's independent newspaper, and his stand for the liberty of the
press.

THROUGHOUT the seventeenth century there had been
constant intercourse between England and the Palatinate,
sanctioned and stimulated by the royal marriage of Elizabeth, daughter of James I, with the Elector Palatine,
Frederick V, already referred to as the Winter King.
Their son, the wise ruler Karl Ludwig, Elector Palatine,
was the cousin of Charles II and James II, kings of
England. There was also between the two countries the
common bond of the Protestant faith. England was
instrumental in effecting the Religious Declaration of
1705, that granted the Reformed Church toleration in the
Palatinate.

The war of the Spanish Succession in 1707 devastated
a portion of the Palatinate on the left bank of the Rhine,
whereby hundreds of Palatines were rendered homeless.
Among these was Joshua von Kocherthal, who, in January, 1708, applied to an English agency in Frankfort-on-
the-Main, for passes and money to go to England. He
included in his request several other families, in all sixty-

one persons, who, when no help could be obtained, together left their home without the consent of the Elector Palatine, and on their own resources traveled by way of Holland to London. Arriving there, they were too poor to live without aid, wherefore the generous Queen Anne allowed each Palatine a shilling a day for his support. The charitable deed of the crown was imitated by several Londoners, and when Kocherthal applied for the means of transportation to the American colonies, the Lords of Trade decided to send the immigrants to the colony of New York. There it was thought they might be used to settle on the frontier, as a buffer against the Indians, or else be employed in the manufacture of naval stores. Before sailing they were naturalized as British subjects,[1] and then placed upon a royal transport under Lord Lovelace, the newly-appointed governor of New York.

The colonists sailed about the middle of October, 1708, and arrived at New York during the last days of that year. Lord Lovelace gave them land on the Hudson to the north of the Highlands, beginning at the mouth of the Quassaick. The colonists called the settlement "Neuburg," after the city of the same name in the Upper Palatinate (*Oberpfalz*). This is the beginning of the busy and prosperous city of Newburgh, the county-seat of Orange County, New York, rivaling in beauty of landscape more venerable cities on the Rhine and Danube. Tracts of land of one hundred to three hundred acres were portioned out

---

[1] The names of the Palatines naturalized August 25, 1708, were, besides Kocherthal : Lorenz, Schwisser, Rennau, Volk, Weigandt Weber, Plettel, Fischer, Gülch, Türk, Rose, Weimar, Faber, Fiere, and Schünemann. Most of these were men between twenty-five and forty years of age; only one man was fifty-two. They were vine-growers, weavers, smiths, carpenters, or representatives of other trades. Among those given lands, not mentioned in the naturalization list, were Lockstädt and Hennicke. Kapp, *Geschichte der Deutschen im Staate New York*, p. 80.

to the settlers, fifty acres to each individual, whether man, woman, or child. Five hundred acres were reserved for the building of a church, forty acres for roads and highways.[1]

Lord Lovelace died in May, 1709, — a great misfortune for the colonists. He was their friend, and had advanced money for their support.[2] The Palatines were compelled to petition the colonial government for the maintenance promised them the first year, but as they happened to mention the fact that nineteen of their number had withdrawn from Lutheranism and turned Pietists, the discriminating government excluded the latter from its benefits. After an investigation, however, of the meaning of *Pietism*, by a special committee, supplies were furnished to them also, just as to the other colonists. Support was a necessity for all colonists during their first year, the first season being spent in clearing the forest and building rude habitations, essential labors before a crop could be raised. "The Palatine Parish by the Quassaick" was the name given to the whole settlement included in the *German Patent*, as constituted about ten years later (1719). The land in this region was not as fertile as was hoped for, the stony hillsides and rocky soil giving no rich returns, and in consequence many of the original inhabitants of Newburgh sold their lands to "Dutch and English New-comers" and departed for Schoharie County to the north, or to the Pennsylvania valleys of the Swatara and Tulpehocken. In this way Newburgh lost its distinctly German character.

Kocherthal was a man of unusual power over his constituents, of versatile occupation, being minister, farmer,

---

[1] Cobb, S. H., *The Story of the Palatines*, chap. iii, p. 66, etc. Putnam, 1897. Kapp, *supra*, pp. 82 ff.

[2] His widow did not receive a repayment from the government until many years later.

man of affairs, leader of men, whose sturdiness of character impressed its stamp upon an entire community, — an exceptional individual, one might say, if the exception were not of so frequent occurrence in German colonial history, with such examples as Pastorius, Conrad Weiser, Giessendanner, Joist Hite, and a succession of others down to the more recent Missourians, Follenius and Friedrich Münch. Kocherthal returned to England for a short visit, and then, accompanying Governor Hunter, sailed again for New York, in 1710, with the great migration of the Palatines. He organized a Lutheran church at West Camp and probably one also on the other side of the river. A Lutheran himself, he was acceptable nevertheless to the Germans of the Reformed church, and was regarded with reverence by the Germans on either side of the Hudson. He was frequently consulted by the provincial authorities for advice and assistance, when entanglements occurred with the German colonists. He died and was buried in 1719 at West Camp on the Hudson.[1]

The settlement on the Quassaick was but the forerunner of the extensive immigration that followed shortly after. The records are scant as to the inception and initial progress of that movement, but in addition to the impelling forces enumerated in the last chapter, an immediate cause must have been the extraordinary severity of the winter of 1708–09. In the words of Conrad Weiser,

---

[1] The story of the Newburgh church bell is an interesting little episode in connection with Kocherthal. It seems that the good Queen Anne presented Kocherthal, before his departure (and on his request), with a church bell for a Lutheran house of worship. Colonial conditions never permitted rapid realization of devout hopes, and for a long time the bell was loaned to the church of New York City, until the Quassaick Parish might be able to build a church. The bell was returned, probably in 1733, when Quassaick got its church, still known in the memory of the oldest inhabitants as the Glebe School House.

then a boy of twelve years, recorded in his autobiography: " Birds perished on the wing, beasts in their lairs, and mortals fell dead in the way." The success of Kocherthal, in gaining the assistance of Queen Anne, encouraged others to adopt the same course, and seek new homes beyond the sea. Religious persecution, political oppression, and economic ruin had made intolerable their dear native land ; impending ruin, famine, and the hope of aid now quickened their resolution, united their action, and, as if by a sudden common impulse, a vast number of Palatines flocked to the shores of England. The migration was probably one concerted at home, and when large numbers appeared at Rotterdam, the first gathering-place, they were speedily shipped off to London. They began to arrive there in May, 1709, and by the end of June their numbers rose to five thousand. The number was nearly doubled before August, and by October thirteen thousand Palatines were in London. These numbers are by no means exaggerated ; indeed, the popular impression reported was that thirty thousand Palatines swarmed to the English coast, " a migrating epidemic having seized on the stricken people." London, then no modern city capable of harboring hundreds of thousands of strangers without a tremor of excitement, was seriously embarrassed by this influx of foreigners, most of whom were reduced to pauperism, necessarily making an appeal to the charity of the nation. It will always redound to the glory of England that her management of this serious problem under trying conditions was most humane and generous. Starvation staring the needy Palatines in the face, England for months provided them with food. Having no homes, they were sheltered in barns, empty dwellings, warehouses, and a thousand tents taken from the army stores. The queen allowed each ninepence per day, for subsistence, and such lodgings as could best be obtained. The paupers of London grew envious of the provision made for the foreigners, and filed complaints against such exceptional treatment.

What to do with the hordes of foreigners was the next question before the Lords of Trade. The numbers, however, were so large that they could not easily be disposed of. A severe discrimination was made in the first place against the Catholics, who numbered about one tenth of the whole. They were all sent back to their homes, except a few hundred, who chose the alternative of becoming Protestants. The remaining Palatines wished for a settlement in America, and an interesting story, told by Conrad Weiser (reported by Mühlenberg),[1] explains the origin of this fixed idea of theirs. It happened that several Indian chiefs were visiting London, at the time when the Palatine exiles appeared in great numbers. The sight of the homeless and half-starved immigrants mightily engaged the sympathies of the redmen, one of whom, unsolicited, made a free-will offering to the queen of a tract of land on the Schoharie, in New York, for the use and benefit of the exiled Germans. It has frequently been evident in American history that the Indian, in spite of his savage instincts, could on occasion be generous; such, indeed, was to be the experience of the Palatine settlers with the Schoharie Indians.

As stated above, there were reported in London an aggregate of thirteen thousand Palatines, in October, 1709. A large number of them were undoubtedly provided for by their entering various trades and pursuits by land and

---

[1] In *Hallesche Nachrichten*, reprint, vol. i, p. 613. The elder Mühlenberg is very accurate in his reports, and Conrad Weiser had a good memory.

sea. For example, Luttrell[1] states that the merchants of Bedford and Barnstaple who were engaged in the Newfoundland fisheries designed employing five hundred of them in their service. About five thousand must have been disposed of in similar ways, as we can account for only seventy-five hundred persons that were shipped to various colonies. In the first division about thirty-eight hundred persons, five hundred families, were sent to Ireland and settled in the province of Munster. Being provided with land, they built homes and became a sturdy stock, useful and influential in the country.[2] We learn from various travelers that they preserved their native character and even their language for a long time.

The second large contingent of Palatines was shipped to the Carolinas, sailing from England in the early autumn of 1709. This expedition was under the leadership of Graffenried and Michell, natives of Bern, Switzerland. They numbered over six hundred, and founded Newbern, near the mouth of the Neuse River, in the present state of North Carolina.[3] No portion of the Palatines settled in Virginia under the auspices of Governor Spotswood, his settlers at Germanna having come from Siegen, Germany.[4]

A much larger number, over three thousand persons, were destined for the colony of New York. Most of these had in mind the Schoharie region as their promised land,

---

[1] *Diary*, vi, 496; quoted by Cobb, *The Story of the Palatines*, chap. iii, p. 84.

[2] *Pennsylvania Historical Magazine*, vol. x, p. 381. *The Pennsylvania German Society*, vol. vii, p. 335. Descended from this stock were the founders of Methodism in America, Philip Embury (Amberg) and Barbara Heck. Cf. *Ireland and the Centenary of American Methodism*, by Cook (Crook).

[3] See Chapter viii, pp. 213–215.

[4] Cobb and others are here in error. Compare the more recent investigations published in the *Virginia Magazine*, vols. x–xiii. Also below, Chapter vii, pp. 178 ff.

and would not be content, as later events proved, until they had ultimately reached its beautiful meadows and fertile hills. The new governor of the colony, Colonel Robert Hunter, had in mind the employment of the Palatines in the manufacture of tar and naval stores. He accompanied the expedition, sailing in April, 1710, with the commission to settle the Germans on the Hudson or Mohawk. The Palatines were distributed on ten ships, on which they must have been closely crowded, as the mortality among them was enormous. According to the governor's account 470 persons died of ship fever during the voyage, and 250 more after their arrival. There remained 2227 Palatines for the settlements in New York, after a loss of 773 persons, if there were 3000 at the beginning.[1] Governor Hunter speaks of the loss of 1700 among 4000 immigrants, while other official documents mention only 3000, which is probably the correct figure.

One of the ships, the Herbert, was lost on the east end of Long Island. The people seem to have been rescued, but their goods were much damaged. This accident was probably the origin of the legend, immortalized by Whittier, concerning a ship called the Palatine, localized on Block Island (Manisees) and elsewhere. One tradition represents the vessel as laden with treasure, belonging to the Palatines, and by them hidden from view until the time immediately before disembarking, when the sight of their gold excited the grasping greed of the crew, who to accomplish the robbery slew every one of the immigrants. In Whittier's poem, " The Palatine," wreckers on the island decoyed the ship by false lights, caused the death of all on board, and then " they burned the wreck of the Palatine." But the phantom ship reappeared at each anni-

---

[1] Kapp's figures, p. 96. Cf. also Cobb, p. 127.

versary of the crime, and haunted the imagination of the wreckers, never allowing them an opportunity to enjoy the fruits of their ill-gotten gain.[1]

So large a company of immigrants could not be received in the small town of New York, and the Palatines, accordingly, were landed on Nutten Island.[2] A proclamation was made preventing extortionate prices for bread and provisions, and a small government was devised for the colonists. Prominent above all others was Johann Conrad Weiser, father of an equally famous son, a descendant of the magistrate of Great Anspach, Würtemberg. The death of his wife, the care of a large family, and the national calamities induced him to join the emigrating thousands. All his surviving children, save one married daughter, went with him. He was easily the chief among his people through his ability, experience, and independence of character. Governor Hunter and others in authority, complained much of his stubbornness, which indeed resembled that of Martin Luther, being born of the love of truth and faith in ultimate justice. Weiser was a stalwart fighter before the Lord, a willing martyr to the cause of individual rights for the American colonist. The first clash with authority occurred when children[3] were forcibly taken

[1] For still, on many a moonless night,
  From Kingston Head and from Montauk Light,
  The spectre kindles and burns in sight.

  Now low and dim, now clear and higher,
  Leaps up the terrible Ghost of Fire,
  Then, slowly sinking, the flames expire.

  And the wise Sound skippers, though the skies be fine,
  Reef their sails, when they see the sign,
  Of the blazing wreck of the Palatine !

[2] Now Governor's Island.

[3] There were seventy-five boys and girls thus apprenticed, some, by no means all, as was given out, were orphans. In the case of the two sons of

from their parents and apprenticed to people in New York City. Two of the sons of Weiser were thus separated from their father, whose protests were without avail. Among the forty-one boys thus apprenticed was John Peter Zenger, who was given to the printer, William Bradford of New York, and will be mentioned below for the prominent part he took in the struggle for the liberty of the colonial press.

In July, 1710, Governor Hunter despatched the surveyor-general of the province " to survey the land on the Mohaques River, particularly the Skohare, to which the Indians have no pretence." This probably means that the Indians had surrendered their rights (there had been no sale or conquest), and furnishes another link in the chain of evidence, that the Schoharie district had actually been given by the Indians to Queen Anne for the colonization of the Palatines.

In the estimation of the governor, Schoharie possessed good land for cultivation, but an insufficient number of pine forests. He wanted pine forests for the manufacture of tar and pitch, his ambition being centred on providing all the necessary stores for the English navy, even hemp, from the resources and labor of this colony, thus saving the Admiralty's heavy expense in buying from Norway, Sweden, and Russia, a heavy tax also upon English pride. Governor Hunter thought that the two requisites, of pine forest and good land, were combined in a tract which he bought from the crafty Robert Livingston, an area of six thousand acres, on the eastern shore of the Hudson, north

Weiser, their brother, Conrad, said that he never saw them again. The names of the forty-one boys, and their ages (mostly between ten and fifteen, some much below), are given in Rupp's *Thirty Thousand Names of Immigrants*, p. 445. They are also given by O'Callaghan in the *Documentary History of New York*.

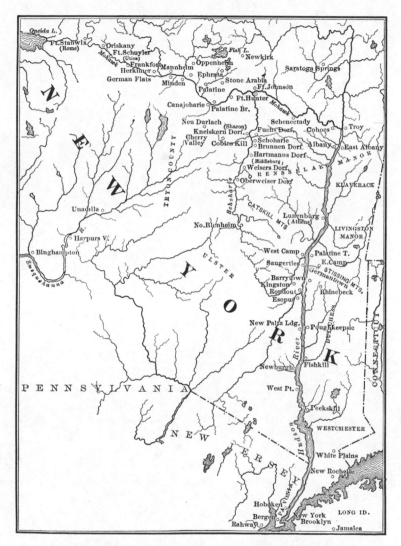

EARLY GERMAN SETTLEMENTS IN NEW YORK

of the present town of Rhinebeck, a part of Livingston Manor. On the opposite side of the river there were some crown lands, probably an additional inducement for the purchase. The colony on that side was called West Camp, in distinction from East Camp, the name given to the principal settlement. The latter was composed of four villages: Hunterstown, Queensbury, Annsbury, and Haysbury, with a total of 1189 colonists in 1711. West Camp was composed of three villages: Elizabethtown, Georgetown, and New Village, with 614 inhabitants, making the total for the two, 1803 colonists.

Over four hundred Palatines were left in New York City (424 out of 2227), most of them widows, single women, and children, not adaptable to the "great and good design" of making tar and pitch. A record of their names is available in the annals of the Lutheran Church of New York City.

The hardships that followed fell solely to the lot of the Palatines in East Camp, on Livingston Manor, no serious effort being made on the west shore toward the manufacture of naval stores. Governor Hunter possessed no qualifications for the great undertaking which he was making his life work, save his enthusiasm. He possessed no technical knowledge, and the overseer, who was expected to fill the gap, proved incompetent. The management was not wise enough to import successful operators from Norway, Sweden, or Russia, who might have produced a far better yield from the trees. Governor Hunter was a soldier, and instituted military methods, demanding implicit obedience from all that were in his employ, particularly from the Palatines, for whom he had apparently no particular sympathy, and who, on their part, believed they were being cheated. Governor Hunter's blunt and tactless manner

roused the prejudices of his laborers against the undertaking, and, instead of making them and their leaders
his main support, he relied on the colonial aristocrats,
who used him merely to advance their own interests. The
shrewdest of them was Robert Livingston, who gained
not only by the sale of a large tract of land, but was
awarded also the profitable contract of feeding the Palatines (adults at sixpence, children at fourpence per day).
It was the opinion of contemporaries on either side of the
water that Livingston grew richer daily on this contract,
and that he was the only man who was benefited at all
by the great scheme of making naval stores. Even Hunter
himself soon wrote in a letter to General Nicholson, that
he had bestowed too much confidence upon Livingston,
the most selfish and ungrateful man in the world.

When the Palatines came to America, the year was
already too far advanced for them to begin work. It was
autumn, and the people had to be fed for the winter and
up to the time when work might begin in the spring. This
enforced period of idleness could not but prove harmful.
Not only was it a financial loss to the management, but
also a great misfortune for the colonists, idleness breeding
discontent, and a paternal régime destroying the independence necessary for the permanent prosperity of a
colony. The Palatines had been promised good land, for
the acquisition of which they would not have felt work
as a hardship; but the labor of serfs in the system now
imposed upon them, without hope of future independence, they felt to be an outrage. Nevertheless, the beginnings were made in good earnest. Overcoming their
dissatisfaction, the colonists cut a large number of trees,[1]

---

[1] Nearly one hundred thousand trees were cut, and even boys and girls
were employed in gathering knots, " that no hands may be idle."

and in return received agricultural implements for the cultivation of their land.

The minister Kocherthal had warned the authorities concerning the irrepressible opposition of the people against the preparation of tar, and of their desire to leave East Camp for the promised land of Schoharie. When therefore an organized revolt began to form, Governor Hunter was ready to apply firm measures. He had ordered a company of soldiers to come from Albany, and on their arrival called the leaders of the colonists before him. In the hearing before the governor they explained the causes of their discontent, being imposed upon, as they thought, in violation of the conditions of their contract. It seems they deceived themselves, or did not understand fully the terms of the contract, for, as we read it, we must concede that the governor's position was correct on the point that the contract required labor from the colonists in the manufacture of ship stores, in return for the expenses of their transportation and sustenance.[1] During the parley three or four hundred of the Palatines came to the rescue of their leaders, thinking that they were in danger. They feigned a desire to speak to the governor, but withdrew when they saw that their leaders were not in captivity or peril. A large troop of armed men had been ordered to reinforce Hunter's soldiers, and with their aid the Palatines were dispersed, and subsequently disarmed in their several villages. Peace was thus restored, but, self-government being taken away from the colonists, they were reduced to the same level as " indented servants."

In June, 1711, the governor established a council to

[1] The governor, however, allowed no weight to be attached to another article of the contract, viz., that after the outlay was repaid, each colonist was to receive forty acres of land in fee-simple, forty acres for each head — man, woman, or child.

take charge of the government of the Palatines and the manufacture of ship stores. This consisted of Robert Livingston, Richard Sackett, the special overseer and expert already referred to, John Cast, Gottfried Wulfen, Andreas Bugge, and Hermann Schünemann. Three of them, provided Livingston or Sackett were present, had the right to inflict punishment for disobedience or misdemeanors, even to the extent of corporal chastisement or imprisonment. For every village there was an executive: on the east side, J. P. Kneiskern for Hunterstown, J. C. Weiser for Queensbury, H. Windecker for Annsbury, G. C. Fuchs for Haysbury; on the west side of the Hudson, for Elizabethtown, J. C. Gerlach, for Georgetown, J. Mauch, and for New Village, P. P. Grauberger.

The Palatines were no cowards, and when in the summer of the same year the province of New York was to furnish a quota of soldiers for the expedition to Canada, it was decided to send three hundred Palatines, in addition to the three hundred and fifty " Christians " and one hundred and fifty Indians of Long Island. The requisite number was easily found and placed under the command of J. P. Kneiskern as captain. Germans in this expedition for the first time served in the same regiment with Indians, the army being under the supreme command of Colonel Schuyler. The Palatines received no pay, though their fitness was acknowledged generally, and on their return, perhaps from fear of revolt, Governor Hunter deprived them of their weapons. In the next winter a number of them served in the garrisons at Albany.

The high-handed treatment of the Palatines by the governor, his utter refusal [1] to encourage their hopes of settle-

[1] In a passion the governor stamped upon the ground and said : " Here is your land " (meaning the almost barren rocks) " where you must live and die." *Documentary History*, vol. iii, p. 424; Cobb, pp. 156-157.

ment in Schoharie, and the greed of Livingston, who made the largest possible profits out of the food supplies, were causes producing the greatest amount of friction, but not necessarily such as to ruin the colony. The disasters that now arose came from the incompetency of the management of the enterprise. The land selected, in spite of the praises that had been sung of it, now proved to be poor in forest growth and unfertile. The trees, after cutting, were not properly prepared, Overseer Sackett not being equipped with sufficient experience or expert knowledge; moreover, after being poorly prepared, the trees were not properly cared for. In consequence, the work done did not bring proportionate returns. Instead of thirty thousand barrels of tar, only two hundred were obtained, by the summer of 1712, out of one hundred thousand trees. At home the Lords of Trade lost confidence in Hunter's ability and particularly in that of his advisers; more especially did they regret his falling into the hands of the ill-reputed Livingston. Altogether Hunter had paid out over thirty-two thousand pounds for the Palatines, and received for his expenses only ten thousand eight hundred, so that the home government owed him over twenty-one thousand pounds.[1] He struggled for more than ten years to get back his outlay, drawn from his private fortune, and it is not known definitely whether he was ever reimbursed for what he had expended.[2] More than twenty thousand pounds had gone into the pocket of Livingston

[1] Cf. Kapp, p. 110 ; Cobb, pp. 181 ff.

[2] When in the year 1722 the Lords required of Governor Hunter, who then had been recalled, that he present the receipts for money paid to the Palatines, the latter were reluctant to give them, fearing some new treachery. The request was made with the usual tactlessness, namely, that if they would not sign the receipts they would be driven from the country. They therefore refused to sign, and waited for the carrying out of the threat. Cf. Kapp, p. 110.

for supplies furnished the Palatines; moreover, his land, bordering on East Camp, increased greatly in value because of the proximity of settlements. On October 31, 1712, Governor Hunter wrote to the Lords of Trade in London saying that, his fortune and credit being exhausted, his appeals for repayment not having been honored by them, he was obliged to abandon the work of manufacturing naval stores on the Hudson; hoping the enterprise would be but temporarily abandoned, he had directed his overseer to announce to the laborers that they must keep in readiness to return to their work. Several hundred Palatines, he states, had made their way to Schoharie, a movement that had been impossible for him to prevent;[1] indeed, he saw therein an advantage, the protection of the frontier against the French and Indians. He speaks hopefully of the manufacture of tar and pitch, and continues to write in this spirit for three years longer. In 1715 the Lords of Trade seemed once more willing to renew the work, but they finally concluded that it was too late, and when the governor himself in 1716 made the confession that the scheme, which at first seemed so advantageous, had been a failure, it was dropped altogether in London.

The consternation wrought in East Camp, when, in September, 1712, John Cast suddenly announced to the settlers that the enterprise was to be abandoned, is difficult to realize fully. Winter was near, with absolutely no provision made for the colonists. They were to shift for themselves, as best they could, and not to look for assistance. At the same time they were reminded of their obligations, warned to remain in the province or even in the settlement, to be within call for the renewal of the

---

[1] He had forbidden it. See following pages.

manufacturing scheme. In their distress the hope that had almost been abandoned, that of reaching the promised land, Schoharie, loomed up brightly before their mental vision. They took counsel and decided to send a group of their leaders to the Indians, asking their permission to settle in the Schoharie region. Johann Conrad Weiser and Captain Kneiskern were among those who beat their path from Schenectady through the woods to Schoharie in execution of the plan. They were well received, and their request was granted. They were told that no one should hinder them from settling there, and that the Indians would help them in proportion to their means. Accordingly a fifteen-mile trail was cut through the woods, and about a dozen families were sent in advance to Schoharie. Upon their arrival a message from the governor overtook them, forbidding their settlement in Schoharie, and declaring that any refusing to obey should be treated as rebels. But after some deliberation the Palatines determined to remain, starvation seeming the other alternative.

In March, 1713, the rest of the Palatines who had decided to migrate appeared in Schoharie. The snow lay three feet deep, the travelers struggled against hunger and cold, but two weeks' hardship brought them to the land of promise. Some citizens of Albany tried to anticipate their purchase of the land, but the Palatines received the preference at the hands of the Indians, who sold them what they wished for the equivalent of three hundred dollars. The privations of the newcomers during the winter were intense, and, had it not been for the friendly aid of the Indians, most of them would probably not have survived. A graphic account of their sufferings is given in the journal of Conrad Weiser, son of Johann Conrad, in which due acknowledgment is made of the services of the

Indians, who "showed the settlers where to find edible roots." "Many of our feasts were of wild potatoes and ground beans."[1] In the spring they "broke ground enough to plant corn for the use of the next year. But this year our hunger was hardly endurable." In March, 1713, "did the remainder of the people (tho' treated by the Governor as Pharaoh treated the Israelites) proceed on their journey, and by God's assistance travel'd in a fortnight with sledges thro' the snow, — which there covered the ground above three foot deep, — cold and hunger, Joyn'd their friends and countrymen in the promised land of Schoharie."

The majority of the Palatines remained at or near the original settlements on the Hudson, and when left to their own resources began to thrive. About thirty families on the Manor, for instance, moved a few miles to the southward, and settled on Beekman's land. Henry Beekman sold them lands in fee-simple, which Livingston apparently would not do, and the town of Rhinebeck was founded. It was originally spelled " Rheinbeek " in honor of their home on the Rhine and Beekman (Beek), their generous patron.

The original settlement of six thousand acres on Livingston Manor also went into the hands of Palatines, but not earlier than 1724. Three of them, Scherb, Hagedorn, and Schumacher, in that year asked Governor Burnet, Hunter's successor, for a title to their lands for themselves and their people. Sixty-three of the families were prepared to remain, ten ready to leave, as reported by Surveyor Colden. The patent was signed by the governor in 1725, allow-

[1] Quotations from the *Journal* of Conrad Weiser. This diary has been edited by D. I. Rupp, in *Der deutsche Pionier*, vol. ii, pp. 182 ff., etc. Cf. also : *The Life of Conrad Weiser, Pioneer, Patriot and Patron of Two Races*, by C. Z. Weiser. 2d ed., Reading, 1899.

ing the above-mentioned men with Heiner and Kollman to act as trustees in distributing the land. Forty acres were left for a church.[1]

The two German ministers, Joshua Kocherthal and Johann Friedrich Häger, on request of the Board of Trade, near the close of Hunter's term, made a census of the Palatines in New York. They reported the following statistics for 1718 in the province of New York: On the east side of the river (in the district now known as Germantown), including Rhinebeck, 499 persons, 126 families; on the west side of the river, including Kingsto(w)n, Esopus, West Camp, etc., 272 persons, 68 families; New York City, 150 persons, 30 families; Schoharie, 680 persons, 170 families; total, 1601 persons, 394 families. Curiously enough Kocherthal and Häger say they have not included widows and orphans, leaving an error in their notation of perhaps several hundred persons. According to this table there were four persons to a family. This is a very low average for frontier conditions, that commonly favor the growth of families. The original number of Palatines landed at Nutten Island being about 2500, the natural increase by 1718 ought certainly to have overcome the death-rate, which is nowhere recorded as having been large, with the exception of the first sojourn on Nutten Island.[2] Kapp estimates that there must have been as

---

[1] The following names, besides those mentioned, are found among them: Stoppelbein, Lauer (changed to Lawyer), Schenk, Hann, Kiszler, Schmid, Lauffmann, Mann, Salbach, Dietrich, Mühler, Rauch, Haubach, Buck, Winder, Schenkel, Schauz, Schöffler, Klein, Bartels. Among those that would not remain were: Schmidt, Schneider, Hausser, Wernershöfer, Wist, and Dirk. Cf. Kapp, p. 115.

[2] The mortality there was 250, as we know from the petition in September, 1711, of an undertaker who prayed for payment for 250 coffins supplied to the Palatines. This number, 250, was already deducted in the estimate of 2227, on p. 83.

many as two thousand to twenty-five hundred Palatines in New York State in 1718. Scheff, who, with
Weiser, was sent to London as an envoy of the Palatines
in defense of their rights, in his separate petition to the
Board of Trade estimated that there were at that time
(1718–20) about three thousand Palatines in the state of
New York. He gives the number of Palatines in Schoharie as one hundred and sixty families or one thousand
souls, making an average of over six persons to a family,
contradicting Kocherthal's estimate of four to a family.
Scheff was pleading a case, while Kocherthal no doubt
shared the experience of all early census-takers in getting
too low an estimate. The truth lies somewhere between,
i. e., for the total number, somewhere between three
thousand and eighteen hundred, plus widows and orphans,
i. e., close up to twenty-five hundred, which is Kapp's
highest figure.[1]

From the middle of the twenties the Germans maintained a sure footing south of Germantown (Columbia
County) and Clermont, and settled also the northern part
of the present county of Dutchess. Germantown and
Rhinebeck [2] became points of attraction for German immigration and the stopping-place for those who desired
to go either north or west in the province. Intimate ties
of both blood and religion existed between these settlers
and those on the Schoharie and Mohawk. Migrations
were frequent, as for instance in 1760, when a number of

[1] Kapp, pp. 114, 115.

[2] Among the first settlers of Rhinebeck were : Häbner, Schufeld,
Hagedorn, Wiederwachs, Staats, Berner, and Elsasser. Some of the names
in Germantown were Coon (Kuhn), Coons (Kuntz), Crysler (Kreisler),
Salbagh (Salbach), Kleyne or Clyne (Klein), Schutts (Schutz), Shoemaker
(Schumacher), Snyder (Schneider), Smith (Schmidt), Freats (Fritz), Shu-
felt (Schufeld), Meghley (Michle), Younghance (Junghans), Wagenaer
(Wagener). See Kapp, pp. 115, 116.

inhabitants of Rhinebeck settled in the Schoharie Valley and founded New Rhinebeck.

The original site of the Schoharie settlement was on the Little Schoharie, beginning somewhat south of the present town of Middleburg, and extending northward to the entry of Fox Creek and the Cobleskill into the main Schoharie River, an area of about two thousand acres. Seven villages were founded on both sides of the Schoharie River, and named after the leaders of the colonists. Weisersdorf was the southernmost village, located where now is Middleburg. Two miles to the north was Hartmannsdorf, named after Hartmann Windecker, soon to become the largest of all the villages, with sixty-five houses, and noted for its fruit trees, and particularly its apple trees, which, as early as the first quarter of the eighteenth century, became a staple product. Then came Brunnendorf, named after its springs, and a thousand paces to the north, Schmidtsdorf, of obvious derivation, the smallest of the villages. Fuchsdorf, at the mouth of Fox Creek, was named after Wilhelm Fuchs, who established the first mill. Two miles to the north was Gerlachsdorf, and beyond that Kneiskerndorf, on the east side of the river, opposite the mouth of the Cobleskill, named respectively after Gerlach and Captain Kneiskern.

The difficulties encountered in the beginning of the settlement were increased by the want of cattle and agricultural implements.[1] For salt it was necessary to journey nineteen miles, to Schenectady. The first crop of grain, however, that sprang from the soil surprised the colonists with its richness and quality, and strengthened them in their determination not to give up their new homes, what-

---

[1] They could not take along those they had used at East Camp ; that would have been theft.

ever the commands of the governor. In general appearance the country reminded them of their native land between the Hardt and Taunus mountain ranges, with its picturesque valleys and hills rising in moderation. In their first year, when Lambert Sternberg bought the first bushel of wheat in Schenectady and brought it on his back to Schoharie, he little thought that forty years thereafter Schoharie would annually send thirty-six thousand bushels of wheat to Schenectady. In the earliest days fifteen to twenty Palatines would be obliged for safety to journey together on their long trip to Schenectady, there to have their sacks of grain ground in the mill. Wilhelm Fuchs soon shortened the distance by setting up his mill on Fox Creek. In Weisersdorf nine inhabitants joined in the purchase of their first horse, using it in common, by taking turns. When, ten years later, some of them migrated to Pennsylvania, they drove large herds of cattle and horses before them. After the first necessities were provided, many of the men in the colony plied their respective trades and thus turned an additional honest penny. This also made their progress more rapid.

The relations of the Palatines with the Indians of the Mohawk tribes were very friendly, to such a degree that Governor Hunter grew suspicious, as will presently appear. Conrad Weiser, by consent of his father, Johann Conrad, lived with the Mohawk Indians,[1] when a boy. He learned their language and their customs, and on his return to the white settlements became ever after the mediator between the two races. An instance of the cordial relations existing between them is furnished by one of the festivals in

---

[1] The Mohawk chief, Quagnant, took a special liking to Conrad, then sixteen years of age, and proposed to take him to his own country and teach him the Indian language.

the early days, the crowning feature of which was a series
of athletic sports. The chief event was a mile race between
the fleetest of the Indian youths and Conrad Weiser. The
speed of the two contestants was about equal for most of
the distance, and they ran neck and neck near the finish,
when Conrad Weiser, by accident or design, collided with
his rival, causing his fall, and in the next moment reached
the mark before his adversary could recover. The Indians,
who had watched the race with breathless interest, complained vehemently of unfair treatment, when Conrad
Weiser, going quickly from chief to chief, explained that
his act was unintentional, and that he certainly was not
deserving of the prize of handsome deerskins, that were
to go to the victor. This pleased the Indians so much
that they, in turn, were not to be outdone as sportsmen,
and insisted on Weiser's taking the prize, the festival
winding up in peace and good will, though at one time
a dangerous antagonism was threatened.

Very different were the relations of the Palatines with
the original Dutch settlers, called frequently Low Dutch,
to distinguish them from the High Dutch, or Germans.
Being older settlers and therefore more well-to-do, they
looked down upon the poor Palatines, or tried to worst
them when business affairs brought them in contact. This
feeling, continuing until the Revolutionary War, was not
due to national hatred, the two types being closely related
by blood and geographical location in their European
homes, but rather to class prejudice existing between rich
and poor, patrician and plebeian, and subsequently between
Tory and Patriot. Violent outbreaks occurred between
them at times, as when, in the year 1714, Adam Vrooman, a well-to-do Dutch farmer of Schenectady, sent his
son Peter to settle in the neighborhood of Weisersdorf.

The estate contained about fourteen hundred acres, and prevented the Germans from spreading out westward beyond the Schoharie. If young Vrooman's statements can be relied upon, Palatines drove their horses over his fields at night, tore down his buildings, and were abusive with "rebellious speeches." Johann Conrad Weiser was accused of being the ringleader in all disturbances, and his son of "telling the Indians all sorts of lies."

The resentment against the Weisers was shared by the governor and all aristocrats, but they were afraid to seize or arrest the Palatine leader, the champion of the rights and independence of the German colonists. The prosperity of the Schoharie settlements aroused the cupidity of the earlier settlers, who now became actively engaged in reviving Governor Hunter's grudge against the Palatines. Overstepping his prerogatives, the governor granted to the Seven Partners [1] of Albany at a very moderate selling-price [2] the identical territory, between the Little Schoharie and the Cobleskill, on which the Palatines had squatted. He might have bestowed upon his friends some of the equally valuable lands on the Mohawk, but his purpose was evidently to drive the Palatines out of the fertile valley of the Schoharie, choosing to forget the original instructions of Queen Anne, in accordance with which he was to engage the Palatines in the business of preparing pitch and tar, but also to have special concern for "the comfort and advantage of the Palatines." It was not so easy a matter for the Seven Partners to gain actual possession of the territory granted them. The Palatines in-

---

[1] The grant was dated,.Fort George, November 3, 1714, and made to Meyndert Schuyler, Peter van Brugh, Robert Livingston, Jr., John Schuyler, George Clark, Dr. Staats, and Rip van Dam. Kapp, p. 127; Cobb, p. 231.

[2] Ten thousand acres for fourteen hundred pistoles. See Kapp, p. 231.

sisted on their right of possession by purchase from the Indians, and by special assignment of Queen Anne. Governor Hunter's only excuse could be that so long as the Palatines had not produced ship stores in sufficient quantity,[1] he would not carry out the other part of the contract, in virtue of which the Palatines as colonists were entitled to grants of land at the rate of forty acres per head.

The Seven Partners soon sent an agent, Bayard, to acquaint the German settlers with the new order of things, and graciously to offer them the lands they had cultivated, at a small rental. Bayard was lodged in Schmidtsdorf, located centrally among the seven villages, and when his purpose became known, men, women, and children, armed with clubs, sickles, knives, and guns appeared before the house where the agent was stopping. Bayard owed his life to his host, Schmidt, who restrained the angered people long enough to allow him to escape. The Seven Partners then sent the sheriff of Albany, named Adams, to renew the offers and drive from the land those unwilling to accept their terms, particularly Johann Conrad Weiser. According to the sheriff's own account, as he tried to seize one of the refractory colonists, he was struck down, dragged through all the dirty pools of the streets by the women of the village, then set upon a fence-rail and carried about for an hour. He lost an eye and had two of his ribs broken, but managed, four days after, to creep or crawl back to Albany. After that either side waited, and the Schoharie people, on their part, were very cautious about appearing in Albany. In time they grew bolder, and a number of young men, including the son of Weiser, ventured to go to Albany to get salt. They were

[1] The failure of the enterprise, however, released the Palatines from their obligations.

captured and put into prison, for how long we do not know, but since no legitimate charges could be brought against them, they had to be set free.

The Seven Partners, being unable to dislodge the Palatines, next applied to the governor. In 1717 he summoned three men from each village to appear in Albany, including Johann Conrad Weiser. When they were assembled, Governor Hunter, in a passion declaring that he would have Weiser hanged, put three questions to the Palatines whom he had summoned : —

(1) Why had they gone to Schoharie without his permission ?

(2) Why would they not make any compromise with the gentlemen of Albany ?

(3) Why had they so much to do with the Indians ?

These questions the deputies answered as follows : —

Firstly, they had been compelled by necessity to shift for themselves, the governor having told them to do so when the manufacture of tar was discontinued. They were compelled to go somewhere and provide against starvation, hoping to gain later the approval of the king and governor. When the speaker, probably Weiser, mentioned the king, Hunter grew angry, and Livingston added, " Here is your king," pointing to the governor.

To the second question the deputies answered that they had nothing to do with the gentlemen of Albany ; that the Indians had presented the land to the crown for the good of the Palatines ; that they had since that time bought the land from the Indians ; that the king had not given it to the Seven Partners ; and that if they must serve any one, they would serve the king and no private person.

In answer to the third question they said that if they did not live on good terms with the Indians, they would constantly be exposed to hostile attacks of both the Indians and the French.

Hunter commanded them either to agree with the Albany gentlemen or to leave the valley, and forbade them to plow and sow the ground until they had come to an agreement. The deputies returned with these behests, none of which were obeyed. The following winter the people sent three men to New York, asking the governor's permission to cultivate their land. Hunter did not change his position, nor did the Palatines theirs, on the return of the delegates. As Weiser says in his subsequent account: "They were forced for their own preservation to transgress these orders, and sowed some small corn and fruits, or else they must have starved." In the spring of 1718 the Palatines concluded that they must appeal to a higher power, and appointed three of their best men to go to London and lay their grievances before the king.

Their envoys were Johann Conrad Weiser, Scheff, and Wallrath. They secretly boarded a ship in Philadelphia, but while at sea misfortune overtook them, they fell into the hands of pirates, and were robbed of all their possessions. Weiser was tied to the mast three times and pitifully beaten, to yield up more money, though he had given his last. The ship was forced to land at Boston, in order to purchase supplies for the remaining passage, and when it arrived in London, the German envoys were bereft of all their means. Friendless and poor in a foreign city, they were compelled to contract debts, in consequence of which Weiser and Scheff were put into the debtor's prison, while Wallrath returned homeward, dying on the way. The others remained in prison almost a year, until a check of seventy pounds from their friends in Schoharie released them. Each then presented a petition inde-

pendently, rehearsing their history and numerous grievances, from the very beginning, their arrival at New York,
to the attempted expulsion from Schoharie, their land of
promise, given them by the crown, that had received it
from the Indians. The documents showed particular
strength in argumentation, and proved that their authors
were by no means ignorant men such as the Palatines are
frequently set down for, but on the contrary men of ability,
particularly Weiser, and both of a higher intellectual type
than commonly found on the frontier. Although they were
supported in their plea by both pastors of the Royal German Chapel, Böhm and Robert, they did not get a satisfactory hearing. Governor Hunter, then in England, after
his recall from office, being questioned as a witness, gave
some damaging accounts of the Palatines, saying among
other things that they had "settled against his will on
other people's lands." He was thus begging the very point
at issue, but his testimony weighed heavily with the Lords
of Trade, and the result was that Hunter's grant of the
lands to the Seven Partners of Albany remained intact.

Scheff left earlier than Weiser, having disagreed with
him on the point of the advisability of threatening to
leave the colony of New York, if their rights were not maintained. Such a step, Scheff thought, transcended the terms
of their commission. Weiser remained at least until 1722,
hoping against hope, determined to make the right of the
Palatines victorious, but in 1723 he was again at home in
Schoharie. There the people were no longer in agreement,
but were discussing [1] the adoption of one of three separate
courses : first, remaining in Schoharie and arriving at an

---

[1] It is said also, that a portion of the younger element of the Palatines
were persuaded or bribed by the Partners of Albany to subscribe to a petition undermining the good work of Weiser and Scheff.

agreement with the Albany proprietors; second, settling in the Mohawk Valley on land assigned them by the new governor, Burnet; and third, migrating to the neighboring colony of Pennsylvania.

Governor Burnet treated the Palatines with more tact than his predecessor. He reasoned with them, and apparently persuaded most of them that it was to their advantage to yield. He offered them equally good lands on the Mohawk, a proposition the acceptance of which he knew would also result in a gain for the province, extending the frontier forty miles westward and thereby protecting the older settlements. The petition of Weiser, after all, probably had had a good effect, for now the home government was commanding Burnet to take action in behalf of the Palatines. The governor had some trouble in getting the squatters to believe that he was fair-minded, in urging them to accept his propositions. His impression of the Palatines he gave in the words, " a laborious and honest, but headstrong ignorant people." At one time he speaks of them as ungrateful, but governing he found a thankless task and the criticism does not apply any more to the Palatines as a people than to others. The latter had been treated very harshly, and a forced migration, even under favorable conditions, was after all an injustice to them.

About three hundred persons remained in Schoharie, making an agreement with the new landlords, on easy terms.[1] They were subsequently joined by additional settlers from Germantown and Rhinebeck, so that at the time of the Revolution the whole of the Schoharie country was settled. The German farms extended twenty-five or thirty miles beyond the original seven villages. The in-

---

[1] Conrad Weiser says, however, the best lands were not available for the Palatines.

dustrious and thrifty settlers made a garden of the country, and peace and plenty entered their lives. They were active in the frontier struggles and in the war of the Revolution, but after that led quiet lives, leaving no particular mark upon the history of the state, yet harboring latent forces, which occasionally came to the surface, as in the career of William C. Bouck, prominent in politics through his native good sense and honesty, and serving as governor of the state of New York from 1843 to 1845.

The leader of the Palatines who settled in the Mohawk Valley was Gerlach. The settlements were made on either side of the Mohawk in the present counties of Montgomery, Herkimer, and beyond. Fort Hunter was the easternmost point, and fifty miles west, at Frankfort, was the western limit. The whole distance between Frankfort and Schenectady is seventy English miles, of which area the Germans settled more than two thirds. In this location they protected the frontier of New York throughout the French and Indian and the Revolutionary wars, the Schoharie Germans forming the other side of the wedge running into the western territory of New York. The district soon became the granary in time of peace and war, and the labors of Governor Burnet were well rewarded. In number the Palatine settlers of the Mohawk Valley, about the middle of the eighteenth century, amounted to from twenty-five hundred to three thousand, inhabiting about five hundred houses. Indian traders advanced as far as Oswego and Niagara, which marked the borders also of the territory of the Six Nations. Even to-day the Mohawk Valley is Palatine territory, indexed with German names, as Palatine, Palatine Bridge, Mannheim, Oppenheim, Newkirk, etc. The level meadows extending along the south side of the Mohawk, unsurpassed in cultivation and fertility, are still known as the German Flats. On the opposite side of the Mohawk lies the town bearing the name of General Herkimer (or Herkheimer), the hero of the battle of Oriskany, described in the chapter below on the Revolutionary War.[1]

Not only Gerlach, who led his hosts to the Mohawk Valley, but another of the seven chiefs would not listen to the compromise of the Albany landlords. Johann Conrad Weiser chose rather to leave the lands he and his people had cultivated for twelve years than suffer injustice. For some time past a number of the Palatines at Schoharie had looked in the direction of Pennsylvania for settlement, receiving encouragement from Governor Keith, who promised them freedom and justice. A petition had been addressed to him from fifteen heads of Palatine families, that recited their experiences in New York, spoke of the generous treatment always shown their countrymen in Pennsylvania, and begged that lands might be set aside for them on the Tulpehocken, which they would be ready and able to purchase. This petition was acted upon favorably, and an immigration to Pennsylvania resulted on invitation of Governor Keith. To carry out the plan, steps were taken in the assembly to satisfy the claims of Chief Sassouan, who protested against the occupation of the Tulpehocken district. The Indians were given compensation satisfactory to them, and the relations between the Palatines and aborigines became as cordial in Pennsylvania as they had been in Schoharie.

The migration was made in two bodies, the first starting in the spring of 1723, and the second in 1728. About sixty families, or three hundred persons, left Schoharie.

---

[1] Chapter XI, pp. 307-314.

This time they had a large train of cattle, abundant supplies, and money to make a good beginning. They ascended the Schoharie, and under the conduct of an Indian guide crossed the mountains southwestwardly to the headwaters of the Susquehanna. They constructed canoes and followed the Susquehanna River to the mouth of the Swatara. Ascending the river, they reached the undulating country that lies between the sources of the Swatara and Tulpehocken, and made it the site of their permanent settlement. Heidelberg was the name given to their first town. Word was sent back to Schoharie of the success of the expedition and settlement, and five years later came Conrad Weiser, with his people, who had been hoping in vain that by some chance they might still get a clear title to their possessions. The Weisers founded the settlement of Womelsdorf, which rapidly gained in importance. Conrad Weiser, the younger, was soon recognized as the head of the new German settlements in Berks County, his public service as a soldier and mediator in Indian affairs making his name respected throughout the land. The elder Weiser lived with his son almost a score of years longer, seeing increase and prosperity all about him, and peace at last. He had been one of the most stubborn fighters for justice and independence in all colonial history, what with the determined stand he took against Hunter, and the defense of his people's rights before the very throne of Great Britain, ever undaunted by poverty, chastisement, imprisonment, and the law's delay.

The number of Palatines in the Tulpehocken district was very soon increased by accessions from Germany. Reports of their kind treatment in Pennsylvania went home through letters and personal messages, with the result that the main stream of German immigration now went into Pennsylvania and avoided New York. The Swedish traveler and naturalist, Peter Kalm, comments upon this fact, and says that even when immigrants were forced to take ships bound for New York, " they were scarce got on shore when they hastened to Pennsylvania in sight of all the inhabitants of New York." Within twenty years of the settlement of Tulpehocken, the Germans in the Pennsylvania counties had increased to nearly fifty thousand. The colony of New York lost inestimably through the diversion of this main current of immigration, and it is largely due to this fact that New York in colonial times ranked but fourth in importance, being exceeded by Massachusetts, Pennsylvania, and Virginia.

The name of probably the most lasting fame among the Palatine settlers of New York State is that of the printer, John Peter Zenger. He made the first good fight in the history of the American colonies for the liberty of the press. When a youth of thirteen years he was apprenticed to William Bradford, then the only printer of New York. He was one of the Palatine orphan boys, separated from the other colonists, and left behind in New York City; but great was his fortune to serve under a man of such high character as Bradford. The latter was an English Quaker, who had come over with William Penn, but in 1685 removed to the colony of New York. In 1725 he had given New York City its first newspaper, "The New York Gazette." With him Zenger learned the trade of printing and the art of editing a newspaper. His rise had been speedy from apprentice, to employer, to partner. In 1733 Zenger left the partnership and started an independent newspaper called the "New York Weekly Journal." Bradford's paper was the organ of the governor's party, Zenger's that of the opposition.

The beginnings of an epoch of severe party strife in New York came with the appointment of Governor Cosby, who had been governor of Minorca and there made an unenviable reputation for avarice. He did not immediately come to New York, but resided in London a year before entering upon his duties. In the interim Rip Van Dam, as president of the council, conducted the affairs of the colony. Cosby claimed that one half of the salary paid to the president of the council was due to himself. Van Dam agreed to this, but demurred when Cosby claimed also one half the fees the former had received. A lawsuit arose which divided the colony into two camps, popular sympathy naturally being on the side of Rip Van Dam. When Cosby dismissed Chief Justice Morris and set in his place a man amenable to his designs, popular discontent rose to white heat. The case naturally was won by Cosby, but it was a victory dearly bought, savoring of bitter defeat. Bradford's "New York Gazette" being the faithful instrument of the government, Zenger thought the auspicious moment had arrived for the founding of a paper voicing the sentiments of the people. The "New York Weekly Journal" obtained as supporters and contributors some of the ablest men in the province, such as Rip Van Dam, Judge Morris, and the lawyers Smith and Alexander. Bradford's stately pages were no match for the bold, truth-telling, satirical columns of Zenger.

Now there appeared in the "Journal" a number of articles, which inveighed against the high-handed actions of the governor, and complained of his driving residents of New York away to other colonies. The following is a brief quotation from the paper: —

We see men's deeds destroyed, judges arbitrarily displaced, new courts erected without the consent of the legislature, by

Numb. I.

THE
New-York Weekly JOURNAL.

Containing the freſheſt Advices, Foreign, and Domeſtick.

MUNDAY November 5, 1733.

Mr. Zenger,

UNDERSTANDING you in-
tend ſhortly to publiſh a Weekly
Paper, I recommend to your diſpo-
ſal the incloſed Verſes upon Wiſdom ;
which is ſo noble a Theme, that whoever
takes the Pains ſeriouſly to reflect thereon,
will find himſelf happily loſt in the bound-
leſs Ocean of Benefits and Satisfaction attending it. It is without Diſpute the chief
Wood of Mankind ; the firm Bank that
conſtantly ſecures us again the impetuous
Raging of that turbulent Sea of Paſſions,
which inceſſantly daſh againſt the Frame
of human Nature. It is a Fort impregna-
ble by all Aſſaults of Vice, Folly, and Miſ-
fortunes, and a ſecure Rock againſt all the
Caſualties of Miſery. It is a Guide and Security to Youth, Health, and Vigour to
Old Age ; and a Remedy and Eaſe in Sick-
neſs and Infirmity. It is Comfort in Ad-
verſity, it is Plenty in Poverty, and a con-
ſtant Source of true Joy and Delight. It is
infinitely beyond all that the feigned *For-
tunatus* ever could wiſh, or *Gyges's* Treaſures
purchaſe ; *For her Ways are Ways of Plea-
ſantneſs, and all her Paths are Peace.*
She is of eaſy acceſs to all that diligently
ſeek her ; and refuſes none that with Sincerity apply to her, and is always a ready
Help in Time of Need : Therefore pray
continue to recommend the earneſt Purſuit
of Her to all Mankind ; and you will particularly oblige.

PHILOSOPHIA.

On WISDOM.

Victorious Wiſdom whoſe ſupreme Command
Extends beyond the Bounds of Sea and Land ;
'Tis thou alone that doſt reward our Pains,
With Pleaſures that endure, and ſolid Gains.

But Oh ! What art thou, and where doſt thou dwell?
Not with the Hermit in his lonely Cell ;
The ſullen Fumes of whoſe diſtemper'd Brain,
Make the dull Wretch torment himſelf in vain :
Whilſt of the World affectedly afraid,
He ſhuns the End for which Mankind was made.

Not with the Epicure in all his Pleaſures,
Nor with the Miſer in his Bank of Treaſures,
The one's a Slave bound faſt in golden Chains,
The other buys ſhort Joys with laſting Pains.

Not in the vain Purſuit of partial Fame,
The gaudy Outſide of an empty Name ;
When mowed by Chance, not Merit common Breath,
Gives the falſe Shadow ſudden Life or Death.

Honour, when meritoriouſly aſſigned,
The noble Actions of a God like Mind,
Is then indeed a Bleſſing from Heaven,
A bright Reward for human Labour given.

But when 'tis Fame's miſtaken Flattery,
A popular Applauſe of Vanity,
The worthleſs Idol ought to be abhor'd,
And is by none but Knaves and Fools ador'd.

Thus as I'm ſearching with the feeble Light
Of human Reaſon, in dark error's Night,
For what has oft eſcap'd the curious Eye,
Of lofty Wit, and deep Philoſophy,
From the bright Regions of eternal Day,
Methinks I ſee a ſmall but glorious Ray,
Dart ſwift as Lightning throug the yielding Air,
To an unſpotted Breaſt, and enter there,

This is the Wiſdom I ſo much adore ;
Grant me but this, kind Heaven, I ask no more ;
This once obtain'd, how happy ſhall I be ?
Kings will be little Men, compar'd to me :
They in their own Dominions only great,
I Conquer of the World, my ſelf and Fate.

Thus arm'd, let Fortune uſe me as ſhe will,
I ſtand prepar'd to meet with Good or Ill,
If I am born for Happineſs and Eaſe,
And proſp'rous Gales ſalute the ſmiling Seas ;
This Path I'll tread, (the Bleſſings to repay)
Where Virtue calls and Honour leads the Way,

But if the Weather of my Life prove foul,
Though Storms ariſe that makes whole Kingdoms
rowle.

Yet

which it seems to me trials by jury are taken away when a governor pleases; men of known estates denied their votes contrary to the recent practice of the best expositor of any law. Who is there in that province that can call anything his own, or enjoy any liberty longer than those in the administration will condescend to let them, for which reason I left it, as I believe more will.

This was plain speaking, unheard of in the colonial papers up to that time, yet it represented the exercise of a newspaper's noblest function, that of giving free and fearless expression to public opinion.

The governor left no stone unturned to close the mouthpiece of the people's party. First he directed the grand jury to indict Zenger for libel. They did not see any cause for accusation. The governor tried the jury again, and failed. He then brought the matter before the colonial assembly, who refused to order the burning by the hangman of certain numbers of the "Weekly Journal." The colonial council (upper house), under pressure from the governor, then passed an order, by which the hangman was to burn publicly certain designated articles, while the burgomaster and magistrate of the city should witness the act. The latter both refused to obey, and when, four days later (November 6, 1734), the sheriff made a motion in court to carry out the order, they forbade the hangman, who was a city official, to act in accordance with the demand. The objectionable numbers of the newspapers were then burned by a black slave of the sheriff in the presence of some officers of the garrison.

Soon after, on the 17th of November, followed the arrest of Zenger, but he was set free on bail, through the efforts of his lawyers, James Alexander and William Smith. In January, 1735, the grand jury again found no cause for indicting Zenger. The attorney-general next took the matter in hand. The lawyers of Zenger attacked the constitutionality of the court over which Delancey (successor to Morris) presided, but this was followed by the latter's disbarring Alexander and Smith from practice in New York for contempt of court. Thus Zenger lost his legal defenders, and his case seemed hopeless in the face of the criminal procedure instituted against him, August 14, 1735.[1] But Zenger's cause had become more than a personal contest; it was now the cause of the people of New York and with them of all the American colonists. The friends of Zenger summoned to his aid Andrew Hamilton of Philadelphia, the most noted and respected advocate of the colonies. He was a Scotch-Irishman, who had settled in the Quaker City in the beginning of the century and had come by his reputation justly through his able and honest public service.

In this trial he admitted at once that his client had published the paragraph in question, whereupon the court claimed a verdict for the crown. But Hamilton maintained that the question for the jury to decide was not whether the paragraph in question had been printed or not by Zenger, but whether the paragraph which Zenger had printed was a libel or not. The paragraph had been described as "false, scandalous, malicious, and seditious." Hamilton declared that there was nothing false in the paragraph, but that it was a statement of plain and well-known facts. The chief justice ruled that the truth of a libel could not be admitted in evidence according to English law. But Hamilton impressed upon the jury, by the very force of his character and eloquence, the justice of his own view, that what the jury was to decide was

[1] Kapp, p. 176.

whether the paragraph of Zenger, if true, could properly be condemned as a libel. Hamilton created a precedent for the future, and this very case of the Zenger trial was referred to in 1792, when the Fox Libel Act became a law in England.[1]

The peroration of Hamilton was a remarkable performance, and won the jury unanimously. In conclusion the able advocate said: —

The Question before the Court, and you, Gentlemen of the Jury, is not of small nor private Concern, it is not the Cause of a poor Printer, nor of New York alone, which you are trying: No! It may in its Consequence, affect every Freeman that lives under a British Government on the Main of America! It is the best Cause, it is the Cause of Liberty, and I make no Doubt but your upright Conduct, this Day, will not only entitle you to the Love and Esteem of your Fellow-Citizens, but every Man who prefers Freedom to a Life of Slavery will bless and honor You, as Men who have baffled the Attempt of Tyranny; and by an impartial and uncorrupt Verdict, have laid a noble Foundation for securing to ourselves, our Posterity and our Neighbors, That, to which Nature and the Laws of our Country have given us a Right — The Liberty — both of exposing and opposing arbitrary Power (in these Parts of the World, at least) . . . by speaking and writing *Truth!*

Judge Delancey delivered a charge to the jury which fell upon deaf ears. They returned very shortly with the verdict of "not guilty." The scene that followed outside of the court-room, when the acquittal of John Peter Zenger became known, had had no equal in the history of New

[1] Fiske, *The Dutch and Quaker Colonies*, vol. ii, p. 244. Cf. also Kapp, chap. ix, — a complete report of the trial, with the speech of Hamilton, in a German translation, is given on pp. 178–199. Cf. also *John Peter Zenger: His Press, His Trial and a Bibliography of Zenger Imprints*, by Livingston Rutherford. New York, 1904. The text is accompanied by abundant illustrations. Zenger's verbatim report of 1736 is given complete, in its original form.

York. There was no greater rejoicing on the day of the inauguration of George Washington. By threats the judges tried to subdue the shouting, but they might as well have tried to stem the flow of the tides. An English naval officer made an allusion to the acquittal of the Seven Bishops, which renewed the popular demonstration. The aged Hamilton, whose bodily infirmities could not keep him from serving his people and nation, was the hero of the hour, and on leaving, he was accompanied by an escort and martial music.

Zenger also deserves a large share of the glory in this brilliant victory. He was the one to provoke the fight for the freedom of the press, and then he added to his services by giving in his newspaper a complete verbatim account of the trial, a valuable piece of legal and historical literature.[1] He possessed the genuine newspaper instinct and persistence. When in prison, his bail having been fixed at so high a sum, eight hundred pounds, that it was impossible to procure release, he went on publishing his newspaper energetically. He communicated with and dictated to his assistants, availing himself, it is said, of a crack in the door of his prison, and his newspaper appeared without interruption. Peter Zenger was no mere typesetter, but a live and fearless journalist of the modern stamp. The Zenger trial laid the foundation of the liberty of the press in America, and Peter Zenger himself was the founder of the first independent newspaper in the country.

[1] This report, printed in full in the works of Kapp and Rutherford, named in the footnote above, puts to shame the charge of ignorance sometimes made against the "Palatine apprentice." Equally unfair is the statement that the "poor printer" knew not the importance of the stand he was taking. We might in the same way find fault with Luther or Columbus because they did not realize at the time the full consequences of the radical steps they were taking.

(handwritten annotations in top margin)

A brief Narrative of the Case and Tryal of *John Peter Zenger*, Printer of the *New-York weekly Journal*.

AS There was but one Printer in the Province of *New-York*, that printed a publick News Paper, I was in Hopes, if I undertook to publish another, I might make it worth my while; and I soon found my Hopes were not groundless: My first Paper was printed, *Nov.* 5th, 1733. and I continued printing and publishing of them, I thought to the Satisfaction of every Body, till the *January* following, when the Chief Justice was pleased to animadvert upon the Doctrine of Libels, in a long Charge given in that Term to the Grand Jury, and afterwards on the third *Tuesday* of *October*, 1734. was again pleased to charge the Grand Jury in the following Words.

'*Gentlemen*; I shall conclude with reading a Paragraph or two out of the 'same Book, concerning Libels; they are arrived to that Height, that they 'call loudly for your Animadversion; it is high Time to put a Stop to them; 'for at the rate Things are now carried on, when all Order and Government 'is endeavoured to be trampled on; Reflections are cast upon Persons of all 'Degrees, must not these Things end in Sedition, if not timely prevented? Lenity, 'you have seen will not avail, it becomes you then to enquire after the Of- 'fenders, that we may in a due Course of Law be enabled to punish them. 'If you, *Gentlemen*, do not interpose, consider whether the ill Consequences 'that may arise from any Disturbances of the publick Peace, may not in part, 'lye at your Door?

'*Hawkins*, in his Chapter of Libels, considers three Points. 1st. *What shall* '*be said to be a Libel.* 2dly. *Who are lyable to be punished for it.* 3dly. *In what* '*Manner they are to be punished.* Under the 1st. he says, §. 7. Nor can there be '*any Doubt, but that a Writing which defames a private Person only, is as much* '*a Libel as that which defames Persons intrusted in a publick Capacity, in as much* '*as it manifestly tends to create ill Blood, and to cause a Disturbance of the publick Peace;* '*however, it is certain, that it is a very high Aggravation of a Libel, that it tends to* '*scandalize the Government, by reflecting on those who are entrusted with the Ad mini-* '*stration of publick Affairs, which does not only endanger the publick Peace, as all other* '*Libels do, by stirring up the Parties immediately concerned in it, to Acts of Revenge,* '*but also has a direct Tendency to breed in the People a Dislike of their Governours,* '*and incline them to Faction and Sedition.* As to the 2d. Point he says §. 10. '*It is certain, not only he who composes or procures another to compose it but* '*also that he who publishes, or procures another to publish it, are in Danger of being* '*punished for it; and it is said not to be material whether he who disperses a Libel,* '*knew any Thing of the Contents or Effects of it or not; for nothing could be more*

A   *easy*

FIRST PAGE OF ZENGER'S TRIAL

CHAPTER V

THE GERMANS IN PENNSYLVANIA

The various religious sects — The Lutherans, German Reformed, and United Brethren, the three most influential denominations — Statistics, and characteristics of the Pennsylvania German farmer, and the sixteen points enumerated by Dr. Rush, the "Tacitus" of the Pennsylvanians — Industrial activity of the Pennsylvania Germans — Their printing-presses, newspapers, schools.

THE principal port of entry for German immigrations before the Revolution was Philadelphia. Some Germans, as will be seen, entered at northern ports; after the ill-starred arrival of the Palatines, however, only a few immigrants landed at New York; Baltimore[1] and Charleston received more Germans, though the exact number is difficult to ascertain; but probably all ports combined did not surpass Philadelphia. The immigrations before the Revolution may be divided into three periods. The earliest, from 1683 to 1710, is the least in amount, and represents the initial movement. An increase came between 1710 and 1727, the latter being the year when records of the immigration were begun, with names of persons and generally of the country whence they came. The reason for recording the immigration was its great increase, sometimes amounting to from five to eight thousand a year, and the consequent fear that this swelling German population, together with the large Scotch-Irish immigration, might change the character of the state

[1] Including Annapolis and Alexandria, i. e., all the Germans coming by way of Chesapeake Bay.

politically and socially. Though there recurred from time to time a nativistic agitation, nothing was done prohibitive of immigration.

After the settlement of Germantown, in 1683, and its subsequent accessions, the second strong current of German immigration into Pennsylvania was that of the Swiss Mennonites, about 1710. They were of the same religious faith as the original settlers of Germantown, who had been Mennonites before joining the Quakers, and whose favorable reports from Pennsylvania no doubt induced their brethren to try their fortunes also in the land of Penn. The movement gained strength in 1711, when the Mennonites of Bern were offered free transportation down the Rhine, the privileges of selling their property and taking their families with them, provided they would pledge themselves never to return to Switzerland. The Mennonites of Holland offered them a helping hand, especially the Dutch ambassador, Runckel. The Swiss Mennonites selected as their settlement a tract of ten thousand acres on Pequa Creek, Conestoga, in what is now Lancaster County (organized in 1729), their patent being made out in the names of Hans Herr and Martin Kundig.[1] The industrious and gentle Mennonites lived on good terms with the Conestoga and Mingo Indian tribes, and with the help of the later German immigrants, that soon poured into the county, Lancaster became the

[1] Some of the names of the Lancaster County Swiss are the following : Aeschlimann, Brubacher, Baumgartner, Brechbühl, Bucher, Bühler, Bürki, Ebersold, Egli, Fahrni, Flückiger, Frick (from Zurich), Galli, Gäumann, Gerber, Goshnauer, Graf, Gut, Haldimann, Hauri, Huber, Jeggli, Krähenbühl (Krehbiel), Kuenzi, Landis, Maurer, Meili, Neukomm, Oberli, Ringer, Rohner, Rubeli, Rubi, Ruegsegger, Rupp, Schallenberger, Schürch, Stähli, Strahm, Wenger, Wisler, Zürcher. Cf. Kuhns, *The German and Swiss Settlements of Colonial Pennsylvania: a Study of the So-called Pennsylvania Dutch*, pp. 46, 47. Holt & Co., 1901.

garden spot and pride of Pennsylvania. Another very old settlement of the Mennonites was that at Skippack in Montgomery County, where a number of the old Germantown Mennonites settled as early as 1702. One hundred acres were presented by Van Bibber for a church, erected about 1726.

In doctrine the Mennonites resembled the Quakers closely. They would not bear arms, they believed in the separation of church and state, the freedom of conscience, simplicity of dress and life. They refused to take oaths, and baptized only on the profession of faith. Their founder was Menno Simons (1492–1559) of Friesland. In the seventeenth century there was a schism, dividing the sect into Ammenites [1] (or Upland Mennonites) and Lowland Mennonites. The former were the more conservative and rigorous in doctrine and in dress. The use of buttons, for instance, was considered a vain thing, and hooks and eyes became the substitute. They are also called Amish, and their number in the United States to-day is about fifteen thousand. [2]

Another sect which chose Pennsylvania as a place of refuge very early in the history of the province was that of the Dunkards or Tunkers. Their name is derived from their method of baptism, dipping (in German, *eintunken*).

---

[1] After the founder, Jacob Ammen, of the Canton Bern, Switzerland. There were other divisions in the Mennonite Church, such as the formation of the Reformed Mennonites. On this subject, see Kuhns, *German and Swiss Settlements of Pennsylvania*, pp. 178 ff. The chapter on "The Religious Life of the Pennsylvania Germans," pp. 153–192, is an excellent presentation of the subject of the German sectarians of Pennsylvania.

[2] The last census (1900) reports the number of Amish as . 13,413
Of old Amish as 2,438
Together 15,851

The total number of Mennonites in the United States, including the Amish, is 59,892.

HUNT LIBRARY
CARNEGIE MELLON UNIVERSITY

As in the case of the Mennonites, there was with them no infant baptism, they refused to take oaths or bear arms, and to accept public office. They would not institute a lawsuit against brethren of the order, and they lived the simple life. Alexander Mack was the founder, in 1708, establishing a congregation at Schwarzenau in Westphalia. In course of time all of the Dunkards came to Pennsylvania, the first group of twenty families arriving in 1719. They were distributed among the settlements of Germantown, Skippack, Oley (in Berks County), and Conestoga. Their leader, Peter Baker (Becker), sometime minister under Mack, made a tour of all the Tunker settlements in 1723, instituted among them a revival of their religion, and succeeded also in gaining many new members. One of the most prominent Tunkers was the printer Cristopher Sauer, the publisher of a German newspaper with a wide circulation throughout the province. The paper made him one of the most influential men among the German settlers, and gave prominence to religious principles that the Tunkers had in common with the Mennonites, Quakers, and Anabaptists, such as rigorous simplicity in dress and habits, refusal to bear arms, take oaths, or accept public office, principles which were opposed to the more strenuous and militant rule of life exhibited by the patriarch of the Lutheran Church, Mühlenberg, and his friend of the Reformed Church, Schlatter, who was soon to appear in Pennsylvania.

Conrad Beissel had been chosen assistant to Baker, in the fold of the Tunkers, but, " being wise in his own conceit," Beissel soon caused trouble in the church, on the issue of Sabbath observance. He declared that the day of rest should be celebrated on the seventh day, and when a council held at Conestoga, where the founder, Alexander Mack, who had come to visit Pennsylvania, was present,

REAR VIEW OF SAAL AND SISTER HOUSE

SOUTH VIEW OF THE BROTHER HOUSE

EPHRATA MONASTERY

decided against him, he determined to secede. With a few followers he organized a society of "Seventh-Day Baptists" on the Conestoga, but some years later, desiring even greater seclusion from the world, he fled to the Cocalico and there founded the Cloister of Ephrata.[1] Its successful administration, peculiar customs, and devotion to music, rendered it unique and picturesque. There was a home for the brothers and one for the sisters, with such names as Kedar, Bethania, and Saron, and some of their buildings have lasted even to our day. Tonsure and monkish robes were introduced, asceticism prevailed, and devotion to the order characterized them from the beginning, when the brethren balked not at becoming their own plow-horses. All property was owned by the order, which grew rapidly in wealth through the self-sacrificing toil of its members. The cloister owned a printing-press, from which there are still extant many of the mystical writings of Conrad Beissel ("Vater Friedsam Gottrecht"), and some of the religious songs chanted by the choirs. The literature of Ephrata reminds one strongly of the Mystic Kelpius and his brotherhood, of which the Ephrata Community, as has been observed above, is the logical successor.

Another sect that built its altar in the forests of Pennsylvania was that of the Schwenkfelders. They were founded by a contemporary of Luther, Kaspar Schwenkfeld, of Ossing, Silesia. They suffered persecution at the hands of Protestants and Catholics alike, until in 1726 they were hospitably received by Zinzendorf. In 1733–34 they immigrated and settled for the most part in Montgomery County, being most numerous in the neighborhood of Goshenhoppen.

[1] Cf. Seidensticker, *Bilder aus der deutsch-pennsylvanischen Geschichte*, pp. 169–250: "Ephrata. Eine amerikanische Klostergeschichte."

The three most important religious denominations, however, were the Lutherans, the German Reformed, and the
United Brethren (Moravians). They were not prominent
in the earliest history of the German settlements in Pennsylvania, though they may have been represented. Being
far more numerous in the mother country, they were
bound to become more and more prominent as the current
of German immigration grew in volume. This applies
especially to the Lutherans and Reformed, the Moravians
finally yielding to the former in numbers, power, and influence, retaining, however, the most prominent place in
the field of missionary work. The first Lutheran preacher
ordained in America was Justus Falckner, who entered
the ministry under the auspices of the Swedish Lutheran
church of Wicacoa (now Southwark, a part of Philadelphia). Undoubtedly he was one of the first, if not the
first German Lutheran preacher in America. Soon after
ordination (1703) he preached to the Germans in Falckner's Swamp (New Hanover), the land which his brother,
Daniel Falckner, had acquired for the Frankfort Company.[1] Soon Justus Falckner was called to serve the Lutheran churches in New York and Albany, leaving Falckner's Swamp without a preacher. Another old Lutheran
settlement before 1729 was that called Trappe (New
Providence), located south of New Hanover, between the
Schuylkill and the Perkiomen, in Montgomery County.
The other Lutherans were located in Germantown and
Philadelphia. It was very common in the early days
for the Lutherans and Reformed to use the same building for worship, sometimes even to retain the same min-

---

[1] As previously noted, it was the remaining portion of the 25,000 acres
after 2675 had been deducted for Germantown and 300 for a tract on the
Schuylkill above the Wissahickon, leaving 22,025 acres.

ister, as was the practice in Philadelphia. In Germantown the Lutherans laid the foundation of their church in 1730.[1]

Under these circumstances the Lutheran Church could not prosper. Therefore three congregations, those of Philadelphia, New Hanover, and Providence, in 1733, united to petition the Lutheran court preacher of London, Reverend F. M. Ziegenhagen, for assistance. A minister was asked for, and contributions in money for the building of a Lutheran church. The matter was much delayed, because of the dishonesty of two of the delegates, who had been sent abroad for the purpose of getting financial assistance. In 1741 a fortunate choice was made in the selection of Heinrich Melchior Mühlenberg, as pastor for the three Pennsylvania congregations. Mühlenberg had studied at Göttingen and prepared himself for his profession at Halle, where Pastor August Hermann Francke was the head of the Lutheran Church, or more strictly of the Pietistic wing. Mühlenberg did not proceed at once to Pennsylvania, but preferred first to visit Pastor Bolzius, the leader of the Salzburg colony in Georgia, in order to get from him some information as to conditions in America. This was done on the advice of the Reverend Mr. Ziegenhagen and was fortunate for him, preparing the young man well for coming events in Pennsylvania and helping him to understand a very intricate problem in the southern colony, which he was subsequently called to solve. In Charleston, before he reached Ebenezer in Georgia, he heard that Count Zinzendorf had arrived in Philadelphia under the name of von Thürnstein, and that he was making a great stir in the church. Mühlenberg there-

---

[1] Other German denominations, that were more numerous, had meeting-houses long before this.

fore hastened his departure, boarded an inferior sloop, but arrived safely on November 25, 1741, in Philadelphia.

When he landed, he was told that one part of the Lutherans favored Count Zinzendorf, and that the others held to Valentin Kraft, the Lutheran preacher who had been deposed by the church authorities in Germany. He heard also that in his prospective home at New Hanover, a dentist named Schmidt was serving as preacher. With such prospects before him, Mühlenberg. on a raw, cold, wintry day at the end of November, rode to New Hanover, thirty-six miles distant, in order to present himself to his congregation. The confusion resulting on his arrival drew from Mühlenberg the comment in a letter, " that he was obliged to undergo a moral seasickness after his physical one!" The people in Trappe counseled him to make a compromise with Mr. Kraft, but that was impossible for such a man as Mühlenberg, not given to halfway measures, particularly when he knew that he was right. The firm position he took, demanding without stint the office for which the three congregations had called him, had a lasting good effect. The battle was fought to a finish at once. Kraft was expelled and Mühlenberg had a clear field ever after.

There was also considerable difficulty with the Moravians, who claimed to be a part of the Lutheran Church, with Zinzendorf as its proper head. Mühlenberg's course of action was characterized by tact and firmness, and he was soon made more secure in his position by a favorable decision in the courts. Combining piety and learning with clear vision and rare gifts of organization, he gave the Lutheran Church in America such a good beginning that in course of time it surpassed in size and influence the

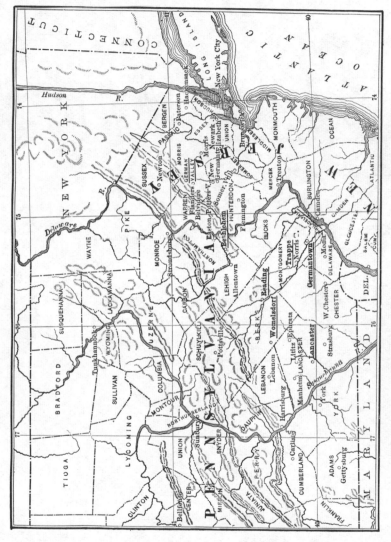

AREA OF EARLY GERMAN SETTLEMENTS IN PENNSYLVANIA AND NEW JERSEY

German Reformed Church, which, when Schlatter first arrived, possessed a larger number of preachers and churches. The steady growth of the Lutheran Church can be followed in detail in the so-called "Hallesche Nachrichten,"[1] a large collection of reports and letters sent to the Lutheran ministerium of Halle in Germany, by Lutheran preachers in America. Most instructive are the numerous reports of Mühlenberg, stating in detail the facts of his arrival, his initial difficulties and every subsequent step taken ; how he at first was the pastor of the three churches of New Hanover, Providence, and Philadelphia, until, the duties becoming too burdensome, it was necessary to get assistance, the Reverend Mr. Brunnholtz being then assigned to Philadelphia and Germantown, Mühlenberg having chosen New Hanover and Providence ; then follow the plans for building a church in Philadelphia, the cost seeming at first an insurmountable barrier, overcome at last with unexpected ease " mit Gottes Hilfe "; the formation of new congregations in Lancaster, York, Reading, Tulpehocken, Easton, and many other places where " parched souls were crying in the desert." The Halle reports, somewhat pedantic in style, and weighted down with a mass of material, give us a realistic picture of the times, from the ministerial point of view. The accuracy of the reports cannot be questioned, since they were written by men of learning and strict regard for the truth. The variety of qualifications necessary for such a post as Mühlenberg's cannot be well understood without a perusal of his reports. He was minister, helper, and adviser in social and spirit-

---

[1] *Nachrichten von den vereinigten Deutschen Evangelisch-Lutherischen Gemeinen in Nord-Amerika, absonderlich in Pennsylvanien.* Halle, in Verlegung des Waisenhauses, 1787. 1 Bd. Allentown, Pa., 1886 ; 2 Bd. Philadelphia, 1895 ; reprints in German. The work has been translated, and published in two volumes by the Lutheran Publication Society, Philadelphia, 1880–81.

ual matters, diplomatist, man of affairs, and frontiersman. Hardships, discomforts, or bodily fatigue never could swerve him from his purpose, adventure and hairbreadth escapes added zest to the sum of his existence. An experience such as the following, at the river crossing in midwinter, was not uncommon.

Returning from service in Philadelphia, in November, 1749, Mühlenberg had twenty miles to ride to his residence. Night overtook him and his companion, and they reached the Perkiomen Creek at eleven o'clock. This was still two miles distant from Mühlenberg's home, and, to his great surprise, he found the river frozen over. His companion had a small horse, unshod, and the minister, therefore, rode in advance to make a path in the ice. To accomplish this, he had to force his horse to rear, so that on coming down the animal would break holes in the ice with his fore feet. They got over safely, but in the darkness missed the outlet on the other side, and came to a bank that was high and almost perpendicular. Not daring to venture back, they took their saddles off their horses, and, with the aid of the bushes, clambered up on land. They tied the girths to the bridle of the small horse, and, forcing him to stand on his hind feet, enabled him to reach the top of the bank with his fore feet. Being pulled vigorously, the horse helped himself bravely, and reached the top in safety. But when the same method was applied to Mühlenberg's horse, which was old and stiff, the bridle broke and the unfortunate beast fell backward with its full weight upon the ice. The ice gave way, and the poor animal lay in the water on its back with legs turned up, and must have drowned, had not the men given it some help; but the horse broke through again and started for the other side obliging them to abandon it, to be looked for next day, and fortunately to be rescued. Saddles and baggage were placed on the other horse, and the men wandered about for some time in the dark thickets, in a circle, until the stars happening to shed light for a short while, allowed them to find their home, about three o'clock in the morning.

The Lutheran church built in Philadelphia, the St. Michaelskirche, was found to be too small after twenty years' occupancy. A new one, the famous Zion Church, was begun in 1766 and consecrated in 1769. It was for many years the largest church in Philadelphia, and because of its spacious interior (108 feet long and 70 feet broad) frequently served as a gathering place for large assemblages, some of them noted in American history. Thus the memorial meeting in honor of Benjamin Franklin, who died the year before, was held in Zion Church in 1791 under the auspices of the Philosophical Society. On December 26, 1799, in the same church, Congress held the funeral services of George Washington, and on that occasion, those ringing words, "First in war, first in peace, first in the hearts of his countrymen," pronounced in the eulogy by Henry Lee, were heard for the first time.[1]

The German-Lutheran congregation of Philadelphia

---

[1] In the Revolutionary War, during the occupation of the British, the church was used as a hospital for soldiers (1778), while the older German church, St. Michael's, served as a place of worship for the British, the German congregation being allowed to retain it for service only one half the time. The British destroyed or removed all the seats of Zion Church, and hence the curious injunction, after the departure of the invaders (found in *Hallesche Nachrichten*, vol. ii, p. 731), that the congregation should bring their chairs with them. The church served about one hundred years, when it was torn down and succeeded by the New Zion Church on Franklin Street; the large congregation was divided into several smaller ones. Cf. *Hallesche Nachrichten*, §§ 1241, 1245, 1408, 1424–26. Also Seidensticker, *Bilder*, etc., p. 254, and *Der deutsche Pionier*, vol. viii, pp. 190–192. "Das alte Philadelphia" (Seidensticker).

numbered nine hundred souls,[1] the most numerous in the capital city at the time of the Revolution. In 1762 Mühlenberg took charge of the Philadelphia congregation, because it needed a firm hand, and he continued until 1776, when, on account of his age, he preferred to go back to his old charge in the rural Trappe district, where he spent the last ten years of his life. During his long career he was frequently called to arbitrate church difficulties, as near by in New Jersey, or in distant Georgia,[2] or to inspire confidence among scattered congregations in Pennsylvania, Maryland, and Virginia. In the summer of 1751 and again in 1752, in order to strengthen the Lutheran church in New York, he resided there as its pastor. Mühlenberg cultivated friendly relations with the Lutheran Swedes, who had been on the Delaware before the arrival of William Penn ; he was on a cordial footing also with the German Reformed pastors, particularly Schlatter. There was likewise an intimacy between the Lutherans and Episcopalians, another instance of which appeared in South Carolina.[3] Strange as it may seem at the present day, a hard and fast line was drawn between Lutherans and Moravians. This was probably due in part to the personality of Zinzendorf, in part also to the fact that the Moravians claimed to be Lutherans, accepting the dogmatic principles laid down in the Augsburg Confession. The rivalry as to who truly represented Lutheranism occasioned bitter antagonism.

As the Lutherans had a great leader in Mühlenberg, so the German Reformed congregations found an organizer

[1] The charter, see *Hallesche Nachrichten*, vol. ii, pp. 629–632 (§§ 1256–60), mentions " about 500 heads of families," in 1765.

[2] See Chapter VI and Chapter IX, respectively.

[3] Cf. Chapter VII. Some of the Lutheran Swedes of Pennsylvania also joined the Episcopal Church.

HEINRICH MELCHIOR MÜHLENBERG

in Michael Schlatter. Most of the Palatines probably belonged to the German Reformed Church, which was akin to the Lutheran, but followed reforms instituted by Calvin and Zwingli. They were very close in their religious doctrines to the Presbyterians, and the Dutch Reformed Church. Schlatter was sent to America by the synods of Holland, the Reformed ministerium in the Palatinate being too weak and humble to extend its influence to foreign parts. When he arrived, in September, 1746, he found only four preachers of the Reformed Church in Pennsylvania, while the number of communicants was estimated at fifteen thousand. He hastened from one settlement to another, to Whitpen, Germantown, Goshenhoppen, Tulpehocken, Lancaster, Falckner's Swamp, and Indian Field, to gather his sheep into folds. He seems to have obtained assistance more easily than Mühlenberg, for in 1748 four other preachers came to help him, in addition to those already present. In 1751 Schlatter reported to the Dutch synods that there were fifteen Reformed parishes in the country, with forty-six churches (thirteen parishes with thirty-eight churches being located in Pennsylvania). Most of them, he declared, were without preachers or teachers, and he appealed earnestly to the Dutch synods to send ministers. The same cry went up from Mühlenberg and all other representatives of denominations, showing that if the frontiersmen were irreligious, a mitigating circumstance was their inability to get religious instruction. Schlatter was not as fortunate in his own career as Mühlenberg. There were misunderstandings with the synods in Holland, and, perhaps in part through his own fault, his position in his own congregation was undermined. He resigned as preacher in Philadelphia,[1] and became army

---

[1] The German Reformed Church was also once used on a public occasion.

chaplain under Colonel Loudon in the Royal American Regiment, fourth battalion, which was mainly composed of Germans. He was chaplain in the campaign against Nova Scotia and Louisbourg. He held a similar position during the Revolutionary War.

The fact of Schlatter's serving as army chaplain is significant, likewise his cordial relations with Mühlenberg. As to their principles of life, their views on religion and the social order, the two men were very much alike, fighting shoulder to shoulder. Together they represented the strong counter-current in Pennsylvania, opposing the views on state and religion held by Quakers, Mennonites, Pietists, Moravians, and numerous other non-resistant, non-office-holding sectarians. Mühlenberg and Schlatter were fighters, vigorous men, whose influence later fell heavily in the balance for armed resistance against British oppression, and who always favored strenuous, virile principles in church and state government.

Totally different was the influence of the Moravians, or United Brethren. The name Moravian is not a happy one. It serves to commemorate one fact in history, but only one, namely, that originally a number of the brethren lived in Moravia (Austria), where they had descended from the Hussites (Utraquists) of Bohemia and Moravia.[1]

On February 19, 1776, the Honorable Dr. W. Smith delivered a eulogy on General Montgomery, who fell at Quebec. The number of hearers was estimated at four thousand. Apart from the German Zion Church and the German Reformed Church, Philadelphia possessed very few public structures. Cf. Seidensticker, *Der deutsche Pionier*, vol. viii, pp. 190–191.

[1] Followers of John Huss, born 1369, burned at the stake in Constance, in 1415. He was the great religious reformer before Luther, descended from Czech peasants, influenced by doctrines of Wyclif, who wished to bring about a reformation without separation from the Catholic Church. He was summoned before the Council of Constance and, in spite of a safe-conduct of the Emperor, was arrested and burned as a heretic. His martyrdom greatly

Suffering persecution at home, the remnant, in 1722, settled in Herrnhut, Saxony, on the estates of the Count of Zinzendorf at his invitation. It is questionable whether many of the brotherhood, as constituted in the eighteenth century [1] or at the present day, ever saw Moravia, or whether they were ever descended from Moravians. The German name given them is "Herrnhuter," while the members themselves adopted the name "Unitas Fratrum," or "United Brethren."

The United Brethren are most noted as missionaries, and at the very earliest period set up as their goal the conversion of the Indians. With this purpose in view they had selected Georgia as their appropriate field, in 1735–36 settling with the Salzburgers at Ebenezer. But when during the war with Spain they were expected to bear arms in defense of the colony in opposition to their religious principles, they left Georgia and betook themselves to Pennsylvania, 1738–39. David Nitschmann, son-in-law of Zinzendorf, bought five hundred acres on the Lehigh (Lecha), "in a barren wooded region." Count Zinzendorf, who visited the spot shortly after his arrival in 1741, gave it the name of Bethlehem. In the same year they bought nearly five thousand acres from George Whitefield, the Methodist, who had made this purchase in order to found

increased the spread of liberal doctrines in Bohemia and Moravia. The fierce Hussite wars arose in 1419, and lasted until 1434.

[1] Queerly enough, the name Moravian has clung to them in the United States, though there is documentary evidence showing that the members themselves fought against this appellation in the eighteenth century. "We are Lutherans," said one (Brother Leonhard Schnell, "Diary," 1747, *Virginia Magazine*, vol. xii, pp. 55 ff.) of the traveling missionaries, and "there are now [1747] not ten in Bethlehem who were born in Moravia." We can say with positiveness that the so-called "Moravians" that appeared in Pennsylvania were Germans, the exceptions being generally brethren not from Moravia, but from their other European home, namely, England.

a negro school, a scheme doomed to failure financially. On this place Nazareth was founded. The immigration of Moravians to Pennsylvania numbered from seven to eight hundred between 1741 and 1762. Zinzendorf, on his arrival, had distinctly in mind the realization of two ideals: first, the conversion of the Indians, secondly, the union of all Protestant churches in a bond of the spirit. Endowed with a vast amount of optimism and energy, Zinzendorf proceeded to invite delegates of all Protestant denominations and sects to meet in Germantown on January 1, 1742. A number of conferences were held in different places under "the Congregation of God in the Spirit." At first there seemed to be hope of accomplishing something, but it soon appeared that few were willing to give up anything, or yield a point. Zinzendorf and his followers held the sway, and the others grew suspicious and withdrew, thinking that Moravian influence and doctrine would overpower them. Those that remained entered the Moravian Church, when it was organized as a separate denomination in the Twenty-eighth Synod, held in Bethlehem, October 23–27, 1748. Zinzendorf's scheme was too grand for realization, and it failed as completely as the similar earlier[1] attempt by Kelpius. The religious sects had come to Pennsylvania to worship in their own way, not to give up their idiosyncrasies, and time alone would be able to put them into the mood of compromise.

Zinzendorf made three journeys into the Indian country, and then returned to Europe, in 1743. His successor was August Gottlieb Spangenberg, who for twenty years was the able head of the United Brethren. He was seconded by Cammerhoff and Peter Böhler. The missionary work among the Indians was continued, and with very

[1] See the close of Chapter II, p. 50.

great success, first in the states of New York and Connecticut. After the Christian Indians were driven away from the colonies by the hostility of the white settlers, a new Indian settlement, Gnadenhütten, was begun at the junction of the Mahoney Creek and Lehigh River. Other missionary posts were built out into the wilderness, and such devoted missionaries as Rauch, Heckewelder, Zeisberger, Jungmann, Post, and Sensemann gained for the Moravians the well-earned reputation of having been the most successful Indian missionaries in the history of the United States.[1]

Another important influence of the Moravians was wrought by their educational institutions. Their day- and boarding-schools in ten different localities, particularly in Bethlehem, Litiz, and Nazareth, were among the best in Pennsylvania. The young ladies' seminary at Bethlehem is still in existence and of very great usefulness. It was founded in 1749 and claims in its modern advertisement to be the oldest school of its kind in America. Similar in purpose is the Moravian Ladies' Seminary in Salem, North Carolina, which also was of very early foundation.

In doctrine the United Brethren avoided dogmatic teaching, adhering to the Scriptures for the ethical principles of life. This was shown by those early missionaries who, about the middle of the eighteenth century, made extensive tours along the frontier settlements, starting from Pennsylvania, proceeding through the mountains of Virginia, then overland through North Carolina and along the seacoast of the Carolinas to Georgia, taking every opportunity to preach the gospel, saving souls and

---

[1] Some of their missions in the Middle West will be spoken of in succeeding chapters. Cf. Chapter XIII, " The Settlement of the Ohio Valley." The United Brethren also sent missionaries to the Danish West Indies.

giving encouragement by word and deed. It is difficult to understand why they occasioned so much opposition on the part of other denominations, unless it be that their preaching was so good, so simple and effective.[1]

The German Catholics were not numerous in Penn-·sylvania. There were congregations in Goshenhoppen (Berks County), in Lancaster, and in Philadelphia, where they built their Trinity Church in 1788. In the year 1757 there were nine hundred German Catholics in Pennsylvania, distributed among the congregations named.

It is difficult to estimate the number of Germans in Pennsylvania before the Revolution, but an approximation at least can be made, far more satisfactorily than for the other colonies. From 1727 on, the immigration at the port of Philadelphia was recorded. A careful computation of the number of Germans landed at Philadelphia between 1727 and 1775 was made by Kuhns,[2] based on the records, and compared with similar estimates by Rupp,[3] with the result, that 68,872 Germans arrived between 1727 and 1775. Kuhns assumes that before 1727 there were almost twenty thousand Germans in Pennsylvania, bringing the total up to 88,872. For the natural increase of several generations he adds a little over twenty thousand, making a grand total of about one hundred and ten thousand Pennsylvania Germans in 1775. This figure represents one third of the population, which agrees[4] with statements

---

[1] For a fuller account of their journeys see Chapter VII, pp. 203 ff.

[2] *German and Swiss Settlements of Pennsylvania*, p. 57, etc.

[3] I. D. Rupp, *Thirty Thousand Names of Immigrants*.

[4] The agreement, however, is accidental. Kuhns takes no account of the migrations of the Germans after their arrival in Pennsylvania. One third or more probably went into Maryland, Virginia, or North Carolina. But the estimate of the number of Germans in Pennsylvania as one third of the entire population is undoubtedly safe, since it was made by so many contemporary authorities. Kuhns's rate of increase is taken at too low a figure.

made by Benjamin Franklin, Dr. Rush, the historian Proud, and others,[1] to the effect that the Germans in Pennsylvania numbered about one third of the population.

We have found the Germans settling in Philadelphia and the neighboring counties, Montgomery, Lancaster, and Berks. They then pushed northward and westward to Lehigh, Northampton, and Monroe counties, and to Lebanon and Dauphin; reaching the Susquehanna they crossed and settled the counties of York, Cumberland, and Adams, then following the slopes of the mountains they went southward through Maryland into Virginia, ascending the Shenandoah Valley and settling it from Harpers Ferry to Lexington, Virginia. Using this main avenue for their progress, they settled in North Carolina and Virginia and later in Kentucky and Tennessee. Pennsylvania, therefore, was the distributing centre for the German immigrations, whence German settlers spread over all the neighboring provinces.

Though living in various parts of the United States, the pre-revolutionary Germans all belonged to the same general type, since they came from a common stock and home, mainly from the Rhine countries and Switzerland,

The increase was probably such as to double every twenty-three years, or nearly so.

[1] Mühlenberg (*Hallesche Nachrichten*, vol. i, p. 411) estimates the population of Pennsylvania in 1752 as follows : Schlatter gives the number of German Reformed in Pennsylvania as 30,000 (46 congregations, 16 parishes), and concedes that the German Reformed are only one third of the total German population of Pennsylvania. Mühlenberg estimates the Lutherans at twice the number of the Reformed. The result would be, according to Schlatter's estimate, that there were 90,000 Germans in Pennsylvania, and according to Mühlenberg 90,000 plus the Germans of various sects, making over 100,000 in 1752. The natural increase would in either case bring the number to at least 110,000 at the time of the Revolution. For larger estimates by Ebeling and Governor Thomas, see *Hallesche Nachrichten*, vol. i, p. 462, note 144.

and on their arrival met similar conditions in the American colonies. They were not paupers, though a great many of them, to pay for their transportation, were compelled to pledge themselves to several years of servitude. They were not wealthy, though many of them brought with them sums of money that they had realized from the sale of their lands at home. The later they settled in America the farther west they were obliged to move, not being able to purchase the land where it had become expensive, i. e., along the coastline. Therefore, whether in Pennsylvania, New York, Maryland, Virginia, or the Carolinas, they constantly became the settlers of the frontier, which they defended, and assisted in pushing farther and farther to the westward. The German settler became a recognized type of frontiersman, and because most numerous in Pennsylvania, or most frequently coming from there, he received the name Pennsylvania Dutch, or Pennsylvania German. His language was the dialect of the Palatinate and the Upper Rhine, mixed with a large number of common English words. His peculiarities of speech and customs made him distinct from the other colonial types, but his individuality was marked by far more noteworthy traits of character. One of the earliest writers on the subject of the Pennsylvania Germans was Dr. Benjamin Rush, the noted Philadelphia physician, one of the signers of the Declaration of Independence, surgeon in the Revolutionary Army, member of Congress, treasurer of the United States Mint, distinguished essayist on medical, social, and literary topics. Dr. Rush was a keen observer and possessed a judicial mind. He noticed that the prosperity of Pennsylvania was largely due to the Pennsylvania Germans, and began to examine into the causes of their success. He seems consciously to have imitated the example of the historian,

Tacitus, who described the virtues and vices of the ancient Germans, perhaps with a view to holding them up as an example for his own people.[1] Dr. Rush wrote what might be called the "Germania" of the Pennsylvania Germans, giving it the title: "An Account of the Manners of the German Inhabitants of Pennsylvania, Written in 1789." [2]

The author enumerates "a few particulars (under sixteen heads) in which the German farmers differ from most of the other farmers of Pennsylvania." No better characterization of the Pennsylvania Germans has ever been written than that of Dr. Rush, and his little essay, covering about twenty-five pages, is a classic in its way, certainly an historical document to be treated with due seriousness. The following are his sixteen specifications in order:—

(1) (Housing horses and cattle.) In settling a tract of land the Germans always provide large and suitable accommodations for their horses and cattle, before they lay out much money in building a house for themselves. The next generation builds a large and convenient stone house. The maxim exists among them: "A son should always begin his improvements where his father left off." The Pennsylvania German farmer has even been reproached for taking better care of his stock than of the members of his family,[3] but certain it is that sleek and well-fed

[1] Scholars of to-day have generally abandoned the theory that Tacitus had an ethical, satirical, or political purpose in the *Germania*. This, however, does not affect Dr. Rush's position, who had been brought up on the old theory. Tacitus wrote on a subject which was a burning question of the day. His view was pessimistic as to many phases of Roman life, and he welcomed an opportunity to emphasize what he considered in the Germans superior traits. Similarly Dr. Rush.

[2] Notes added by I. D. Rupp, Philadelphia, 1875. Published also among Benjamin Rush's *Essays, Literary, Moral, and Philosophical* (Philadelphia, 1798), pp. 225–248. This volume also contains the essay bearing partly on the subject: "An Account of the Progress of Population, Agriculture, Manners, and Government in Pennsylvania, in a letter to a friend in England."

[3] Meyer, *Deutsche Volkskunde*, p. 212, cites a saying of German peasants in the Palatinate: "Eine gute Kuh deckt viel Armut zu"; also

Weibersterbe isch ka Verderbe!
Aber Gaulverrecke, des isch e Schrecke!

cattle were a source of the greatest pride to him. The housing of them brought far better results than leaving them to run wild.

(2) (Good land.) "They always prefer good land, or that land on which there is a large quantity of meadow ground. By attention to the cultivation of grass, they often grow rich on farms, on which their predecessors have nearly starved. They prefer purchasing farms with some improvements, to settling on a new tract of land." Rush places the German farmer in what he calls the third class [1] of settlers, that is, the permanent kind. The first is hardly better than the hunter and savage, whose mode of life he has adopted, the second class makes a few shoddy improvements on the land, which he is glad to leave (going westward) as soon as civilization draws near. The question of the Germans' selecting good land is one frequently discussed since Dr. Rush's time. It is quite definitely settled that the Germans commonly occupied wooded land ; [2] they knew that where there was rich forest growth, good soil was to be found underneath. The Scotch-Irish and Irish preferred land that lay along navigable rivers, or such as was well watered, which was generally not as fertile. In Pennsylvania the Germans settled mostly on the great limestone areas, while the Irish colonized slate formations. This process of settling the limestone areas the Germans continued throughout Pennsylvania, Maryland, and Virginia

[1] See Rush's essay already cited : "An Account of the Progress of Population, etc., in Pennsylvania," *Essays* (1798), pp. 213–220.

[2] In the West a similar tendency is apparent. The Germans in Wisconsin have extensively settled in the wooded sections, leaving the prairies for Americans. They had harder work and a slower rise, while the Americans could cultivate larger areas and get quicker and larger returns. But the Americans more quickly drained the resources of the land, prairie land being sooner exhausted, while the Germans, with their slower and more even progress, could at a later day get more steady yields from their smaller farms. The scorn of the native American, accustomed to luxurious living, gave place to envy of his successful competitor, the frugal German farmer. Instead of the mortgaged farm, the German farmer in Wisconsin steadily grows on capital that he develops slowly by his own industry. It is again the story of the evolution of the stone house, built by the next generation. Cf. Emil Rothe, *Der deutsche Pionier*, vol. ii, p. 53.

(the Shenandoah Valley), and, as will be seen also, in the Blue
Grass region of Kentucky. The limestone areas contain the
most fertile soil, and the Germans developed it to its fullest extent.

(3) (Methods of clearing land.) " In clearing new land they
do not girdle or belt the trees simply, and leave them to perish
in the ground, as is the custom of their English or Irish neighbors ; but they generally cut them down and burn them." Under-
wood and bushes they would pull out by the roots, "grub them
out of the ground." The advantage was that the land was as fit
for cultivation the second year as in twenty years afterward.
The expense of repairing a plow, often broken by small stumps
concealed in the ground, is greater than grubbing the field completely at the first clearing.

(4) (Good feeding.) They feed their horses and cows well,
thereby practicing economy, for such animals perform twice the
labor or give twice the yield of the less well fed. " A German
horse is known in every part of the state. Indeed, he seems to
feel with his lord the pleasure and pride of his extraordinary
size and fat."

(5) (Fences.) "The fences of a German farm are generally
high and well built so that his fields seldom suffer from the inroads of his own or his neighbor's horses or cattle." This is a
mark of the German's adaptability. He was not accustomed to
fences at home, but saw their usefulness in the new country
where there was no scarcity of wood, but scarcity of labor, i. e.,
of men to watch cattle.

(6) (Use of wood.) " The German farmers are great econ-
omists of their wood." They do not waste it in large fireplaces,
but burn it in stoves, using about one fourth to one fifth as much.
They thus save their horses the great labor of hauling wood
in midwinter, which so often unfits them for spring plowing.
Their houses are very comfortable with their large stoves [1] in

---

[1] These large stoves were patterned after the German " Kachelofen."
Undoubtedly many were imported, but later they were made in this country,
e. g., by Baron Stiegel. As a result of the use of stoves, the German-built
house commonly had one chimney from the middle of the roof, while the
English or other houses had two chimneys, one at either end of the roof.

the centre of the room, around which the family can get a more equal chance than when burning their faces and freezing their backs before the fireplaces. Dr. Rush believed that habits of industry, e. g., spinning and repairing farm utensils were encouraged in this way. He also mentions that the Germans frequently protected their trees with a view to saving their wood, putting fences around them,[1] or letting saplings grow for later usefulness, and in general giving attention to the principles of forestry.

(7) (Comfort of cattle.) "They keep their horses and cattle as warm as possible in winter, by which they save feed, for those animals when they are cold eat much more than when they are more comfortable."

(8) (Economy.) "The Germans live frugally in their homes with respect to diet, furniture and dress." They sell the profitable grain, which is wheat, and eat the rye and corn, thus saving what is equal to the price of a farm for one of the children. They eat sparingly of boiled meat, but large quantities of all kinds of vegetables. They use few distilled spirits (whiskey and rum) in their families, preferring cider, beer, wine, and simple water. Their feather beds and homespun garments are likewise economical. When they use European articles of dress, they prefer those of best quality and highest price. They are afraid of debt, and seldom purchase anything without paying cash for it.

(9) (Gardens.) Kitchen gardening the Germans introduced altogether. Their gardens contained useful vegetables at every season of the year. Turnips and cabbage at one time were the principal vegetables in Philadelphia. A greater variety was brought in by the German gardeners in the neighborhood of Philadelphia, " and to the use of these vegetables in diet may be ascribed the general exemption of the citizens of Philadelphia from diseases of the skin." (The testimony of an experienced physician is extremely valuable on this point.) " Pennsylvania is indebted to the Germans for the principal part of her know-

---

[1] Large trees were often kept in pasture land to afford shade for the cattle, cool retreats to escape from the sun's heat. The fence served to protect the tree from the cattle.

ledge in horticulture." Though Dr. Rush apparently means a
particular branch of horticulture, the raising of vegetables, we
find from other sources that the Germans planted orchards
in abundance (e. g., apples in Schoharie), and that they were
very fond of planting flowers on the edges of their gardens and
houses.

(10) (Few hired men.) The Germans seldom hire men to
work upon their farms. The wives and daughters of the German
farmers frequently forsake for a while their dairy and spinning-
wheel and join with their husbands and brothers in the labor of
the fields.[1] The work of the gardens is generally done by the
women of the family. Hired help was procured only in harvest
time. Slaves were particularly objectionable to the Germans,
because the latter did their own work and thus would be compelled to work side by side with a race instinctively repulsive to
them.

(11) (Wagons.) "A large and strong wagon covered with
linen cloth is an essential part of the furniture of a German
farm. In this wagon, drawn by four or five large horses of a
peculiar breed, they convey to market over the roughest roads
2000 or 3000 pounds of produce. In September and October
on the Lancaster and Reading roads it is no uncommon thing to
meet from fifty to one hundred of these wagons on their way
to Philadelphia, most of which belong to German farmers."
The breed of horses referred to is probably the heavy stock
called sometimes the Conestoga horses,[2] and the wagon the
famous Conestoga wagon, "the ship of inland commerce." These
wagons are described in the county histories of Pennsylvania as
of a particular pattern. The body of the wagon was built strong
but not clumsy, was painted blue and mounted upon sturdy
wheels, painted red, masterpieces of the wheelwright's art. A
cover of white linen was drawn tightly over the arched frame-
work of the top, lower near the middle and projecting like a
bonnet in front and at the back. The horses were equipped with

---

[1] Cf. Whittier's poem, "Maud Muller."

[2] Derived and improved from a stock brought over by English immigrants. — Note by Rupp.

good harness, sometimes with sleigh-bells,[1] and were invariably possessed of sleek skins and round bodies. The railroads ended the régime of the Conestoga wagons in the East, but then they gained a new life under the name of "prairie schooner," the vehicle of overland passage that carried untold numbers of pioneers across the western deserts.[2]

(12) (Children.) "The favorable influence of agriculture, as conducted by the Germans, in extending the most happiness, is manifested by the joy expressed at the birth of a child. No dread of poverty or distrust of Providence from an increasing family depress the spirits of this industrious and frugal people." As elsewhere on the frontier the birth of a child meant a helper, and as the children became of age they wandered westward and built homes of their own, being no care to their parents.

(13) (Love of labor.) "Germans produced in their children not only the *habits* of labor but a *love* of it. When a young man asks the consent of his father to marry the girl of his choice, he does not inquire so much whether she be rich or poor, or whether she possess any personal or mental accomplishments, but whether she be industrious, and acquainted with the duties of a good housewife." Rupp in his notes gives a number of proverbs illustrative of the consequences of idleness,[3] etc.

(14) (Patrimony.) "The Germans set a great value upon patrimonial property." The idea prevails that a house and home should be possessed by a succession of generations. This had the effect of making an estate a matter of family pride, and we shall see later that the Germans elsewhere, for instance in Missouri, always kept their land in the family.

(15) (Superstition.) "The German farmers are very much influenced in planting and pruning trees, also in sowing and reaping, by the age and appearances of the moon." Of course

---

[1] They were often tuned in harmony, the rear horses carrying bells of lower pitch, to distinguish them from the forward pair.

[2] Ellis and Evans's *History of Lancaster County*, p. 350 Also, *Americana Germanica*, vol. v, p. 1 ; an illustration of the Conestoga wagon is there given.

[3] e. g., "Müssiggang ist des Teufels Ruhebank."

"Wie einer den Zaun hält, halt er auch das Gut."

"Mit Futtern ist keine Zeit verlorn."

this was a matter of superstition, but Dr. Rush believes that it resulted in their giving close attention to the climate of the country, and therefore was an aid to success. The Pennsylvania Germans were as careful as seamen in observing the position of the heavenly spheres and the signs of the seasons. They consulted the mystics,[1] or other people believed to possess occult power. The divining-rod was expected to show them the presence of water in the ground, and old women with the reputation of witches (they were never burned) furnished talismans, incantations, and magic formulas. The different phases of the moon were carefully observed in the almanac, for planting was better done in the waxing of the moon than in the waning. The moon in the sign of the twins made the best time for sowing. Not only sowing and planting, but slaughtering and building were carefully planned with reference to mysterious influences. Even more curious were their magic arts of healing, and concerning these Dr. Rush, the physician, could not repress some words of complaint. But in general it may be said that the German frontiersmen were not worse than their contemporaries elsewhere, they were not as fanatical as the witch-burners, nor was their folklore more extravagant than in other sections of the country.

(16) (Barns.) " A German farm may be distinguished from the farms of the other citizens of the state by the superior size of their barns,[2] the plain but compact form of their houses, the height of their enclosures, the extent of their orchards, the fer-

---

[1] See Chapter II, p. 50.

[2] The Pennsylvania German barn (sometimes called the "Swisser" barn) is recognizable in all localities where the German farmers have settled. It is of a peculiar type, largely imitated from that used in their European home. The following is a description in detail : " They are two stories high, with pitched roof, sufficiently large and strong to enable heavy farm-teams to drive into the upper story to load or unload grain. During the first period they were built mostly of logs, afterward of stone, frame, or brick, from 60 to 120 feet long, and from 50 to 60 feet wide, the lower story, containing the stables, with feeding passages, opening on the front. The upper story was made to project 8 or 10 feet over the lower in front, or with a forebay attached to shelter the entries to the stables and passageways. It contained the threshing-floors, mows, and lofts for the storing of hay and grain. The most complete barns of the present day have in addition a granary on the

tility of their fields, the luxuriance of their meadows, all of which have a general appearance of plenty and neatness in everything that belongs to them."

The opinion of Rush agrees with other contemporary accounts, and also with that of subsequent European travelers, such as Bernhard of Saxe-Weimar and others. They affirm the superiority of the German farmers over the agriculturists of other nationalities. The significance of this superiority should not be overlooked. Professor F. J. Turner[1] says: "The limestone farms of the Germans became the wheat granary of the country." In the year 1751 there were exported 86,000 bushels of wheat, 129,960 barrels of flour, 90,743 bushels of Indian corn. The total exports of 1751 exceeded in value one million dollars.[2] An interesting account of the milling industry of Lancaster County, the very core of the great farming country of Pennsylvania, can be seen in an article based on researches on the spot by G. D. Luetscher.[3] By the time the Revolutionary War began, the yield of the Pennsylvania farms was enough to feed the American and French armies during the entire period of the war. Indeed, the Pennsylvania German

upper floor, a cellar under the driving-way, a corn-crib and shed, wagon with horse-power shed attached." See Kuhns, pp. 94, 95, who quotes this passage from Ellis and Evans's *History of Lancaster County*, p. 348.

Professor M. D. Learned has made extensive investigations on the subject of the Pennsylvania German barns, and has given his results in a number of illustrated lectures, to be published under the title: "The German Barn in America."

[1] *Studies of American Immigration*, by Frederick Jackson Turner, in the *Record-Herald's* "Current Topics Club," *Record-Herald*, Chicago, August 28 and September 4, 1901, "German Immigration in the Colonial Period."

[2] Rupp's notes to Rush's *Manners of the Pennsylvania Germans*.

[3] G. D. Luetscher, "Industries of Pennsylvania after the Adoption of the Federal Constitution, with special reference to Lancaster and York Counties," *Americana Germanica*, vol. v (*German-American Annals*, i), pp. 135-155, and pp. 197-208.

baker, Christoph Ludwig, who provided all the bread for the patriot army, drew his supplies of grain directly from the Pennsylvania German farms. Dr. Rush says the Pennsylvania farms produced millions of dollars, which after 1780 made possible the foundation of the Bank of North America (chartered 1781). Besides the cultivation of staples, the German farmers raised crops of a varied kind, disposing of the surplus in neighboring large cities. As Turner says, it was a necessary step in the development of the industrial self-dependence of the United States.

Pennsylvania German colonists, though for the most part farmers, were also noted as mechanics. Of them Dr. Rush says: "Their first object is to become freeholders; and hence we find few of them live in rented houses. The highest compliment that can be paid to them on entering their house is to ask them, 'Is this house your own?' They are industrious, frugal, punctual, and just." They adapt themselves to new conditions and retain the arts they brought from Germany. There were also merchants in the coast cities that acquired great wealth by foreign and domestic commerce. "The Bank of North America has witnessed," says Rush, "from its first institution, their fidelity to all their pecuniary engagements." A few additional traits are mentioned by Dr. Rush. With his model, the "Germania" of Tacitus, in mind, he speaks a word concerning hospitality, giving an instance where the host would not accept pay for board and lodging, because he had himself on some occasion been treated thus kindly before, saying: "Do you pay your debt to me in the same way, to somebody else." The Germans, according to Dr. Rush, were little addicted to so-called "feeding parties," by which we are to understand, no doubt, such feasting as Mrs. Trollope described in her

"Domestic Manners of the Americans."[1] In spite of Dr. Rush, we know from numerous other sources that the Germans, as well as their neighbors in agricultural communities, were given to holding frolics, log-rollings, quilting parties, and husking-bees, to cider- and apple-butter-making in social coöperation, and we know that drinking and gorging were also indulged in beyond the canons of good taste and health, at weddings and funerals. The Reverend H. M. Mühlenberg regrets that the latter ancient Teutonic custom was brought over to the New World. In regard to their customs in general, we may accept Dr. Rush's criticism of the entire people of his own state, and let it apply also to the Pennsylvania Germans: "If they possess less refinement than their Southern neighbors, who cultivate their land with slaves, they possess also more Republican virtue."[2]

As manufacturers, the Germans of Pennsylvania likewise made distinct contributions. The weavers of Germantown gave their industry firm root on American soil, while the establishment of the first paper-mill in the country was likewise an achievement of Germantown. Grist- and saw-mills ground and groaned, wherever Germans turned the sod. Glass-blowing and iron manufactures were also introduced by the Germans as early as colonial conditions would allow.

A bit of romance clings to the establishment of the first iron foundry, by Baron Stiegel. He was by no means the vain and erratic dreamer or the adventurer he is frequently represented to have been. Little is known of his early career. He seems to have been sent to America on his own request by well-to-do relatives, who were glad to get rid

[1] Though her descriptions of the frontier are of a much later date (1832), still customs are conservative. Cf. e. g., vol. ii, pp. 129–132.

[2] Rush, *Essays, Literary, Moral, and Philosophical*, p. 220.

of him. He possessed a genial mind, his ruling passion being to embark in grand enterprises. Arriving in Philadelphia, the repose of the Quaker City was not in accordance with his temperament. He journeyed to Lancaster, whence he drifted to Ephrata. Müller and Beissel received him kindly, and finding that he was interested in iron, told him to go to Schäferstädtel, in the neighborhood of which iron ore had been found. Stiegel, accompanied by his faithful body-servant, Jacob of Ettenheim, found the place, returned to Philadelphia for more capital and laborers, and soon established an iron foundry that gave him a limited amount of credit. According to one account, he had some means himself, having come from Europe supplied with "much money and good recommendations." It was about 1758 when he founded Mannheim in Lancaster County, laying it out after the checkerboard plan of his native city. He named his works the *Elizabeth* Iron Foundry and Smelters, in honor of his wife. The town rose as if by magic ; a smithy, a wagon-factory, and, most important of all, a factory for stoves, were all built near the foundry. Iron plates for stoves were manufactured in great numbers and the stoves of Stiegel brought high prices. They are said to have borne the inscription :

> " Baron Stiegel ist der Mann
> Der die Oefen giessen kann." [1]

Another great achievement of Stiegel was the founding of his glassworks, by which he astonished both Germans and Americans, and which, it was rumored, yielded him annually five thousand pounds.

---

[1] L. A. Wollenweber claims to have seen one of these stoves a century later (shortly before 1870), with its inscription, in Lebanon, Pennsylvania. Cf. *Der deutsche Pionier*, vol. ii, p. 28. See also, for an account of Baron Heinrich Wilhelm Stiegel, *ibid.*, vol. xii, pp. 82–87; and *Pennsylvania Magazine of History and Biography*, vol. i, pp. 67 ff.

The indulgence of some of his extravagant tastes made Baron Stiegel a unique figure among the German colonists, inured as they were to plain living. About a mile from Schäferstädtel, on a high hill commanding a view of the whole region, he built a castle with a watch-tower. The story goes, that a cannon-shot announced the master's arrival or departure; two shots, the coming of visitors; and a band of music, trained from among the musically gifted of his laborers,[1] greeted his guests at meals, while Rhenish and French wines and hunting-parties were not lacking for their entertainment. These eccentricities were, of course, derived from his birth and early environment.

The Baron's ambitious ventures were doomed to ultimate failure. The moralizing age in which he lived generally attributed the failure to his extravagant habits, but by looking a bit more deeply into the matter, we cannot but arrive at a more favorable view. Baron Stiegel spent much money, but he made much also. Most of his factories were successful and brought him good returns. The great mistake which he made was to purchase the land interests of Stedman, who held two thirds of the land in Mannheim, against one third originally held by Stiegel, the latter having invested most of his money in the factories. This immense real estate speculation must have deprived the factories of the necessary working capital. Stiegel's faith in the continued prosperity of Mannheim would, in course of time, have been rewarded, had not another unforeseen event occurred. It was the Revolutionary War, and, worse than that, the numerous precedent tyrannical measures of the British Parliament which ruined the commerce and in-

---

[1] The German army has no trouble in equipping its musical corps from the rank and file of the German soldiers. Dr. Rush comments upon the " strong propensity for vocal and instrumental music among the Germans of both sexes." " Manners of the Pennsylvania Germans," *Essays*, p. 239.

dustries of the colonies. No one was hit harder than Baron Stiegel, especially since he had purchased the entire property in Mannheim at a high figure. He writes appealing letters to his lawyers, pleading for time, and speaks gratefully of the successful attempts of his wife, who more than once influenced his creditors to wait. In letters to the Honorable Jaspar Yates he pleads in pathetic language (though a foreigner's English) for help and influence to weather the storm, the burden of his letters being, "If I am given time I will pay every debt." And finally he cries in despair : " Can it be possible that my former friends in Lancaster wish to drive me to ruin, when I have increased the wealth of the country at least 150,000 pounds ! " All the letters [1] were written in the autumn of 1774, showing that his final difficulties came in the storms of the Revolutionary outbreak, and inducing us to believe that, had not uncommon occurrences prevented, he would have met all his obligations and made real his beautiful dream. The family of Stiegel became destitute, and he himself died in great poverty, it is not definitely known how or where, probably in the neighborhood of the smelters. Stories are told of a debtor's prison and death by starvation, but these seem legendary. Speculators in Philadelphia who purchased the works at Mannheim at a low figure, undoubtedly reaped the benefit of Stiegel's ventures, so well begun.

Another industry in which the Germans were very active was that of printing, and most famous of all was the printing-press of Sauer, in Germantown. His was in fact a publishing-house for two generations, established in 1738 and lasting for forty years, until the war put an end to it. One hundred and fifty books or pamphlets and three

---

[1] The letters were reprinted in *Der deutsche Pionier*, vol. xii, pp. 85–87.

quarto editions of the German Bible were published by Christopher Sauer and his son. The honor of printing the first German books in America belongs to Benjamin Franklin ;[1] Sauer was the first, however, to use the German type. Christopher Sauer was born in Laasphe (Wittgenstein, Prussia) in 1693. He left Germany for religious reasons, coming to America with his wife and son in 1724. For some time a farmer in Lancaster County, he subsequently settled in Germantown, and there established his press, importing all of his materials from Germany. His High German Calendar was issued in 1738 and appeared regularly thereafter. In the next year he received an important order to print a hymn-book for the monks of Ephrata, with the pompous title: "Zionitischer Weyrauch-Hügel oder Myrrhen-Berg," 820 pages. Difficulties soon arose between Sauer and Beissel, the two devout religionists. Sauer began to write in a satirical manner, comparing the monk to the apocalyptic beast, commenting upon his virtues, derived from all of the planets: from Mars, severity; from Venus, power to attract the fair sex (a reference to Sauer's wife, who ran away from home and lived in the monastery at Ephrata as Sister Marcella); from Mercury, his clownish tricks. Beissel revenged himself by getting his books printed in Germany, or Philadelphia, afterwards setting up his own printing-press.

The greatest product of Sauer's press (or of the entire colonial press) was the printing of the Lutheran Bible in German, with 1272 pages, quarto form. As the preface stated, it was the first edition of the Scriptures printed in

---

[1] Franklin furnished three volumes of mystical songs in German for Conrad Beissel, 1730–36. The *Göttliche Liebes und Lobesgethöne*, 1730, is noteworthy, because Benjamin Franklin's name as a printer appears on it for the first time without the name of his partner, Meredith.

BIBLIA,

Das ist:

Die

Heilige Schrift

Altes und Neues

Testaments,

Nach der Deutschen Uebersetzung

D. Martin Luthers,

Mit jedes Capitels kurtzen Summarien, auch
beygefügten vielen und richtigen Parllelen:

Nebst einem Anhang

Des dritten und vierten Buchs Esra und des
dritten Buchs der Maccabäer.

Germantown:

Gedruckt bey Christoph Saur, 1743.

TITLE-PAGE OF SAUER BIBLE OF 1743

the Western Hemisphere in a European language.[1] The excellent paper of the edition came from the paper-mill of Rittenhouse in Germantown ; the types were imported from Frankfort-on-the-Main. This first edition appeared in the summer of 1743, a second edition in 1763, and a third in 1776. In addition to these, Sauer printed the New Testament and Psalter in separate editions, and any number of hymn-books for the various sects in Pennsylvania. Most influential of all was the newspaper which he printed, entitled : " Der Hoch-Deutsch Pennsylvanische Geschicht-Schreiber, oder Sammlung wichtiger Nachrichten aus dem Natur- und Kirchen-Reich," a name that was altered several times. At first the journal appeared monthly, then semi-monthly, and from 1773 on weekly, without a rise in price, while the size was constantly increased. The newspaper was sold not only in Pennsylvania, but also in the Carolinas, Maryland, Virginia, and Georgia. It supported Sauer's principles, the pacific policy of the Quakers, and was generally opposed, as already indicated, to the militancy of Mühlenberg and Schlatter. Sauer also established a book-bindery and paper-mill, and manufactured printer's ink and types, the latter being the first attempt in America. The younger Sauer was accused of being a Tory, and therefore his whole estate was confiscated. This was unjust to him,[2] though two sons of his (Christoph and Peter) did establish a Tory newspaper [3] (in

[1] Only once before had a Bible been printed in America ; it was the New Testament in the Indian language for the converted Indians of Eliot in Massachusetts. No Bible had been printed in the English language in the colonies before the German Bible of 1743. A copy of the Sauer Bible, in any edition, is now regarded as a rare treasure.

[2] Cf. Seidensticker, *Bilder*, etc., pp. 158–166, "Christoph Saur, der Jüngere, und die amerikanische Revolution."

[3] A number of this paper, May 6, 1778, is reprinted in Schlözer's *Briefwechsel*, vol. iii, pp. 260–267. Göttingen, 1778. See Chapter XI.

German) in Philadelphia, when General Howe occupied the city.

There were other printing-presses that followed Sauer's. That at Ephrata for the most part printed religious literature. In Philadelphia Joseph Crell printed a German newspaper in 1743, which did not live long. He was followed by the Armbrüsters (1746) and Johann Böhm. Böhm had been associated with Franklin in printing Johann Arndt's "Sechs Bücher vom Wahren Christenthum" (8vo, 1388 pp.), a book which, next to the Bible, was read most by the German immigrants. Heinrich Müller (Miller), from 1760, was for twenty years the best German printer and publisher in Philadelphia. He was the printer of Congress, and published a large number of books in the English language. In 1762 he founded the "Philadelphischer Staatsbote," first a weekly and then a semi-weekly paper. He apparently sold out, in 1776, to the German firm Steiner and Cist, who represented the Revolutionary doctrines. Thomas Paine's "The Crisis" was issued by their press,[1] and Cist, in 1776, started the "Columbian Magazine." Steiner paid more attention to his German newspaper, "Philadelphia Correspondenz." All these German printers fled from Philadelphia during the English occupation, but returned immediately afterwards. Before the close of the century there were also German presses in Lancaster, Reading, and Easton. "Der Reading Adler," a weekly newspaper, started in 1796, is still in existence.

The Pennsylvania Germans have frequently suffered the rebuke of being neglectful in matters of education. It was a charge made during nativistic epochs, and has made by

---

[1] They printed a German edition of Paine's *Common Sense*, and were the first printers of *The Crisis* in English.

far too strong an impression. The main origin of the charge was the tenacity with which Germans held to their own language and customs. The German settlers brought with them their school-teachers and preachers. Schools were invariably established by them, and sometimes before churches. The schools were, however, rarely separated from the churches, and when a movement began for establishing public schools in their districts, the Germans opposed it.[1] They viewed the movement with suspicion, as if its purpose were to deprive them of their religion, the influence of their preachers, or the use of their language. Along with that went a degree of pride (*Bauernstolz*) in their ability to pay for the instruction of their children. They did not wish to inflict this burden upon the state, failing altogether to see the benefits derived from a common school system. It was long before the church school could be replaced by a public school in their counties. An attempt was made to train a body of teachers among the German population, giving instruction in the English language and the rudiments of American law and politics, by the establishment of a college. This foundation was located in Lancaster County, in 1787, and was named after Benjamin Franklin. Henry Mühlenberg was chosen the first head of Franklin College.[2] The charge of ignorance against the Pennsylvania Germans was frequently due to their lack of proficiency in the use of the English language. Education in that day did not go beyond the three R's, or the practical necessities of life, and to the native population the first of these necessities seemed, of course, the ability to use the English language. Younger generations,

---

[1] Sauer was a leader in this opposition.

[2] The subject of the college and education in Pennsylvania will be treated more fully in the chapter on "Educational Influences." See Volume II, Chapter V.

however, unless inbred, found no difficulty with the English language, and many of the descendants of the Pennsylvania Germans shone [1] brilliantly in the professions at an early date, as testified by Dr. Rush.

The Germans, as seen in the present chapter, during the eighteenth century became more numerous in Pennsylvania than in any other colony, numbering at least one third of the total population. They were the best farmers of the colony, laying the foundations of its economic wealth. They developed industries, milling and weaving, iron and paper manufacture, glass-blowing. Their industry, thrift, and steadiness furnished an example to the rest of the population. From Pennsylvania the Germans spread to the south and west.

[1] Examples are David Rittenhouse, the astronomer ; Caspar Wistar and Joseph Leidy, eminent in medicine ; H. E. Mühlenberg, in botany ; S. S. Haldemann, as a naturalist and philologist.

SGRAFFITO PIE PLATE (1786)

SGRAFFITO DISH (1762)

TULIP WARE OF THE PENNSYLVANIA-GERMANS

CHAPTER VI

THE EARLY GERMANS OF NEW JERSEY AND OF MARYLAND

NEW JERSEY : Germans in New Jersey at the beginning of the eighteenth century — German Valley — Settlements spreading over Hunterdon, Somerset, Morris, and over parts of Sussex and Warren counties — Eminent descendants of the early Germans — A church quarrel arbitrated by Mühlenberg, etc. — The Moravian settlements.

MARYLAND : Sporadic cases of German settlers in the seventeenth century — In the eighteenth century Germans numerous and influential in Baltimore — The Germans of Western Maryland ; Frederick County ; Hagerstown — Distinguished Marylanders descended from the early Germans.

THERE is a tradition that the northern counties of New Jersey, the region between the Raritan and the Passaic, were favored by an accident in getting their first German settlers. In 1707 a number of Germans of the Reformed Church, residing originally between Wolfenbüttel and Halberstadt, embarked for New York, but by adverse winds were carried into Delaware Bay. In order to reach their destination among the Dutch of New York, they took the overland route from Philadelphia through New Jersey. As they entered the beautiful valley of the Musconetcong[1] and the Passaic River country, they were so well pleased with the goodly land that they resolved to go no further. They settled in the region of German Valley (Morris County), whence they spread to Somerset, Bergen, and Essex counties.[2]

---

[1] A tributary of the Delaware forming the boundary line between Morris and Hunterdon counties on the east side, and Sussex and Warren on the west, and then flowing into the Delaware.

[2] I. D. Rupp, *Thirty Thousand Names of Immigrants*, pp. 2, 3.

While it is possible that Germans arrived in these
parts as early as 1707–08, the first authentic record of
the presence of a German in that region is that of the
baptism of a child of John Peter Appleman and Anna
Magdalena, August 1, 1714. This event occurred at the
house of Ari de Guinea (Harry from Guinea, a Christian
negro). The child had been born on March 25, and the
parents had come into the state at least a few months
previously. The date, 1713, is therefore adopted by the
Germans of New Jersey as the beginning of their history.[1]
Another event on record is the first religious service in
German Valley, which took place in 1743 (or 1744),
according to a letter addressed to Michael Schlatter by
the people of Fox Hill, Lebanon, and Amwell (German
Valley), in 1747, which speaks of the service as having
taken place three or four years before. A religious service
of this kind naturally presupposes a settlement of some
dimensions, and therefore the first settlers must have come
to German Valley long before. The first German Lutheran
church in New Jersey was opened for worship in 1731
in what is now Potterstown, about a mile east of Lebanon
(Hunterdon County).[2] There were Holland Lutherans in

---

[1] The facts above and following on the early German settlements of New
Jersey are very largely taken from Chambers, *The Early Germans of New
Jersey, their History, Churches, and Genealogies*, Dover, 1895. The work is
based on careful and accurate historical researches, on examination of church
records (particularly in German Valley and its neighborhood), land records
at the county-seats, books of wills at Trenton, county and family histories,
and finally tombstones in old graveyards.

[2] The church at Potterstown (Rockaway) was dedicated Saturday, September 11, 1731. Berkenmeyer and two elders from New York were present,
also the Reverend D. Falckner. On Sunday, the 12th, communion was
administered to about thirty persons, at which Berkenmeyer and Falckner
officiated. Sachse, *The German Pietists of Provincial Pennsylvania*, p. 330,
takes this note from Berkenmeyer's *Diary*. See also *Archives of the Lutheran Seminary*, Gettysburg, Pa.

the state, settled earlier, in the region of Hackensack, Bergen County.

There is evidence also that some of the Palatine immigrants of 1710 settled in New Jersey, records[1] of baptisms and marriages kept by the First Lutheran Church of New York furnishing the proof. The parish of the Reverend Justus Falckner, who began his ministry in New York City in 1703, extended over a vast area, from Albany in New York to the Raritan region (Hunterdon County) in New Jersey. The Germans of New Jersey would be justified in taking 1710 as their beginning, or three years before the date they selected when they celebrated the one hundred and eightieth anniversary of their first settlement.[2]

In South Jersey there were Germans who came with the Swedish settlers long before 1700, but they lost their identity amid the predominant race. In Salem County, not far from the sources of the rivers Cohansey and Alloway, where now stands the little town of Friesburg, there was a German Lutheran congregation. Jacob M. Miller had settled there in 1732 with Pastor Johann Christian Schultze.[3]

[1] The names given by Chambers (p. 35) are : Schneider, Lorentz, Müller (widow), Hoffman, Schmidt, Henneschild (Hendershot), Fuchs (Fox), Vogt, J. and N. Jung (Young), Klein, Cramer (widow), Lucas.

A road survey in 1721, in the vicinity of Amwell Township, Hunterdon County, makes mention of "the Palatines' land." This is another evidence of the early settlements of Palatines in New Jersey, in Hunterdon County.

[2] This memorable event occurred in 1893 under the auspices of the early German settlers of German Valley, among whom are many men distinguished in the service of church and state. The Reverend Theodore Frelinghuysen Chambers was one of the moving spirits.

[3] *Hallesche Nachrichten*, vol. i, pp. 184, 269. They were served by the Swedish pastor Tranberg, 1726–40, later by Lutheran ministers from Philadelphia. In 1760 Pastor Handschuh baptized twelve babes and had one hundred and twenty communicants, when there was a great assemblage. They built and rebuilt churches, one of brick, bearing the date 1768, the "Emanuel Church."

The bulk of the early German settlers were located within the present boundaries of the counties Hunterdon, Somerset, Morris, and parts of Sussex and Warren. The towns of Newton and Lambertville would mark the boundaries on the north and south; Bound Brook and the Delaware River on the east and west respectively. Some of the names of the settlements which may serve to denote the locality more definitely are: German Valley, Fox Hill (once the name of the whole region now centring in German Valley; Fairmount Presbyterian Church is the successor of the old Fox Hill Church), Lebanon, New Germantown, Unionville, Flanders, Spruce Run, Schooley's Mountain, Pleasant Grove. Each place had its church, Lutheran or German Reformed (sometimes both), the latter often taking a step in conformity with prevailing religious conditions in New Jersey and becoming Presbyterian, the differences in dogma not being considered important, and the necessity of hearing sermons in English being strongly felt. The Lutheran churches were more tenacious of their denominational identity, owing to their stronger organization and their greater numbers.

Chambers[1] gives about three hundred German family names, compiled mainly from church records before 1762, within the above-named district, giving evidence of quite a large population. The German settlers of Passaic, Bergen, and Essex counties may have come from the region of German Valley or may have entered from Hudson County, i. e., they were new immigrants coming from New York City.

Like the early Germans elsewhere, those of New Jersey were industrious and thrifty. They were mainly of the agricultural class, and converted German Valley and

[1] On pp. 34–37, and in the appendix of his book.

neighboring districts into garden-like farm-lands.[1] They were religious, building churches and schools and enjoying above most other districts the reputation of liberality toward their preachers, a fact which is dwelt upon by both Mühlenberg and Schlatter. An instance of such a spirit is found, for example, in 1760, when the sum of one thousand pounds, munificent for that period, was bequeathed to the church of New Germantown for the purpose of its support and that of its school.

Though the New Jersey Germans kept their German speech and customs for a long time, they were public-spirited and patriotic, bearing their full share of the burdens of the colonial wars and particularly of the Revolutionary War, the latter raging in New Jersey probably longer and more fiercely than in any other district. Instances of exemplary devotion to the patriotic cause were those of Nevelling and Frelinghuysen. John Wesley Gilbert Nevelling, who served the Amwell church at the beginning of his ministry, converted all his property into money, amounting to five thousand pounds. He loaned it to the Continental Congress, and, losing the certificate of receipt of the government, he never recovered any of the amount. He served as chaplain in the army, was highly esteemed by Washington, and a large reward was offered for his capture by the British government.[2]

General Frederick Frelinghuysen, grandson of the Reverend Theodore J. Frelinghuysen (who also spelled his name Frelinghausen, and was born at Lingen, East Friesland, within the present limits of Prussia), was prominent

---

[1] They also improved agriculture; e. g., a man by the name of Fuchs introduced a new and superior variety of wheat, and the people from a great distance bought wheat of him. "They went to Foxenburgh" (Fairmount). Chambers, p. 128.

[2] Chambers, p. 40.

as a soldier in the Revolutionary War. He took part in the battle of Trenton, where he shot the Hessian colonel Rahl. Afterwards in command of militia, he took part in the skirmishes at Springfield and Elizabeth, and in the battle of Monmouth Courthouse, June, 1788. He was a member of the Continental Congress, of the Convention of 1787, and of the United States Senate, 1793–96. In 1794 he was major-general of the forces of New Jersey and Pennsylvania that served during the Whiskey Insurrection of Pennsylvania.

Some distinguished descendants of the early New Jersey German settlers are found in the Werts family. The Reverend John Conrad Wirtz, born in Zurich, Switzerland, was the first German Reformed preacher in Lebanon and German Valley, before 1750, of whom there is any record. The Honorable George Theodor Werts, governor of New Jersey, 1893–96, is a great-great-grandson of the Reverend John Conrad. The man noted as the wealthiest capitalist in the world, John D. Rockefeller, the founder of the Standard Oil Company, is a direct descendant of the early Germans in New Jersey. But recently (1906), Mr. John D. Rockefeller erected a monument to the memory of his ancestor Johann Peter Rockefeller,[1] "who came from Germany about 1733 and died in 1783." The monument[2] is erected in the village of Larrison's Corner, near Flemington, Hunterdon County, New Jersey, on a piece of land

[1] Spelled also Rockefellar. See Chambers, *Early Germans of New Jersey*, appendix. John Peter Rockefeller had two sons, Peter and John (naturalized 1730). Some of the Rockefellars settled at the camp in New York (Saugerties).

[2] It was erected in 1906, and bears an inscription stating that the monument is dedicated to Johann Peter Rockefeller by his direct descendant, John Davison Rockefeller. At a recent family reunion it was stated that the family had descended originally from a Huguenot ancestor, who had immigrated to Germany.

which Johann Peter Rockefeller gave as a burial-ground for his family and his neighbors. This giving instinct was not exceptional among the early Germans, — it has grown in modern times, and culminated in such magnificent endowments as the University of Chicago, that of the General Education Board,[1] and the Rockefeller Institute for Medical Research, New York. There is probably no modern benefactor whose vast and numerous gifts have been more wisely distributed.

As an illustration of the seriousness with which church and religious matters were treated by the early Germans, the following narrative may be of service. It is the story of a church feud, taken from the letters written by the Reverend Mr. Mühlenberg[2] to the church fathers at Halle, published in the "Hallesche Nachrichten."[3]

During the lifetime of Justus Falckner, who was the able head of the Lutheran Church in New York from 1703 to 1723, his brother, Daniel Falckner, served the German Lutheran churches in the Raritan district. But after the death of Justus Falckner in 1723, and when Daniel Falckner had become too old for service, the German churches in New Jersey applied to the Reverend Mr. Berkenmeyer, successor to Justus Falckner, for a new preacher to be imported from Germany. A call, duly sealed and signed by the members of three congregations, was forwarded to Germany in 1731. Nothing came of it, however, until three years

---

[1] The recent gift of $32,000,000 to the General Education Board, by John D. Rockefeller, "is the largest sum ever given by a man in the history of the race for any social or philanthropic purposes." (Words quoted from the letter of acceptance by the Board.)

[2] The character and career of the great organizer of the Lutheran Church in America, the Reverend Heinrich Melchior Mühlenberg, has been sketched in the preceding chapter.

[3] German Reprint: Allentown, Pa., 1886. See vol. i, pp. 113 ff., 119 ff., 123 ff. The translation appeared earlier : Reading, Pa., 1882.

later, when the home church ordained August Wolf, and
sent him to America at a stipulated salary and expenses
paid. The call was given by three congregations, "on the
mountain" (about one mile from Pluckamin), Rackaway,
or Rockaway (Potterstown), and Hanover (probably Fox
Hill). The Reverend Mr. Wolf was received with love
and hopeful expectation, which very soon, however, gave
place to disappointment, for the new pastor, according to
Mühlenberg, proved "a wolf in sheep's clothing." To
quote the story as told in the "Reports" : —

They then fell into strife with one another, which Pastor
Berkenmeyer and Mr. Knoll from New York have again medi-
ated. But Mr. Wolf does not look at his office rightly, for he is
not willing or able to preach without his written sketches. Having married a farmer's daughter, he lived with her amid contin-
ual blows and quarreling. This quarrelsome life and inefficiency
in preaching made the congregation dissatisfied, so that they did
not pay him his promised salary. They offered him his traveling expenses, if he would return home again, but he would not
consent to do so. He boasted then that he had brought his
written call and seal from Hamburg. Mr. Berkenmeyer and Mr.
Knoll interfered and complained to the governor, of the un-
scrupulousness of the congregation. The governor ordered that
the congregation pay and support him. The congregation complained that the minister was not efficient. The matter then
came to trial before the court. When a year had passed Mr.
Wolf swore before the authorities that he had performed his
duties according to contract. The members were then served
with writs of execution upon their property, and many of them
were arrested upon the highway. In short, the office of preacher
was by these causes brought into disrepute, the young neglected,
the holy communion not administered, the sick not visited, indeed, there was such a desolation, that it was made among the
Germans a subject of street songs. Finally, the matter came
before the supreme court and caused a heavy expense to the con-

gregation. The lawyers found their advantage in it. Part of the members sold their property and moved away.[1]

This condition had endured for many years. Mühlenberg had often been implored to help the congregations, but his duties kept him in Pennsylvania. Finally a board of arbitration was chosen, consisting of four preachers. Mr. Wolf named on his side the ministers Berkenmeyer and Knoll of New York; the congregations named the ministers Mühlenberg and Brunnholz of Pennsylvania. For the latter the Reverend Mr. Wagner was afterward substituted. Mr. Berkenmeyer absented himself. Thus with three judges the examination and deliberations went on, continuing four days and four nights and proving an arduous task. The board found "that Mr. Wolf had been the primary cause of all the contention and scandal," and, as Mühlenberg also reports: "He had not shown official and paternal fidelity enough to teach his children the Ten Commandments."[2] The board was ready to set the congregation free, when a compromise was agreed to, yielding Mr. Wolf a sum of money, for which he would release the congregation absolutely. The famous document (the call) bearing the signatures of the congregation, was handed over, and Mr. Wolf received ninety pounds, from which the court costs were deducted. The Reverend Mr. Mühlenberg had once more done his church and countrymen a noble service. Thus ended the most bitter of all the colonial German church quarrels, with the exception perhaps of the one in Georgia,[3] which Mühlenberg also arbitrated.

[1] *Hallesche Nachrichten*, vol. i, p. 119.
[2] The discovery of this neglect no doubt weighed heavily in the balance against Wolf.
[3] See Chapter IX.

The church difficulty was not completely settled after the decree of the ministerial judges had gone into effect. The congregations were unwilling to sign another call, having had the one unfortunate experience, and they hesitated also because of the rivalry between the Lutheran ministeriums of Halle and Hamburg, each of which wanted to fill the vacancy. But Mühlenberg was equal to all emergencies, becoming the patron of the Lutheran congregations of New Jersey for a number of years, frequently serving them for months at a time. He healed all schisms and brought about a period of prosperity. Sometimes, to be sure, he was disappointed in the choice of assistants, and he writes mournfully to the church fathers at Halle: " The lack of faithful, steady, and experienced laborers is a great hindrance to the spread of the kingdom of Jesus Christ. May the Lord have compassion upon us and send faithful laborers into his harvest." Mühlenberg remained the patriarch of the New Jersey congregation (from 1757 to 1775), with assistants to serve the various churches, among whom for some time were his sons Peter and Henry.

An interesting product of prevailing colonial conditions was the Reverend Mr. Caspar Wack. He was called to Great Swamp Church in 1771. When he first came to German Valley, the preaching was all in German, but under changed requirements in the latter part of his ministry, he preached only occasionally in German, to please the old people. The jargon of the transition period between the German and English sermons probably did not offend in those days as it might now. On the contrary, on one occasion it had a very pleasing effect. An English army officer, having heard that the Reverend Mr. Wack was a German, went to his church in order "to hear what a German sermon would sound like." He came away rejoicing. "He never knew before that German was so much like English; he could understand a great deal of what Mr. Wack said." On that day Mr. Wack had preached an English sermon, or at least what he took to be English. In later days, however, the Reverend Mr. Wack is said to have been in command of good English, at least of correct English, faulty only in accent, and somewhat in pronunciation, though as to the latter it is known that he carefully marked his manuscript with the dictionary's pronunciation.

Mr. Wack was musical, taught a singing-school, carried on a farm, and drove an oil- and fulling-mill, using for power the stream on his land. He became a well-to-do member of the community. No eight-hour laws prevailed with him, and he was out on his fields before the first peep of day. When the breakfast-bell was heard, he would say: "Now, boys! a race," and he was rarely beaten.[1] Stories are told of the quickness of his wit. While on one of his long journeys, a young man asked him for a ride. "Certainly," said Mr. Wack, "get up behind me." Now this young man was not one that had walked straight in the paths of church virtue, nor had the shepherd ever had an opportunity to lead back this recalcitrant member of the flock. The opportunity had come, and the minister poured into the ears of the sheep such an amount of wholesome admonition that the latter remembered it as an experience in his life. The young scapegrace declared, when he was released, that it was the hardest ride he had ever taken. Mr. Wack later removed to Stone Arabia in the Mohawk Valley, and served as chaplain in the War of 1812.

Besides the settlements in German Valley and sur-

[1] Chambers, pp. 112 ff.

rounding counties, there are records of a few other German colonies. At Elizabethtown, where the first English settlement was made in 1664, there were many German settlers prior to 1734, as we learn from the Urlsperger "Reports."[1] Other German settlers were located at a place called Hall Mill, some thirty miles from Philadelphia.[2] In addition to these we get information about others from the reports of the Moravian preachers. The latter had regular preaching stations in the more southerly counties of New Jersey, at Maurice River, Penn's Neck, Raccoon, Cohansey, Middletown, Trenton, Maidenhead, Crosswicks, Crawberry, and Princeton. These stations presuppose the existence of German settlers in considerable numbers, for the Moravian preachers commonly preached in German, many of them not knowing English well enough to preach in that language, as we learn from the diaries of Moravian missionaries who passed through Virginia.

A prosperous Moravian colony, at least for a period, was the Hope Settlement, located in Warren County. American travelers,[3] passing through, commented on "the strong, neat, and compact Moravian houses, mostly of stone, the mechanics' shops, the stores, and above all a mill, one of the finest and most curious mills in America." The same mill is described in the travels of a French soldier,[4] in 1778, one of the members of La Fayette's staff:

Mr. Colver treated us with an anxiety and respect more German than American, and led us first to see the saw-mill which

[1] Von Reck, *Urlsperger Nachrichten*, p. 159.

[2] The Reverend Michael Schlatter preached there in 1746. *Magazine of German Reformed Church*, vol. ii, p. 266.

[3] The Honorable William Ellery and the Honorable William Whipple, two signers of the Declaration of Independence, in 1777, wrote about it in their diary, from which the above quotation is taken.

[4] *Travels in North America*, pp. 307 ff., published 1780–82, by the Chevalier de Chastellux.

is the most beautiful and best contrived I ever saw. A single man only is necessary to direct the work; the same wheels which keep the saw in motion serve also to convey the trunks of trees from the spot where they are deposited to the workhouse, a distance of 25 or 30 toises (making a total distance of over 150 feet): they are placed on a sledge, which, sliding in a groove, is drawn by a rope, which rolls and unrolls on the axis of the wheel itself. Planks are sold at six shillings, Pennsylvania currency, the hundred. If you find the wood, it is only half the money.

In 1807 the properties[1] at Hope were sold by the Moravian Brethren, and the members of the settlement removed to Bethlehem or other Moravian towns. All their settlements were managed on the coöperative plan, and if any proved less advantageous, it was abandoned or sold so as not to be a burden for the others.

We have seen that the Germans settled within the present boundaries of New Jersey as early as the first and second decades of the eighteenth century. They soon massed in great numbers in the district known as German Valley. Their settlements were most prosperous within the boundaries of the present counties of Hunterdon, Somerset, Morris, and in portions of Sussex and Warren. Many distinguished Americans have descended from the old New Jersey Germans.

Maryland: In the province of Maryland some few Germans had settled as early as the seventeenth century. There was Cornelius Commegys from Vienna, who settled in Cecil County with four other Germans, among them Augustin Herman (Harman), before 1660. There was Martin Faulkner (Falkner), who received one hundred and fifty acres in Anne Arundel County (1680), which he

---

[1] There were also a tannery, pottery, oil-mill, besides a saw-mill and farms.

called " Martin's Rest." Robert Sadler in 1689 received a grant of land in Baltimore County. There were a number of others in various counties, as the records in the state capitol at Annapolis show.[1] Most of the immigrants landed at Annapolis, called " The Port of Severn," then of much greater importance as a seaport than Baltimore, the latter being incorporated as a city not until 1796 (though laid out about 1730), Annapolis having been made a city in 1696, one hundred years earlier.

There were a number of Germans with the Labadists,[2] the sect of communists who settled (1684) on the Bohemian River, within the present state of Delaware. The founder and leader of the Labadist settlement on Bohemia Manor was Peter Sluyter, born at Wesel in the Rhineland. His original name was Vorstmann, but just before his immigration he assumed the name of Sluyter or Schluter. His co-worker, Jasper Danker, had also changed his name, from Schilders. They had been sent by the mother colony at Wieuwerd in Westfriesland to discover a suitable place for a colony in America. The place selected was that already named, on Bohemia River, on the land of Augustin Herman. Herman even promised to erect the necessary buildings for the colony, and his oldest son, Ephraim, became a convert to the society.[3] Danker soon withdrew

---

[1] J. A. Weishaar, " The German element in Maryland up to the year 1700," *Fifteenth Annual Report of the Society for the History of the Germans in Maryland*, pp. 13–34. The author has carefully worked through the old court records at Annapolis and brought to light a quantity of interesting facts regarding the earliest Germans of Maryland.

[2] They were followers of Jean de Labadie, Christian communists. They denied the observance of the Sabbath on the ground that life is a perpetual Sabbath. They believed in marriage as a holy ordinance, and denied original sin. The sect disappeared about the middle of the eighteenth century, and even earlier in America. In 1698 besides Sluyter only eight male members remained in the Labadist settlement of Bohemia Manor.

[3] The deed conveyed the land, August 11, 1684, to Sluyter and Danker

and left Sluyter sole leader of the community with the
rank of bishop. The latter became a successful tobacco
planter, and it is said a slave trader, dying a wealthy man.

The most noted of the Germans in this section was,
however, Augustin Herman[1] (born at Prague, 1621), the
founder of Cecil County, patron at one time of the Labadists, and defender of the rights of Maryland against
neighboring colonies.[2] He drew a map[3] of the state of
Maryland for Lord Baltimore, which was "applauded for
its exactness even by His Royal Majesty, the King," and
about the same time he was chosen representative of
Baltimore to the General Assembly.

No considerable number of German settlers arrived in
Maryland before the eighteenth century, even not before
the second quarter. From its very beginning (1730) Germans were active in the settlement and commercial progress of Baltimore. Many of them, enterprising Germans
or descendants of Germans, came down from Pennsylvania,
and with "capital and industry employed here, contributed
essentially to aid the original settlers."[4] G. M. Meyer

from Friesland, Bayard from New York (the Huguenot ancestor of a line of
American statesmen, the last of them Thomas Francis Bayard, secretary
of state, 1885–89, ambassador to England, 1893), John Moll and Arnold de
la Grange from Delaware.

[1] Augustin Herman was naturalized in Maryland by act of legislature in
1663, with two sons and three daughters ; with them a family by the name
of Hack, also of German stock. One John Hack traded with the Indians
and was well known in Maryland and Virginia, in 1647.

[2] Augustin Herman had previously lived in New Amsterdam, and was
there distinguished as a trader in tobacco, a representative of the popular
party and a diplomatist. Though not a friend of Stuyvesant, the latter
used him on many important embassies, the last becoming the occasion of
Herman's settling in Maryland. *Deutsch-amerikanisches Magazin*, pp. 202 ff.
and 524 ff.

[3] Cf. Weishaar, p. 28.

[4] Cf. Colonel J. G. Scharf, *The Chronicles of Baltimore*, pp. 37, 202. Baltimore, 1874. See also *Der deutsche Pionier*, vol. xviii, p. 179, article by
E. F. Leyh.

erected a mill, D. Barnetz and Leonard from York, Pa.,
together established the first brewery, Valentin Larsch
built an inn at the southwest corner of Baltimore and Gay
streets, Andrew Steiger was the first butcher, who, before
1759 and after, purchased large tracts of land in the bend
of Jones's Falls and beyond, for the feeding of his cattle,
his purchases covering a large part of East Baltimore and
being known as Steiger's Meadow. German Street, parallel to Baltimore Street, and one of the thoroughfares for
the wholesale trade, was once covered with the kitchen-
garden and tobacco plantation of a German farmer. After
Baltimore was incorporated, in 1796, there were three Germans among the first seven aldermen of the new city, viz.:
Engelhardt Yeiser, Peter Hoffmann, and George Linden-
berger, the latter a public-spirited man, magistrate, founder
of a fire company and a militia officer during the Revolutionary War. As early as 1758 a German church was built
in Baltimore, and four years later a second one.[1] Both
were Protestant, the German Catholics being not numerous enough as yet to build a church of their own, or finding it more advantageous to join the prominent English
Catholic congregations.

At the time of the Revolutionary War the Germans
of Baltimore sent many volunteer companies into the
patriot army, a fact that proves the existence of a large
German population in that city. Washington's purchasing

---

[1] Cf. *Second Annual Report of the Society for the History of the Germans
in Maryland*, pp. 60 and 64. Also : *A History of Zion Church of the City
of Baltimore*, 1755–1897, pp. 9, 10, 14. By Pastor Jul. Hofmann. Baltimore,
1905. The Germans held union services (including the Lutheran and Reformed) in Baltimore very soon after the town was laid out (1730). The
Lutherans founded a separate organization as early as 1755 (Zion Church).
Their first church, however, seems to have been built a few years after the
church of the German Reformed (1758), who were at first more numerous

agent, Jake Keeport (Kuhbord), was a Baltimore German. When the Continental Congress, after its flight from Philadelphia, sought refuge in Baltimore, they held their meetings in a hall owned by the German merchant, Veit.[1]

Many of the noted families of the city and state are of German origin, among them those bearing the names of Albert, Appold, Baer, Diffenderfer, Friese, Frick, Hoffmann, Keyser, King, Levering, Mayer, Miller, Miltonberger, Reeder, Schley, Schmucker, Steiner, Stricker, Uhler,[2] Van Bibber, Yeiser, and a large number of others.[3] The ancestor of the Alberts came from Würzburg, Bavaria, in 1752. The family were prominent as merchants and organizers of financial and charitable institutions in the city. Peter Hoffmann came from Frankfort-on-the-Main in 1742, settled first at Frederick, then became a drygoods merchant in Baltimore, his descendants expanding into business operations of many kinds, in and beyond the state. George Hoffmann is noted for once owning the finest residence in Baltimore called "Hoffmann's Folly," at the corner of Franklin and Cathedral streets. The Leverings are descended from an ancestor born in Germany, who settled first in Roxborough township, in the county

---

[1] *Der deutsche Pionier*, vol. xviii, pp. 179 ff.

[2] The name Uhler appears very early, in Uhler's Alley, 1730, when the town was laid out.

[3] C. F. Raddatz, "German American Families in Maryland," *Sixth Annual Report of the Society for the History of the Germans in Maryland*, 1891–92, pp. 43-50. Also *Fifth Annual Report*, "Family Records," pp. 91-96. Also *Sixth Annual Report*, E. F. Leyh, "Baltimore's Deutsch-Amerikaner im Handel u. Industrie," pp. 77-85. The Calendar of 1795 contains a very large percentage of German names, among them representatives of prominent business houses : Peter Hoffmann, Falck, Focke, Albert, Mayer, Schwarz, Schäfer, Bohn, Slingluff, Brantz, Waesche, Raborg, Schroeder, Benziger, Reinecker, Diffenderfer, Stauffer, Stark, Seekamp, Ratien, Könicke, Zollikoffen, Clemm, Eichelberger, Sadler. Governor Sharpe in 1753 comments on the prominence of well-to-do Germans in Baltimore.

of Philadelphia, about 1685, and later removed to Baltimore. His name appeared in a deed as Weekhart Lieber-
ing, and he lived to the age of 109 years.[1] His great-
grandchildren, Aaron and Enoch, through the influence of
their brother-in-law, John Brown, a native of Belfast, Ireland, removed to Maryland and became the founders of
the Levering family in Baltimore. Aaron became a soldier
in the Revolution, one of the captains of the flying camp,
and was honorably discharged with the rank of colonel.
As merchants the Leverings became distinguished by
their coffee trade with South America.[2] More reputed as
a soldier was General John Stricker, born in Frederick,
Maryland, 1759, the son of Colonel George Stricker of
Revolutionary fame. He fought in the Revolution, later
became a merchant of Baltimore, and during the attack
on the city in 1814 by the English under General Ross,
commanded the brigade which was sent forward to check
the enemy's advance. A street in Baltimore bears his
name. Christian Mayer[3] and his partner, Louis Brantz,
emigrated from Germany in 1784 and were intimately
connected with Baltimore's commercial development. They

[1] He died in 1744, as stated in the *Pennsylvania Gazette*, no. 844.

[2] Joshua Levering was the prohibition candidate for the presidency of
the United States, 1896. The Leverings were the donors of the Y. M. C. A.
building of the Johns Hopkins University.

[3] Francis B. Mayer, ex-president of the Baltimore & Ohio Railway Com-
pany, gives some interesting items of family history, published by the Soci-
ety for the History of the Germans in Maryland (*Fifth Annual Report*). The
Mayers came from Ulm, Würtemberg, first went to Ebenezer in Georgia,
thence to Maryland, bearing a letter from Cecil Calvert to Benjamin
Tasker, first in the council of the state, "recommending Mr. Christopher
Bartholomew Mayer to Civilitys on his arrival in Maryland" (1752). C. B.
Mayer led a group of Palatines to the Monocacy settlement in Frederick
County. They had come on the ship *Patience* from Georgia. A branch
of the Mayer family later removed to Baltimore, as was the case with many
Frederick County Germans, e. g., the Schleys and Steiners.

established a tobacco trade with the Netherlands, and founded marine insurance companies. There were prominent also the Appolds, leather merchants, the Fricks, men of affairs and lawyers, and Jac. Brusstar, one of the first shipbuilders of Baltimore, when that industry was the pride of the state. The Bremen and Hamburg ship companies soon established agencies in Baltimore, as, for instance, the firm Kapff and Ansbach in 1795, succeeded by others later. These German ship-lines going regularly back and forth to Europe, and visiting also South American ports, had much to do with raising Baltimore to a high rank as a seaport in the nineteenth century.

Just as important is the part the Germans took in the settlement and development of Western Maryland. Generally the settlers of Western Maryland were Pennsylvania Germans who, on their way to Virginia (Spotsylvania), were attracted by the good land and prospects on the way. The route of travel from Lancaster County to Virginia was over an Indian trail, now broad enough to be used by travelers and settlers moving with packhorses. It extended across York and Adams counties, Pennsylvania, to the Monocacy River near the point where it crosses the boundary between Maryland and Pennsylvania, followed the river for a time, then went westward across the Blue or South Mountains, at Crampton's Gap, and thence to the Potomac River. On this route the first Germans arrived in Maryland about 1729, and settled near the Monocacy River. They built the first German church in Maryland between 1732 and 1734. The Indian trail in 1739 was widened by action of the Lancaster County Court and the Maryland Assembly, and became known as the Monocacy Road, being used as a part of the great highway from the East to the South and Southwest. On this road one hundred and fifty wagons and two hundred packhorses, secured in Pennsylvania, were brought to the camp at Frederick in 1755, preparatory to the campaign of General Braddock.[1]

Charles, Lord Baltimore, seeing the generous propositions made by neighboring provinces to German settlers, tried to do better than the governor of Virginia. Accordingly in 1732 he made an exceedingly liberal offer to colonists: two hundred acres of land in fee (subject to the rental of four shillings sterling per year, for every one hundred acres, payable at the end of three years) to any person having a family who should within three years actually settle on the land between the rivers Potomac and Susquehanna, and to each single person, male or female, between the ages of fifteen and thirty, one hundred acres of land on the same terms, with the assurance that they should be as well secured in every particular in Maryland as in any part of the British plantations in America, without exception. This offer guaranteed land at the rental of one cent an acre, and no rent to pay for the first three years. It is not surprising that many Pennsylvania Germans, seeing the good land in what is now Frederick and Washington counties, Maryland, dug their spades into the earth then and there, set up their hearthstones, and forgot all their intentions of going farther.

The earliest settlement was that called Monocacy,[2] near the present site of Creagerstown, about ten miles north of the present city of Frederick. The location of the old log church of Monocacy and of the graveyard near by, has been fixed as less than a mile distant from Creagerstown.

[1] The road was macadamized in 1808.

[2] Cf. E. T. Schultz, "First Settlements of Germans in Maryland," a paper read before the Frederick County Historical Society, etc. Published by request, D. H. Smith, Frederick, Maryland, 1896.

The latter place was a later settlement, founded by a German, either Cramer or Creager, between 1760 and 1770. This town was located on more elevated ground, doubtless an advantage over the older village, which declined and possibly was even abandoned. Creagerstown might well have adopted the name Monocacy, and then could claim the honor of being the oldest town in Western Maryland.

The successful rival of the Monocacy settlement was Frederick Town. In 1735 there arrived about one hundred families from the Palatinate by way of Chesapeake Bay, landing either at Annapolis or Alexandria,[1] presumably at Annapolis, because the German immigrants settled on lands owned by Daniel Dulaney of Annapolis, located in Western Maryland. There a town was laid out in 1745, on both sides of Carroll Creek, three miles from the Monocacy River. It was called Frederick Town in honor of Frederick, son of Lord Baltimore, then a boy of fourteen.

The leader of the immigrants was Thomas Schley, their schoolmaster, the ancestor of a prominent family with branches in Maryland and Georgia. He seems to have been, like Ulmer of the Waldo settlement in Maine, every inch a leader, capable of taking the initiative in all important activities of the colony, besides being the teacher, and reader in the absence of a minister. Schlatter reports of him: " It is a great advantage for this congregation[2] that they have the best schoolmaster I have

[1] Both of these towns were more important seaports at that time than Baltimore. Large numbers of Germans landed at Annapolis, as the following record will illustrate, taken from the entries at Annapolis. Between 1752 and 1755, 1060 immigrant Germans arrived. In 1752, 150 arrived ; in 1753, 460 ; and in 1755, 450. Cf. " Memoranda in reference to early German Immigration to Maryland," by F. B. Mayer, *Fifth Annual Report of the Society for the History of the Germans in Maryland*, 1890–91, p. 19.

[2] The Monocacy congregation embraced Frederick and the straggling settlements in the neighborhood.

met with in America. He, Thomas Schley, spares neither labor nor pains in instructing the young, and edifying the congregation according to his ability, by means of singing and reading the word of God, and printed sermons, on every Lord's Day." Germans continued to arrive in the Monocacy district in a steadily flowing stream. Before 1750 German families of the following names had built their homes in this valley: Zimmerman, Kolb, Hoffman, Beckenbaugh, Bickel, Tradane, Devilbiss, Wetzel, Eckman, Cramer (Kramer), Brinker, Crise (Kris), Gushorn, Dohlman, Blumingshine, Protsman, Shrump, Stull, Culler, Creiger (Krieger), Poe (Poh), Eichelberger, Shriver, Weinbrenner, Shryock, Wilnide, and many others. Most of these can be recognized as good Pennsylvania German names.[1] A few settlers of English extraction intermingled with the Germans, the Campbells, Grimes, Hammetts, Heads, and others. The first church-rolls of the Reformed and Lutheran congregations in the Frederick district furnish an abundance of names known from Pennsylvania to Carolina in addition to those mentioned, such as Baltzell, Brunner, Baer, Getzendenner, Michael, Holtz, Kemp, Sinn (or Zinn), Steiner (Stoner), Wolff, Thomas, Gephardt, Mantz, Doll, Hauer, Lingenfeld, Schwartz, Schriner, Schultz, Rohr, Kunkle, Kuntz (Kuhns, Coons, etc.), Fauble, Webber, Witman, Wetzel, Bentz, Weiss, Staley (Stehli), and numerous others.

Most of our information concerning Monocacy and

[1] The Albaughs, Zollers, Harbaughs, Stauffers, Stimmels, Smiths, Cronises, Millers, Derrs, Delaplanes, Shanks, Hauvers (Hoover, Huber), Dudderers, Fogles, Adamses, Weavers, Barracks, Hedges, Crimms, Wiers, Kellers, Snooks, Reamers, Snyders, Clems, Ramsbergs, Shaefers, Lettermans, Wormans, Houcks, and Heffners were also settlers prior to 1760 in what are now the districts of Hauvers, Lewistown, Woodsboro, Liberty, and Mechanicstown. Schultz, *First Settlements of Germans in Maryland*, p. 24, etc.

Frederick is derived from reports of Schlatter and Mühlenberg, who organized congregations, preached to them, and supplied them as far as possible with ministers. Both of them comment on the fact that there were few sectarians in Maryland. There was only one other denomination besides their own, namely, the Moravian, and that gave Mühlenberg some trouble. The missionaries, Ninke and Nyberg, between 1745 and 1749 collected a number of believers about them and founded the settlement of Graceham, about twelve miles northwest of Frederick Town. Graceham is the seat of the first Moravian church in Maryland, and for a long time was a noted centre of religious worship.

Michael Schlatter, with the purpose of organizing the German Reformed congregations, arrived in Maryland in 1747, and repeated his visits subsequently. On his first tour he baptized twenty children and administered the Lord's Supper to eighty-six communicants. He comments upon the purity of the settlement, meaning the absence of "religious errors," i. e., sects, and says that if this congregation were united with Conogocheague, lying thirty miles distant, the two would be able to support a minister (a union which was effected some years later). The settlement at Monocacy in the earlier years was undoubtedly more important than Frederick Town, since both Schlatter and Mühlenberg always made the former their headquarters, going to Frederick Town, ten miles distant, for their religious work and coming back the same day to lodge at Monocacy. The first regular pastor of the Lutheran church at Frederick was the Reverend Bernard Houseal, in 1753, the son-in-law of Christopher B. Mayer (who arrived with the company of Palatines at Annapolis). Between 1748 and 1753 as many as twenty-eight hundred

Palatines came to Maryland seaports directly from Germany. These settled in Frederick or in Baltimore County.[1]

Another noteworthy settlement in Frederick County was that of Fleecy Dale. John Frederick Amelung came from Bremen in 1784 with a colony of from three to four hundred persons, — bakers, blacksmiths, doctors, shoemakers, tailors, etc. They settled on Bennett's Creek, near the Monocacy, in what is now the Urbana district of Frederick County. The noteworthy fact about the settlement was the founding of an establishment for the manufacture of glass. President Washington, in a letter to Jefferson, referring to these works, says : " A factory of glass is established upon a large scale on Monocacy River near Frederick in Maryland. I am informed it will produce this year glass of various kinds to the amount of ten thousand pounds." A claim is made that this factory was the first in America that manufactured hollow glassware. Amelung presented in person to Washington "two capacious goblets made of flint glass, exhibiting the General's coat of arms." The story goes, that the presentation was made at Mount Vernon, Amelung appearing in full court costume. Crossing the lawn he addressed a man mounted on a ladder, who, in his shirt-sleeves, was fixing the grape-vines. The ornamental gift of crystal almost dropped from Amelung's hands, when he found that the person addressed on the ladder was Washington himself. A large number of pieces of Amelung's manufacture are still in the possession of the Masonic Lodge at Alexandria, of which Washington was a member and the first Master. Some others of Amelung's decanters, punch-bowls, and wine-glasses are preserved by the old Holland Masonic Lodge of New York. The quality

[1] Complete ship lists of immigrants to Maryland have, unfortunately, not been preserved.

of his mirrors is said to be unsurpassed even at the present day.[1]

The names of other large settlements of Germans, not already mentioned, in Frederick and neighboring counties, were Middleton, Sharpsburg, Taneytown, Tom's Creek, Point Creek, Owen's Creek, Union Bridge, Emmettsburg, Woodsboro, Hauvers, and Mechanicstown. During the period of westward migration the Germans of Western Maryland found Ohio, Indiana, and Illinois very easy of access. Tiffin and Dayton, Ohio, were long the favorite points for settlement by the Germans of Frederick County.

The westernmost settlements of Maryland were Conogocheague and Hagerstown, both of them German colonies. Conogocheague was near the present town of Clear Spring, seven or eight miles southwest of Hagerstown, in Washington County. The first regular German Reformed pastor was the Reverend Theodore Frankenfeld, who served this, as well as the congregation at Frederick Town, from 1753 to 1755. The founder of Hagerstown was another of those strong personalities of the settlement period, Jonathan Hager,[2] who emigrated from Germany prior to 1739. He

---

[1] Schultz, p. 17. Amelung removed his plant to Baltimore in 1796. See *Sixth Annual Report of the Society for the History of the Germans in Maryland*, p. 81.

[2] A good account of Jonathan Hager's public services in advancing the economic interests of his section of country is found in an article by Basil Sollers, "Jonathan Hager, the founder of Hagerstown," in the *Second Annual Report of the Society for the History of the Germans in Maryland*, 1887–1888, pp. 17–30. Very interesting also is the contest over the question, whether Hager should be permitted to take his seat in the assembly of Maryland, after being duly elected by his district. He was at first declared ineligible (being foreign born, though a naturalized citizen) by a vote of twenty-four to twenty-three. A new law was made for him, representing the cause of naturalized citizens, whereupon he was permitted to take his seat in the first assembly, to which he had been elected. Hager was reëlected, and the contest was renewed the following year, but no action was taken removing him. He was placed on several committees.

took out land patents aggregating in all twenty-five hundred acres, two hundred of which he obtained December 16, 1739. In 1762 he laid out a town which he named Elizabeth in honor of his wife, which name he used in all legal documents. The popular name, Hager's Town, however, displaced the founder's favorite. In 1775 the place contained over one hundred houses, in 1807 they were increased to three hundred, exclusive of the public buildings, courthouse, jail, etc., Hagerstown being the county seat. Among the names of the pioneer settlers in these westernmost colonies were the following : Prather, Poe (both families famed as Indian fighters), Startzman, Snevely, Stull, Wolgamot (probably Wolgemut), Burhartz, Elwick, Kendrick, Shryock, Hauser, etc.

An interesting historical situation was developed in connection with the disputed boundary between Maryland and Pennsylvania.[1] Lord Baltimore claimed correctly that his territory extended to the fortieth parallel, and accordingly issued grants included in this territory. Difficulties arose, culminating in border warfare. The fierce Indian fighter, Cresap (he who was accused subsequently of murdering the family of the Indian chief Logan), made an organized attempt to drive back the German settlers from Pennsylvania, who had settled west of the Susquehanna. These settlers, believing that they belonged to Pennsylvania, organized for resistance, and, aided by the Pennsylvania government, captured Cresap, who, when taken to Philadelphia a prisoner, said scornfully : "This is the finest city in the province of Maryland." Though Cresap was right at the time, the charter of Maryland clearly

---

[1] Cf. Hennighausen, " Die Revolte der Deutschen gegen die Regierung in Maryland," *Third Annual Report of the Society for the History of the Germans in Maryland*, pp. 45–59.

defining the fortieth parallel as Maryland's northern
boundary (and Philadelphia being to the south of the
fortieth parallel), still the case was soon decided otherwise by the boundary survey known as Mason and Dixon's
Line (1766), which deprived Maryland unjustly of two
million acres.

Some of the German colonial families were especially
influential in the affairs of the state and of the nation.
Such were the Schleys. One of the sons of Thomas Schley,
the schoolmaster, was Jacob, a captain in the Revolution.
A grandson, William Schley, was a member of Congress
and governor of Georgia, where Schley County was named
after him. John, his brother, sat upon the supreme bench
in Georgia, while another brother rose likewise to eminent
judicial positions. Henry Schley, father of Dr. Fairfax
Schley (in Baltimore), was born in Frederick in 1793
(died 1871); he participated in the battles of Bladensburg
and North Point in 1814, and then returned to Frederick
as one of its foremost citizens. William Schley, born in
Frederick, 1799, removed to Baltimore and became a distinguished member of the Baltimore bar. He preferred
the profession of the law to public office, and after his
retirement from the state senate, took no active part in
politics. The family has reared also a national hero, Winfield Scott Schley, the rescuer of the Greely Arctic Expedition, commander of the flying squadron in the Spanish
War, and at the battle of Santiago in immediate command
of the fleet that destroyed Cervera's squadron. Concerning the Brunner, Steiner,[1] Getzendanner (Kitchadanner),

[1] The Baltimore branch of the Steiner family furnished the first librari-
ans of the Enoch Pratt Free Library. Dr. Louis H. Steiner was the first
librarian, and his son, Bernard C. Steiner, succeeded him. Under their
charge the library has become one of the most useful circulating libraries
in the country.

Kemp, Albaugh, and Poe [1] families, who were numerous and influential in Western Maryland, Baltimore, and throughout the state, local histories furnish abundant materials.

It has been shown in the preceding pages that in the eighteenth century the Germans of Maryland were grouped mainly about two centres, Western Maryland and Baltimore. In the latter they advanced materially the commercial and industrial interests of the city, contributing largely to Baltimore's passing her rival, the older port of Annapolis. In Western Maryland the Germans were mainly devoted to agricultural pursuits, forming a link in the chain of German farms between Pennsylvania and the Valley of Virginia. Others founded the westernmost settlements in the state, becoming the defenders of the frontier.

[1] The Poe family were noted, as before mentioned, as Indian fighters on the frontier ; in Baltimore City, members of the family are leaders of the Baltimore bar. A relic of the fighting spirit survived in the young Poes, who on the football field, always playing for Princeton, annually filled Yale sympathizers with terror ; their combination of pluck, daring, and skill frequently snatched victory from defeat during the last few minutes of play.

CHAPTER VII

THE GERMANS IN VIRGINIA

Earliest settlement at Germanna, 1714 — Governor Spotswood's iron-works — Settlements at Germantown, Virginia, and elsewhere on the Piedmont Plateau — Expedition of Governor Spotswood to the mountains — German settlements in the Valley of Virginia, beginning in 1726-27 — The Shenandoah Valley receives the tide of immigration coming from Pennsylvania — Settlements pushing toward the southern slope of the Valley, and through the gaps in the mountains — Germans in other parts of Virginia — The journeys of Moravian missionaries along the frontier.

ACCORDING to the popular impression Virginia was settled entirely by the English stock. It is indeed true that the latter form a larger percentage in the population of Virginia than they do of most other states, and that the people of Tidewater Virginia are almost exclusively of English origin. But on the other hand, there are, even in Virginia, districts, such as the Piedmont slope, and the whole area of the Valley of Virginia, where the percentage of the English stock among the early colonists was very small, the German and Scotch-Irish predominating. Kercheval,[1] the historian of the Valley of Virginia, long ago called attention to the large Pennsylvania German settlements in the Shenandoah Valley, and Schuricht,[2] more recently, showed that the early Germans of Virginia, as well as the German immigrations of the nineteenth

[1] Samuel Kercheval, *History of the Valley of Virginia.* (Woodstock, Va., 1850, second edition.)

[2] *History of the German Element in Virginia.* By Hermann Schuricht. 2 vols., published by the Society for the History of the Germans in Maryland. (Baltimore, 1900.)

century, had a far more important share in the development of the state than was ever thought possible. Schuricht's work, however, is full of inaccuracies, and has been revised, supplemented, and in some measure done over by several more recent writers on the history of the German element of Virginia.[1]

The earliest German settlement in Virginia was made under the auspices of Governor Spotswood, favorably disposed toward colonists, and appreciative of the value of the Germans as settlers. In imitation of *Penn*sylvania, a large county of Virginia was named *Spot*sylvania in honor of the governor. Within this district (now in Orange County) he founded the town Germanna. The first colonists consisted of twelve German families of the Reformed Church, who arrived in Virginia in April, 1714. They came on the solicitation of Baron de Graffenried,[2] to establish and operate for Governor Spotswood the ironworks which they built about ten miles northwest of the present town of Fredericksburg. The names of the heads of the families were John Kemper,[3] Jacob Holtzclaw, J. and H. Fischback, Hoffman, Otterback (Utterback), Dil-

---

[1] Their articles have appeared in the *Virginia Magazine*, vols. ix-xiii, and are continuing to appear. Most important are the articles of J. W. Wayland, "The Germans of the Valley," in the *Virginia Magazine of History and Biography*, vol. ix, pp. 337–353; vol. x, pp. 33–48 and 113–130. (Richmond, 1902.) Also the articles of C. E. Kemper, and the notes of William G. Stanard, the editor of the *Virginia Magazine:* On the basis of these researches we can come to very definite conclusions about the early Germans in Virginia, though the investigations made are not exhaustive. Much remains to be done, while a great deal undoubtedly has sunk into hopeless obscurity.

[2] See Chapter VIII, pp. 213 ff.

[3] John Kemper was born at Muesen, and died in Virginia between 1754 and 1759. We are indebted for the facts about the Germanna settlement to W. M. Kemper. Cf. Kemper and Wright, editors, *Genealogy of the Kemper Family in the United States, descendants of John Kemper of Virginia, with a short historical sketch of his family and of the German Reformed colony at Germanna and Germantown, Virginia*, (Chicago, 1899.)

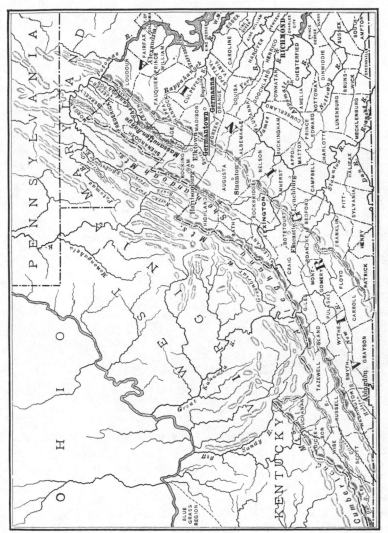

THE VALLEY OF VIRGINIA

man Weber (Tillman Weaver), Merdten (Martin), Hitt, Counts (Coons), Wayman, Han(d)bach. The colonists came from Muesen and Siegen, Nassau-Siegen, in West-phalia. They had been skilled iron-workers for generations past, Muesen having been an important iron centre since 1300. Several groups of German settlers followed : twenty families, about eighty persons, in 1717, and forty families between 1717 and 1720. Governor Spotswood built small houses to shelter the colonists, and apparently pushed the work at the mines. The latter have been described in bright coloring by the pen of Colonel Byrd.[1] A recent statistical work confirms the antiquity of Governor Spots-wood's enterprise : " The oldest furnace of which we have any certain knowledge was 'Spotswood' in the County Spotsylvania." [2] Whether the governor lacked capital, or whether there were unforeseen difficulties, is not known, but the mining operations did not continue long. In the middle of the eighteenth century, Colonel Byrd informs us, " Germanna consisted of the residence of Governor

[1] *The Westover Manuscript*, printed by Edmund and Julian Ruffin, Peters-burg, Va., 1841. Colonel Byrd, the founder of Richmond, Va., was interested in procuring German colonists for a section of country on the Roanoke River. For this purpose he wrote a book in praise of the "New Garden of Eden," as he called it, and had it translated into German and circulated abroad. Its title was *Neu gefundenes Eden, oder ausführlicher Bericht von Süd u. Nord Carolina, Pennsylvania, Maryland und Virginia*. In Truck ver-fertigt durch Befelch der Helvetischen Societät 1737. Republished in *Der Westen*, Chicago, Illinois, November 6, 1892, and January 29, 1893.

On Colonel Byrd's testimony, the wife of Governor Spotswood was a Ger-man woman born in Hannover, named Theke, which would give another motive for Spotswood's interest in the Germans. The historian Campbell denies that Spotswood married a German wife, but gives her name as Anna Butler Bryan. Cf. also *Dictionary of American Biography*, vol. xiii, p. 388.

[2] *Handbook of Virginia*. By the Commissioner of Agriculture. (Fifth edi-tion, p. 82, Richmond, Virginia, 1886.) At the present time iron ore is still produced here by the Wilderness Mining Company, five miles south from Parker Station.

Spotswood and a dozen and a half of half-decayed houses, formerly occupied by German families." The records show that some of the German colonists, being engaged in a lawsuit with the governor, prayed for an attorney to represent their side of the question. Spotswood explained his position at length, declaring that the colonists owed him money for their transportation and keep; the colonists, on the other hand, held that their period of service was ended, and claimed land.[1] We have no information as to the adjustment of the matter, but we know that all the German colonists, except three families, had departed from Germanna in 1748, the year in which the Moravian missionary, Gottschalk, visited the Great Fork of the Rappahannock.

Two important German settlements were established by the immigrants from Germanna, the first being called Germantown. The original colonists of the German Reformed faith founded this village about 1721, "because Governor Spotswood refused to sell them the land on which they were settled at Germanna." A deed dated August 22, 1724, was made out by the proprietors of the Northern Neck of Virginia in favor of Jacob Holtzclaw, J. Fischback, and J. H. Hoffman. Germantown was located along the Licking Run, about ten miles from the Little Fork of the Rappahannock, where there had settled another group of the original Germanna settlers, the German Reformed who had originally come from Westphalia. Both places in 1748 had built churches and schoolhouses, the

---

[1] The petitioners, Zerichias Fleschman and Georg Utz (for themselves and fourteen other High Germans), belonged to the second colony, which came to Germanna in 1717. They were Lutherans, who subsequently, about 1724, settled in Madison County. They begged for an attorney, on the governor's order for their arrest. They stated that the governor refused to give them a copy of the agreement they made with him.

reader[1] of Germantown being old Mr. Holzklo (Jacob Holtzclaw), and of the Little Fork, John Jung. They could not afford a minister in these early days and the Moravian missionaries naturally found an "open door."[2] Brother Gottschalk speaks of these places in a much more kindly manner than of the Lutheran settlements, which, being supplied with ministers, did not receive the missionaries so cordially. "A very fine, neighborly, and friendly people"; and "the people did not look so much upon religion, but rather that Christ be preached to them," were Gottschalk's comments on the Germantown settlers. Brother Schnell, another Moravian missionary, visited Holzklo in 1734. On Sunday the Reverend Mr. Schnell preached to about one hundred persons, in a "neat church." He was offered a parsonage, one hundred acres of land and a garden, and the promise that they would not allow him to suffer want in other directions if he would only stay and preach. Germantown was situated in the present Fauquier County, about nine miles south of Warrington, on the Licking Run.

The German Lutherans of Germanna who came in 1717, migrated to what is now Madison County, Virginia, forming the second important settlement. These "upper Germans" were more numerous. In 1748 there were eighty families, mostly from Würtemberg, within a circle of a few miles, that had "a beautiful large church and school and also a parsonage and a glebe of several hundred acres

---

[1] Readers were frequently schoolmasters, who, in the absence of ministers, would at regular intervals read to the settlers printed sermons, or passages from the Scriptures, in lieu of preaching a sermon.

[2] A phrase used by the missionaries. Cf. *Moravian Diaries of Travels through Virginia*, edited by the Reverend W. J. Hinke and Charles E. Kemper, published in the *Virginia Magazine*, vols. xi and xii. These diaries are documents of historical value, preserved in the archives of the Moravian church at Bethlehem.

with seven negroes who must cultivate the minister's land."
These colonists removed from Germanna prior to 1724,
and settled in the forks of the Conway and Robinson
rivers. In 1737 they numbered three hundred souls, and
in 1740 built Hebron Church, one of the oldest churches in
Virginia, used by the Lutherans continuously. It stands on
a beautiful eminence in the forks of the Robinson River
and White Oak Run. Reverend John Caspar Stoever was
their first minister.[1] He went abroad to procure funds
for the building of his church, and was very successful.
He collected about three thousand pounds, and after the
building of the "Hopeful Evangelic Lutheran Church"
at Hebron, a surplus was left for which seven hundred
acres of land were purchased and a number of slaves.
This latter circumstance has frequently been looked upon
as a blot on the history of the early Germans of Virginia,
for everywhere else they stanchly opposed slavery. Probably this purchase was made under the influence of the
Reverend Mr. Klug, the successor of Pastor Stoever, the
latter not being destined to reap the fruits of his labors.

The Reverend Mr. Klug was a very energetic individual,
extending the Lutheran affiliation far into the Shenandoah
Valley. A very different type of man from Mühlenberg
or Schlatter, he was given to the evil habits of his time,
particularly to drinking, for which, no doubt, he found
plenty of examples among his well-to-do friends, the
colonial gentry, with whom he consorted. He was not
accustomed to plain living as an incentive to high thinking, and confessed generously to one of the Moravian
missionaries that he was no Pietist, gratuitous information,

---

[1] Cf. Dr. Slaughter's *History of St. Mark's Parish*, pp. 45–46; Bishop
Meade's *Old Churches and Families of Virginia*, vol. ii, pp. 74–76; *Journal
of the Presbyterian Historical Society*, vol. ii, nos. 1, 2, and 3.

in the face of stories current about the minister's tipsy rides homeward from functions not ministerial. Mr. Klug was not an eloquent preacher, but a worldly-wise man of affairs, whose actions were directed by policy, who clung to the strong and successful element. His predecessor, the Reverend Mr. Stoever, had already made good beginnings, providing church organization and joining the Virginia German Lutheran communities of Fredericksburg, Newmarket, Strasburg, Winchester, Woodstock, etc., with the Lutheran Synod of Pennsylvania. The Hebron Church in Madison is still in existence, and prizes among its rare possessions some antique sacred vessels received from friends in Germany, and, more highly still, an organ constructed about 1800 by the German organ-builder David Tannenberg of Lititz, Pennsylvania.[1] A succeeding clergyman, William Zimmerman, introduced the English language into the German service at Hebron, and anglicized likewise his own name into Carpenter.

We shall now leave the settlements on the Piedmont Plateau to consider another and stronger current of immigration, namely that into the Valley of Virginia. Strange as it may seem, there was no movement from east to west, from the lowlands of Virginia to the western or higher portions, as there was in some other states, but the migration came from the north, from Pennsylvania, moving southwestwardly through the mountain valleys of Virginia, and growing in such proportions as to be forced to send tributaries in an easterly direction.

Alexander Spotswood, governor of Virginia from 1710 to 1723, during which period he greatly improved the condition of his province by wise legislation and able ad-

---

[1] For an account of Tannenberg's work in the Moravian settlement of Lititz, see *The Pennsylvania German*, vol. x, no. 7 (July, 1909), pp. 399 ff.

ministration, made the first organized effort to extend the frontier line beyond the Appalachian Mountains. He was not the first white man to see the Valley. The topography was surely known in 1705,[1] and even earlier through Lederer's explorations in 1670. But the great range of mountains that stretched from northeast to southwest seemed like an impassable barrier to American colonists. What lay beyond, no one was certain of. Governor Spotswood was determined to increase his knowledge of the geography of his colony, entertaining the vain hope perhaps of finding one of the Great Lakes within view of the summits of the Blue Ridge. Accordingly he gathered about him an exploring party consisting of nine of his personal friends, a band of tried rangers, and four Indian guides. They were well provided with provisions and plentifully also with invigorating drinks. They frequently encamped to lighten their baggage, and made great fires and hunted game. The itinerary of the party was presumably as follows: From Germantown, ten miles below the Falls of the Rappahannock, they started on the 29th of August, 1716; then proceeding to Germanna, and following the left bank of the Rapidan. They crossed that river near Peyton's Ford, passing by the present site of Stanardsville, in Greene County. They entered the foothills of the Blue Ridge by way of Swift Run Gap. On a bright day of early Septem-

---

[1] The general topography of the Valley being known as early as 1705, Governor Spotswood and his party were not the first white men to enter or look upon that region. (*Virginia Magazine*, vol. xiii, p. 113.) The first legislative recognition of the country beyond the Blue Ridge appears to have been in 1705, when the General Assembly of Virginia passed an act for free and open trade with the Indians, and, among other provisions, it was enacted that any person who should make discovery of "any town or nation of Indians situated or inhabiting to the westward of or between the Appalachian Mountains, should have, for the space of fourteen years, the sole right to trade with them." *Hening's Statutes*, vol. iii, pp. 468–469.

ber, from a mountain height which had just been ascended, the view of the Valley suddenly broke upon the governor, who was riding somewhat in advance of his troop. The broad Valley, untouched by human hand, lay before him, in its original splendor, the Shenandoah[1] River winding its silvery course through groves and tall grasses, and toward the north, spurs of the Massanutten Range projected into the Valley. The governor and his merry company were well satisfied with the view, descended to the Shenandoah and forded the stream several miles below the historic village of Port Republic. That the party crossed the Valley and passed on westward to the Alleghany Range, striking it where now is Pendleton County in West Virginia, is a matter of conjecture.[2] The company at all events, did not tarry long in the Valley. On their return, the governor, so the story is told, founded the order of the "Knights of the Golden Horseshoe,"[3] bestowing upon each of his fellow travelers a miniature golden horseshoe, with the inscription, "Sic juvat transcendere montes," "which signified that it would help to pass over the mountains."[4] No immediate results followed, though

[1] The translation of Shenandoah, "Daughter of the Stars," is probably incorrect. It is an Iroquoian name, derived from the name of an Oneida Indian chief. *Virginia Magazine*, vol. xiii, p. 119.

[2] The only early account of this expedition known to be in existence is contained in the journal of John Fontaine, which appears in the work entitled "Memoirs of a Huguenot Family," reprinted in Slaughter's *History of St. Mark's Parish*, pp. 39–41.

[3] For historical confirmation of the foundation of the order see *Virginia Magazine*, vol. xiii, p. 125. Another translation of the inscription reads: "Thus it is a pleasure to cross the Mountains."

[4] This expedition is notable because it was the first organized effort made by any of the colonies to extend the frontier line beyond the Appalachian Mountains. Governor Spotswood desired to check the rising power of the French in the West, and also to discover the sources of the Virginia rivers. He likewise wished to establish friendly relations with the Indians to the westward. *Virginia Magazine*, vol. xiii, note to p. 114.

all the knights that took part in the jaunt were loud in their praises of the new country. The trip had been seriously undertaken by the governor in the hope of extending the frontier and encouraging immigration toward the western part of the colony of Virginia. Ten years elapsed, however, before the first settler arrived in the Valley.

The Valley of Virginia lies between two mountain ranges, the North Mountain or the Alleghanies, and the South Mountain or Blue Ridge, both ranges running from northeast to southwest, and forming the westernmost physiographical section of the state of Virginia. The Valley is divided into two sections with a slope to the north and another to the south, the highest portion being in the present county of Rockbridge, and the divide approximately denoted by a line running through the town of Lexington. The more fruitful section toward the north is drained by the Shenandoah River, whose two forks nearly surround the picturesque Massanutten Range, until they unite at Front Royal, and after a total course of one hundred and seventy miles, empty into the Potomac near Harper's Ferry. The Massanutten range does not divide the Valley equally; it lies nearer the Blue Ridge, and is about forty miles in length, ending at Strasburg. Then the Opequon River becomes the boundary-line of counties, separating Frederick and Berkeley from Clarke and Jefferson, as the Massanutten Range had separated Shenandoah from Warren and Page. Farther up the Valley are the counties of Rockingham, Augusta, and Rockbridge, extending from mountain to mountain. The southern slope of the Valley is drained on the east by the headwaters of the James and Roanoke, on the west by the New River, a tributary of the Great Kanawha, that opens the territory of West Virginia toward the Ohio. Still farther to the south the Valley is drained by the headwaters of the Tennessee, by the Clinch and Holston rivers, where the first settlements of Tennessee were located, affording a gateway to the territory beyond the Alleghanies.

The average breadth of the Valley is from twenty to thirty miles, and the length over three hundred. It is the natural avenue of communication between north and south, between Pennsylvania and Tennessee or Kentucky, and had long been so, before those territorial names were known. The Indian hunters and war-parties had long ago beaten a trail through the Valley, the white hunters following in their tracks; then came the men of axe and rifle; and finally the patient settler, whose toil made the earth luxuriant with grain, fruit, and flowers. A great highway for the development of the West, and Southwest, by way of Kentucky and Tennessee, was thus opened before the war of the Revolution, and continued with ever greater usefulness thereafter. The fertile Valley, also in the later days of the railroad, was destined to play a prominent part in the affairs of the nation. Its importance as a granary for armies was seen alike by the armies of the North and South in the Civil War, the Valley of the Shenandoah becoming the bone of fiercest contention and consequently the scene of some of the bloodiest fighting in the whole war. The possession of the Valley meant subsistence; it was the key alike to both capitals, Washington and Richmond (through Lynchburg).

It is now established beyond any doubt that at least the portion of the Shenandoah Valley sloping to the north was almost entirely settled by Germans. There was but a sprinkling of the Scotch-Irish and of French Huguenots, an English settlement being claimed only for the diminutive Clarke County. Many Germans settled on the southern slope of the Valley, but it is a commonly accepted fact that among the early settlers in that area there were more Scotch-Irish and Huguenots. The story of the first settlement of the Valley is typical, full of interest, and, since not generally known, worthy to be followed in some detail. All of the first settlers were Germans,[1] starting almost without exception from Pennsylvania and Maryland, following the trails to the Potomac, crossing at or near the mouth of the Shenandoah or the Opequon (a little higher upstream), and then ascending the Valley between the two mountain ranges.

An exception to this course of settlement was the first of the pioneers, Adam Müller (Miller), who, following the line of Governor Spotswood's march, entered the Valley through Swift Run Gap, and in 1726–27[2] settled near the present site of Elkton. Adam Müller was born in Germany,[3] about 1700, located first in Lancaster County, Pennsylvania, but after living there for several years, de-

---

[1] The first Scotch-Irish settler in the Valley was John Lewis, who in 1732 located far up the Valley near Staunton. The first deed of William Beverly, who was very instrumental in getting Scotch-Irish settlers about his manor (Staunton District), was made to John Lewis in 1738. (*William and Mary College Quarterly*, vol. iii, p. 226.) The numerous settlements of the Scotch-Irish in this county are largely due to him.

[2] The claim has been made that Jost Hite was the first white settler of the Valley, but the naturalization papers of Adam Miller prove that he settled in the Shenandoah in 1726 or 1727. (Cf. *William and Mary College Quarterly*, vol. ix, p. 132.) The first step to secure land in the Valley of Virginia by due process of law was taken by Colonel Robert Carter. The record of a tree bearing the inscription "R. C., 1729," in the Shenandoah district, proves that the land was surveyed as early as that. Robert Carter was the agent for many years of the Fairfax estate, and acquired lands second in extent only to his principal. He was familiarly called "King Carter," and was one of the foremost men in Virginia. He died in 1732.

[3] The place of birth is given in the *Virginia Magazine* (see references below) as Schresoin. There is no such place. It may have been: Schretzheim in Bavaria, Schrezheim in Würtemberg, or Schriesheim in Baden.

termined to try his fortune in Virginia. He embarked at the head of Chesapeake Bay, and, coming to Williamsburg, he heard, presumably from the mouth of a " Knight of the Golden Horseshoe," of the wonderful country beyond the Blue Ridge. This he determined to see with his own eyes, and was so well pleased with it that he went back to Pennsylvania to fetch his family. He then settled near Swift Run Gap, his final abode being on the Shenandoah some few miles distant from his first location. Upon his representations, his former neighbors and friends in Pennsylvania joined him and became settlers at Elkton. Such were undoubtedly Abram Strickler, Mathias Selzer, Philip Lang (Long), Paul Lang (Long), Michael Rhinehart, Hans Rood, Michael Kaufman, and other Pennsylvania "Dutchmen" so-called, who with Adam Müller (Miller) in 1733 petitioned for a clear title to their lands at Massanutten (Indian name), which they claimed to have bought for a sum of money amounting to upwards of four hundred pounds (five thousand acres), from Jacob Stover.[1] The latter was a later settler, but more fortunate in securing a large land grant. Previous to that Müller and his associates had been squatters merely. The petitioners were located in the southeastern portion of what is now Rockingham County, or the southwestern part of Page County, along the Shenandoah River, near the Massanutten Mountain, and in that year (1733) counted fifty-one persons, young and old, on nine plantations.[2]

[1] They claimed that they had bought this land four years before (1729–1730). They were apparently granted their claims, and the suit of William Beverly was dismissed. Kemper gives convincing evidence from court orders that the settlement at Massanutten was the first permanent white settlement in the Valley of Virginia and that its date was 1730 or 1729. *Virginia Magazine*, vol. xiii, pp. 121 ff.

[2] The facts about the first settler in the Valley of Virginia have been set forth by a descendant of Adam Müller, Charles E. Kemper, of Washington,

Some distance above Harper's Ferry there is an ancient ford over the Potomac, once called "The Old Packhorse Ford," the link between the north country and the Shenandoah Valley. Indian hunters and warriors had passed and repassed before the packhorse forded the stream, and numerous encounters must have taken place there between the red-skinned warriors, of which the innumerable arrowheads found in the vicinity bear witness. Probably as early as 1726 or 1727 a number of Pennsylvania Germans crossed the ford, and near by, twelve miles above Harper's Ferry, founded a village which they called New Mecklenburg.[1] When the place was incorporated in 1762, it was named Shepherdstown, in honor of Thomas Shepherd (Schaefer), who had settled there in 1734. Many of the most respected families of Jefferson County, West Virginia, trace their descent from these original settlers, land grants dating as far back as 1729 being in possession of some of them. The settlers were generally at first squatters, but in course of time they were compelled to buy the lands they had cultivated, from some fortunate individual who had received a land grant. Thus in this settlement a number of settlers bought the lands they had improved from a Welshman, Richard A. Morgan, who received a large land grant about 1730.

In 1732 came Justus Heid (Joist or Yost Hite)[2] *via*

D. C. This family, like so many of the pre-revolutionary German Virginians, have been closely linked with the weal and woe of the state throughout its history and are looked upon with pride and respect no less than the descendants of the cavaliers. *Virginia Magazine*, vol. x, pp. 84–86; vol. ix, pp. 351–352. (James Lawson Kemper, governor of Virginia, 1873–78, was a member of this family.)

[1] Noted as the place where James Rumsey built the first steamboat in 1788.

[2] Joist Hite was born in Strassburg, and the town of that name in the Valley was probably named by him. He died in 1760, leaving a numerous

York, Pennsylvania, with his family, his three sons-in-law with their families, and a few others, among whom was Peter Stephan (Stephens), in all sixteen families. They crossed the " Cohongoronta " (a spelling used in the treaty of Lancaster, the Indian name for Potomac), and settled on the Opequon River. Joist Hite settled five miles below where Winchester now stands, his home being on the great Indian trail leading to the upper parts of the Valley, the same which is now transformed into the macadamized Valley turnpike. Jacob Chrisman (Christmann) selected for his location a spring, two miles further south on the same trail, the site being known as Chrisman's Spring. Another son-in-law, George Baumann (Bowman), settled still further up, on Cedar Creek, and the third, Paul Frohmann (Froman), several miles to the west of Bowman, also on Cedar Creek. Peter Stephan with others founded Stephansburg, which, after several changes in name, is now called Stephens City. About the same time the first house of Kernstown was built on the land of Adam Kern. One of the landmarks of that early period is a limestone house near Winchester (Frederickstown) built in 1753, by Colonel John Hite (a son of Joist Hite), distinguished for bravery in the Indian wars. At that time it was considered one of the most elegant houses west of the Blue Ridge, and it is still standing in good preservation.

Joist Hite and his followers purchased their lands from a Dutchman, John Vanmeter, of whom the story is told that he accompanied a war-party of the Delawares against their old enemies, the Catawbas. A fierce battle was fought about where Franklin, the present county-seat of Pendle-

and highly respected posterity. Joist Hite was responsible himself for the confused spelling of his name. He is said to have signed it three different ways on the same day, in the execution of three different deeds.

ton County, West Virginia, now stands. The Delawares were defeated. On the retreat Vanmeter beheld the rich land of the Valley and obtained a large grant from Governor Gooch, forty thousand acres in the lower part of the Valley, which he sold later to Joist Hite. The Vanmeters settled on the southern branch of the Potomac in West Virginia, Hampshire and Hardy counties.

A large grant of land was obtained as early as 1729–30 by another prominent German settler, Jacob Stauffer (Stover), a shrewd man. It is said that, in order to procure a large quantity of land, he represented every head of horse or cattle that he possessed as the head of a family ready to settle on the land. His lands extended from the forks of the Shenandoah southwestwardly along the main branch to Page County, comprising portions of three counties as constituted at present. He chose as his own location the northern end of the Massanutten Range, where he founded Staufferstadt, later renamed Strasburg by two Germans from Alsace.

The German, Robert Harper, in 1734, settled at the Great Falls, the junction of the Shenandoah and Potomac, and founded the historical town of Harper's Ferry, named in his honor and describing his vocation. Many others settled near by: Winchester had settlers as early as 1738, Woodstock (Millerstown) was founded two years later by Jacob Müller (Miller), and "originally laid out upon a larger scale than any other of our ancient villages" (Kercheval).[1] Ruffner's Cave (near Luray Cave) commemorates the name of the settler Ruffner (1745), the son of a German baron who lived in Hannover.

---

[1] "Woodstock," Kercheval says, " like most of our towns, was settled exclusively by Germans, and German (Pennsylvania German) was the language heard on the streets up to 1850." The same is said to be true of Strasburg.

A tide[1] of immigration swept up the Valley as soon as its fertility became known. Most of the settlers came from Pennsylvania, an additional incentive being the growing hostility of the Indians on the Pennsylvania frontier. The settlers believed they would be better protected in the Valley, which was guarded by mountains on two sides. After Braddock's defeat in 1755, the migrations became still more numerous, reaching their height after the Revolution. Villages were founded and towns incorporated in large numbers by the inflowing population. Thus Harrisonburg, in Rockingham County, was established by law in 1780 and five years later had twenty persons owning lots. Front Royal (Warren County) was incorporated in 1788, and likewise received a strong German population. Keezletown (the German Keizell's Town) was established in 1791, near Harrisonburg in Rockingham County, and became the keen rival of the latter.[2] Mr. Keizell laid out one hundred acres of land in lots and streets — double the size of Harrisonburg — and offered inducements to purchasers who would build on these lots. During the years 1781–84 there appear to have been more deeds recorded for lots in Keizell's

---

[1] Some of the names of German settlers during the early half of the century were : William Millars, William Strope, Israel Friend, Edward Lucas, James Foreman, John Lemon, the Schmuckers, the Koiners, the Benders, Beckers (Bakers), Westerhoefers, Sauers (Sowers), Von Webers, Casselmanns, Finks, Funkhousers, Molers, Weiers. Bernhard Weier, a hunter, discovered the beautiful Weyer's Cave (1804). The commissioners who valued the lands of Rockingham County in 1782 found 860 landowners in the county. Among the largest landowners were the following Germans : the Bowmans, Conrads, Coffmans, Chrismans, Clicks, Crotzers, Fitzwaters, Bransbergers, Kisers, Kislings, Kooglers, Kaylors, Millers, Minnicks, Michaels, Messicks, Pences, Rollers, Rimels, Sheetses, Shumakers, Shavers, Shanks, Vanpelts, Wines, Wingers, and Weavers. Cf. Wayland, "The Germans of the Valley," *Virginia Magazine*, vols. ix, x.

[2] Wayland, "The Germans of the Valley," *Virginia Magazine*, vol. x, p. 43, etc.

Town than in Harrisonburg. The consideration for conveyance of a lot was that the purchaser should build a dwelling-house twenty by eighteen feet, with stone or brick chimneys, and make an annual payment of four shillings.

The Germans developed the country not alone in a material way, i. e., by making the Valley a garden; they were in the front rank also in every other form of activity. For example, among the prominent families of Shenandoah County were the German families the Neffs, the Kageys, and the Henkels, who settled in or near New Market. The Reverend Paul Henkel was the first of the family in Shenandoah, coming soon after the close of the Revolution. Born near the present city of Salisbury, North Carolina, he was the grandson of the Reverend Gerhard Henkel, who, previous to his coming to America, was a German court preacher. In 1806 the Reverend Ambrose Henkel, son of Paul Henkel, established a printing-house at New Market, which is still in the hands of the Henkel family. The oldest press of the Valley was distinguished also for the large amount of Lutheran theological works issued.[1] The Neffs, of Swiss German descent, came from Pennsylvania and many members of the family were distinguished in civil and military life.[2] The Kagey family likewise had their origin in German Switzerland. Hans Kagey settled in Pennsylvania in 1715. Henry Kagey removed from Lancaster County in 1768 and a few years later located two miles east of New Market. Others of the family fol-

---

[1] The Henkel Press supplied Bibles, hymn-books, catechisms, tracts, etc., for the North and South Carolina and Tennessee Lutheran synods, besides the less remote congregations of Virginia.

[2] Cf. Neff (Elizabeth Clifford), *A Chronicle, together with a little romance regarding Rudolf and Jacob Näf, of Frankfort, Pennsylvania, and their descendants including an account of the Neffs in Switzerland and America.* (Cincinnati, Ohio.)

lowed. John Kagey, eldest son of Henry, was a plain Dunker preacher, who led a pious and exemplary life. It is said that "almost as good as John Kagey" has been an adage in Rockingham and Shenandoah counties for the last three generations. "Nobody could make John Kagey do wrong, or break his word," was an article of faith in the generation in which he lived. It is likewise interesting to note that this family of strong virtue produced an abolitionist, in spite of its Southern environment, in the person of John Henry Kagi, John Brown's secretary of war, who was killed at Harper's Ferry in 1859. He was a great-grandson of Henry Kagey.

The tide [1] of immigration from Pennsylvania and Maryland that swept up the Valley before and at the close of the Revolution, produced a thickening of settlements and a pushing on farther up the Valley. There resulted also a crowding out through the gaps of the South Mountain into the neighboring counties of Virginia on the Piedmont Plateau.

The southern slope of the Valley of Virginia, below the line of Lexington, which was at first but sparsely settled by Germans, began to be invaded after the Revolution by the steadily flowing stream of Germans from Pennsylvania and Maryland. Representatives of all denominations, German Lutherans, and Reformed Mennonites, Dunkers, etc., forced their way up the Valley and down the other side, supplying with an agricultural population the counties of Augusta, Rockbridge, Botetourt, Roanoke,

---

[1] Names of settlers in Shenandoah County toward the close of the Revolution were: the Tirkles, Hesses, Garbers, Wines, Myerses, Pences, etc., located in the neighborhood of Forestville ; the Faltzes, Halsleys, Coffelts, Clines, Kellers, Benders (Painters), Bowmans, Rinkers, Tysingers, Empschillers, Lantzes, Stouts, Wilkinses, Frys, Rosenbergers, and Lindamoods, settled in the vicinity of Hamburg.

Craig, Montgomery, Pulaski, and Wythe. In Wythe, Pulaski, Montgomery, and Craig counties the Germans probably met a number of Swiss who emigrated from North Carolina to Virginia. Captain R. B. Moorman, of Roanoke, says:[1] "Rockbridge, Botetourt, Roanoke, Craig, Montgomery, and Pulaski present a grateful field to the German American historian." The German Lutherans were for many years in almost exclusive possession of Salem, and it is supposed that many chapels and meeting-houses, at one time existing in the more remote valleys of the mountains, are now lost to history.

Concerning the settlements on the southern slope, Judge B. Simmons says:[2]

The earliest deeds to the German element in Botetourt County bear date from 1783. The first, or among the first German settlers were the Graybills, Simmons, Keplers, Gishs, Broughs, Sniders, Harshbergers, Bechmers, Amens, and others. The Amens now spell their name "Ammen." All came in the eighties. These Germans came into this county directly after the Revolutionary War, from Pennsylvania and Maryland,— mostly from Pennsylvania. The German element I think you will find came into Virginia about the same time all along up the Valley, a great many of them stopping in what are now Rockingham, Shenandoah, and Augusta, and the lower counties. I do not think many of them stopped in what is now Rockbridge. The Germans looked for good land, and have as a general rule held on to it. They *evidently had money* and seem to have *paid cash for their lands*, and paid as much for their lands then as the same lands are worth now. As a rule the German element are frugal, sturdy, honest folk. For many years they made the mistake of not educating[3] their children; but for some years

---

[1] Quoted by Schuricht, *History of the German Element in Virginia.*

[2] Quoted by Wayland, *Virginia Magazine*, vol. x, pp. 38–39.

[3] Wayland writes a note stating that the criticism pertains only to the Dunkards and Mennonites, and that most of the Botetourt Germans were

many of them have been educating their children, many of whom are filling the various professions with ability.

While the writer quoted is guilty of several inaccuracies, particularly that concerning the settlement of the entire Valley at about the same time, still he records another impression which is striking and of very great value. "The Germans did not stop in Rockbridge, they were looking for better lands," and secondly, "they had the money to pay for them." Their cash in hand furnishes an additional explanation of their ability to get a choice of lands, to dispossess former settlers on good lands and give to their own settlements greater stability. Coupled with that, on the road to success, was their skill and experience as farmers, which made of indifferent land good land, their economy, industry, and clean methods of conduct, which gave their settlements permanence and tone.

Fincastle, the county-seat of Botetourt County, was incorporated in 1772. A German, Israel Christian, at that time made a present of forty acres of land to the justices of the Botetourt court for the use of the county, an act worthy of commendation for its public spirit. Near Fincastle, and probably about the date of its settlement, the village of Amsterdam was founded by Pennsylvania German Dunkards.[1] The official survey of Amsterdam was made in 1796. Deeds of conveyance to certain lots are from George Stoner and wife " in Stonertown," but the

Dunkards. Moreover that now they have a college at Daleville, Botetourt County. It should also be added that the native population generally was not well educated when the Germans were not, and also that ignorance of the English language was regarded as tantamount to illiteracy. The frontiersmen, of whatever nationality, were never in the front rank in matters of education and religion ; they should not be judged harshly, however, in view of their difficulty in getting either teachers or ministers to serve them.

[1] The same as Tunkers or Dunkers.

surveyor calls the plan of the town " A Map of Amsterdam." George Stoner was a German who bought his land on December 29, 1794, of John Snider, who had bought it two years before.[1]

In 1795 or thereabouts Dr. George Daniel Flohr was pastor among the German settlements on New River and primarily at the Swiss colony of New Berne, Pulaski County. In Wythe County, to the southwest adjoining, a German Lutheran church was established in 1792, on land donated by Stophel Zimmerman and John Davis, and owned jointly by the Lutherans and Reformed. The early Germans of Wythe County had some means, and were equally divided between Lutheran and Reformed. Costly Bibles were preserved by them as heirlooms.[2]

The above facts show that there was a larger percentage of Germans settled on the southern slope of the Valley than is generally supposed, and that the number constantly increased after the Revolution. This district is the one which was so important in the early settlements of Tennessee and Kentucky, which, Theodore Roosevelt explains,[3] was the germ-centre of the new life which was to flow into the great undeveloped territory of Indian fame, the dark and bloody ground. Neither the Indian tribes of the North nor of the South dared to claim that No Man's Land as their own, and as a result, the peerless hunting-grounds became the booty of the white man, — but not

---

[1] See Wayland, *Virginia Magazine*, vol. x, p. 42.

[2] Additional churches were St. John's Lutheran Church, one mile north of Wytheville, and twelve miles west, St. Paul's Church. In 1796 the Reverend Leonard Willy became pastor of Cedar Grove Church, in Smyth County, and of Kimberling, St. Paul's, and St. John's in Wythe County. In 1799 the Reverend Dr. Flohr was called and located in southwestern Virginia several miles north of Wytheville. *Virginia Magazine*, vol. x, p. 123. See also Schuricht, p. 93 (vol. i).

[3] *The Winning of the West*, vol. i, pp. 134 ff.

until after one of the fiercest struggles known to mankind, not one of pitched battles, but of daily combat between settler and savage. The part played by the German settler in this struggle has been underestimated. He was, if not the very first [1] in the land, — a distinction claimed by the Scotch-Irish and Huguenot elements, — at least closely on the heels of the first colonists, and very well represented among the first *permanent* settlers of Kentucky and the Southwest.

Customs and speech the Germans brought with them into the Valley, and for a time held to them tenaciously. When the Germans and Irish met, there was often friction, such as Kercheval describes, e. g., in the town of Winchester, the capital of Frederick County. Winchester had a mixed population of Germans, Irish, and a few Scotch and English. " It was customary for the Dutch on St. Patrick's Day," says Kercheval, " to exhibit the effigy of the saint, with a string of Irish potatoes around his neck, and his wife Sheeley, with her apron loaded also with potatoes. This was always followed by a riot. The Irish resented the indignity offered to their saint and his holy spouse, and a battle followed. On St. Michael's Day the Irish would retort, and exhibit the saint with a rope of sauerkraut about the neck. Then the Dutch, like the Yankee, 'felt chock full of fight,' and at it they went, pell-mell, and many a black eye, bloody nose, and broken head was the result. The practice was finally put down by the rigor with which the courts of justice punished the rioters." But as the two elements lived longer together, with common interests, they began to appreciate one

[1] In Chapter xii, below, it will be seen that the Germans sent quite a considerable number even among the first settlers, i. e., hunters, adventurers, and soldiers, into Kentucky.

another and frequently intermarried. The Revolutionary War cut down mightily the barriers of nationality.

As the Valley became more thickly settled, the current of immigration flowed not only southwestwardly between the mountain ranges, but also eastwardly through the gaps of the mountains, into the counties lying at the base of South Mountain. The counties that received a strong German element were Loudoun, Fauquier, Rappahannock, Madison, Greene, Albemarle, Louisa, Orange, Culpeper, and Prince William. Fairfax may have received some German immigrants from the port of Alexandria, where small accessions to the German population entered, coming directly from Germany. The counties Madison and Fauquier had been settled by Germans even earlier than those of the Valley, and no doubt possessed the largest German population of all the surrounding counties. One of the most important elements of the population in Madison County at this day is constituted by the descendants of the original colonists around Hebron Church from Germanna.[1] The same can be said of the descendants (fewer in number) of the other group of Germanna colonists who settled along the Licking Run in Fauquier County.[2]

Among the settlers in the present Culpeper County were the Waggener brothers, five in number. They joined Colonel Washington against Fort Duquesne in 1754, and were members of the First Virginia Regiment when Braddock met his defeat, Edward Waggener being among the slain. Andrew Waggener was commissioned captain and placed in command of Fort Pleasant, to defend the frontier against the Indians. He then settled in Berkeley County, West Virginia (Bunker Hill), where he remained until the Revolution, when he joined the army at once and served

[1] Cf. pp. 178 ff., 181–182, and 204.   [2] Cf. pp. 180–181, and 204.

from the beginning to the end of the war. In Louisa
County Schuricht found a number of German names
among the first entries in the land registers, such as Boe-
sick, Hesler, Hehler, Arndt, Armistead (Armstaedt), Flem-
ming, Kohler, Brockman, Buckner, and Spiller. Into Prince
William County a number of Tunkers migrated from the
Valley, there selling at high prices and buying at a low
figure in Prince William, then "improving and making
former waste fields to blossom."[1]

The statement is often repeated that the current of
immigration from the mountains met, in Midland Virginia,
another coming northward from the Carolinas. There
seems so far to be no definite verification for this tradition. Apparently some North Carolina Germans settled
on the southern line of Virginia, on the Dan and Roanoke
rivers, in the counties of Pittsylvania, Halifax, and Mecklenburg.[2] The Moravian missionary, Schnell, met the
Swiss settler, Zollikoffer, on the Roanoke, and concerning
the same region we find a statement made, "there gained
considerable wealth in a short time a few Swiss and some
Frenchmen — by cultivating hemp and flax."[3] The Hel-
vetian Society also made the record : "Many French re-
formists, representative people from Alsace and Lorraine
(at present within the borders of Germany), owned large
plantations along the James River, particularly above the
James River Falls (Powhatan and Goochland counties),

[1] Thomas Whitehead, Commissioner of Agriculture in Virginia, *Report
of the State Board of Agriculture of Virginia*, p. 142. (Richmond, Virginia,
1888.) The Commissioner encourages others to do the same.

[2] Some perhaps also settled in Wythe, Pulaski, Montgomery, and Craig
counties, i. e., along the mountain ranges. Cf. above, pp. 196–198.

[3] *Neu gefundenes Eden, oder ausführlicher Bericht von Süd und Nord
Carolina, Pennsylvania, Maryland und Virginia*. In Truck verfertigt durch,
Befelch der Helvetischen Societaet, 1737. Republished in *Der Westen*, Chi-
cago, Illinois, November 6, 1892, to January 29, 1893.

who had left France, fugitive on account of their religious faith."

Scattered German settlers appeared in a great many towns of Virginia at or near their period of foundation. In Richmond it seems that the first sale of land by Colonel Byrd was to a German and that the oldest building in the city, " the old stone house on Main Street," still standing,[1] was built by a German about 1737. The lot was sold by the son of Colonel Byrd to Samuel Sherer, who afterwards deeded it to Jacob Ege, the property remaining in the possession of this German family until a few years ago. The " stone house " is the oldest building in Richmond, and its erection probably antedates the laying-out of the town. There were a number of German names among the first settlers of Petersburg, Norfolk, and Portsmouth. Smithfield, in the county Isle of Wight, was founded by Germans who built a Lutheran church there in 1772. It is claimed that the first owner of the land upon which Lynchburg (Campbell County) was built was a German Quaker, who sold it to John Lynch, an Irishman, after whom the city received its name.

Such scattered details show that much remains to be done before the history of the Germans in Virginia can be finally written. One fact is very clear, viz., that the German settlements were far more numerous toward the west or higher portions of Virginia than elsewhere. The desirable German immigrant, a farmer, artisan, or day laborer, was repelled by the presence of negroes in Tidewater Virginia, and would not work by their side. Neither his worldly estate nor his natural inclination allowed the German to be idle. He did not therefore fit into the society of Eastern Virginia. Where the German settle-

---

[1] Schuricht (1898), vol. i, p. 80.

ments were numerous, there were very few negroes, a fact
that remains true to the present time.[1]

There remain to be noticed a few settlements in the
extreme west of the colony of Virginia, established before
the Revolutionary War, at the very outposts of civilization.
They were located within the present borders of West
Virginia, within the Alleghany Mountains. Two of them
were situated respectively on Patterson's Creek and on
the South Branch of the Potomac, the third settlement
was on the New River, which with the Greenbrier forms
the Great Kanawha, tributary of the Ohio. These remote
settlements are brought nearer to us by the diaries of the
Moravian missionaries Schnell, Gottschalk, and Spangenberg (deposited in the Archives of the Moravian church
at Bethlehem).[2] The Moravian missionaries made annual
or sometimes semi-annual trips through the frontier settlements, in order to keep the spark of religious life from
going out in the barren outposts of civilization. The
earliest trip recorded is that of Schnell in 1743. The common route taken was from Bethlehem by way of Lebanon,
Lancaster, and York in Pennsylvania, to Frederick and
Hagerstown in Maryland. A stop was made with old Hager,
who would probably take the missionaries for safety to
Prathor or to Cresap, the latter, though reputed ferocious
as an Indian, being gentle to the envoys of the "Lamb."
They would cross the North Mountain, the last and highest ridge being called High Germany; thence they pro-

---

[1] According to statistical reports in 1877, the negro population in the
Alleghany district amounted to nearly seven per cent, in the Valley sixteen
per cent, but in the Piedmont and Coast districts from forty-seven to fifty-
one per cent of the total population. Schuricht, vol. i, p. 97.

[2] Translated in the *Virginia Magazine*, vol. xi, pp. 113 ff., 370 ff. ; vol. xii,
pp. 55 ff., 62 ff., etc. All of the missionaries named above were of German
or Swiss birth (not Moravian).

ceeded to the Potomac, sometimes stopping at the Hot
Springs (now Berkeley Springs, Morgan County, West
Virginia), and sometimes going upward by the Potomac
toward Cumberland, Maryland, and then proceeding up
Patterson's Creek, in West Virginia.

Brother Gottschalk in 1748 names as the German stations, where there was an open door for the Word of God,
eleven German settlements: first, Patterson's Creek; second, the South Branch of the Potomac; third, Shenandoah;
fourth, Cedar Creek (the settlement of Joist Hite); fifth,
Massanutten; sixth, the Upper Germans (Madison County);
seventh, the Great Fork of the Rappahannock (Germanna);
eighth, the Little Fork of the Rappahannock (a branch of
the Germantown settlement); ninth, Germantown (Licking Run, Fauquier County); tenth, Newfound River
(Dunkards); eleventh, New River. If the whole round
were made, namely, beginning with West Virginia, going
southwestwardly through the mountains to the New River,
and thence northeastwardly, through the Shenandoah Valley, back through Maryland and Pennsylvania, the whole
distance was about one thousand miles.

Not all the settlements were visited on every tour. The
remote New River settlement was sometimes omitted, and
as the Reverend Mr. Klug in Madison County and the
Lutherans at Shenandoah did not generally lend a willing
ear, they also were often left unvisited by the missionaries.
Opposition to the Moravians was increased by the proclamations of Governor Gooch against lay preachers,
aimed primarily at the Whitefieldians and Methodists,
the Episcopal and Lutheran churches uniting against
their so-called heresies. The purpose of the missionaries,
however, was never to separate Christians from their denominational affiliations: they preached no dogmas, but

desired merely to impress the spirit of Christianity in its most elemental forms. Everywhere they came upon people thirsting for an uplifting word and their preaching proved wonderfully inspiring because so simple, unselfish and pure.

Patterson's Creek flows into the North Branch of the Potomac about twelve miles below Cumberland, Maryland. On both sides of the Creek, Brother Gottschalk tells us, in 1748, there lived Germans interspersed with English, for a distance of twenty or thirty miles. He says there is in this district not only an opportunity to preach among the Germans, but the English seem even more eager for it than the Germans. Brother Schnell put down in his diary July, 1748: "We came to William Degart, whom I asked, whether I could preach in his stable, for the houses are all very small and poor. He sent out messages that evening to announce the service." High Germans, English, and Low Germans assembled for his sermon.

The settlements on the South Branch of the Potomac were next visited by the missionaries. The description which Gottschalk gives, holds good for to-day. "It is a large and long river extending over one hundred and fifty miles and rising high in the Alleghany Mountains. Most of the German people live along the river, but also many English settlers, because it is an extraordinarily beautiful and fertile country. This river, the South Branch, has above it a long fork called the South Fork. About forty-five miles below the South Fork, the country becomes thickly populated, and thus it continues upwards to the upper part of South Fork." Gottschalk preached along the South Branch at two places, below at the house of an Englishman named Collins, who requested more sermons in English. Above, at the South Fork, he preached in English and German at the home of Matthias Joachim. Schnell and Spangenberg also stopped with Joachim, and Spangenberg with Urbanus Kraemer and the Dutchman Van Meter (from Esopus, New York). Gottschalk in 1748 was influenced to stay at least two weeks. " In all Virginia I did not find another place like the South Branch where I felt that the gospel had such free course among the people. They were exceedingly well satisfied with my sermon. They liked Brother Schnell very much " (he was there the year before, in 1747, and in 1749). The following is a typical entry in the diary of the missionary Schnell; he is speaking of the South Branch : —

July 17th (1747), a considerable number of people assembled towards noon, to whom I preached from John vii. 37, "If any man thirst, let him come unto me and drink." After the sermon the people complained about their poor condition, that they had no minister, while in Pennsylvania there were so many. They asked me to stay with them. Then they brought me about six children, whom I should baptize, but I had to refuse. [There was objection to baptizing by itinerant preachers.]

July 20th. At noon we stopped with an Englishman. He complained that for two years he had heard no sermon, although he had been compelled every year to pay for the county minister.

July 21st. Came to a place where they had just eaten the last bit of bread. We waited for a woman who baked some for us. [This was an uncommon experience ; generally there was no bread to be had on the frontier.]

Brother Joseph (Bishop Spangenberg's name among the Brethren), in 1748 continued along the South Branch almost to the place where it rises and where the last settlements of the Germans are located, i. e., the extreme southern part of Pendleton County, West Virginia, near the northern border of Highland County, Virginia.[1] They lodged with a German, Christian Evi, and there Brother Joseph preached in German, also in English because many English settlers lived there. These were the first sermons which "a mundo condito" had been preached in this locality. The missionaries (Spangenberg was accompanied by Mathew Reutz) lost their way, but, aided by an elk trail, they got out of the mountains at the settlement of Adam Rader in the vicinity of Timberville, Rockingham County, Virginia.

Brother Schnell, in 1749, visited the New River settlement, accompanied by Brandmueller. They had great difficulty in finding it, proceeding from the source of the South Fork of the South Branch of the Potomac. They were on the very outskirts of civilization, in dense forests infested by wolves. They slept on bear skins in settlers' huts, received plenty of bear meat, but no bread and cheese. The ministers entered the present Highland County, Virginia, followed the Cow Pasture River, and reached the James, through which they swam. They arrived at the Irish settlements not far from Fincastle, — in the words of the diary : " Then we came to a house where we had to lie on bear skins around the fire like the rest. The manner of living is rather poor in this district. The clothes of the people consist of deer skins, their food of Johnnycakes, deer and bear meat. A kind of white people are found here, who live like savages. Hunting is their chief occupation." [2] The missionaries found no bread even at

---

[1] In the neighborhood was Seybert's Fort, the scene of an Indian massacre in 1758.

[2] *Virginia Magazine*, vol. xi, p. 123. Editor's note: Counties of Bath and Alleghany, Va. "The settlers were on the last outpost of civilization with the Indians as their only neighbors on the west. The wolves were numerous, a price was fixed upon their heads — 256 heads were presented in 1751."

Justice Robinson's, who owned a mill. Thirty miles more the missionaries journeyed onward without seeing a house until coming to the New River. There they found a number of Germans settled within the present limits of Montgomery and Augusta counties. The missionaries stayed at the house of Jacob Hermann, who was subsequently killed by the Indians, in 1756.[1]

Brother Schnell continues to say that they were only a few miles distant from the Seventh Day Baptists, who lived at that time on the New River. "But we had enough with the description which the people gave of them," meaning, no doubt, that their preaching would not change them. The people referred to were a part of the Ephrata Community, S. and I. Eckerlin, Alexander Mack and others who left Ephrata in 1745. According to the "Ephrata Chronicle," they "fled about four hundred English miles toward the setting sun — to the New River (which ran toward the Mississippi). They spent their time amid the dregs of human society, who spent their time hunting wild beasts." The Moravian diaries prove that the two colonies on the New River were distinct, with little or no intercourse between them. The Sabbatarian settlement was given up in 1750.

One of the bravest deeds in the history of the American frontier was the journey made by Brother Schnell, lasting from November 6, 1743, to April 10, 1744, and extending from Bethlehem, Pennsylvania, through Maryland, Virginia, and the Carolinas to Georgia. It was a mission tour, for a long distance marking the frontier line of the

[1] Presumably many of the settlers were killed by the Indians in 1755–56, but the settlement may have risen again after the blow, as in most other places. Cf. Waddell's *Annals of Augusta County*, pp. 154–158 (1902). The editor of the *Virginia Magazine* surmises that these German colonists on the New River came from North Carolina.

American wilderness. Leonhard Schnell was accompanied by Robert Hussey (born in Wiltshire, England), a teacher of the Moravian school in Oley, Pennsylvania. They traveled on foot, except when occasionally a kind-hearted pioneer would lend them a horse to convey them to the next settler, and they went unarmed, except for the Indian hatchet that they used to cut a path through the dense brushwood. They took the regular road from Bethlehem to Maryland, there stopping at the Monocacy settlements with Abraham Mueller, among " plain people," and "felt very happy among them." The stalwart Schnell carried his companion over the Monocacy, the latter being very tired, for they had already walked forty miles. Perhaps the West Virginia settlements did not yet exist,[1] for the missionaries went up the Shenandoah Valley, stopping with Joist Hite on the Opequon, where they disclosed their purpose of going overland to Georgia. Joist Hite told them of a route through the Irish settlements, in the present Augusta and Rockbridge counties, but the missionaries did not wish to take that course. The German Catholic Schmidt directed them on another way, and as a result they left the Shenandoah Valley, going to Germantown, next to the German settlements of Madison County, and then directly southward almost in a straight line, taking the sun as a guide, through Louisa, Goochland, Powhatan, Amelia, and Brunswick counties, to the Roanoke River near where it intersects the state boundary. There they met Zollikoffer, the Swiss settler. Thence they went southeastwardly, crossing the Tar River, the Neuse, and entering Craven County, North Carolina. Striking the offshoots of the New Bern settlement, they

[1] This was in 1743. By 1747–48 the settlements were numerous and prosperous, as described above.

were feasted by Abraham Bossert. They heard many reports about new Swiss arrivals, and Germans were strewn
all along their path. They made their way to Wilmington,
North Carolina (called Williamstown), arriving December
17, and finding snow and ice. They crossed Cape Fear
River, paying fifteen shillings for the passage (one shilling sixpence, sterling), which they could well afford,
having been supplied with funds from the German settlers
just visited. Then they passed over to South Carolina,
December 20, and journeyed along the ocean over the
sand of the beach at low tide. They had to hurry from
station to station before the tide should return, otherwise
their lives would be in danger. They made Winyal Bay
on December 22, were taken across the Santee River,
and on Christmas Day arrived at Charleston. Hearing that
there were not many Germans in the city, they hurried
on to Purysburg, and remained with Brother Beck at
White Bluff, where the Germans lived on about forty
plantations. Schnell preached and worked, though several
had threatened to stone him if he did. Subsequently he
visited Savannah and Ebenezer in Georgia, and on February 15, boarded a sloop for New York, arriving in
Bethlehem April 10, 1744. The deeds of the Moravian
missionaries have never been heralded as great achievements in American history, but in justice to them it must
be admitted that in their exhibition of courage, endurance,
and humanity they rank higher than many of the great
feats of war.

The Germans in Virginia during the eighteenth century carried onward the work which the Pennsylvania
Germans had been noted for. As agriculturists their
main achievement was to make the Valley of Virginia
and the adjacent lands to the east, at the base of the

mountains, the richest farming country in the state. They had settled on the western frontier, and were ready to take part, in the front rank, in the permanent settlement of Kentucky and the Southwest.

CHAPTER VIII

THE GERMANS IN NORTH AND SOUTH CAROLINA DURING THE EIGHTEENTH CENTURY

First settlement at Newbern, North Carolina, in 1710 — Indian war — Germans in Charleston, South Carolina — Purysburg, South Carolina, 1732 — Settlements in the Orangeburg and Lexington Districts (Saxe-Gotha), South Carolina, 1735 — The Giessendanners — Zauberbühler — Counties of South Carolina with early German settlers — The fifteen churches of South Carolina — German settlers from Pennsylvania in the interior of North Carolina, 1750 — The Reverend A. Nussmann — Moravian settlements in the "Wachovia" tract, North Carolina, 1753 — Bethabara, Bethany, Salem.

THE first German settlements[1] in the Carolinas were naturally along the seacoast. North Carolina received its first quota of German settlers from the mass of Palatines who arrived in England in 1710. Christoph Graffenried (also known as Baron Christopher de Graffenried) of Bern, Switzerland, arrived in London with some Swiss emigrants

[1] Much of the early history of the Germans in the Carolinas is still obscure, as in the case of Virginia, and undoubtedly a great deal is lost forever. The best available sources are Bernheim and Urlsperger. Bernheim's *History of the German Settlements and the Lutheran Church in North and South Carolina* (Philadelphia, 1872), gives a fairly complete account of the Germans in both North and South Carolina, based on facts gathered from the archives of the Lutheran churches, the church record books kept by Giessendanner, and other founders of congregations, and from *Journals* of the Council of the Province of South Carolina (in manuscript form in the office of the Secretary of State). The voluminous work edited by Urlsperger is described in its title : Samuel Urlsperger : *Amerikanisches Ackerwerk Gottes; oder Zuverlässige Nachrichten, den Zustand der Amerikanisch-englischen und von Salzburgischen Emigranten erbauten Pflanzstadt, Ebenezer in Georgien betreffend, aus dorther eingeschickten glaubwürdigen Diarien genommen, und mit Briefen der dasigen Herren Prediger noch weiter bestättigt.* (Augsburg, 1754–67, 5 vols.) Both of these works are reliable as sources of information.

just at the time when London was so much concerned about the disposal of the thirteen thousand Palatines. In London Graffenried met Louis Michel (frequently spelt Mitchell), also a Swiss, who had spent several years in America to examine the conditions of American colonists.[1] Graffenried and Michel thought the time opportune for planting a colony in the Carolinas. They accepted the liberal terms of the proprietors, paying twenty shillings sterling for each one hundred acres of land and binding themselves to a quitrent of sixpence yearly for every hundred acres. An additional one hundred thousand acres were to be laid off and reserved for twelve years. They induced about six hundred and fifty Palatines to go with them, filling two vessels. They received permission to locate in one body, on or between the Neuse and Cape Fear rivers or their tributaries, and arrived in December, 1710, at the confluence of the Neuse and Trent, North Carolina, where they founded New Bern (Newbern), named after the capital of Switzerland.

Their first year was calamitous, for in 1711, not many months after their arrival, an Indian war broke out. The white settlers had lived on friendly terms with the Indians, admitting them into their houses as friends, frequently as domestics, and all threatening troubles had been adjusted amicably. As usual the premeditated Indian massacre was concealed beneath a stratagem. At the appointed time many hundred Tuscaroras appeared, some in small divisions entering the houses of the colonists as often before, and others as night approached coming in larger numbers to the villages as if to gather provisions, —not numerous enough, however, to occasion alarm. They awaited the sunrise as a signal for attack. Then the In-

---

[1] He was an explorer. Cf. Chapter I, pp. 28–29.

dians, in the houses, and without, gave the war-whoop, awakening the response of the Indians lying out in the woods. The settlers were completely taken by surprise; an indiscriminate slaughter of men, women, and children followed. One hundred and thirty whites were butchered in the settlements of North Carolina; sixty or more Swiss and Palatines around Newbern were among the victims. The torch was applied to dwellings in which colonists had concealed themselves, and they were forced from their hiding-places to meet death or torture.

Graffenried, with no suspicion of coming hostilities, was absent on an exploring tour with the surveyor-general, Lawson. Expecting to spend their first night in an Indian village, they were taken captive instead of being hospitably received. Graffenried escaped by declaring he was a king of the German Palatines, demanding by what authority they could put a king to death, who had committed no offense against them. He was kept in custody, but spared, on the promise that the Palatines should be kept from waging war against the Indians. The promise was kept, in the subsequent war of revenge by the whites, much to the latter's displeasure. The Palatines, however, were of assistance in acquainting the whites as to the plans and movements of the Indians.[1]

As a result of the war of revenge, the Indians were reduced in numbers and removed to more remote parts, the Palatines being on the whole benefited by the war. Graffenried left the colonists,[2] serving them an ill turn by

---

[1] Lawson was tortured to death in the most savage manner, sharp splinters of pine being put into his flesh and set on fire. A land surveyor never received quarter on falling into the hands of the Indians, who always considered him the cause of the land robberies.

[2] Whether Graffenried returned to America is not known; descendants of his name still reside in various parts of the Carolinas.

withholding from them the titles of their lands, which the two Swiss leaders had sold to their own creditors. The victims of the speculation sent a petition to the Carolina Council, November 6, 1714, asking for a grant of four hundred acres for each family and two years' time to pay for it. The petition was granted, and the colonists undoubtedly spread over what is now Craven County, where they were found extending over a wide area by the missionary Schnell in 1743.[1]

In South Carolina the first German settlers are found in the city of Charleston, the immigrant port of the South. It is quite possible that there were some Germans among the Dutch Lutherans that settled on James Island, southwest of the Ashley River and opposite Charleston, in 1674. They had fled from the intolerance of their own countrymen of the Protestant Reformed Church, at New Amsterdam. Certain it is that there were some Germans at Charleston when Bolzius landed with his Salzburgers in 1734. They had settled at Charleston at a time when the lands inland, on the Congaree River, were not yet occupied, being too far west. When Mühlenberg visited Charleston in 1742 on his way to Ebenezer, and was detained waiting for a vessel, he labored for the spiritual welfare of the Germans at Charleston from October 20 to November 12, 1742. He lived with the family of a painter named Theus, the brother of the German Reformed minister in Saxe-Gotha, South Carolina, along the Congaree River. Charleston, however, was not at first favored as a place of settlement, serving more as a distributing centre for the inland counties, Saxe-Gotha and Orangeburg, a verification of which is found in the fact that the inland rural districts had a regular German pastor as early as 1737,

[1] See Chapter VII, pp. 209–210.

while Charleston did not until 1755. The Reverend Mr. Friedrichs built the first Lutheran church in Charleston in 1759.

Next in chronological order among the settlements in the Carolinas is Purysburg, 1732, in Beaufort County, South Carolina, some thirty miles inland from the seacoast, on the east bank of the Savannah River. The settlement was due largely to the enterprise of John Peter Pury (Purry) of Neufchatel, who received liberal inducements from the Carolina proprietors. In 1731 he closed a contract with the English government by which he received four hundred pounds sterling for every hundred able-bodied men that he might bring from Switzerland.[1] To make his harvest good, Pury advertised extensively in Switzerland, according to the methods employed for luring immigrants.[2] One hundred and seventy Switzers composed the first expedition, and forty thousand acres were assigned to them.[3] Not long afterwards two hundred more settlers arrived. They were described as "zealous workers, whose intention it was, besides the necessary husbandry, to plant the vine and rear and manufacture silk." The soil was considered good for the grape-vine and the white mulberry tree, on which the silkworm feeds. The manufacture of silk at Purysburg represents another industry which Germans inaugurated in America. Of their other activities we learn something from the journal of Bolzius, who says (May, 1734): "This town is built on the more elevated banks of the river, and has

---

[1] *South Carolina Resources and Population, Institutions and Industries*, p. 383. (Published by the State Board of Agriculture of South Carolina, Charleston, South Carolina, 1883.) Three hundred and seventy men came out of Switzerland to Purysburg in the first year.

[2] Cf. Chapter III, pp. 63 ff.

[3] The other leaders besides Pury were: James Richard, of Geneva, Abraham Meuron and Henry Raymond, both of St. Sulpy.

many wealthy people residing here; it is hoped that in a short time it will become a considerable town. The inhabitants labor industriously in their gardens and fields, and persons can already procure here fresh meats, eggs, garden vegetables, even more than in Savannah. We were shown all kindness, and several of the inhabitants besought us to return soon again, and administer the communion." They brought their own pastor with them, the Reverend Joseph Bügnion, a German Reformed minister, who later was induced to receive the Episcopal ordination. Purysburg played some part in the Savannah campaign in the American Revolution, and was taken by the British under Prevost. A large number of Swiss settlers of Purysburg sought homes in other parts of Carolina, both before and after the Revolution, leaving to Purysburg very little more than a name in history. The westward movement in South Carolina seems to have begun earlier than in most other colonies, the attractions of a higher country, a healthier climate, and abundant land proving irresistible.

As in other colonies, the Germans of South Carolina were defenders of the frontier. Their settlements began in the present Orangeburg and Lexington counties, extending along both sides of the Edisto and Congaree rivers, and spreading into neighboring counties to the westward, viz., Barnwell, Newberry, Abbeville, etc. The Germans were practically the first settlers in the Orangeburg district.[1] They did not all arrive at the same time. The

---

[1] The first white inhabitant was Henry Stirling, presumably a trader located at Lyon's Creek, where he received a grant of land in 1704. The next were three or four individuals who settled at the Cowpens, northwest of the white settlements in the Low Country. These and the Cherokee and Catawba Indians were all the inhabitants who had preceded the Germans. Cf. Bernheim, pp. 99–100. (Bernheim quotes Mills's *Statistics of South Carolina*, pp. 656–657.)

first colony came in 1735, another in 1736, and their first
pastor, the Reverend John Ulrich Giessendanner, Senior,
arrived with a third group of colonists in 1737.[1] They
were tillers of the soil, and soon were blessed with the
fruits of their labors in the fertile districts of South Carolina. A considerable number of mechanics were among
them, a circumstance favoring the independence of their
settlement. In comparison with these permanent colonists,
Purysburg was merely a station, the residents of which
soon removed to a more favorable location.

The Giessendanners, of Swiss nativity,[2] kept a church
record[3] which is very valuable historically and genealóg-
ically. A neighboring German Lutheran settlement in
Amelia Township, along Fourhole Swamp and Creek, was
also served by Giessendanner. On the death of the elder
Giessendanner in 1738, his nephew, John Giessendanner,
succeeded him. The Journals of Council of the Province
of South Carolina[4] give an interesting account of a church
difficulty, in which an adroit young man by the name of
Zauberbühler (Zuberbühler)[5] attempted to displace John
Giessendanner. The latter was not a member of the
established church in the province, and Zauberbühler
hoped, by becoming an ordained minister of the Episco-

[1] Mills, in *Statistics of South Carolina*, tells us that immigrants arrived in
Orangeburg district as late as 1769, only a few years before the Revolution.

[2] Bernheim argues that the Giessendanners were Lutherans, until they
joined the Episcopal Church.

[3] This church record has been published in *The History of Orangeburg
County, South Carolina*, chap. ii, pp. 91–216. By A. S. Salley, Jr. (Orangeburg, 1898.)

[4] Vol. x, pp. 395 ff. ; xi, pp. 74–76, 139–143, 152. Quoted by Bernheim,
pp. 110–119.

[5] The Reverend Bartholomew Zauberbühler should not be confused with
Sebastian Zouberbühler (Zauberbühler) who was prominent in connection with
the German colonies of Waldoboro (Maine) and Lunenburg (Nova Scotia).

pal Church, to gain an advantage over the Lutheran pastor. Accordingly, he addressed a petition to the Council of South Carolina, stating that many people at Orangeburg, feeling the need of instruction in the true religion, desired that he be ordained by the Bishop of London ; wherefore he prayed for support and payment of the expenses of the voyage, in consideration of which he would bring back a large number of German settlers. He was asked to produce documents, showing that he was qualified to receive orders, and that the people of Orangeburg desired a preacher. He obtained a number of signatures, and the council was ready to grant the petition, voting five hundred pounds.[1]

A counter-petition was prepared (March 6, 1743) by the friends of John Giessendanner in the Orangeburg district. This testified that Giessendanner had visited Charleston to get orders, and had received advice to go to an Assembly of the Presbytery, who, after some time, presented him with orders to preach, —

which he has since done in German constantly for the space of five years, to the inexpressible satisfaction of the congregation at Orangeburg ; and about two years ago your said English petitioners being fully sixty miles from any other place of divine worship, some of whom had not been favored with the opportunity of hearing a sermon in the space of seven years, observing the said Mr. John Giessendanner to be a man of learning, piety, and knowledge in the Holy Scriptures, prevailed with him to officiate in preaching once every fortnight in English, which he hath since performed very articulate and intelligible, to the entire satisfaction of the said English petitioners, and always behaves himself with sobriety, honesty and justice, encouraging

[1] Colonists sometimes left for other provinces, where they could get the services of a preacher. This fact undoubtedly weighed heavily with the council. Cf. Bernheim, p. 193.

virtue and reproving vice. And the said Mr. John Giessendanner, lately observing great irregularities and disorders being committed almost every Sabbath Day by some wicked persons in one part of the township, publicly reprimanded them for the same, which reproof so exasperated them, that they threatened to kick the said John Giessendanner out of the church if he offered to preach there any more and have lately sent for one Bartholomew Zauberbühler, a man who not long ago pretended to preach at Savannah town; but, as your said petitioners are informed was soon obliged to leave that place and a very indecent character behind him, etc., etc.

This was addressed to the governor, who was asked to interpose with authority, and signed by John Harn and above fourscore more subscribers, i. e., in all ninety names, some few being English names.

Certificates of good character for Zauberbühler were obtained from various places, among them from the Ebenezer pastors, whose judgment, beyond question, was fair in the matter. The bitterness of the quarrel had no doubt caused mutual criminations. The governor settled the trouble in a judicial manner, retaining Giessendanner at Orangeburg absolutely, and in an interview with Zauberbühler threatening to cut him down to one-half the five hundred pounds voted for his trip abroad, unless he would bring the foreign Protestants over with him. It seems Zauberbühler returned to Carolina after his trip to London, bringing colonists with him, but little is known definitely concerning him.[1]

Reverend J. G. Friedrichs, who was the first preacher of the Lutheran church in Charleston, subsequently became the pastor in the Orangeburg district. During his ministry there settled in Orangeburg a colony of Germans from Maine, accompanied by their pastor, the Reverend Mr.

---

[1] See *ante*, p. 218, note 5 ; also p. 225.

Silly. According to one account sixty-three families were there in 1763, but according to another most of these colonists returned to Maine.[1]

Giessendanner's congregation must have been large, since the petition written in his behalf was signed by ninety persons, heads of families. Their church was built in 1743, only a few years after the settlement began. Giessendanner[2] labored there for ten years, after which he went to London, in 1749, to receive Episcopal ordination, his church becoming Episcopalian in the same year (with one hundred and seven communicants ordinarily and on Whitsunday, twenty-one more).

The next German settlement in South Carolina began very soon after the founding of the Orangeburg colony, in the so-called Saxe-Gotha district, a name that originated in Queen Anne's time (before 1714). The benevolent queen had probably intended the Saxe-Gotha district as a place of refuge for German and other Protestant exiles in the South, as Schoharie had been in the North, but no colony was established there in her time, Saxe-Gotha being then still too far west for settlement.

The Journals of Council[3] of South Carolina fixed the

---

[1] See Chapter IX, p. 260.

[2] Giessendanner died in 1761 and was probably buried in the "Old Graveyard" near the Edisto River.

[3] Vol. viii, p. 69, May 26, 1742. A petition of J. J. Gallier and family, J. C. Gieger (Geiger) and family, J. Shalling and family, Abram Gieger and family, J. Liver and family, J. Gredig and family, Caspar Fry and family, Conrad and Caspar Küntzler (Kinsler), J. J. Bieman and family, H. Gieger and family, Elizabeth Shalling and family, shows that they had settled since 1737 in Saxe-Gotha township. Again under date of 1744, J. J. Gieger, arrived seven years ago, prays for one hundred acres of land over against the Santee River, opposite Saxe-Gotha, where he has already begun to clear ground and almost finished a house. The petition was granted. Cf. Bernheim, pp. 126–127; cf. also: A. S. Salley, *The History of Orangeburg County, South Carolina* (1898), pp. 70–71.

date of settlement of Saxe-Gotha by the Germans as 1737. This district was located farther west, and therefore colonized some time later than Orangeburg. It embraced the whole of the present Lexington County, a name which it received in 1872. It was one hundred English miles distant from Charleston, on the road which passed through Orangeburg, and was "settled by German people." [1] They were not from Saxe-Gotha but from the Rhine country, Baden, Würtemberg, and Switzerland. Their first minister was the Reverend Christian Theus, of the German Reformed Church. Interesting is the frank statement he made to the government of South Carolina, that if the latter desired to keep the colonists, they must be provided with churches and schools; otherwise the colonists would do what many had done before, migrate to Pennsylvania, where all those advantages existed.[2] The government gave five hundred pounds to assist in the erection of a church, which was built under the ministry of Theus, at a location a short distance below the confluence of the Saluda and Broad rivers (forming the Congaree River). It was St. John's Church,[3] a few miles from the present capital, Columbia, of the state of South Carolina. The church was probably destroyed during the Revolutionary War, since it was not mentioned in the incorporation act of the united German churches, passed by the legislature of South Carolina in 1788. About eight miles from Columbia, near Sandy Run, there is a tombstone bearing the inscription : " This stone points out where the remains of the Reverend Christian Theus lie. This faithful divine labored through a long life as a faithful servant in his Master's

---

[1] *Urlsperger Nachrichten*, vol. iii, p. 1791.

[2] This seems to support the tradition existing in Virginia, that there was an emigration northward from the Carolinas.

[3] Found on the map, *Carroll's Collections*, 1771–75.

vineyard and the reward which he received from many for his labor was ingratitude." The stone was erected by Abraham Geiger (Gieger), parishioner, at his own expense. We probably ought not to take the inscription too seriously, except for the statement regarding his long life and excellent service. Theus never labored for rewards. As an octogenarian he probably had to endure the consequences of old age, indifference and neglect, and the frequent separation of union congregations[1] into Lutheran and Reformed probably disturbed him greatly.

During the years 1744–50 Saxe-Gotha received a large influx of German settlers. *The St. Andrew*, Captain Brown, commander, was a good ship, on board of which passengers for the Carolinas were treated well,— when they paid their passage. Captain Ham was another of the sea-captains who brought over many new recruits for Orangeburg, some also for Saxe-Gotha.

From 1759–60 the people of Saxe-Gotha suffered greatly from the Cherokee War, instigated by the French. The German settlements were as far out as any. The Congaree and Fork settlements were greatly exposed to attacks, and, we are told by Bolzius, many settlers took refuge at Ebenezer, Savannah, Charleston, and Purysburg, until the Indian hostilities were over. The damage done, however, was merely temporary.

[1] The *Urlsperger Reports*, vol. iv, p. 672 (1750) : " The Reformed church (a congregation of about two hundred and eighty souls) have received five hundred pounds, Carolina currency, from the government for this church, but no one is interested in the Lutheran, unless I would do something in their behalf. They live with the Reformed in great disunion, at which I showed my displeasure in my former letter. Several people have left us for other settlements, who might have obtained land here. They even built both a saw-mill and a grist-mill, and expected to build more of the kind. Here then should they be enabled to erect a house of worship if they were sincerely in earnest."

A number of other German settlements in South Carolina, mostly later than Orangeburg and Saxe-Gotha, were the following : First, the German Lutheran colony at Hard Labor Creek, 1763–64, in the present county of Abbeville, quite a little to the westward, bordering on Georgia. This colony had its own peculiar history. A German officer, named Stümpel, having applied to the British ministry for a tract of land in America, and having received some encouragement, returned to Germany and brought between five and six hundred people over to England. When they were there, Stümpel was unable to fulfill his promises. A German clergyman published the facts in a newspaper, and a bounty of three hundred pounds was given by the government. Tents were ordered from the Tower and money was sent for the relief of the immigrants. They were sent to South Carolina, an additional inducement being the bounty allowed to foreign Protestants by the Provincial Assembly, in consequence of which, when their source of relief from England would be exhausted, another would become available upon their arrival in America. Two ships were equipped, and one hundred and fifty stands of arms were ordered from the Tower for their defense, to be used after their arrival in South Carolina, which occurred in April, 1764. The government of South Carolina (under Governor Boone) voted five hundred pounds sterling to be distributed among the "Palatines." Captain Calhoun with a detachment of Rangers conducted them to their location, Londonderry Township, in Abbeville County, where the captain owned an estate. As usual these settlers brought their own (Lutheran) pastor with them, and built St. George's Church in 1788. What frequently happened on the frontier among Presbyterian, Reformed, and Lutheran congregations, occurred here, viz.: they transferred[1] their allegiance to the Methodist, or to the Baptist Church, emotional preaching appealing more strongly to the frontiersmen.

A second county with German settlers was Barnwell. This settlement was doubtless formed, by the breaking-up of the Dutch colony on James Island (below Charleston), by gradual absorption of the German and Swiss colony at Purysburg, and by the influx of other German settlers from Orangeburg County on the northeast.

Third: settlements were made along the boundary-line of Richland and Fairfield counties on Cedar and Dutchman's creeks, probably from Saxe-Gotha and Orangeburg counties. On Cedar Creek there was once a German church, incorporated in 1738, the "German Protestant Church of Apii-Forum," later absorbed by the Methodist congregation.

Fourth: the Newberry County Germans, who were mostly descendants from the original Germans in Saxe-Gotha Township, with occasional additions from North Carolina and Virginia.

Fifth: the New Windsor colony, located in the southern part of Edgefield County along the Savannah River, opposite the city of Augusta, Georgia. A number of Germans located here, who were brought over under the leadership and perhaps at the solicitation of the Reverend Bartholomew Zauberbühler, once of Orangeburg County.[2] John Jacob Riemensperger brought over a later group, under commission of the provincial government of South Carolina, and also took some colonists to Saxe-Gotha. The

---

[1] The Lutheran missionary, R. J. Miller, visited the settlement at Hard Labor Creek in 1811, and preaching at what was once the German Meeting House, said: "Here the Methodists and Baptists have pulled each other out of the pulpit."

[2] See above, pp. 219–221. Cf. Bernheim, p. 169.

226 THE GERMAN ELEMENT

people of German descent now located in the central part of Edgefield County, came originally from New Windsor and from Saxe-Gotha Township.

A sixth settlement, Old Indian Swamp, was probably located in Barnwell County, where there are Lutheran churches at present. Philip Eisenmann said to Mühlenberg in 1774 that he was a resident of Old Indian Swamp, fifty miles from Charleston, where "he and his neighbors had accepted as a preacher a young man lately arrived from Germany and who might answer for a schoolmaster."[1] The church called the German Protestant Church of St. George on Indian Field Swamp was incorporated in 1788.

The extent and progress of the German settlements in South Carolina are well illustrated by the act of incorporation of the fifteen German churches of the interior of South Carolina in 1788. They formed a union, and the constitution of their "Corpus Evangelicum" was signed by nineteen ministers and candidates for the ministry.[2]

[1] Cf. Bernheim, pp. 169–170.

[2] The Reverend Frederick Daser was chosen senior of the ministry, the Reverend Wallberg, secretary. The seven German ministers were: F. Daser (Lutheran), Christian Theus (Reformed), J. G. Bamberg (Lutheran), F. A. Wallberg (Lutheran), C. F. Froelich (Reformed), F. J. Wallern (Lutheran), M. C. Binnicher (Lutheran).

The names of the churches were as follows: —

(1) Frederician Church of Cattel's Creek.
(2) The German Calvinistic Church of St. John, on the Fourhole.
(3) The German Lutheran Church of St. Matthew, in Amelia Township.
(4) The German Lutheran Church of Salem, on Sandy Run.
(5) The German Lutheran Church of Mt. Zion, on Twelve-Mile Creek.
(6) The German Lutheran Church of Bethel, on High-Hill Creek.
(7) The German Lutheran Church of St. Peter, on Eighteen-Mile Creek.
(8) The German Lutheran Church of St. Martin.
(9) The German Lutheran Church of Bethlehem, on Forest's (Fust's) Ford.
(10) The German Protestant Church of Bethany, on Green Creek.
(11) The German Protestant Church of Apii-Forum, on Cedar Creek.

These fifteen churches probably comprised the entire German element in the interior of South Carolina in 1788, i. e., five years after the close of the Revolutionary War. Since no large additions came during the war, we may suppose that the German population of South Carolina in 1775 was not much less than here represented.

It is curious to note that the German church of Charleston did not belong to this union, though it was by this time large and influential. The German population in Charleston had increased greatly and had immortalized itself by several coöperative foundations. The first, the " German Benevolent Society," Mühlenberg praises as the "flower and crown of the German nation in this place." It was founded in 1766, and in a little more than eight years had upwards of eighty members. The association had a funded capital, at first of four hundred pounds sterling, the interest of which was applied for the relief of every needy member (or of his widow or orphans), who had been connected with the society for seven years, and had paid his contributions. The other foundation was the German Fusileer Company, which served in the Revolutionary War.[1] The fact of Charleston's being excluded from the church organization of the interior of South Carolina furnishes an illustration of an interesting histor-

(12) The German Protestant Church, dedicated to Queen Charlotte, on Slippery Creek.

(13) The German Lutheran Church of St. George, on Hard Labor Creek.

(14) The German Lutheran Church of St. Jacob, on Wateree Creek.

(15) The German Protestant Church of St. George, on Indian Field Swamp.

Of these fifteen churches nine were Lutheran, and seven of the nine Lutheran churches are in existence at the present day. All of the Reformed churches ceased to exist, partly due to the fact that they were not cared for by ministers, the congregations then joining other churches; frequently also the record was lost. Bernheim, pp. 300 ff.

[1] See Chapter XI, p. 340.

ical fact, that the frontier chose to settle its own affairs, independent of and sometimes in opposition to the seacoast. Moreover the people at the sea knew very little about what was going on at the frontier. In the journal of the Reverend Arnold Roschen we find the statement : "We heard such dreadful reports of the people where my congregations are situated" (Rowan County, North Carolina), "which, however, God be praised, arose from the fact, that in Charleston the citizens are as badly informed as in Germany concerning this country."[1] The overland journey of the pastor to his flock lasted fourteen days.

There were also a large number of German colonists in the interior of North Carolina. They did not, however, as in South Carolina, come from the seacoast, that is, directly from Europe, but they had treked from Pennsylvania. They arranged themselves on vacant lands to the eastward and westward of the Yadkin River, while the Scotch-Irish from Pennsylvania, who had lived on friendly terms with the Germans in that province, soon followed them southward and occupied vacant lands mostly to the westward or southward of the German settlers, along the Catawba River. The Germans on the Yadkin, in course of time, went westward and settled also on the Catawba, becoming quite as numerous as the Irish, and with them going westward again from there.

The Germans usually left their home, i. e., Pennsylvania, in autumn, after all the harvesting was over and the proceeds of the year's labor were in hand. They arrived at the new settlements just before the commencement of the winter season, bringing with them the means of passing through the winter without great hardship. The first of the pioneer trains came about 1745; the large migrations did not be-

---

[1] Bernheim, pp. 319–320.

gin until 1750. Their history is partly to be gleaned from
tradition, partly from family records contained in old German Bibles ; it is safely established in the records of land-
purchases, which, however, always appear some years after
actual settlement. The settlers were industrious, economical, and thrifty farmers, who generally avoided settling in
towns. They were well informed in their own branch of
industry, shrewd to recognize their own advantage ; they
despised the business of the merchant, barter and trade,
as beneath them, though many of their descendants at later
periods became very successful in mercantile pursuits.
Like all Pennsylvania Germans they were religious, well
read in the Bible and devotional books. Their German
school-teachers, in the absence of ministers, read prayers
to them and sermons on Sundays, buried the dead and
baptized children. For a decade or more no regular pastors,
occasionally only a missionary, appeared to preach among
them and, if he would, baptize the children.

Since there came no increase from the seacoast, but
from Pennsylvania alone, it took a score of years, or until
the seventies, before the congregations became numerous
enough to build churches. Then they seriously felt the
need of ministers, but Mühlenberg in Pennsylvania had
none to spare. Characteristic [1] it is, that the German
settlers of the interior of North Carolina then decided to
act for themselves. In 1772 Christopher Rintelmann from
Organ Church in Rowan County, and Christopher Layrle
from St. John's Church, Mecklenburg County (now Cabarrus), were sent as a delegation to Europe for the purpose of applying to the Consistory Council of Hanover
for ministers and school-teachers to supply the various
Lutheran congregations then organized in North Carolina.

---

[1] Showing again the independence of the frontier.

They applied at Hanover and not at Halle, because the American colonies were under the jurisdiction of the king of England, who was also the elector of Hanover. They succeeded in getting at least one minister, the Reverend Adolph Nussmann, and as their school-teacher, Gottfried Arndt. Both [1] arrived safely in North Carolina in 1773, and more would probably have come had not the Revolutionary War cut off all intercourse with Europe. Nussmann was the right man for the place. He served Organ Church (Salisbury, Rowan County), and St. John's in the present Cabarrus County, and made mission tours into Davidson, Guilford, Orange, Stokes, and Forsyth counties, "strengthening what remained." These tours tell us also where the German settlers were located. Schoolmaster Arndt was subsequently ordained and became an efficient helper. After the Revolution the Lutheran Church organization was strengthened and the number of settlers greatly increased.

The cause for the migration to North Carolina was mainly the difficulty of getting land in Pennsylvania. It could be bought from the Indians in small parcels only on the frontier, and these were quickly taken, while in the easterly sections no land could be got at all cheaply. Before the Revolution the settlers did not cross the Alleghany Mountains, but when seeking new land, they followed the mountain ranges to the south and west, keeping on their eastern slope. [2] Speaking of the interior of North Carolina, Bernheim says : "Had a traveller from Pennsylvania visited, about forty or fifty years ago (1820–1830), portions of the present counties of Alamance, Guilford,

---

[1] The names are spelled Nüszmann, and Arnd, in *Hallesche Nachrichten* (reprint), vol. i, p. 32.

[2] Cf. also Williamson's *History of North Carolina*, vol. ii, p. 71.

Davidson, Rowan, Cabarrus, Stanly, Iredell, Catawba, Lincoln, and some others in the State of North Carolina, he might have believed himself to have unexpectedly come upon some part of the old Keystone State." Pennsylvania German was still spoken about 1820–30.[1]

An interesting chapter in the history of the German settlements in North Carolina is that of the Moravian foundations in Forsyth and Stokes counties. In 1751 the Moravians purchased one hundred thousand acres of land in North Carolina from Lord Granville, president of the Privy Council of the government of Great Britain. Bishop Spangenberg was commissioned to locate and survey the land, and accordingly he journeyed with some friends, during the month of August, from Bethlehem, Pennsylvania, to Edenton, North Carolina. He first visited the head-waters of the Catawba, New, and Yadkin rivers, but after many hardships, decided to locate farther eastward, in Forsyth County, to the east of the Yadkin River. The deed was made out for 98,985 acres, signed and sealed August 7, 1753, and the land received the name "The Wachovia Tract," in honor of one of the titles of Count Zinzendorf, who was lord of the Wachau Valley in Austria. In the autumn of 1753, twelve single brethren with a wagon and six horses, some cattle and necessary household utensils for husbandry, made the long journey from Bethlehem through the Shenandoah Valley to North Carolina.[2] Seven new colonists arrived in 1754. They

[1] Many of the family names found in Montgomery, Berks, Lehigh, and Northampton counties, Pennsylvania, are also found in the North Carolina counties, e. g., Klein (Cline), Trexler, Schlough, Seitz (Sides), Reinhardt, Bibers (Beaver), Kohlman (Coleman), Derr (Dry), Berger (Barrier), Behringer (Barringer), etc. Schwartzwälder (Blackwelder), a family of seven sons, had four of them (two killed) in the battle of Camden, South Carolina. Bernheim, p. 247, etc.

[2] Their journey is described in a diary kept in the Archives of the Mora-

founded the town of Bethabara (the house of passage) which was to be a temporary abode until the central settlement should have been built. Bishop David Nitschman visited them in 1755 and consecrated the first meeting-house. In 1758 the Cherokee and Catawba Indians, who went to war against the Indians on the Ohio, marched through Bethabara in large companies, often several hundred. The Cherokee Indians seem to have been pleased with the treatment received, for they described Bethabara to their nation as "the Dutch Fort, where there are good people and much bread."

In 1759 the town of Bethany was laid out, three miles to the north of Bethabara, which in 1765 contained eighty-eight inhabitants, while Bethany had ten less. In 1766 the beginning was made in the building of Salem, the principal settlement of the "Unitas Fratrum" in North Carolina, five miles southward from Bethabara. Ten new colonists came over direct from Germany by way of London and Charleston, a sign of growing prominence. As at Herrnhut, Niesky, and Bethlehem, separate buildings were erected for men and women. Intermarriage was not permitted until some years after. Two other settlements followed in the Wachovia tract, one, Friesburg, in 1769–70, receiving a considerable number of settlers from Germany and Maine. The other, the Hope settlement, was founded in 1772 by colonists from Frederick, Maryland. During the Revolutionary War the Moravians

vian Congregation at Salem, North Carolina, translated in the *Virginia Magazine*, vol. xii, pp. 134 ff. The original is printed in *German American Annals*, vol. iii (*Americana Germanica*, vol. vii), pp. 342 ff. and 369 ff. The following is the list of Moravian brethren who located in Wachovia and founded the village of Bethabara : Grube, Meekly, Feldhausen, Lung, Pfeil, Beroth, all of Germany ; Kalberlahn and Ingebretsen of Norway ; Peterson of Denmark ; Loesch of New York ; Loesch of Pennsylvania, and Lischer of unknown origin. The last three have German names.

of Wachovia were exempted from military duty by the payment of a triple tax. In 1804 the Salem Female Academy was founded, which has educated the daughters of prominent families of North and South Carolina, Virginia, and other Southern States. The Moravian settlement at Salem-Winston is still the centre of the Moravian denomination in the South. Their quaint customs and beautiful music, particularly at Easter, attract a large number of admirers from all the surrounding country.

The Carolinas, as shown in the preceding pages, received a good share of early German settlers in the eighteenth century. Newbern in North Carolina was the earliest German colony, 1710, but Charleston, South Carolina, became the distributing centre of the German immigrants in the South. Germans became most numerous in the so-called Saxe-Gotha district, the present Orangeburg and Lexington counties of South Carolina, and thence spread to neighboring counties and to the westward. The interior of North Carolina likewise received an ever increasing number of German settlers, who came from Pennsylvania, beginning about 1750. The Moravians established a colony at Salem-Winston, which has flourished ever since its foundation.

CHAPTER IX

GEORGIA, the farthest south of the American colonies,
became the home of the Salzburgers, immediately after
the earliest settlement at Savannah. They were German
Protestants[1] exiled in 1731 by a decree of Archbishop

[1] Among the Salzburgers there were descendants of the Waldensians,
named after their founder Waldo, a citizen of Lyons in southern France.
The sect was formed about 1170, and its chief seats were in the Alpine valleys of Piedmont, Dauphine, and Provence. They have often been included
under the name Albigenses (from Albi, a district in Languedoc). These first
Protestant sects in Europe, in the twelfth and thirteenth centuries, represented a purer form of Christianity than the dogmatic mother church. Wars
of extermination were waged in their homes, and popes preached crusades
against them (Pope Innocent III, in 1208). The Waldensians welcomed the
Reformation of the sixteenth century, and as a result again suffered terrible
persecutions. A portion of them were supposed to have settled in the Alpine
district of Salzburg in the secluded glens and valleys of the Deferegger
Mountains (now in the extreme eastern part of the Tyrol).

Leopold, Count of Firmian, who with fanatical zeal drove out from his domains all who were not Catholics. More than thirty thousand Protestants were forced to leave the Austrian archbishopric of Salzburg, but after many hardships they were welcomed in Protestant countries, notably in Prussia, where seventeen thousand of them found homes.

About the same time, in 1732, King George II of England empowered twenty-one gentlemen to colonize the southern part of the Carolinas, to be known as the colony of Georgia. They were to select only worthy immigrants, and under such a category were named Scotch Highlanders and German Salzburgers. In the same year General James Edward Oglethorpe sailed with the first transport of English colonists and on January 20, 1733, arrived at the Savannah River, where he founded the city of that name. The Society for the Promotion of Christian Knowledge[1] in London coöperated with the Georgia land company for the benefit of the Salzburg exiles. Liberal contributions were made by the land company, and the religious society undertook to pay the expenses of the immigrants to Rotterdam and support a minister for them. A first group of Salzburg immigrants destined for America was formed at Berchtesgaden,[2] and under the leadership of Baron von Reck they reached Rotterdam, November 27, 1733. There the ministers Bolzius and Gronau awaited them. The former had been the superintendent of the

---

[1] "Societas promovenda cognitione Christi." Influential friends of the Salzburgers were the Reverend Dr. F. M. Ziegenhagen, Lutheran chaplain of the court of St. James London ; the Reverend Dr. G. A. Francke, son of the founder of the orphan asylum in Halle (Prussian Province of Saxony) ; and the Reverend Dr. Samuel Urlsperger, pastor of St. Anna Lutheran Church in Augsburg (Bavaria).

[2] Then included in the archbishopric of Salzburg.

Lutheran orphan asylum in Halle, and the latter a teacher in the same institution. The immigrants celebrated their Christmas in England, and set sail a few days after under the guidance of their two ministers and Baron von Reck. They arrived at Charlestown (Charleston, South Carolina), in March, 1734, and soon after at Savannah, where the entire population, among them a number of Germans, awaited them at the landing, while cannons booming bade them welcome. General Oglethorpe allowed the Salzburgers to select the site for their colony. Von Reck and several others, after a tour of inspection, chose land on the right bank of the river, about twenty-five miles from the settlement of Savannah. It was at the mouth of a small river flowing into the Savannah, about forty miles distant from the sea. The devout colonists, " after singing a psalm [1] set up a rock which they found upon the spot, and in the spirit of the pious Samuel named the place Ebenezer (the stone of help), for ' hitherto hath the Lord helped us.' " [2] The usual difficulties of early colonists were increased by the absence of carpenters and mechanics, until this deficiency was removed by the second shipload of immigrants, bringing fifty-seven additional Salzburgers. The Georgia company was liberal in every respect, furnishing boards for houses and other colonists' supplies. Von Reck returned to Germany with the purpose of bringing a still larger number of immigrants. This resulted in what has been called the " great embarkation," bringing eighty Salzburgers, twenty-seven Moravians [3]

---

[1] P. A. Strobel, *The Salzburgers and their Descendants*, p. 63. (Baltimore, 1855.) Strobel's work is authoritative on the subject.

[2] 1 Samuel, vii, 12.

[3] The Moravians made no permanent settlement in Georgia. Those that came with the Salzburgers (who were Lutherans), remained but a short time until the troubles with Spain forced the colonists to armed resistance.

(under the leadership of Nitschmann), and a number of English and Scotch Protestants.

They arrived at Savannah in the beginning of February, 1736, after a voyage that has become memorable for an occurrence of great importance. On board the ship were John Wesley, founder of Methodism, and his brother Charles. The former, on the invitation of General Oglethorpe, was on his way to Georgia with the twofold purpose of preaching the Gospel to the Indians, and improving the religious condition of the colony. The German passengers on board had attracted John Wesley's attention by evidences of their strong faith and humble piety. On the Sabbath day, about noon, while the Salzburgers and other Germans were assembled in religious worship, a storm suddenly arose, greater in violence than any other that they had experienced even on that tempestuous voyage. Amid the commotion of the elements every heart trembled with fear, and even Mr. Wesley was confessedly alarmed. But it was very different with the Salzburgers and Moravians. While the raging waters threatened to carry the worshipers to an instant doom, they calmly sang praises of their Creator, exhibiting perfect self-control, and utter absence of fear for themselves. When the storm had spent its fury, Mr. Wesley inquired of one of the Germans, "Were you not afraid?" He replied, "I thank God, no." "But were not your women and children afraid?" He replied mildly, "No, our women and children are not afraid to die." [1] The impression made upon Mr. Wesley by the conduct of these people, so great in

Bearing arms being contrary to their religion, they withdrew from Georgia and founded Bethlehem, Pennsylvania, in 1741. Bancroft, in his history of the United States, erroneously calls the Salzburgers Moravians.

[1] Quoted from the *Journal of the Reverend John Wesley*, under date of Sunday, January 25, 1736.

faith, was strengthened upon his arrival at Savannah. There he was introduced to the Reverend Mr. Spangenberg, later bishop of the Moravian Church, and to the Moravian pastor, Boehler, from whom, John Wesley subsequently declared, he had derived more light than from any other man with whom he had ever conversed. " I was ignorant of the nature of saving faith, apprehended it to mean no more than a firm assent to all the propositions contained in the Old and New Testaments," remarked John Wesley. Two years after his first visit to Georgia, having returned to England, he wrote the following note in his journal: " It is now two years and nearly four months, since I went to America to teach the Georgia Indians the nature of Christianity; but what have I learned of myself in the meanwhile? Why (what of all I least expected) that I, who went to America to convert[1] others, was never myself converted to God." The voyage to America, with the impressions received from the pious Salzburgers and from interviews with the Moravian pastors, became to John Wesley one of the important epochs of his life, and this fact is worthy of record, as one of the influences of colonial America upon ancient Europe.

Governor Oglethorpe wished to plant a new colony farther to the south, for the defense of the older settlements against Spanish America. A fort was therefore projected on St. Simon Island, and some newly arriving Salzburgers were asked to become its defenders. Most of

---

[1] John Wesley, the founder of the Methodist churches, was converted ("felt my heart strangely warmed") at a meeting which he attended among the Moravians in Aldersgate Street, London, during the reading of Luther's preface to Paul's Epistles to the Romans, in which the great reformer has given such a clear exegesis of the doctrine of justification by faith. Cf. Strobel, pp. 79, 81, 82. Also C. T. Winchester, *John Wesley*. (New York : The Macmillan Company, 1906.)

them, however, believing that their religion forbade the
use of arms, preferred to locate at Ebenezer, and Oglethorpe did not force his will upon them. Nevertheless a
goodly number of others among the arriving German
immigrants agreed to go to the projected fort under their
captain, Hermsdorf. Their settlement was called Frederica,
a German church was founded there, and the colony was
prosperous in 1743, when a traveler spoke of it as " a quiet
village of the Salzburgers, rurally charming, the improvements everywhere evincing the greatest skill and industry,
considering its late settlement." The village declined, however, after 1749, and in 1751 it presented " the melancholy
prospect of homes without inhabitants, barracks without
soldiers." [1]

Two years after the foundation of Ebenezer the Salzburgers found that its site was very badly chosen. Strobel
says, " it was a region which is composed of hills and plains
that are sterile, and upon which no one, having a correct
knowledge of the character of the soil, would ever think
of settling a farm." [2] The location was about four miles
below Springfield, the present seat of justice for Effingham
County. To add to their disappointment came diseases incident to exposure and excessive fatigue in a warm climate.
The mortality which existed at Ebenezer was heart-rending. [3]

At this time there seem to have been about two hundred Salzburgers settled at Ebenezer. These expressed their
dissatisfaction with the location of the colony before Governor Oglethorpe, who counseled them to remain, since

---

[1] Strobel, p. 119. The name St. Simon Island is still used for the coast
section of Glynn County, Georgia. Brunswick is the largest city near by.

[2] Strobel, p. 67.

[3] Characteristic in the reports of the Reverend Mr. Bolzius were the records, that disease and death were endured with Christian resignation, and
earthly pilgrimages were closed with joy and triumph.

their troubles were such as befell all new colonists when
the ground had just been cleared of forests, and since the
good work already done, in case of removal, would all be lost.
The governor allowed them to act according to their choice,
however, and the result was that they changed their abode
to another, about eight miles distant, lower on the Savannah River. The site of New Ebenezer was located on a
high ridge within a short distance of the river, and because of the peculiar color of the soil, called Red Bluff. [1]
The Savannah River was on the east, Little (Lockner's)
Creek and a lake (Neidlinger's Sea) on the south, and on
the north the meandering course of Ebenezer Creek. The
surrounding country was covered with a fine growth of
forest trees, but unfortunately for the permanent prosperity of the town, there were low swamps on three sides of
it, that at times became generators of disease.

The town was not laid out like Germantown in Pennsylvania on two sides of one long street, but in the checkerboard style, with streets at right angles, three from east
to west crossed by four from north to south. City lots
were portioned out and market-places measured off.[2]
Spaces for a church, parsonage, school-house, public
storehouse, and orphan asylum were laid out. Pastures
were on the outskirts of the town, and beyond Little
Creek were the farms, each of fifty acres. The country
to the north beyond Ebenezer Creek was occupied by the
Uchee Indians, with whom the settlers seem always to have
lived in peace. New Ebenezer was on the opposite side of
the river from Purysburg, an earlier settlement,[3] whence
some Germans came over to join the Salzburgers. Some

[1] In the present Effingham County.
[2] Strobel, pp. 91 ff.
[3] See Chapter VIII, pp. 216 ff.

JOHN MARTIN BOLZIUS

of the newcomers were growers of silk. At a time when silk manufacture in all other colonies had been abandoned (i. e., 1750) the Salzburgers still persevered, and every year they became more skilled in this industry.[1] In 1751 they sent over to England a thousand pounds of cocoons and seventy-four pounds two ounces of raw silk, yielding them the sum of one hundred and ten pounds sterling.

A traveler[2] described the settlement in the following way : " The people live in the greatest harmony with their ministers and with one another, as one family. They have no drunken, idle, or profligate people among them, but are industrious, and many have grown wealthy. Their industry has been blessed with remarkable and uncommon success, to the envy of their neighbors, having great plenty of all the necessary conveniences for life (except clothing) within themselves ; and supply this town (Savannah) with bread-kind, as also beef, veal, pork, poultry, etc." Up to the year 1741 over twelve hundred[3] German Protestants had arrived in Georgia, most of them becoming landowners at once, receiving support from friends for the journey and for a start in the New World, in fewer cases coming as redemptioners.

The colony was governed by its pastors, the Reverend John Martin Bolzius, and the Reverend Israel Christian Gronau, who in turn were under the superintendency and advisorship of the English trustees for the Society for the Promotion of Christian Knowledge, and the Evangelical Lutheran Church in Germany. The church council of

---

[1] Cf. Strobel, pp. 129–130. The Salzburgers began to plant mulberry trees in 1736. See below.

[2] In a letter by Thomas Jones, dated Savannah, 1740. See Strobel, pp. 111–112.

[3] According to a statement made by Mr. Benjamin Martyn, Secretary of the Trustees. Cf. Strobel, p. 115.

Ebenezer subscribed to a code of regulations[1] drawn up by the European Lutheran ministers, Urlsperger, Ziegenhagen, and Francke. One of the regulations required the support of school-teachers as well as ministers, another the care of those in need, such as widows and orphans. For the latter an orphan asylum[2] was built after the model of the Halle institution, and strangely enough was completed earlier than the church. It served as a church for the many years before a house of worship could be erected. The two pastors formed a tribunal governing matters spiritual as well as temporal, and were most unselfish and just in their rulings. Their judgments seem always to have been satisfactory, and no appeals were ever taken from their decisions.

The Salzburgers of Ebenezer, like the German Quakers of Germantown, proved their high moral standard by their opposition to slavery. The trustees of the colony as well as the ministers were opposed to the introduction of negro slaves, and their determined stand through many years threatened to cause difficulties with the larger landowners of the province, who, as elsewhere in the South, were interested in the extension of the slave-trade. The two reasons assigned by the citizens of Ebenezer against African slavery were firstly, that the colony was an asylum for the oppressed, and secondly, that negro slaves starved the poor laborer. Another argument used against the purchase of negroes was the danger of a servile war, aggravated by the proximity of the Spaniards.[3] Pastor Bolzius was one

---

[1] Strobel, pp. 167–180.

[2] About 1738 there were seventeen children and a widow in the orphanhouse. George Whitefield on his visit was very much pleased by the "little lambs that came and shook me by the hand one by one." Strobel, pp. 110–111.

[3] These arguments were stated by Baron von Reck. Cf. Strobel, p. 103.

of the very last to yield his opposition, and reproved Mr. George Whitefield for his complacent policy, expressed in Alexander Pope's maxim : " Whatever is, is right." To relieve themselves of their embarrassment, the Salzburgers referred the slavery question to the Reverend Mr. Urlsperger of the parent church in Augsburg. The latter very diplomatically advised the Salzburgers to yield : " If you take slaves in faith, and with the intent of conducting them to Christ, the action will not be sin, but it may prove a ' benediction.' " The Reverend Mr. Bolzius thereupon, on behalf of himself and the Salzburgers, withdrew his opposition to the repeal of the law prohibiting negro slavery.[1]

Pastor Gronau died in 1745, mourned by the whole colony, but by no one more sincerely than by his colleague, the Reverend Mr. Bolzius. The latter's ministerial labors were thereby increased, causing his numerous other burdens to be felt all the more heavily. These duties were administrative, including the trusteeship of the funds that had been collected in Europe for the benefit of the congregation at Ebenezer. He invested the sums received in lands and mills, which he superintended himself for the benefit of the colony. The necessary building stones and other equipments were imported from Germany or received from General Oglethorpe. There were erected two gristmills, a saw-mill, and a rice stamping-mill, all the property of the church, the income from which was devoted to the payment of ministers and charities. Bolzius was also interested in the manufacture of silk. In 1733 Mr. Nicolas Amatis of Piedmont was induced to remove to Georgia to instruct the colonists in the rearing of silkworms and the manufacture of silk.[2] Mulberry trees were planted in 1736

[1] Strobel, p. 105.
[2] Stevens's *History of Georgia*, quoted by Strobel, p. 129.

under the direction of the pastor, and his people became very successful in the culture of the silkworm. In 1742 five hundred trees were sent to Ebenezer and a machine was erected for the preparation of silk. To encourage the Germans to persevere in their efforts, the trustees (for the settlement of Georgia) gave a reeling-machine to each woman who would master the art of spinning, and in addition two pounds in money.[1] The Salzburgers, as above mentioned, persevered longer in the production of silk than any other colony.

The successor to Pastor Gronau was the Reverend Hermann H. Lembke, sent over from Germany at the request of Pastor Bolzius for assistance. The choice was a judicious one, and the church interests prospered. Four churches besides the one at Savannah were now included in the "Parish of St. Matthew," viz.: Jerusalem, Zion, Bethany, and Goshen. It was a large territory for two pastors to serve, extending over more than thirty miles, in part through a difficult country. The German settlements covered even a wider area, their farms being located on both sides of the road leading from Savannah to Augusta, a distance of about one hundred miles, and were spread out on the banks of the Savannah River, and on Lockner, Ebenezer, and Mill creeks. The patron of the Georgia churches in Germany, the Reverend Mr. Urlsperger, sent over an additional minister in 1752, making an excellent choice in the Reverend Christian Rabenhorst. With him came a colony of immigrants from Würtemberg, whom Bolzius was more inclined to welcome than a third minister. He very soon con-

---

[1] "Many mulberry trees are still standing at Ebenezer, which no doubt have sprung from the original stock ; many of the descendants of the Salzburgers continue to raise silk, which they manufacture into fishing-lines and sell very readily in Savannah." Strobel, p. 130. (Published 1855.)

fessed his error, however, when his strength began to show signs of declining, and the three pastors lived in great harmony for twelve succeeding years. Mr. Rabenhorst brought with him a capital of six hundred and forty-nine pounds, sixteen shillings and fivepence, from the interest of which he was to derive his support. The trust funds and the mill properties in which they were invested were in 1757 given over by the Reverend Mr. Bolzius to his brother-in-law, the Reverend Mr. Lembke, the former fearing his advancing age and wishing to introduce his colleague into the routine connected with the management of the properties. Ten years after, or two years after the death of the Reverend Mr. Bolzius, Pastor Lembke acted in accordance with his predecessor's example, assigning the trust to Rabenhorst. The most notable event under the Reverend Mr. Lembke's administration was the building of Jerusalem Church, a brick structure erected at Ebenezer in 1767.[1]

The successor of Lembke, Christopher F. Triebner, proved to be not well selected; a young man of "fine talents, but very impetuous in his character, and possessed of a very small share of the humility and piety which characterized his predecessors."[2] A church quarrel arose, which, like that in New Jersey,[3] was finally settled by the patriarch of the Lutheran church, the Reverend H. M. Mühlenberg. The latter arrived at Ebenezer in November, 1774, and at once proceeded with characteristic tact and wisdom. He called on each of the pastors personally, and after a friendly interview requested each to furnish in writing a statement of his grievances. Mr. Rabenhorst, the senior pastor, complained mainly of the charges and in-

---

[1] A picture of the church is found in Strobel, after p. 148.
[2] Strobel, p. 151. [3] Cf. Chapter IV, pp. 156–158.

trigues of his brother in office. Mr. Triebner made accusations of a more bitter kind, assailing the ability and character of the Reverend Mr. Rabenhorst. Mühlenberg decided virtually in favor of Rabenhorst, of whom he wrote in his diary, "most heartily would I have regarded myself as fortunate, if the Lord had lent us in Pennsylvania a laborer like Mr. Rabenhorst, and I would rejoice even in my last days to be the adjunct of such a man. . . . Although he was most grossly wronged he was the first to extend his hand to the offender."[1] The result of the Reverend Mr. Mühlenberg's arbitration was to exonerate Mr. Rabenhorst completely from all charges, to place him at the head of the parish of St. Matthew, and Mr. Triebner in a more subordinate position, with the latter's prerogatives very narrowly defined.

The restoration of peace in the church was not the only service of the Lutheran patriarch. He took an inventory of the properties of the church,[2] and examined carefully the deeds and grants. He found that the property had not been ceded definitely to the Lutheran church, but that under the conditions of the deed the established church of the colony (which was the Church of England) might claim the property. Mühlenberg succeeded in having the matter rectified in the courts of Savannah. He preached in all five churches, Savannah, Jerusalem, Bethany, Goshen, and Zion, and drew up a discipline of church government and conduct, which was signed by one hundred and twenty-four male members of the Jerusalem

---

[1] Of the Reverend Mr. Triebner Mühlenberg said : " A young man who, although well-meaning and gifted, was nevertheless inexperienced, passionate, and a dangerous novice."

[2] Strobel, pp. 190–191, gives eight items which made up the valuable property of the church. He estimates that the value could not have been less than twenty thousand dollars.

JERUSALEM CHURCH, EBENEZER, GA., ERECTED 1767

Church.[1] Mühlenberg remained in Georgia about four months to complete his important work in behalf of the parish of St. Matthew.

The Reverend Mr. Triebner was an ardent Tory during the Revolutionary War, and invited the British, after they had captured Savannah, to take possession of Ebenezer, which lay on the turnpike between Savannah and Augusta. Triebner probably carried a portion of his small congregation with him, but by far the majority of the Salzburgers joined the patriotic cause and were vigorous supporters of the party that advocated independence. This will receive comment in a later chapter.

The town of Ebenezer, at about the period of Mühlenberg's visit (1774–75), had attained the height of its importance. The population numbered about five hundred, live intercourse was maintained with Savannah and other towns, an export and import trade of limited extent was carried on with Europe, silk being exported to Europe and drugs and medical supplies being received from Germany. The population increased rapidly throughout the parish, spreading westward to the Ogeechee River, and remaining most numerous along the Savannah River between Savannah and Augusta.

The German settlements of the eighteenth century in New England were not numerous, yet their history, though not of the same importance as elsewhere, is nevertheless of interest. The beginnings of German colonies in New England are associated with the name of Waldo. Jonathan Waldo, of Swedish Pomeranian nobility, came to

---

[1] Cf. Strobel, p. 180, where their names are given. For a list of the names of the principal residents of Ebenezer in 1741 (i. e., thirty years earlier, at the beginning of the colony's history), see Strobel, p. 112.

Boston at the close of the seventeenth century as the agent of a Hamburg house. He rose to be one of the leading merchants of the city, and his business often took him to Germany and England. On one of these trips a son, Samuel Waldo,[1] was born in London. Samuel Waldo when a young man was sent to Harvard College, and afterwards to Germany, to complete his education. Like Peter Mühlenberg, a generation later, he was fascinated by the soldier's career, and entered the Hanoverian service. He was a member of the elector's body-guard when the latter ascended the English throne as George I, and advanced to the rank of major in the English service, remaining in London until 1724, when his father's death called him to Boston to take charge of the paternal estate. On his departure from England he was made a colonel of militia of Massachusetts Bay, and, residing in Boston, he soon gained the repute of energy and enterprise in business affairs.

Samuel Waldo became interested in a land speculation within the present state of Maine, which then was a part of the colony of Massachusetts. Ten proprietors — to whom later twenty associates were added — purchased lands on the Muscongus River, a tract situated in the present counties of Knox, Lincoln, and Waldo (Maine). They could not get a clear title from the crown, and therefore commissioned Waldo, *persona grata* at St. James's, to represent their interests in London. By " untiring application at court " Waldo was successful in adjusting the case, and as a reward the Thirty Proprietors surrendered to him one half of the Muscongus Patent.[2]

---

[1] His mother was also German. See *Collections of the Maine Historical Society*, series 1, vol. ix, p. 75, "General Samuel Waldo," by Joseph Williamson. Cf. also, Eaton's *Annals of Warren*, p. 109, and *Der deutsche Pionier*, vol. xiv, pp. 7–9.

[2] Cf. *Collections of Maine Historical Society*, series 1, vol. vi, pp. 321–322.

Waldo had his land surveyed in 1732, and prepared to colonize it at once. The first settlement was made in 1736, principally by Scotch-Irishmen on St. George's River, but he wished to secure a larger agricultural population. In 1738 the enterprising merchant went to Germany to secure colonists. Circulars [1] were distributed and arrangements made for transportation. In 1740 he succeeded in inducing forty German families from Brunswick and Saxony to accept his imposing offers to settle in the Broad Bay district of Maine.[2] They founded Waldoborough (Waldoburg) on both sides of the Medomak River, but led a wretched existence until larger numbers of German settlers joined them. They did not understand the art of fishing, which might have saved many of them, and they complained much of disappointment in their expectations; for even if the promises were "kept to the ear, they were broken to the hope." [3]

Waldo found his business affairs too engrossing to allow him much time for the colonists. He therefore employed an agent named Sebastian Zauberbühler (Zuberbühler), who had had some experience in other colonies. The

[1] A book was printed subsequently describing the new land, entitled: *Kurtze Beschreibung derer Landtschafft Massachusetts-Bay, in Neu Engellandt. Absonderlich des Landstrichs an der Breyten Bay, so dem Königlichen Britischen Obersten, Samuel Waldo, Erbherrn des Breyten Bay, zugehörig, sampt denen Hauptbedingungen nach welchen sich fremde Protestanten daselbsten ansiedeln mögen.* Speyer, 1741. Cf. *Der deutsche Pionier*, vol. xiv, p. 10.

[2] The most valuable contribution to the history of the Germans in Maine has been made by H. A. Rattermann, who visited the sites of the old colonies and studied their documentary history; published in *Der deutsche Pionier*, vols. xiv, xv, and xvi : " Geschichte des deutschen Elements im Staate Maine, deren Ursprung, Entwickelung u. Verfall, vom Jahre 1739 bis zur Gegenwart." The writer is deeply indebted also, for suggestions and corrections, to the Reverend Henry O. Thayer, A.M., former secretary of the Maine Historical Society and author of *The Sagadahoc Colony*, to whom the manuscript was submitted for revision.

[3] Eaton, *Annals of Warren*, p. 62.

agent succeeded in inducing from one hundred and fifty to one hundred and sixty Germans, all that remained after exasperating and costly delays, to cross the Atlantic with him in August, 1742, with the object of settling on Waldo's land in Maine. They were well received at Marblehead near Boston, and Waldo accompanied them to the Scotch-Irish settlement on St. George's River. Then they sailed into the mouth of the Medomak River, where, on the bay-like harbor called Broad Bay, a few log huts or sheds marked the site of their new homes. Zauberbühler remained with them until December, to help them in the selection of their lands, then went to Boston never to be seen by them again.[1] Waldoborough [2] (Waldoburg) remained the name by which the settlement was known. School-master John Ulmer acted as preacher and faithful leader of the colonists. The time of year for their arrival was badly chosen, for, though they saw the Maine forests in all the beauty of their autumnal foliage, and rejoiced in the experience of an Indian summer, a severe winter stood before them, destined to bring untold suffering. They could not sow until spring, and supplies, long awaited, had to be sent from Boston. Log huts were rudely constructed without windows or chimneys; unfamiliar hardships had to be endured before the settlement could become habitable. The few German colonists already located there could not give much assistance, needing help themselves and suffering from the fevers so common among first settlers.

---

[1] Sebastian Zauberbühler (in Massachusetts official documents spelt Suberbuhler and Zouberbuhler) was of Swiss birth, and probably came over with John Pury, founder of Purysburg, in 1732. The latter's example inspired him to similar ventures. After leaving Maine, Zauberbühler reappeared in Nova Scotia as magistrate of Lunenburg. He should not be confounded with the Reverend Bartholomew Zauberbühler of Orangeburg, South Carolina.

[2] The present spelling is Waldoboro.

When the spring came, the colonists were in such straits that it was impossible for them either to better their condition or migrate. They therefore petitioned Governor Shirley and the assembly of Massachusetts, setting forth their sufferings and begging that they be taken out of the country and be "employed in such business as they are capable of for the support of themselves, their wives and children." [1] The General Court Assembled had the matter investigated, and their commission reported that the complainants (Dr. Kast in behalf of himself and his Palatine brethren) had suffered greatly, and that, if not soon relieved, they might "stand in need of the Compassion of this Government." But since Waldo was absent from Boston, a settlement of the matter was deferred until the next meeting of the court. The committee of investigation then reported that each party had violated the contract, the Palatines in not paying the passage-money, Zauberbühler in not providing shipping in due time, Waldo in not paying the officers' wages, etc.; and recommended that some suitable person or persons be appointed to settle their accounts, and that "a sum of money be granted to be laid out in provisions and clothing to help them (the Palatines) thro' the winter." The report was read before the House and Council September 17, 1743, but was voted down, and the colonists were left to shift for themselves. The second winter must have been one of even greater trials, since the supplies of Waldo failed them after October, his contract requiring him to serve them only the first winter. But this was only the beginning of their troubles, and it was shown here even more than elsewhere that the lot of early colonists was not a happy one.

[1] May 25, 1743. See *Massachusetts Records* (MS.), vol. 15 A, pp. 33 ff. Printed in *Der deutsche Pionier*, vol. xiv, pp. 95–98 (Rattermann).

In the following year (1744) war broke out between
France and England, which drew into its vortex the colonies of the Western Hemisphere and threatened also the
insecure foundations of the German settlement in Maine.
In the spring of 1745 an expedition was made against the
French fort, Louisbourg, the "Gibraltar of America," on
Cape Breton Island, Nova Scotia. The force was under
the command of William Pepperell. Samuel Waldo, brigadier-general, was third in command of the New England
forces, and rendered conspicuous service.[1] A large German
contingent was enlisted under the captaincy of Johannes
Ulmer, "priest, prince, and military commander."[2] Those
of Waldoboro who did not accompany the expedition went
for protection to the forts on the Pemaquid and St.
George's rivers, and after the successful termination of
the campaign returned to their settlements.

The Indians, heretofore peaceable, had become dissatisfied because of the increase in the number of colonists
and their taking possession of territory above the Falls
of St. George. For a time they were bought off with presents, and it seemed as if the German settlements, friendly
to the red men, would be spared. But the quiet proved
to be only the lull before the storm. The new war had
changed conditions entirely, and the Indians were planning the extermination of the white settlers. On the
morning of the twenty-first of May, 1746, they surprised
the peaceful settlement of Waldoboro and destroyed it
entirely, only a few of the colonists escaping, making
their way to neighboring blockhouse forts or to Louisbourg, where they remained until the end of the war. In
spite of this terrible setback, the survivors returned in

---

[1] Collections, Maine Historical Society, series 1, vol. ix, p. 82.
[2] Eaton's Warren, p. 175.

1748, after the peace of Aix-la-Chapelle, in order to build
up their village again. Waldo made strenuous efforts to
get new colonists. He succeeded in bringing about twenty
or thirty families of German immigrants from Philadelphia, and thus infused new life into Waldoboro. Grist-mills
and saw-mills were erected, and soon also a church spire
pointed skyward to mark the progress of the colony.

About the same time the government of Massachusetts
became cognizant of the advantages which other colonies,
particularly Pennsylvania, had gained through German
immigration. When Joseph Crellius[1] in 1750 presented
a memorial to the General Court of Massachusetts, pro-
posing to bring over German Protestants, providing they
could be given sufficient inducements, Lieutenant-Governor
Spencer Phips used his influence in support of the plan,
urging that "they [the Protestants] would introduce
many useful manufactures and arts."[2] In 1749 the
General Court of Massachusetts appropriated four townships for the accommodation of foreign Protestants, two
in the eastern and two in the western part of the province.
Two of the townships were located in the extreme northwestern part, near Fort Massachusetts, west of the Connecticut River, in what is now Franklin County, and
extending into Vermont. The area included the present

---

[1] Crellius (or Crell, born in Franconia) came from Philadelphia, where
for a time he had published the second German newspaper in America, *Das
hochdeutsche Pennsylvania Journal* (1743), and translated into German
Benjamin Franklin's *Plain Truth.* Through his journalistic work he probably became acquainted with the publishing house of Luther in Frankfort-
on-the-Main. He was also interested in immigration schemes, and in 1748
induced a shipload of immigrants, that he had conducted to Philadelphia, to
accept Waldo's offers to settle in Maine. Seeing great profits in the venture,
he then decided to deal directly with the Massachusetts government, and
offered his services. See *Der deutsche Pionier,* vol. xiv, pp. 142 ff.

[2] Williamson, *History of Maine,* vol. ii, p. 285.

towns of Adamsville, Beaver Meadow, Bernardstown, Coleraine, Leyden, West Northfield, and Shattuckville. Adamsdorf, Bernardsdorf, and Leyden are names that date back to the German settlements.

The other two townships were to be located far east (in the extreme western part of Maine, the present Cumberland County), from "Sebago Pond to the head of Benirck." Crellius was to be granted a reserve of two hundred acres in each township, provided he imported and settled one hundred and twenty Protestants in each township within three years.[1] He was not able to carry out the conditions, and therefore the grants were revoked, but he succeeded in bringing over a number of families who settled in various localities. None went to the Sebago Lake region, and not until after three years had elapsed did some settle around Fort Massachusetts. It is probable that Crellius had previously sold his claims in Maine to the Plymouth Company ("The Company of the Kennebec Purchase").

Crellius, in his numerous advertisements, not only declared himself to be the authorized agent of the Massachusetts Bay Colony, but also implied that the British government was supporting his ventures. This called out a denial, and antagonized a host of other agents, interested in the immigrations to Pennsylvania, Carolina, and Nova Scotia. Mutual criminations and recriminations resulted, which could not but discredit all parties and open the eyes of the rulers of German principalities to the nefarious practices of the "newlanders." To Crellius belongs the credit of advocating an act passed by the Massachusetts House of Representatives in 1750, the first of its kind,

---

[1] *Massachusetts Records* (MS.), vol. 15 A, pp. 49–51; January 25, 1749. Printed in *Der deutsche Pionier*, vol. xiv, p. 177 (Rattermann).

"regulating the Importation of German and other Passengers," preventing crowding and other abuses.[1] Crellius thought to gain an advantage thereby, but the result was that the ship-companies, their profits being interfered with, refused to let their vessels go to the Massachusetts colony. A most valiant battle for reform was fought by Hofrat Heinrich Ehrenfried Luther, of Frankfort-on-the-Main, who sought to legitimize German emigration by getting the several American colonial governments to control the transportation and settlement of colonists, and to assume responsibility for their safety.[2] Thereby the emigrants would have been rescued from the clutch of the newlanders and ship-companies. The latter saw their danger, and fought successfully against the ruin of their profitable trade. Luther for some time supported Crellius, until the latter proved to be engaged in the emigrant traffic solely for his own pecuniary advantage, no better than other newlanders.[3]

Crellius succeeded by the spring of 1751, with the aid of Luther, in getting together twenty or thirty families in two transports and taking them down the Rhine to Rotterdam. There and in London his enemies did all they could to prevent his procuring ships, but he finally succeeded, after many delays, in carrying his people across the Atlantic. They stopped two weeks in Boston, and in December, 1751, some proceeded on the frigate of the province to new homes on the Kennebec River. On the left bank of the river, about twenty miles from its mouth, they founded Frankfort (now Dresden). Their land lay

---

[1] *Massachusetts Records* (MS.), vol. 15 A, pp. 52–55. Printed in *Der deutsche Pionier*, vol. xiv, pp. 177–179 (Rattermann).

[2] See, e. g., the letter of Luther to Lieutenant-Governor Phips of Massachusetts, *MS. Records*, pp. 67–80 ; *Der deutsche Pionier*, vol. xiv, pp. 179–187.

[3] Cf. *Der deutsche Pionier*, vol. xiv, pp. 428–429.

twelve to fifteen miles directly west of Waldoboro, having
for its eastern border the Sheepscott River, and being a
part of the territory held by the Plymouth Company. A
large number of the settlers of Frankfort were from
the borderland of Germany and France, and French Protestants were accordingly numerous among the original
settlers. The settlement, though German in name, seems
not to have been purely German like Waldoboro.[1]

A portion of the German colonists whom Crellius
brought over, in 1753 located on the western frontier of
Massàchusetts, near Fort Massachusetts. The later date
is explained by their coming over as redemptioners, therefore being obliged to serve several years to pay off the
cost of their transportation. When this period was over,
they settled in the region described above, and others
following them, they founded several villages, among them
Leydensdorf, to commemorate the trials of their passage
over the sea and their servitude on land.[2]

Nova Scotia had received a large number of German
immigrants through the activity of John Dick of Rotterdam and his sub-agent Köhler in Frankfort. They succeeded in deflecting a strong current of German settlers
who would otherwise have gone to Pennsylvania and
Carolina. Almost an entire brigade of Brunswick-Lune-
burg troops, who had come to America in the English
service, settled in Nova Scotia on government invitation
and liberal offers of land.[3] Lunenburg (in the earliest

---

[1] Cf. *Collections of the Maine Historical Society*, series 1, vol. viii, pp.
213, 214 (William Gould); also *ibid.*, series 2, vol. i, pp. 313 ff. and vol. iii,
pp. 351 ff. (Charles P. Allen).

[2] Another explanation of the name Leydensdorf or Leyden would be that
there were some Dutch settlers among them, who named the town after the
Dutch city of Leyden.

[3] The plan of offering land in Nova Scotia to soldiers was originated by
Lord Halifax, in 1749. See *Der deutsche Pionier*, vol. xiv, pp. 148–149 (Rattermann).

church records appearing with the German spelling, Lüne-
burg), the second oldest county of Nova Scotia, bordering
on Halifax (the oldest), was settled by them and many
shiploads of Germans and "foreign Protestants." The first
group, of one hundred and thirty persons, embarked at
Rotterdam in the good ship *Anne*, John Spurrier, master,
and arrived at Halifax in 1750. Between this first date
and 1753 large accessions were brought over in the *Pearl*,
Gale, *Sally*, *Betty*, *Murdoch*, *Swan*, and other ships,
bringing the total number of immigrants to 1615,[1] mainly
Germans, with a sprinkling of French and Scotch Protestants. Prominent men in the earliest days of the town of
Lunenburg were the Germans Leonard Christoph Rudolf
(judge and assemblyman), Dettlieb Christoph Jessen (justice of the peace), Sebastian Zouberbühler (magistrate),[2]
Captain John Rouse (whose name lives in Rouse's Buckel,
the "Plymouth Rock of Lunenburg"), and Caspar Wol-
lenhaupt (whose name appears as a signer of the mortgage upon the town of Lunenburg exacted by American
privateersmen, when they *brand-schatzed* the town in
1782).[3] In the list of land grants of 1761 more than nine
tenths of about two hundred names appear to be German.[4]
A contemporary local historian[5] estimates that the German

[1] M. B. Des Brisay, *History of the County of Lunenburg*, p. 23. (Toronto,
1895.)

[2] He had been Waldo's first agent. When Zouberbühler died, in 1773, he
seems to have been quite wealthy. His estate and the effects of his daughter,
on her death, are inventoried in Des Brisay, pp. 57–59.

[3] Cf. Agnes Creighton : " Relics of the History of Lunenburg " (paper read
before the Canadian Historical Society); also by the same author : " A Plea
for Remembrance," *Acadiensis*, vol. vii, no. 1, January, 1907 (containing
copies of inscriptions on tombstones of old Lunenburg settlers, church records, etc.).

[4] They are published in Des Brisay, pp. 69–72.

[5] The author of " Relics of the History of Lunenburg," to whom and to
Professor Archibald MacMechan of Dalhousie College, Nova Scotia, I am
deeply indebted for suggestions, and answers to my queries.

element of the present day in Lunenburg County is about
one half, in the city of Halifax about one tenth of the
total population. The latter is a conservative estimate
and perhaps disregards the fact that a large number of
Germans took a prominent part in the early settlement
of Halifax. In 1753 the immigration to Nova Scotia was
checked by the English government, after an investigation
which showed that more immigrants had been sent there
than the country could support, and that therefore unde-
sirable conditions of poverty and disease resulted, giving
good cause for complaint on the part of the colonists.
The testimony of greatest influence was that given by
Colonel Edward Cornwallis, up to that time governor of
the province.

The checking of the immigration to Nova Scotia was
advantageous for the New England settlements. Waldo
now strained his efforts to make the best of the opportunity, advertising in England, Scotland, and Germany.[1]
Exactly how far he was successful, we do not know. He
went to Germany in person, accompanied by his son. The
father was received as a distinguished man at many of the
small German courts, and from some of them he gained
permission to advertise for immigrants. In other principalities such privileges were withdrawn by legal action,
the result, perhaps, of the controversies among the newlanders. Waldo left his son in charge of an immigration
bureau in Frankfort-on-the-Main, where he lived at the
house of Luther. Count Nassau was one who favored the
plans of Waldo and even appointed an agent, Karl Leistner, who should accompany the colonists to America and
see to their wants. Leistner, reported to be a man of edu-

---

[1] Waldo's circular is published in an English translation : *Collections of
the Maine Historical Society*, series 1, vol. vi, pp. 325–332.

cation, gathered together about sixty families in the moun-
tainous districts of the Taunus, and brought them to the
Broad Bay settlements. This was in all probability a later
group than that reported by the "Annals of Warren"
(1753)[1] to have been housed in a shed unfit for habitation,
many freezing to death, or dying of diseases induced by
privations, many of the newcomers being "fain to work
for a quart of buttermilk a day," or "considered it a boon
when they could gain a quart of meal for a day's labor."
Certainly under Leistner's magistracy conditions changed,
and many families of local distinction sprang from the
immigration of 1753. Joseph Ludwig was a prosperous
agriculturist, Peter Mühler (Miller) built a house "distinguished among its neighbors," and George Varner (Wer-
ner) built a grist-mill partly in his own, partly in Waldo's
interest.[2] A meeting-house was built in 1760, dedicated
in 1763 (Eaton). A church fifty by seventy feet, with a
gallery, probably dating from 1790, still stands in good
preservation, and a commemorative service is held in it
every summer (Thayer).

As a result of natural growth and the work of recruiting colonists abroad, the settlements in Maine, at Broad
Bay and on the Kennebec, spread over a wider area, the
village later known as Bremen being an offshoot of Waldoboro, and Fort Frankfort (also called Fort Shirley)
spreading over the settlement Dresden and later taking
that name.[3] After the death of Waldo the rights of the
settlers on his own estate (not the claims of the colonists
of Frankfort) and on the lower Kennebec became a matter of dispute. About fifty to sixty families in the year

[1] See Eaton's *Annals of Warren*, p. 82.

[2] *Ibid.*, p. 83.

[3] The fact that the final name, adopted in 1794, was Dresden, again seems
to indicate a strong German population.

1763 bought their land a second time from the supposed rightful owners ; then it was found that still another party had older claims. Wearied of these experiences, a number of the German colonists sold their land and claims at a low figure, about 1770–73, and migrated to the settlements of their countrymen in the Orangeburg district, South Carolina, whence had come enthusiastic reports. Some returned subsequently, making a settlement with the proprietors, and " were received with open hearts and arms." [1]

One other settlement in Massachusetts, little known, but of much interest, was caused indirectly by the others. Germans who were destined for the Massachusetts colonies, in the east or west, frequently remained in Boston, serving their time as redemptioners, or tarrying for good reasons before selecting a permanent abode. In this way, quite a number had in course of time settled down as gardeners or truck-farmers in the neighborhood of Boston. There were some merchants also, commonly North Germans from Hamburg, who remained in or near Boston, and like the farmers were industrious, thrifty people, who gained the respect of the English population. The good impression the German settlers had made matured a plan in the minds of some Boston promoters, to establish a German town near Boston ; others interested were Waldo and the Kennebec proprietors, who welcomed a station from which they might draw settlers for their colonies. The result was the foundation of (New) Germantown about ten miles south of Boston (in the present neighborhood of Braintree, Quincy). On August 21, 1750, the ship *Thomas* brought a great

---

[1] *Collections of the Maine Historical Society*, series 1, vol. v, pp. 403–406, "Germans in Waldoborough," by the Reverend Mr. Starman. He estimates that about fifteen hundred German immigrants settled at Broad Bay (p. 404). He gives an account also of the churches and ministers of Waldoboro.

number of Germans to settle in New Germantown.[1] Some immigrants arrived in 1757, and twelve families engaged to go to the Germantown glassworks, for the settlement distinguished itself by establishing various manufactures. Undoubtedly some of the families brought over by Crellius, in 1751, settled there, and it was reported that in the following year over one hundred houses had been built.[2] Benjamin Franklin, then a printer of Philadelphia, bought eight building lots in the village, in 1751, proving that he had considerable faith in the future of New Germantown.[3] In 1757 twenty names represent those liable to military duty, and in many ways Germantown seemed a rival of Waldoboro. But by 1760 the manufacturing enterprises of Germantown seem to have declined or failed, the colony broke up, and a large part went to the Broad Bay settlements in Maine.

It has frequently been affirmed that the inhabitants of Waldoboro and the parts where the old German settlements of Maine were located, have preserved many traits distinct from the surrounding Yankee element. That would be a surprising phenomenon in a locality where intermarriages have been so very frequent. A correspondent,[4] well acquainted with Waldoboro, judges, however, that by conservative estimate ninety per cent of the population are of German descent. Very common names are such as: Schenck, Schwartz, Benner, Kaler, Waltz, Bornheimer, Ludwig, Creamer (Krämer), Kuhn, Hahn, Hoffses, Schuman. As late as 1840 sermons in German were occa-

[1] *Frankfurter Ober-Post-Amts-Zg.* no. 140, August 31, 1751, quoted in *Der deutsche Pionier*, vol. xv, pp. 208–210. See also *Frankfurter Ober-Post-Amts-Zg.*, no. 98, June 19, 1752, etc.

[2] This statement is contained in an advertisement in a German paper, and is probably extravagant.

[3] Cf. *Der deutsche Pionier*, vol. xv, p. 209.

[4] For this information I am indebted to the Reverend Henry O. Thayer.

sionally heard in the church of Waldoboro.[1] During the
Revolutionary War the Maine Germans were heartily patriotic. When to their great indignation their Tory minister refused to read the Declaration of Independence, a
layman, A. Schenck, translated and read it to the people.

The foregoing chapter intended to show that even at
the extremities of the American colonies, Georgia and
Maine (Massachusetts), the Germans took firm root early
in the eighteenth century, almost at the time of the formation of those colonies. Geographically Ebenezer and Waldoboro are the Alpha and Omega in the history of the
German element before the period of the Revolution.

[1] Judge Groton's statement, *Collections of the Maine Historical Society*,
series 1, vol. v, pp. 403–411.

CHAPTER X

THE LOCATION OF THE GERMAN SETTLERS BEFORE 1775;
THEIR DEFENSE OF THE FRONTIER; AND AN ESTIMATE
OF THEIR NUMBERS

The location of the Germans before the Revolution marked by counties
(present boundaries) — Two facts impress themselves: (1) that the
Germans occupied the best farming-lands and (2) that they were almost
directly on the frontier from Maine to Georgia — Their defense of the
frontier; on the Mohawk; and during the French and Indian War —
The services of Conrad Weiser and Christian Frederick Post, as envoys
to the Indians, etc. — An estimate of the number of settlers of German
blood in the thirteen colonies in 1775.

To see at a glance the location of the German settlements
before the Revolution, a map has been prepared (following this page), based upon a study of the population by
counties, according to their present boundaries, that were
inhabited by Germans.[1] As far as our present sources of
information tell us, the counties inhabited by Germans
were as follows: In the province of Massachusetts, the
counties of Lincoln, Knox, Waldo, of the present state of
Maine; and the county of Franklin, in the northwestern
part of the state of Massachusetts. In the province of
New York the Germans inhabited portions of Dutchess,
Ulster, Columbia, and Greene counties along the Hudson;
Schoharie, and the counties along the Mohawk, Montgomery, Fulton, Herkimer, and portions of Oneida, Saratoga,

[1] Where the population was about one half (or more) German, the shading is dark; where about one third, a lighter shade appears. If a German
population existed less than one third, but still of importance and influence,
the shading is faint.

and Schenectady. The German counties of Pennsylvania, exclusive of Philadelphia, were Montgomery, Berks, Lancaster, Lehigh, Lebanon, Dauphin, York, Chester, Northampton, Monroe, Cumberland, and Adams; of Maryland they were Baltimore, Frederick, Washington, and (in part) Carroll counties. New Jersey was thickly settled by Germans in Hunterdon, Somerset, Morris, less so in Sussex, Passaic, Essex, and (in the southern part) Salem counties. All the counties of the Valley of Virginia had strong German populations; in West Virginia, Jefferson, Berkeley, and Morgan counties; in Virginia, Clarke, Frederick, Warren, Shenandoah, Page, Rockingham; also, though fewer in number, Augusta, Rockbridge, Bath, Botetourt, Montgomery, Wythe, and others. East of the mountains in Virginia the following counties: Madison, Fauquier, Rappahannock, Loudoun, Prince William, Albemarle, Greene, Louisa, and Orange; scattered settlements existed in the Isle of Wight and Henrico counties, and elsewhere. In the Alleghanies Germans had located in the counties of Hampshire, Mineral, Hardy, Grant, Pendleton, all in West Virginia, along Patterson Creek, and the South Branch of the Potomac. In North Carolina the westerly counties, then on the frontier, along the Yadkin and Catawba rivers, viz., Davidson, Stanly, Cabarrus, Rowan, Iredell, Catawba, and Lincoln were populated by Germans from Pennsylvania; the counties of Forsyth and Stokes were settled by German Moravians; earlier settlements existed on the seacoast, in Craven (Newbern) and Brunswick (Wilmington) counties. German settlers in South Carolina filled the counties of Orangeburg and Lexington; portions of Barnwell, Newberry, Abbeville, Fairfield, Richland, Edgefield, Beaufort (Purysburg), and Charleston. In Georgia the Germans were most numerous in

GERMAN SETTLEMENTS AND FRONTIER LINE IN 1775

Effingham County, spreading along the Savannah River into Screven, Burke, and Chatham counties, i. e., between Savannah and Augusta.

As we study on the map the location of the Germans before the Revolution, two facts impress themselves. In the first place, the Germans were in possession of most of the best land for farming purposes. They had cultivated the great limestone areas reaching from northeast to southwest, the most fertile lands in the colonies. The middle sections of Pennsylvania were in their possession, those which became the granary of the colonies in the coming Revolutionary War, and subsequently the foundation of the financial prosperity of the new nation. The Shenandoah and Mohawk valleys were the rivals of the farm-lands of Pennsylvania, while the German counties of North and South Carolina pushed them hard for agricultural honors. The Germans in these sections supplanted all other nationalities through their superior industry, skill, and material resources acquired through habits of economy.

Even before the Revolution the value of the midland Pennsylvania counties as provision-houses for armies was recognized by the following incident. In 1758 an army was raised for the taking of Fort Duquesne, near which Braddock had met disaster three years before. The question arose whether the army starting from Pennsylvania should go straight through the woods, hewing a new road, or should march thirty-four miles southwestwardly to Fort Cumberland in Maryland and thence follow the road made by Braddock. It was in accordance with the interests of Pennsylvania that the new road be made, while Virginia was unwilling to see a highway cut for her rival that would lead into the rich lands of the Ohio, claimed by Virginia. Washington, who was then at Fort Cumberland with a part of his regiment, earnestly advocated taking the old road, while the quartermaster-general, Sir William Sinclair, advised in favor of the Pennsylvania route. The generals in command, Forbes and Bouquet, decided for a particular reason to take the straight course. "It was shorter and when once made *would furnish readier and more abundant supplies of food and forage;* but to make it would consume a vast amount of time and labor."[1] As later events proved, it was not British success in battle, but mainly the advantage of position, the possibility of getting supplies and holding out longer, advantages beyond the reach of the French, that forced the latter to evacuate Fort Duquesne.[2]

The second striking fact which impresses itself in a study of the map is the occupancy by the German settlers of almost the entire frontier area from Maine to Georgia. On the accompanying map the frontier has been indicated by a line representing the farthest points of settlement toward the west. Sometimes forts aided in determining the position of the line.[3] The farms of settlers generally

[1] Parkman, *Montcalm and Wolfe*, vol. ii, p. 134. (Boston, 1901.) Bouquet did justice to Colonel Washington, writing to Forbes : " Colonel Washington is filled with a sincere zeal to aid the expedition, and is ready to march with equal activity by whatever way you choose."

[2] In actual fighting the French and Indians had the better of it, — witness the defeat of Grant and his Scotch Highlanders.

[3] The task of drawing the frontier line was one of considerable difficulty. Contemporary maps were used to determine its position, such as those found in William Russell, *The History of America* (London, 1778) ; and Thomas Jeffreys (geographer to the king), *The American Atlas ; or a Geographical Description of the whole Continent of America* (London, 1778). The frontier line, as drawn on the map, follows the one hundred-foot line (U. S. Map, Geological Survey) of the coast of Maine, extending with it up the Penobscot and Kennebec rivers, and retreating again toward the coast ; when the present boundary of Maine and New Hampshire is reached, it is made to extend due west to Stevens's Fort on the Connecticut (about midway between the forty-third and forty-fourth parallels) ; then northwestward on the path

did not reach the forts; the forts, therefore, represent outposts beyond which the settlements did not go.

The credit for defending the American frontier has very commonly been accorded to the Scotch and Irish settlers.[1] From the map here presented, based upon a careful study of the location of the German settlers, it appears that the Scotch and Irish could not have had a larger share in the defense of the frontier than the Germans, when the whole extent of the frontier line is considered. In New England the English element no doubt stood the brunt of the Indian attacks. In New York the Mohawk and Schoharie regions, so largely inhabited by Germans, were pushed out farthest into the territory of the Six Nations. In Pennsylvania the Germans shared with the Scotch and Irish the distinction of defending the permanent settlements of the midland counties. In Maryland there were no Scotch and Irish farther west than the German settlers of Washington County, except perhaps in isolated instances (as that of Cresap). In Virginia the Germans were more numerous than any other element, in

to Crown Point at the southern end of Lake Champlain ; then southward to Fort George (Fort William Henry) and to Saratoga ; from that point westward to the farthest limit, Fort Stanwix (now Rome); then the line retreats to Cherry Valley and farther eastward some distance ; then southwestward to Port Jervis ; southwestward again to Fort Penn (Stroudsburg), and westward to Fort Augusta (Sunbury) on the Susquehanna ; then extending along the edge of the Blue Ridge (Tuscarora Mountains) to the Potomac, following this river to Fort Cumberland ; thence the line runs southwestward along the Alleghany mountain-range to a little east of the point where the present boundaries of North Carolina and Tennessee meet Virginia ; from that point the line passes southwestward to the point where the Catawba River cuts the boundary of North and South Carolina (at the western boundary of Mecklenburg County, N. C.) ; thence southwestward to Fort Charlotte (opposite the entrance of the Broad into the Savannah River) ; from there the line runs parallel to the Savannah River to the sea.

[1] Cf. Hanna, *The Scotch-Irish, or the Scotch in North Britain, North Ireland, and North America.*

the Valley, from the Potomac to Rockingham County; beyond that the Irish and Scotch-Irish outnumbered them; far in the southwest, even before the French and Indian War, there were for a time German settlements on the New River, and Germans appeared among the earliest settlers at the headwaters of the Great Kanawha. In West Virginia along Patterson Creek and the South Branch of the Potomac, the Germans were mingled for the most part with English settlers in about equal numbers, according to the diaries of the Moravian missionaries. In North Carolina the Scotch and Irish were farther to the southwest for at least half of the frontier line, although the Germans were close at their heels. In South Carolina the Germans occupied the larger part of the frontier area; in Georgia they formed a large portion of the population between Savannah and Augusta.

There were certain reasons why so large a percentage of the German immigration settled on the frontier, similar causes operating for the bulk of the Scotch, Irish, and Huguenot immigrants. They were poor, and were obliged to go where land was cheap or where squatters could maintain their independence. Redemptioners were commonly placed as far out on the frontier as possible, as for instance in the province of Massachusetts, where the German settlers that could pay for their land were sent to the Kennebec and Waldo districts in Maine, considered more desirable, and the others, after completion of their service-period, were sent to Fort Massachusetts on the northwestern frontier of the province. The Germans, being commonly of the permanent class of settlers who made the best of their land,[1] suffered greatly from the

---

[1] They frequently combined in one generation the three classes of settlers, the hunter, the squatter, and the permanent settler. Cf. Chapter v, p. 132.

attacks of hostile Indian tribes. Being at work in the fields they could easily be taken unawares, and their abundant cattle and crops tempted the predatory invader. The Indians rarely attacked the forts, well protected by stockades; even when the forts were badly equipped, "the enemy rarely molested even the feeblest of them, preferring to ravage the lonely and unprotected farms." [1] The Mohawk Valley Germans suffered as frequently and as terribly as any pioneers on the American frontier. In 1746 the French and Indians, led by a Jesuit, Peter Cœur, traversed the valley, reaching Schenectady, and even Albany. This war-party was in search of bigger game and did not seriously molest the farms of the Mohawk, giving them merely a foreboding of coming events. The German Flats (the present Herkimer) were surprised in 1757 by the French captain Belêtre. Sir William Johnson,[2] the defender of the Mohawk settlers, and of great influence among the Indians, was incapacitated at the time by illness. Belêtre fell upon the defenseless farms north of the Mohawk, killing about forty men, women, and children, and taking about one hundred prisoners. He did not dare

---

[1] Parkman, *Montcalm and Wolfe*, vol. i, p. 423 ; *Ibid.* p. 422 : " Meanwhile the western borders were still ravaged by the tomahawk. New York, New Jersey, Pennsylvania, Maryland, and Virginia all writhed under the infliction. Each had made a chain of blockhouses and wooden forts to cover its frontier, and manned them with disorderly bands, lawless, and almost beyond control."

[2] Sir William Johnson was born in Ireland. He married a German woman, a Palatine, who was the mother of two sons, who figured subsequently as Tories. The second wife of Johnson was a sister of the Indian chief Brant. Sir William Johnson was the leader of the forces against Crown Point, and was created a baronet for his services in that campaign. The distinguished honors which the family received and the wealth acquired under the protection of the crown, undoubtedly made them loyal to the English government. The family became ardent Tories and with their great influence over the Indians became the worst possible enemies of the Mohawk settlers during the Revolution, as they had been their best friends during the French and Indian and the preceding wars.

to attack the house of Herkimer (Herckheimer), on the south side of the Mohawk, because it was reported to be in a condition for defense. An extravagant report was sent by Vaudreuil to the Ministry of France, in which it was pretended that three thousand head of cattle, three thousand sheep, fifteen hundred horses, and personal property amounting to more than one million five hundred thousand livres were carried away from the German Flats.[1]

Although the population on the German Flats numbered only about three hundred at that time, and their wealth could not have been so enormous, nevertheless the report probably would not have been so extravagant if the booty taken had not been large. The exaggerated account illustrates the fact that the Mohawk Germans were prosperous and owned fine herds of live stock. The next year (1758) the enemy came in greater numbers and attacked the southern side of the Mohawk. Captain Nicholas Herkimer was in command of the defenders, and acquitted himself honorably, as he did subsequently also in the Revolutionary War. According to custom, when attacked by greater numbers, the colonists gathered in a protected palisade fort, whence the Indians could not dislodge them. The farms and produce, however, had to be abandoned, a prey to the robbers, while settlers living in remote localities were left to their fate. Men, women, and children were killed and scalped, the men often tortured to death and the women taken to Canada as prisoners, while their houses and crops were burned before their eyes. The Indians never tarried long, but after inflicting severe damage to life and property, escaped as rapidly as they had come, suffering but slight loss themselves.

---

[1] Parkman, *Montcalm and Wolfe*, vol. ii, p. 7, note ; and Kapp, *Geschichte der Deutschen im Staate New York*, p. 162.

In the province of Pennsylvania the troubles between governor and assembly occasioned neglect of measures for the defense of the frontier. The spirit of vacillation and non-resistance which characterized the Quaker government at Philadelphia resulted in untold hardships for the frontiersmen. After Braddock's defeat in 1755 the whole country was open to Indian attacks. News came that the settlement of Tulpehocken, only sixty miles distant, had been destroyed, that the Moravian settlement, Gnadenhütten, was burned and nearly all its inhabitants massacred. Bodies of men, gathered together from many places, appeared in Philadelphia to compel the governor and the assembly to defend the province. Among them four hundred Germans marched in procession to demand measures of defense. A band of frontiersmen presently arrived, bringing in a wagon the bodies of friends and relatives lately murdered, displaying them at the doors of the assembly, amid curses and threats of vengeance.[1] Tardy measures were taken for defense. The province of Pennsylvania, aided by the home government, in control of William Pitt, adopted the plan of taking Fort Duquesne, and fitted out the expedition already referred to, under the command of General Forbes and Colonel Bouquet. Washington commanded a division of Virginia troops, among whom there were Virginia Germans of the Valley. Another division was that under the command of Henry Bouquet, a native of Switzerland. It was called the Royal American Regiment, and was a new corps raised in defense of the colonies, largely composed of Germans of Pennsylvania.[2]

On the southern frontiers, in the Carolinas, the Chero-

---

[1] Parkman, *Montcalm and Wolfe*, vol. i, p. 348.
[2] Parkman, *Montcalm and Wolfe*, vol. ii, pp. 132–133.

kees began hostilities, though more serious ravages occurred farther northward in the New River and Great Kanawha districts where the settlements were, for a time at least, totally destroyed.

During these Indian wars there were two Germans who rendered conspicuous service. Their names were Conrad Weiser, the son of Johann Conrad Weiser, the Palatine leader,[1] and Christian Frederick Post, the Moravian missionary. Weiser, who had lived among the Mohawk Indians when a boy, acquiring their language and also kindred dialects, was famous as an interpreter. The Indians reposed confidence in him, and his presence in council insured justice, they thought. He addressed them in the oratorical manner that gave them delight, and the story of his youth made his personality pleasing to them. His services brought him into contact with all the tribes of the Iroquois Nation and even with the distant Indians of the Ohio Valley. In the year 1737 he undertook a long journey to Onondaga in New York, under commission from Governors Logan of Pennsylvania and Gooch of Virginia, with the purpose of inducing the chiefs of the Six Nations to make a truce and then an alliance with the Cherokees and Catawbas. The Indians at the North and South had waged destructive wars against one another, disturbing the peace also of the pioneer settlements. The mission was completely successful and was carried out in the severity of winter. In the summer of 1742, Weiser was again one of the principal figures, when seventy chiefs and warriors of the Six Nations met in council with Governor ·Thomas of Pennsylvania. The parley lasted ten days, July 2 to 12. The two difficult objects to be attained were, firstly, to appease the Indians for land robberies

[1] See Chapter IV, pp. 94–95, etc.

committed, and secondly, to get their help against the threatened French invasion. Contemporaries reported that without Weiser's tactful mediation the matter would not have been so quickly and happily brought to a conclusion. In 1745 the Six Nations threatened to overrun the Mohawk Valley settlements. Land robberies again had incensed them, and French agents had kindled their revengeful spirit. Governor Clinton of New York sent Weiser, accompanied by several friendly Indian chiefs, to Onondaga, and from there to Oswego, with the result of not only pacifying the Indians but of regaining their friendship. In 1748, under orders from the governor of Pennsylvania, Weiser traveled through the mountains of Pennsylvania to the Ohio, and on the Ohio to Logstown,[1] bringing presents to the Indians to keep them from an alliance with the French. At the same time he observed closely the character of the French settlements in the Ohio Valley, the location and strength of their forts, and gathered information concerning the intentions of the enemy. This experience served him in good stead in 1754, when representatives of seven colonies met in council with the chiefs of the Six Nations, to form a common plan of resistance against the French. That was an important moment in colonial history. It was altogether necessary to retain the friendship and to secure the alliance of the Six Nations against the French and their allies, the hostile Indians of the Ohio. Weiser was able to repeat in the language of the Mohawks his experiences with the French and the haughty Indians of the Ohio Valley, and he roused the animosity of the Six Nations against them, taking advantage of the Indians' greed for land.

[1] Directly west of Pittsburg, near the Ohio state line.

When the French and Indian War broke out, Weiser was already an old man. Nevertheless he served as a lieutenant-colonel of the militia, and as Mühlenberg, his son-in-law, reports, he was absent much on consultation in Philadelphia with European soldiers concerning Indian affairs. Conrad Weiser died during the war, in 1760.[1]

The other German who nobly served the colonies during the Indian troubles was the missionary Christian Frederick Post, a member of the Moravian Brotherhood.

Post [2] spoke the Delaware language, knew the Indians well, for he had lived among them and married a converted squaw. He was a plain German, upheld by a sense of duty and a single-hearted trust in God; alone, with no great disciplined organization to impel and support him, and no visions and illusions such as kindled and sustained the splendid heroism of the early Jesuit martyrs ; yet his errand was no whit less perilous.[3]

The Moravian envoy made his way to the Delaware town of

[1] Conrad Weiser's autobiography, already referred to, is one of the most curious documents of its kind, not only valuable for the life-history which it gives, but interesting also for the many sidelights on religion and politics. Cf. also J. H. Walton, *Conrad Weiser and the Indian Policy of Colonial Pennsylvania.* (Philadelphia, Jacobs & Co., 1908.)

[2] This whole passage, containing the thrilling narrative of Post's mission to the Indians, resulting in their breaking their alliance with the French, is quoted from Francis Parkman's authoritative work, *Montcalm and Wolfe,* vol. ii, pp. 144–150.

[3] "Here we may notice the contrast between the mission settlements of the Moravians in Pennsylvania and those the later Jesuits and Sulpitians had established at Caughnawaga, St. Francis, La Présentation, and other places. The Moravians were apostles of peace and they succeeded to a surprising degree in weaning their converts from their ferocious instincts and warlike habits, while the mission Indians of Canada retained all their native fierceness and were systematically impelled to use their tomahawks against the enemies of the church. Their wigwams were hung with scalps, male and female, adult and infant ; and these so-called missions were but nests of baptized savages, who wore the crucifix instead of the medicine-bag, and were encouraged by the government for purposes of war." Parkman, *Montcalm and Wolfe,* vol. ii, pp. 144–145.

Kushkushkee, on Beaver Creek, northwest of Fort Duquesne, where the three chiefs known as King Beaver, Shingas, and Delaware George, received him kindly and conducted him to another town on the same stream. Here his reception was different. A crowd of warriors, their faces distorted with rage, surrounded him, brandishing knives and threatening to kill him; but others took his part, and order being at last restored, he read them his message from the governor, which seemed to please them. They insisted, however, that he should go with them to Fort Duquesne in order that the Indians assembled there might hear it also. Against this dangerous proposal he protested in vain. On arriving near the fort the French demanded that he should be given up to them, and being refused, offered a great reward for his scalp; on which his friends advised him to keep close by the camp-fire, as parties were out with intent to kill him. " Accordingly, " says Post, " I stuck to the fire as if I had been chained there. On the next day the Indians with a great many French officers came to hear what I had to say. The officers brought with them a table, pens, ink, and paper. I spoke in the midst of them with a free conscience,[1] and perceived by their looks that they were not pleased with what I said." The substance of his message was an invitation to the Indians to renew the old chain of friendship, joined with a warning that an English army was on its way to drive off the French, and that they would do well to stand neutral.

He addressed an audience filled with an inordinate sense of their own power and importance, believing themselves greater and braver than either of the European nations and yet deeply jealous of both. " We have heard," they said, " that the French and English mean to kill all the Indians and divide the lands among themselves," and on this string they harped continually.[2]

After waiting some days the three tribes of the Delawares

---

[1] Parkman quotes from the journal of Christian Frederick Post here and elsewhere, dated July, August, September, October, November, 1758.

[2] Parkman says that if they had known their true interest they would not have made peace with the English, but would have all united to form a barrier of fire against their farther progress.

met in council, and made their answer to the message brought by
Post. It was worthy of a proud and warlike race, and was to the
effect that since their brothers of Pennsylvania wished to renew
the old peace-chain, they on their part were willing to do so, provided that the wampum belt should be sent them in the name,
not of Pennsylvania alone, but of the rest of the provinces also.

Having now accomplished his errand, Post wished to return
home; but the Indians were seized with an access of distrust,
and would not let him go. This jealousy redoubled when they
saw him writing in his notebook. "It is a troublesome cross and
heavy yoke to draw this people," he says; "they can punish
and squeeze a body's heart to the utmost. There came some together and examined me about what I had wrote yesterday. I
told them I writ what was my duty. 'Brothers, I tell you, I am
not afraid of you. I have a good conscience before God and
man. I tell you, brothers, there is a bad spirit in your hearts
which breeds jealousy and will keep you ever in fear.'" At last
they let him go; and eluding a party that lay in wait for his
scalp, he journeyed twelve days through the forest and reached
Fort Augusta with the report of his mission.

As the result of it, a great convention of white men and red
was held at Easton in October. The neighboring provinces had
been asked to send their delegates, and some of them did so;
while belts of invitation were sent to the Indians far and near.
Sir William Johnson, for reasons best known to himself, at first
opposed the plan; but was afterwards led to favor it and to induce tribes under his influence to join in the grand pacification.
The Five Nations, with the smaller tribes lately admitted into
their conference, the Delawares of the Susquehanna, the Mohe-
gans, and several kindred bands, all had their representatives
at the meeting. The conferences lasted nineteen days, with the
inevitable formalities of such occasions and the weary repetition
of conventional metaphors and long-winded speeches.

When their difficulty was settled, the governor of Pennsylvania addressed the assembled Indians and

gave them the wampum belt, with the request that they would

send it to their friends and allies and invite them to take hold also of the chain of friendship. Accordingly all present agreed on the joint message of peace to the tribes of the Ohio.

Frederick Post, with several white and Indian companions, was chosen to bear it. A small escort of soldiers that attended him as far as the Alleghany was cut to pieces on its return by a band of the very warriors to whom he was carrying his offers of friendship; and other tenants of the grim and frowning wilderness met the invaders of their domain with inhospitable greetings. The young warriors said: "Anybody can see with half an eye that the English only mean to cheat us; let us knock the messengers in the head." I said: "As God has stopped the mouths of the lions, that they could not devour Daniel, so he will preserve us from their fury." The chiefs and elders were of a different mind from their fierce and capricious young men. They met during the evening in the log house where Post was to be lodged; and here a French officer presently arrived with a string of wampum from the commandant, inviting them to help him drive back the army of Forbes. The string was scornfully rejected. "They kicked it from one to another as if it were a snake." . . . There was a grand council at which the French officer was present; and Post delivered the peace message from the council at Easton with another with which Forbes had charged him. The messages pleased all the hearers except the French captain. He shook his head in bitter grief and often changed countenance. . . . After the Indians began to mock him, he went out. The overtures of peace were accepted, and the Delawares, Shawanoes, and Mingoes were no longer enemies of the English.

The loss was all the more disheartening to the French, since a few weeks before they had won a victory over a part of the army of Forbes, because of which they hoped to hold their wavering allies. Major Grant, in command of the Highlanders, had prevailed upon Colonel Bouquet to allow him to detach eight hundred men from the advancing army, in order to reconnoitre Fort Duquesne.

The troops, consisting of Highlanders (Scotchmen), Royal Americans (Germans of Pennsylvania), and Provincials (Virginians), started together from the camp at Loyalhannon, but, owing to the bad generalship of Grant, who divided his forces so that they could not support one another, the expedition met with disaster. The enemy outnumbered them even when united; Grant's force was completely routed, five hundred and forty, however, out of the eight hundred and thirteen returning safely. In spite of this defeat, which had happened a few weeks before, the mission of Post was successful. He was *persona grata* among the Indians, beloved and respected by many, and no better messenger could have been chosen for this dangerous embassy. The selection of Post, as well as the plan of the meeting at Easton, was the work of General Forbes, as the next in command, the tactful Colonel Bouquet explained in a private letter.[1] Fort Duquesne was evacuated by the French, after they were left in the lurch by their Indian allies and by the troops from Louisiana and the Southwest. These desertions becoming known, the army of Forbes made forced marches over the mountains, and took the fort without opposition shortly after its evacuation.

In the defense of the frontier during the French and Indian War, the Royal Americans made a glorious record.

---

[1] Bouquet to Chief Justice Allen, 25 November, 1758. Quoted by Parkman, *Montcalm and Wolfe*, vol. ii, p. 161 : " After God, the success of this expedition is entirely due to the general, who by bringing about the treaty with the Indians at Easton struck the French a stunning blow, wisely delayed our advance to wait the effects of that treaty, secured all our posts, and left nothing to chance, and resisted the urgent solicitation to take Braddock's road, which would have been our destruction. In all his measures he has shown the greatest prudence, firmness, and ability. " General Forbes was a martyr to this work. He suffered from a severe illness during the whole campaign, and died shortly after its completion.

This regiment consisted of four battalions, of one thousand men each. Fifty of the officers were to be foreign Protestants, while the enlisted men were to be raised principally from among the German settlers in America. The immediate commander was Colonel (later General) Bouquet, a Swiss by birth, an English officer by adoption, and a Pennsylvanian by naturalization, the last a distinction conferred upon him for his campaign in Western Pennsylvania, where he with Forbes wiped out the disgrace of Braddock's defeat.[1] The rank and file of the regiment were German and Swiss settlers of Pennsylvania, young men enlisted for three years, and they saw service in all parts of the colonies. A list of their campaigns is as follows:[2]

1757. First Battalion in Indian wars.
    Five companies under Stanwix in Pennsylvania.
    Third Battalion at Fort Hunter and Fort William Henry.
    Second and Fourth at Louisbourg.
    First Battalion under Bouquet in South Carolina.
    First and Fourth at Crown Point and Ticonderoga.
1758. Second and Third Battalions at Louisbourg.
    First and Fourth under Bouquet and Forbes at Fort Duquesne.
1759. Fourth Battalion under Prideaux at Fort Niagara.
    Second and Third under Wolfe at Quebec.
    Fourth under Haldiman at Oswego.
    First under Amherst at Lake Champlain.
    Fourth under Sir William Johnson, Bouquet, Stanwix, and Wolfe at Quebec.
1760. First, Second, and Third at Quebec.

[1] Cf. Rosengarten, *The German Soldier in the Wars of the United States*, pp. 16–22. (Philadelphia, 1890.) A history of the Royal American Regiment is found in *A Regimental Chronicle, and List of Officers of the Sixtieth, formerly the Sixty-second, or the Royal American Regiment of Foot*. By N. W. Wallace. (London, 1879.)

[2] Rosengarten, *supra*, pp. 19–20.

1761. First in Virginia.
1762. Third at Martinique and Havana.
1763. First under Bouquet at Bushy Run and Pittsburg.

These campaigns made veterans of the Pennsylvania boys and prepared a nucleus of self-reliant soldiers for the coming war of the Revolution.

The story of the sufferings of pioneer settlers, who were constantly exposed to the inroads of savages during more than "half a century of conflict," is too distressing a narrative for detailed depiction. History repeated itself during the Revolutionary War, and therefore instances of heroism on the part of German frontiersmen will be cited in the following chapter (xi). The Germans of Pennsylvania, until the Revolutionary War, were left more at peace than many of the other frontier settlers, a circumstance probably due to the missionary work of the Moravians and to the pacific policy adopted toward the Indians by the Quaker government. The Virginians, the "Long Knives," would never admit this to be the fact, claiming that the reason of the Indian preference was that the Virginians were settlers and the Pennsylvanians only traders. Such a view, however, contradicts the facts, the Pennsylvanians being preëminently settlers.

The question as to how large was the total number of German settlers in the colonies before the Revolutionary War is one which cannot be determined with accuracy. There are no exact statistics extant concerning the population of the thirteen colonies. The Continental Congress of 1776 made an estimate of the population as a basis from which to apportion the expenses of the war.[1] The figures of this congressional conjectural census are as follows: —

---

[1] Pitkin's *Statistics*, p. 583 ; *Harper's Magazine*, vol. li, p. 399.

New Hampshire	102,000
Massachusetts (including Maine)	352,000
Rhode Island	58,000
Connecticut	202,000
New York (including Vermont)	238,000
New Jersey	138,000
Pennsylvania	341,000
Delaware	37,000
Maryland	174,000
Virginia (including Kentucky)	300,000
North Carolina (including Tennessee)	181,000
South Carolina	93,000
Georgia	27,000
Total white population	2,243,000
Slave population	500,000
Grand total	2,743,000

This estimate is generally considered too large, since the census of 1790 showed a total white population of only 3,172,006. New Hampshire took a state census in 1782 to lessen its proportion of the general taxes, and as a result of that census reported its population at 82,000, which figure was probably as far below the true number as the congressional estimate was above it. Bancroft estimated the total white population of the colonies in 1775 at 2,100,000.[1]

For the Scotch and Irish, Hanna[2] makes an estimate of 385,000, which he derives in the following way: Leaving New England out of consideration (assigning to it one third of the population, viz., 700,000), since its population was almost purely English, he takes Bancroft's figures for

[1] *History of the United States*, vol. iv, p. 62. (1888.)

[2] See Charles A. Hanna, *The Scotch-Irish, or the Scotch in North Britain, North Ireland, and North America*, vol. i, pp. 82–84. (New York and London, Putnam, 1902.)

the territory west of the Hudson and south of the St. Lawrence district, which are as follows : —

New York (excluding Vermont)	202,000
New Jersey	109,000
Pennsylvania	273,000 [1]
Delaware	30,000
Maryland	134,000
Virginia (including Kentucky)	325,000
North Carolina (including Tennessee)	206,000
South Carolina	90,000
Georgia	34,000
	1,403,000

Hanna estimates the inhabitants of Scotch and Irish blood or descent to have been one eighth of the whole white population in New York; one fifth to one fourth in the states of New Jersey, Maryland, and Virginia; more than one third in Pennsylvania, Delaware, North Carolina, and Georgia; and one half in South Carolina, resulting as follows : —

New York	25,000
New Jersey	25,000
Pennsylvania	100,000
Delaware	10,000
Maryland	30,000
Virginia	75,000
North Carolina	65,000
South Carolina	45,000
Georgia	10,000
	385,000

To get at the approximate number of inhabitants in 1775 who were of German blood is just as difficult. In

[1] This estimate for Pennsylvania is extremely low, as compared with the congressional census, viz., 341,000.

New England the settlements of Maine, those around Fort
Massachusetts, and near Boston, probably together contained about fifteen hundred Germans. For New York
State we can get nearer a correct estimate. The census
made by the Reverend Mr. Kocherthal of the Palatines in
New York State in 1718 estimated the Germans at about
two thousand. This, as we have seen, was a low estimate,
and corrected, as explained in Chapter iv,[1] would in
1720 make about twenty-five hundred. The natural increase, doubling in about twenty-three years (three per
cent a year), added to the new arrivals at the port of
New York, would make about twenty-five thousand. Pennsylvania's German population, as has been explained in
Chapter v,[2] was about one hundred and ten thousand.
Judging by the numerous German churches in the northern counties of New Jersey, by the proximity to the seaports of Philadelphia and New York, the German population in New Jersey must have been no less than fifteen
thousand. Maryland was thickly settled by Germans in the
western counties of Frederick and Washington, and in
the neighborhood of Baltimore; giving Delaware five
hundred, the German population of the two states together
can be estimated at about 20,500. More numerous was
the German population of Virginia and West Virginia.
The German colonies visited by the Moravian missionaries
in the Valley and on the South Branch, about 1744–50,
represented about three to five thousand settlers. The
natural increase and the German settlements in other
counties, enumerated in Chapter vii, probably made a total
of twenty-five thousand. South Carolina's German population can be estimated in the following way: In the year
1788 fifteen German churches were incorporated under

[1] See p. 92.   [2] See p. 128.

the laws of the state (Chapter VIII, see pages 226–227). These churches were in existence before the Revolution, and probably were more numerous at that time, many being burned and pillaged and their congregations scattered during the war, by Tory raids. The question arises, how large a population does a single church represent? Some light on that subject is afforded by the estimate of Schlatter. He counted the number of the German Reformed in Pennsylvania as thirty thousand, distributed among forty-six congregations, sixteen parishes, to be served by as many pastors.[1] If forty-six congregations represent thirty thousand people, fifteen churches would represent at least ten thousand people, since congregations were frequently not large enough to build churches. The fifteen churches did not include the church in Charleston nor numerous other smaller settlements, nor the non-church-going Germans scattered beyond the interior, i. e., on the frontier where no ministers were available. The estimate of fifteen thousand is therefore not excessive. North Carolina had quite a large German population before 1775, as has been seen in the account of settlements in the central part of the state (Chapter VIII), and as is also evident from the tradition that there were immigrations of Germans from North Carolina into Virginia. We may estimate the population at about one half that of South Carolina, viz., eight thousand. Georgia had twelve hundred Salzburgers in 1741 according to documentary evidence. The natural increase up to 1775, added to the new arrivals, could not have been less than five thousand. This is a very small estimate in view of the political importance of the Salzburgers during the Revolutionary War. A summary of estimates will appear as follows:—

[1] *Hallesche Nachrichten* (Reprint), vol. i, p. 411.

New England	1,500
New York	25,000
Pennsylvania	110,000
New Jersey	15,000
Maryland and Delaware	20,500
Virginia and West Virginia	25,000
North Carolina	8,000
South Carolina	15,000
Georgia	5,000
Total	225,000

This estimate is very conservative, being based upon estimates of the numbers in known German colonies. The number of scattered German settlers in the large cities, and the number of settlements of which there is no record, must have been quite large. An estimate of two hundred and twenty-five thousand inhabitants of German blood at the outbreak of the Revolution must therefore be regarded as a minimum. It would mean that a little more than one tenth of the total white population at the beginning of the war of independence was of German blood. In certain localities, of course, the German population was much larger in proportion to the total population, notably in Pennsylvania, where it was one third of the total number. Future researches in the colonial history of the Germans will undoubtedly reveal larger numbers than have been given above, but the attempt has been made here to confine the estimate within limits that are clearly incontestable.

CHAPTER XI

THE GERMANS AS PATRIOTS AND SOLDIERS DURING THE WAR OF THE REVOLUTION, 1775-1783

Activity of Germans at the beginning of the Revolutionary agitation — Services of sectarians in the war — The Tories — Resolutions of the Virginia Valley Germans — The Salzburgers as patriots — The German regiments — Armand's Legion — Washington's body-guard — Two types of German patriots : Peter Mühlenberg and the baker, Ludwig — The Mohawk Germans— Battle of Oriskany — Herkimer — Results of the battle — Heroism on the frontier — German officers in the American army : Baron Steuben, his services ; John Kalb ; F. H. Weissenfels ; Ziegler ; Lutterloh ; Schott, etc. — The Hiester and Mühlenberg families — German families of Charleston, etc. — Individuals, Dohrmann, etc. — Germans in the French service — Siege of Yorktown — The Hessians.

THE French and Indian War was the training-school for the Revolutionary struggle. The extensive service of the Royal American Regiment, described in the foregoing chapter, laid the foundation of military experience among the German settlers of Pennsylvania. In the Mohawk Valley Herkimer gathered the people together, and in the Valley of Virginia German military companies were quickly organized. There existed in the colonies a large number of German sectarians, Mennonites, Quakers, Dunkards, Seventh-Day Baptists, and others, whose religion forbade the use of arms. They, like the English Quakers, represented the spirit of non-resistance, which inflicted much suffering upon the frontier settlers during the French and Indian War. The newspaper of Sauer gave expression to this pacific attitude, which should not, however, be mistaken for Toryism. The Mennonites and other

religious sects, though they did not bear arms, furnished
in supplies and taxes the equivalent of trained eyes and
limbs. They would not at any time have been unwilling
to lay down their lives for their country. The Moravians
of North Carolina submitted cheerfully to a triple tax
levied upon them by the province, in lieu of military service.

The more vigorous and manly virtues of the Germans,
who as a race from the beginning of their history proved
themselves good warriors, were represented by such men
as Mühlenberg and Schlatter. The latter was the army
chaplain of the Royal Americans in the French and Indian War, and served in a similar capacity during the
Revolution. The Reverend H. M. Mühlenberg was proud
of the military achievements of his son Peter (to be noted
below), and his directing hand was evident from the very
beginning. In 1775 the vestries of the German Lutheran
and Reformed churches in Philadelphia sent a pamphlet
of forty pages to the Germans of New York and North
Carolina, stating that the Germans in the near and remote
parts of Pennsylvania had formed not only militia companies, but a select corps of sharpshooters ready to march
wherever they were required, while those who could not
do military service were willing to contribute according
to their abilities.[1] An earnest appeal was made to the Germans in other colonies for armed resistance against the
" oppression and despotism " of the English government.
With the sanction of Mühlenberg back of it, this appeal
must have produced a thrill of enthusiasm among the German population. The volunteers of Pennsylvania were
called " Associators " ; those who were Germans had their
headquarters at the Lutheran schoolhouse in Philadelphia.

[1] Rosengarten, *The German Soldier in the Wars of the United States*, p. 29.
(Second edition, Lippincott, Philadelphia, 1890.)

There were very few German Tories in Pennsylvania, though there were many sectarians. One notable exception was, not the printer Sauer himself, but his two sons, who during the occupation of Philadelphia by General Howe published a newspaper voicing Tory sentiments. It was the only case on record of a German Tory paper printed in the colonies. Its influence could not have been of any importance at all, and its pages were perused more seriously abroad than on this side of the water. Schlözer prints a complete copy of one of the issues of the paper (May 6, 1778); it is a curious jumble of local items, advertisements, misstatements, and flamboyant verses.[1] The social condition of the Germans in the colonies forced them as a necessary consequence into the Democratic party. They were not members of families that had been in favor at court for generations; they were not owners of estates

[1] August Ludwig Schlözer's *Professors in Göttingen*, etc. *Briefwechsel, meisthistorischen u. politischen Inhalts*, Dritter Theil, Heft XVII, pp. 260–263. (Göttingen, 1778.) The paper is called a weekly: *Der Pennsylvanische Staats-Courier oder Einlaufende Wöchentliche Nachrichten*. Alle Wochen herausgegeben von Christoph Saur jun. und Peter Saur. Of curious interest are the verses describing a caricature of King George bending one knee before Washington and directed to bend the other, followed by an exhortation to loyalists : —

Der König liegt vor ihm (Washington), auf einem Knie gebogen.
Ist dieses würklich wahr ? Herr, es ist nicht gelogen ?
Und was noch ärger ist, er soll mit Fingern zeigen
Der König möge doch das andre Knie auch beigen.
Ist das nicht unverschämt ? den Frevel muss man strafen,
Heiszt das ein freies Volk ? Nein — Sie sind Congresz Sklaven.
Auf ! Auf ! ihr Britten auf ! Ihr Hessen frischen Mut !
Marschirt nur hurtig vor ; des Königs Sach steht gut ! etc.

An amusing couplet found in the same issue, written by some aspiring poetaster, called " Eine Satire," is as follows : —

Ich will — ich mag — ich kann nicht schweigen !
(Wiewohl ich weisz, die Thoren wollen mich nicht *gleichen*.)
(These verses are quoted as specimens, recommending the book of verse.)

that were gifts of the crown; they felt no national sentiments binding them to a British prince. They were men
who had hewn their own farms out of the wild forest, had
maintained their independence against its savage inhabitants, and now claimed as their own the soil on which
their battles had been won. Frontiersmen — and most of
the Germans were or had been such — gained from their
mode of life a degree of independence which often set
them in opposition to the policies of the seaboard. The
conservative easterly settlements were better satisfied with
the *status quo*, the frontiersmen looked beyond, aspired
to new conditions, and were ready to make a bold venture.
The frontier turned the balance toward independence.

In the opinion of John Adams, the people of New York
and Pennsylvania were very equally divided between the
Tory and Democratic parties, and nearly one third of the
whole population of the colonies, at the time of the Revolution, were Tories. "New York and Pennsylvania were so
nearly divided, if their propensity was not against us, that
if New England on one side and Virginia on the other
had not kept them in awe, they would have joined the
British."[1] This opinion was affirmed in a letter to Thomas
McKean, chief justice of Pennsylvania, sometime president of Congress, and signer of the Declaration of
Independence, who wrote in reply: "You say that about
one third of the people of the colonies were against the
Revolution. It required much reflection, before I could
fix my opinion on this subject; but on mature delibera·
tion I conclude you are right, and that more than one
third of influential characters were against it."[2] In subse·

[1] *Works of John Adams*, vol. x, p. 63. The letter is dated, "Quincy, 31
August, 1813."
[2] *Adams's Works*, vol. x, p. 110. (Letter to James Lloyd dated, "Quincy,
January, 1815.")

quent letters (1780) he speaks of the Tories as constituting not a twentieth of the population, which may mean that the Tories decreased in numbers as the war progressed. At the outbreak of the Revolution the Tories were undoubtedly more numerous; it would be no exaggeration to assume that, at the beginning, in New Jersey, Pennsylvania, and Delaware one third of the population were opposed to the war; in New York, Georgia, and the Carolinas, two fifths; in Maryland and Virginia, one sixth.[1] Moses Coit Tyler[2] says: "In Virginia, especially after hostilities began, the Tories were decidedly less in number than the Whigs. In North Carolina, the two parties were about evenly divided. In South Carolina, the Tories were the numerous party ; while in Georgia their majority was so great that, in 1781, they were preparing to detach that colony from the general movement of the rebellion." A Hessian officer,[3] writing from New Hampshire, estimated that the population was one sixth loyal, one sixth neutral, and two thirds rebel, agreeing with the estimate of Adams and McKean.

All contemporary accounts and sources of information seem to indicate that in the German population the proportion of Tories was by no means as great as the averages mentioned. There were a few loyal Germans serving under the Hessian colonel, Knyphausen, during his New Jersey campaign, but they would by no means represent

[1] Hanna, *The Scotch-Irish, or the Scotch in North Britain, North Ireland, and North America*, vol. i, p. 84.

[2] *American Historical Review*, vol. i, p. 28, "The Loyalists in the American Revolution " (pp. 24-45).

[3] He wrote from Castle Town, New Hampshire (now probably Castleton, Vermont), July 20, 1777. The style of the letter is such as to inspire confidence in the writer's statements. Printed in Schlözer's *Briefwechsel*, vol. iii, pp. 275-282. Schlözer's *Briefwechsel*, 1777-1782, contains many letters from Hessian officers serving in the American colonies during the Revolution.

one third or even one sixth of the German population. Benjamin Franklin, when queried before the English Parliament concerning the dissatisfaction of the Americans with the Stamp Act, was asked how many Germans there were in Pennsylvania. His answer was: "About one third of the whole population, but I cannot tell with certainty." Again the question was put whether a part of them had seen service in Europe. He answered, "Many, as well in Europe as in America." When asked whether they were as dissatisfied with the Stamp Tax as the native population, he said: "Yes, even more, and they are justified, because in many cases they must pay double for their stamp paper and parchments."

The German newspaper in Philadelphia called the "Staatsbote," published by Henry Miller, later the printer of Congress, was one of the papers that fanned the flames of rebellion.[1] In the conventions held in Philadelphia in June and July, 1774, and January, 1775, to adopt measures of sympathy and union with Massachusetts, the Germans were represented by Christopher Ludwig, Schlosser, Engel, and Hillegas; by Hubley, Barge, Rosz, Ferree, Slough (Schlauch), Erwin, Schultz, Potts, Küchlein, Arndt, Weitzel, Hasenclever, Melcher, Wagner, Graf, Kuhn, Eichelberger, Smyser, Levan, and Gehr, who were residents of Philadelphia and of the Pennsylvania German counties of Lancaster, Berks, Northampton, Northumberland, York, etc.[2] This representation shows that the

[1] His paper was read as far as the Valley of Virginia. Heinrich Ringer, at Winchester, and Jacob Nicolas at Peaked Mountain, Augusta County, were the agents of the paper. The edition of March 19, 1776, contains an appeal to the Germans beginning: "Remember that your forefathers immigrated to America to escape bondage and to enjoy liberty." *Virginia Magazine* vol. x, pp. 45 ff.

[2] Cf. Seidensticker, *Bilder aus der deutsch-Pennsylvanischen Geschichte*, p. 259. (New York, 1886.)

Germans were aggressive patriots at the very beginning of the Revolutionary movement.

Among the merchants of Philadelphia who fixed their signatures to the document bidding them to refrain from importing English goods, there were the Germans, Keppele (senior and junior), Steinmetz, Deschler, Wister (Daniel and John). "In the Valley of the Blue Ridge the German congregations, quickened by the preaching of Mühlenberg, were eager to take up arms."[1] Even before the outbreak of hostilities the Germans of the Valley of Virginia were among the first to adopt resolutions which smacked of treason to the British king. On June 16, 1774, a meeting took place at Woodstock, Virginia, in which initial revolutionary steps were taken. The Reverend Peter Mühlenberg was chosen moderator of the meeting, and afterwards chairman of the committee on resolutions. The resolutions were bolder than public opinion at that time was prepared to sanction. The following extracts show the spirit pervading them: —

That we will pay due submission to such acts of government as His Majesty has a right by law to exercise over his subjects, and to such only.

That it is the inherent right of British subjects to be governed and taxed by representatives chosen by themselves only, and that every act of the British Parliament respecting the internal policy of America is a dangerous and unconstitutional invasion of our rights and privileges.

That the enforcing the execution of said acts of Parliament by a military power will have a necessary tendency to cause a civil war, thereby dissolving that union, which has so long happily subsisted between the mother country and her colonies;

[1] George Bancroft, *History of the United States of America, from the Discovery of the Continent,* vol. iv, p. 318. The author's last revision. (N. Y. Appleton, 1884.)

and that we will most heartily and unanimously concur with our suffering brethren in Boston and every other part of North America, who are the immediate victims of tyranny, in promoting all proper measures to avert such dreadful calamities, to procure redress of our grievances, and to secure our common liberties.

The lovers of liberty closed by "pledging themselves to each other, to our country," and promising "inviolably to adhere to the votes of this day." The committee of safety and correspondence appointed for the county consisted of Peter Mühlenberg, chairman, Francis Slaughter, Abraham Bird, T. Beale, J. Tipton, and Abraham Bowman, at least half of whom were Germans.[1]

The British traveler Smyth,[2] while in Fredericktown, Maryland, in 1775, had some trouble with the armed "Associators." He had been invited before the Revolutionary committee, but preferred to leave town, going by way of Middletown and Funkstown to Hagerstown. Everywhere he found Germans, and he describes in a grotesque manner, how, after his first escape, he was seized again. "One said, 'Got tamn you, how darsht you make an exshkape from this honorable committish?' 'Fer flucht der dyvel,' cried another, 'how can you shtand so shtyff for King Shorsh akainst dish Koontery?' 'Sacramenter,' roars out another, 'dish committish will make

---

[1] These resolutions are printed in the *Virginia Magazine*, vol. x, p. 46. The editor of the magazine states that similar resolutions were adopted in meetings in Virginia, as follows: Fredericksburg, June 1 ; Prince William County, June 6 ; Frederick County, June 8 ; and then very shortly after occurred the meeting at Woodstock, June 16, 1774. The proceedings of the meeting are published in full in the *Virginia Gazette* for August 4, 1774 (Library of Congress). The spurious Mecklenburg (N. C.) declaration, it was claimed, occurred in May, 1775 (one year later).

[2] Smyth, *A Tour in the United States of America*, vol. ii, chapter lxv, pp. 274 ff. (London, 1784.)

Shorsh know how to behave himself'; and the butcher exclaimed, 'I would kill all de English tieves as soon as Ich would kill van ox or van cow.'" Smyth's experience, though his imitation of Pennsylvania German does not quite meet the rigorous demands of modern philology, proves at least that the Frederick County Germans were patriotic. The farmers and small tradesmen in the western counties were almost without exception favorable to the Revolutionary cause, a few exceptions to the contrary notwithstanding. What matters it if John Brake, an old German of considerable wealth on the South Fork of the South Branch, who had no friends but his gold-pieces, became a Tory from selfish interests? General Morgan soon took Brake prisoner and quartered his German sharpshooters at the old gentleman's house, to live on the best that his farm, mill, and distillery afforded. A few Germans in this section, who had become Tories, drawn over by the Scotchman, John Claypole, repented, and are known to have fought subsequently against Cornwallis at Yorktown.[1]

In North and South Carolina, where the Tories in many places outnumbered the Revolutionists, to be a patriot meant a greater risk or sacrifice. Many Germans in the central or western districts of those states suffered greatly from Tory raids.[2] Among the few Germans loyal to the crown probably the most noted was the Reverend John Joachim Zubly, for many years the most prominent Reformed minister in the South. He was educated in Switzerland and followed his father to America in 1774. In September, 1775, he was elected a member of the Con-

---

[1] *Virginia Magazine*, vol. x, p. 113.

[2] Cf. Bernheim, *History of the German Settlements, etc., in North and South Carolina*, pp. 269–273.

tinental Congress, but he turned Royalist, was expelled, and lost to memory.[1]

Concerning the Germans of Georgia we can say with assurance that by far the majority of them were patriotic, the German Tories amounting by no means to two fifths of the German population.[2] When in 1775 the provincials assembled in Savannah, to adopt measures to protect the province against the arbitrary legislation of the mother country, St. Matthew's parish was represented in that congress by the Salzburgers, — John Stirk, John Adam Treutlen, Jacob Waldhauer, John Flerl, and Christopher Cramer. An evidence of the prominence of the Salzburgers among the patriots of Georgia was the election of John Adam Treutlen to the office of provincial governor. In his youth Treutlen had been instructed by the worthy minister of the Salzburgers, the Reverend Mr. Bolzius, in Latin, French, English, and mathematics, and by virtue of his broad education and natural abilities he became the centre of influence in the German congregation. He was an opponent of the mischief-maker, the Reverend Mr. Triebner, and the most ardent supporter of the minister Rabenhorst in the church quarrel which the Reverend H. M. Mühlenberg arbitrated and settled. Among his own people and beyond he took a strong initiative for the party of liberty. In a commonwealth where there was much Toryism and neutrality he soon became the leading patriot. In May, 1777, the first legislative body of the state met in Savannah and under the new constitution Treutlen was elected the first governor. In the following year dictatorial powers were conferred upon him by act

[1] *Virginia Magazine*, vol. xi, p. 392, note.
[2] As estimated above, two fifths to one half the population of Georgia were Tories.

of the Georgia Council.[1] One of his appointees, Colonel Elbert, took possession of the fortress Frederica in April, 1778, a brilliant victory whereby two English warships and a large amount of supplies fell into the hands of the captors. The most prominent German Tory in this section, the Reverend Mr. Triebner, an old enemy of the governor, welcomed the British to Savannah and advised them to garrison Ebenezer. The home and farm of Treutlen were made a special object of vengeance, his movable property was confiscated, and his dwelling and stores were burned to the ground. He fled to Elbert County, and though fifty-three years of age[2] joined the army of General Wayne, and served throughout the war as quartermaster-general. Other Salzburgers prominent were Samuel Stirk, rebel secretary; William Holsendorf (Holzendorf), rebel councilor; John Stirk, rebel colonel; and many others who served under General Wayne in the war for independence. Among those notorious on the royalist side, for marauding parties, were the Germans Eischel and Dasher, whose evil work, however, was counterbalanced by the military services of the sons of Frederick Helfenstein, and of George Wysche, John Schneider, and other " proscribed rebels."

A number of German regiments were raised at the very beginning of the war for service wherever needed. Congress decided on May 22, 1776, to raise a German regiment, consisting of four companies levied in Pennsylvania and four in Maryland, to which, by resolution of July 9, 1777, was added a ninth company recruited from Pennsylvania. The officers and men were entirely German or of German

---

[1] Stevens's *History of Georgia*, vol. ii, pp. 300–301, 304.

[2] Treutlen was born, in 1726, at Berchtesgaden, in the Salzburg district.

descent.[1] The colonel of the regiment was originally Nicholas Haussegger, who was succeeded by Ludwig Weltner. The regiment was engaged in Sullivan's division during the New Jersey campaign and took part also in the latter's campaign against the Indians. The German regiment served also to protect the city of Philadelphia against the enemy and the disaffected during Howe's campaign in New Jersey; subsequently it joined Washington's army, taking part in the battle of Trenton that so revived the hopes of the patriotic party. The regiment took part also in the battles of Princeton and Brandywine, and spent the winter of 1777–78 at Valley Forge, suffering privations with the rest of the American army.

The regiment called Armand's Legion was originally recruited by Baron von Ottendorff as a troop of light infantry, but on account of the need of well-disciplined cavalry, it was changed into a dragoon corps. Ottendorff was from Saxony and had served in the Seven Years' War under Frederick the Great. He was directed by Congress December 5, 1776, to raise an independent corps of one hundred and fifty, of which he was put in command with the rank of major. His command was filled in Pennsylvania and remained in service from 1777 to 1780, when it was merged into Armand's Legion, while Ottendorff is supposed to have returned to Europe.[2] This happened after the battle of Savannah, in which Pulaski suffered death, and in which Ottendorff's company also met many losses in the

---

[1] Cf. Rosengarten, pp. 100–101. Also *Pennsylvania in the Revolution, 1775–1783*, 2 vols. (Harrisburg, 1880.) Edited by Linn and Engle. Full lists of officers and men serving in Continental forces are there given. For a list of the captains and lieutenants see Seidensticker, pp. 263-264. The first, third, fifth, seventh, and ninth companies were Pennsylvanians. Maryland deserves great credit for furnishing so large a proportion, four ninths of the regiment.

[2] Rosengarten, pp. 103–104.

attack. Schott's dragoons, recruited in the Pennsylvania-German districts, were also for a time in Armand's Legion. The regiment did gallant service in the South, at Yorktown, and at the siege of New York. Several hundred names of officers and men belonging to this regiment are given in "Der deutsche Pionier."[1] The same source-book for German-American history gives the names of hundreds of soldiers who served during the Revolution in the Continental regiments I to XIII of Pennsylvania.[2]

One of the interesting facts concerning the military history of the Revolution is that Washington's body-guard was largely made up of Germans. There had been Tories, or at least suspects, in the first body-guard appointed, and plots were revealed by which the person of the commander-in-chief was to be seized. On the advice of Washington's private secretary and adjutant, Reed, who was of German descent,[3] a troop was formed consisting entirely of Germans, called the Independent Troop of Horse, and placed under the command of Major Barth. Van Heer, a Prussian, who had served as cavalry lieutenant under Frederick the Great in the Seven Years' War. Of Washington's good opinion of German soldiers we find a proof in his letter to the president of Congress, dated June 30, 1776 :[4] " The battalion of Germans which Congress has ordered to be raised will be a corps of much service, and I am hopeful that such per-

[1] Vol. viii, pp. 450–456.

[2] *Der deutsche Pionier*, vol. viii, pp. 133–142, 181–187, 275–282, 333–336 (Seventh Continental Regiment of Pennsylvania, formerly the Sixth Battalion, Dr. William Irvine, commander, under whom served Rose, mentioned below), 496–499; vol. ix, pp. 276–278, 329–333; vol. x, pp. 158–161. The lists were verified by comparison with the statistics of the Pension Bureau at Washington. The investigation was made by H. A. Rattermann, editor of *Der deutsche Pionier*.

[3] *Der deutsche Pionier*, vol. vii, p. 217.

[4] *American Archives*, series ix, vol. vi, p. 1142.

sons will be appointed officers as will complete their enlistment with all possible expedition."

Van Heer recruited most of his men in the Pennsylvania German counties, Berks and Lancaster. They began to serve in the spring of 1778, and were honorably discharged at the end of the war, twelve of them serving longer than any other American soldiers, having the honor of escorting the commander-in-chief to his home at Mount Vernon. These twelve men each received presents of arms, accoutrements, and a horse, as we learn from a written record in the possession of the family of one of the twelve, Ludwig Boyer, discharged December 10, 1783.[1] Washington's mounted body-guard consisted of fourteen officers and fifty-three men, nearly all Germans,[2] — exclusively Germans, according to the testimony of Colonel John Johnson, sometime president of the Historical and Philosophical Society of Ohio, and personal friend of Washington.[3] In the pension lists of 1828 a number of names of soldiers belonging to Van Heer's troop are given. Boyer was granted a pension, one hundred pounds annually; Jacob Fox (Fuchs), who had lost his discharge, brought as witnesses two former comrades, Burckhardt and Trischer,

[1] The descendants of Boyer lived in Piqua, Ohio. The discharge of Boyer was in the handwriting of Washington's aide-de-camp, David Cobb. Most discharges were printed formulas. A facsimile of the original is found in *Der deutsche Pionier*, vol. vii, p. 469. The father of Ludwig Boyer (or Beyer) was a Palatine or Rhine Hessian, who landed in Philadelphia in 1752 and settled in Berks County.

[2] Rosengarten, p. 139.

[3] Colonel John Johnson was by birth an Irishman, who came to the United States after the Revolution. He seems to have had no reason for a prejudiced view. His acquaintance with Washington and distinguished men of the Revolutionary period gives his statements some weight. He said that not a single officer or soldier of this troop understood a word of English, and that it was commanded by Major Van Heer, a Prussian. For a discussion of the whole subject, see *Der deutsche Pionier*, vol. vii, pp. 215–221, and 469–485 (Rattermann).

who both swore that they had belonged to Van Heer's corps and that that troop was the body-guard of Washington.

As representatives of two classes of German patriots, differing as to origin and social position, but one in motive and enthusiasm, there may be selected the two men, Peter Mühlenberg and Christopher Ludwig (Ludwick). The former, born in America, educated in Germany, the eldest son of the patriarch of the Lutheran Church, Henry Melchior Mühlenberg, was destined to hold high offices in military and civil affairs; the other, born in Germany, without the advantages of scholarly training, but beaten about in the world until matured and ripened, was a representative of the sturdy middle-class element among the Germans, that sometimes causes amusement by its foreign smack, but has frequently inspired admiration for its old-fashioned virtue and power.

Peter Mühlenberg was destined by his father for the ministry, and was sent to Halle as a student of theology. But there flowed in Peter's veins the blood not only of the ministerial Henry Melchior Mühlenberg, but that also of the adventure-loving Conrad Weiser.[1] In Mühlenberg's family there were also some soldier ancestors. The inclinations of Peter therefore swerved between the serious purpose of the preacher and the danger-haunted life of the soldier. Being born under a lucky star, it happened that he was able to gratify his tastes for both vocations. His father had misgivings when the young man preached his first sermon, and well he might, for Peter had not been an ideal student, — but the elders of the church grouped about his father afterwards, congratulating him upon the initial achievement of his son. Peter accepted

---

[1] His mother was a daughter of Conrad Weiser.

a call in 1772 to the Lutheran church at Woodstock, in the Shenandoah Valley. His frank and manly bearing made friends within the congregation and without. An intimacy arose with Patrick Henry and Colonel George Washington. With the former he laid deep plans of sedition, with the latter he shot bucks in the Blue Ridge Mountains.

Peter Mühlenberg was made the chairman of the Committee of Safety and Correspondence in Dunmore County, within which Woodstock was located. In the state's convention of 1774 at Williamsburg, and in the next session at Richmond in March, 1775, he supported Patrick Henry eloquently and gave assurance of the support of his large constituency in the Valley. Patrick Henry renewed his motion of arming the province of Virginia, and Mühlenberg seconded him. In accordance with the wishes of Washington and Patrick Henry, Mühlenberg was put in command of the Eighth Virginia Regiment. The German-Americans, Abraham Bowman and Peter Helfenstein, were his lieutenant-colonel and major respectively. Quite typical of Peter Mühlenberg was the little romance connected with his last sermon. The news that the favorite minister was to preach his last sermon brought crowds of hearers from far and near, filling not only the church, but also the churchyard roundabout. It was in January, 1776, when the atmosphere was charged with potentialities. At the close of his sermon the minister spoke of the duties we owe our country, saying with a fervor born of conviction that "there was a time for preaching and praying, but also a time for battle, and that such a time had now arrived." He pronounced the benediction, then threw off his clerical robe, and behold, minister no more, he stood in the uniform of a colonel of the Continental Army. As he slowly descended from the pulpit the drums were beaten outside the church, for the mustering of soldiers in the cause of freedom. Enthusiasm blazed up spontaneously, carrying men away to a step before which they had long hesitated and trembled. Three hundred recruits were at once taken into the regiment of Mühlenberg, and on the following day the numbers increased to over four hundred.

The regiment of Mühlenberg was always more numerous than others, and its colonel was chosen several times to restore the numbers of other colonial regiments. His regiment was first used in South Carolina, then brought to the North. On February 21, 1777, Congress raised Colonel Mühlenberg to the rank of brigadier-general, in command of the First, Fifth, Ninth, and Thirteenth Virginia regiments. Mühlenberg's and Weedon's (Wieden's) brigade formed General Greene's division, distinguished for bravery and discipline in the battles of Brandywine and Germantown. At Brandywine Mühlenberg's brigade was used by General Greene in his famous manœuvre, covering the retreat of the American army, and preventing its annihilation by Cornwallis. It was a difficult position to hold, against picked Hessian troops and the Guard regiments of the British. At the battle of Germantown Mühlenberg's division divided the right wing of the enemy in a brilliant bayonet attack; the errors of that unfortunate battle were made in other quarters. The regiment was at Valley Forge during the winter, and subsequently sustained its good reputation in the battle of Monmouth.[1]

Christopher Ludwig was an aggressive advocate of the Revolution. From the very first he maintained, in popular meetings, that no compromise measures would be effective,

[1] Mühlenberg's operations in the South will be mentioned below.

and spoke for war with England even if it be one of long duration. When Governor Mifflin made a motion that a collection be made for the purchase of arms and ammunition, and several voices were heard in opposition, Ludwig rose and said in badly accented but very plain English: "Mr. President, I am of course only a poor gingerbread baker, but write me down for two hundred pounds." Ludwig's move closed the debate and the proposition was adopted unanimously. In the summer of 1776, though fifty-five years of age, Ludwig became a volunteer in the militia. He was well acquainted with the soldier's and sailor's life, for he had served against the Turks in Austria, had been in the army of Frederick the Great, then with the English in the East Indies, and from 1745 on, he had been for seven years at sea. He had settled in Philadelphia since 1754 and had followed the trade of a baker, which he had learned in his native city of Giessen. He was tall in stature, erect in carriage and of commanding presence, so that he was nick-named the "Governor of Laetitia Court" (where his Philadelphia bakery was located). He impressed his fellow men at once with his capacity for managing affairs. He was a member of the "Powder Committee," as we know from his advertisement for a man "skilled in the art of manufacturing powder." In May, 1777, Congress appointed Ludwig superintendent of bakers and director of baking for the entire army.[1] It was demanded of him to furnish one hundred pounds of bread for every one hundred pounds of flour. "No," said he, "Christopher Ludwig does not wish to become rich by the war. He has enough. Out of one hundred pounds of flour one gets one hundred and thirty-five pounds of

[1] With the salary of seventy-five dollars a month and a daily supply of two rations. Two rations presumably for himself and his wife.

bread,[1] and so many will I give." His predecessors, grafters of an early day, had always given themselves the benefit of the ignorance of the legislators. General Washington was in the habit of referring to Ludwig as his "honest friend." Meeting difficulties in securing men to help him, Ludwig was sent to Philadelphia by order of the commander-in-chief to apply to the supreme executive council of Pennsylvania to furnish him with such number of journeymen bakers out of the militia as he might want. One of Ludwig's notable achievements was the prompt execution of Washington's order, immediately after the surrender at Yorktown, to bake bread for the army of Cornwallis; Ludwig baked six thousand pounds of bread in one day. In the company of officers Ludwig showed good humor and wit. A beautiful punch-bowl of porcelain, which he had brought from Canton, China, served the officers on festive occasions. Washington is said to have drunk many a toast from it, and was fond of closing with the couplet, "Health and long life, to Christopher Ludwig and his wife."

The occupation of Philadelphia by the British inflicted heavy losses upon Ludwig, as also upon the printer Miller and other "notorious" rebels.[2] Ludwig recovered, however, after the war, and when he died in 1809, eighty-one years of age, he left several bequests, — not large, to be sure, according to modern standards, but very well be-

---

[1] The added water increases the weight.

[2] The printing-press and property of Heinrich Miller (printer of Congress) were confiscated. The British robbed the house of Jacob Schreiner, a member of the Revolutionary Committee, destroyed the sugar refinery of David Schäffer (senior and junior, father-in-law and brother-in-law respectively of F. A. Mühlenberg), plundered the house of the Reverend Mr. Schlatter in Chestnut Hill, and damaged the property of the following Germans: Keppele, Kuhn, Hogner, Zautzinger, Bärtch, Sprögel, Eckert, Graff, Gressler, and Knorr, most of whom were well-to-do merchants of Philadelphia.

stowed. His benefactions were extended to the Deutsche Gesellschaft, the University of Pennsylvania, and to two churches that were to award the income to poor children. The residue of his estate, three thousand pounds, was given to found a free school, which in 1872 was named in his honor Ludwick's Institute.[1]

The German settlements in the Mohawk Valley and the Schoharie district suffered more from Indian attacks during the Revolution than any other frontier area. They were the outposts of American civilization in the territory of the Six Nations, the most warlike of all the Indian tribes. The Six Nations had for the most part been friendly during the French and Indian War; now the English had succeeded in persuading them that their king across the water was the stronger master, and in consequence they served the English. An additional incentive was the great opportunity for rewards from the British, combined with the certainty of plunder from the colonists. The English at one time placed a price of eight dollars upon every scalp brought in. The rich farms and fat herds of the Mohawk and Schoharie valleys were their legitimate prey, if the Indians chose to join in the war against the American colonies.

The family of Sir William Johnson, in Tryon County, who had been so influential in keeping the Indians loyal during the French and Indian War, now became Tories, and carried the Indians of their section with them. Sir William Johnson had married the sister of the Indian chief Brant, whom he had given a good school education.[2]

---

[1] Dr. Benjamin Rush thought Ludwig worthy of a biography by his own distinguished pen: *Life of Ludwick*. (Philadelphia, 1801; reprinted, 1831.) Cf. also *Der deutsche Pionier*, vol. viii, pp. 18–25; and Seidensticker, *Bilder aus der deutsch-pennsylvanischen Geschichte*, pp. 261–262.

[2] Brant was sent to the school of Dr. Wheelock, of Lebanon, Connecticut.

Captain Joseph Brant became the scourge of the Mohawk Valley, and the Schoharie district. He was superior in intelligence to his own tribe and to a large portion of the frontiersmen, and was one of the most terrible foes the frontiersmen at any time or place had the ill fortune to encounter.

The Germans of the Mohawk Valley could not wait until they might receive aid from the New York state government. The Committee of Safety in Tryon County organized four battalions in the summer of 1775. All four of the colonels were Germans, Nicholas Herkimer (Herckheimer), commanding the first battalion (Canajoharie), Jacob Klock the second (Palatine district), Frederick Fisher the third (Mohawk), and Hanjost Herckheimer the fourth (German Flats and Kingsland).[1] The whole force was put under the command of Nicholas Herkimer, who by pressure and persuasion made the whole district loyal to the American cause.

In the middle of June, 1777, General Burgoyne began his march from Canada. He wished to cut off the New England states from the rest of the colonies by establishing a line from Lake Champlain down the Hudson to New York. He was to be aided by a British expedition up the Hudson from New York. Colonel St. Leger was to come from the westward, joining Burgoyne at Albany, after having subdued the whole of the Mohawk Valley and robbed it of its rich harvests, which were to supply Burgoyne's army with food. St. Leger left Montreal about the end of July, and on the third of August ar-

His Indian name was Thay-en-da-ne-gea, signifying a bundle of sticks, the symbol of strength.

[1] Kapp, *Geschichte der Deutschen im Staate New York*, pp. 239 ff. (New York, 1867), furnishes a list of all the staff and company officers; almost all were Germans.

rived in the neighborhood of the present city of Rome, on the narrow plateau which forms the watershed between the Hudson and St. Lawrence.

In the mean time General Herkimer had summoned to arms all the men, between sixteen and sixty years of age, in Tryon County; even the members of the Committee of Safety were not excused from service in the ranks. Four battalions, about eight hundred men, under the commanders named, advanced in the direction of Fort Stanwix (its location was near what is now Rome), where a garrison had been stationed under Colonel Gansevoort. The latter had with him about six to seven hundred men, and had put the fort into a condition of defense. General St. Leger, after surrounding Fort Stanwix, demanded its surrender, and was greatly surprised when he met a stern refusal. The militia under Herkimer crossed the Mohawk at Fort Schuyler (the present Utica), and on the evening of the fifth of August encamped near the confluence of the Oriska and the Mohawk, where Oriskany is now located. The inexperienced troops were aflame with eager desire to meet the enemy. The general, who had experienced the dangers of border fighting in the French and Indian War, wisely advised caution, and wished to select a secure position in which to wait for an attack. Just as Daniel Boone's advice a few years later was scorned before the disastrous battle of the Blue Licks,[1] and the Kentucky militia, inflamed by Major McGarry's taunts, advanced contrary to Boone's wishes, so here the undisciplined bravado of the raw militia could not be restrained. The brave commander was denounced as a coward and Tory by his brother officers, Fischer (Visscher), Cox, and Paris,

[1] Cf. Roosevelt, *The Winning of the West*, vol. ii, pp. 200–201. The battle was fought August 19, 1782.

who carried the eager masses with them. "I am placed over
you as a father and guardian," said Herkimer calmly,
"and I will not lead you into difficulties from which I
may not be able to extricate you." But the confusion and
dissatisfaction becoming unbearable, Herkimer exclaimed,
"If you will have it so, the blood be upon your heads,"
and yielding, he gave the command to move on.[1]

Colonel St. Leger had received information concerning
the approach of General Herkimer and preferred to meet
him in the field rather than await him. He detached
eighty men of Sir John Johnson's Royal Greens under
Major Watts (Sir John's brother-in-law), and the entire
body of Indians under Joseph Brant, the whole under the
command of Johnson, to intercept Herkimer's approach.
On the advice of Brant the plan followed was to draw the
Americans into an ambuscade. A position was selected,
admirably adapted for this purpose, about two miles west
from Oriskany, and about six miles distant from Fort
Stanwix. The road led through a ravine, and sloped to a
swamp bottom, that was made passable only by a corduroy
road, constructed for the benefit of supply-wagons going
to Fort Stanwix. On the other side the road sloped upward
and opened toward the west. The country on either side
was wooded and afforded good opportunities for observing
the corduroy road. About eleven o'clock in the morning,
Herkimer, riding at the head of his column on a white
horse, reached the ravine. His people followed him slowly,
going into the ravine and deliberately ascending the western height where Herkimer waited for them.

The small force had in part ascended the western slope,

[1] Cf. W. M. Reid, *The Mohawk Valley, Its Legends and its History* (The
Knickerbocker Press, N. Y. 1901), p. 418. A good description of the battle
follows, pp. 419–429.

THE HAND TO HAND CONFLICT

HERKIMER DIRECTING THE ORISKANY BATTLE

BAS-RELIEFS FROM THE ORISKANY MONUMENT

a greater part was still in the ravine, while the baggage-train had just entered. Only the rear guard, consisting of Colonel Fischer's regiment, was still on the eastern slope. Suddenly at a given signal the Tories and Indians broke forth from the forests and thick brushwood, and with tremendous noise and hideous yells fell upon the unsuspecting militiamen. As Herkimer had predicted, Colonel Fischer and his men were seized with a panic and made a hasty retreat, deserting the baggage-train and the rest of the force of Herkimer, whom they had so loudly denounced as cowards.

Though taken by surprise, Herkimer's men rallied under his noble example, and after firing their guns, met the onslaught of the Indians with their knives and the butts of their guns. Noticing that the firing from along the eastern slopes of the ravine was irregular, the commander ordered Colonel Bellinger and the soldiers who had not yet crossed the causeway to retake the hill. Dashing through the hail of lead on both flanks the stalwart Palatine Germans stormed the hillside, firing to kill as they went. Regaining the hilltop they formed into circular squads, leaving the bottom of the fatal ravine to the dead and dying and the prowling savages with painted skins, who were in search of scalps and plunder. It was about noon, after Herkimer had succeeded in getting the regiment stationed in some sort of order on the plateau, when he was hit below the knee by a bullet which shattered his leg and killed his horse. Immediately he had his saddle brought to the foot of a large beech tree, and taking his seat upon it, directed the fight from that position. He lighted his pipe and continued to order the progress of the battle with firmness and composure, until the final retreat of the enemy. The tactics on either side varied, in formation and style, from fighting under cover to bayonet attacks in mass. The Palatines grouped around their leader at the vantage-point on the plateau, and resisted every charge with dauntless courage.

The day had been hot and sultry, the distant rumblings, indications of a coming storm, had not been heard amid the roar of battle. So intent were the contestants upon the struggle that they did not take notice of the thunderstorm until it broke forth with great violence. The heavy downpour of rain, the swaying of the trees in the wind, and the great darkness arrested the work of death for about an hour. But hardly had the skies become clear again when the rage of battle once more rivaled the fury of the elements. The pause was of advantage to the Palatines. They recovered their composure completely, had kept their powder dry and reloaded their guns. Herkimer again showed his skill in tactics. He had noticed that the Indians always watched the tree from which a shot came and immediately afterwards leaped toward it in order to tomahawk the marksman before he could reload. Herkimer now placed two men behind each tree. As soon as one had shot his gun, the other was ready with his, giving the first man time to reload. The second man regularly shot the approaching Indian. In this manner the Indians began to suffer severe losses, causing their courage to droop and dwindle. Heavy punishment the Indians could never endure, and as soon as it occurred they became disheartened.

Johnson's Royal Greens now hastened to repair the losses sustained. A large number of the Royalists were recognized as former residents of the Mohawk Valley, former neighbors now met face to face as enemies. The contest grew in bitterness and stubbornness. The rage of the patriots increased to white heat as they recalled what they had suffered from Tory treachery. The terrible hand-to-hand struggle lasted longer than half an hour, until the Royalists were gradually pushed backward. Colonel Cox fell during this close fighting; his clear commanding voice had long overtopped the hissing of the rifle-balls, and the wild battle-cry of the Indians. His loss was balanced by the loss of Major Watts and many others of the Royal Greens. Suddenly the thundering of cannons was heard from the direction of Fort Stanwix, and the British, fearing to be attacked in the rear, left the battle-field in possession of the brave peasants of Tryon County. The sortie from the fort was due to a plan of Herkimer's. He had sent a messenger to Gansevoort, directing him to attack the British force in the rear at the same moment when he himself should meet the enemy in the front. The messenger, however, did not arrive at the fort until one o'clock in the afternoon, having with difficulty eluded capture. Gansevoort at once sent Lieutenant-Colonel Willet forward with two hundred and fifty men. They attacked the camp of General Johnson, took possession of his baggage and papers, captured five British flags, and all the presents which had been intended for the Indians. Hearing that Herkimer's advance had been arrested, they retreated to the fort without loss.

The effect of this sortie was of great importance. In the first place it decided the retreat of the British force, and in the second it increased the discontent of the Indians. They had sustained the loss of a large number of their chiefs and best warriors, and now, on returning to camp, they found themselves deprived of all their comforts. Being accustomed to go into battle naked, and finding no blankets, they suffered severely from cold during the night, and even the tortures of their prisoners could not comfort them in their misery. To revenge themselves they plundered the baggage of English officers and took possession of the boats on Wood Creek. The battle of Oriskany thoroughly discouraged and demoralized the Indians and made them unfit as allies. When they returned to their villages they mourned the loss of their chiefs, and whatever presents they had received did not appear to them an adequate compensation.

The losses of the Palatines were great also, to be sure. About two hundred, one fourth of the number that had gone into battle, had been slain or were severely wounded. Colonels F. Bellinger and Cox, Majors Eisenlord, Klappsattel, and Van Slyck, Captain Helmer, and Lieutenant Petrie were among the dead. Most of the subaltern officers were killed, some captured with Colonel Bellinger and Major Frey. There was hardly a house in the Valley which was not put into mourning by the death of a father, brother, or son.

The English force retreated toward Fort Stanwix, to which they laid siege. On the day after the battle Willet and Stockwell stole through the besieging force and brought news to General Schuyler. Arnold was sent to the assistance of Gansevoort with a handful of regulars and a number of volunteers collected in the Mohawk Valley. Extravagant reports being spread about in the camp of the British, concerning the size of the reinforcements, a panic seized the camp of St. Leger, aggravated no doubt by the restlessness of the Indian allies. On August 22, 1777, St. Leger hastily raised the siege, leaving his tents and ammunition behind.

The most severe loss to the patriot cause was the death of General Herkimer, which followed shortly after the battle. He had paid little attention to his wounds, attending to the business of reorganizing the militia, until nine days after the battle, when his leg had to be amputated. It was done in the most unskillful manner, the leg being cut off square without allowing flesh enough below the bone to cover the wound. Colonel Willett called to see him soon after the operation and found him sitting up in his bed, cheerful as ever, smoking his pipe. A hemorrhage followed, and toward evening of the same day Herkimer felt that his end was near. He called for his Bible, and in the presence of his family read the thirty-eighth Psalm. His voice gradually grew weaker, the book slipped from his fingers, and death overtook him.[1] "It was Herkimer," said George Washington, "who first reversed the gloomy scene" of the Northern campaign. The pure-minded hero of the Mohawk Valley "served from love of country, not for reward. He did not want a Continental command or money." "Before Congress[2] had decided how to manifest their gratitude he died of his wound; and they decreed him a monument. Gansevoort was rewarded by a vote of thanks and a command; Willett, by public praise and an 'elegant sword.'"

The results of the battle of Oriskany were far greater than the small number of men engaged might indicate. Had not the Palatines of the Mohawk Valley stopped the advance of St. Leger, the rich harvests of their farms would have been used to feed the army of Burgoyne. St. Leger's auxiliary forces, with the Mohawk Valley

[1] Nicholas Herkimer (correctly spelled Nikolaus Herckheimer), though twice married, had no children. He was very wealthy and left his estate to his relatives, who were numerous and influential in the valley. In the genealogical work of P. S. Cowen, *The Herkimers and Schuylers*, an historical sketch of the two families with genealogies, etc., the descendants of George Herkimer (the ancestor who arrived in 1721 from the Palatinate) are enumerated.

[2] Bancroft, vol. v, p. 170.

accessible to them, would probably have prevented Burgoyne's surrender. The other far-reaching result was the effect the battle had on the Indians. They had not expected such obstinate resistance nor such severe losses. They grew discontented with their allies, the British, and the latter considered their Indian allies a failure. Official information went home to the effect that the red men "treacherously committed ravages upon their friends; they could not be controlled; they killed their captives; that there was infinite difficulty to manage them; that they grew more and more unreasonable and importunate." [1]

During the whole of 1777 and until the summer of 1778, the Valley of the Mohawk was not troubled by the Indians and Tories. The farmers could peacefully till their fields and bring in their harvests. But their repose and unpreparedness invited new troubles. The numbers in the militia companies had shrunk since the battle of Oriskany from nine to seven companies. Fort Stanwix lay thirty miles distant from the last German settlements, so that it could easily be passed by small war-parties. An enemy like Joseph Brant, the Mohawk chieftain, was quick to see the defenseless condition of the Valley and arouse in his warriors their natural lust for booty. Even when subsequently Fort Stanwix was given up, and the main defensive strength was placed in Fort Dayton (the present Herkimer), Brant, who knew every trail and opening in the Valley, could easily pass in and out as he pleased. The Mohawk chief opened hostilities in 1778, attacking the small settlement of Andrustown, in the southeastern part of present Herkimer County. Four men were killed, others led off captive. The inhabitants of the German Flats

[1] Bancroft, vol. v, p. 170.

started in pursuit, but succeeded only in taking revenge upon a Tory friend of Brant. The next expedition, more ambitious, was directed against the German Flats, protected on the north side by Fort Dayton and on the south by Fort Herkimer. The German Flats were at that time inhabited by about one thousand Palatines, men, women, and children. They were no match, however, for the large band of Tories and Indians mustered by Brant. The settlers had just gathered in their harvests, an opportune moment chosen by Brant for his attack. Three of the four messengers whom the Germans had stationed as scouts were killed, and only one, Helmer, brought the news of Brant's approach. The attack was so sudden that the settlers could only retreat hastily to their forts, leaving their possessions a prey to the marauders. Sixty-three houses, seventy-five barns, three grist-mills, and two saw-mills with their contents were set on fire by the invaders, who drove off with them two hundred and thirty-five horses, two hundred and twenty-nine head of cattle, two hundred and sixty-nine sheep, and ninety-three oxen. Brant did not attack the forts, and escaped as suddenly as he had come, eluding the three to four hundred soldiers who started in pursuit. This story of sudden attack, robbery, and escape was repeated month after month and year after year along the whole frontier of New York. No help was received of an effective kind until the punitive expedition under Sullivan devastated the villages of the Six Nations. This happened in 1779 after the Wyoming massacre[1] (July 3, 1778) in

---

[1] One of the German settlers of Wyoming County was Judge Matthew Hollenbach. He refused offers of British agents to play the traitor, and joined the patriot army as lieutenant in New Jersey. He was very successful in getting recruits from the Wyoming Valley. At the time of the massacre of the Wyoming settlers Hollenbach suffered severe property losses. Cf. *Der deutsche Pionier*, vol. i, pp. 262 ff.

Pennsylvania, and that of Cherry Valley (December 10, 1778) in Otsego County, New York. In both of these massacres the German settlers suffered with the rest.[1] It would be wearisome to rehearse the agonizing details of border warfare on the Mohawk.[2] A striking proof of the monstrous cruelty of the Indians at this time, and of the stoic sufferings of the frontier settlers during the Revolutionary War, is furnished by the following inventory of scalps taken by the Seneca Indians, which accidentally fell into American hands.[3] There were eight items as follows: Lot 1, forty-three scalps of soldiers of Congress killed in battle, also sixty-two scalps of farmers who had been killed in their houses; lot 2, ninety-eight scalps of farmers killed in their houses surprised by day, not by night as the first lot. The red color applied to the hoops of wood, which were used to stretch the scalp, indicated the difference; lot 3 contained ninety-seven scalps of farmers killed in their fields, different colors denoting whether killed by tomahawk or rifle-ball; lot 4 contained one hundred and two scalps of farmers, most of them young men; lot 5 contained eighty-eight scalps of women, those with blue hoops cut from the heads of mothers; lot 6 contained one hundred and ninety-three scalps of boys of different ages killed with clubs or hatchets, some with knives or bullets; lot 7 contained two hundred and eleven scalps of girls, large and small; and lot 8, one hundred and twenty-two scalps of various

[1] In 1769 there were about forty or fifty families, mostly of those called Scotch-Irish, and as many more in the vicinity consisting of Germans and others. See "Four Great Rivers," the *Journal of Richard Smith*, 1769. Edited by F. W. Halsey. (New York: Scribner's Sons, 1906.)

[2] Kapp, *Geschichte der Deutschen im Staate New York*, chap. xii, pp. 255–279, gives a very good account of this terrible struggle, basing it upon authentic records.

[3] Kapp, *supra*, pp. 276–279. Based on Campbell's *Annals of Tryon County*, pp. 67–70 (appendix).

kinds, among them twenty-nine babes' scalps carefully stretched on small white hoops. The entire bundle, including the total of 1062 scalps, fell into the hands of a New England expedition against the Indians, and a prayer was found, accompanying the inventory, addressed to the British governor (Haldimand): "Father, we wish that you send these scalps to the Great King that he may look at them and be refreshed at their sight — recognize our fidelity and be convinced that his presents have not been bestowed upon a thankless people." The scalps represented the work of the three years preceding February, 1782, and were taken from the frontier settlers of New England, New York, Pennsylvania, and Virginia.[1]

Among the numerous stories of heroism on the frontier there is none more memorable than that told of Johann Christian Schell. He lived with his wife and six sons about three miles to the northeast of Fort Dayton, in what was called Schell's Bush. It was in August, 1781, when most settlers had retreated for safety to the forts, or to more easterly settlements. He decided to breast the storm, relying upon his sure eye and brave arm. Schell's blockhouse was strong, well built, and well adapted for defense against ordinary attacks. His house was stored with weapons and ammunition. He was at work in the field with his sons one day when the enemy appeared. The two youngest sons, twins eight years of age, could not follow their father and elder brothers fast enough, were taken captive, and dragged off to Canada. It was two o'clock in the afternoon when about forty-eight Indians and sixteen Tories attacked the house. Their leader was Donald Mac-

---

[1] Cf. Kapp, p. 278. Kapp and others were misled by this newspaper account long believed to be authentic, but proved to be an invention of Benjamin Franklin. See note to this page in the *Appendix*.

Donald. While Schell and his four sons shot off their rifles, his wife reloaded them. Almost every shot hit its mark, but the enemy were so numerous as not to feel their losses. Finally MacDonald himself succeeded in reaching the door, which he tried to pry open with a lever. During the attempt he was shot in the leg. Quick as a flash Schell unbolted the door and pulled the wounded captain into his house. This success rescued the besieged from the danger of fire, for MacDonald would in such an event have been burned also. MacDonald's ammunition also fell into the hands of Schell, which was fortunate, for he had only a few shots left. The last effort of the enemy having failed, the brave family were given a respite from their bloody labors. While father and sons were getting their rifles ready for another attack, the mother began to sing the battle hymn of the Reformation, "A Mighty Fortress is our God." The men fell in and Luther's martial hymn echoed through the woods with tremendous power. The words—

> "Und wenn die Welt voll Teufel wär,
> Und wollt uns gar verschlingen,
> So fürchten wir uns nicht so sehr,
> Es muss uns doch gelingen!" —

inspired them to their last great effort. The Tories and Indians now pushed some of their guns through the shot-holes of the house, at a moment when the men had withdrawn to load. The courageous mother, seeing the danger, seized an axe and struck in upon the guns, bending their bores, and giving her men time to reload. Darkness soon set in, and the besieged family sang with lusty voices, as if they were confident relief were coming from the neighboring Fort Dayton. The attacking party, not being able to see through the woods, and discouraged by the loss of their leader, withdrew into the forest, taking with them the two youngest sons of Schell. During the night the latter with his family wisely withdrew to Fort Dayton. The next morning MacDonald was brought into the fort and remained a hostage for the two sons. This courageous defense, with its inspiring singing, stands out as one of the bright spots in the long tale of suffering which the Mohawk settlers were called upon to endure. Not always was bravery so well rewarded. Even Schell himself, a year later, died from the effects of a wound received from another marauding party of Indians.

As a result of the constant border fighting, the Palatines of the Mohawk and Schoharie sections became skillful in the methods of Indian warfare.[1] Individuals who gained a reputation throughout the state for their prowess as Indian fighters and hunters were Johann Adam Hartman, Timothy Murphy, Nicholas Stoner, and Nathaniel Foster. Hartman was born in 1743 at Edenkoben, in the Palatinate. There, when arrested for poaching, giant that he was, he struck down the officers that apprehended him and fled to America. Hunter and trapper, best shot of the Mohawk Valley, he became the most fearless of the Indian fighters at the opening of the Revolutionary War. He was looked upon as the defender of the settlements, and though without house and home himself, he was welcome everywhere. The lonely farmer knew that when Hans Adam (Hartman) was around, he could work in the fields without danger, mothers could do their housework with-

---

[1] Cf. Jephtha R. Simms, *History of Schoharie County and Border Wars of New York*, etc. (Albany, 1845.) Also F. Kapp, *Die Deutschen im Staate New York*, chap. 12, "Für Haus und Hof," pp. 255–279. Also Jephtha R. Simms, *Trappers of New York, or a Biography of Nicholas Stoner and Nathaniel Foster, together with anecdotes of other celebrated hunters, and some account of Sir William Johnson and his style of life.* (Albany, 1850.)

out anxiety, and children play unharmed before the block-house. If danger approached, the crack of Hans Adam's rifle would give warning, his unerring eye and sinewy arm afforded protection. True, he was not of the law-abiding sort, but the cause of the settler was a law unto him. He died a cripple at the great age of ninety-two.

Timothy Murphy, no doubt an Irishman, was a bold spirit concerned in every daring undertaking. He proved his character even in his wooing, for he eloped with the only daughter of the wealthy Schoharie farmer, J. Fick (or Feeck). Murphy was then a soldier in the Revolution-ary army, and receiving very good reports from Murphy's superiors, the wealthy German father-in-law finally accepted a penniless son-in-law and made a stable citizen of him. Intermarriage between the Germans and Irish was of frequent occurrence on the border, each nationality showing reluctance at first, but soon yielding gracefully to the inevitable.

The struggle for liberty in the American colonies attracted soldiers from foreign lands, some of them adventurers, who proved troublesome to the commander-in-chief and Congress, but others again of an entirely different stamp. They had served in European wars, and through their experience added just that element of discipline and self-confidence which was necessary to make the military struggle successful. Of all the distinguished foreigners who aided the American cause, none did more real service than Baron Steuben, the drill-master of the American forces.[1] In the words of Hamilton, quoted by Bancroft:

. [1] The standard biography of Friedrich Wilhelm Freiherr von Steuben (1730–94) is by Friedrich Kapp, entitled: *Leben des amerikanischen Generals Fried. Wilh. v. Steuben.* (Berlin, 1858.) A translation was published in New York (Mason Brothers, 1859). Another biography was published by Francis Bowen, *The Life of Baron Steuben*, in Sparks's *Library of American*

" He benefited the country of his adoption by introducing into the army a regular formation and exact discipline, and by establishing a spirit of order and economy in the interior administration of the regiments." [1] Baron von Steuben, born at Magdeburg, Prussia, belonged to an ancient and distinguished family, and following good traditions he became a soldier. He fought in the war of the Austrian Succession, and during the Seven Years' War distinguished himself at Rossbach. He became an aide of Frederick and was a favorite pupil of the great general. After the war he held a lucrative position, but was not satisfied with inactivity. When on a visit to Paris the French secretary of war, Saint-Germain, spoke to him of a glorious opportunity existing in America, that of introducing Prussian military discipline into the raw American militia. Benjamin Franklin, whom Steuben met at Paris, made no promises, but friends in France strongly advised Steuben to undertake the venture. Steuben soon came to a favorable decision. He gave up his assured and comfortable position at home, asking the king of Prussia to transfer his income, yielding him 4600 livres annually, to his nephew the Baron von Canitz.

It was a difficult matter for Steuben to determine in what capacity to enter the American army, but he settled the question by offering his services as a volunteer, ready to perform any duty which the commander-in-chief might assign him. Commissions for his aides and the payment of his actual expenses were the only conditions stipulated for, leaving the question of ultimate compensation to be

---

Biography, vol. ix. (1838.) Cf. also G. W. Greene, *The German Element in the War of American Independence*. (New York, 1876.) The latter book contains a sketch of Steuben, Kalb, and the Hessians, based on the three works of Kapp on the same subjects.

[1] Bancroft, vol. v, p. 220; quotes Hamilton's *Works*, vol. ii, p. 229.

decided by the success or failure of the struggle. The Continental Congress was then in session at York, Pennsylvania, whither Steuben repaired with his letters from Franklin, Saint-Germain, and others. General Gates, who was then intriguing against Washington, oppressed the newcomer with civilities, but Steuben, with keen insight into human character, refused his dangerous hospitality. Steuben's offer was accepted, and he was sent to Washington at Valley Forge. On his way he passed through Lancaster County, and was greeted with ovations throughout the German farming country. At Valley Forge Washington received him in accordance with his rank and experience as a soldier, and by these outward marks of respect at once installed him in the high position of authority which the general-in-chief wished to establish for the army's schoolmaster.

At no time was the condition of the army at a lower ebb, not only through lack of supplies and equipment, but also through the absence of discipline and military spirit. Through desertion and disease the original force of seventeen thousand had dwindled down to a little more than five thousand men who could be called out for duty. Even these were poorly armed, and clothed in rags. Yet there were capabilities in these men which the trained eye of Steuben recognized. After the intriguing and incapable Conway had been removed from the inspector-generalship, Steuben received a free hand. With the assistance of Greene, Hamilton, and Laurens, and the French aides which he had brought with him, Steuben's first plan was to institute a system of inspectorship. He drafted from the line one hundred and twenty men to form a military school. He drilled them twice a day and frequently took a musket into his own hands, showing

BARON VON STEUBEN

them how he wished them to handle it. At every drill his several inspectors were required to be present, and doubtless many officers were present without requisition. " In a fortnight," said Steuben, "my company knew perfectly well how to bear arms and had a military air, knew how to march, and to form in column, to deploy and execute some little manœuvres with excellent precision." Steuben showed his superiority by not making too much of the manual exercises. He was no mere martinet. Very soon he passed to manœuvring and thereby really interested the men. He studied the capacities of the militia before him and adapted his rigid discipline to the circumstances. Every scholar of his school became an apostle of reform. Those who looked on admired and longed to be permitted to share in the lessons. Battalions came next, then brigades, and then divisions. Within a month the American troops, for the first time since the opening of the war, were able to execute the manœuvres of a regular army. On the fifth of May Steuben was appointed by Congress inspector-general with the rank and pay of major-general.

A reform in drill was but a small part of the real work to be done. The whole organization of the army required reform in all its parts. The necessity of internal administration of a regiment and a company was then entirely unknown. The number of men in a regiment or company had been fixed by Congress, but there were some who were three months' men, some six, some nine. They were constantly coming and going, and when they went they commonly took their rifles with them, so that Congress had to buy thousands of new rifles every year. Sometimes a regiment was stronger than a brigade, sometimes it contained but thirty men. The men were scattered about everywhere and frequently they were drawing pay long after they had left the ranks. Leaves of absence and dismissals were given out promiscuously. All of these abuses had to be corrected, and exact records of every detail were now instituted. In the inspections there was no trifling, no hurrying over details. "Every man not present was to be accounted for; if in camp, sick or well, he was produced or visited; every musket was handled and searched, cartridge-boxes were opened; even the flints and cartridges counted; knapsacks were unslung and every article of clothing was spread on the soldier's blanket and tested by his little book." It took little to move Steuben's anger; undue delay, hesitation, were sure to do it, and out came a storm of oaths, German first, then French, and then both, ludicrously mingled; when the stock was exhausted, turning to his aide he would say, "My dear Walker," or "My dear Duponceau, come and swear for me in English. These fellows will not do what I bid them." The sonorous voice of Steuben, however, was respected and it received the backing of the highest authority.

Events very soon proved the excellence of his work. In the spring campaign of 1778, Lafayette, seeing himself outnumbered and cut off from the main body, was able to save his men by an orderly retreat; Washington at the same time could get his whole army under arms and ready to march in fifteen minutes. At Monmouth, not long after, the sound of Steuben's familiar voice rallied Lee's broken columns. They wheeled into line under a heavy fire as calmly and precisely as if the battlefield had been a parade-ground. In this style of manœuvring Steuben was adapting established principles to American conditions. But in the formation of the light infantry he became an inventor and sent back a lesson from the New World to the Old. These bodies of skirmishers fought in

Indian fashion under cover, as the American backwoodsman was accustomed to do, using his rifle to the best
advantage and according to his own judgment, always
being careful to keep his body sheltered as much as
possible. Frederick the Great adopted a similar body of
skirmishers and sharpshooters into his military system.

In order to make the principles of military discipline
accessible in all quarters, Steuben published a manual,
long known in the army of the United States as "Steuben's Regulations" or "the Blue Book." The printing
of the book was a trial and tribulation, but when that
difficulty was overcome, the work was sent to governors
of states, and distributed through the army. For the
first time since the war began, American officers had a
clear and definite guide for the performance of their military duties.[1] The economies of the service resulting from
Steuben's work were enormous. A single instance of this
was that the War Office, instead of having to count upon
an annual loss of from five to eight thousand muskets,
could enter upon its record that in one year of Steuben's
inspectorship only three muskets were missing and that
even these were accounted for. His example of indefatigable industry was contagious, as was also his democratic
manner of personally instructing the common soldier with
necessary details, which the American officer, following
the English model, had considered beneath him. Jealousies and opposition were overcome because of the excellent
results of Steuben's discipline.

[1] Cf. also the Reprints : F. W. Steuben, *Regulations for the Order and Discipline of the Troops of the United States ; Prefixed, the Laws and Regulations
for the Militia of the United States and of New Hampshire.* (Published by order
of the General Court of New Hampshire, Portsmouth, 1794.) And F. W.
Steuben : *Regulations for the Order and Discipline of the Troops of the United
States.* (Boston, 1802.)

Next to the inspectorship, Steuben's most valuable services were his work in Virginia, in the winter of 1780–81, and during the siege of Yorktown. General Greene had been appointed to command the Southern army after the fatal battle of Camden, where General Gates had deserted his troops. Steuben went with Greene because "an army had to be created." Virginia was relied upon as the main field for recruiting, but the militia was thoroughly demoralized, their ignorance of military discipline and "plundering proclivities" were appalling. Thomas Jefferson, the democratic governor, could not remove any of the obstructions which the generals had to encounter. Steuben frequently lost his temper and strained his authority to the utmost while creating an army for Greene. Nevertheless, through his hard work and good judgment Arnold's invasion was checked, and Lafayette was enabled to score successes.

At Yorktown Steuben was the only American officer who had ever been present at a siege,[1] and his experience was of great service. He was in command of a division, and fortune willed that his division should be in the trenches when the first overtures for surrender were made. He had the privilege, therefore, so highly prized by all the superior officers, — and notably by Lafayette, who wished to claim the honor, — of being in command when the enemy's flag was lowered. No one was more deserving of the distinction than Steuben, the schoolmaster of the army. During the last two years of the war the discipline of the regular American troops could well be compared to that of European soldiery.

[1] Steuben was a volunteer at the siege of Prague when a boy of fourteen ; the last siege in which he had participated was that of Schweidnitz at the close of the Seven Years' War. He was then Frederick's aide.

Steuben continued to be of service to the country after the war. He formulated the plans for building a military academy, and in his project provided for full professorships of history, geography, civil and international law, eloquence and belles-lettres, showing that he would insist that an officer be a broadly educated man. It is quite probable also that he gave the first suggestion for the formation of the order of the Cincinnati.

At the close of the war, Steuben, having before coming to America yielded his revenues abroad to his nephew, remained in straitened circumstances for eight years, until Congress voted him a pension of $2500 and the legislature of New York State a gift of 16,000 acres of land in the neighborhood of Utica, Oneida County, New York. This settlement, though tardy, showed that republics are not always ungrateful. To his last years Steuben identified himself closely with all military interests of the country, as for instance his proposing a plan of fortifications for New York. He was chosen a regent of the University of New York, was one of the original members of the Cincinnati, and the president of the German Society of New York (for the benefit of immigrants) from 1785 to 1794. He died in 1794, leaving generous gifts to friends and his former aides. Though Steuben's deeds did not shine forth in the reports of battles, they were such as prepared and assured permanent victories. He was the creator of the discipline of the regular army and the organizer of its military system and economy. His influence lasted long beyond his life. The system of drills and manœuvres which he drew up in 1779 remained authoritative for several generations. "His system of reviews, reports, and inspection gave efficiency to the soldier, confidence to the commander, and saved the treasury not less than $600,000." If men are classed according to their services, no one in the military history of the Revolution, after Washington and Greene, stands so high as Steuben. Some other generals have received more praise in our histories because of valor shown on the field of battle; such opportunities never came to Steuben, though he frequently felt a longing for them. Lafayette, for instance, a youthful enthusiast who came to America in 1777 with an open purse, a warm heart, and the inexperience of twenty winters, was given rare opportunities in the field. He received as much as he gave, and if the amount of his indispensable service be weighed, though much to be appreciated, it will be found light in comparison with that of the veteran Steuben, who trained the army, created its discipline, prepared its victories, and subsequently identified himself closely with the new-born republic as a public-spirited citizen.

One of the fighting generals that Germany supplied in the Revolutionary forces was John Kalb, so frequently called the Baron de Kalb. He was the son of a Franconian peasant, born in 1721 in Hüttendorf (not the son of a Dutch nobleman). He was employed some ten years before as the emissary of Choiseul and secret agent of the French government (1768), to inspect the condition of the British colonies. After his return he married the daughter of a Dutch millionaire and occupied an assured position of influence and comfort in Europe. Nevertheless he came to America in 1777, with Lafayette. He was asked to present the offer of the Count of Broglie, who insinuated his willingness to become the William of Orange of America, — for a period of years, or longer, if his distinguished services could not be dispensed with. The messenger soon wrote to the French count that there was no possibility of his filling Washington's place. John Kalb then offered his

own services to Congress, writing : " General Washington
has perhaps friends or deserving officers to whom he would
give the preference. In such a case I should be sorry my
coming in did in the least cross him or prevent his dispo-
sitions in this and in other respects. I will gladly and entirely submit to his commands and be employed as he shall
think most convenient for the good of the service." He
was appointed major-general and served under Washington
in New Jersey and Maryland. In 1780 he was dispatched
to South Carolina in command of the Delaware and Maryland troops. Kapp says[1] that of all the foreign officers
Kalb was the most "experienced, calculating, and cautious." He had served in the Seven Years' War, knew
America from a previous visit, and was energetic, ambitious,
and duty-loving. He was a specialist in matters of topography and engineering.

In the Southern campaign he very soon noticed the incapacity of General Gates. When stationing his troops in
the battle of Camden, Gates placed the rawest of Virginia
militia, who had just arrived and did not yet understand
the use of bayonets, opposite the veteran regiments of
Cornwallis. The centre proved little better in the fight, for
they yielded almost as quickly as the militia. In the words
of Gates the Virginia militia " ran like a torrent," " and
the General ran with them," says Bancroft, " and faster,
for he outdistanced the most terrified of the militia and
was altogether ignorant of the fate of his army." Concerning what remained, Bancroft says,[2] "The division which
Kalb commanded continued long in action, and never did
troops show greater courage than those men of Maryland

---

[1] Friedrich Kapp, *Leben des amerikanischen Generals Johann Kalb*. (Stuttgart, 1862.) Translated into English, *The Life of John Kalb, Major-General
in the Revolutionary Army*. (New York, 1884.)

[2] Bancroft, vol. v, pp. 388–89.

and Delaware. The horse of Kalb had been killed under him and he had been badly wounded; yet he continued to fight on foot. At last, in the hope of victory, he led a charge, drove the division under Rawdon, took fifty prisoners, and would not believe that he was not about to gain the day, when Cornwallis poured against him a party of dragoons and infantry. Even then he did not yield until disabled by many wounds. The victory cost the British about five hundred of their best troops; 'their great loss,' wrote Marion, 'is equal to a defeat.' Except one hundred Continental soldiers whom Gist[1] conducted across swamps through which the cavalry could not follow, every American corps was dispersed. Kalb lingered for three days. Opulent, and happy in his wife and children, he gave to the United States his life and his example. Congress decreed him a monument."

Another German general, who had already served in the French and Indian War in America, as lieutenant in the Royal American Regiment, was George Weedon, or Gerhard von der Wieden. He was born in Hanover, served in the war of the Austrian Succession, 1742–48, distinguished himself in the battle of Dettingen, served with Colonel Henry Bouquet in Flanders and America. When the French and Indian War was over, he settled at Fredericksburg, Virginia,[2] so largely populated by Germans, and when the Revolution broke out he became lieutenant-colonel of the Third Virginia Militia, colonel

[1] The Maryland regiment of Gist was a German regiment. Cf. Rosengarten, p. 144.

[2] Smyth says of him: "We arrived at Fredericksburg, putting up at an inn, or public house kept by one Weedon, who is now a general officer in the American army, and was then very active and zealous in blowing the flames of sedition." *Smyth's Tour*, vol. ii, p. 151. (London edition, 1784.) Cf. *Ibid.*, p. 197 : "Weedon and his banditti ran down to the riverside (Rappahannock), ordering me to land immediately," etc.

of the First Virginia Continental, and finally in 1777 brigadier-general, taking a leading part in the battles of Brandywine and Germantown. He left the service for a time, then in 1780 reëntered it under Mühlenberg and commanded the Virginia militia before Gloucester Point at the siege of Yorktown.

General Weissenfels, or Friedrich Heinrich, Baron von Weissenfels, was an officer in the British army in New York, but as soon as the Revolution broke out he offered his services to Washington. He had served in the French and Indian War, was engaged in the attack on Fort Ticonderoga, and the taking of Havana in 1762. With the brave Wolfe he mounted the Heights of Abraham and "saw him fall in the arms of victory." After the peace of Versailles he was an English officer on half-pay living quietly in New York. At his wedding with Elizabeth Bogart, General Steuben was his best man. In the Revolution he was with General Montgomery in the attack on Quebec, and on his return served as lieutenant-colonel in command of the Third Battalion in the Second New York Regiment of which he was soon in complete command. He defeated the enemy at White Plains, accompanied Washington over the Hudson and through New York to Pennsylvania and took part in the battles of Trenton and Princeton. He was with his regiment at the capture of Burgoyne at Saratoga. In the attack at Monmouth Court House the formidable British regulars were for the first time driven off the field at the point of the bayonet by his regiment and under his command. As second in command under General Sullivan, in 1779, a victory was again won by his bayonet charge in a hot battle with the Indians at Newton on the Chemung (near Elmira). Weissenfels was honorably discharged by Congress at the end of the war, and died in 1806 at New Orleans. He was the first vice-president of the New York *Deutsche Gesellschaft*, of which Steuben was for many years president.

Prominent in the Revolution, but even more so in the subsequent Indian wars, where he will be spoken of again, was David Ziegler. Born in Heidelberg, in 1748, he served in the Russian campaign against the Turks under the Empress Catharine, and subsequently settled at Lancaster, Pennsylvania. He served as adjutant in a Pennsylvania regiment, and as the second to enlist for the war under Washington, he became the senior captain of the First Pennsylvania Continental Regiment, serving with distinction.

Another noted German officer was Heinrich Emanuel Lutterloh, major of the guard of the Duke of Brunswick. He became acquainted with Franklin in London, and through the latter's influence came to America at the beginning of the Revolutionary War. He was the first assistant quartermaster, with the rank of colonel on Washington's staff in 1777. Not until the following year, when Baron Steuben was made inspector-general, the evil influence of General Conway being set aside, was it possible to bring some degree of order out of chaos. Lutterloh's work was especially appreciated by Washington, who in May, 1780, made him quartermaster-general of the army, in which capacity Lutterloh served to the end of the war. The responsible positions of inspector-general (Steuben), quartermaster-general (Lutterloh), and superintendent of bakers (Ludwig), were thus held by Germans.

Early in 1776 there arrived in New York City a young man of culture, engaging manners, and military appearance, who carried letters of introduction to Governor Tryon, introducing him as a first lieutenant in the service

of Frederick the Second, king of Prussia, and adjutant of
Prince Ferdinand of Brunswick. The bearer of the letters was Johann Paul Schott. Though coming with the
purpose of serving the English king, he soon changed
his mind, being greatly impressed by the serious purpose
of the patriots. He noticed that they lacked guns and
ammunition, and since he was well-to-do, he determined
by a daring stroke to furnish them with the sorely needed
supply. In the summer of 1776 he sailed to St. Eustache,
an island of the Lesser Antilles belonging to the Dutch,
where enterprising Netherlanders had established a station
for blockade-runners, whom they were prepared to furnish
with goods and contraband of war. There Schott hired a
schooner, loaded it with weapons and war materials at
his own expense, and steered for the coast of Virginia.
At the mouth of the Chesapeake he found the English
fleet blockading the entrance to Hampton Roads. Schott
deceived them by hoisting a British flag; he had also
dressed his entire crew in the uniform of English seamen.
The English warships at first took the schooner for a
transport belonging to their own fleet, until they saw
Schott cross their line. Their signal to return was not
heeded, but the shot and broadside that followed did no
harm to the swift schooner. When they reached their
destination, Schott's men were again in danger, owing to
their disguise, for although they hoisted the flag of the
colonies they had not had an opportunity to change their
uniforms. They were fired upon, when Schott raised a
white flag and the schooner then anchored in the harbor
of Norfolk amid great rejoicing. The supplies were gladly
bought by the colonists and a vote of thanks was given
him. His petition for an officer's rank in the Continental
army was granted soon after in 1776. He was made cap-

tain and sent to General Washington in New York, in active service.

A story is told connecting a bit of romance with his entry into the army. General Washington was stationed at the Battery, in order to observe the movements of the British fleet. A large frigate tried to go up North River, whereupon Washington gave command to fire upon it. At the same time his own battery was being bombarded from Governor's Island and there was particularly one gun which troubled the Americans. Schott, who had had no opportunity to approach General Washington because he was in council with his staff, noticed a cannon that was not being served. Thereupon he called several of the men who stood about idly, bade them help load the gun, and then sighted it himself. The first shot silenced the troublesome piece on Governor's Island. Washington, who had observed the movement, turned to Schott and asked him whether he was a trained artillerist. The latter assented, and delivered to the general his papers. Washington turned to Colonel Knox, commander of the artillery, asking him whether there was a vacancy among his captains. There proved to be one, owing to the illness of one of the captains, Schott was put in his place, and at the battle of White Plains commanded the Third Battery in Knox's artillery. It will be remembered that it was principally due to the artillery of Colonel Knox that the Americans were able to get off their entire baggage in the face of the enemy.

Schott proved serviceable in another way. At a time when Washington had great difficulty in retaining soldiers about him, their periods of service being over, and when the English forces were constantly being increased by mercenaries from the Continent, Washington sent Schott to the Pennsylvania districts to recruit an independent

German troop of dragoons (July 31, 1777). Schott had
permission to appoint his own officers and give commands
in German. Subsequently there were three more companies who were put under his command, whom he led in
the battle of Short Hills. Given the post of covering the
retreat, he was severely wounded and taken prisoner. It
was a queer whim of fate that he, who had been fêted by
the Tories on his arrival at New York, should now for
six months become their prisoner. They offered him a
place in the British army, but he refused.[1] He was in
prison under the notorious Cunningham, and after being
exchanged in 1779 was in the army of General Sullivan,
commanding the right wing in the brigade of General
Hand. The Indians were attacked at Newton (near the
present Elmira, New York), their forces were annihilated,
and their villages destroyed.

Generals Sullivan and Hand recommended Schott for
promotion, which no doubt would have been acted upon
favorably if his wounds, received in the battle of Short
Hills, had not made active service very difficult for him.
Schott was therefore made commandant of the forts in
Wyoming, which position he held to the end of the war.
After that he settled down in Wilkesbarre. In 1787 he
was elected to the state legislature and was one of the
most earnest advocates of the union of the colonies. He
was active in all the public affairs of his constituency and
figured also in the Wyoming trouble between Pennsylvania
and Connecticut.

[1] In a letter to the Honorable Richard Rush (June 28, 1828), *Archives of
the Pension Office*, 1828, vol. ii, no. 179, MS., Schott says : "I had chosen
America as my fatherland, and nothing could induce me to desert her just
cause." He also states that he was born in Prussia, in 1744. In the pension
lists of 1828 he is credited with an annual pension of $1200, payable until
his death. Cf. *Der deutsche Pionier*, vol. viii, pp. 49–57 (Rattermann).

It will be impossible in these pages to do justice to the great number of German soldiers who fought with distinction during the Revolutionary War. The order of the Cincinnati, consisting of officers who were engaged on the patriot side in the Revolution, had among its membership a very large number of Germans. For the state of New York alone — and we know that the German population of New York was not so large as that of some other colonies — the roll of the Cincinnati includes the following names: Major-General Steuben, Colonel H. E. Lutterloh, Colonel Nicholas Fish, Colonel F. von Weissenfels (Second New York Regiment), Major Sebastian Baumann[1] (Second New York Artillery Regiment), Captain H. Tichout (First New York Regiment), Captain G. Sytez (First New York Regiment), Lieutenant Peter Anspach (Second New York Artillery Regiment), Lieutenant Henry Demler (Second New York Artillery Regiment), Lieutenant Joseph Freilich (Second New York Regiment), Lieutenant Michael Wetzel (Second New York Regiment), Lieutenant John Furmann (First New York Regiment), Lieutenant C. F. Weissenfels (Second New York Regiment), Captain-Lieutenant Peter Neslett (New York Artillery), and Captain-Lieutenant Peter Jaulmann.[2]

Families of German descent frequently gave every able-

---

[1] Sebastian Bauma. n was major in Colonel Lamb's regiment of artillery. He served from 1777 to 1784, was a well-trained officer of German birth, and resident in New York long before the war. He took part in the siege of Yorktown, and in 1782 published the only American map or survey of that important field of operations. He was postmaster of New York after the war, and died in 1803. Cf. Rosengarten, p. 136.

[2] Rosengarten, pp. 136–137. For a list of the German officers in the First to the Thirteenth Pennsylvania Continental Regiments, see *Der deutsche Pionier*, vols. viii, ix, and x. Hundreds of names of German officers, subalterns, and common soldiers are there given.

bodied man into the service of the cause. Such a family were the Heisters (Hiesters). At the outbreak of the Revolution their names were on the list of "Associators," a military company that rendered important service in the campaigns of New Jersey, New York, Delaware, and Pennsylvania. Daniel Heister's four sons all entered as officers, — Daniel, the oldest, as colonel; John and Gabriel as majors; and William, the youngest, as leader of a company. The most distinguished of the family was Joseph Heister, a son of John Heister. He became captain of the " Flying-Camp," organized in Reading and environs. Joseph at that time was twenty-three years of age. He was highly esteemed by his fellow citizens and possessed a gift of speech and persuasion which could fire others with enthusiasm. He recruited first a company and later a regiment, using frequently his own means to effect his purpose. He was a modest man, and though the soldiers wished him to be their colonel, he refused in favor of others, offering rank as an inducement to win them for the service of the country. Accordingly he used his influence among the soldiers to appoint Haller colonel and Edward Burd major. He was himself content with the rank of captain. They marched off to join Washington, but when they learned that they were to serve far beyond the limits of their state, and that the result was much in doubt, the militiamen were near a mutiny. Heister gathered them in a compact group, then appealed to their patriotism and sense of honor. He declared that he would go alone if no one would follow. When the drum was sounded, all but three obeyed the command of " Forward! march," and a moment later the three skulkers also joined the moving ranks.

On Long Island they were united with the regiment

of Lord Stirling and fought bravely with him and his Maryland regiments until captured. The First Pennsylvania Battalion sustained the heaviest loss, and a contemporary estimate reads : " Lord Stirling's brigade sustained the hottest of the enemy's fire ; — they were all surrounded by the enemy and had to fight their way through the blaze of their fire. They fought and fell like Romans." [1] Among the German officers that fell were Lieutenant-Colonels Piper, Lutz, and Kächlein, and Major Burd. Joseph Heister languished for some time in an English prison-ship, under Cunningham, and after being exchanged had to lose more time at his home in Reading, to regain his health. He then returned to the army and rose rapidly to the rank of brigadier-general, on Washington's own recommendation. He served to the end of the war, and afterwards, with the Mühlenbergs and Albert Gallatin, became a leader of the Germans in Pennsylvania. He was for fourteen years representative of his district in Congress, after which he was elected by a large majority to the governorship of the state. After serving for three years he would not allow his name to be used again for candidacy.

No Pennsylvania family furnished more eminent men for the public service than the Mühlenbergs. Three of the sons of the Lutheran patriarch, who himself was an ardent patriot, rose to distinction in the service of the republic, and the oldest (John) Peter (Gabriel) was Pennsylvania's choice when a statue of its representative citizen was to be placed in the capitol at Washington. His career has already in part been sketched. As a soldier he won distinction at Charleston, Brandywine, Germantown, Mon-

---

[1] *American Archives*, series v, vol. i, p. 1212, — a letter from New York dated August 29, 1776.

FREDERICK AUGUSTUS MÜHLENBERG   PETER MÜHLENBERG

JOHN CHRISTOPHER KUNZE   G. H. ERNST MÜHLENBERG

mouth, Stony Point, and Yorktown. In Virginia he was the right-hand man of Steuben in creating an army, and fought desperately against superior numbers to check the advance of Arnold in Virginia. He represented Pennsylvania in the United States Congress from 1789–91, 1793–95, and from 1799–1801. He was vice-president of the state of Pennsylvania under Franklin, and owing to Franklin's age and infirmities became practically the head of the government. In the year 1788 he and his brother left no stone unturned to secure the adoption of the Constitution of the United States.

The brother was Frederick August Mühlenberg, who had likewise been trained in theology at Halle, but when the war began became interested in the politics of his country. In 1779–80 he was a member of the Continental Congress, and during the next three years a member and speaker of the Pennsylvania state legislature. He called the Convention of 1790 which drafted the constitution of Pennsylvania; was a member of the First, Second, Third and Fourth United States Congresses, and possesses the distinction of having been the first Speaker of the House of Representatives. He was reëlected Speaker of the House during the Third Congress. Another brother, Henry Ernest Mühlenberg, was likewise intended for the ministry by his father, studied theology at the University of Halle, as did his brothers, and on his return became a Lutheran minister in Lancaster, Pennsylvania, and elsewhere. He was the foremost scholar of the family, a naturalist and botanist, member of the American Philosophical Society (Philadelphia), and of learned European societies. His son, Henry August Mühlenberg, was a member of the United States Congress for nine years, a supporter of President Jackson, was nominated for governor of Pennsylvania by the Democratic party, but died before the election.

In Charleston, South Carolina, there was organized in 1775 a German regiment called the German Fusileers, which by 1776 counted over one hundred Germans in its ranks. Its captain was Alexander Gillon, its first lieutenant Peter Bouquet (brother of the general of that name), and its second lieutenant, Michael Kalteisen. At the storming of the fortress at Savannah, in 1779, where Pulaski lost his life, the German Fusileers were under the command of the German colonel, Laurens. They lost their captain, Karl Scheppard (Schaefer), and the first lieutenant, Joseph Kimmel. Michael Kalteisen was a moving spirit in the formation of the German Friendly Society (already referred to), which by the time of the Revolution had a membership of one hundred, and advanced two thousand pounds to the state for defense against the crown, a sum surely not inconsiderable at that time.

At the battle of King's Mountain (or Cowpens), October 29, 1781, which did so much toward reviving the hopes of patriots in the South, Colonel Hambright, of German descent, and in all probability representing a southern branch of the Pennsylvania family of the same name, rendered excellent service. The North and South Carolinians of the American forces were under command of Williams, Lacey, Hambright, Chronicle, and others.[1] Hambright and Chronicle were in command of the South Fork men from the Catawba. Chronicle was killed and Hambright wounded. In spite of his wounds, the latter kept in the saddle and continued in the battle. The tactics of the fight consisted in retreating before a bayonet attack by the enemy, but returning immediately upon him after

[1] Roosevelt, *The Winning of the West*, vol. ii, pp. 276, 282.

the charge. Staying qualities such as shown by Hambright were therefore needed to carry out the plan of ultimately surrounding and annihilating the enemy. Tarleton's much-feared raiding bands were on this day almost totally destroyed.

An interesting group of soldiers were the sharpshooters under General Morgan. Among them there were a large number of Germans gathered from the Valley of Virginia and from the frontier settlements of the Carolinas. The names of a number of German Virginians from Winchester and vicinity who were in Morgan's famous band of riflemen, have come down to us:[1] Johann Schultz, Jacob Sperry, Peter and Simon Lauck, Frederick Kurtz, Karl Grimm, Georg Heisler, and Adam Kurz. Six of these formed the so-called "Dutch Mess." They messed together during the entire war and survived all their severe campaigns. They acted as aides-de-camp, but never received or accepted officers' commissions. After the war they obtained lands near Winchester, Virginia, and their descendants live in that locality to-day.

An interesting individual, reminding one of the "Marketenderin" in Schiller's "Wallenstein's Lager," was Moll Pitcher. She had served as a maid in Dr. William Irvine's family in Carlisle, Pennsylvania, and was generally called Molly, her real name being Maria Ludwig. About the time of the beginning of the war she married William Hays. Her husband became a gunner in an artillery company, and Molly returned after a time to serve in General Irvine's family. She got news that her husband had been severely wounded, whereupon she started out immediately to find him. She nursed him when found, and after that, for seven years, she accompanied him from

[1] Cf. *Der Westen*, Chicago, 1892, reported by Andreas Simon.

battlefield to battlefield. She was utterly fearless, brought water and food to the soldiers, and helped to carry away the wounded and care for them. " Here comes Molly with her pitcher," was a refreshing sound in the heat of battle, that made her known throughout the army as Moll Pitcher. At the battle of Monmouth she is said to have served in exemplary fashion. At a moment when her husband was wounded and no assistance seemed available for serving the cannon, she herself set about putting the piece in order and loading it, while those about her were apparently in doubt whether to stand or retreat. It was a trying moment, but the company held out until sustained by reinforcements.[1]

A patron of American sailors was the German merchant, Dohrmann, located at Lisbon, Portugal. He frequently supported American privateersmen who were stranded or in trouble on the Continent of Europe. By selling weapons and munitions of war to American cruisers, which he sometimes accomplished on the high seas by means of his own ships, he exposed himself to the hostility of the British government, who finally succeeded in inducing the court of Lisbon to banish Dohrmann from the country. This happened in the year 1782. Leaving his business

[1] *Der deutsche Pionier*, vol. viii, pp. 187–190. One of her grandchildren describes her as of short, thick-set stature, blue eyes and reddish hair, and almost masculine features. She was possessed of great strength of character, and according to the same source of information had mannish manners, was often feared, and would sometimes swear. (Correspondence of editor H. A. Rattermann with surviving granddaughter, Mrs. Malester, of Carlisle, in 1876.) E. S. Ellis, after careful researches under the eye of General Wm. S. Stryker, declares that Molly Pitcher was the daughter (Mary) of John George Ludwig. This name is unquestionably German. If the family of Ludwig came from Ireland, as the historian Lossing states, they may have been Palatines settled in the north of Ireland about 1710. J. Zeamer (see *The American Catholic Historical Researches*, N. s. vol. v, no. 4, October, 1909) regards the Molly Pitcher exploits as altogether untrustworthy, and claims to be in possession of proofs that Molly Pitcher was a myth.

and extensive banking interests in the hands of a brother, he made his way to New York. Washington, in a letter to the Honorable Samuel Chase, July 9, 1785, introduced him in the following manner: Dohrmann "who at an early period of the war (when our affairs were rather overshadowed) advanced his money very liberally to support our suffering countrymen in captivity. He has some matter to submit to Congress which he can explain better than I. I am persuaded he will offer nothing which is inconsistent with the strictest rules of propriety and of course that it will merit your patronage."[1] Mr. Dohrmann's private fortune had in the mean time met severe reverses because of the failure of his partners in Lisbon. The plea before Congress was to permit Dohrmann to realize on the heavy advances he had made for the benefit of American seamen. Congress, on the report of the treasurer, awarded the sum of $5806, with interest for expenditures according to vouchers examined. Resolutions were made as follows: —

Whereas the claims of Arnold Henry Dohrmann against the United States of America amounted to $20,277 over and above the sum of $5806, as above stated, in support of which important documents are offered by Mr. Dohrmann, whose own house was frequently the asylum of whole crews of captive American seamen, who were fed, clothed, and relieved in sickness through his benevolence, and that at a time when his attachment to the cause of America was dangerous both to his person and property:

And whereas Congress are disposed to acknowledge in the most honorable manner the eminent services rendered by Mr. Dohrmann and to make him further compensation:

Resolved unanimously: That the said A. H. Dohrmann be

[1] *Der deutsche Pionier*, vol. ix, pp. 52 ff., 109 ff., 201 ff. Heinrich Arnold Dohrmann was born in Hamburg. He was naturalized as a citizen of the United States December 18, 1787.

allowed, as agent from the United States at the Court of Lisbon, the sum of $1600 per annum, and that said salary be computed from the period at which his expenditures commenced to the present day.

Resolved unanimously : That one complete and entire township . . . surveyed in the western territory of the United States, be granted to A. H. Dohrmann, free from all charges of survey, and with choice of the three ranges last surveyed.[1]

Dohrmann was instrumental in negotiating loans for the United States, e. g., in 1783 for John Adams during his visit to Holland with the bankers Van Staphorst and others in Amsterdam, leading to a loan of two million guilders.[2] The later loans, of June 1, 1787, and March 13, 1788, of one million Dutch guilders each, were negotiated by the house of Dohrmann in New York, though they bear the signature of John Adams. In 1789 came the financial crash at Lisbon. James Madison and Thomas Jefferson, then in Paris, were Dohrmann's lawyers. Dohrmann paid his debts, but the loss of three ships in 1808 with valuable cargoes broke his fortunes. Even the land given him by Congress, located in Tuscarawas and Harrison counties, Ohio, went into the hands of land sharks. Dohrmann settled finally at Steubenville, Ohio, where he died in 1813 of a broken heart. His wife in 1817 received a pension from Congress.

It is not commonly known, though all historical documents agree as to the fact, that the French troops under Rochambeau, who were sent over to aid the American cause, contained a large number of German soldiers,[3] and

[1] These resolutions were dated Monday, October 1, 1787, *Journal of Congress*, vol. iv, pp. 783–84.

[2] Consummated March 9, 1784. *Journal of Congress*, second edition, appendix of vol. iv, p. 25.

[3] Cf. *Der deutsche Pionier*, vol. xiii, pp. 317 ff., 360 ff., 430 ff.

some German regiments. The German-French auxiliary troops were as follows: —

First: The regiment called Royal Allemand de Deux Ponts. This was the Royal German Regiment of Zweibrücken. The colonel and commander of this regiment was Prince Christian of Zweibrücken-Birkenfeld; the lieutenant-colonel was Prince Wilhelm von Zweibrücken-Birkenfeld; the major was Freiherr Eberhard von Esebeck (Baron d'Esbech), and the captain was named Haake. The regiment served in America from 1780–83.

Second : A battalion of grenadiers of Kur-Trier, of the Regiment Saar, which appears as " Détachement du Régiment La Sarré," and which was incorporated with the regiment "Saintonge," under the command of Colonel Adam Philipp, Count of Custine of Lothringen.

Third: Several divisions of Alsatians and Lotharingians joined with the regiments " Bourbonnais" and "Soissonnais" as yagers.

Fourth: A large part of the "Independent Horse" under the command of the Duke of Lauzun, of which legion a list is found in the archives of Harrisburg, Pennsylvania.

Fifth : Several German officers served in responsible positions in the French army, such as Freiherr Ludwig von Closen-Haydenburg, adjutant of Rochambeau; Captain Gau, commandant of artillery ; and the Strassburg professor, Lutz, interpreter for the marquis. Whether the regiment called Anhalt (six hundred men) mentioned in connection with the siege of Savannah, 1779, in the forces of Count d'Estaing, was composed of Germans, is a matter of doubt; detailed information is lacking.

Knowing which were the German regiments among the French troops, and which were German in the Colonial army, it becomes manifest that the German soldier rendered conspicuous service in the final campaign which culminated in the siege and capture of Yorktown. The only sortie which was made during the siege, namely, that of Tarleton at Gloucester, was beaten back by the Legion of Armand, about twelve hundred militia under General Weedon and the men under the Duke of Lauzun, all together between three and four thousand men, over half of whom must have been German. The enemy were defeated at all points and Tarleton escaped capture with difficulty.

When the second parallel of trenches was drawn about the city of Yorktown, two redoubts stood in the way. On the fourteenth of October the American batteries directed their fire all day against the abatis and salient angles of these two advanced redoubts, and breaches were made in them sufficient to justify an assault. The redoubt on the right near York River was garrisoned by forty-five men, that on the left by three times as many. The storming of the former fell to the lot of the Americans under the command of Lieutenant-Colonel Alexander Hamilton; that of the latter to the French.[1] On the left about four hundred grenadiers and yagers were selected and placed under the command of Count William de Deux Ponts. He was no other, as we have seen, than Prince Wilhelm von Zweibrücken, and his grenadiers and yagers were selected from the regiment of Zweibrücken (entirely German), Gatinois, and Agenois, among whom also were Germans. We are told by a contemporary account[2] that there was joy and confidence before the start, quiet and energy in overcoming the dangers of the attack, and order and

---

[1] Bancroft, vol. v, pp. 519 ff.

[2] That of the Baron of Viomenil, who had the supreme command in the attack on the redoubts.

humanity in victory. According to a well-founded tradition, commands were given in the German language on either side when the redoubt was captured,[1] showing that German regiments in the French service were attacking and Hessians were defending the fortification.[2] The redoubt was defended by one hundred Hessians and thirty English and they defended themselves bravely, inflicting heavy losses; 56 of the Gatinois regiment, 21 grenadiers and yagers of the Zweibrücken regiment, 6 of Agenois, and 9 others killed or wounded. Prince Wilhelm von Zweibrücken was slightly wounded in the face. At the head of the Royal Grenadiers of Zweibrücken there was Captain Henry de Kalb, a cousin of the German-American general who fell at Camden. He was the first of the attacking party to enter the redoubt. Tradition has it that he lost one of his shoes in climbing the parapet, which evidently did not impede his progress, for he immediately took a British officer prisoner.[3]

The Marquis of Rochambeau rewarded the soldiers who had taken part in the storming of the redoubt with two days' extra pay. Washington presented them with two of the brass cannons they had taken, one each to Zweibrücken and to Gatinois as a remembrance of their bravery. The other redoubt was not so well defended and

---

[1] Cf. *The Diary of Johann Conrad Doehla in Zell*, "Marschroute und Beschreibung der merkwürdigsten Begebenheiten in und aus Amerika" (1811). Cf. *Der deutsche Pionier*, vol. xiii, pp. 422 ff. Also Kapp, *Life of Steuben*, p. 459.

[2] Eelking was evidently in error when he spoke of the use of German commands as "eine Kriegslist." He wrote from the Hessian point of view. Max von Eelking, *Die deutschen Hülfstruppen in Nord Amerika im Befreiungskriege*, 1776–83 (Hanover, 1863), two volumes, is a work giving a very complete account of the campaigns of the Hessian soldiers in the United States. The work was translated: *The German Allied Troops in the North American War of Independence*, 1776–83, by Rosengarten. (Albany, 1893.)

[3] Kapp, *Life of Steuben*, p. 459.

was taken without loss by the American force under the
officers Hamilton, Fish, Gionat, Laurens, and Mansfield.
The importance of the capture of the redoubts was very
soon evident. Steuben included them in the second parallel and on the morning of October 17 the regiments Zweibrücken, Bourbonnais (containing divisions of Alsatians
and Lotharingians), on the French side, went into the
trenches, while the division of Baron Steuben was ordered
into the works on the American side. All resistance soon
proved ineffective against the impenetrable chain of fortifications which was now enclosing Yorktown. The brigade of Steuben consisted of Wayne's Pennsylvania
regiment, Mühlenberg's Virginians, Gist's Marylanders,
the whole brigade being at least one half German. The
German element was thus very fortunate in occupying
the most honorable position, namely, that in the trenches,
at the time when the crisis came. There it was that Steuben received the first overtures of peace from Cornwallis.
Lafayette requested that he be permitted to supersede
Steuben, but the latter, knowing that by the etiquette of
military custom he was entitled to the place until the surrender, referred the matter to Washington. Washington
decided in favor of Steuben. The latter was not impelled
by personal vanity, nor did the Prussian feel antagonistic
to the Frenchman, but he possessed a large measure of
pride in his Americans. He wanted the American soldiery,
his pupils in military tactics and discipline, to be honored
as the recipients of the enemy's suit of surrender. Similarly, when shortly before the capitulation the Count Deux
Ponts (Zweibrücken) offered to support Steuben's forces
in the trenches, he refused any aid whatsoever. When
the Count Deux Ponts had gone away, Wayne remarked
that Steuben had only one thousand men in his entire

division. The latter said, "If I was guilty of a certain amount of gasconade with regard to the number of my men, it was for the honor of your country," whereupon Wayne took him by the hand, and addressing himself to the officers present said: "Now, gentlemen, it is our duty to make good the exaggeration of Baron Steuben and to support him just as if he had double the number of the troops that he has." [1]

The popular impression about the Hessians who served in the English army is that they were a species of Nibelungs, or devils. Time ought to be allowed to heal the wounds that Hessian bayonets once inflicted; the lover of his country should understand before casting judgment. The Hessians were the victims of the tyranny of their rulers, who sold the lives and services of their subjects to the highest bidder. The English government was at that time the best customer. Large profits were realized by the petty princes who were willing to sell mercenaries for the war in the American colonies, as can be seen by examination of the contracts between the parties on either side, contracts which were not kept secret. An estimate of the returns derived by several of the princes is as follows: [2]

Hesse-Cassel	in 8 years	£2,959,800
Brunswick	in 8 years	750,000
Hesse-Hanau	in 8 years	343,130
Waldeck	in 8 years	140,000
Anspach-Bayreuth	in 7 years	282,400
Anhalt-Zerbst	in 6 years	109,120

Kapp estimates that, all told, the expense to England for the German mercenary troops was at least seven million pounds sterling, the equivalent at present of one hundred and twenty to one hundred and fifty million

[1] Kapp, *Life of Steuben*, p. 458.   [2] Rosengarten, p. 63.

dollars.[1] Mercenary soldiers existed among the Germans from time immemorial. They served the Romans in order to learn the art of war, and subsequently applied the teaching against their former masters. They served in the civil wars of Rome on either side of the contests; they were participants perhaps in every European war down to 1870. The Thirty Years' War, the age of the *Landsknechte,* was an epoch that deprived the mercenary soldier of any national principles that he may have had.[2] One day he would fight for the Empire, the next for the Swede, then for the French, always going with the best pay and largest booty.

In the eighteenth century the German armies were not composed of the whole body of citizens as now. They consisted of recruits frequently drafted or forced into the army against their will. The system of recruiting soldiers was developed to an art and had its rules and regulations, all to the disadvantage of the recruit. Kapp has furnished us with extracts from a book of regulations giving suggestions to recruiting officers.[3] The recruit must be disarmed and searched carefully, lodged only in hotels that keep rooms specially fitted for the purpose. If on the march he is under suspicion of running away, the buttons of his trousers or his suspenders are to be cut, so that he must carry his trousers with his hands. If he has made an attempt to escape, he must be put in irons or the

---

[1] This estimate is found on page 212 of Friedrich Kapp's authoritative work, *Der Soldatenhandel deutscher Fürsten nach Amerika.* (Berlin, 1874.) Reviewed by the *New York Nation,* September 10, 1874. Kapp estimates one hundred and twenty to one hundred and fifty million thalers; according to the present value of money we may estimate dollars at least.

[2] The *Landsknechte* were recruited from adventurers of all nations.

[3] Kapp, *Soldatenhandel,* pp. 13–17. The book is Prussian, showing that the abuses of recruiting existed in a country where soldiers were not sold nor mercenaries tolerated.

thumbscrews must be applied. It is unfortunate if the officer in charge has to make use of his gun and wound the recruit, or be obliged to kill him. If the recruit is of particular strength, it is well to have two officers accompany him, etc., etc. Young and vigorous men were always in danger of being kidnapped, but no exception was made for fathers of families or travelers distant from their friends. Men of any station in life were in danger of being impressed into the service, as was for instance the German traveler and poet Seume, who has written a delightful autobiography, containing his experiences as a kidnapped trooper in the English service.[1] As a result, the military service, for which the German has no innate abhorrence, became roundly hated, and desertions were very frequent. The Margrave Anspach, for instance, in order to make sure that the soldiers he had sold would arrive at their destination, acted as their driver, taking "his children" on board the ship and even marking their beds. The attitude of the recruits was by no means such as depicted by the Duke of Walbeck in a letter to the Earl of Suffolk,[2] when he described his regiment as consisting of six hundred men "composed of officers and soldiers who, as their prince, did not wish for anything better than to find an occasion of sacrificing themselves for his British Majesty." If the parents of the kidnapped sons complained, the father was sent to the iron-mines and the mother to jail. A deserter was compelled to run the gauntlet twelve times a day for two days in succession, sometimes being beaten to death by switches during the ordeal. Schiller's depiction, in "Kabale und Liebe," of the soldier's parting from home was no exaggeration.[3] What the poet says of

[1] J. G. Seume, *Mein Leben.* (1813.) [2] Kapp, *Soldatenhandel*, p. 244.
[3] Schiller's *Kabale und Liebe*, Act II, Sc. ii.

the excesses at the petty courts and the small valuation put upon a human life was literally true. The Margrave of Anspach, in order to please his mistress, had a chimney-sweep shot down from the roof of the castle of Bruckberg. She had uttered a wish to see the man fall. The widow, who besought His Grace for some means of support, was given five guldens as a compensation. Human life became only valuable in the foreign service; it was not rated at five guldens there. The Landgrave of Hessen, for example, in spite of stupendous extravagance, was able at his death to leave sixty million guldens in the treasury as a result of his barter in human flesh.

The greatest of the German princes did not allow his subjects to be sold. Frederick the Great used his influence against the sale of recruits in other German states and refused to allow mercenaries who were intended for the American service to pass through his domains. He said on one occasion: "If that crown [the English] would give me all the millions possible, I would not furnish it two small files of my troops to serve against the colonies." Frederick encouraged France in a war against England for the defense of the colonies, and made promises to do all in his power to prevent the purchase of mercenaries.[1] In 1778 Frederick's minister Schulenburg wrote officially to one of the colonial commissioners in Paris: "The king desires that your generous efforts may be crowned with complete success. He will not hesitate to recognize your independence, when France, which is more directly interested in the event of this contest, shall have given the example."

In view of the system of mercenary soldiery it is not surprising to find that on many of the American battle-

[1] Bancroft, vol. v, p. 240.

fields there were Germans opposing Germans. Dieskau in the French and Indian War served the French and fought against the Mohawk Germans under Colonel William Johnson. In the New Jersey campaign, during the Revolution, Knyphausen was at times pitted against Steuben, both of these officers having served in the Seven Years' War, as comrades under Frederick the Great.[1] In the siege of Yorktown Tarleton led his Hessians against the German Colonial troops under Armand, the left redoubt was taken by Germans under Zweibrücken against Hessian defenders, and other instances might be cited.

As soldiers the Hessians behaved like veterans and were not exultant in victory. Their officers, Riedesel, Heister, Knyphausen, Donop, Specht, Baum, Breimann, and Rahl, were all brave and capable men (possibly with the exception of the last mentioned). When in captivity they proved amiable companions; Thomas Jefferson, for instance, enjoyed their music. Riedesel, who was captured at Saratoga, and his wife, who wrote the delightful letters,[2] were especial favorites of their captors. The Germans in the English service who were made prisoners at Yorktown fraternized with the German Colonial regiments. General Mühlenberg commanded the small escort which accompanied the German prisoners to their winter quarters at Winchester in the Shenandoah Valley. Later they were sent to Frederick, Maryland, where they also found a hearty welcome on the part of the German farmers of that region. Others were sent to Lancaster, Pennsylvania,

---

[1] Knyphausen gave out a special order by which Steuben's life was to be spared if ever endangered by an attack of the Hessians. Cf. Rosengarten, pp. 78–79.

[2] *Briefe der Generalin von Riedesel*. (Berlin, 1800.) Translated by Wallenstein; also by Stone. Cf. also Von Riedesel, *Die Berufsreise nach Amerika*. (1788.)

and in all these places, because the Hessians were good
fellows, houses were opened to them, home comforts were
provided, and the German tongue was used to the delight
of their ears. In consequence many of them settled permanently in Pennsylvania, Maryland, or Virginia. We
read that at Frederick the salute in honor of the close of
the war, in April, 1783, was fired by Hessian soldiers
under a Bayreuth artillery captain. He also prepared the
fireworks for the evening, and the German regiments
furnished the music for the ball. Instances of Hessian
officers serving as school-teachers, and of still a larger
number becoming farmers, can be noted all the way from
New York to South Carolina.[1] In the Carolinas desertions
of Hessians were particularly numerous, following the
example of John Yost Mütze, who deserted near Charleston, then located in the Saxe-Gotha district, and became
the father of an influential family.

Desertions had occurred very early in the war and were
encouraged. The baker, Christopher Ludwig, declared his
policy in the following words: " Bring the captives to
Philadelphia, show them our beautiful German churches,
let them taste our roast beef and homes, then send them
away again to their people and you will see how many will
come over to us." Congress was not averse to the idea,
and their committee wrote to Washington advising not to
exchange the Hessians captured at Trenton. Washington
agreed, and the provision and transportation of the German prisoners was put into Ludwig's hands, who brought
them first to Berks, Lancaster, and Lebanon counties.
There were many deserters among the Hessians who were

---

[1] e. g., the ancestor of General Custer, Indian fighter, and cavalry
leader in the Civil War, was a Hessian soldier who settled in Pennsylvania. See below, Chapter XVI.

ready at once to volunteer for the American service. A movement was instituted to establish a regiment of Hessian deserters, but the plan was not countenanced by Washington.

The exact number of Hessians who made the united colonies their home will never be known. They commonly located in the German settlements, being disliked as a rule by the English settlers, who harbored resentful feelings against them. They never settled in groups large enough to form separate colonies, and were therefore lost in the German population. We depend for information upon insufficient records, such as those of a traveling Rhinelander, who reports that he found many Hessians located in the city of Baltimore, where, he says, one third of the population was German.[1] In accordance with the tendency of locating with other earlier German settlers, a number of Hessians located at Lunenburg, Nova Scotia. Several of the Hessians were men of learning, such as Julius von Wangenheim, captain of yagers, who wrote a description of American trees and bushes (Göttingen, 1781), and Dr. Johann David Schöpf, military surgeon of Bayreuth, who made a careful study of plants useful in medicine.[2]

Eelking[3] gives the names of twenty-eight officers and sub-alterns of the Brunswick auxiliary troops who remained in the United States at the close of the Revolutionary War,

---

[1] *Nachrichten und Erfahrungen über die Vereinigten Staaten von Amerika, gesammelt auf seiner Reise in den Jahren 1806 bis 1808.* Von einem Rheinländer. (Frankfurt-am-Main, 1812.)

[2] He traveled through the United States as far as Florida after the war, became acquainted with G. H. E. Mühlenberg, the botanist, who rendered some assistance to Schöpf in his work, published in Germany in 1787, entitled *Materia Medica Americanis Septentrionalis Potissimum Regni Vegetabilis.* Cf. Rosengarten, pp. 91-92.

[3] In the work already cited, *Die deutschen Hülfstruppen in Nord Amerika im Befreiungskriege,* 1776-83.

or deserted previously, or who returned to America after having gone back to Europe with their companies.[1] Kapp furnishes a careful tabulation of the number of German auxiliary troops in the English service, giving the number that arrived in America and returned to Europe,[2] as follows : —

	Number sent	Returned	Lost
Brunswick	5,723	2,708	3,015
Hessen-Kassel	16,992	10,492	6,500
Hessen-Hanau	2,422	1,441	981
Anspach	2,353	1,183	1,170
Waldeck	1,225	505	720
Anhalt-Zerbst	1,160	984	176
Total	29,875	17,313	12,562

Twelve thousand five hundred is therefore the careful estimate of the number of Hessian soldiers who remained in the United States, dead or alive. Certainly one half of the number can be counted as survivors and settlers within the precincts of the United States. If they were all like those of whom we have record, they made good citizens of their adopted country.

[1] The list is reprinted in *Der deutsche Pionier*, vol. **xv**, pp. 285–287.
[2] Kapp, *Soldatenhandel* (chap. xi), pp. 209–210.

CHAPTER XII

THE WINNING OF THE WEST

I. THE GERMAN SETTLERS IN KENTUCKY AND TENNESSEE

The early history of the Kentucky settlements — Germans among the colonists from the Carolinas and the Valley of Virginia — Favorable location of the Germans for early colonization — Migratory spirit — The question as to whether any particular national type was superior on the frontier — The frontier creates types — Many instances of Germans as hunters, trappers, and Indian fighters — The three classes of settlers — The Germans' share in the permanent settlement of the Blue Grass Region of Kentucky — Statistics gathered from land-records and the United States Bureau of Pensions — The Germans settled mainly in the central and western portions of the Blue Grass Region — Evidences of early settlements by Germans in Tennessee.

THE next four chapters will follow the progress of Western settlement from the period succeeding the Revolutionary War to the time when the frontier line disappeared from the map of the United States. The German immigrants of the nineteenth century, just as their predecessors of the eighteenth, followed the frontier line closely, aiding materially in the advance of American civilization to the westward, regardless of the hostility of savage races, or adverse conditions of soil and climate.

The settlement of the great Middle West, the present centre of population of the United States, proceeded through two channels: first, by way of the early settlements in Kentucky and Tennessee, and secondly, by way of the Ohio River.[1] As the opening from the southwest came earlier, that will be considered first.

The early history of Kentucky is inseparably linked with the name of Daniel Boone.[2] He was born in Bucks County, Pennsylvania, and migrated in his eighteenth

[1] All roads from the Atlantic States converged upon two points, Fort Pitt (Pittsburg) and Cumberland Gap. There was a road from Philadelphia through the upper and central points of Pennsylvania, by way of Juniata Creek and Fort Ligonier to Pittsburg; another led out from Baltimore, passing Old Town, and Cumberland Fort on the Potomac River, and along Braddock's road to Redstone Old Fort (now Brownsville, Pennsylvania), on the Monongahela River, thence to Pittsburg. The distance from Philadelphia to Pittsburg was about three hundred and twenty miles. From the latter place the settlers boarded a flat-boat and floated down the Ohio River. But the dangers of the water route were so great that if the travelers had little baggage it was far better for them to take the road through the Valley of Virginia to Cumberland Gap. The distance from Fort Washington (now Cincinnati) to Philadelphia by this so-called "Wilderness Road" was almost eight hundred miles, but the traveler was protected for most of the distance, though led through wild country. A military order of 1792 calls this the most direct route between Fort Washington and Philadelphia, i. e., by way of Lexington and Crab Orchard (Kentucky); Cumberland Mountain, Powell Valley, Abingdon, Botetourt, Lexington (Virginia), and Staunton; Martinsburg (West Virginia) and Hagerstown (Maryland); York and Lancaster (Pennsylvania). See *Filson Club Publications*, no. 2 (1886); Thomas Speed: *The Wilderness Road; a description of the routes of travel by which the pioneers and early settlers first came to Kentucky*, pp. 10 ff., 23 ff.

In 1792 the Wilderness Road was improved by private enterprise, the following German names appearing among the subscribers: Jacob Froman (who was the only one, besides Isaac Shelby, who subscribed so large an amount as three pounds), Peter Troutman, Isaac Hite and Abraham Hite, George M. Bedinger, George Muter, George Teagarden (Theegarten). See *Filson Club Publications*, *supra*, pp. 48–49.

[2] It was claimed for some time by writers on the Germans in the United States that Boone was of German origin. His birth in a county of Pennsylvania where there were many Germans, and the fact that he spoke Pennsylvania German fluently, seem to indicate more than mere acquaintance with Germans. The spelling of his name, ending in *e*, and resembling "Bohne," a frequent German name, seemed to give some further basis for the supposition. Biographers generally (e. g., Thwaites, *Daniel Boone*) give English ancestry. Cf. *Der deutsche Pionier*, vol. x, p. 273.

MISSISSIPPI FLAT-BOATS

CONESTOGA WAGON

year to North Carolina, where for some years he lived as
a hunter and farmer. About 1769, in company with several frontiersmen, he made a journey to the West for
adventure and discovery, and returned after an absence
of two years. He had visited the great hunting-grounds,
lying between the Ohio on the north, and the Tennessee
and Cumberland rivers on the south. That territory the
Indians, both of the north and of the south, claimed as
their own, but neither dared to have and to hold it. They
called it Kan-tuck-kee, "the dark and bloody ground,"
for it was the scene of battle and bloodshed whenever
rival hunters met. Into the struggle for possession of this
No Man's Land, the white race soon forced an entrance,
Boone's journey, in 1769, marking the beginning of the
stubborn war of conquest. After his return, Boone determined to make a settlement in the rich country that he
had seen. With his wife and children, and two of his
brothers and their families, he migrated to Kentucky. On
the way they met five other families and forty well-armed
men,[1] who joined the company. Near the Cumberland
Gap they were attacked by Indians, and driven back to
the Clinch River, a tributary of the Tennessee.

Several years later the Transylvania Company was
founded for the settlement of Kentucky, and Boone was
chosen to lead the surveying party. They cut the Wilderness Trail, went far into the interior of Kentucky, and
built a stockade fort, called Boonesborough. In 1775
Boone brought his wife, children, and friends, who had
remained on the Clinch River, to the settlement on the
Kentucky River, named in his honor. Other fortified
stations, as Harrodsburg (1774), Logan's Fort, Bryant's

---

[1] It is more than probable that some of these were pioneers of German
descent.

Station, Lexington, were founded. Bloody Indian wars followed, which drove back almost all of the early colonists, — who had settled in Kentucky immediately before or during the first years of the Revolutionary War. But when hostilities between the American colonies and Great Britain practically ceased, in 1782, a vast influx of pioneers appeared in Kentucky. The treaty that followed was not fairly kept by either the white or the red men, with the result that the Indian war was renewed with treble violence.

Boone was not the earliest hunter to explore Kentucky. A few years before Boone went to Kentucky, Stoner (Steiner) and Harrod, two hunters from Pittsburg,[1] who had passed through the Illinois territory, went down to hunt in the bend of the Cumberland, where Nashville now stands, and found game very abundant. In 1774 some forty men, led by Harrod and Sodowsky,[2] founded Harrodsburg, where they built cabins and planted corn.[3] This was the earliest settlement in Kentucky, and while its beginnings were ill-starred, it still exists, as the county-seat of Mercer County. George Yeager (Jäger), the "long Dutchman," had visited Kentucky with the Indians, when, as a boy, he was their prisoner. In 1771 he fell in with Simon Kenton and George Strader (possibly

[1] So stated in Roosevelt's *The Winning of the West*, vol. i, p. 144. Stoner (Steiner) was a Pennsylvania German, a schoolmate of Boone, and his companion in many adventures.

[2] There were a number of men of German blood in this expedition, e. g., Abraham Hite, grandson of Joist Hite, one of the earliest settlers in the Valley of Virginia. Cf. *Der deutsche Pionier*, vol. ix, pp. 262 ff. Sodowsky was a German Pole who was very successful as an Indian trader. The spelling of his name is also Sandusky.

[3] The corn was planted and harvested by John Harman (Johannes Hermann) in 1774, the first crop of a white man in Kentucky. Cf. L. Collins, *Historical Sketches of Kentucky* (1847), p. 452. Cf. *Der deutsche Pionier*, vol. x, p. 274.

the German name Sträter), and they proceeded down the Ohio to the mouth of the Kentucky River, looking in vain for the rich cane-lands, which Yeager remembered to have seen, in the land which the Indians called Kantuck-kee. In 1775, after Yeager had been killed by the Indians, Kenton and Williams accidentally discovered cane-lands inland, south of the Ohio River, in what is now Mason County (within the Blue Grass Region), presumably the same which Yeager had praised with great warmth, kindling Kenton's enthusiasm for the quest.[1]

The following is a glowing tribute to the unnumbered hunters and pioneers, whose strength was spent and whose blood was shed that others might follow: "The West was neither discovered, won, nor settled by any single man. No keen-eyed statesman planned the movement, nor was it carried out by any great military leader; it was the work of a whole people; of whom each man was impelled mainly by sheer love of adventure; it was the outcome of the ceaseless strivings of all the dauntless, restless backwoods folk to win homes for their descendants and to each penetrate deeper than his neighbors into the remote forest hunting-grounds where the perilous pleasures of the chase and of war could be best enjoyed. We owe the conquest of the West to all the backwoodsmen, not to any solitary individual among them; where all alike were strong and daring, there was no chance for any single man to rise to unquestioned preëminence." [2]

It has generally been conceded, in a vague manner, that the Germans had some part in the winning of the West, but the great importance of their share, from the very beginning to the end, has never been awarded full

---

[1] Cf. Collins, *supra*, pp. 383, 384 ; *Der deutsche Pionier*, vol. ix, p. 186.

[2] Roosevelt, *The Winning of the West*, vol. i, pp. 145–146.

recognition. At the period of the Revolutionary War, and immediately after, when the first strides forward were made, the Germans stood in great numbers at the very gateways of the Western territory, ready to press out into the new country as soon as the barriers could be lowered. The map illustrating the location of the German pioneers about 1775 (Chapter x) shows at a glance that the Germans were settled directly on the frontier line for most of the distance between Maine and Georgia, and that they were most advantageously located for the first plunge into the Western wilderness. The two sections that took the most prominent part in the early settlement of Kentucky and Tennessee were the Valley of Virginia, and the central, then western counties of North and South Carolina. In the Valley of Virginia, taking it throughout its length, the Germans were more numerous than the Irish, or any other element taken singly. In Botetourt, Wythe, and the southwestern counties of Virginia, German settlers became ever more numerous about 1775, and in the New River section and along the Kanawha, as far as our meagre information goes, they were about as well represented as any other national stock. In North Carolina they first settled in the Yadkin River district, while the Scotch-Irish were a little to the southwest of them on the Catawba, but by 1775 the German settlers had mingled with the Irish on the Catawba, thus reaching the farthest western borders. Their position on the Yadkin was quite as near, however, to the gateways of the West. In South Carolina the German settlers were from the start as far west as any. "In the Carolinas the Germans seem to have been almost as plentiful on the frontiers as the Irish," such was the opinion of contemporaries.[1]

[1] Adair, p. 245 ; and Smyth's *Tour*, vol. i, p. 236. Quoted by Roosevelt,

In Pennsylvania the Germans occupied the best lands of
the middle sections, and they also mingled with the borderers, the more adventurous among them, or the young,
wishing to build new homes, seeking the frontier. The German pioneers were a prolific people; large families never
appeared a burden to them. Children would very quickly
become helpers in the field or in the woods. As soon as
they reached maturity they would marry and seek homes
farther west, if they could not conveniently be provided
for at home. Their future depended entirely upon their
own energy and industry, as had that also of the parent
stock. These facts of early marriage and constant migration
we find recorded repeatedly by the ministers of the Lutheran and other German churches, from Pennsylvania to
Georgia. Mühlenberg says:[1] "I have noticed that within
the five years of my being here, hardly half of the original members of my congregations in the country remain.
Of the other half some have died, but for the most part
they have gone away, forty to one hundred English miles
[in the manuscript of his journal Mühlenberg says more
correctly, one to two and three hundred miles], to the
boundaries of Pennsylvania, to Maryland and Virginia.
In the mean time the congregations have not become less
in number, but have grown, because every year more Germans come in, and the others settle their children about
them, as many as can find room and subsistence." No

vol. i, p. 107. Smyth says : "It was also unlucky for me that the inhabitants on the plantations [frontier of North Carolina], where I called to enquire my way, being Germans, neither understood my questions, nor could
render themselves intelligible to me ; and the few I chanced to find that
did understand English, being chiefly natives of Ireland, most wretchedly
ignorant and uncivilized, could give me no directions to ascertain the right
way."

[1] *Hallesche Nachrichten* (Reprint), vol. i, p. 342, § 217, written from Providence, Pennsylvania (1747).

more authentic or striking proof of the migratory spirit of the German colonists could be found than this statement of the patriarch of the Lutheran Church. It shows us that migration took place westward and southwestward not only from the border-lands, but also from the midland counties.

In regard to the survival and success of pioneer settlers of different national stocks, a contemporary observer in Kentucky estimated that, " of twelve families of each nationality, nine German, seven Scotch, and four Irish prospered, while the others failed." [1] " The German women worked just as hard as the men, even in the fields, and both sexes were equally saving. Naturally such thrifty immigrants did well materially ; but they never took a position of leadership or influence in the community until they had assimilated themselves in speech and customs to their American neighbors. The Scotch were frugal and industrious ; for good or for bad they speedily became indistinguishable from the native-born. The greater proportion of failures among the Irish, brave and vigorous though they were, was due to their quarrelsomeness and their fondness for drink and litigation ; besides [remarks this Kentucky critic] they soon took to the gun, which is the ruin of everything." [2]

The good impression which the German settlers made upon influential men is illustrated by George Washington's plan of settling Germans upon his ten thousand acres, south of the Ohio, — lands that had been granted him for service in the French and Indian War. He wrote in February, 1774, to James Tilghman, in Philadelphia,

[1] *Description of Kentucky*, 1792, by Harry Toulmin, president of Transylvania Seminary, 1794–96 ; Secretary of State, 1796–1804. Quoted by Roosevelt, vol. iii, p. 17. (Should be ascribed to Crèvecœur.)

[2] Roosevelt, vol. iii, pp. 17–18.

concerning the possibility of settling Palatines on his lands,[1] inquiring whether he should send an intelligent German to the Old Country, for the purpose of recruiting colonists and transporting them. He also addressed Henry Riddle in Philadelphia, promising to give the German peasants free transportation to the Ohio, sustenance up to the first harvest, and four years' free rental on unimproved land. But the Revolutionary War made an end of his plan for the settlement of the Ohio Valley. Governor Glenn of South Carolina, in the middle of the eighteenth century, wrote concerning the Germans: "Our trade with New York and Philadelphia was of this sort, draining us of all the little money and bills that we could gather from other places for their bread, flour, beer, hams, bacon, and other things of their produce, all of which, except beer, our new townships began to supply us with, which were settled with very industrious and thriving Germans. This no doubt diminishes the number of shipping and the appearance of our trade, but it is far from being a detriment to us."[2] The German settler not only survived among the fittest, wherever he went, but he also established the economic independence of his colony.

The best frontiersmen were undoubtedly those born on the border. "Colonists fresh from the Old World, no matter how thrifty, steady-going, and industrious, could not hold their own on the frontier; they had to settle where they were protected from the Indians by a living barrier of bold and self-reliant American borderers."[3] The native-

[1] Sparks, *The Writings of George Washington*, vol. ii, pp. 382–383.

[2] Weston, *Documents connected with the History of South Carolina*, p. 61 ; quoted by F. J. Turner, *The Significance of the Frontier in American History*, p. 29.

[3] Roosevelt, *The Winning of the West*, vol. i, p. 124. The rule here stated had many exceptions.

born American possessed distinct advantages over the European as a border fighter, and he loved his work and manner of life. In that class of self-reliant frontiersmen the native-born of German descent were probably as numerous as any other stock. Impressions have been recorded, principally by writers on the Scotch-Irish element, giving the latter preëminence over other nationalities in the struggle with the forests and Indians. Any claim of that sort rests upon very uncertain foundations. The borderers were of mixed descent, English, German, Scotch-Irish, Scotch, Irish, Huguenot, and Welsh. The advantage of numbers after all lay with the Germanic stock,[1] taking both the English and Germans together as distinct from the Celtic. At all events, as time went on, the balance of advantage must have inclined more and more in favor of the Germanic race, because the latter, as contemporaries all agree, were in the end more stable, prosperous, and their permanent increase was larger.[2]

[1] An opposing view is the following : " The backwoodsmen were Americans by birth and parentage, and of mixed race ; but the dominant strain in their blood was that of Presbyterian Irish, — the Scotch-Irish, as they were often called. They were in the West almost what the Puritans were in the Northeast, and even more than the Cavaliers were in the South. Mingled with the descendants of many other races, they nevertheless formed the kernel of the distinctively and intensely American stock who were the pioneers of our people in their march westward, the vanguard of the army of fighting settlers, who with axe and rifle won their way from the Alleghanies to the Rio Grande and the Pacific." Roosevelt, *The Winning of the West*, vol. i, pp. 102 ff.

[2] One of the few available tests of the comparative rates of increase of various nationalities is furnished by the work of R. R. Kuczynski, " The Fecundity of the Native and Foreign-born Population in Massachusetts," *The Quarterly Journal of Economics*, November, 1901, and February, 1902. While the fecundity of the Irish Population is shown to be great, their permanent rate of increase stands behind the German and most other nationalities. Cf. also the statements recorded by Toulmin (see above, p. 364), that of a dozen families of each nationality, nine German, seven Scotch, and only four Irish survived.

The question of superiority of any particular national type over others, in the fight with the wilderness and the savages, is rendered all the more difficult because of the wonderful leveling influence of the frontier upon all national elements. A new type of American was evolved as a result of frontier conditions. Physically he approached the ideal of the red man, with his gaunt and sinewy frame inured to hardships and incapable of fatigue. His intellectual characteristics have been described as follows:[1] "That coarseness and strength combined with acuteness and inquisitiveness; that practical, inventive turn of mind, quick to find expedients; that masterful grasp of material things, lacking in the artistic but powerful to effect great ends; that restless, nervous energy; that dominant individualism, working for good and for evil; and, withal, that buoyancy and exuberance which come with freedom, — these are traits of the frontier, or traits called out elsewhere because of the existence of the frontier."

Germans or men of German descent, that came under the influence of frontier conditions, became hunters, Indian fighters, backwoodsmen, miners, or whatever later types the prevailing conditions made of them. They became indistinguishable from other frontiersmen. Great numbers of hunters of German blood were found among the early explorers and settlers of the "dark and bloody ground." There was Johann Salling, the German Indian, who under the name of Menou, "the Silent," was made a member of the Cherokee tribe. He fought their battles, hunted their game, and wooed their maidens until 1742, when he was captured by the French and taken to Canada, sub-

[1] F. J. Turner, *The Significance of the Frontier in American History*, published in the *Fifth Yearbook of the National Herbart Society*, Chicago, 1899, p. 40. Also in the *Annual Report of the American Historical Association for 1893*, pp. 199–227.

sequently to be set free.[1] With Daniel Boone there were Germans on most of his expeditions. Michael Stoner (Steiner) was the forefather of the numerous Kentucky Stoners of the present day. Kaspar Mansker, or Mansko, was one of the most famous of the Indian fighters. A wonderful marksman and woodsman,[2] he was made a colonel of the frontier militia. The crack of his deadly rifle, "Nancy," haunted his foes like a message of doom. Though not a native German, but of German descent, he spoke only broken English. He knew the cries of the beasts and birds and could never be deceived by Indian imitations of them. Stories of his Indian fights are told without number by Tennessee writers.

"Every old Western narrative contains many allusions to 'Dutchmen,' as Americans very properly [?] call the Germans. Their names abound on the muster-rolls, pay-rolls, lists of settlers, etc., of the day; but it must be remembered that they are often anglicized, when nothing remains to show the origin of the owners."[3] A "Dutch" station was established on Beargrass Creek (Jefferson County, Kentucky), in 1780.[4] At Estill's Station and Hart's Station (1779), there were "principally families from Pennsylvania — orderly, respectable people, and the men good soldiers, most of whom became victims of the Indian wars."[5] Lawrenceburg, the county-seat of Anderson County, was first settled by an "old Dutchman by

[1] *Der deutsche Pionier*, vol. ix, pp. 401–408. F. W. Hess, *Johann Salling, der deutsche Indianer*.

[2] Roosevelt, vol. i, pp. 150–153 ; Carr's *Early Times in Middle Tennessee*, pp. 52, 54, 56, etc. (Nashville, Tenn., 1859.)

[3] Roosevelt, pp. 107 ff. Reference is made to Blount MSS., State Department MSS., McAfee MSS., *American State Papers, etc.*

[4] *Filson Club Publications*, no. xi, p. 26.

[5] Collins, *Historical Sketches of Kentucky*, p. 421.

the name of Coffman" (Kaufmann), who was killed by the
Indians.[1] Another "Dutchman" is praised for his good
sense,[2] who, in company with Kenton, Haggin, and others,
would not wantonly fire into an Indian camp, remained
seated on his horse, and cantered off much at his ease,
when the others were hard-pressed in consequence of their
rash acts. There was an enterprising "Dutchman" named
Myers, a land-agent and general locator in the Ohio Valley, "in whose name more land was entered than in that
of almost any other man in the West."[3] These examples
might be multiplied. Last but not least should be mentioned the "Dutch" woman, who with Mrs. Mary Ingles
escaped from captivity in the Indian camp at Big Bone
Lick (Boone County, Kentucky), and successfully made
the journey, mostly on foot, and without provisions, for
hundreds of miles, through the wilderness of Kentucky,
following the Ohio River, then the Great Kanawha from
its outlet up to the New River country, where they found
rescue. The Dutch woman was crazed by the hardships
and privations of the journey, almost at its end, and attacked Mrs. Ingles, according to the latter's account, in
a life struggle.[4] Mrs. Ingles secured a canoe and abandoned her companion; both, however, completed the journey and survived. They were, in all probability, the first
white women who saw Kentucky.

When in 1784 the separatist spirit gained the upper

[1] Collins, p. 169. His wife said in her affliction : "I always told my old
man that the savage Ingens would kill him ; and I 'd rather lost my best
cow at the pail than my old man."

[2] Collins, p. 385.

[3] Collins, p. 217.

[4] As Mrs. Ingles declared, with cannibalistic intent (by agreement). It is
more than likely, however, that the struggle occurred for possession of the
canoe, which was only large enough for one. For a detailed account, see
J. P. Hale, *Transallegheny Pioneers*, pp. 41 ff.

hand in the Tennessee area, owing to disappointing legislation by the United States government, concerning
the navigation of the Mississippi, the settlers founded the
new state of Frankland or Franklin, with Sevier as
governor. His adjutant-general was the German, Major
Elholm,[1] who organized the militia with unusual skill. He
became very popular on account of his imperturbable
good humor, and his musical talent likewise won the
young people, who looked upon a campaign under him as
a recreation.

A more typical man of the frontier was Henry Crist
(Heinrich Christ),[2] born in 1764 of German parents, in
Virginia. In 1788 he made a trip in a flat-boat, from
Louisville, on the Ohio, to Bullitt's Lick, for the purpose
of preparing salt. The expedition consisted of twelve armed
men and one woman. They were on the way to Mud Garrison, situated midway between Bullitt's Lick and the falls
of the Salt River, almost where the town of Shepherdsville
now stands. Arriving in the Salt River, they were attacked·
by Indians, about eight miles below Rolling Fork. The
battle which ensued was costly. Of the whites, Crist alone[3]
survived, but he was frightfully wounded. Being unable
to walk, he bound his moccasins to his knees, and crawled
in the direction of the Licks. He almost succumbed from
exhaustion when but a few miles distant from his destination. Bleeding from many wounds, his clothes torn to
shreds by briars and thorns, he was discovered by a negro.
The latter, fearing this bleeding piece of humanity to be

---

[1] *Der deutsche Pionier*, vol. ii, p. 368 ; J. A. Wagener, *Frankland und
Franklin.*

[2] Collins, *Historical Sketches of Kentucky*, pp. 217–220.

[3] Collins, *Historical Sketches of Kentucky*, p. 219. Crist's companion Crepps
(German name Krebs), who had fought like a lion and made his escape,
died shortly after reaching Long Lick.

an indication of an Indian attack, rode back to camp at full
speed and gave the alarm. Crist was carried in safety to
the salt camp, but it took a full year for him to recover
completely from his wounds. The woman of the party
was taken captive by the Indians and later exchanged,
after General Wayne's victories. She reported, what seems
incredible, that of the Indian party, consisting of one
hundred and twenty warriors, about thirty were killed;
her story seems to indicate, at least, that the twelve whites
in this battle made the Indians pay dearly for their victory.
Crist some years after became prominent in politics, being
chosen a member of the legislature of the state of Kentucky, and in 1808 elected to the United States Congress.
He died in 1844 at the age of eighty.

One of the most prominent Indian fighters in border
history was Ludwig Wetzel, whose career concerns chiefly
the settlement of the Ohio Valley.[1] The two Sanduskys
(Sodowskys), German Poles from the Prussian province
of Posen, already referred to, were typical hunters and
traders. Jacob Sandusky, in a canoe, paddled down the
Cumberland into the Ohio River, then made his way into
the Mississippi, and followed its interminable course all
the way to New Orleans. He was the first white man on
record to do this, exclusive of the French and Spaniards.[2]
Jacob Sandusky died in Jessamine County, Joseph, in
Bourbon County, Kentucky.

The most brilliant military achievement originating in
Kentucky was the expedition of George Rogers Clark in
1778–79 against Kaskaskia (Illinois) and Vincennes (Indiana). Clark was the master spirit in the undertaking,
and was a Virginian of English descent, but his two ablest

---

[1] It will therefore be given attention in the next chapter.
[2] *Der deutsche Pionier*, vol. ix, p. 262.

lieutenants were Virginians of German descent, namely, Captain Leonard Helm (Fauquier County) and Major Joseph Bowman (Baumann, of Frederick County). Joseph Bowman was next in command to General Clark, and served with distinction in this campaign.[1] Other Virginia Germans among the volunteers were Captain Johann Holder, Major George Michael Bedinger (adjutant of Bowman), Johann Hager (of Ruddle's Station), Hans Sauter and Johann Pleakenstalber (Blickenstalwer). Colonel *John* Bowman, as county lieutenant, in May, 1779, commanded one hundred and sixty Kentuckians in an expedition against the Ohio Indian town of Chillicothe. The Indian town was surprised, many cabins were burned, and horses captured. The Indians rallied in a blockhouse, and drove off their enemies. When the Indians pursued, they were in turn driven back. The loss was nine killed and two or three wounded, of the whites, and two killed and five or six wounded, of the Indians. The attack was of great benefit to the Kentuckians, who were inclined to blame Bowman for defeat. It kept the Indians from making an inroad into Kentucky. The Indians were very badly frightened. " The expedition undoubtedly accomplished more than Clark's attack on Piqua next year." [2]

[1] The expedition of Clark will be described more fully in a succeeding chapter (xiv), on the settlement of the Northwest. It will be seen there that Bowman and Helm were the two lieutenants intrusted with the largest responsibilities.

[2] Cf. Roosevelt, vol. ii, pp. 96–97. We learn that "Logan, Harrod, and other famous frontier fighters went along." The Germans Johann Bulger and George M. Bedinger (later United States Congressman) were also among those that took part in Bowman's expedition. Cf. *Der deutsche Pionier*, vol. ii, p. 56. Two other German names appear prominently in the conquest of the Northwest : Honaker and Chrisman. Cf. *The Virginia Magazine*, vol. x, p. 47. Cf. also W. H. English, *The Conquest of the Northwest of the River Ohio, 1778–83*, and *Life of General Clark*.

In every important engagement, whether of discovery or warfare, we come upon German names. Thus in the fatal battle of the Blue Licks, August 19, 1782, in which the rashness of Major McGarry prevailed over the prudence of Boone, Major Benjamin Netherland (Niederland) was a "man of the hour." [1] "The majority of the men who escaped from the destructive conflict owed their preservation to Benjamin Netherland, — a fearless man, fruitful in resources, and the impersonation of nobleness and courage." Like many men of his stock, he was not a man of bravado, and therefore was sometimes suspected of cowardice. He was born in Powhatan County, Virginia, of German or Dutch descent, served under Lincoln in the Southern army in the Revolutionary War, and after coming to Kentucky in 1787 was one of the most prominent men in the Indian wars. In the battle of the Blue Licks, at the age of twenty-seven, he exhibited wonderful coolness and judgment. Being well mounted on the retreat, he gained the ford and crossed the stream in advance of many others. Looking back, he saw that his comrades, swimming and struggling in the water, were at the mercy of their ferocious enemies. "He dismounted and commanded the fleeing horsemen to halt, and fire upon the Indians. His splendid presence — he was six feet two inches high — restored the spirit of the fear-stricken riders. A dozen or twenty men instantly obeyed his call, and facing about with Netherland, they opened a fatal and deadly fire upon the foremost of the pursuing savages. The counter-attack was so sudden and unexpected that it checked the fierce pursuit of the Indians, and they instantly fell back from the opposite bank."

[1] *Filson Club Publications*, no. xii, pp. 183 ff., 186–187. K. T. Durett, *Bryant's Station.*

Another Virginia German [1] in this battle was Major George Michael Bedinger, born in Schäfersdorf, Virginia, of German parents. He came to Boonesborough at the age of twenty-four, and was one of ten to settle on Muddy Creek [2] (Mason County, Kentucky). In 1779 he served with distinction under Colonel John Bowman in the expedition to Old Chillicothe. In 1792 he was a member of the legislature of Kentucky for Bourbon County, and from 1803 to 1807 was a member of the United States Congress.

In the development of the West, three classes of settlers have commonly been enumerated [3] as representing successive waves of pioneer conquest. First comes the hunter or trapper, frequently combining with the pursuit of game the functions of an Indian trader. He would build a rude hut, do little with the soil, and for a livelihood rely mostly on hunting. In Kentucky and Tennessee most of the first settlers were hunters, rather than trappers or traders. Daniel Boone was of this class, and his descendants went ever farther westward, repeating the same service for advancing civilization. Immediately after came the hunter-settler. He was rather a cattle-raiser and ranger than farmer. He did his work roughly, and lived in a cabin destitute of the meanest comforts. His field was imperfectly tilled, blackened stumps and girdled trees stood all around, showing desperate and hasty efforts. He was restless, adventurous, shiftless, and when more in-

[1] Several others are also named in *Der deutsche Pionier*, vol. xi, p. 182 ; Jesse Jocum, Ludwig Rose, Peter Harget.

[2] Two other Germans accompanied him, Johannes Haller and Thomas Schwearingen.

[3] Turner, *The Significance of the Frontier in American History*, pp. 26–27, who quotes also Peck's *New Guide to the West* (Boston, 1837) ; Roosevelt, *The Winning of the West*, vol. iii, pp. 208 ff. Cf. also Dr. Rush's similar views, as given in Chapter v, above.

dustrious neighbors came about him, he felt uncomfortable and would escape before the advance of civilization. He sold his claim, gathered his cattle and scanty household goods, and went westward into the wilderness, to establish another advance post. "The Lincolns, the forebears of the great President, were a typical family of this class."[1]

The third class of settlers were the thrifty farmers. They understood the business of farming, possessed better tools, and were more conservative. They came to possess the land and bequeath it to their children. They raised big crops and big families, cut better roads through the forests, threw strong bridges over the streams, built mills of all kinds, established industries, laid out towns, and planted the institutions of civilized government. They had come for economic reasons, — because they were children of large families seeking an independent position for themselves, or they had found that their former location was not so good as they hoped their new location might become. But they had no intention of remaining pioneers all their lives. Some few of the first and second class of settlers would remain with the advance of the third class. There were also settlers that combined the characteristics of all three classes, starting as hunters, and becoming ultimately prosperous farmers, but that was the exception rather than the rule.

A foregoing chapter (v) has shown to what class of the three the German settlers commonly belonged. Dr. Benjamin Rush did not hesitate to put them into the class of permanent settlers. While such a disposal of them reflects the greatest amount of credit upon the Germans, since authorities agree that the only settlers of permanent value

[1] Roosevelt, vol. iii, p. 209.

are those of the third class, still we should be unjust to the German frontiersmen if we should deprive them of their part of the glory of having subdued the forest and the Indian with axe and rifle. Perhaps a greater amount of that glory belongs to other nationalities, but the more deeply investigation goes, the more convincing become the evidences of the large share of the German pioneers in overcoming the rage of the warring elements and savage men. Many instances have just been given of hunters, traders, and Indian fighters of German blood in Kentucky. Settlers of the third class, who located near or on the frontier, suffered more than any of the others, because their goods and cattle attracted predatory bands. The Irish and Scotch elements in general possessed a temperament more given to the love of fighting for the fight's own sake, while the German fought as fiercely and as well when his house and home were in peril, or when he saw some definite object to be attained.[1] When the fighter who fought merely for the love of it was born among them, such as Ludwig Wetzel, he was rather the exception than the rule.

It is not generally known how very extensive was the share of the German pioneers in the permanent settlement of the best farm-land of Kentucky, namely, the Blue Grass Region. This section embraces an area in the northern part of the state, the eastern boundary of which is a line drawn from the Ohio River opposite Portsmouth, extending south-westwardly to the confluence of the Red River (on the boundary between Clark and Estill counties) and the Kentucky River. The southern and western boundaries are

---

[1] It is interesting in this connection to note, as is explained in the chapter on the Civil War (Chapter XVI), that the German element, and the English also, exceeded the Irish element in the enlistments, in proportion to their numbers. Since the Germans were more numerous than the Irish, their total enrollment also was larger.

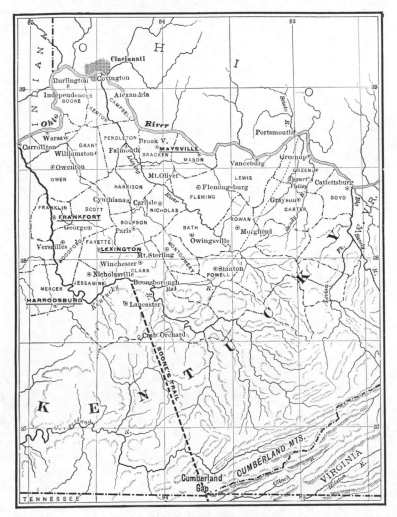

THE BLUE-GRASS REGION

formed by the Kentucky River, the northern boundary by the Ohio River. The bluish-green color which the grass shows here, and which the same grass loses when planted elsewhere, has given the region its name. The whole area is very fertile, tobacco, wheat, maize, flax, and hemp being the best products; the horses and cattle of this region are famous. From the earliest time the Germans from Virginia and the Carolinas, or their descendants, were attracted, as were the other settlers, by the offers of cheap land. The building of a block-house and one harvest, however small, secured the possession of four hundred acres of land and a preëmption of one thousand acres more.[1] This system, valid under the laws of Virginia, was to terminate in 1780. The desire to enter under these privileges before the time had elapsed brought crowds of settlers to Kentucky. The Indians noticed this influx of settlers with resentment, and troubles broke out at once, but the tide of immigration could not permanently be held back.

Among the eight men chosen to lay out the city of Lexington, in 1781, were John A. Seitz and George Tegersen. A plan was completed on September 26 of the same year, and sixty-two building-lots were sold, among others to the following Germans: Nickolaus Brobsten, William Martin, senior, and his three sons, John and William Niblich, Karl Seemann, Joseph Weller, and Johannes Weimar. Between 1782 and 1783 there settled also the following Germans in Lexington: Christopher Kistner and his mother, George Schäfer, Bernard Niederland, and the brothers Adam, Jacob and Christopher Zumwald.[2] The first pioneer hunters

---

[1] See specimens of certificates of Michael Stoner and others in H. Marshall, *The History of Kentucky*, vol. i, p. 100. (Frankfort, Ky., 1824.)

[2] *Der deutsche Pionier*, vol. xi, pp. 65–72, etc. These names were taken from land records by H. A. Rattermann, editor of *Der deutsche Pionier*. Cf.

of Lexington, Kentucky, and in the Blue Grass Region had been: George Jäger (Yeager), Michael Stoner (Steiner), John Harman (Hermann), John Haggin (Hagen), Joseph and Jacob Sodowsky (Sandusky), Peter Nieswanger, Michael Schuck, Leonard Helm, Abraham Hite, Abraham Schöplein (Chaplin).[1] Some of these became permanent settlers. Among the Germans at Bryant's Station were Jacob Böhler, who had a good house and farm in 1780,[2] and also the two friends Philip Niederland and Balthazar Kurz.[3]

In 1783 Kentucky was by act of the Virginia legislature made an independent court district. One of the first three judges was George Muter, son of a German father and a Scotch mother. He was born in Madison County, Virginia, and played a prominent part in the organization of the state of Kentucky. He made a decision against Simon Kenton in the matter of land claims (McConnell against Kenton), favoring the strict interpretation of the law. His decision occasioned a storm of opposition, since most titles in Kentucky were not clear. An attempt was made by the legislature to remove the judges, Muter and Sebastian, but without success. Muter resigned in 1795. Partisanship was violent in those days, but Muter had

his articles entitled : " Die deutschen Pioniere von Lexington, Kentucky, nebst Notizen über die ersten Ansiedler der Blue Grass Region." *Der deutsche Pionier*, vols. x and xi. Other articles of Rattermann on the Kentucky Germans are contained in volumes ix and xii. Rattermann has proved, what was not known before, that the German element participated largely in the early settlement of the Blue Grass Region, though a good many of his statements in detail must be viewed cautiously.

[1] *Der deutsche Pionier*, vol. x, p. 273.

[2] He was the same that lost two sons in the battle of the Brandywine.

[3] Cf. Didaskalia, *Die ersten Kentuckier.* (Baltimore, 1848.) The descendants of Böhler spell the name Baylor, those of Niederland, Netherland. Kurz was changed to Short. (Not all of the name Short, of course, are of the Kurz family.) Collins, *History of Kentucky*, vol. ii, pp. 173 and 772 ; *Der deutsche Pionier*, vol. x, p. 373.

fearlessly done his duty as he saw it. In consideration of
his services to the state, Muter was voted a pension in
1806 by the legislature of Kentucky, but this was recalled
in 1809. With Judge Muter as presiding officer, a meeting was held in Lexington, May 24, 1794, when resolutions were passed almost revolutionary in character. They
furnish an illustration of the spirit of separatism that existed on the western frontier. The resolutions maintained
that the protection of the frontier was a duty of the
United States government, and demanded for Americans
the right of free passage on the Mississippi (denied by the
Spaniards), though such a right be obtainable only by
force.[1] Muter was a member of the German Reformed
Church in Lexington and the first president of the Cale-
donian Society, the latter office showing his descent from
a Scotch mother.

The first college in the Valley of the Ohio, Transylvania Seminary, the first higher institution of learning
west of the Alleghanies,[2] received its first charters in 1780
and 1783, by act of the General Assembly of Virginia.
In 1792 the school was permanently located at Lexington,
and, uniting with the Kentucky Academy in 1798, the
institution received the name, " Transylvania University."
Colonel John Bowman, first military governor of " the
county of Kentucky," George Muter, and Jacob Froman
were among the first trustees of Transylvania Seminary.
John Lutz, A.M., a professor of the institution, was
during a short period president *pro tem.* Benjamin Gratz,
whose father, born in Silesia, was a prominent merchant
of Philadelphia, became a trustee and patron of Transyl-

---

[1] *Der deutsche Pionier*, vol. xi, p. 427, gives the resolution, quoting the
Centinel of the Northwestern Territory, June 14, 1794.

[2] The University of Tennessee (Nashville) dates from 1785.

vania. The Bowman family were very energetic promoters of the cause of education in Kentucky. Three brothers were the first three patrons of Kentucky University, starting the subscription with one thousand dollars each. John B. Bowman devoted more than twenty years, without salary, to the building up of Kentucky University, raising the endowment to two hundred thousand dollars, and through his exertions Transylvania was consolidated with Kentucky University in 1865.[1]

The Lexington Immigration Society printed their circulars also in German, to get immigrants of that nationality. The first record-books of Lexington were destroyed by fire, and the oldest existing volume dates from 1796. A number of Germans, owners of land, in that year sold their property, while others were purchasers.[2] The first lottery in Kentucky was established by Germans, to found a German Reformed Church near Lexington. In December, 1792, the following men composed the vestry of the so-called Dutch Presbyterian Society (which meant a congregation of the German Reformed Church): Schmidt (Smith), Schwab (Swope), Kerstner (Carsner), Kassel (Castle), Keyser (Kiser).[3]

The counties bordering on Fayette (in which the town

---

[1] *Filson Club Publications*, no. xi, *Transylvania University*, by Robert Peter and Johanna Peter, p. 20, etc. (1896.) Cf. also Ranck, *History of Lexington*.

[2] German names recorded under the sale of lands were: Reybolt, Wilking, Keyser, Hartmann, Rochus, Kruse, Helm, Schiner, Lischmann. Under purchasers of land in and about Lexington: Franks, Lützel, Georg Jung, Kühn, Lingenfetter, Gärtner, Poyzer, and Weibel. (*Deed Records*, vol. A.) Poyzer was the first drygoods merchant in Lexington. Cf. *Der deutsche Pionier*, vol. xi, p. 430.

[3] The following were German settlers belonging to the congregation: Lemkert (Lamkard), Springel (Springle), Keyser (Kiser), Weber (Webber), Adam(s), Hagert (Haggard), Böshardt (Bushart), Howe (of North German origin), and Meyer (Myers).

of Lexington is situated) likewise contained early German
settlers. So it was with Jessamine,[1] Woodford,[2] Scott,[3]
and Harrison counties.

The counties opposite the present city of Cincinnati,
Boone, Kenton, and Campbell, had early German settlers.
In Boone County there settled, in 1785, on the left bank
of the Ohio a family by the name of Tanner. Its head was
Johannes Tanner, a name once spelled Danner (or Gerber),
as the descendants in Boone County believe.[4] Johannes
Tanner was a Dunker preacher who had settled in Virginia.
Friction with the other denominations (the preachers Stöver
and Henkel) led to his removal to Pennsylvania, and subsequently to Kentucky. Both of his sons were kidnapped
by the Indians, which caused him to migrate once more,
in 1798, to New Madrid, in Missouri. Before Tanner removed to Missouri several German Dunker families had
settled at Tanner's Station (later called Bullittsburg),
among them the families Dewees, Matheus, and Schmidt
(Mathews and Smith). Many other German settlers, from
Lancaster, Pennsylvania, down to Madison County, Virginia, were attracted by the good reports from the original settlers. In 1800 Ludwig Rausch made his way to
Boone County, and his journey induced many others to
follow[5] a few years later. The city of Florence was

[1] The Priors, Millers, Poythress', were among them. Francis Poythress
was one of the pioneers of German Methodism in Kentucky. *Der deutsche
Pionier*, vol. xii, p. 298.

[2] Collins, vol. ii, p. 767, says Woodford County was settled by emigrants
from Virginia and West Virginia, but there were also several families from
North Carolina, Maryland, Pennsylvania, and New Jersey, as well as a respectable number of Irish and Germans.

[3] There were not many Germans in Scott County; among them were
Jacob Stucker, who had a farm on the North Elkhorn River, and from
whom the Indians in 1788 stole three horses.

[4] *Der deutsche Pionier*, vol. xii, p. 68.

[5] The following names denote heads of families settled in 1805, and after,

founded in 1820 by Wilhelm Wilheut (the descendants write the name Wilhoyt), Heinrich Crysler (Kreusler), and Jacob Kohnmer (Conner). The settlement grew and had a Lutheran preacher, William Carpenter,[1] who served the congregations in the Ohio Valley below Pittsburg.

The neighboring county of Kenton contains the town of Covington, opposite Cincinnati. The name Covington came from Leonhard Covington, who was born in Maryland. His father was of a noble family, from the neighborhood of Neubreisach, in Upper Alsace, who in 1697 wrote their name Korfingthan or Kurfingthan. The father came over before the Revolution, as an officer of the French, was captured, settled in Maryland, and later fought in the War of Independence.[2] One of the early governors of Kentucky was Christopher Greenup, after whom a county has been named. It is claimed that he was of German Virginian origin, his name having been Grönup.[3] One of the earliest settlers of Kenton County was Edmund Rittenhouse, a relative of the famous German-American astronomer, David Rittenhouse. Wilhelm Martin married Rittenhouse's daughter Marguerita, and

in Boone County : Hoffmann, Rause (Rouse), Tanner (several heads of families), Haus, Zimmermann (commonly changed to Carpenter), Ayler (Eiler), Biemann, Rausch, Holsklaus (Holzklo). and Utz ; most of these came from Virginia, as the names indicate. Holzklo will be remembered as the name of the old schoolmaster-preacher of Madison County, Virginia. Cf. *Der deutsche Pionier*, vol. xii, p. 71 ; Rattermann, *Eine alte deutsche Gemeinde in Kentucky.*

[1] His father, Wilhelm Zimmermann, was a Palatine who arrived in 1720. His son served in the Revolutionary War under Mühlenberg, from whom he received the suggestion to enter the ministry. Carpenter was a prominent minister, from 1813. The first vestrymen were Daniel Biemann, Rausch, and Tanner. One hundred and seventy-seven members signed the church document. They are named in *Der deutsche Pionier*, vol. xii, pp. 97–98. Carpenter founded a school at once.

[2] Cf. *Der deutsche Pionier*, vol. ix, p. 261.

[3] *Der deutsche Pionier*, vol. ix, p. 261.

their child, Isaac Martin, born May 4, 1798, is supposed
to have been the first white child born in Kenton County.
Another early settler was Johannes Piper, who arrived
in 1795 (his parents, coming from North Germany, had
settled in Savannah, Georgia, in 1742), and still another,
G. M. Bedinger, adjutant of Colonel Bowman, whose
descendants still live around Covington. Between 1810
and 1825 a number of German settlers took up their
abode in the county, among them the Schinkels.[1]

In Campbell County the Germans were active in the
first settlement of Newport, and the building of the roads
and mills on the banks of the Licking, as well as improving the land by cultivation. Johann Busch received the
right to run a ferry[2] across the Ohio opposite North Bend.
In 1795–96 Heinrich Brascher was judge of the court
in Campbell County, and Johannes Bartel, brewer, inn-
keeper, and farmer, in 1796; Franz Spielman followed as
judge in 1799.[3] To the south Gallatin, Grant, and Pendleton counties all had early German settlers, the descendants of whom were influential in state politics.[4]

In Franklin County the settlement of Frankfort, the
county-seat, and capital of the state of Kentucky, is of
interest to Germans. Its name implies German settlers,
but its early history is obscure. Collins[5] names the following as the founders: General Jacob Wilkinson, Daniel
Gano, and Daniel Weissiger, and the date as 1787. In

---

[1] A list of names can be seen in *Der deutsche Pionier*, vol. ix, pp. 309–315.

[2] Germans were frequently the ferrymen at river-crossings. Thus Harper
on the Potomac, at Harper's Ferry. See also, below, the ferry at Maysville.

[3] *Der deutsche Pionier*, vol. ix, p. 191.

[4] Steven Drescher in 1822 was a member of the state legislature, Samuel
T. Hauser in 1832, Samuel F. Schwab (Swope) from 1837 to 1841 (and
state senator 1844–1848), and William W. Dietrich (Deadrick) from 1871
to 1873. *Der deutsche Pionier*, vol. xii. p. 446.

[5] Collins, *History of Kentucky*, vol. ii, p. 707.

the register of 1802 Rattermann found a large number of English, Irish, and German names. Weissiger gathered about him a large number of Germans [1] and descendants of Germans in Frankfort (many of them from Frankfort-on-the-Main). Little is known of Weissiger; there is a record that in 1797 he was the possessor of a billiard-table, for which he paid taxes; he was the owner of one of six wagons in Frankfort. Frankfort seems to have been a gay town according to the frontier notion, possessing a theatre for a time. In order to check the passion for gambling, the establishment of a library was attempted, which, however, proved a failure. Whether or not the French and German population had anything to do with the gayety of the town is a moot question.

In Bracken County the towns: Germantown, second in size in the county, Berlin, and possibly Augusta, Milford, and Foster are of German origin. The county has its name from Matthias Bracken (a German name), a surveyor who came to Kentucky with Captain Thomas Bullitt, and laid out Frankfort. [2]

Maysville (in Mason County) is the oldest town on the Ohio below Pittsburg. Among its earliest settlers were Hans and Edward Waller. The father of Waller, commonly called "Old Ned," is claimed to have been one of the early settlers of Germanna, Spottsylvania County, Virginia. His son brought him to Kentucky about 1785. They had had difficulties at Germanna and withdrew to the Shenandoah Valley in 1770, whence they migrated

---

[1] Such names are given by Rattermann as Braun, Cammach, Casselmann, Hickmann, Jünger, Rauling, Rennick, Saltzmann, Schmidt, Vorhees, Melanchton, and Springer. *Der deutsche Pionier*, vol. xii, pp. 300–301. Dr. Louis Marschall was the first physician of Frankfort and father of Humphrey Marshall, noted in both the civil and military history of Kentucky. Cf. Rosengarten, *The German Soldier in the Wars of the United States*, p. 158.

[2] *Der deutsche Pionier*, vol. xii, p. 447.

again to the Opequon River. There young Waller met Simon Kenton and went with him to Kentucky. The two Wallers and George Lewis were the real founders of Maysville,[1] which up to 1800 bore the name of Limestone Point. In 1784 Hans Waller, in company with Johannes Müller, went to the Middle Fork of the Licking River, near the Upper Blue Licks. They settled thirteen miles south of the Blue Licks and founded Miller's Station. In 1797 the court of Mason County allowed Edwin Martin to run a ferry from Maysville across the Ohio.[2] Martin bought of the heirs of John May, who gave the name to Maysville, all purchasable lots, and remained in charge of the ferry until 1829. In 1818 Joseph Ficklin also received the privilege of running a ferry across the Ohio from Maysville.[3]

In addition to searching through the land records of the Blue Grass Region, H. A. Rattermann, editor of "Der deutsche Pionier," examined the pension lists at Washington of the years 1818, 1828, and 1832, mentioned in the reports of 1835. He there noted the names of the officers and men of the German regiments of the Revolutionary War, who received land-grants in lieu of cash payments. It appears that a large number of the German soldiers of the Revolution, particularly of the Virginia line, availed themselves of the privilege of obtaining lands in the Blue Grass Region of Kentucky, in the counties of Jessamine, Woodford, Franklin, Scott, Owen, Grant, Boone, Campbell, Pendleton, Bracken, and Mason.[4]

---

[1] *Der deutsche Pionier*, vol. xi, pp. 72 and 181.

[2] The first to do this had been Benjamin Sutton. *Der deutsche Pionier*, vol. xii, p. 448.

[3] *Ibid.*

[4] Many pages of German names of officers and men, in the Continental army and the militia, during the Revolutionary War and the War of 1812,

These statistics furnish a most convincing proof that the central and western areas of the Blue Grass Region were settled very early by Germans. From another source we learn that the Germans had also settled in the eastern edge of the Blue Grass Region. In 1813 the Lutheran ministers Scherer and Göbel found Germans settled in Tygart's Valley, "who had united themselves with the Baptists and Methodists." [1] Thus it appears that also in the great trans-Alleghany limestone area, that of Kentucky, the German farmers arrived early and took a strong hold.

An interesting view of the spread of the German settlements to the westward is furnished by the reports of the Lutheran missionaries of the North Carolina Synod, which was organized in 1803. The Reverend R. J. Miller [2] journeyed southwestwardly from Abingdon, Washington County, Virginia. In Sullivan County, Tennessee, he reports having found German congregations in charge of the Reverend Mr. Smith. Before his arrival they had been attended, as he says, by the Reverend Mr. Sink (Zink), now gone to Kentucky. The fact is very worthy of note

who received land-grants in the counties named above, are given by Rattermann, in *Der deutsche Pionier*, vol. xii, pp. 298–305, 444–450. The investigation might well be renewed and supplemented by researches in the archives of the War Department.

[1] Cf. Bernheim, *History of the German Settlements and of the Lutheran Church in North and South Carolina*, p. 389, etc. The latter work is based upon the Urlsperger and Helmstädt reports, church records, minutes of synods, and private journals. The facts contained in the succeeding paragraphs are derived from Bernheim.

[2] The Reverend Robert Johnson Miller, a Scotchman by birth, fought in the patriot army during the Revolutionary War, and after peace was declared lived in the South. He was licensed to preach by the Methodist Conference, yet, not having the authority to administer the sacraments, his people of White Haven Church in Lincoln County, North Carolina, sent a petition to the Lutheran pastors of Cabarrus and Rowan counties, praying that he might be ordained by them, which was accordingly done. He was probably the first

that he found several congregations on the Holston[1] River as early as 1803. They must have settled there long before, to have become so numerous. The fact also is significant that Mr. Sink, the preacher, went to Kentucky, undoubtedly to German congregations who had settled there. This shows the drift of the times. Miller wrote in his reports : " I preached in all congregations and in other places, particularly in Blountsville [county-seat of Sullivan County]; met Reverend Smith, an honest, upright man. Both he and his congregations are glad to be connected with our ministerium [of North Carolina]. Preached at Cove Creek October 11, to large and attentive congregations." Concerning the use of the German language in the western settlements,[2] the Reverend Mr. Miller remarks : " Among the old Germans there is a standing still; their youth learn and speak English; if a teacher speaks German, it is to them like the sound of a church-bell. But the affair is the Lord's."

In 1813 the Reverend Jacob Scherer, accompanied by another German minister, the Reverend Mr. Göbel, was sent on a missionary tour to Ohio, Kentucky, and Tennessee. After leaving Ohio they arrived in Powell's Valley, where there were many people from North Carolina and " several congregations could be formed." Scherer preached in Grassy Valley, and the next day arrived at the Reverend Mr. Smith's (on the Holston River), who accompanied him from the thirteenth to the nineteenth of July, for Mr. Göbel had left him there. On the twenti-

Lutheran clergyman who preached in English in the South or Southwest, and was selected as a missionary for his ability to preach in English.

[1] The name of this river is frequently spelled " Holstein." There may be some significance in this German spelling, which occurred very early.

[2] The missionary says this of the western settlements of South Carolina, but his point is undoubtedly applicable to the settlements of Tennessee, Kentucky, and elsewhere, as well.

eth he formed another congregation on the fork of the Holston (he calls it Holstein), and on the next day preached in "Rössler's" church. He preached also in " Bueller's " church, and in a new church on the middle fork of the Holston in Washington County, Virginia; then before another isolated congregation which had never yet been visited, on the north fork of the Holston. He soon arrived in the district of the Reverend Mr. Flohr, who was the Lutheran minister for a very large portion of western Virginia (including portions of present West Virginia). In conjunction with the Reverend Mr. Miller, he (Scherer) altogether organized thirteen congregations consisting of eleven hundred and seventy-five members (1813).

The great sweep of immigration to the Southwest did not take place before the Louisiana Purchase in 1803. Then it was that glowing reports of the fertility of the lands in the Southwest were spread broadcast, and advantageous offers were made to the settlers to secure for themselves homes "without money and without price." Many, accordingly, sold their possessions in North Carolina and Virginia, and migrated to Tennessee and Kentucky and to the Southwest, or otherwise, to the north of the Ohio River. In April, 1812, the North Carolina Synod admitted nine congregations in Tennessee as follows: Zion's and Roller's, in Sullivan County; Brownsboro and another (name not mentioned), in Washington County; Patterson, Sinking Spring, and Cove Creek, in Greene County; Lonax and Thomas, in Knox and Blount counties.[1] In succeeding years petitions for preachers came to the North Carolina Synod from Sevier County, Tennessee,

---

[1] These nine congregations were under the pastoral care of the Reverend C. Z. H. Smith, after whose death, in 1814, the Reverend Philip Henkel took his place.

and subsequently from Franklin, Lincoln, and Bedford counties, Tennessee. The Lutherans had become so numerous in eastern and southern Tennessee, in the second decade of the nineteenth century, that in 1820 a separate synod was formed, namely, the Tennessee Synod. At the first meeting, July 17, German was made the business language of the synod, and all of its transactions were to be printed in that language. In 1825 the minutes of the synod were printed also in English; during the first three days of the synod of 1827 German was the official language, but ever afterwards English. The leaders of Lutheranism found that the church grew much more rapidly when the English language was used in divine service and in the affairs of the denomination. Before 1820 a Lutheran seminary on a small scale had been begun in Greene County, Tennessee, under the supervision of Henkel and Bell. Theology, Greek, Latin, German, and English were taught. When the Lutheran seminary was established at Lexington,[1] South Carolina, the Greene County institution in Tennessee had long ceased to exist.

With these evidences of settlement and activity by the Germans in Tennessee, and a far greater number in the state of Kentucky, it is clear that the German element was very largely concerned with the great initial movement of Western development at the Southwest, which preceded the opening of the Ohio Valley. The location of the German settlers on the frontier, as illustrated by

---

[1] The theological seminary and classical school of Lexington, South Carolina, went into operation on the first Monday in January, 1834. The Reverend E. L. Hazelius, D.D., a native of Silesia, Prussia, was the first professor of theology, and he served for twenty years, until his death. The influence of the seminary was quickly felt in the Lutheran Church of the Carolinas. A larger number of ministers of good training were soon available for the Southern and Southwestern states. Cf. Bernheim, pp. 507 ff.

the map of German settlements in 1775 (after p. 263), and their migratory spirit, as described in the reports of the Reverend H. M. Mühlenberg, might have been accepted without further evidence as a proof that the German pioneers crossed the Appalachian Mountain ranges at every possible point and at the earliest opportunity. Yet they have never received credit for this historical fact. The materials brought forward in this chapter have long remained hidden in places difficult of access, such as the volumes of "Der deutsche Pionier," or in the obscure corners of local and state histories. It was necessary, therefore, to present a large amount of detail for the purposes of proof, at the risk frequently of wearying the reader.

CHAPTER XIII

THE WINNING OF THE WEST

II. THE SETTLEMENTS OF THE OHIO VALLEY

German traders, hunters, and missionaries in the Ohio territory — Causes for slow development — Pontiac's War — Colonel Bouquet — The first permanent white settlement in Ohio that of the Moravian missionaries on the Muskingum, Gnadenhütten, Schönbrunn, etc. — David Zeisberger — The massacre of the Christian Indians at Gnadenhütten — Continuous Indian wars — Settlements on the Ohio River, at Marietta, Losantiville (Cincinnati), etc. — St. Clair's defeat — General David Ziegler — The Indian fighter Lewis Wetzel — Expedition of General Wayne against the Indians opens the country for settlement — Ebenezer Zane, founder of Zanesville — German sectarians in Tuscarawas County — The "Backbone Region" of Ohio — The Scioto Valley — Martin Baum of Cincinnati, pioneer of Western commerce — Chr. Waldschmidt in the Little Miami Valley — Dayton and Germantown in the valley of the Great Miami — Distribution of German settlers throughout the larger towns of Ohio — The traveler Sealsfield's observations — Mission tours of the German Methodist Heinrich Böhm.

BEING more difficult of access, the territory north of the Ohio was not settled as early as Kentucky and Tennessee. It was inhabited by warlike Indian tribes, who proved to be quite as capable of resistance as their conquerors, the Six Nations, had been in the East. The first Germans to penetrate the Ohio country were the two men prominent for their exceptional services in Indian affairs, Conrad Weiser and Christian Frederick Post. Weiser several times served as envoy to the Indians of the Ohio Valley, in 1748 visiting the Indian village called Logstown, due west of Fort Pitt, near the Ohio state-line. The important mission, during the French and Indian War, of the

Moravian, C. F. Post, to the Indians of the Ohio Valley, in which he succeeded in separating them from their French allies, has been described in a preceding chapter.[1]

Post had established for himself the reputation of being a friend of the red man, and his marriage with a Delaware squaw increased the Indians' confidence in him. The marriage, however, was contrary to the wishes of the Bethlehem church fathers, and deprived him of the privilege of laboring in the mission service of the Moravians. This circumstance induced him to work independently among the Indians, in the spirit of the Moravians, though no longer as their ordained missionary. In 1761 he became the first white settler in the Ohio district, locating among the Tuscarora Indians in the upper Muskingum Valley, in what is now Stark County, Ohio. His was the first dwelling erected by a white man in the Ohio region, exclusive of the stations of the Jesuit missionaries and the huts of traders. Desiring to found a mission for the Indians, he applied for assistance to the brothers at Bethlehem. The young John Heckewelder thereupon volunteered to go to Post's settlement, and he soon became a worthy disciple, learned in the Indian tongues. At first they had some difficulty in obtaining permission from the Indians to cultivate the land, but soon after they laid out a garden (in 1762), gave instruction to the Indian children, and preached the Gospel to the more mature. But their presence in the Indian territory seemed to be viewed with disfavor, and involved danger to themselves. Judging from the signs all about them, something mysterious was brewing. Post had gone eastward, when Heckewelder found that he was in danger of assassina-

[1] See Chapter x, pp. 274–278.

tion. The latter immediately fled to Fort Pitt, and meeting Post on the way, notified him of the danger. Post would not be convinced until he had returned to the settlement, when he also concluded that his only chance for safety lay in flight.

The storm that was gathering resulted in what is known as Pontiac's War, which followed immediately after the French and Indian War. The Indians had found that they had merely changed masters when the French had given up their claims to the territory west of the Alleghanies. A more formidable adversary was facing them, and it was now their time to crush him before he had grown too strong. The Indians were fortunate in having a leader of great ability, Chief Pontiac, of the Ottawa tribe. Imposing in physique, eloquent and magnetic, he was endowed with all the qualities of the ideal Indian warrior. Going from tribe to tribe along the frontiers of New York, Pennsylvania, and Virginia, he convinced his hearers that the time had come when they might, by a bold stroke, crush the advancing white settlers, and regain all the hunting-grounds which the red men had lost. They were told that the Great Spirit was angry with them because they were cowards, and they were shown how all could be accomplished in a short time. The genius of Pontiac conceived the plan to attack all the frontier forts at the same moment, depriving them of the opportunity of assisting one another. Since the Indians were never desirous of storming fortifications, Pontiac planned to take the forts by stratagems. For each outpost a different scheme of surprise was devised, and complete secrecy was charged upon all the Indian allies. At one place the Indians, laden with furs, entered a fort, apparently to engage in trading. At a given signal the unsuspecting whites were cut down

almost to the last man.[1] At another the king's birthday
was celebrated with an Indian game of ball. The Chippewas and Sacs were engaged on opposite sides, and when
the game was at the hottest the ball was thrown over the
fortifications. All the players, numbering several hundred,
instantly leaped over the walls after the ball, and having
thus gained entrance, killed the defenders and took possession of the fort.[2] By most clever tricks and surprises all
the forts of the entire western frontier fell into the hands
of the Indians, with the exception of Detroit and three
forts in Pennsylvania : Bedford, Ligonier, and Pitt. Detroit
was saved by an Indian squaw, who revealed the plan to
Major Gladwyn. The three Pennsylvania fortresses owed
their safety to the watchfulness and discipline enforced by
Colonel Henry Bouquet, who in the French and Indian
War had served as colonel of the German regiment, the
Royal Americans, and as second in command in the expedition against Fort Duquesne. The Indians laid siege to
the Pennsylvania forts until Colonel Bouquet came to their
relief, who gained a victory in the battle of Bushy Run.

As was their wont, the Indians quickly wearied of the
struggle, deserted Pontiac, and lent a willing ear to pro-
posals of peace. Two punitive expeditions were immediately organized to invade the Indian territory, one at the
north under General Bradstreet, in the direction of Lake
Erie and Niagara, the other farther south into Ohio,
under Colonel Bouquet. Colonel Bouquet arrived in the
upper Muskingum region in the autumn of 1764, and
established a camp. Thither he summoned the chiefs of
the Seneca, Delaware, and Shawnee tribes, and their allies.

---

[1] The stockade at St. Joseph's River, in the northern part of Indiana.

[2] Fort Michillimackinac. Cf. Francis Parkman, *The Conspiracy of Pontiac,
and the Indian War after the Conquest of Canada*, vol. i, p. 338. (Boston, 1880.)

Before he would listen to any suggestions of peace, he demanded that within twelve days from the seventeenth of October, the Indians should deliver into his camp all white prisoners whatsoever who were in their hands, whether they be English or French, women or children, whether they be adopted by a tribe, united by marriage, or held on any other pretense. They were required also to furnish the prisoners with clothing, food, and horses, as far as Fort Pitt. After that, he declared, he would be ready to dictate terms of peace.

This bold manner of treating the Indians had the desired effect. They brought to the camp at Wakatamake two hundred and six persons whom they had taken prisoners, — eighty-one men, and one hundred and twenty-five women and children. The prisoners and their relatives at home were duly thankful for their release.[1] Those prisoners whose relatives or friends had not come with the army were taken to Carlisle, Pennsylvania, to be identified there. It is recorded that a German woman, Frau Hartmann, from eastern Pennsylvania, came to Carlisle, eagerly searching for her daughter. When found, the child did not recognize the mother. Bouquet asked the latter whether she could not recall some melody that she had sung to the girl in her childhood. Frau Hartmann sang the old church hymn, —

> " Allein und doch nicht ganz alleine
> Bin ich in meiner Einsamkeit,"

the child listening intently, and when the words were uttered, —

> "G'nug, dasz bei mir, wann ich allein,
> Gott und viel tausend Engel sein,"

---

[1] A few, it is said, had become so thoroughly accustomed to the Indian manner of life that they longed to get back to it, and were permitted to return.

the girl remembered them, and fell about her mother's neck.

We have seen that the attempt of Post and Heckewelder, in 1761, to found a mission in Stark County, Ohio, had failed on account of Pontiac's War. In the autumn of 1767 Post returned to his Western Indian congregation and remained there, the first pioneer. In the following year David Zeisberger founded an Indian congregation at Goshocking, on the Allegheny River, in western Pennsylvania. The Indian braves looked with suspicion upon an organization which converted their warriors into peaceable settlers, and several unsuccessful attempts were made to assassinate Zeisberger. By 1770 the congregation had greatly increased in numbers and they decided to move farther west, selecting a site on the Big Beaver River, about twenty miles from its confluence with the Ohio, and founding a settlement which they named Friedensdorf. But when this section was sold to the whites, the Christian Indians found refuge among the Delawares, Mingos, and Wyandots, of Ohio, who invited them to settle on the Muskingum. There Zeisberger settled with twenty-seven of his red-skinned disciples and founded Schönbrunn. The greater part of the Indians from Friedensdorf arrived in several groups during the summer, and a municipal code for the government of the Indians was committed to writing.[1] The regulations included a discipline, and also a summary of the fundamental doctrines concerning non-resistance.[2] The settlements were governed by the elders, Zeisberger, Ettwein, Heckewelder,

---

[1] Cf. Heckewelder, *A Narrative of the Mission of the United Brethren among the Delaware and Mohigan Indians, from its commencement in the year 1740 to the close of the year 1809.* (Philadelphia, 1820.)

[2] Paragraph 19: "He who goes to war, i. e., will shed human blood, he may no longer live among us."

and several other white men, together with the Helpers (National Helfer), who were Indians. In the following spring the remaining converted Indians on the Susquehanna and Big Beaver rivers came to the upper Muskingum region and founded Gnadenhütten and Salem, Brother Johannes Roth being the spiritual guardian of the former and Brother Gottlieb Sensemann of the latter.

These three Christian Indian villages lay at that time about five miles distant from one another, grouped about the confluence of the Tuscarawas and Muskingum rivers. To the north were the villages of the Mingos and Delawares, to the west those of the Mohawks, and to the south of the Shawnese. Northwest, on the Sandusky River, the Senecas had their hunting-grounds, while the Miamis and Wyandots were located still farther to the west. In the forks of the Muskingum, not far from Gnadenhütten, lay the Mohawk village Goshocking (Coshocton), in which lived the chief, White Eye. He was very friendly to the missionaries, and begged them to found another Christian village in the neighborhood, with the result that, in 1776, Lichtenau was built on the east bank of the Muskingum, about three miles below Goshocking. Thither Zeisberger and Heckewelder wandered, leaving Jacob Schmick at Gnadenhütten. This period was perhaps the most prosperous in the history of the settlements. A book,[1] printed in the Delaware language, was used by the converted Indians,[2] which taught them to read and write their own language, and gave them instruction in English and German. The

---

[1] *Buchstabir-und Lesebuch*, of Zeisberger, printed in Philadelphia; *Grammar of the Language of the Lenni Lenape, or Delaware Indians*; translated from the German manuscript by P. S. Du Ponceau, with a preface and notes by the translator. (Philadelphia, 1827.) Published by order of the American Philosophical Society in the third volume of the new series of their *Transactions*.

[2] Within the present Coshocton County, Ohio.

congregations numbered four hundred and fourteen persons toward the close of 1775. The Delawares lived in Schönbrunn and Salem, the Mohawks from New York in Gnadenhütten, and the Mohawks from the Muskingum region at Lichtenau. The journal of Zeisberger[1] shows that the Indians were capable of being trained in the peaceable pursuits of civilization. Had the Moravians been given a chance to develop the experiment more fully, it is probable that permanent results, of far-reaching consequences, might have been obtained. But the warlike spirit of the time and the unalterable prejudices of the contending races were in opposition to the peaceful methods of the Moravians. The converted Indians were destined to become the victims of a brutal massacre that will forever stain the annals of pioneer history.

When the Revolutionary War broke out, the Indians were invited to become the allies of the British, and from their point of view they decided correctly that such an alliance was their only hope against the advancing colonists. Soon even the tribes more friendly disposed joined the British alliance, while every neutral tribe was looked upon with suspicion. To the American borderers all Indians seemed equally noxious; to them the only good Indian was a dead Indian.

The Christian Indians were wedged in between two great war-parties, their own race urging them to join them and the British, and their few friends among the colonists advising them to go to the American forts for protection. In spite of these invitations they remained in their settlements, trusting in the protection of a Higher Power, and as they

---

[1] *Diary of David Zeisberger, A Moravian Missionary among the Indians of Ohio* (1781–98). (2 vols. Cincinnati, 1885.) Translated from the origina German manuscript and edited by E. F. Bliss.

thought, observing a strict neutrality between the two great rival parties. Nevertheless, on account of their location, being on the road to Fort Pitt and the eastern forts, they were forced to provide food and shelter to traveling war-parties. Thus they fell under suspicion, on the one hand, of being a relay station of the Indian warriors,[1] while on the other, the British and the renegade Simon Girty declared that Zeisberger and his companions were spies of the Americans.

The Six Nations, urged on by the British agents, directed the Chippewas and Ottawas to destroy the settlements of the peaceable Indians,[2] but the Western Indians felt no inclination to massacre the Moravian Indians, many of whom belonged to their own races. Finally the Wyandots were prevailed upon to act. Under their half-king, Pomoacan, the Wyandots, accompanied by groups of Delawares and other Indians, appeared in the Muskingum settlements in September, 1781. They were entertained by the Christian Indians for some time, until the guests began to act wantonly, killing pigs and cattle to no purpose. The demand was then made that all the converted Indians go with them and abandon their settlements. On their refusal, the white missionaries, who had great influence over their flock, were seized, and the entire body of Indians of Schönbrunn, Salem, and Gnadenhütten were forced to accompany their oppressors to the northward. According to Zeisberger,[3] the

[1] They were compelled from time to time to furnish food and shelter for both parties. On several occasions the shelter given the Indians, who had just surprised and attacked American frontier settlements, was bitterly remembered against the Christian Indians.

[2] Zeisberger's *Diary* gives the message of the Iroquois as follows : " Wir schenken euch die Christengemeinde, macht Suppe daraus ! " i. e., " We will make you a present of the Christian congregations. Make soup of them ! "

[3] *Diary of David Zeisberger, 1781–98.* (2 vols. Cincinnati, 1885.) Abstracts from the journal are found in *Der deutsche Pionier*, vol. v, pp. 284 ff.

missionaries were stripped of their clothing, and the whole village was robbed of all provisions and goods. The peaceful Indians were not even allowed to gather their crops. They saw the warriors parading about in clothing stolen from them, yet they proceeded cautiously throughout, fearing that resistance would bring death. An Indian woman, who had come with the warriors, being distressed by the evil treatment of the missionaries, stole the Delaware chief Pipe's horse, the best in the whole company, and rode it to Pittsburg. Her flight made the Indian warriors suspicious of the missionaries. Their fear of armed interference from Fort Pitt was not without foundation, for the American commander at the fort, Colonel Gibson, had endeavored to get the Christian Indians to come into the American lines, where he might protect them.[1]

It was soon apparent that the Wyandots were under positive orders from the Six Nations to bring the peaceful Indians away, dead or alive. The Wyandots had been attracted by the opportunity for plunder, and the hope also of increasing their fighting strength from the captured Indians. They had suffered severely from war and pestilence, and the half-king was troubled, because he could hardly get one hundred braves together. For greater safety the Wyandots had got other tribes to support them in this expedition.

Before the Moravian Indians left the settlements where they had prospered so well, they listened to a parting sermon and sang their German hymns. Then they journeyed for many days to the Sandusky region, near the southern shore of Lake Erie. They built rude huts, so that they might endure the winter's cold, but they were almost reduced to starvation. After earnest entreaties, some were

---

[1] Roosevelt, *The Winning of the West*, vol. ii, pp. 144–145.

finally permitted to go back to the Muskingum to harvest their corn and bring it to their new abode. About one hundred and fifty, men, women, and children, arrived in the abandoned villages at the beginning of February, 1782. In the mean time bands of Wyandots, under the Scotch-Irish renegade, Simon Girty, had ravaged the American settlements on the upper Ohio and Monongahela. Evil tongues had spread the report that the Christian Indians who had come back to the Muskingum had taken part in these savage raids.[1] Some of the border settlers conspired to destroy the Moravian villages, and accordingly a company of volunteers gathered together early in March, 1782, under the command of Colonel David Williamson.

The Christian Indians had just completed their work of gathering up the harvest, they had filled their sacks with corn, and were preparing to leave for the Sandusky region the next day. But the conspirators approached stealthily and rapidly. Finding a few peaceful Indians on the outskirts of Gnadenhütten, they slew them, so that the settlement was completely taken by surprise. The Indians were told that they would be brought to Fort Pitt, to be there protected against Simon Girty's savage bands, and that they should now summon the settlers from the other places, Salem and Schönbrunn. The Indians of Schönbrunn did not obey the summons and fled, but those of Salem came to Gnadenhütten, when they were seized and herded like sheep, along with the Indians of Gnadenhütten. They were placed in two large barns, the

---

[1] There were backsliders among the Christian Indians, young braves who joined the Indian war-parties that passed through their villages. These runaways were as cruel and savage as their associates, and, when they were recognized, the whites would blame the whole congregations for the apostasy and crimes of these few men. Roosevelt, vol. ii, pp. 151 ff.

men in one and the women and children in another. A mock trial was held by Williamson, in which the question was put, whether the captives should be taken to Fort Pitt or murdered. Williamson asked those who wished to spare the Indians to step out of the ranks, but only eighteen men out of the whole number showed any inclination toward mercy and humanity. The majority voted for cold-blooded butchery. In justice to American frontier history, it should be said that not one of the more noteworthy borderers was among them — no man of military distinction or reputation as an Indian fighter.[1] The cowards next decided upon the plan of massacre. Some were for setting flames to the blockhouse with its living prisoners; others, greedy for scalps, preferred to act as executioners. The latter method prevailed, and after giving the prisoners a brief spell to prepare themselves for death, the assassins entered the prison-houses and with club and knife dispatched every man, woman, and child. The only survivors were two boys;[2] one had concealed himself under the floor, and the other revived after being partially scalped. A detachment which was sent to Schönbrunn found that the Indians there had received warning and escaped.

The better element of the frontier was certainly not concerned in the expedition: the lowest and most bloodthirsty alone took part; nevertheless it is impossible to excuse the massacre under any consideration. It gave evidence of the savagery of the frontier, the inhuman cruelty resulting from the frequency of bloody scenes.[3]

[1] Cf. Roosevelt, vol. ii, pp. 157, etc.

[2] Klauprecht, *Deutsche Chronik in der Geschichte des Ohio-Thales und seiner Hauptstadt, Cincinnati. Zusammengestellt nach authentischen Quellen,* p. 92. (Cincinnati, Ohio.)

[3] Roosevelt's *Winning of the West,* which speaks with indignation of this massacre, contains a paragraph and footnote (vol. ii, p. 157) which

The person most to be blamed was Williamson, the leader, who drifted along in obedience to the popular wishes, without having character enough to lead or restrain. He and many of his men who had taken part in the massacre were shortly after called to a reckoning, not by the laws of the colonies, but by the fate of battle, in the wilds of Ohio. Williamson, to be sure, escaped with his life, but many others of the butchers met their death in the woods or were even tortured to death in Indian camps. A body of four hundred and eighty Pennsylvania and Virginia militia gathered at Mingo Bottom on the Ohio (near Steubenville), for the purpose of destroying the towns of the Wyandots and Delawares, in the neighborhood of the Sandusky River. The object was to punish them for their repeated raids on the Pennsylvania and Virginia frontier settlements. Their having taken in charge so large a part of the converted Indians had nothing to do with the

might seem to imply that the German element had some share in this massacre. The name of but one German is recorded as having taken part in this expedition. His name was Karl Bilderbach, who murdered the young Schebosch, the half-breed Moravian, immediately before the expedition arrived at Gnadenhütten. Bilderbach seems to have been as coarse and cold-blooded as the rest of the company. There is no evidence that any other Germans were in the expedition. The fact that the expedition was formed on the headwaters of the Ohio does not prove that there were Germans in it. If the German element was at fault at all, it was in a different way. Zeisberger and his Moravian missionaries had converted the Indians to a pacific Christian mode of life, out of keeping with the savagery of frontier conditions, to a non-resisting group of settlers destined to be ground to pieces between two millstones. In the footnote on page 157 appear the lines: "The Germans of up-country North Carolina were guilty of as brutal massacres as the Scotch-Irish backwoodsmen of Pennsylvania. See Adair, 245." This statement by no means accords with the reports we have by Lutheran ministers in the Carolinas on the general character of the German settlers, e. g., "Never has a German stood in the pillory in Salisbury; nor has ever a German been hung in this place." From a report by the Reverend Mr. Roschen. Cf. Bernheim, *History of the German Settlements and the Lutheran Church in North and South Carolina*, p. 332.

movement. Colonel William Crawford, a just and upright man, but with no special fitness for the undertaking, was elected to command the expedition. He was successful, by only five votes, in securing the leadership over Williamson, who had been in command of the forces at the Moravian massacre.[1] The borderers advanced to the Indian towns of the Wyandots and Delawares in the neighborhood of the Sandusky River. The battle that followed showed that the murderers of the peaceful Indians were no match for the Indian warriors, when roused in defense of their homes. The Americans were defeated, their retreat being soon changed to a rout. Crawford unfortunately was cut off from his men, taken captive and tortured to death by the Indians, a fate that Williamson should have met, who on the retreat took command when Crawford could not be found. An officer, John Rose, is mentioned as having been a tower of strength on this expedition. He was the soul of the fight in the battle with the Indians, and on the retreat was opposed to the separation of the army into small parties, which the commander Williamson advocated with such disastrous results. Even Williamson in a letter to General Irvine was unreserved in his praise of Rose.[2] The latter, whose real name was Rosenthal, was of German blood, born in the Baltic province of Livland. A duel had led to his exile. He served in the Revolutionary War in General Irvine's Pennsylvania regiment, and with greater distinction in the succeeding Indian wars. He went back to his native land upon hearing from his friends that he might safely return.

[1] Cf. Roosevelt, vol. ii, p. 159. The author notes that Williamson's command of votes indicated that public opinion on the border was not, as it should have been, outraged by the massacre.

[2] C. W. Butterfield, *The Historical Account of the Expedition against Sandusky under Colonel William Crawford, 1782*, pp. 206–207. (Cincinnati, 1873.)

JOHANNA MARIA HECKEWELDER

In spite of their misfortunes, the honor of having made the first settlements in the state of Ohio belongs to the Moravians in Tuscarawas County. In the village of Gnadenhütten the first white child[1] of Ohio was born July 4, 1773. Its name was Johann Ludwig Roth, son of the Moravian missionary of that name. The first white girl born in Ohio was in all probability Johanna Maria Hecke-welder, daughter of the missionary John Heckewelder, born April 16, 1781, in Schönbrunn. The settlement in Tuscarawas County struck new roots after the Revolutionary War, as will be seen below.

The frequent disasters attending expeditions against the Indians retarded the settlements in the Ohio Valley, Generals Harmar and St. Clair lost their reputation in successive Indian campaigns, and not until General Anthony Wayne, in 1794, made his thorough-going campaigns in Ohio, was the backbone of Indian resistance broken. Disasters, however, did not check completely the daring and enterprise of colonists moving toward the Ohio. The river itself gradually became the avenue of approach, in spite of the dangers of its wooded shores, where savages lay in wait for an opportunity to shoot down all whom the current brought within range, or, for the sake of plunder, to lure the boatmen into ambush by imitating the sounds of game.

[1] This statement is based upon the official journal of Gnadenhütten found in the Moravian archives of Bethlehem. The father was born in Branden-burg, Prussia, 1726, arrived at Bethlehem, Pennsylvania, 1756, and three years after entered the service of the Indian mission. Cf. *Der deutsche Pionier*, vol. vii, pp. 66–70. The honor of being the first white child born in Ohio had been claimed by Millehomme, the child of French traders, born in 1774. There is a tradition that among the captives surrendered in 1764 to Colonel Bouquet, there was a white woman from Virginia with a baby that had presumably been born in Ohio. That is a mere supposition, however, since the child could have been born elsewhere before captivity. The nationality of the Virginia woman is not known.

Settlements began to be made along the Ohio at the mouths of the rivers, and they soon proceeded upward along the courses of the larger tributaries. Marietta was the first settlement, in 1788, at the mouth of the Muskingum River. It was built for the protection of the border settlers, and a company of regulars under General Harmar was stationed there. The settlers were almost exclusively from New England. About the same time a few settlements were made farther below on the Ohio River, in the Miami region. Columbia, now within the precincts of the city of Cincinnati, was founded by Major Benjamin Steitz, an officer of the Revolutionary War. It was not known that he was of German blood (his name being spelled Stites) until Heckewelder's journal appeared. The Moravian missionary was a guest of Major Steitz in the year 1792, and says among other things that his host had bought twenty thousand acres from Judge Symmes and founded the town of Columbia, in October, 1788. At the time at which the note is made in the journal (June, 1792), Heckewelder states that Columbia had 1100 inhabitants.[1] The year after, in 1789, Losantiville was founded close by on the Ohio, opposite the mouth of the Licking River. John Filson[2] gave the name to the settlement: "L" being for Licking, "os" the mouth of the river, "anti" opposite,

---

[1] Columbia and the larger part of Steitz's land are at present within the first ward of Cincinnati. Heckewelder's journal was first published in 1797 at Halle, with the title *Sammlung von ausländischen, geographischen und statistischen Nachrichten. Herausgegeben von Sprengel.* It was published separately as already mentioned: *A Narrative of the Mission of the United Brethren.* etc. (Philadelphia, 1820.)

[2] He taught school at Lexington, Kentucky, in 1782, and was the first historian of Kentucky. His history appeared also in a German edition at Frankfort-on-the-Main, 1789. The Filson Club, which has published a valuable series of historical monographs, mainly on Kentucky history, honored him in the adoption of his name.

and " ville" the city; therefore "the city opposite the mouth of the Licking." The author of this queer conceit left his partners, among them Denmann,[1] a German-American from Strasburg (in Pennsylvania), to carry forward the project. Denmann was a land speculator and had bought from Judge Symmes eight hundred acres at five shillings an acre, now the very centre of the city. In 1790 the name Losantiville was changed to Cincinnati, in honor of the Society of the Cincinnati.[2] About fourteen miles below Cincinnati, Judge Symmes had projected the city of Cleves. The three localities, Columbia, Losantiville, and Cleves, were for a time rivals in the ambition to become the emporium of the Miami Valley. At first Columbia seemed to be a little in the lead, although Cleves undoubtedly had " the pull," Symmes being the influential man. But the third rival, Losantiville, or, as it was re-named, Cincinnati, ran off with the bone. Much depended on the location of the defensive fort of this region. Symmes wanted to have it at Cleves, but contrary to his wishes Fort Washington was built at Cincinnati, on the choice of Ensign Lutz. Tradition has it that his choice turned upon his desire to be near his mistress, who had removed from Cleves to Losantiville.[3]

[1] Another of the partners had been Colonel Robert Patterson ; Colonel Ludlow took the place of Filson. Judge John Cleves Symmes and his associates in 1787 bought from Congress a tract of land along the Ohio and Miami rivers. It originally contained one million acres, which was reduced later to 248,540 acres, because of the partial failure of the colonization plans. Its location was approximately between the Little and Great Miami rivers from the Ohio River on the south to the city of Dayton and beyond on the north. Cf. Jameson, *Encyclopædic Dictionary of American Reference*, vol. ii, p. 276.

[2] As described in a previous chapter (xi), a society consisting of officers who had fought in the Revolutionary War.

[3] See Eickhoff, *In der neuen Heimat*, p. 272. The chapter in which the story is told : " Die Deutschen in Ohio und Indiana," pp. 272 ff., was writ-

The Scioto River was ascended early for the establishment of land claims, but no settlements could prosper during the period of Indian wars, while the American armies were meeting galling defeats, and the Indians, confident and arrogant in victory, even threatened the settlements on the Ohio River. The Miamis, Wyandots, Ottawas, and others were by no means willing to give up their lands, merely because the Six Nations had by treaty resigned their claims to the Northwestern Territory. The Indians had inflicted irreparable losses upon the untrained armies of Harmar and St. Clair. General Harmar had in 1790 conducted an expedition to the Indian towns, destroying the dwellings and provisions of the Miami tribes, but on the retreat he was made to pay the penalty. His blow was only severe enough to anger and unite the Indians, not to cripple and crush them. Banding together, their vengeful forays on the frontier gained in frequency and ferocity. Attacks followed on all the Ohio settlements from Marietta to Louisville.[1] When, a year after, General St. Clair made his ambitious campaign against them, the Ohio Indians were ready to meet a more formidable foe than the raw militia and untrained regulars whom the brave but imprudent general gathered about him. Not taking the requisite precautions against his hidden and skillful foe, St. Clair's camp on the eastern fork of the Wabash was surprised by a force consisting of the "picked warriors of the Delawares, Shawnees, Wyandots, and Miamis, and all the most reckless and adventurous young braves from among the Iroquois and the Indians of the

ten by H. A. Rattermann, the editor of *Der deutsche Pionier*, whose important researches in German-American history have repeatedly been cited in other places.

[1] Roosevelt, vol. iii, p. 310.

upper lakes, and many of the ferocious whites and half-breeds who dwelt in the Indian villages." [1]

Their manner of attack was that which was generally employed with such terrible effect. They would shoot from under cover, from which they would appear only to tomahawk a victim or to escape when a bayonet attack was made. In this battle the Indians were numerous enough to surround a company which would charge with the bayonet, if lured on by fleeing savages. To escape annihilation St. Clair gathered about him what remained of the fourteen hundred men who had begun the fight, and charged desperately toward the road by which they had come. The Indians gave no quarter to the wounded that fell into their hands, and had they been less intent on plunder, they might have inflicted even greater losses on the retreating army. [2] From the rich spoils each tribe received everything they could desire in the way of horses, tents, guns, axes, powder, clothing, and blankets. Their insolence and savageness were increased tenfold and the conditions on the frontier became worse than ever before. St. Clair hastened to Philadelphia to defend his military reputation. His courage in battle and his honorable career in the Revolutionary War gained him a merciful judgment on the part of Congress and of President Washington, who had, however, earnestly warned him against being taken by surprise.

During St. Clair's absence his place on the frontier was taken by David Ziegler. General Ziegler took command at Fort Washington and reëstablished a sense of security

[1] Roosevelt, vol. iv, p. 37.

[2] A mere handful of the army reached Cincinnati. "Six hundred and thirty men had been killed and over two hundred and eighty wounded. Less than five hundred, only about a third of the whole number engaged in the battle, remained unhurt." Roosevelt, vol. iv, p. 47.

among the settlers. Every inch a soldier, and the ablest of the officers under St. Clair, he was the latter's choice for the position of defending the frontier at this trying period. In the Revolutionary War he [1] had been among the very first to enlist, serving in the first regiment of Pennsylvania in the Continental line, which became the second [2] regiment to be enrolled under Washington's banner. In the Revolutionary service he had the reputation of being second to none as a disciplinarian. [3] His subsequent career as an Indian fighter was noteworthy. He took part in the defense of Fort Harmar (Marietta) at various times; of Fort Finney at the mouth of the Great Miami; he was in the expedition of General George Rogers Clark against the Kickapoos on the Wabash; and, in 1790, in Harmar's expedition on the upper Miami. He was not present in the fatal encounter on the Wabash; having been detached for special service. After the battle, through watchfulness and enforcement of discipline, Ziegler succeeded in getting the remnants of the retreating army back into Fort Washington. The woods being full of Indians, he began at once the task of clearing them, at the same time adopting energetic measures for the protection of the inhabitants of the Ohio Valley. He thereby became the hero of the day and the favorite officer of the army in the Ohio district.

St. Clair had, by his assignment of Ziegler to this office, placed the latter over the heads of the ranking officers, Wilkinson, Butler, and Armstrong. This created bad feeling against Ziegler, particularly on the part of Wilkinson,

[1] A native of Heidelberg, Germany (born, 1748), he had served in the Russo-Turkish wars, and then immigrated to America, settling at Lancaster, Pennsylvania, in 1775.

[2] The first was a Massachusetts regiment.

[3] Major Denny's *Diary*. Cf. Eickhoff, p. 266.

whose resourcefulness at intriguing became notorious subsequently in the affair of Aaron Burr. Ziegler was made the victim of false charges, accused of drunkenness, and insubordination to the Secretary of War (General Knox). Ziegler thereupon resigned from the army, but retained his enviable place in the hearts of the settlers of the Ohio Valley. When Cincinnati was incorporated, he was elected the first mayor, or president, in 1802. In the following year he was reëlected unanimously, in recognition of his able defense of the settlement in 1791 and 1792, and as a recompense for unjust treatment on the part of the government.[1]

During the Indian wars a number of Germans gained renown as scouts and Indian fighters, either on their own account, or as members of the expeditions of Harmar, St. Clair, and Wayne. On the Scioto were the Indian hunters, George Ruffner,[2] David Bolaus, and Frederick Behrle. Without any special location lived as scouts and hunters, Peter Nieswanger, Jacob Miller, Johann Warth, and the

---

[1] Cf. Judge Burnett, *Notes on the Settlement of the Northwestern Territory.* Quoted by Eickhoff, p. 268.

[2] Ruffner was a German Virginian. Ruffner's Cave was named after the original settler in the Valley. Members of the family also settled in the Kanawha district in present West Virginia. In J. P. Hale's *Trans-Allegheny Pioneers* appear the notes (pp. 279, 280) : "1797. — The late General Lewis Ruffner was born October 1, in the Clendenin blockhouse, probably the first white child born within the present limits of Charleston" [West Virginia]. Also: "1817 — David and Tobias Ruffner first discovered and used coal here." Numerous other items occur concerning the Ruffners. They were one of the most prominent families in the district, as men of affairs, politicians, and preachers. Another important family were the Bowyers. In 1798 Peter Bowyer, father of the late Colonel John Bowyer, of Putnam County, made the *first* settlement in the New River Gorge, and established a ferry at Sewell. These items show that in the Kanawha district German pioneers came as early and were as active and prominent as those of any other nationality. Compare the numerous German names in Hale's *Trans-Allegheny Pioneers.*

brothers, Christopher and Joseph Miller. The most famous of the Indian fighters on the Ohio was Ludwig
(Lewis) Wetzel. " As a hunter and fighter there was not
in all the land his superior." [1] Lewis's father, Johann
Wetzel, [2] was born in the Palatinate, emigrated to Pennsylvania, and became one of the first pioneers of the West,
settling probably near Wheeling, in the county of West
Virginia which bears the family name. The Wetzel family consisted of four sons and four younger daughters.
The latter, together with one boy and the mother, had
one day gone to Wheeling to visit friends. Martin was
out hunting, Lewis and Jacob with the father, when they
were attacked in their blockhouse by a band of Indians.
They slew the father and made the two boys captives,
Lewis being wounded in the breast. He was then thirteen
years of age. The Indians encamped on the Blue Lick,
about twenty miles up the Muskingum. They neglected
to bind the captives, and when the Indians were sleeping,
Lewis whispered to his brother, " Jacob, let us escape and
go home." After they had gone a few hundred steps they
sat down upon a tree stump. Lewis again whispered to
his brother, " We cannot go barefooted. I shall go back
and get two pairs of Indian moccasins." After he had come
back with them, they thought it might be better to be
armed. Lewis went back to the Indian camp a second
time, taking two guns and a hunting-knife. Thus armed
the two boys fled homeward, taking the moon as a guide.
The Indians in their search passed the boys, and the latter then followed their pursuers' trail, which showed them
the path homeward for a distance. They again skillfully

[1] Roosevelt, vol. ii, p. 138.
[2] The name Wetzel in the original German records of the family appears
as Wätzel or Watzel. Roosevelt, vol. ii, p. 138.

eluded the Indians on their return from their vain hunt, and got back safely to the blockhouse, in the charred ruins of which they found the lifeless body of their father, mutilated and scalped. Then and there they swore to kill every Indian they should lay eyes on, and the vow was as faithfully kept as Hannibal's against the Romans.

Lewis became wonderfully skilled in the handling of his rifle. He could load and fire while running at full speed. In the use of a tomahawk and scalping-knife no Indian was his better. Of medium height, broad-shouldered, thick-set, his frame like his heart was of steel. His eyes were black and shot fire, his face was covered with the scars of smallpox, his complexion was dark from exposure, almost like that of an Indian. He was a true friend and a dangerous enemy, taciturn in mixed company, but communicative, oven eloquent, in a small circle of friends. Numerous are the adventures told of him. In 1782, shortly after Crawford's death at the stake, Wetzel happened to go in search of a horse with his friend Thomas Mills in the neighborhood of St. Clairsville. Near the so-called Indian Spring they met a company of forty Indians, who were watching for the stragglers of Crawford's expedition. The Indians and the whites caught sight of one another at the same moment. Lewis fired first and killed his Indian, while Mills had the misfortune to be wounded, overtaken, and scalped. Four Indians threw away their guns and pursued Wetzel at full speed. After running half a mile one of his pursuers was only ten steps away from Wetzel. The young man turned, shot his pursuer, and bounding away again, reloaded his rifle as before. Very soon the second Indian had come so near that when Wetzel turned to shoot him, the Indian took the muzzle of the gun in his hand, and forced a desperate struggle for

possession of the rifle. Wetzel succeeded in bringing the
mouth of the gun against the breast of the Indian, fired,
and the Indian fell. In the mean time Wetzel, as well as
his two remaining pursuers, was nearly exhausted. The
fugitive succeeded, however, in reloading his gun, and
now remained standing to await the two Indians. One of
them stepped behind a young tree, which gave his body
only poor protection, for he fell a victim to Wetzel's sure
aim. Thereupon the last Indian, believing that his adversary had diabolical resources at his command, gave up the
chase, shouting : " Can't catch that man; rifle always
loaded." The Indians on one or more occasions got close
enough to Wetzel to strike him with their tomahawks,
but desiring to capture him alive, so that he might be put
through a series of tortures befitting his great record,
they always missed their opportunity to rid themselves of
him. In the neighborhood of Wheeling alone, Wetzel is
said to have killed twenty-seven Indians. Another account credits him with no less than fifty Indians slain by
his own hand.[1] He slew more Indians than were killed
by either one of the two large armies of Braddock and St.
Clair during their disastrous campaigns.[2]

To punish the Indians for an attack below Steubenville,
the white inhabitants offered a reward of one hundred
dollars for the first Indian scalp secured. Major McMahon,
who had frequently led the whites in bloody encounters,
took twenty men from the Ohio and pressed on to the Muskingum. They there encountered a much larger body of
Indians and decided to retreat. Wetzel, however, would not
hear of retreating without having taken a single scalp,
and, concealing himself on the edge of the Indian camp,

[1] *Encyclopædic Dictionary of American Reference*, vol. ii, p. 364.
[2] Roosevelt, vol. ii, p. 140.

lay in wait for stragglers. He was successful in surprising two Indians in their sleep, killed one, and was much chagrined that the other succeeded in escaping. He arrived at home only a day later than the rest of the party and claimed the reward. He would frequently go off alone on an Indian hunt. On one occasion he was bold enough to attack four Indians who were asleep. He leaned his rifle against a tree, his plan being to kill one Indian after another with his tomahawk. He killed three in the moment of their awaking, and the fourth only saved his life by flight.

Wetzel was utterly without fear, and a good friend of the white settler, but his ferocity toward the Indians at times endangered the sacredness of treaty obligations. When peace had been made with the Indians in 1789, Wetzel would not recognize any restraint, and killed an Indian who had a safe-conduct from General Harmar. The latter succeeded in capturing Wetzel for this crime, but the law-breaker planned an escape. He asked to be allowed to walk about freely, by the river (the Muskingum). The privilege was granted and Wetzel frisked about like a colt, then returned to his guard. After repeating the trick several times, ever increasing the distance, he suddenly, by a tremendous effort, effected his escape into the woods, although his hands were tied. He was recaptured in Maysville and brought back to General Harmar at Cincinnati. When the prayers for his release were of no avail, the pioneers on both sides of the Ohio River determined to set him free by force, for Wetzel was as much an idol of the American frontiersmen as an object of superstitious dread on the part of the Indians. The news of the storming of the Bastille by the people of Paris had just reached Cincinnati. Incited by the reports, the pioneers planned to storm Fort Washington, where Wetzel was imprisoned. In order to prevent bloodshed, Judge Symmes issued a writ of *habeas corpus*, whereupon Wetzel, giving bond, was set free.

Enraged at his treatment by Harmar, Wetzel soon migrated to Spanish territory. In Natchez he was again the popular hero of the settlers, but became the victim of a treacherous plot. Though he could neither read nor write, and attached little value to money, he was arrested as a counterfeiter and sentenced to lifelong imprisonment in the calaboose at New Orleans. After being imprisoned four and a half years in a dark, damp cell, Wetzel was set free through the aid of influential friends, including the governor. In order that Wetzel's liberation might not come into conflict with royal instructions, a stratagem was resorted to. The prisoner pretended sudden illness and death; his body was placed in a coffin and was given over to his friends for burial. In the evening Wetzel arose from his tomb and the empty coffin was buried in the river. Under an assumed name he then went to Natchez, where he lived a few years in the family of his cousin, Siks. After the Louisiana Purchase he migrated to Texas, but his long imprisonment had undermined his constitution, and he soon died on the banks of the Brazos, in Texas, in the primeval forests that he loved.

The brothers of Lewis, Martin and Jacob Wetzel, were likewise good Indian fighters. An interesting encounter of Jacob with an Indian chief is told, in which the combat culminated in a wrestling-match. There was an accidental fall, whereby the Indian landed on top, and Jacob was saved only by his faithful dog, that sprang at the throat of the Indian, whom Wetzel was then able to dispatch. By a timely bit of good luck, he found a canoe, in which he crossed the river, and made good his escape, while he could distinctly hear the savage cries of his pursuers, who could not cross the river and who were bewailing the loss of their chief.[1]

Every type of backwoodsman was fashioned out of the German clay by the prevailing conditions of the frontier, and it is not strange therefore that we also meet the desperado. Mike Fink was a frontiersman of the half-horse, half-alligator type, a boxer, a gouger, a drunkard, and gross wit. His nickname was " Bang-all." He was a boatsman, having a keel-boat on the Ohio and the Mississippi. One of his favorite pastimes was to practice shooting with his bosom friend Carpenter. A glass of whiskey was put on the head of either and the other would shoot it off.[2]

After the defeats of Harmar and St. Clair, the constant Indian attacks threatened the very existence of every settlement in the Ohio Valley. The United States government was finally roused from its indifferentism. Men and resources were placed at the command of General Anthony Wayne, who had received the name " Mad Anthony " for his dash and fearlessness, but who in the Revolutionary War had also learned the value of caution. Contrary to the example of his predecessors, he would not enter upon his campaign until his army was well drilled in the practices of Indian warfare. Nor did he ever on the advance neglect to send out scouts and sentries in all directions. The result was an overwhelming defeat of the Indians,[3] in

---

[1] *Der deutsche Pionier*, vol. vi, pp. 173–174, "Bilder aus dem Hinterwald."

[2] *Der deutsche Pionier*, vol. vi, pp. 129, 135.

[3] The Indians numbered fifteen hundred to two thousand, Shawnees, Delawares, Wyandots, Miamis, Ottawas, Pottawatamies, Chippewas, and Iroquois, besides Detroit rangers and refugees. Wayne's forces were more numerous, two thousand regulars and one thousand mounted volunteers from Kentucky. Roosevelt, vol. iv, pp. 85–86.

the battle of Fallen Timbers, in the Maumee River district. This led to an Indian treaty the following year, and an era of new settlements on the Ohio and its tributaries on the north, the Muskingum, Scioto, the Little and Great Miami.

On the upper Muskingum the Pennsylvania German, Ebenezer Zane (Zahn), founded Zanesville. In lieu of payment for his lands, he contracted to cut a pack-horse trail from the Ohio River at Wheeling by way of Chillicothe to Limestone Point, i. e., Maysville, Kentucky. The United States mail was carried over this path for the first time in 1797. In the latter year Zane [1] laid out New Lancaster (now Lancaster), through which town the road also passed. The road and the towns upon it grew in importance and were for a long time the connecting link between the East and Kentucky. In New Lancaster appeared the first German newspaper west of the Alleghanies, "Der Lancaster Adler" (1807), printed in Pennsylvania Dutch.

Jefferson County, on the right bank of the Ohio River, just beyond its sharp turn southward, and opposite the "panhandle" of present West Virginia, was organized in 1797 by a proclamation of Governor St. Clair. Many Germans settled there and founded the city of Steubenville in honor of General Steuben. On the opposite side of the river, the area of western Pennsylvania around Pittsburg and south and west of it, including the district around Wheeling, West Virginia, there settled numerous Germans in a mixed population. In the Wheeling dis-

---

[1] Zane came from Lancaster, Pennsylvania, and named the new town in Ohio New Lancaster, in honor of the old. He first located in the neighborhood of Wheeling, West Virginia. See the account in the succeeding paragraph.

trict were located the famous Wetzels, the father, John Wetzel, being one of the earliest of the settlers in this region. A county near by, in West Virginia, commemorates the name of Wetzel. The settlements were exposed to Indian attacks, and many instances of heroic defense might be cited. The most noted case was that of the German family Zane (Zahn). Ebenezer Zane had established the first permanent foothold on the Ohio River, in 1769, building a blockhouse [1] on the present site of Wheeling. The fort was attacked in 1782 by a band of forty British soldiers and one hundred and eighty-six Indians. The particular hero of the siege was Elizabeth Zane, sister of Ebenezer Zane. The latter at the time lived about forty yards distant, in a house which was used as a magazine for the fort, which was left in command of Silas Zane. The ammunition of the fort being exhausted, it was proposed that one of the swiftest runners get a new supply from the magazine. Elizabeth Zane insisted on being allowed to go instead. "You have not one man to spare," she said; "a woman will not be missed in the defense of the fort." She rushed out when an opportunity presented itself, and reached the house. There Colonel Ebenezer Zane fastened a tablecloth about her waist, into which he emptied a keg of powder; then, with her precious burden, she succeeded in safely returning to the fort amid a shower of bullets, several of which passed through her clothes.[2]

[1] Its original name, Fort Fincastle, was afterwards changed to Fort Henry. During the Revolutionary War it was the object of frequent attacks by the British and Indians.

[2] This is the account given in the *National Cyclopædia of American Biography*, vol. xi, p. 90. Elizabeth Zane lived for many years near Martinsville, on the Ohio River. She was twice married. Her first husband was named McLaughlin; her second, Clark. A poem was written by Kara Giorg, commemorating her heroism. Cf. *Der deutsche Pionier*, vol. i, pp. 33–35. A monument has been erected in honor of Elizabeth Zane in the city of Wheeling.

Within the precincts of Pittsburg the Germans built the first Christian church west of the Alleghanies. Named "Die Smithfieldische deutsche evangelische protestant- ische Gemeinde," it celebrated the hundredth anniversary of its foundation July 9, 1882. Perhaps a Catholic church, founded by Father Weber, antedated this, but otherwise the English and Irish had no churches that were earlier.[1]

The first settlement in Ohio, that of the Moravians in Tuscarawas County, destroyed by the massacre of Gnaden- hütten, was revived when in 1797 Congress granted the Indian Moravian congregation three tracts of land, of four thousand acres each, in the same location as the de- stroyed settlements of Gnadenhütten, Salem, and Schön- brunn. It was an attempt at reimbursement for the losses inflicted by the brutal mob under Williamson, over which the government had had no control. Zeisberger had in the mean time wandered about for fifteen years in Ohio and Michigan. He had founded new villages (e. g., New Gnadenhütten, Pilgerruh, etc.), but the old distrust and hatred of the Indian race prevailed everywhere. In 1798 Heckewelder and another missionary were officially sent to the Moravian congregations abiding at Fairfield on the Thames River in Canada, to bring them back to their old homes on the Muskingum. They came and settled about three miles distant from New Philadelphia, and founded the village of Goshen. Zeisberger, the first town-builder in the Ohio Valley, died at Goshen in 1808. His tomb- stone records his age (eighty-seven years), and the glory of his life, his service as a missionary among the Indians during the last sixty years of his life.

[1] *Geschichte der ersten deutschen vereinigten evangelischen protestantischen Gemeinde zu Pittsburg, Pa. Anlässlich ihres hundertjährigen Jubiläums, nach Quellen bearbeitet.* (Pittsburg. Verlag von Louis Holz.)

The Moravian congregations in Tuscarawas County prospered, though the Indian element declined. Numerous settlers arrived, beginning with Jacob Busch in 1799.[1] An enterprising German, whose name was Knifely (spelled also Knisely), laid out New Philadelphia, since then the county-seat. Tuscarawas County attracted other sectarians. Mennonites came, and Zoarites settled in Lawrence Township. The latter were from Swabia, about one hundred and fifty landing at Philadelphia in 1817, with Joseph Bäumler as their leader. He was a weaver by trade, became their schoolmaster, and showed considerable talent for organization. The whole county received a definite stamp from its sectarian settlers. Its population was industrious, developed good farms and prosperous industries, but took little part in the affairs of the world about them. More than half of the present inhabitants are estimated to be of German descent.[2]

North of the forty-first parallel, and extending one hundred and twenty miles westward from Pennsylvania, there lay the territory called the Western Reserve, because it had been reserved by Connecticut when she ceded her other Western land claims. Its settlers were almost exclusively from New England, and they came by way of central New York and Lake Erie. There were some German islands, e. g., in Cuyahoga County, principally in the city of Cleveland, where many Germans and Bohemians settled when the Ohio Canal was opened; some Alsatians

[1] In the same year Peter Greer, Edmonds, Ezra and Peter Warner, from Gnadenhütten, in Pennsylvania, and several others arrived. Some of the names among them were : Uhlrich, Blickersdorfer, Peter, Rehmel, Romig, Stoker, Demuth, Lehn, Walton, Keller, etc. *Der deutsche Pionier*, vol. ii, p. 310.

[2] This estimate was made about 1870, but will undoubtedly hold for the present day. Cf. *Deutsch-Amerikanisches Conversations-Lexikon* (Schem), vol. xi, p. 51. (1874.)

and Lotharingians in Lorain County; and some in the northwestern corner of Erie County, in the neighborhood of Sandusky. These islands did not exist before 1826.[1] Immediately south of the Western Reserve, with its New England population, there was a broad belt of German farmers. The territory was called the " Backbone Region " of Ohio, because it formed the watershed of the state and lay somewhat elevated. The district is about fifty miles broad and extends westward across the state. It is distinctly the Pennsylvania-German part of Ohio, and its principal business was farming, mainly the growing of grain, while the Western Reserve raised more cattle; wherefore the Germans called it the cheese district. Even to this day Stark and Wayne counties are said to be the best wheat districts in Ohio. Stark, Tuscarawas, Wayne, and Holmes form the centre of the German agricultural area.[2] The settlement by the Germans began at the very beginning of the nineteenth century. While most of the names of the towns and townships were assigned without discrimination or special significance, still it is noticeable that a large number of the place-names are German, indicating thereby a German population, as, for instance: Berlin, Winesburg, Saxon, Hanover, Strasburg, Dresden, Osnaburg, Frankfort, Spires, Potsdam, Freeburg, etc. A

---

[1] There was one exception, namely, William Hollenbeck, the first German who settled in the Western Reserve of Ohio. He tramped from Pennsylvania to Wayne County, where he arrived in 1800. He then settled at Akron, Summit County. Cf. *Der deutsche Pionier*, vol. vi, pp. 200, 224 ff. There were also isolated cases of German settlers in 1801 and 1806.

[2] Richland County was a part of the German district. In Mansfield there settled, in 1818, the Swiss, John Jacob Weiler, who died in 1881, over one hundred years old. He was the richest man in central Ohio, not without culture, and had done much for the development of the whole region, especially by the building of railroads. He was the Martin Baum of the inland country.

German township occurs in almost every county, and the towns with scriptural names, such as Bethlehem, Salem, Nazareth, Goshen, Canaan, were for the most part settled by German Moravians, Dunkers, Amish, or other German sectarians. The towns of Canton, Massillon, Alliance, and Minerva were to a great extent founded and developed by Germans. Their industrious hands transformed the country from prairie and forest to rich farm-lands; their skill and enterprise quickened the development of industries, as the agricultural implement factories of Canton bear witness.[1]

In the Scioto Valley, in the present Ross County, were made some of the earliest settlements in Ohio. The German hunters, Ruffner, Bolaus, and Behrle, had already for a time lived in the neighborhood of Chillicothe. When in 1802 this town was incorporated, two Germans were elected to civic offices, Eberhard Herr and J. Brink. Chillicothe was for a time the capital of the state, and a convention for drafting the state constitution was held there. In this convention sat two Germans, Grubb and Op den Graff. Dr. Tiffin, an influential settler of the Scioto Valley, who was elected the first governor of Ohio (1802), turned to the Philadelphia immigration agent for colonists. A large number of German redemptioners, contracting for three years' service, were sent to Ohio. After securing their freedom they made good settlers. About seventy heads of German families, mostly tradesmen and mechanics, arrived between 1798 and 1818, settling for

---

[1] Ephraim Ball and Cornelius Aultman (Altman) laid the foundation for the prosperity of Canton with their two great factories devoted to the manufacture of threshing and harvesting machines, plows and bridge-building materials. *Der deutsche Pionier*, vol. iii, p. 218, etc. See also, *The German Element in the United States*, Volume II, Chapter III.

the most part at Chillicothe. One of them established the
first iron-works at the falls of Paint Creek.[1]

The earliest history of Cincinnati has already been
sketched. In the early settlement Germans were not numerous, but the few who were there were very influential.
David Ziegler's defense of the settlement has already been
noted, and his being elected the first mayor of the town.
He at one time established a grocery store in Cincinnati, but not possessing mercantile ability, he was glad to
sell out. A merchant of the highest type, however, was
Martin Baum, for a long time one of the richest men,
and the most daring and successful promoter of the West.
He was born at Hagenau, in Alsace, migrated to America
before the Revolutionary War, studied medicine in Baltimore in accordance with the wishes of his father, and
came to the West with General Wayne. After the war he
settled down in Cincinnati as a merchant. He kept a general store and rapidly grew rich. He used his means for
the promotion of great enterprises. In 1810 he built the
first iron foundry in the West, and about the same time
imported the German expert, Gülich, from Baltimore, to
build the first sugar refinery. Textile factories and steam
mills were also set up by him. He founded the first bank,
and was for many years the agent of the United States
Bank in Cincinnati. With another German, Captain
Bechtle, he introduced sail-boats on the Ohio and Missis-

[1] Quite a number of these Germans took part in the War of 1812–14. Colonel A. Hagler, Captain Joachim, and the names Funk, Keil, Kramer, Müller,
Hester, J. and V. Schob, Henness, Schumacher, and many others are on the
records. They were all of the Northwest army assembled at Chillicothe,
and had greater hardships to endure than the Eastern army. After the surrender of General Hull, some were transported to Canada, those escaping
running the gauntlet of Indian tomahawks through the Ohio woods. All the
interior settlements of Ohio were in danger of Indian ravages after Hull's
defeat. *Der deutsche Pionier*, vol. vii, pp. 144, 455, etc.

sippi, supplanting the flat- and keel-boats used up to that time. His vessels made regular trips between Cincinnati and New Orleans. He was a public-spirited man, interested in every important undertaking. He was mayor of Cincinnati in 1807, was reëlected in 1812, and served as recorder from 1816 to 1819. With his brother-in-law, Judge Burnet, and the physicians, Drake, Sellmann, and Busch, Baum labored to give Cincinnati a start also in matters of art and literature.[1] He was interested in schools and museums, helped to found the Cincinnati College in 1818, and the Western Museum in the year before. In his numerous undertakings he needed reliable laborers, and brought many German redemptioners to Cincinnati, whom he treated well. In his beautiful home, which was famous for its gardens and vineyards, he was the host of many German scholars and cultivated travelers.[2] In conjunction with some of the wealthiest men of Cincinnati, he met reverses in 1821–22, arising from the failure of the Cincinnati Exporting Company, which they had founded. Baum sold a great part of his property to Nicholas Longworth, like Drake and Burnet giving up his house in payment of bank debts. He recovered from his reverses and lived nine years longer to foster the commerce of the West, though he was not able to support great and daring enterprises with as large capital as before. One of his last undertakings on a large scale was the establishment in 1829 of a cotton trade with Liverpool. He was also the first land-owner and projector of the present city of Toledo, near Lake Erie (it was in 1817 called Port Lawrence), which he regarded as the

---

[1] He was one of the founders of the Cincinnati Literary Society, 1818 ; the Apollo Society, 1824 ; and the Society for Vocal and Instrumental Music.

[2] Cf. Eickhoff, pp. 278–279, where their names are given.

terminus of a line of communication from Cincinnati, through the Miami district, to the Lakes. His financial reverses, however, compelled him to sell his interests. He died in 1831, with the distinction of having been, in his generation, the greatest pioneer of Western commerce.[1]

Though Cincinnati did not contain a large number of Germans during her beginnings, it is very different at the present day. The great increase of the German population began about 1830. In that year only five per cent of the population was German; in 1840, twenty-three per cent; in 1850, twenty-seven per cent; in 1860, thirty per cent; in 1869, thirty-four per cent; in 1900, over forty-one per cent.[2] The Germans always remained influential. The manufacturers, Gross and Dietrich, who had come to America in 1828, built on their own resources the Dayton and Michigan Railroad from Dayton to Toledo, a distance of one hundred and forty-three miles, at a cost of nearly three million dollars. They thus executed the plan which Baum had dreamed of, and which he started to realize by his purchase at Port Lawrence.

An interesting German settlement was the first colony in the Miami Valley, on the banks of the Little Miami (1795).[3] The founder was Christian Waldschmidt, who in 1785 had lived at Gengenbach in Baden. He was a Separatist, and though well-to-do, refused to pay church taxes. He finally sold all his property, including a paper-mill, and in 1786, with about twenty families, sailed for the United States. He first settled in Montgomery County, Pennsylvania, then sent a party to examine the Miami

---

[1] *Der deutsche Pionier*, vol. x, pp. 42 ff. Cf. also Eickhoff, pp. 277–279.

[2] The total population in 1900 was 325,902 ; the total of persons of German parentage (including those with one parent German, the other native or foreign) was 136,093.

[3] *Der deutsche Pionier*, vol. x, pp. 346 ff.

country, and getting a favorable report, the whole company went westward. The site chosen was near the present postal station of Milford. It extended three miles north and south, was about two miles broad, and lay in a fruitful valley. Barns, mills, forges, and comfortable homes were soon built. There an industry, then rare in the West, the manufacture of paper, was established by Waldschmidt, who had already been familiar with this art in his native land. His was the first paper-mill in Ohio. The "Western Spy," which in April, 1800, had had to shut down because no paper could be obtained, even from the East, encouraged Waldschmidt to build the mill. On May 27, 1800, the "Western Spy" was enabled to reappear, printed on paper made in the mill of the Miami settler. Advertisements like the following appeared in the "Western Spy" : "Storekeepers and printers may be supplied with all kinds of paper at the store of Baum & Perry, Cincinnati, or at the mill."[1] (1811.)

Numerous groups of German settlers followed the first of 1795, coming in 1796–97 and 1798. A number of the later settlers came from Pennsylvania; the earliest were from Baden.[2] Christian Waldschmidt (Wallsmith) died in 1814 a rich man, leaving a property valued at $48,914, in those days considered a great fortune. The settlement called "Germany" was prosperous until 1861, when the United States military camp, called Camp Dennison, was

[1] The oldest mill in the West was in Virginia, at Brownsville, called the Red Stone Paper Mill (of Jonathan Sharplus). This mill, however, could not supply the large demand.

[2] The various groups are named in *Der deutsche Pionier*, vol. x, pp. 346–351. The changes of name are interesting. Waldschmidt becomes Wallsmith ; Freiberger, Frybarger ; Harmar, Horne ; Freis, Ferris ; Laudon, Langdon ; Bohne, Boone ; Bechenbach, Peckinpaugh ; Späth, Spade ; Rüthi, Reedy ; Orth, Orr ; Bockenheim, Buckingham ; Prisch, Parrish or Price ; Montag, Montauk.

established there by General Rosecrans. The camp ruined the town, and the old settlers migrated to neighboring counties or larger cities.

On the Great Miami, the German settlements were thickest in the present county of Montgomery, centring in two places, Dayton and Germantown, which as late as 1825 were rival cities, each hoping to surpass the other. Immediately after the treaty of General Wayne, in 1795, German settlers came to Dayton, among them Georg Neukomm.[1] Germantown was laid out in 1814, by Philipp Gunkel. In 1845 all of its five churches used the German language in divine service. In 1820 the town promised to outstrip Dayton. In 1825 it still maintained the same rank, but three years later the building of a canal from Dayton to Cincinnati gave Dayton a decisive advantage. Miamisburg, Pyrmont, and numerous other towns were founded by Germans. On the whole the German element preponderated throughout the county. German names are seen in all the public books and documents of the county, and in the maps of the villages.[2] Much of the German character is noticeable in the rural population of the district : industry, domesticity, frankness and merriness, along with the petty jealousies and quarrels, perhaps incident to village life more than to nationality.

All of the counties on the line between Cincinnati and Toledo received German pioneers between 1820 and 1835.

---

[1] He was the son of Christian Neukomm of Zweibrücken, who came to America in 1754–55, adopting the name Newcomer, and later Newcom. The Newcoms were not Irish, the mistake probably arising from the marriage of one of the boys with Margaret McCarthy. Other names among the earliest settlers were Gosz, Hammer, Glaszmeier. *Der deutsche Pionier*, vol. xi, pp. 127 f., 170 f. Other lists of names are found in the same volume, pp. 219, 254, etc.

[2] Names not previously mentioned are Gottesburg, Snydersburg, Philippsburg, Bachmann, Harschmannville, etc.

In Miami County,[1] Piqua has a large German population. Auglaize County had numerous German settlers at Wapakoneta, Minster, and New Bremen.[2] A little later, Germans settled Glandorf in Putnam County, and Delphos on the border between Allen and Vanwert counties. Germans from Frederick, Maryland, settled in the twenties at Tiffin, on the Sandusky River, in Seneca County. The city of Toledo, as all the large cities of Ohio, including the capital, Columbus, received an ever-increasing German population. In the south, Highland, Brown, and Hamilton counties had early German settlers.

An interesting record of the distribution and numerical strength of the German settlers throughout Ohio is found in the works of German travelers. Charles Sealsfield, in 1825, journeyed from Kittanning, Pennsylvania, about thirty-five miles north of Pittsburg, to New Orleans. He described the Moravian colony in Tuscarawas County, and was impressed by the number of Germans in Zanesville, Lancaster, Canton, and Dayton.[3] The early pioneers of Ohio did not have opportunities for regular church service, but were visited by traveling preachers with greater or less frequency. The Moravian missionary, Zäslein, was eagerly listened to, just as subsequently the Methodist, Heinrich Böhm.[4] The Pennsylvania German pioneers, and

---

[1] The earliest settler of Miami County was the German named Knoop. Eickhoff, p. 274.

[2] This settlement was made from Cincinnati. Cf. *Der deutsche Pionier*, vol. i, pp. 84 ff.

[3] *Die vereinigten Staaten von Nordamerika nach ihrem politischen, religiösen, und gesellschaftlichen Verhältnisse betrachtet*, von C. Sidons (Charles Sealsfield). Cotta: 1827. Zweiter Band, zweites und drittes Kapitel, pp. 20–54.

[4] Heinrich Böhm was the real apostle of German Methodism in the United States. He was born in Lancaster County, Pennsylvania, in 1775. His great-grandfather was a Swiss by birth, a Pietist who settled in the Palatinate and became a Mennonite. Jacob Böhm immigrated to America in 1715 and settled in Lancaster County, where Martin Böhm and also his son Heinrich

the Germans who came directly from abroad, preferred to hear preaching in German. In Ohio, so Bishop Asbury writes in his journal, "Brother Böhm has the largest body of hearers, because he preaches in German." In 1808 began the missionary travels of Böhm, in company with Bishop Asbury. They visited the states of Ohio, then only just beginning to be settled, Kentucky, Tennessee, the two Carolinas, Virginia, Maryland, New Jersey, Pennsylvania, New York, New England, and Canada. It is noteworthy that wherever they went they met Germans, and Brother Böhm had to preach in all places in the German language. It seems that he was selected to accompany Bishop Asbury for that very reason. Whenever their journey took them to pioneer settlements, they found Germans. Böhm preached in the German language at Pittsburg, Pennsylvania; at Wheeling, West Virginia; in the state of Ohio at Zanesville, Lancaster, Chillicothe, Circleville; in Kentucky at Louisville, Lexington, and Frankfort; in several places in Tennessee[1] and North Carolina, and at Charleston, South Carolina. This will give some notion of the more populous German areas. In Cincinnati, Böhm preached the first German sermon that had been heard there. It was September 4, 1808. "The village," he writes in his journal, "promises to grow very

were born. The young Heinrich received a good education from Rosmann, a Hessian soldier who had been captured with Rall's regiment at Trenton. To him Heinrich owed his good German. Böhm's father belonged to the United Brethren, becoming a bishop of the sect, but Heinrich received his inspiration at the Methodist conferences of Baltimore and Philadelphia.

[1] In East Tennessee he remained for some time on Pigeon River to preach to the Germans there. This was in the neighborhood of Sevierville. The German preacher Hemminger had already preached in German there (1808), which is a clear indication of a large and early German settlement in this region. Cf. *Der deutsche Pionier*, vol. viii, pp 25-35. It is interesting that Böhm found Germans even in New England. In Boston he stayed at the house of the Reverend Bernhard Othemann.

rapidly. It has almost 2000 inhabitants."[1] After the general conference of 1812, Böhm discontinued his missionary travels, settling down to work among the Germans in Pennsylvania. Subsequently he was assigned to New Jersey, locating in Jersey City. In 1859, though over eighty years of age, he made another tour of the West, this time crossing the mountains by rail. On June 8, 1875, he reached his centenary, and a great celebration was held in his honor in Trinity Church, Jersey City. His fivescore years did not prevent Böhm from preaching a sermon on this occasion. He died, January 15, 1876, in his one hundred and first year. During his tours he had traveled over one hundred thousand miles on foot and on horseback, and had seen prosperous cities rise spontaneously on what had once been prairie and forest. He had shared in all the joys and sorrows of the land, had seen all the presidents of the United States from Washington to Grant, and had voted in all the presidential elections from 1796 to 1872.

Historical records, as well as the accounts of travelers and preachers, prove that in the first decades of the nineteenth century the German element was very largely represented in the Ohio Valley by permanent settlements. The great immigrations from Germany into the Middle West were destined soon to follow.

[1] He apologizes later in his autobiography for calling the " Queen City of the West " a village.

CHAPTER XIV

THE WINNING OF THE WEST

III. THE ADVANCE OF THE FRONTIER LINE TO THE MISSISSIPPI AND MISSOURI RIVERS

(A) Westward progress of the frontier line, shown by the census maps — Descendants of Germans and foreign-born Germans as frontiersmen — Two centres of distribution on the Mississippi, (1) New Orleans, (2) St. Louis — Early Germans in Louisiana and Alabama (Mobile) — German settlements along the Missouri River — Duden's farm and description of Missouri — The "Giessener Gesellschaft," Follen and Münch — German towns and counties in Missouri.

(B) Beginning of the advance of the frontier line toward the Northwest; the Illinois territory opened by George Rogers Clark — Sketch of his expedition and of the work of his German lieutenants, Bowman and Helm — Settlement at Vevay, Indiana — The Harmony Society (Rappists) on the Wabash in 1815 — St. Clair County, Illinois ; Belleville, Highland, Madison County — Chicago — German settlements in Iowa : Dubuque, Davenport, Des Moines, etc. — Germans in Michigan ; the missionary Baraga ; settlers in Detroit, Ann Arbor, and Westphalia (Ionia County).

THE two foregoing chapters described the first two stages in the winning of the West with reference to the part taken by the Germans and their descendants. The Virginia and Carolina Germans were found stationed on the advance line and among the reserves that opened Kentucky and Tennessee for settlement. Coming from Kentucky on the south and from Pennsylvania on the east, they pushed forward for the conquest of the Valley of the Ohio. The pioneers of German blood arrived as early as any, and were surpassed by none in securing a permanent foothold in the newly settled areas.

One of the most glorious chapters in American history has been outlined in the report of the Eleventh Census of

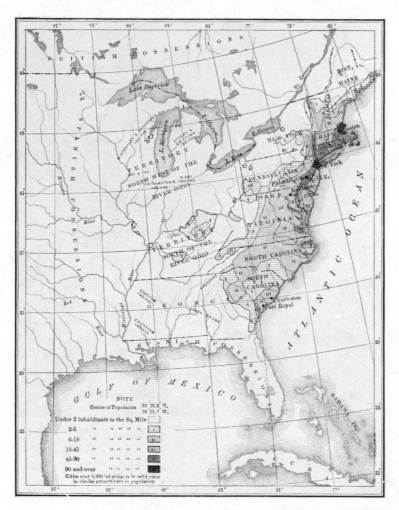

DISTRIBUTION OF THE POPULATION IN 1790

the United States in the volume on population.[1] It is the history of a century of conquest, 1790–1890, a conquest of the vast territory lying between the Atlantic and Pacific oceans, the Great Lakes and the Gulf of Mexico. The chapter is sketched by the aid of maps illustrating the density of the population of the United States at each successive census period. The frontier line in 1790 ran parallel to the Appalachian Mountain Range, crossing the latter only in a few places, — the Mohawk Valley, the Pittsburg district, the Holston and Kentucky lines of settlement. Slowly the frontier advanced to the westward, scarcely reaching the Mississippi by 1820, showing that a desperate struggle was going on between the white settlers on the one hand and the aboriginal inhabitants, aided by wild nature's barriers, on the other. Sometimes the line is involved and complex, but decade upon decade it steadily moves on, beyond the Mississippi, onward to about the ninety-fifth meridian in 1850, reaching the one hundredth (the beginning of the arid region) in 1880, with scattered settlements meanwhile leaping beyond, making a new frontier on the Pacific coast and in the Rocky Mountains. The next census report in 1890 announced the momentous fact that the frontier line had disappeared from the map of the United States.[2]

[1] *Report on Population of the United States at the Eleventh Census*, 1890, part I, pp. xviii to xxix.

[2] " Up to and including 1880 the country had a frontier of settlement, but at present the unsettled area has been so broken by isolated bodies of settlers that there hardly can be said to be a frontier line. In the discussion of its extent, its westward movement, etc., it cannot, therefore, any longer have a place in the census reports." *Bulletin of the Superintendent of the Census for 1890.* F. J. Turner, in his essay, *The Significance of the Frontier in American History* (p. 9), adds the following comment : " This brief official statement marks the closing of a great historical movement. Up to our own day American history has been in a large degree the history of the colonization of the West. The existence of an area of free land, its continuous recession,

For the historian of the German element in the United States no more gratifying field of labor will be found than the location of German settlements in the Western areas. He will find the German element on the frontier line at every stage of its progress westward, securing and defending it, or pushing it onward as did the Palatines before the Revolutionary War. Just as in the eighteenth, so in the nineteenth century, two classes of the German element must be reckoned with, those who through one or more generations were native Americans, and secondly, those who were born in Germany. The latter either came to better their condition, or they were refugees, oftener political than religious in the nineteenth century.

The native German element, except where it had dwelt in a distinctly German environment, showed complete assimilation and was undistinguishable from the native stock. Nevertheless the fact of its existence should not be overlooked. It had the advantage of position, also of familiarity with the modes of pioneer life, when compared with the European representatives of the same stock. This native element was abundant in every one of the three great currents of westward movement: (1) That along the Mohawk River through central New York to Lake Erie and northern Ohio. This was the road for the New Englanders to the Western Reserve district, but it was also the road west for the German element in the Mohawk Valley or on the Hudson, or even in New Jersey. (2) That proceeding through central Pennsylvania to Pittsburg, or the lower road following the southeastern border of the Pennsylvania mountains into Maryland, then westward on the North Branch of the Potomac River, thence to

and the advance of American settlement westward, explain American development."

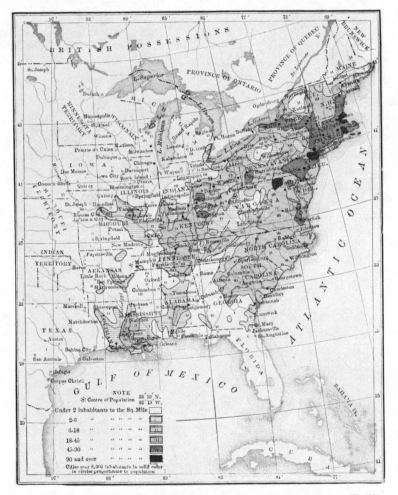

DISTRIBUTION OF THE POPULATION EAST OF THE 100TH MERIDIAN IN 1820

Pittsburg or Wheeling. (3) That of the Valley of Virginia, following its slope upward from the Potomac River and down after reaching Lexington, always proceeding southwestwardly to the narrow arm of Virginia in the neighborhood of Abingdon (Washington County, Virginia), thence to the Clinch and Holston rivers, which afforded an opening into Tennessee, — or to Cumberland Gap, opening a gateway into Kentucky.

But if in the eighteenth century immigrants from Germany could be numbered by hundreds of thousands, in the nineteenth they were numbered by millions. About the middle of the nineteenth century the German immigration grew to be larger than that of any other European stock, surpassing even the Irish. In the nineteenth century Germany's addition to the population of the United States was the largest single contribution of any foreign nation. The great bulk of the new foreign element settled in the growing West. The principle underlying the movement was the same as that apparent in the eighteenth century. The newcomers, who as a class were not wealthy, were looking for betterment of their condition, and migrated to those districts where the land was most available and cheap. Consequently they settled largely on the Western frontier. Being particularly well adapted to the work of the agriculturist, the town-builder, and small trader, and possessing the advantage of numbers, the Germans can claim the honor of having contributed a larger share toward winning the great Western territory for civilization than any other single foreign element. Their nearest rivals in numbers, the Irish, were not as well distributed over the Western areas, settling, as the census reports show, more largely in the populous towns.

An examination of the geographical location of the German immigration according to the statistics of the last census (1900)[1] will show that the Germans have located in the West in greater numbers than elsewhere. Of the total number born in Germany, 2,666,990, who were living in the United States in 1900, there were 883,908 located in the North Atlantic division; 72,705 in the South Atlantic; 1,461,603, or more than one half, in the North Central division, including Ohio, Indiana, Illinois, Michigan, Wisconsin, Minnesota, Iowa, Missouri, North and South Dakota, Nebraska, Kansas; while in the South Central and Western divisions there were 109,743 and 135,459 respectively. This shows that the Germans in the Western far outnumber those of the Eastern areas, however great may be their fondness for the larger cities of the Atlantic coast. They have advanced into every new state in numbers proportionate to the resources of the section. The settlements described in the twelfth and thirteenth chapters bring us to the decade 1810–20. On the maps of the census reports[2] we notice that settlements on the Mississippi River were begun by 1810, and until 1820 increased principally in two localities: (1) around St. Louis to the north and south, on both shores of the Mississippi, and westward on the Missouri; (2) around New Orleans and the rivers near by, that flow into the Mississippi. After the Louisiana Purchase had been made in 1803, the Valley of the Mississippi was open for settlement, but New Orleans did not immediately increase in population to any large degree. Not until after the battle of New Orleans, in 1815, did immigration advance more rapidly toward

[1] *Twelfth Census of the United States,* 1900, vol. i, "Population," part I, pp. clxxiii – clxxiv, table LXXXII.

[2] Preceding pages xxi and xxiii of the *Report on Population of the United States at the Eleventh Census,* 1890, part I. The maps of 1790, 1820, 1850, and 1890 have been inserted in the present and succeeding chapters.

DISTRIBUTION OF THE POPULATION EAST OF THE 100TH MERIDIAN IN 1850

Louisiana, receiving serious setbacks, however, by the inroads of yellow fever.

There had been German settlers shortly after the foundation of New Orleans by the French under Bienville in 1718. The speculator, John Law,[1] had founded in Paris a Western Company for the settlement of the lower Mississippi. His tract lay on the Arkansas River, not far from its mouth, and he sent out agents for his colonizing scheme to France, Germany, and Switzerland. In the Palatinate, owing to conditions described in a previous chapter, the recruiting agents were very successful. About two thousand persons are said to have accepted the inducements of free passage, land, and citizenship, for three years' service in the "earthly paradise of Louisiana." On their arrival it was found that no preparations had been made to receive them on the Mississippi, and they were therefore landed on the coast at Biloxi, near Mobile Bay. In that locality they are said to have remained five years, most of them becoming victims of Southern fevers. Their camps became heaps of graves, where remained a few ghastly spectres that yet stole from place to place.[2] Some sought food in the woods, others made their way to the English and Spanish settlements, only a few saw their fatherland again. Those who remained, about three hundred in number, were settled, in 1722, west of the Mississippi in Attakapas, Southern Louisiana. They

---

[1] John Law (1671–1729) established a private bank in Paris in 1716. His plan of a national bank and the issue of paper money was adopted by the French Regent. In 1719 depreciated national currency was received at its par value in payment of shares in Law's scheme for colonizing the Mississippi Valley. Speculation and inflated currency caused a panic in 1720. *Encyclopædic Dictionary of American History*, vol. i, p. 386.

[2] Morbois, *History of Louisiana ;* quoted by Eickhoff, *In der neuen Heimat*, p. 316.

are said to have become prosperous, and undoubtedly they were immune against disease.

A Swedish captain, Karl Friedrich D'Arensbourg, likewise induced by Law's promises, settled some Alsatians and Würtembergers about twenty miles above New Orleans, in the St. Charles District. They were more fortunate, and in 1750 their settlement was still the most important in that region. The names, Lac des Allemands, the river Bayou Allemand, and the village Allemand, found in the region of their settlement, still bear witness of their existence.

Germans from abroad did not again come to New Orleans until about 1830. At that time a large number were transported to the upper Mississippi by way of New Orleans.[1] Many German immigrants tarried at New Orleans and remained, as often happened in the seaports where immigrants landed. A little after 1840 the city is said to have numbered ten thousand Germans among its inhabitants. For the most part they were not wealthy, and because they had not the means to leave during the unhealthy period, great numbers filled the wet graves of the city. In 1843 almost a thousand are said to have perished. Many dwelt in Algiers, opposite New Orleans, and were described as prosperous and gay. In the city proper the Germans commonly lived in the English quarter, only a few in the French, and none in the

[1] An evidence of the immigration was the founding of the "Deutsche Gesellschaft" of New Orleans, June 2, 1847, for the protection of German immigrants. At the time of its foundation it had one hundred and fifty-two members. Between June, 1847, and May, 1887, over 284,900 Germans landed at New Orleans. Cf. the pamphlets of J. Hanno Deiler, *Zur Geschichte der Deutschen am unteren Mississippi.* (New Orleans, 1901.) Also, *Louisiana ein Heim für deutsche Ansiedler,* p. 4. (1895.) The important discoveries by the same author, contained in his *Settlement of the German Coast of Louisiana, and the Creoles of German Descent* (see *German American Annals,* 1909, N. s. vol. vii), appeared too late to be incorporated above.

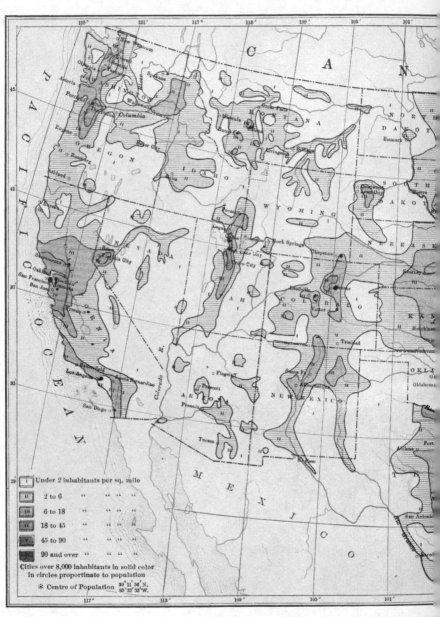

Spanish quarter. There were also German settlements in St. Peters, Baton Rouge, and on the Red River; also in the towns of Alexandria, Natchitoches, and Shreveport.[1] In general the lower Mississippi, because of its treacherous climate, was not favorable to German immigration. The German settler throve better in a climate more closely resembling his own, though, to do him justice, he fared no worse in tropical latitudes than other North Europeans.

Examining the map of 1820, we notice an uninhabited tract along both shores of the Mississippi north of the present state of Louisiana. The western shore was colonized first, the Arkansas River territory attracting settlers. In the year 1836 sixty families from Rheinhessen immigrated to Arkansas, settling near Little Rock. Their leader was the Reverend Mr. Klingelhöffer,[2] the friend and host of the German traveler and novelist, Friedrich Gerstäcker. The latter wrote a number of fascinating romances, e. g., "The Regulators of Arkansas," "Pirates of the Mississippi," "Hunting Tours," etc.,[3] based upon his experiences in this wild territory, and he undoubtedly owed Klingelhöffer a debt of gratitude for having introduced him to many of the scenes he later portrayed so vividly.

St. Louis was the other centre of distribution on the Mississippi River for the Western territory. Settlements soon extended to the north and south on the Missouri and Illinois sides of the Mississippi River, and then along

---

[1] Cf. Löher, *Geschichte und Zustände der Deutschen in Amerika*, pp. 208, 323. (Göttingen (2d edition), 1855.)

[2] The name is so spelt by Löher, and Eickhoff; Körner writes "Klingenhöfer."

[3] *Die Regulatoren in Arkansas* (1845), *Die Flusspiraten des Mississippi* (1848), *Streif u. Jagdzüge* (1844), *Mississippi-Bilder* (1847–1848), etc.

the Missouri upstream like a long index finger pointing to the West (see map following p. 436). In these early settlements native Americans of German blood were numerous beyond any doubt. They came from the Ohio Valley or from Kentucky and Tennessee, the districts that had struggled and waited for the opening of the Mississippi. Some came from Maryland and Virginia, or other Eastern states, as, for instance, Henry Geyer from Frederick, Maryland, who became a noted jurist and later a United States Senator from Missouri. In 1817 Missouri had 60,000 inhabitants, and in 1821 it was admitted as a state, but no Germans from abroad had as yet settled there. Soon after, in 1824, two Germans, Gottfried Duden, a graduate in law and medicine, accompanied by Eversmann, an agriculturist, came to the United States with the purpose of founding a home in the Missouri territory. They landed at Baltimore, journeyed by way of Wheeling to St. Louis, where on making inquiries at the land office, they were provided with charts of available land on the Missouri River. On their search they lodged overnight on the farm of a Pennsylvania German, who called their attention to some vacant congressional land in the neighborhood, and offered to take care of them until they had chosen their location. Duden acquiesced, and purchased about two hundred and seventy acres[1] above the Femme-Osage River, about fifty English miles above the mouth of the Missouri. Being possessed of means, he had his land cleared and cultivated for him, while he em-

[1] Most of it was congressional land, bought at $1.25 an acre. Duden's companion purchased about 130 acres adjoining. It is interesting to note that Daniel Boone had lived in the immediate neighborhood from 1795 to 1804, after leaving Kentucky. For want of a title he lost his land again after the United States acquired possession in 1803. But in consideration of his services Congress confirmed his title to another tract in 1812.

ployed his leisure hours writing a romantic description of his journey to America and the attractions of a life spent in the primeval forests of the Far West. His book was published in Germany and went through many editions.[1]

His skillful pen mingled fact and fiction, interwove experience and imagination, pictured the freedom of the forest and of democratic institutions in contrast with the social restrictions and political embarrassments of Europe. Many thousands of Germans pondered over this book and enthused over its sympathetic glow. Innumerable resolutions were made to cross the ocean and build for the present and succeeding generations happy homes on the far-famed Missouri.

At first there came a large number of farmers and laborers from Westphalia and Hannover. They were followed by many people of a higher social class, who settled in the neighborhood of Duden's farm in Warren (then Montgomery) County, Missouri. The latter group consisted of counts and barons, scholars, preachers, gentlemen-farmers, officers, merchants and students, all of them possessing some means and therefore unaccustomed and not willing to do the work of laborers. The plain farmers, after years of toil, prospered almost without exception, but the others as constantly went backward. When they had completely exhausted their means of support, they

---

[1] *Berichte über eine Reise nach den westlichen Staaten Nordamerikas und einen mehrjährigen Aufenthalt am Missouri (in den Jahren 1824, 1825, 1826, und 1827) in Bezug auf Auswanderung und Uebervölkerung, oder: Das Leben im Innern der Vereinigten Staaten und dessen Bedeutung für die häusliche und politische Lage der Europäer dargestellt, (a) in einer Sammlung von Briefen, (b) in einer politischen Abhandlung, (c) in einem ratgebenden Nachtrag. Gedruckt zu Elberfeld im Jahre 1829 ; zweite Original-Ausgabe, mit vielen Zusätzen* (Bonn, 1834) ; *Auf Kosten der Schweizerschen Auswanderungsgesellschaft gedruckt.* (St. Gallen, 1832.)

would either go to ruin utterly,[1] or begin life anew with the determination to labor and succeed. Owing to the fact that so many of the colonists had been educated in the German gymnasia, and there received thorough instruction in Latin and Greek, their abode was called the "Latin settlement." The epithet, "Latin farmers," has commonly been applied to the scholarly German settlers, who became quite numerous about the revolutionary periods of 1830 and 1848, a class of cultivated men, yet frequently unpractical, for whom manual labor proved a hard school of experience.

The next German settlement of some size in Missouri was made under the auspices of the so-called "Giessener Gesellschaft." It was an ambitious plan to concentrate German immigration upon some territory of the West which had not yet been admitted as a state. We shall observe similar ventures planned here or in Germany and directed to other localities; for instance, to Texas and to Wisconsin. The idea of immigration on a large scale to the Mississippi territory started with two young men of great ability, Paul Follenius and Friedrich Münch. They were idealists, who began the fight for political liberty in their own country, but saw every effort foiled by the reactionary policy of the German governments. They felt keenly the degradation of paternalism exercised by incapable and tyrannical autocrats, and they were hunted down by an Argus-eyed system of espionage. It was about 1830, a period of blasted hopes, when the day for constitutional government had not yet come for Germany. Münch suggested immigration to Follenius, but the latter shook his

---

[1] Many committed suicide, some died as beggars on the street; the latter was the experience of a Hannoverian count known to Friedrich Münch (see below).

head, for he considered such a course tantamount to deserting the flag, in their glorious fight for liberty. When he began to see the hopelessness of the cause that animated his youthful ambition, he took refuge in a plan of the following kind, which he concocted together with Münch:[1] "We must not go from here [Germany] without realizing a national idea or at least making the beginnings toward its realization; the foundation of a new and free Germany in the great North American Republic shall be laid by us; we must therefore gather as many as possible of the best of our people about us when we emigrate, and we must at the same time make the necessary arrangements providing for a large body of immigrants to follow us annually, and thus we may be able at least in one of the American territories to establish an essentially German state, in which a refuge may be found for all those to whom, as to ourselves, conditions at home have become unbearable, — a territory which we shall be able to make a model state in the great republic." Paul Follenius, gigantic in stature, impressive in personality, of keen wit, sure tact, and indomitable will, was a man born to take the lead in popular movements.[2] Münch, of a more conservative and practical turn of mind, though pleased with the idea, was aware of the difficulties of so grand an undertaking.

Such was the beginning of the "Giessener Auswanderungsgesellschaft." The company, centralized in and

[1] Cf. the "Reminiscences" of Friedrich Münch in *Der deutsche Pionier*, vol. i, pp. 188–189. Paul Follenius (or Follen) was the brother of Carl Follen, professor of German literature at Harvard.

[2] Unfortunately he died, at the prime of life, from a nervous fever contracted in 1844 at a time of floods and great hardships in Missouri. He was buried under a group of sugar maples, his favorite place on the farm, the same on which Duden had lived for several years, when he lodged with the Pennsylvania German. *Der deutsche Pionier*, vol. i, p. 187.

depending for its membership mostly upon the grand-duchy of Hessen, expected first to select for its German state the territory of Arkansas,[1] but, receiving unfavorable reports from those that had gone before, the later bodies of immigrants went to Missouri, settling in various parts of the state. The larger part of them in 1834 settled with Münch and Follenius on the north bank of the Missouri River, in the present Warren County, where Duden had passed his idyllic existence ("das Dudensche Idyll"). This was destined to become the centre of the most widespread settlement of Germans west of the Mississippi. On both sides of the Missouri River, from its mouth, a little to the north of St. Louis, upward a distance of about 125 miles, all is German territory. In all towns from St. Louis to Jefferson City, such as St. Charles, Washington, Hermann,[2] Warrenton, Boonville, and even beyond and including Kansas City, the Germans are very numerous, generally constituting over one half of the population. In 1870 St. Charles, with seven or eight thousand inhabitants, was more than three fourths German. On the north side of the river the Germans numbered nine tenths of the population in Warren County, in St. Charles County over one half. In the latter county Germans from Osnabrück and Oldenburg had settled in the beginning of the twenties, before the arrival of Duden. On the south side of the Missouri Germans formed one half the population of Franklin and Gasconade counties. In St. Louis, Lincoln, Montgomery, and Osage counties innumerable German

---

[1] Münch suggests in his reminiscences that Iowa would have been the best location. *Der deutsche Pionier*, vol. i, p. 189.

[2] For a history of the settlement of Hermann (1837) by the German Settlement Society of Philadelphia, its subsequent independence, and the development of its important industry, the production of wine, see the work of William G. Bek, *The German Settlement Society and its Colony, Hermann, Missouri*, Americana Germanica Press, Philadelphia, 1907.

communities were found. In Cole County (Jefferson City), in Moniteau,[1] and to the west and southwest in Morgan, Pettis (Sedalia), and Benton counties, large groups of German immigrants established permanent homes. Westphalia, in Osage, and Deepwater, in Henry County, were German towns. Kansas City and St. Louis owed a large part of their prosperity to their German citizens.

The Germans of the Missouri Valley differed in religion, but that was to them no cause for dissension.[2] Catholics, Protestants, and Sectarians, living in harmony, cultivated the soil side by side. In material resources they developed with the times, their initial difficulties and hardships being relieved somewhat by the better times that followed the Mexican War and the discovery of gold in California. Every acre of the country was soon under cultivation. Neat cottages of frame or brick, large barns and farm buildings, dotted both banks of the Missouri. Like the Pennsylvania farmer, the Missouri German took good care of his cattle and horses, and planted gardens. In course of time the farmers used modern agricultural machinery and put larger areas under cultivation. They took particular pride in keeping the land in their possession generation after generation. German settlers acquired the best land,

[1] Tipton, Missouri, 162 miles from St. Louis, in Moniteau County, with 1000 inhabitants in 1870, was nearly one half German. *Der deutsche Pionier*, vol. ii, p. 8.

[2] *Der deutsche Pionier*, vol. i, pp. 269–273, contains an article bearing on this point by J. G. Brühl, a prominent German settler. He was a Catholic, and the German townships about him were Protestant. It is curious to note that Brühl served all the colonists, of whatever denomination they might be, as a sort of minister-teacher, in the manner of Holzklo, of Madison County, Virginia. (Cf. Chapter VII, pp. 180–181.) Since they had no minister, he was accustomed to act as leader in prayers and scriptural reading. When the Lutherans became very numerous they appealed to the patriarchal Brühl to get them a Lutheran minister, which he did on one occasion, and on another listened to the trial sermon of a candidate for a Lutheran pulpit in his district, and gave a favorable opinion (p. 270).

as when they bought the valuable estate of Daniel Boone in the beautiful valley of the Femme-Osage in St. Charles County.

The Germans almost to a man were opposed to slavery, and, as will be seen in a later chapter, turned the tide of sentiment in Missouri in favor of the Union cause. The dream of Follenius[1] and Münch was realized in a manner different from their plans. No German state was formed, — such a scheme was nowhere successful, — but Germans accomplished what earlier settlers had not done: they gained a permanent foothold for themselves, their descendants, and thousands of their countrymen, and they nobly served the land of their adoption. Friedrich Münch is a conspicuous example of the high grade of German settlers that appeared in the nineteenth century. He was a "Latin farmer," completely successful. Leaving brilliant prospects behind, he chose not to sacrifice his republican principles, and sailed with Follenius to America. With his own hand he cleared the ground and tilled the soil on his Missouri farm,[2] and adapted himself to every condition of life in the new country. He became a leader of his people, noted for his frankness and clearness of speech. He took a prominent part in politics during the agitations that preceded and accompanied the Civil War, and in 1862 was elected to the state senate. Throughout his political career he was always of the people and for the people, and his intelligent conservatism and plain-spoken honesty made

---

[1] The widow of Follenius was still living in 1869, and had six married children and about twenty grandchildren. Friedrich Münch was likewise blessed with a numerous progeny.

[2] Münch's settlement was near Dutzow, in Warren County. Cf. *Der deutsche Pionier*, vol. vii, pp. 53–59 (Rattermann, "Ein Besuch bei Friedrich Münch"). *Ibid.*, vol. xi, pp. 316–319 ("Eine deutsche Niederlassung am Missouri," von Fr. Münch).

him stand out prominently in the Missouri assembly. He was a frequent contributor to German newspapers, on political, religious, and social topics, and there also he appeared sane, sound, and public-spirited.[1]

The Missouri Germans as early as 1835–36 made expeditions to the Far Western plains. Captain John A. Sutter, later prominent as the pioneer of California, and August Laufkötter made an expedition into the country of the Apaches for the purpose of trading. Their ventures were not very successful financially, but they made noteworthy explorations ; for instance, when Laufkötter, starting from the camp of the Apaches with several Delaware Indian guides, pressed onward to the confluence of the Gila and the Colorado rivers, in the southwestern corner of Arizona.

The site of St. Louis attracted Germans in great numbers. St. Louis was the terminus of the steamboat lines from New Orleans, the starting-point for navigation to the upper Mississippi, Illinois, the Missouri, and, most important of all, to the Ohio River. Before the days of the railroad, Chicago, the metropolis of the Northwest, could not compete with St. Louis. Immigration had not as yet found its way in that direction. St. Louis was then about four times the size of Chicago. About 1845 two German

[1] *Der deutsche Pionier* (vol. ii, pp. 230–235) gives a list of the early settlers of the "Giessener Gesellschaft." Among them was Professor David Göbel, from Coburg. He settled with his family six miles west of Washington, Missouri, and was prominent as a teacher of mathematics and lecturer on astronomy in St. Louis, and as a mathematical expert in the surveying service of the Western States. His son, Gert Göbel, was born in Coburg in 1816, assisted his father as a surveyor, was a successful farmer, hunter, and surveyor. At the outbreak of the Rebellion, he was very active in organizing the "Home Guards" of Washington County. He was elected to the state legislature in 1862, and was an ardent advocate of the emancipation of the slaves. He served six years as a member of the Missouri state legislature. Cf. Gert Göbel, "Länger als ein Menschenleben in Missouri," *Der deutsche Pionier*, vol. x, pp. 333 ff. and 361 ff.

newspapers were issued in St. Louis daily. The city was a distributing-centre of the German population for Missouri and the land west of the Mississippi, just as Philadelphia had been for Pennsylvania, Maryland, and Virginia.

An interesting group of German settlers arrived at St. Louis in 1839. They were the Saxon Lutherans who came under the leadership of their bishop, Martin Stephan. They left Germany for religious reasons, being dissatisfied with the reforms introduced into the established Protestant churches, and they called themselves Alt-Lutheraner.[1] Since most of them came from Saxony, they received the name Saxon Lutherans. Stephan in Dresden, with marked gifts of eloquence and shrewdness, was the natural leader. His defects of character, not his principles, were severely attacked abroad. His many followers, however, were not concerned about these charges, but followed his plan of emigration, which, under the spell of Duden's book, brought them to Missouri. They settled in Perry County, one hundred and ten miles south of St. Louis. It developed that the accusations abroad concerning Stephan's private life had been justified, and he was accordingly deposed.[2] Among the Saxon Lutherans were the Walthers, who became very prominent in the Missouri Synod. Six settlements were founded on the property of the company in Perry County: Wittenberg, Seelitz, Dresden, Altenburg, Frohna, and Johannesberg, none of them, however, becoming important towns.[3]

---

[1] The reforms meant a greater degree of nationalization, uniting the two Protestant churches, the Lutheran and the Reformed, under one state organization called the Union.

[2] The leaders of the congregation, May 27, 1839, published in the St. Louis paper, *Anzeiger des Westens*, the fact of the deposition and its causes.

[3] Cf. *Der deutsche Pionier*, vol. vi, pp. 157–159 (F. Schnake " Die Einwanderung der Sachsen ").

Germans soon found their way into the more southerly counties of Missouri. Iron, Washington, and St. François contain a mixed population with a good representation of Germans. In Scott County were the German towns New Hamburg, Dommüller, Duhlstadt, Morley, and Commerce. Cape Girardeau County, though originally settled by French people, later received a very large German population. Others located in Bollinger, Mississippi, and Butler counties. None of the southeastern counties were affected by the early German immigrations, except perhaps Cape Girardeau (1838). The movement of Pennsylvania Germans to Missouri is illustrated by the fact that on the 25th of March, 1843, a steamer stopped at St. Louis with two hundred and fifty German passengers from Pittsburg, the forerunners of a company of three thousand that were to settle in the neighborhood of Hannibal, Missouri.

(B) BEGINNING OF THE ADVANCE OF THE FRONTIER LINE
TOWARD THE NORTHWEST

Looking again at the census map of 1820, we observe that the Northwestern States including northern Indiana and Illinois, Michigan, Wisconsin, and Minnesota, were at that time practically undiscovered territory for the American pioneer. The southern part of Indiana (along the Ohio and Wabash rivers) and the southern and southwestern parts of Illinois (along the Ohio and Mississippi rivers) had already begun to receive permanent settlers. The main current of migration, however, had gone southwestward, following the river courses to the Mississippi and thence along this great avenue of trade toward the Gulf. The immigration northwestward toward the Great Lakes had not yet begun, though George Rogers Clark and his brave followers had opened the Illinois territory over forty years before.

It is not remote from our subject to recall for a moment the deeds of that gallant leader and his band of adventurous pioneers. Though Clark appealed for aid to the government of Virginia and elsewhere, the entire work of recruiting his army was left to the originator of the plan. Thomas Jefferson and Patrick Henry foresaw indeed great advantages for Virginia and Kentucky in a successful outcome of the Illinois venture ; still, few men could be spared by Virginia from the forces that were defending the liberties of the colonies against the British king. Great secrecy had to be maintained by Clark concerning the real purpose of his expedition. The recruits that were attracted by his name and by the prospects of large land grants in the conquered country were led to believe that they were marching for the defense of Kentucky. With great difficulty one hundred and fifty men were gathered together by May, 1778, when they started from Pittsburg, down the Ohio, touching at Wheeling for stores. Though few in number, the men in this command were a picked lot of young border settlers, acquainted with the woods and Indian warfare. At the falls of the Ohio (now Louisville, Kentucky) Clark built a fort and was there joined by a few Kentuckians with Simon Kenton. Some of his men were left behind at the fort to guard Kentucky, the rest advanced, to conquer Illinois.

The vast territory of Illinois was at that time inhabited by warlike Indian tribes, except here and there on the rivers, where a few French settlements were located, some of them over a hundred years old. It was Clark's purpose to win over the French inhabitants, and through them check the Indian tribes. As he was about to start, he was rejoiced at hearing that the French alliance with the American colonies had been proclaimed, for he knew that that would help him with the Creoles. Since his plan was to take the French settlements by surprise, he avoided the Mississippi River and continued on the Ohio to the mouth of the Tennessee; from there he started overland to the Illinois towns on the Mississippi. He was fortunate in getting correct information from American hunters, who declared that Kaskaskia could easily be taken by surprise. The latter settlement, the most important of the Creole towns, was commanded by the Frenchman Rochblave, who was faithful to the British flag. The latter had two or three times as many men as Clark, but they were not of the same stamp as the American backwoodsmen. From the Indians the timid Creoles had heard monstrous accounts of the savagery of the "Long Knives," as the Kentuckians and Virginians were called. This unsavory reputation gave prestige to Clark's handful of men, who arrived suddenly, like demons rising from out of the earth. They effected a complete surprise, and put the Creoles into a state of panic, in which conditon they eagerly accepted any terms. Clark diplomatically invited them to become citizens of the American Republic, and thus he converted them into his allies against Great Britain. The light-hearted Creoles were well satisfied, all except Rochblave, who was therefore sent a prisoner to Virginia. The Creoles of Cahokia, the settlement situated opposite St. Louis, followed the example of Kaskaskia,[1] taking the oath of allegiance.

The priest Gibault volunteered to go to Vincennes, and

---

[1] Kaskaskia was situated on the Kaskaskia River, near its confluence with the Mississippi. It was founded in 1673, over a hundred years earlier than the first white man settled in Kentucky. It was the capital of the Illinois territory until 1818.

succeeded there in winning the inhabitants for the American cause. Since no garrison could be spared to go to Vincennes, Captain Leonard Helm was sent thither alone to take command.[1] This mission, which was of great importance, shows that Clark had a high estimate of Helm's ability. The other three captains of Clark's forces were John Montgomery, Joseph Bowman, and William Harrod. Of these four, Helm and Bowman were German Virginians. They were always assigned the tasks of greatest responsibility, obviously being the two ablest and most reliable commanders under Clark. Captain Helm acquitted himself well at Vincennes, training the young Creoles in military service, winning the population over to the cause of American liberty, and keeping the Indians at peace.[2] His position, like that of his commander, was precarious. Clark's own men were so anxious to return home that he succeeded only in inducing a hundred Americans to serve eight months longer. When he made a pretense of leaving Kaskaskia, the inhabitants begged him to stay for their own protection. This gave him an excuse for drilling the native Creole population. By force, firmness, and diplomacy he kept the Indians pacified, and he also cultivated friendship with the Spanish commandant at St. Louis.

Henry Hamilton, the English commander at Detroit, had planned an attack on Fort Pitt, but Clark's movements put him on the defensive, and he now organized an expedition to recapture Vincennes, which, he heard, was but

---

[1] Cf. Roosevelt, *The Winning of The West*, vol. ii, p. 49. For a graphic account of the expedition of Clark, see the same work, vol. ii, chaps. 2 and 3, pp. 31–90, on which the above account is based.

[2] "Some volunteers — Americans, French, and friendly Indians — were sent to the aid of the American captain at Vincennes, and the latter, by threats and promises, and a mixture of diplomatic speech-making with a show of force, contrived, for the time being, to pacify the immediately neighboring tribes." Roosevelt, *supra*, vol. ii, p. 55.

poorly garrisoned. In December, 1778, with five hundred men, of whom one hundred and seventy-seven were whites, the rest Indians, Hamilton appeared before Vincennes, after capturing Helm's scouts, and a messenger who carried a note written by Helm informing Clark of what was happening. "Helm showed so good a front that nothing was attempted until the next day. . . . Poor Helm was promptly deserted by all the Creole militia. The latter had been loud in their boasts until the enemy came into view, but as soon as they caught sight of the red-coats, they began to slip away and run up to the British to surrender their arms. He was finally left with only one or two men, — Americans. Nevertheless he refused the first summons to surrender ; but Hamilton, who knew that Helm's troops had deserted him marched up to the fort at the head of his soldiers and the American was obliged to surrender, with no terms granted, save that he and his associates should be treated with humanity." [1] Hamilton remained for the winter at Vincennes, believing himself secure against all attacks, because of the impassability (as he thought) of all avenues of approach. In the following spring he expected to complete the re-conquest of Illinois.

He was forestalled, however, by the genius of Clark, who, hearing that Hamilton had kept but a small garrison of eighty men in Vincennes, planned to take him by surprise before reinforcements could arrive. The distance overland from Kaskaskia to Vincennes, situated on the eastern bank of the Wabash (in Indiana), was two hundred and forty miles. The roads were well-nigh impassable and the country was flooded, but nothing could daunt the spirit of Clark. He drew together a little garrison from the French towns, and with some accessions of

[1] Roosevelt, vol. ii, p. 63.

young Creoles, he started on February 7, 1779, with one
hundred and seventy men. After hardships that would
have discouraged any other leader, and which, indeed,
the energetic Hamilton had considered insurmountable,
Clark's expedition arrived in the neighborhood of Vincennes, exhausted from the march, numb with cold, and
wet to the bone from fording swollen rivers. The example of their leader, however, inspirited the men. They
were organized in two companies, Clark leading the first,
consisting of two companies of Americans and the Kaskaskia Creoles. The second, led by Bowman, contained
his own company and the Cahokians.[1] Vincennes was
taken by surprise, the fort resisting some time longer
than the town, the Creole population being ever ready to
yield to the superior force.

After the fort had surrendered, and Captain Helm,
who had remained a prisoner, gained his freedom, he was
at once used for important service. Clark sent Helm and
fifty men in boats up the Wabash to intercept a party of
French volunteers from Detroit, who were bringing to
Vincennes bateaux heavily laden with goods of all kinds,
to the value of ten thousand pounds sterling. In a few
days Helm returned, completely successful, and the supplies, together with the goods taken at Vincennes, were
distributed among the soldiers, who " got almost rich." [2]

The expedition of Clark, opening the Illinois territory
and making possible the American claim to the whole
Northwest Territory bordering on the Great Lakes, was one
of the grandest achievements in the history of the winning of the West. The fact that in this expedition the
two ablest captains of Clark were Bowman and Helm may

[1] This proves that Bowman was considered the second in command.
[2] Cf. Roosevelt, vol. ii, pp. 85–86.

always remain a source of gratification to the Germans of this country and particularly to Germans of the great Northwestern Territory, in which fertile and progressive area they were destined to outnumber every other national element.

Small colonies of American settlers soon gained a foothold about the conquered French towns in Illinois and Indiana, as we see indicated on the census map of 1790, but it took a score of years before that territory received permanent settlers in large numbers. The sections along the Ohio River were settled first, and in those early settlements there were some Germans. In Indiana the Swiss settlement of Vevay was founded, in 1796. In that year a number of wine-growers had been sent from the Canton of Vaud (Waadt) to produce vintages on the Ohio, "the Po of the New World."[1] The settlement (in present Switzerland County, Indiana) perhaps dates from 1802, when Dufour and a number of others bought thirty-seven hundred acres, and started vineyards. A number of German farmers followed the original French Swiss, and in 1810 the colony pressed their first good vintage, of twenty-four hundred gallons. In 1817, five thousand gallons of wine were produced. Extravagant hopes of supplanting the French wines were not realized, however, either in the quality or the quantity of the American product. The colony made no great progress, and many of its best men left Vevay for Cincinnati.[2]

Very successful as long as it lasted was the commun-

---

[1] A metaphor of Freiherr D. von Bülow, who had traveled in the West shortly before. For an account of the German settlements in Indiana, see W. A. Fritsch, *Zur Geschichte des Deutschtums in Indiana. Eine Festschrift zur Indiana-Feier im Jahre 1900.* (New York : Steiger, 1896.)

[2] Among them was Captain Weber, the founder of the William Tell Hotel, in Cincinnati, which once had a considerable reputation. Cf. Eickhoff, *In der neuen Heimat*, pp. 276–277.

istic settlement of the Rappists, who in 1815 located on the Wabash, in Posey County, Indiana. This society had been founded by Johann Georg Rapp, a native of Würtemberg, a weaver and tiller of the soil, who in his native land had founded a religious sect called the Harmonists. He left Würtemberg in 1803, and sought refuge for himself and his community in America. In 1805 he founded the colony of Harmony in Butler County, Pennsylvania, where he continued until 1815.[1] In the mean time the farms and property of the Rappists had increased enormously in value, and Rapp was enabled to realize $100,000 from their sale. He then bought thirty thousand acres on the Wabash, where in a few years, through industry and thrift, the colony rose to still greater prosperity. Another sale was effected in 1824 to Robert Owen,[2] and this time fully $200,000 was the price, exclusive of seven thousand acres sold to William McClure for his reform school. The Rappists then returned to Pennsylvania, where they established their third colony, at Economy (Beaver County), and where the properties of the sect increased to the value of millions.[3] The Rappists in Indi-

---

[1] Rapp was a benevolent autocrat, who held the material and religious affairs of his communistic order firmly in hand. Industry and economy were the secret of the extraordinary success of his model farms and mills. Rapp died in 1847, at the age of ninety. When there were withdrawals from the order, property was restored or services paid for; generally the members were fanatically devoted to the founder.

[2] Robert Owen, founder of English socialism, established his socialistic community at New Harmony in 1825. It failed in 1827.

[3] An excellent account of the Harmony Society is to be found in the German-American Annals, vol. ii, pp. 274, 339, 403, 467, 571, 597, 665 ; The Harmony Society ; a Chapter in German-American Culture History, by John A. Bole. Many illustrations accompany these articles. The membership of the order reached its highest point in 1827, when there were 522 members. There was a defection in 1832, when 175 members withdrew in a body with Count Leon, receiving $175,000. In 1844 the membership rose again to 385, but since celibacy was enforced from the beginning, the order was not self-

ana did not isolate themselves entirely, as did many of the other communistic societies. Friedrich Rapp, adopted son of the founder, and from an early period head of all the industrial activities of the Rappists, was one of the representatives of the county in the political affairs of the territory. He was, in 1820, one of the ten commissioners of the state who chose a site for the state capital. Their choice was Indianapolis, a city which subsequently received a very large German population.[1]

In Illinois there were some Germans who settled in St. Clair County before 1820. L. Schönberger was a grand juryman in 1792; Friedrich Gräter in 1796 bought the first piece of land sold by the sheriff in Cahokia. In the latter place lived also the German Kramer, whose French neighbors changed his name to Cramour.[2] Julius A. Barnsbach (Bärensbach) settled with his family in Madison County as early as 1809, and many of his relatives located near by. Dutch Hill, in St. Clair County, had its suggestive name before 1816, and was farmed by several Swiss families, under the leadership of Leonhard Steiner, from Aargau. The large current of German immigration, however, came after 1830, the possibilities of the Northwest Territory having been discovered during the Black Hawk War.[3]

perpetuating. Few new members joined, and in 1894 there remained but eighteen, in 1903 but four members (of whom three were women), who are the owners of a vast property.

[1] Cf. Eickhoff, p. 286. Evansville (Posey County) and Fort Wayne (Allen County) likewise received large German populations. Tell City on the Ohio (Indiana side) was founded by Swiss Germans.

[2] Cf. the researches of E. B. Hoffmann in *Der deutsche Pionier*, vol. xiii, p. 21. Cf. also E. Mannhardt, " Die ältesten deutschen Ansiedler in Illinois," *Deutsch-Amerikanische Geschichtsblätter*, I Jahrgang, Heft 4, pp. 50–59. Vierteljahrschrift hrg. v. d. D. A. Historischen Gesellschaft von Illinois. (Chicago, 1901.)

[3] The Black Hawk War took place in 1830–32. Under the provisions of

St. Clair County became one of the centres of German influence in Illinois. Across the river from St. Louis, beginning at the north opposite the mouth of the Missouri and stretching southward to the outlet of the Kaskaskia River a little above Chester, there is a stretch of fertile upland about a hundred miles in length and six to ten miles in breadth. The higher portions of this plateau are wooded, and the bottoms, stretching toward the Kaskaskia, are varied with woodlands, prairies, and lakes. Into this territory was poured the German immigration, far outnumbering the few wealthy Virginian and American landholders, the latter often of German descent, coming from Pennsylvania or North Carolina. The German immigrants had among them large numbers of born leaders and "Latin farmers." There were clustered together, notably at Belleville, a large group of men who had been members of the " Burschenschaften," the German student fraternities of a political cast, which had been made special objects of vengeance by the arbitrary governors of the reactionary period. Many friends of gymnasium or university days were now gathered together within the radius of a few miles. Such were Dr. G. Engelmann, Dr. G. Bunsen, Dr. A. Berchelmann, Gustav Körner, Theodor Hilgard, Theodor Kraft, Georg Neuhoff, Theodor and Adolf Engelmann, Karl Schreiber, Karl Friedrich, Ernst Decker, Wilhelm Weber, August Dilg. In 1849 there was added Friedrich Hecker, the leader of the in-

the treaty with the chiefs of the Sac and Fox Indians at Prairie du Chien, July 15, 1830, the land east of the Mississippi was ceded to the whites. The chief Black Hawk refused to submit to the treaty. In 1831 he made an attack on some Illinois villages, but was driven off by a force of militia under General Gaines. The next spring Black Hawk returned with a strong force and renewed his attacks. United States troops were called against him, and upon his defeat on July 21, and on August 2, 1832, the war was ended. *Encyclopædic Dictionary of American History*, vol. i, p. 80.

surrectionary forces in Baden during the revolution of
1848–49. At the university Hecker had fought a duel
with Gustav Körner; now these men extended to one
another the hand of comradeship in their new home.
Besides showing the usual German qualities of industry and thrift, the Germans of St. Clair County were
interested and wide-awake in politics. In Belleville, with
over fifteen thousand inhabitants, it happened that for
years no native American sat in the city council, and
that all civic offices were filled by Germans. The county
officers likewise were generally German, and their influence extended beyond the county limits. Eduard Retz
was three times state treasurer, and Gustav Körner was
lieutenant-governor of Illinois in 1852.[1] Under Julius
Raith[2] a German company was recruited for the Mexican
War, and during the Civil War all men capable of bearing arms fought for the cause of the Union. It is estimated that at present three fourths of the population of
the county are German or of German descent. As early as
1836 a " Deutsche Bibliotheks-Gesellschaft " was formed
in Belleville, which founded a library that in 1879 contained fifty-five hundred volumes, exclusive of public
documents presented by Congress. For that time and in
that section this fact may be recorded as noteworthy.
The appellative " Latin settlement " or " Latin farmers "
was probably first used in connection with the cultivated
settlers of Belleville.[3]

---

[1] In 1862–1865 he was minister to Spain.

[2] Julius C. Raith (b. 1820 in Würtemberg) served as captain in the
Mexican War and in the Rebellion as colonel of the Forty-Third Illinois
Regiment. He was killed in the battle of Shiloh (1862). Cf. Rosengarten,
The German Soldier in the Wars of the United States, p. 231.

[3] Cf. Körner, *Das deutsche Element in den Vereinigten Staaten von Nordamerika, 1818–1848*, p. 265.

Twenty or thirty miles east of St. Louis, in Madison County, Illinois, was founded a Swiss colony named Highland. The plateau, called the Looking-Glass Prairie, was settled by the families Köpfli and Suppiger, in October, 1831. They became the permanent owners, though Americans had settled there ten years before. Proximity to St. Louis was an advantage for the disposal of their products. Alton, in the same county, was the most important commercial city in the state, in the early thirties, and interested enthusiasts predicted that it might sometime surpass St. Louis. It attracted many Germans at that time; indeed all the cities that rose up and gave promise of a great future received a good contingent of German immigrants at the very beginning of their hopeful career. Such were Vandalia, Peoria,[1] Quincy,[2] Springfield, Peru, and Chicago. With the building of railroads the country opened more and more toward the Northwest, and the centre of population moved in that direction. Chicago in 1848 had scarcely ten thousand inhabitants. The Germans were there early[3] and grew in numbers and influence. The "Illinois Staats-zeitung" was started in 1848 as a weekly paper, while St. Louis already had two German dailies in the same year. The years 1850–1854 mark the crest in the wave of the German immigration of the nineteenth century before 1880. The largest part of the flood

---

[1] G. F. Müller was the first German settler in Peoria (1836) ; he was an alderman of the city in 1852.

[2] A Tunker named Georg Wolf, a native of the lower Rhine, settled there in the summer of 1822, a year after the first settler, John Wood (later governor), from whom Wolf bought his land. Cf. Der deutsche Pionier, vol. xi, p. 222, etc. (" Highland, Illinois," von A. E. Bandelier.) Cf. also : Geschichte der Deutschen Quincys, von H. Bornmann. Deutsch-Amerikanische Geschichtsblätter, Erster Jahrgang.

[3] Mannhardt : Die ersten beglaubigten Deutschen in Chicago, Deutsch-Amerikanische Geschichtsblätter, Bd. I, Heft 1, pp. 38, 46.

poured into Indiana, Illinois, Wisconsin, Minnesota, Michigan, and Iowa. In Chicago the German spirit had its first awakening in 1844, when a meeting was held in opposition to nativistic influences. But these beginnings cannot be compared with the political influence of the Chicago Germans in the days of Franz A. Hoffmann, merchant and banker, who, an ardent supporter of Lincoln, became lieutenant-governor of Illinois in 1860.

The settlement of the state of Iowa came late, but was very rapid when once begun. In May, 1842, the newspapers of St. Louis announced that during the first three months of that year 529 steamers had arrived in the harbor of St. Louis with more than thirty thousand passengers destined for Iowa. The causes for this rapid filling-up of the new territory were: the good soil, the fine climate, and the discovery of lead-mines in the neighborhood of Dubuque.[1] Along with native Americans, many Germans were drawn from Missouri and Illinois toward pastures new in Iowa and Minnesota. Since the avenue of entrance was the Mississippi River, there were soon established on its banks the cities Keokuk, Burlington, Davenport, and Dubuque. Iowa City was built on the Iowa River, Des Moines on the river of the same name, and on the Missouri rose the town of Council Bluffs. New cities sprang up like mushrooms and new immigrants were always at hand to link their fortunes with new localities. Dubuque, once first, now second city in size in the state, contained a population more than one half of German blood. There were among them Germans, Swiss, Alsatians, and Luxemburgers. In 1880 there were two large Ger-

---

[1] The first white man to come to Dubuque, after the French fur traders left, was, in 1832, the German, Peter Weigble, whose descendants still reside in Dubuque. A year later came the Swiss, Nikolaus Hoffmann. Eickhoff, p. 352.

man Catholic, one Lutheran, one German Presbyterian, and three or four small German Protestant congregations. Five of the ten state councilmen and two or three county supervisors were Germans. In state politics the latter were likewise very influential, as for example J. H. Thedings (b. in East Frisia, Prussia), who was in turn justice of the peace, mayor, president of the county council, and head of the school system.

Northwest of Dubuque there was the German Catholic town of New-Wien (New Vienna), and to the west of it, on the Mississippi, the town of Guttenberg, founded by Germans from Cincinnati. In Clayton County, on the so-called "Potato Prairie," there was a colony of communists, founded by Heinrich Koch in 1847, after his return from the Mexican War, in which he had served as captain. Another communistic society, the "Icarians," settled at Corning, Iowa, after leaving Nauvoo. They had first bought the deserted properties of the Mormons, who were driven out of their Illinois settlement, Nauvoo, in 1850. The Frenchman Etienne Cabet was their leader until his death in 1856, and their removal to Adams County, Iowa. They called their new settlement, at Corning, the Icaria Commune in reminiscence of Cabet's book "Icarie." Although most of the members were French, the most influential of them after Cabet's death were Germans.

The three leading cities, Des Moines, the capital of the state, Dubuque, and Davenport, the city third in size, received large German populations, Davenport getting a large contribution from Schleswig-Holstein and Denmark. From Davenport as a centre grew a number of German colonies; such as, Avoca, Minden, Walcott, Wheatland, Dewitt, etc.[1]

[1] Cf. Eickhoff, p. 355.

The northern and western parts of Michigan long remained untouched by the American pioneers, because of the cold climate and the presence of hostile Indian tribes. The German blood is nevertheless represented in the early history of Michigan, through the distinguished service of Friedrich Baraga, the Indian missionary. He was born in Carniola, Austria, in 1797. His mother was an aunt of the noted German poet Auersperg (whose pseudonym was Anastasius Grün). Of noble birth and with every advantage of social influence and education (he studied jurisprudence at the University of Vienna), Baraga entered the priesthood, contrary to the counsels of relatives. In 1830 he decided to enter the missionary service among the American Indians. Stopping long enough in Cincinnati to learn the language of the Ottawas from an Indian in a Catholic school of that city, he traveled by way of Detroit to the northern part of the Michigan peninsula, and established himself at Arbre Crochu. There he taught the Indians of the Lake Superior region (including the Ottawas, Pottawottomies, Chippewas, or Ojibwas) how to read, write, and count, and also the simple principles of Christianity. He would not use the books of the French in the Algonquin language, but prepared his own text-books and catechisms in the Chippewa language, with materials from the Old and New Testaments; he wrote a grammar of the Chippewa dialect, and compiled a reader in the Ottawa language. In 1853 Baraga was made bishop of the Northern Indian Missions, his residence being Sault Sainte-Marie, and later Marquette, on Lake Superior. He died at Marquette in 1868.[1]

If we look again at the census maps, we find that, with

---

[1] A sketch of his life can be found in *Der deutsche Pionier*, vol. i, pp. 291-295. ("Ein Vorkämpfer der Civilisation.")

the exception of the district around Detroit, Michigan
was practically uninhabited when the census of 1830 was
taken. In 1840 the region to the north of Detroit and the
area extending westward to Lake Michigan were settled,
though not densely. There are proofs that the Germans
had come during the interval. In 1839 the Catholic priest
and missionary Dr. Hammer wrote concerning the Germans as follows :[1]

Real German life as it is found in many American states, one
can find in Michigan only in three places, for in all other places
our people [meaning the Germans] are too scattered to form
congregations that might support a German preacher : (1) In
Detroit, there are two large German congregations, the stronger
being Catholic and having built a cathedral, the other, also having a church of its own, being Protestant (the Reverend Mr.
Schade). The members of the two congregations live in harmony with one another, and never allow their religious differences to interfere with their social intercourse. At marriages
and baptisms they are never concerned about which preacher
they should choose, but that they should have a good time in
the German fashion. A large number of the Germans remain
in the city only so long as to earn money enough to buy land
outside and establish farms. (2) The second German colony,
and the most prosperous, is that near Ann Arbor. The Germans
there come largely from Würtemberg, and are under the Protestant preacher, the Reverend Mr. Schmid. Their grain and
cattle are unsurpassed in Michigan. (3) The third German
colony is that on the Grand River, in the neighborhood of
Lyons, Ionia County, under the Reverend Mr. Kopp, from
Westphalia. The colony is called Westphalia.

The German traveler, J. G. Kohl (in 1855), adds a few
more facts about the Ann Arbor Germans.

The first were some few who came from the villages near
Stuttgart about 1830. It was just the time when Michigan was

[1] Eickhoff, pp. 376–377.

lauded to the skies, just as twelve years later everybody talked
about Illinois and Indiana, and after another twelve years, it
was Iowa, Wisconsin, and Minnesota. The early settlers helped
to build the city of Ann Arbor, and wrote home about their
prosperity. The word was passed from village to village; first a
dozen men, then a dozen families, crossed the ocean until about five
to six thousand Swabians had settled around Ann Arbor (1855).
The native speculators bought up the land near the prosperous
settlers, but the increased price of land did not stop the purchasers; for the Swabians kept on extending their farms. Detroit's German newspaper, already in existence toward the end
of the forties, did not prosper greatly until the large German
immigration of the fifties was added to the Michigan population.

An interesting episode in the westward movement of
the German element was the settlement of Waterloo
County, in the Province of Ontario, Canada. Waterloo
was settled by German Mennonites from Pennsylvania,
beginning in the year 1800, and became the earliest settled
inland township in the western peninsula of the Province
of Ontario.[1] The pioneers were Joseph Sherk (Schörg) and
Samuel Betzner, who left Franklin County, Pennsylvania,
in the autumn of the year 1799, and spent the winter in
the Niagara Peninsula. The following spring they went
in search of a better location, and penetrated the woods

---

[1] Cf. *The Biographical History of Waterloo Township and other Townships of the County, being a history of the early settlers and their descendants,
mostly all of Pennsylvania-Dutch origin.* By Ezra E. Eby. (Berlin, Ontario,
1895.) Also, *The Consolidated By-Laws of the Township of Waterloo up to
the year 1888, to which is appended an historical sketch of the early settlement
and subsequent development, etc.* By Alex. Shoemaker. (Galt, Ontario, 1888.)
The Romance of Ontario, or the Peopling of the Province. By C. C. James,
M.A. Appendix to the report of the Ontario Bureau of Industries, 1897.
(Toronto, 1899.) *The Ethnographical Elements of Ontario.* By A. F. Hunter.
(Ontario Historical Society.) For the books and materials above-named I
am indebted to Professor G. H. Needler, University College, Toronto, On-
tario, who has carefully investigated the subject of the Germans in Canada.

about thirty miles beyond the limits of human habitation, having heard vaguely of " a fine river traversing that region." Only a few traders had entered these forests, and but one, named Dodge, remained as a " permanent and prominent landmark of the community." Sherk and Betzner, having satisfied themselves as to the quality of the land, bought from Richard Beasley a tract of land on the Grand River, and at once brought their families there. Later in the same year a second party of Mennonites, from Lancaster County, Pennsylvania, settled on the Grand River, coming in their large four-horse wagons filled with farm implements and household effects. Reichert, Gingerich, Bechtel, Rosenberger, Bricker, Kinsey (Kinzie), Biehn (Bien, then Bean), Clemens, were the names of some of the earliest German settlers. They brought their families and possessions, including many horses and small droves of cattle. The journey from Pennsylvania, about five hundred miles, was made with covered wagons,[1] and lasted about ten weeks. The greatest obstruction was found at Beverly Swamp, just before reaching Waterloo, and teams would lie for two weeks at Horning's (the last settlement), until the men had made the road through the swamp passable. The Pennsylvania German pioneer, George Clemens, drove the first team that ever went through Beverly Swamp.

It was found after the country had received quite a number of German settlers (1804), that all of their land, sold to them by Richard Beasley, was incumbered by a large mortgage, of $20,000, duly recorded. Fearing to be dispossessed at a future time, they sought aid of their brethren in Pennsylvania, and, after some vain attempts, succeeded in getting the Mennonites of Lancaster County,

---

[1] Described as Conestoga wagons in a previous chapter (v), pp. 135–136.

Pennsylvania, to form a company and take up the mortgage. This was accomplished mainly through the persuasive powers of Samuel Bricker, who also performed the feat of carrying the coin, $20,000 in silver dollars, in a light conveyance ("leicht pläsier weggli") safely from Lancaster to Niagara, where on June 29, 1805,[1] sixty thousand acres of land were duly conveyed to the representatives of the Mennonites for £10,000 Canadian currency. The immigration from Pennsylvania ceased during the years of the war with England, but after 1815 German settlers came again into Waterloo and neighboring townships, not alone Mennonites, but Lutherans, Reformed, and Catholics in quite as large numbers. As everywhere else the German settlers bought the best land only, and established a reputation for model farming. They were very successful also as manufacturers, the towns of Berlin, Waterloo, Preston, Hespeler, in Waterloo County, and Hanover, Neustadt, and Ayton, in Grey County, becoming thriving German manufacturing towns. In 1846 the town of Berlin had four hundred inhabitants; in 1908, twelve thousand; its wealth is self-made, as that of the farms. The furniture manufacturing industry in Canada is very largely in the hands of Germans.[2] But the limits of this work will not admit of a consideration in detail of the Germans beyond the borders of the United States.

[1] *History of Waterloo*, pp. 30 ff. The Mennonites of Waterloo County were not United Empire Loyalists ; their migration was undertaken in search for good land for settlement. Their brethren in Pennsylvania hesitated to support them because they were in a country belonging to the British crown

[2] H. H. Miller, M.P., "The Germans in Canada," *Busy Man's Magazine*, July, 1908, pp. 17-31.

CHAPTER XV

THE WINNING OF THE WEST

IV. THE NORTHWEST, THE SOUTHWEST, AND THE FAR WEST

(A) The Northwest opened by the Black Hawk War, 1832 — First German settlers in Wisconsin — Milwaukee as a distributing-centre — "Deutsch-Athen " — The causes for Wisconsin receiving so large a share of German immigration : the plan of a German state ; favorable soil ; climate ; reports and literature ; sale of school lands ; commissioners of immigration — Distribution of Germans in Wisconsin — Minnesota's first German settlers from the Red River district — Founding of New Ulm — Indian troubles — The attack on New Ulm by the Sioux.

(B) The Southwest — The earliest settlers in Texas — The " Adelsverein " and its plans of colonization — New Braunfels and Friedrichsburg — Wreck of the " Adelsverein " — Stability of German colonies in Texas — The agricultural area : Seguin, New Braunfels, San Antonio — Germans prominent in Texas : Congressmen Schleicher and Degener.

(C) The Far West — German Mennonites in Kansas and Nebraska — The Pacific Coast : Oregon Germans — H. L. Yesler, founder of Seattle, Washington — John Sutter, pioneer of California ; his career ; gold first discovered on his estate ; cause of his misfortunes — The Germans of California — Sutro and Spreckels of San Francisco.

(A) The Northwest — Wisconsin

THE military expeditions incident to the Black Hawk War in 1832 opened the state of Wisconsin for settlement. The mineral wealth, the fertility of the soil, and the good climate became known for the first time through the militia who took part in these expeditions. The good reports spread eastward and across the ocean. In 1830 the population of Wisconsin was 3635, and the inhabited region belonged to the territory of Michigan till 1836. Soon the population of the new area increased by leaps and bounds: in 1840 Wisconsin had 30,945 inhabitants; in 1850, 305,391; in 1860, 775,881. Every ten years thereafter showed an increase of about 300,000, until at the census of 1900 the population numbered 2,069,042. The same census states that 709,969 of the inhabitants are of German blood, i. e., either born in Germany or having one or both parents born in Germany.[1] In this wonderful increase of population the German immigration contributed a larger share than any other stock. The periods of their greatest immigration were the decades 1840–50, 1850–60, 1880–90. More exactly, the periods were 1846–54 and 1881–84, corresponding to the years of the largest German immigration to the United States. During these two periods Wisconsin probably received a much larger proportion of Germans than any other state.[2] In 1900 the population of German blood numbered 34.3 per cent of the entire population of Wisconsin, very close to fifty per cent of the total population of foreign parentage, the latter numbering 71.1 per cent of the entire population of the state.

Though it is not definitely known when the first Germans settled in Wisconsin, it must have been in the beginning of the thirties. Among the pioneer stations of Green County, there was the " Funk " blockhouse, which existed in the year 1832.[3] At the same time a man by the

[1] Cf. *Twelfth Census of the United States*, vol. i (Population, part I), pp. 812, 820, 828.

[2] Cf. Everest-Levi, " How Wisconsin came by its large German Element," *Collections of the State Historical Society of Wisconsin*, vol. xii, pp. 299–334. For the history of the Germans in Wisconsin see also, *Wisconsins Deutsch-Amerikaner bis zum Schlusz des neunzehnten Jahrhunderts*, vol. i, by Wilhelm Hense-Jensen ; vol. ii, by Hense-Jensen and Ernest Bruncken. Cf. also Eickhoff, *In der neuen Heimat* (chapter contributed by P. V. Deuster), pp. 365–375.

[3] *Annual Report of the Wisconsin Historical Society*, vol. vi, p. 411. Funk

name of Westphall was living in the northern part of Calumet County. The first German to settle in Milwaukee County was Wilhelm Strothmann, in 1835.[1] The German immigration began properly in 1840, when in the summer months there arrived in Milwaukee two to three hundred Germans every week. Milwaukee was at first the point of attraction, and subsequently became the great distributing-centre for the German immigration. A large increase came in 1843–44, when from a thousand to fourteen hundred Germans arrived every week during the summer season. They no longer remained in Milwaukee in such large numbers, but penetrated into the interior of the state. The flood of immigration brought along a number of prominent individuals, such as F. W. Horn, who in 1848 was a member of the first legislature of the newborn state, and in 1851 was Speaker of the House (Assembly). He was a member of the legislature as late as 1882. Dr. Franz Hübschmann, a graduate in medicine of the University of Jena, was one of the delegates to the convention in 1846 which framed the constitution of the prospective state of Wisconsin. Two other Germans, Janssen and Kern, both of Washington County, were also members of this constitutional convention. In 1844 Moritz Schöffler, the printer, founded the first German weekly (later a daily paper), " The Wisconsin Banner "; Schöffler was a member of the second convention for the drafting of the constitution, in 1847. As early as 1843 the Ger-

is also mentioned with a family of seven in the first territorial census of Wisconsin. Cf. *Ibid.*, vol. xiii, p. 260.

[1] A number of other Germans came in the same year : Andreas Eble, Wilhelm Baumgärtner, N. Esling, Walter Shattuck, Alfred Orendorf, Edward Wiesner. In 1836 there came George Hahn, Louis Treyser, George Abert, F. and H. Harmeyer, Henry Bleyer ; in 1837, Mathias Stein, C. W. Schwartzburg, David Knab. Cf. Eickhoff, p. 365.

mans united in a demonstration connected with a public festival in Milwaukee.[1] They soon found it necessary to unite against " Knownothingism," which as it spread over the country also entered Wisconsin.

The foundation of a bishopric[2] at Milwaukee by the Catholic Church aided immigration to the new state, particularly from South Germany. John Martin Henni, a native of Switzerland, was appointed the first bishop of Milwaukee. An Austrian priest, Dr. Salzmann, founded the Catholic seminary of St. Francis near the same city, and subsequently a teachers' seminary was added, which furnished German teachers for various parts of the country. The influence of the German Catholics was exhibited in the choice of a successor to Archbishop Henni. This successor, Michael Heisz, was also chosen from the German element, and two other German bishops were appointed for Wisconsin. The Lutheran congregations were likewise numerous and vigorous, and under the influence of their pastors,[3] churches were built that became centres of moral and educational influence. The Protestants erected two colleges in Wisconsin, Northwestern University at Watertown and the Concordia Gymnasium at Milwaukee, both still existing as denominational institutions. A school which performed continuous and excellent service, not confined to the German population, was the Deutsch-Englische Akademie,[4] founded. in 1851. The

[1] On the occasion of the movement to improve the harbor of Milwaukee.

[2] This was subsequently made an archbishopric, when the population grew larger. Henni was the first archbishop.

[3] Among the earliest there were the Reverends Krause, Kindermann, Dulitz, Streiszguth, Lochner. Very noteworthy was the so-called " Mühlhäuser Kirche" (Gnaden-Kirche), popularly named after the first pastor, the Reverend Mr. Mühlhäuser, a man noted for his charity and devotion. Cf. Eickhoff, p. 368.

[4] This school will be mentioned again in Volume II, Chapter v, "German Influence on Education in the United States."

most noted teacher of this school at the early period was
Peter Engelmann, who taught for the love of it and impressed his character on several generations of pupils.

The Germans of Milwaukee introduced their social life
into the new state, e. g., their "Turnvereine" and their
"Gesangvereine." The first German singing-society began in 1847 with sixteen members, and the famous Milwaukee "Musikverein" was founded May 1, 1850.[1] The
first musical director was Hans Balatka, a German Bohemian, the real founder of the society. In the winter of
1849–50, a dramatic performance was attempted by an
association of amateurs, and a theatre was established in
1852 by Joseph and Heinrich Kurz. The tradition was
begun of having a permanent German theatre in Milwaukee, and even at the present day few other cities have
given the German drama such kindly shelter.[2] In 1852
the first "Turnverein" in Milwaukee was established by
Edward Schultz, a political refugee from Baden. The
years 1853–54 were considered the "flowering-time" of
Milwaukee's musical and literary activities, and from that
period dates the name: "Deutsch-Athen" (German
Athens). The hyperbole is excusable when we compare
the good musical and literary attainments of Milwaukee
with the low plane of culture existing at the time in most
American cities, whether in the East or in the West. The
accounts of cultivated European travelers furnish abundant evidence of the deplorable absence of literary and
musical aspirations.

Among the early influential Germans in Wisconsin,

---

[1] In honor of the fiftieth anniversary celebration of this musical association, a volume containing its history was published, entitled, *Der Musikverein von Milwaukee, 1850–1900 : Eine Chronik*. (Milwaukee, 1900.)

[2] See Volume II, Chapter VII.

there were the orator and poet, A. H. Bielefeld, and the
teacher and advocate, Eduard Salomon. The latter was
elected lieutenant-governor of Wisconsin in 1862, and
when Governor Harvey died in office, Salomon became war-
governor, a great distinction for the first German governor
of the state. As journalists, teachers, and physicians many
Germans became prominent, but even more important for
the development of the state was the share of the German
element in commerce and industrial enterprises. Some of
their establishments became famous all over the United
States. Their breweries, tanneries, tobacco storehouses,
banks, hotels, their trade in iron, lumber, and drugs,
built up the wealth of Milwaukee, and gave the state a commanding position in the commerce of the Great Lakes
and the Northwest.

There were several causes for Wisconsin's receiving so
large a German population. In the first place there was
an effort made, as in the case of Missouri and Texas, to
individualize Wisconsin as a German state. The plan to
found a German state in the Wisconsin territory failed
as it had elsewhere, but as in the other cases the result
was favorable for the state selected, the latter being
thereby rapidly supplied with a desirable and abundant
population. We observed above the foundation of the
"Giessener Gesellschaft" in 1833, and the large consequent immigration entering Missouri. In 1835 a society
called "Germania" was formed on this side of the ocean,
with the purpose of maintaining German customs, speech,
and traditions against all destructive influences, and
assisting German refugees and immigrants arriving in the
United States.[1] After a rebuff met by their memorial to
Congress, asking that land be set aside on easy terms for

[1] Cf. Gustav Körner, *Das deutsche Element in den Vereinigten Staaten von*

German [1] fugitives, their next plan was to direct German immigration to specific areas, of which they might gain control through their numbers, so as to make of them German states. The promoters could not agree on the region to be settled; Texas and Oregon were desired by some, while the majority favored the Northwest Territory, between the Mississippi and the Great Lakes. The society did not have a long life. A similar movement took place in 1836, started in Philadelphia by the German-American Settlement Society,[2] the final result of which was the founding of the town of Hermann, in Gasconade County, Missouri. Franz Löher, perhaps the first German traveler and man of letters who felt sincerely interested in the German-American population of the United States, and who wrote the so-called "romantic history" of the Germans in America,[3] advocated as the best place for German settlers the territory between the waters of the Ohio and Missouri, and thence to the northwest. The Irish, he argued, remained in the East or in the cities, whereas the native Americans were scattered through the Far West. That left the centre and northwest, the real pick of the territory, to the German immigration. He favored concentration, and spoke in favor of Wisconsin and Iowa, for

Nordamerika, 1818-1848, p. 108. (Cincinnati, 1880.) Cf. also Löher, *Geschichte und Zustände der Deutschen in Amerika*, pp. 281-282. (1847.)

[1] There had been a precedent. June 30, 1834, thirty-six sections of public land, in Illinois or Michigan, had been granted to 235 Polish refugees by Act of Congress.

[2] The "Deutsche Ansiedlungs-Gesellschaft," in which J. G. Wesselhoeft, editor of the *Alte und neue Welt*, and many others were interested. Cf. the work already referred to: W. G. Bek, *The German-American Settlement Society of Philadelphia and its Colony, Hermann, Missouri.* (Americana Germanica Press, Philadelphia, 1907.)

[3] The book already referred to: Franz Löher, *Geschichte und Zustände in Amerika.* (2te Ausgabe, Göttingen, 1855.) Cf. pp. 501-505: Länder für deutsche Staatenbildung; and pp. 280-285: Staatenpläne.

German settlement, and if elsewhere, Texas. The same general plan is advocated in numerous other works.[1]

An influence still stronger were the favorable reports sent home by immigrants who were well pleased with their location in Wisconsin. "Nothing succeeds like success" is an adage nowhere more applicable than to immigrations. The climate of Wisconsin was such as to encourage them. Though the winters were cold, the air was dry, and fevers incident to new settlements were not so frequent as elsewhere. The climate and soil closely resembled what the Germans had left at home. The products of the soil were the same as they had raised in Germany for generations, — wheat, rye, oats, and garden vegetables. Moreover there was no competition with slave labor, and, after the period of slavery, with free negro labor, felt to be degrading by the self-respecting German, who had been attracted by the reports he had heard of the dignity of labor in America.

Several other well-marked causes united in bringing Wisconsin so large a foreign and particularly a German population. In the first place, Wisconsin, when admitted to statehood in 1848, was unincumbered by public debts arising from internal improvements on a large scale.[2] No burdens of taxation, therefore, were to be feared by the immigrant In the second place, the constitution adopted

---

[1] Cf. A. E. Hasse's book, published in Grimma, 1841, in which he directly counsels the Germans to settle in Wisconsin, basing his advice on his "own observations and experience." Cf. also Everest-Levi, *How Wisconsin came by its Large German Element*, pp. 303–312. Cf. Theodor Wettstein, *Berichte aus Wisconsin*. (Elberfeld, 1850.) The author regards the state as best suited for Germans because of its natural advantages of soil and climate.

[2] The *Milwaukee Courier*, quoting the *Mohawk Courier* (N. Y.), says, August 31, 1842, "Immigration now turns to Wisconsin, Missouri, and Iowa, for Michigan, Illinois, and Indiana have public debts." Everest-Levi, p. 314. (Reprint, p. 18.)

by the state was very liberal toward foreigners. To secure
the right of voting, only one year of residence was required. This unusual privilege [1] was the result, to be sure,
of a struggle, one in which two Germans had been very
influential. These two were Dr. Franz Hübschmann, the
representative of the Germans in the first convention of
1846, and Moritz Schöffler, their able spokesman in the
second convention of 1847–48. [2]

Another feature favorable to the immigration was Wisconsin's liberal land policy. The land granted her by the
government for the maintenance of schools was sold at
low prices and without delay to the immigrants. Altogether the state received nearly four million acres of land [3]
for the benefit of schools and the University, and the
greater part of these lands were offered for sale at the
minimum government price of $1.25 per acre. Some sec-
tions in remote regions sold for less, others were appraised
higher, but excellent pieces of land were even sold on
credit. Naturally the liberality of this system bore fruit,

[1] Wisconsin was the only state possessing so liberal a franchise in 1848 ;
in 1851 Indiana put a similar clause into her constitution ; Minnesota in
1857. Other states followed in ten or fifteen years. Everest-Levi, *supra*.
(Reprint, p. 18.)

[2] Dr. Franz Hübschmann was a native of Weimar, who settled in Milwaukee as a physician in 1842. He was interested in all public affairs of the
city and state, became instrumental in getting the appropriation for the
harbor of Milwaukee, was leader in all political, social, and musical activities
of the German element, and brought to the city other men of talent, such as
the journalist, Moritz Schöffler. Hübschmann's speech on the franchise was
published in the *Wisconsin Banner*, November 7, 1846. Under the editorship
of Schöffler, the *Wisconsin Banner* became the leading organ in the movement for the liberal franchise for foreigners. The Germans were joined in
their efforts by the Irish element. In the earlier years of the struggle, 1843–
44, the Germans, K. J. Kern, H. Härtel, F. A. Lüning, were also influential.
Cf. R. A. Kosz, *Milwaukee* (Milwaukee, 1871), pp. 231, 258 ; Hense-Jensen,
Wisconsins Deutsch-Amerikaner, vol. i, pp. 103–109.

[3] Everest-Levi, *supra*, pp. 321–322. (Reprint, p. 25.)

for even the poorest immigrant, after some years of honest toil, was enabled to meet the financial obligations thus assumed.

Still another circumstance favoring the Germans was the appointment by the state of a commissioner of immigration. The law passed in 1852 required the commissioner to reside in New York City throughout the year and to give immigrants information favorable to Wisconsin. The first appointee, G. Van Steenwyk, was followed in 1853 by Hermann Härtel. Both men distributed pamphlets, and advertised in German newspapers in the East and in Europe. Leipzig, Kassel, Nuremberg, Basel, Bremen, and other places in Germany were made acquainted with the advantages of Wisconsin's soil and climate. Härtel reported that within eight months he had answered three hundred and seventeen letters from Europe, and that, of the three thousand people who had visited his New York office, two thirds were Germans. Often money was sent to him from settlers in Wisconsin to assist their relatives on arrival at New York. The American consul at Bremen, Dr. Hildebrandt (a German of Mineral Point, Wisconsin), gave valuable assistance in circulating information. Nearly thirty thousand pamphlets were distributed, one half of them in Europe. The third commissioner, F. W. Horn (of Ozaukee County, Wisconsin), appointed in 1854, used similar means of advertising, and of directing immigrants to Wisconsin. A branch office was established in Quebec, though not with satisfactory results.

The existence of the Wisconsin Bureau of Immigration became widely known throughout Europe, and its square dealing strengthened the good name the state had already gained. The office was discontinued in 1855, but in 1867 the state established a board of immigration. The gov-

ernor, *ex officio* a member, was authorized to appoint a
local committee of three citizens in each county to assist
the board, particularly in making out lists of the names
and addresses of European friends of Wisconsin settlers,
so that information in regard to the state might be sent
to them.[1] For some years Bernhard Domschke, a German
editor of Milwaukee, was a member of the board, and
German pamphlets were distributed in large numbers. In
1871 the board was abolished, and the office of a state
commissioner of immigration was created, to be elective
for a term of two years. The incumbent was to reside in
Milwaukee and to appoint a local agent for Chicago. The
duties of the commissioner were to prepare and distribute
pamphlets, giving information about the resources of the
state and the land still available for settlement. In 1879
the experiment of a board of immigration was renewed,
and it was maintained from 1881 to 1887; J. A. Becher
was the well-qualified president of the board. During this
period Wisconsin was well represented in Europe, especially in Germany.[2] The Wisconsin Central Railroad sent
its agent, K. K. Kennan, to Basel, Switzerland. He found
it to his advantage to be under the state authority and to
represent the interests of the whole state of Wisconsin,
rather than those of a private corporation. Through his
efforts and those of the board, about five thousand immigrants were secured, mainly from the forest lands of Bavaria, and were distributed along the line of the Wisconsin Central Railroad from Stevens Point to Ashland.
The inducement held out to them was good wages in the

---

[1] Cf. Everest-Levi, *supra*, pp. 327–328. (Reprint, pp. 31–33.)

[2] Twenty thousand pamphlets and nine thousand copies of a pocket map,
with a description of Wisconsin, were printed in 1882 and largely distributed in Germany. *Ibid.*, p. 33, note.

lumber camps, where they might in a short time earn
enough to buy land and build homes. Some provision was
made by the Wisconsin Central to accommodate the settlers; e. g., in Medford, where a house was used to shelter
from seventy-five to one hundred immigrants for two
weeks free of charge, with the use of a large cooking-
stove.[1]

The German books and pamphlets, published for distribution, and written by travelers in Wisconsin, are too
numerous to enumerate with a view to completeness. A
few of the important titles are as follows: —

A. Ziegler, " Skizzen einer Reise durch Nordamerika und
Westindien mit besonderer Berücksichtigung des deutschen Elements, der Auswanderung und der landwirthschaftlichen Verhältnisse in dem neuen Staat Wisconsin " (Dresden and Leipzig, 1849); Dr. Carl de Haas, "Nordamerika" (Wisconsin,
Calumet, 1848), " Winke für Auswanderer "; Freimund Gold-
manns " Briefe aus Wisconsin in Nordamerika," herausgegeben
von Dr. G. Goldmann (Leipzig, 1849); Wilhelm Dames,
" Wie sieht es in Nordamerika aus? " (1849). Other books
were those of Theodor Wettstein (1848), on the physical features of Wisconsin, and of W. C. L. Koch (Göttingen, 1851),
on the mineral wealth about Lake Superior and the Mississippi
River; also K. K. Kennan's " Der Staat Wisconsin, seine
Hülfsquellen und Vorzüge für Auswanderer " (Basel, 1882);
Gustav Richter, " Der Nordamerikanische Freistaat Wisconsin "
(Wesel, 1849).

The geographical distribution of the Germans in Wisconsin is as follows: They are most numerous in the eastern and north-central counties, which correspond to the
heavily wooded districts of the state. Their preference
was first for the wooded lands near the main routes of
travel, viz., the eastern counties. Thence they spread to

---

[1] Everest–Levi (Reprint), p. 36.

the counties in the north-central parts of the state in the deep forests. This selection was by no means accidental, since the German agriculturist knew that heavy timber grows only on fertile soil. His progress could, of course, not be so rapid as on prairie land, but the results after laborious industry would be permanently good. R. G. Thwaites,[1] secretary and superintendent of the State Historical Society of Wisconsin, makes the following statement concerning the distribution of the Germans in Wisconsin : —

The Germans number seventy-five per cent of the population of Taylor County, sixty-five per cent of Dodge, and fifty-five per cent of Buffalo. They are also found in especially large groups in Milwaukee, Ozaukee, Washington, Sheboygan, Manitowoc, Jefferson, Outagamie, Fond du Lac, Sauk, Waupaca, Dane, Marathon, Grant, Waushara, Green Lake, Langlade, and Clark counties. There are Germans in every county of the state and numerous isolated German settlements, but in the counties named these people are particularly numerous. Sometimes the groups are of special interest, because the people came for the most part from a particular district in the Fatherland. For instance, Lomira, in Dodge County, was settled almost entirely by Prussians from Brandenburg, who belonged to the Evangelical Association. The neighboring towns of Hermann and Theresa, also in Dodge County, were settled principally by natives of Pomerania. In Calumet County there are Oldenburg, Luxemburg, and New Holstein settlements. St. Kilian, in Washington County, is settled by people from Northern Bohemia, just over the German border. The town of Belgium, Ozaukee County, is populated almost exclusively by Luxemburgers, while Oldenburgers occupy the German settlement at Cedarburg. Three fourths of the population of Farmington, Washington County, are from Saxony. In the same county Jackson is chiefly

[1] *Preliminary Notes on the Distribution of Foreign Groups in Wisconsin*, by Reuben G. Thwaites. (Extract from the *Annual Report of the State Historical Society of Wisconsin, 1890*, pp. 58–59.)

settled by Pomeranians, while one half of the population of Kewaskum are from the same German province. In Dane County there are several interesting groups of German Catholics. Roxbury is nine tenths German, the people coming mostly from Rhenish Prussia and Bavaria. Germans predominate in Cross Plains, the rest of the population being Irish. The German families of Middleton came from Köln, Rhenish Prussia, and so did those of Berry, a town almost solidly German.

In Wisconsin, whose population is three fourths of foreign origin, the German element has always predominated. The industrial, agricultural, and commercial prominence of the state is due more largely to the Germans than to all other foreign elements combined. They have also been more successful in maintaining their social life than elsewhere, including their introduction of music, their singing-societies, their Turnvereine, their opposition to the Puritanic spirit. The traveler through Wisconsin is now and then impressed with a similarity in landscape to parts of Germany.[1] This is particularly true of the eastern and north-central counties of the state, where, as before mentioned, the Germans are most numerous. The well-kept farms, the neat houses, commonly of light-colored brick, the generous barns, and the normal appearance of order, cleanliness, neatness, and substantial prosperity are as impressive as they are in Lancaster County, Pennsylvania, while German traditions and German speech, owing to later settlement, are still more live in Wisconsin than in that earlier stronghold of German influence, the Keystone State.

Minnesota

The history of Wisconsin's neighbor on the west also exhibits an extraordinary development within a few years.

[1] Cf. K. Lamprecht, *Americana*, p. 24 (Freiburg i, B. 1906): " An den schönsten Stellen scheint es, als seien wir nach dem Lande gekommen, wie es

Minnesota was organized as a territory in 1849. The census of the following year gives it 6077 inhabitants.[1] In the next decade came the record-breaking increase to nearly thirty times that number, viz., 172,023. By December 1, 1862, Minnesota[2] had sent 11,877 men into the Union army, and Governor Ramsey could truthfully say that Minnesota had sent a larger number of men into the field than it had had inhabitants in 1850; the fact is, she sent nearly twice as many.

The German population of Minnesota has always been large, though not maintaining the same ratio to the remaining population as in Wisconsin. According to the last census, the total foreign population of Minnesota in 1900 was 1,312,019. Of these 289,822 were of German parentage. The German population was larger than that of any other nationality, but second to the Scandinavian element if Norway and Sweden be taken together as one people.[3]

Excepting the men in military stations the earliest pioneers of Minnesota were a company of German Swiss, who migrated from the Red River settlements in British America. In 1822 five families went with the American cattle-drivers who returned from the north to the United States. The Swiss received aid at Fort St. Anthony (later called Fort Snelling), at the confluence of the Minnesota

sich der deutsche Landwirt träumen mag : ein verbessertes Deutschland, eine Gegend, von der der Dichter ahnend sagte : Und wie ein Garten war das Land zu schauen. Das ist deutsches Farmerland, Land deutschen Fleiszes."

[1] They were located almost without exception on the Mississippi River, as far as it was navigable.

[2] Minnesota was admitted as a state in 1858.

[3] Sweden numbered 211,769 ; Norway, 224,892. The total population of the state, including the native element, was 1,751,394, the population of foreign and mixed parentage being 74.9 per cent of the whole. Cf. *Twelfth Census of the United States*, vol. i (Population, part I, pp. 806, 808, 810).

and the Mississippi rivers. There they remained for the
winter, and the next spring settled on the military reservation, selling their farm products to the garrison.[1] In
the spring of 1823 thirteen other colonists with their
families from the Red River country braved the raw climate, the trackless woods, and hostile savages. They used
for transportation the so-called Red River carts, constructed without iron, untanned hides being drawn over
the rudely fashioned wooden wheels, in place of tires.[2]
They tarried for some time at Lake Traverse, about two
hundred miles from Fort Snelling, and then went on, de-
scending the St. Peter (Minnesota) River, in dug-outs.
After a journey of twelve hundred miles through a
country, part of which had never been traversed by white
men, they reached the Mississippi, and at length St.
Louis. The end of their wanderings, however, had not yet
come, for they found the climate of St. Louis unsuitable,
and decided to settle farther north. They finally located
about fifteen miles northeast of La Pointe, where they
found employment in the lead-mines.[3] The large migration
of the Swiss colony on the Red River did not come, however, until 1826. The severe winter of 1825–26 and the
terrible floods of the succeeding spring destroyed the property and food-stores of the Red River colonists and threat-

---

[1] The names of the first pioneers of Minnesota were : Louis Massie, Jacob
Falstrom, Antoine Pepin, Joseph Rösch, Joseph Bisson. Cf. *Der deutsche
Pionier*, vol. xi, p. 15.

[2] Such carts were frequently seen in St. Paul before the opening of the
Northern Pacific Railroad. Cf. *Der deutsche Pionier*, vol. xi, p. 15 (illustration).

[3] The location is about the present town of Galena, in the northwestern
corner of the state of Illinois. A number of others of the Red River colonists settled the towns of Bern and Zurich, in Hay Township, Ontario. The
leaders of this group of about ten families were : Christian Hay, Georg Hess,
and Johann Rothermühl. Cf. *Der deutsche Pionier*, vol. xi, p. 18.

ened them with famine. In June, 1826, two hundred and forty-three people left Fort Garry, and followed the path of their predecessors by way of the Red River to Lake Traverse, thence to Fort St. Anthony, and then by steamer on the Mississippi to their destination, La Pointe, where they were warmly received by the earlier Swiss settlers. They settled mostly as agriculturists, but some became miners. In the Black Hawk War, six years later, almost all of the men volunteered under Captain Schneider. Their descendants spread over the Northwest, but are to be found in the greatest numbers in the lead districts.

The Red River Swiss, though the first settlers, did not select Minnesota for their permanent homes. The German element had numerous other representatives, however, who pushed the frontier line of Minnesota to the westward. There was the German settlement at Henderson on the St. Peter (Minnesota) River, forming a nucleus for log houses scattered through the forests and over the prairies. But the most interesting settlement, historically, was one farther west, called New Ulm, which to-day is a prosperous town of over 5400 inhabitants. An organization of workingmen in Chicago was responsible for the settlement. Their membership having grown to eight hundred in 1854, their ambition was to leave the city's labor market and establish farm homes on cheap land on the western frontier of Minnesota. The pioneers that were sent to settle had some difficulty in finding their destination, but they were fortunate finally in obtaining a good location on the Cottonwood River, a tributary of the Minnesota. They measured off their land in 1855, but their coming occasioned great wrath among the Sioux, who pulled up the surveyors' stakes and annoyed the whites until the latter drove them off. The dispute was referred to the governor at St. Paul, who decided that the settlers would have to move if they were not on congressional land. It was found, however, that the reservation of the Indians began nine miles beyond the new settlement, called New Ulm, and therefore the German settlers were left in possession.[1] A society of Chicago Turners[2] soon united with the first organization, so that by 1857 a considerable number of settlers had arrived, making a respectable village. Two steam-mills were erected, farm-houses spread out in all directions, and in the autumn of the same year New Ulm was incorporated as a town in the territory of Minnesota. The new town proved its virility in 1861, by organizing a company of militia to be sent to Fort Ridgely, about fifteen miles distant, on the Minnesota River, and also by placing many recruits in the service of the Union army. After the departure of most of the fighting element, a disaster befell the settlers which nearly destroyed New Ulm. This was the massacre of 1862, by the Sioux or Dakota Indians.

The Indians had some grounds for discontent, but as frequently happened on the frontier the penalty for the wrongs committed was paid by the innocent pioneers. The annual sums of money which had been promised the Indians by the United States government, for lands ceded by them in 1858 on the north bank of the Minnesota River, were promptly paid out of the United States Treasury, but very rarely reached the Indians. The money went

[1] Cf. *Der deutsche Pionier*, vol. iii, pp. 13 ff.: vol. iv, pp. 122 ff.: vols. viii and ix, "Geschichte von New-Ulm, Minnesota," von Alex. Berghold. The twentieth anniversary of the settlement of New Ulm was celebrated October 11, 1874, making the date of the original settlement 1854. It was at that time the westernmost point of settlement in the territory of Minnesota.

[2] "Der Ansiedlungsverein des sozialistischen Turnerbundes von Nordamerika."

into the pockets of the Indian agents and traders, who resorted to the most varied pretexts for defrauding the Sioux. One method employed by the Indian traders was to set up storehouses, where supplies were sold at enormous rates. The Indians, having no money, were given credit, in consideration of which they were made to sign papers whereby ultimately they transferred their claims to white thieves. The Indians could not read or write, and did not understand the papers which they marked. Again, heavy fines were sometimes imposed upon them; a white man in Sioux City, for instance, received five thousand dollars for stolen horses, which sum was simply taken out of the congressional funds, and charged against the Indians.[1]

Danger from the Indians began as early as 1857, in which year about forty settlers were killed or captured. The insurrection was put down with the aid of friendly Indians, among them Chief Little Crow, who in the succeeding struggles became an implacable foe of the white man. In 1861 the crops of the Indians turned out badly and famine stared them in the face. By the middle of December fifteen hundred of them had to be supplied with food to keep them from starvation. The hope of early hunting was dispelled by the heavy snows. Under these circumstances the pay-day of 1862 was looked forward to with desperate eagerness. The Indians had some knowledge of the progress of the Civil War, and were in fear that the government could not pay. When from five to six thousand Sioux gathered about the agency clamoring for their money, they were told that they would receive it, but that they would have to wait. A great many were on the verge of starvation, and the

[1] Cf. *Der deutsche Pionier*, vol. viii, pp. 229-230.

more reckless element, the young braves, took advantage
of the situation. The older Indians opposed the plan of
an insurrection on a large scale, but the younger warriors
prevailed, and determined to wipe out all the pioneer
settlements at one fell swoop. The plan matured quickly,
and the first deed of violence was committed August 4,
1862, when four hundred mounted Indians and one hundred and fifty on foot broke open the door of the storehouse, shot down the American flag, and took out one
hundred and fifty sacks of flour. The storehouse was re-
taken, but the fact that no Indians were punished made
the latter all the bolder. As mentioned above, the departure of recruits for the war (the McKeeville Rangers)
weakened the resisting power of the pioneers and gave
the Sioux a golden opportunity.

The German settlement of New Ulm, being farthest
west, had to endure the brunt of the attacks. Jacob Nix,
a native of Bingen-on-the-Rhine, was commandant of the
defenses of the town, such as they were, during the first
days of the hostilities. He had much trouble in convincing the people of their danger. He had come from Fort
Ridgely, and had seen the unmistakable signs of Indian
outrages. The outlying Upper Settlement, seven miles
west of New Ulm, was totally destroyed and every inhabitant killed. There was no hope for the farmers in solitary
places. Men, women, and children were slaughtered, or
tortured to death. The Indians employed their usual tactics, approaching in a friendly manner and catching their
victims off their guard. New Ulm was almost taken by
surprise, so quick was the approach of the Indian advance
guard. The story[1] goes that a number of New Ulm citi-

---

[1] This account is based on the articles of Alex. Berghold in *Der deutsche
Pionier*, vols. viii and ix.

zens were making an excursion in wagons to gather in
volunteers for the Union army. With fluttering banners
and cheering music they drove directly in the direction of
the scene of the massacres. The Indians, hearing the
sounds, waited for the wagons to approach and then received them with a murderous volley. Most of those in
the first wagon were killed, but those behind found time
to turn and effect their escape from the Indians, who did
not pursue them. The survivors then gave the alarm,
though they also experienced difficulty in impressing the
citizens of New Ulm with the imminence of their danger.
Settlers from all directions now hastened to the town,
which was surrounded by the Sioux on the seventeenth
of August, 1862. Their attack lasted into the night, and
they advanced into the middle of the city. The settlers
were under the disadvantage of not having their fighting
strength at home and of being poorly provided with arms
and ammunition. They fought from behind barricades
set up in the streets, their desperation making up for
their handicaps. The first attack was probably made only
by the outposts of the Indians, who withdrew next morning, Little Crow taking them westward to Fort Ridgely,
which they then besieged. The defenders succeeded, however, in communicating their danger to the settlement of
St. Peter and they received aid. When the fort proved
its ability to make a stout resistance, the Indians returned
upon New Ulm, laying waste all the country that lay
between the two points.

The second battle at New Ulm occurred on the twenty-
third of August, but the settlers had in the mean time
improved their barricades and had also received a rein-
forcement of seventy-five men under Captain Cox. The
attacks continued Saturday and Sunday, after which the

Indians withdrew to try their fortunes at other places. The losses at New Ulm are variously estimated, but the property loss was no doubt greater than the loss of life.[1] The terrors of the massacres fell more heavily upon the smaller settlements, such as Newton, about six miles north of New Ulm. The experiences of the German pioneers during the Sioux massacres, though of shorter duration, were no less terrible than during the border warfare in the Mohawk or the Ohio Valley, in the eighteenth century. The story of Maria Hartmann rivals that of Mary Inglis and the " Dutch woman," in the pioneer history of the Kanawha, for its harrowing experiences and hairbreadth escapes, continuous for more than a month.[2]

At the direction of the government, the town of New Ulm was deserted by its inhabitants after the second attack, though many settlers were loath to go. A train of one hundred and fifty wagons made its way toward points more easterly, that could be more easily defended. Such as were able to bear arms remained at Mankato, in order to defend that town ; the others went on to St. Peter,[3] where they were well provided for, or even to St. Paul, the capital of the state. Some of the bolder spirits returned to New Ulm as soon as they heard that militia had been sent out in pursuit of the Indians. The new settlers found the farms in good condition, and prosperity quickly followed. The German element continued to predominate, and at the present day New Ulm is still a German town.

[1] One estimate is that New Ulm lost eight killed and seventy wounded, and that one hundred and fifty to one hundred and seventy-five houses in that place were burned by the enemy.

[2] *Der deutsche Pionier*, vol. ix, pp. 106–109.

[3] St. Peter, Mankato, and Fort Ridgely are all located on the Minnesota River.

The punitive expedition [1] which was sent out by the government captured a large number of Indians, three hundred and three of whom were sentenced to death. They were pardoned, however, all but thirty-nine, some of the latter being half-breeds. The thirty-nine were executed publicly December 7, 1862, and the terror which this act inspired brought the Indian attacks to an end. Official reports gave the number of those killed by the Sioux as somewhat over seven hundred, the number of fugitives from outlying settlements as thirty thousand, and the property loss as about $2,000,000. The German pioneers suffered a large part of this loss in life and property, and thereby contributed once more to the defense of the American frontier, a service which the same stock had continuously performed since the beginning of the eighteenth century.

(B) The Southwest — Texas

The history of the German element in the state of Texas presents some important individual traits. The tale is one of increased hardship and suffering, due to the treacherous climate, to unfamiliarity with the products of the soil, and to hostile encounters with warlike Indian tribes; yet the sequel is the same as in other German colonies, — victory hard-earned and prosperity well-deserved. Lured by speculators, dishonest or unsophisticated, German settlers poured into Texas after the revolt of the "Lone Star" against Santa Anna. Before the territory became a part of the United States the German pioneers joined the American forces in their invasion of Mexico, which

[1] Four thousand Sioux were pursued in 1862–63 by an American army under the command of General Sibley. They were brought to a stand at Devil's Lake, Dakota. Little Crow was not captured, but he was killed later in Minnesota, probably by accident.

guaranteed the future of Texas. They were expected to do more by their European promoters, who had unscrupulously cast them upon the fever-ridden swamps or torrid deserts of the Gulf coast. But the extravagant hope of creating a German state in the Far Western territory was doomed to failure a third time,[1] with the resultant gain to Texas of a large German element in her population, easy of assimilation and sturdy in character.

In 1823, when Texas was still a part of Mexico, Baron von Bastrop founded a German colony on the Colorado River. Named Bastrop[2] after the founder, it was the earliest settlement by the Germans in Texas, and until the foundation of Austin was the northernmost white settlement in the valley of the Colorado. The inhabitants were mostly Oldenburgers of the County Delmenhorst. They were often harassed by the Indians, and were compelled from time to time to leave their settlement. Most of them, however, returned as soon as the troubles seemed over. About the end of the twenties and at the beginning of the thirties, many German families had located between the Brazos and the Colorado rivers.[3] The settlers shared the fortunes of the province in which they lived, and when, in 1836, Texas revolted against the dictatorship of Santa Anna, the Germans fought for their adopted country. In proportion to their numbers they assisted in gaining the glorious victory of San Jacinto,[4] in which the

---

[1] The attempts at forming a German state in Missouri and Wisconsin have been described above.

[2] The name has survived for town and county.

[3] Cf. Eickhoff, *In der neuen Heimat*, pp. 321–323.

[4] The historical novelist, Charles Sealsfield (Carl Postl), in his masterpiece, *Das Kajütenbuch*, depicts the Texan war of independence as the historical background of his romance. The book has been translated into English several times, under the title of the "Cabin Book," and is frequently spoken of as the gem of Sealsfield's tales describing American frontier life.

Germanic overcame the Latin races, as they had done before in Canada, Louisiana, and Florida. A number of young Germans had crossed the American border as volunteers in this Texan war of liberation, and an increase of immigration to Texas followed after the war. In New York City there was formed in 1839 a society with the name "Germania," whose aim was to establish a colony in Texas. The first division of settlers, numbering one hundred and thirty persons, sailed from New York on November 2 of the same year, contracting to cultivate in common an area of ground for three years, after which it was to be divided among the members. The company was provided with rations for six or eight months and with implements necessary for building houses. Galveston was to be made the depot for the succeeding immigrations; the first division, however, did not carry out its programme, but dissolved in Houston. Its president and some others of the more well-to-do returned to New York; the others were left to shift for themselves.[1] Such was the fate not only of German immigrants, but of most early immigrants to Texas, who were generally duped by luring advertisements and brilliant prospects. As elsewhere, so in Texas, the German immigration seemed very desirable to promoters. In the early forties a Frenchman, Henri Castro, received a land-grant west of San Antonio, and founded Castroville, in the present Medina County. A number of German, Alsatian, and Swiss immigrants settled there. A proof of the increasing German immigration was the establishment at Austin in 1841 of the "Teutonia-Orden," the purpose of which was to preserve the national German traits, to encourage German immigration, and to carry on a correspondence with Germany in the interests of Texas.

[1] Eickhoff, p. 323.

About the same time, and possibly encouraged by the example of Castro, a plan was matured to arouse German immigration on an unprecedented scale. Count von Castell, an adjutant of the Duke of Nassau, conceived the idea of concentrating the German immigration from Hessen and surrounding countries upon one area. Castell succeeded in interesting a large number of minor princes and influential noblemen. They formed a company,[1] each member depositing a moderately large sum of money. In May, 1842, two representatives, Count von Boos-Waldeck and Victor von Leiningen, were sent over to Texas to inspect the ground. Boos remained in Texas, founding a plantation at Jack Creek (called Nassau), which is still in existence.[2] Leiningen returned in the following year with favorable reports. The "Mainzer Adelsverein," as the company styled itself, then issued its programme [3] advertising Texas as the one desirable place for the German immigrant. The "Verein" was not fortunate in its first purchase of land, from Henry Fischer, a native of Cassel, who had lived several years in Houston, Texas. Fischer sold to them a large stretch of land on the San Saba River for sixteen thousand dollars and a share in the profits. The prospects appeared brilliant for the settlers, and

[1] The members were : the Duke of Nassau, Protector of the Society ; the Duke of Meiningen ; the Duke of Coburg-Gotha ; the Prince of Prussia ; the Landgrave of Hessen-Homburg ; the Prince of Schwarzburg-Rudolstat ; Prince Moritz of Nassau ; the Princes of Leiningen, Neuwied, Solms-Braunfels, Colloredo-Mansfeld, and Schönburg-Waldenburg ; the Princes Alexander and Carl of Solms-Braunfels; Counts of Neu-Leiningen Westerburg and Alt-Leiningen Westerburg (Friedrich, Victor, and Christian) ; Counts Ysenburg-Meerholz, Hatzfeld, Knyphausen, Colloredo-Mansfeld, Carl von Castell, and several others.

[2] Cf. Eickhoff, *In der neuen Heimat*, p. 324.

[3] Cf. Eickhoff, *In der neuen Heimat*, pp. 323–333, for a complete account of the plans and activities of the "Adelsverein." Cf. also Löher, *Geschichte und Zustände der Deutschen in Amerika*, pp. 349–353.

even conservative men like Herr von Wrede spoke favorably of the outlook, and he himself made a second journey to Texas, where unfortunately he was killed by the Comanches. The "Verein" demanded three hundred gulden from a man, or six hundred gulden from a family, and for these sums would furnish their transportation to the place of settlement, and would give them a log house and one hundred and sixty acres [1] of land for every male inhabitant and double the number of acres for every family. Cattle and agricultural implements were to be obtained at cheap rates. Churches, schools, drugs, and hospital care were all to be furnished, provided the settler would cultivate fifteen acres of land for three years and would occupy his house. Concealed beneath these favorable terms was the plan to bring German settlers to Texas in such numbers that by and by the German population should predominate over all other national elements. Texas did not then belong to the Union, and the English government, which opposed the annexation of Texas by the United States, looked with satisfaction upon the ambitious undertaking of the German noblemen.

In May, 1844, Prince Carl of Solms-Braunfels started for the new land, and was followed by about one hundred and fifty families, who sailed in three ships from Bremen. They arrived in December in Lavaca Bay (Indianola), and then were transported in ox-carts through trackless and swampy areas into the interior. In March, 1845, they arrived at the banks of the Comal River, where Solms had bought one thousand acres of land for the site of a city, after finding that the land bought from Fischer was

[1] The "Adelsverein" was granted three hundred and twenty acres for every male settler, and six hundred and forty acres for every family brought over. Retaining one half the land, the organization, if well managed, could have become wealthy.

too remote. The new city was named New Braunfels, in honor of the leader. Each immigrant received a building-lot of one half an acre, besides ten acres in the vicinity, all this independent of the one hundred and sixty acres guaranteed by the company. The people went zealously to work, and a second train of immigrants that followed were also satisfactorily located. But when through neglect of economy the funds of the society had become nearly exhausted, the management proved altogether incapable of carrying forward the difficult undertaking. The " General Commissär," Solms-Braunfels, who had squandered much of the company's resources, resigned and returned to Europe. The colonial council, consisting of his advisers, was dissolved. A successor was appointed, Von Meusebach, who, arriving from Europe in 1845, had little experience and no acquaintance with Texas. He wisely economized wherever he could, but thereby made enemies, especially among the indolent. In the autumn of the year he led an expedition into the Indian country and selected a site for an additional colony, distant about ninety English miles, or three days' journey on horseback, from New Braunfels. This became the city of Friedrichsburg (Fredericksburg).

When he returned he received word that within a short time several thousand immigrants would arrive in Galveston. He repaired thither to make arrangements for their transportation, but when he arrived at Galveston he found that the directors of the " Adelsverein " had sent over several thousands of human beings, but not a cent of money for their future sustenance and transportation. Even the money which the immigrants had deposited in Germany, and which was to be paid out to them on their demand, had not arrived. As a result even people who had been well-to-do at home, and thought they had provided themselves with ample means, remained destitute for months after their arrival, until they could get back their money.

Meusebach hastened to New Orleans to borrow funds, and the immigrants were gradually taken from Galveston to Indian Point, a harbor on Lavaca Bay, whence they were to be transported overland to the place of settlement. We know the facts concerning this ill-fated immigration from the work of Alwin Sörgel,[1] who was on board the *Franzisca*, one of the last ships to arrive.

Their experiences on shipboard remind one of the sufferings of immigrants in the eighteenth century. Their experiences on land would tempt the pen of a Balzac. Of the twenty-five hundred passengers, about twenty-three hundred landed at Galveston. Fifty men were sent in advance to prepare the colony in the interior, while the rest were huddled together at Indian Point, on Lavaca Bay, where under rudely constructed sheds or tents, surrounded by their chests and mounds of baggage, they were exposed to the fevers and excesses of a tropical climate. Many a man vainly sought for work at Galveston, and German barons were glad to push wheelbarrows in the streets of the town to earn the means of mere subsistence. Money could not be had; for that the immigrants were directed to wait until they got to New Braunfels. Nothing could be done for the betterment of their unhappy condition until the spring, and then came swarms of mosquitoes to add to their misery and increase their mortality. The evils

[1] A. H. Sörgel : *Neueste Nachrichten aus Texas, zugleich ein Hülferuf an den Mainzer Verein zum Schutze deutscher Einwanderer in Texas.* (Eisleben, 1847.) Cf. also : Ferd. Römer, *Texas. Mit besonderer Rücksicht auf deutsche Auswanderung und die physischen Verhältnisse des Landes nach eigener Beobachtung geschildert.* (Bonn, 1849.)

of the situation at Indian Point were aggravated, because all means of transportation had been requisitioned by the military authorities. The country was on the eve of the war with Mexico, and forced preparations for the movement of soldiers and supplies interfered with contracts already entered into. Von Meusebach had had such a contract with the merchants of Houston for the transportation of the entire body of immigrants. Several hundreds of the German immigrants, giving up all hope of ever reaching New Braunfels, formed a volunteer company and joined the United States army that invaded Mexico.

Alwin Sörgel and two companions were fortunate in securing means of transportation and getting to New Braunfels.[1] There they found that the town had gone backward since the collapse of the association's treasury. The hostility of the Indians had kept the settlers near together and prevented their spreading out into neighboring territory. Harvests had not been plentiful, and many of the inhabitants, accustomed to receiving supplies from the "Verein," had grown indolent and thriftless. Many would work for a few dollars in the service of those who still had a little money. Some in their desperate plight, surrounded by disease[2] and ruin, sought to enjoy after their own fashion the brief span of life still left them. Resorting to a wooden booth where there was

[1] Along the way they frequently met stragglers, — one, for instance, a German, who had gone from Indian Point to seek employment. He had left his wife and children at Indian Point, and expressed the hope that the "Verein" might transport them to New Braunfels. This is an instance among hundreds of the separation of families.

[2] There was but one physician in New Braunfels, Dr. Köster, and so many died under his hands that the cemetery of the settlement was called "Köster's Plantation." Whether this was due to a lack of skill on his part or to other causes is not stated. He was the physician of the "Verein."

dancing every night, the hale and the sick together
raved in a dizzy reel of enjoyment to the shrill music of a
clarionetist, an individual who was also the professional
grave-digger of the place. This midnight dance of death
was the dreadful culmination of the sights the travelers
had witnessed on their way to New Braunfels, — human
bones, cast-off pieces of clothing, beds, tools, chests strewn
along the desert path between Indian Point and New
Braunfels. But not all the settlers went to destruction,
for the next summer, in 1846, New Braunfels[1] received
additions to its population and gained in stability. The
annex, ninety miles north, called Friedrichsburg, also had
one thousand inhabitants the next winter. Disease became
less frequent and the harvesting of crops placed a pre-
mium on work. As soon as the colonists were made to
stand on their own feet, the sturdy class prospered and
the idlers fell away like frost-bitten leaves in autumn.

Meusebach had contributed much to the welfare of the
colony, though his services were not appreciated. He was
made the scapegoat for all the mismanagement committed
by his predecessors and the home office. At one time a
mob appeared before his house and threatened to kill him.
In spite of all he maintained himself as head of the colonies until the "Adelsverein" sold its properties. The
princes and noblemen of the organization had, through
their incapacity, brought untold sufferings upon the thousands of German settlers whom they had, by fair promises,
induced to immigrate. The "Verein" was no doubt well-
intentioned, but, committing error after error, it fortun-

---

[1] New Braunfels, at present a prosperous town of a little more than two
thousand inhabitants, celebrated its twenty-fifth anniversary in 1870, making
the date of foundation 1845. Fredericksburg celebrated its twenty-fifth
anniversary in 1871. The latter, not so favorably located, has about twelve
hundred inhabitants.

ately came to an end. The German immigration received a setback from the reports of the mishaps of the Texas colonists, yet the check was only temporary.

After 1848 the current of German immigration first turned toward the earlier settlements already described, and then spread northward and westward, yielding additions also to the population of the principal towns, such as San Antonio,[1] Dallas, Galveston, Houston, and Austin. The entire country, almost without exception, in the triangle between Seguin, New Braunfels, and San Antonio is in the possession of Germans, who have upheld what may be called the ancient reputation of German settlers in the United States, that of being the best farmers in their particular state and exemplary as law-abiding and patriotic citizens. The census of 1900 gave Texas a foreign white population of 466,651, of which 157,214, or thirty-three and seven tenths per cent, were Germans. The influence of the German element in the state is seen also in their representation in the United States Congress at various times. The most conspicuous congressmen were Gustav Schleicher and Eduard Degener. Gustav Schleicher was born in Darmstadt, Germany, in 1829, and came to Texas about 1847. With a group of companions he had decided to build on the Rio Grande an "Icarie," after Cabet's plan. Since there were just forty young comrades, they called themselves the " Vierziger," but their existence as a community was shortened through

---

[1] About 1840 the population of San Antonio was almost exclusively Mexican ; about thirty years later its population was about one half German. Cf. *Der deutsche Pionier*, vol. i, p. 282. In Kendall County are the German settlements Börne and Comfort ; in Dewitt County, Yorktown ; High Hill, in Fayette County, was originally called Blum Hill, in honor of Robert Blum, lover of liberty, executed in Vienna in 1848. *Der deutsche Pionier*, vol. i, p. 349.

robbery by the Comanches and deception practiced upon them by speculators. After the colony's failure Schleicher withdrew and became a farmer on his own account. Subsequently he joined some other members of his family at San Antonio, and there was engaged in the practice of his profession as engineer. In 1853 he was a representative in the state legislature, and six years later a member of the state senate, where he was noted for his public spirit, his clear and thorough thinking. He opposed the secession movement in 1861, but when the state decided to join the Confederacy, he went with the majority. He served in the war, principally as an engineer, building several forts, notably Fort Sabine. In 1874 he was elected a member of the United States Congress from Texas, and was twice reëlected, in 1876 and in 1878. He served on some of the most important committees, — on railroads, foreign affairs, and ways and means, — and died in office in 1879. Memorial addresses by James A. Garfield and Thomas F. Bayard prove how deeply his loss was felt by the nation.[1]

Eduard Degener was born in Brunswick, Germany, in 1809. He left Europe in 1850 and traveled in the United States before settling in Texas. Like Schleicher, he was also for some time a " Latin farmer." When the Civil War broke out, Degener remained faithful to the Union, though he incurred the danger of assassination. Both his oldest sons fell in battle against a regiment of Confederates, and he himself was taken as a prisoner to San Antonio, where for some time he languished in a filthy dungeon in an old Mexican house. He was finally released on the bail of two Confederate friends, and became a successful merchant in

[1] Cf. Körner, *Das deutsche Element i. d. Vereinigten Staaten v. Nordamerika, 1818–1848*, pp. 365–368. (New York, 1884.)

San Antonio. In 1866 he was elected (reëlected, 1868) a member of the constitutional convention of Texas, and advocated universal suffrage without distinction of race. The Republican party, in 1869, elected him a member of the United States Congress from western Texas.[1]

(C) The Far West

The settlement of the western highlands of the United States followed rapidly after the Civil War, as is seen by the census map already referred to. Kansas and Nebraska received the earliest immigrations, native as well as foreign. In the other states of the Far West the population centred about the mines, and such other areas where it was possible for human beings to exist and acquire wealth. Germans, Swiss, Scandinavians, and Mennonites (mostly German-Russians), were abundant in those islands of population that were scattered about on the plains and plateaus of the arid West. Their history does not differ from that of the native pioneers, and their national peculiarities were almost immediately lost in the types which the frontier imposed upon all pioneers alike. Miners, ranchmen, cow-boys, hunters, were all similar in appearance and habits, whatever their place of birth, especially after some years of residence on the plains. As for the Mennonites, they kept together, forming large settlements in Kansas, between 1876 and 1878; entire communities of Mennonites also made Nebraska their home. These people originally hailed from West Prussia, and migrated thence to Southern Russia, where they remained until they heard of the prospects in the great republic across the seas. A representative colony is that of Germania, on the Atchison, Topeka & Sante Fé Railroad, in the south-

---

[1] *Deutsch-amerikanisches Conversations-Lexikon* (Schem), vol. iii, p. 573.

western part of Kansas. It is a country of big farms, where wheat, corn, rye, and barley are raised on farms of from sixty to one thousand acres in size. The Mennonites quickly learned to use American machinery and were reliable in the payment of their debts. They also brought fruit-trees — e. g., apricots — from Russia.[1] In larger cities, such as Leavenworth and Topeka, wherever the Germans clustered in larger groups, they preserved much of their nationality. But most of them are scattered over the state, and are engaged in the business of agriculture.

Even on the frontier line farthest west, — that is, on the Pacific coast, — the German pioneers arrived among the earliest. The route to Oregon, over the Rocky Mountains to the Columbia River, by way of the South Pass, was known to American pioneers early in the nineteenth century. The expedition of Lewis and Clark in 1804–05 had opened the way, but for a long time no settlers followed thither. In 1808 the Missouri Fur Company sent some trappers and hunters into that region, and three years later John Jacob Astor, the leading merchant of New York City, founded Astoria, on his own independent means and at his own risk.[2] Astor's brilliant plan

[1] Cf. *Der deutsche Pionier*, vol. x, pp. 147–150 ; C. L. Bernays, *Unter den Mennoniten in Kansas*.

[2] John Jacob Astor was born at Walldorf, near Heidelberg (Baden), in 1763. His parents were poor and he migrated first to England, where he had an older brother. He came to America after the close of the Revolutionary War. While on board ship his attention was called to the possibilities of the fur trade in the colonies, by a fellow passenger. Upon his arrival in New York he exchanged the musical instruments he had from his brother for furs. These he sold in London at a good profit, and thus made his start. He was the first regular dealer in musical instruments in the United States. He speculated in New York real estate, and during the war period of 1812 in government securities. In 1809 he organized the American Fur Company, in which he manifested rare enterprise and courage, and acquired immense wealth. At his death in 1848 his fortune was estimated at the then fabu-

was to connect the fur trade of the Far West by a line of trading-posts extending from the Great Lakes along the Missouri and Columbia rivers to the Pacific. At the mouth of the Columbia, Astor established the new trading-post Astoria, which threatened to take the monopoly of the fur trade out of British hands. That had been the ambition of Astor, but during the succeeding war, in 1813, the British government took possession of the place and named it St. George. Astoria was returned to the United States after the conclusion of the War of 1812,[1] but the American scheme had been financially crippled.

About 1839 began a current of immigration to the Oregon district, and the families that had pushed the frontier line westward steadily from decade to decade reappeared in the valley of the Columbia, to found a new state. They were aided by the foreign element. When the California gold-fever started, in 1848, Oregon for several years lost many of its pioneer settlers. Congress came to the rescue with an act by which every male inhabitant who had settled in Oregon before the first of December, 1850, should receive three hundred and twenty acres of land, and a similar amount for his wife ; each male settler dating from December 1, 1850, to December 1, 1853, should receive one hundred and sixty acres and an equal amount in addition if he were married ; the one condition was, that the settler should remain four years. Offering such inducements, Congress created for Oregon a well-to-do, land-rich class of settlers who were satisfied

lous sum of $20,000,000. He founded the Astor Library, with the gift of $400,000.

[1] Cf. Washington Irving's novel, *Astoria*, which is descriptive of this venture. Irving was a personal friend of Astor, and his regular guest in New York City. Cf. also J. Parton, *Famous Americans of Recent Time.* (Boston, 1867.) Chapter on John Jacob Astor.

to remain permanently in the new territory. Portland, the commercial centre of Oregon, contains a large number of Germans ; they founded German newspapers and introduced their social life, their Turn-, Gesang-, and Schützen-vereine. Travelers describe them as a frank, whole-souled, respectable, and physically fine-looking class of people.

In 1853 the territory north of the Columbia River was separated from Oregon, and called Washington. That territory and the more easterly areas, Montana and the Dakotas, did not receive many accessions to their population until the opening of the Northern Pacific Railroad, the promoter and president of which was a German, Henry Villard. He (Heinrich Hilgard) was born in 1835 at Speyer (Rhenish Bavaria), within the borders of the old Palatinate. With the advantages of a university education (at Munich and Würzburg), he came to this country in 1853, and rapidly fitted himself for the career of a journalist. He gained a mastery of the English language, reported the joint debates between Lincoln and Douglas in 1858, established himself at Washington as the political correspondent of leading Eastern papers, and at the outbreak of the Civil War became a prominent war correspondent in the field, continuing for three years. He revisited Germany during the war periods of 1866 and 1871, and returned as the representative of the foreign bondholders of the Oregon and California Railroad Company, of which he became president in 1875. With the aid of German capital he gained control of the Northern Pacific Railroad, and, completing its western extension, he accomplished the great feat of creating a trunk-line from the Great Lakes to the Pacific. This successful enterprise made him one of the great railway magnates of the country until reverses overtook him in 1883. He recovered, however, and regained control of the Northern Pacific, which opened for settlement the great area of the far Northwest, a magnificent addition to the resources of the American people.[1]

The founder of Seattle, the most important city of the state of Washington, was a Maryland German by the name of Yesler. Henry L. Yesler was born in Leitersburg,[2] Maryland, in 1811. He learned the trade of a carpenter, and at the age of twenty-two followed the stream westward to Ohio, settling at Massillon, where he remained from 1832 to 1851. Industrious and shrewd, he became well-to-do, and when the boom struck the Pacific coast, he resolved to take a look at the country so highly praised. He did not take the tedious and dangerous route across the plains, but sailed from Baltimore to Panama, crossed the Isthmus and took ship to California. He was not induced to stay long among the miners of the gold-lands, nor the boomers of Portland, Oregon, but was fascinated by accounts he heard concerning the region of Puget Sound. There, he was told, was the only real lumber country in the world. Yesler determined to test these reports, and after he had arrived on the spot, his keen eye convinced him that they were true. There lay Alki Point, on Puget Sound, a lumber camp, consisting of three block-

---

[1] He became conspicuous in electrical enterprises, and distinguished through his benefactions, e. g., his gifts to the universities of Oregon, Washington, and to Harvard ; also abroad, e. g., the 'building of a hospital, and training-school at Speyer, an orphan-asylum at Zweibrücken, the endowment of an industrial institution at Kaiserslautern, and the Red Cross Hospital at Munich. He died in 1900. See *National Cyclopædia of American Biography*, vol. iii, p. 498.

[2] Leitersburg received its name from its founder, Jacob Leiter, who was born in Holland, settled first in Pennsylvania, and then trekked to western Maryland. His descendants are the grain merchants of Chicago. Lady Curzon (the deceased wife of the Viceroy of India) was a lineal descendant of Jacob Leiter.

houses, of which one was a store and two were taverns.
A tribe of filthy Indians, dwarfed like Eskimos, dwelling
in ragged tents, would furnish cheap labor. A single acre
would yield scores of straight blocks, over a hundred
feet in length, five or more feet in thickness, which in
the ship-building harbors of the world might bring more
than a hundred dollars apiece. Yesler arrived in the
autumn of 1852; in the summer of the following year he
had built a saw-mill[1] about a mile from Alki Point, on
the present site of Seattle. He availed himself of the government grant of one hundred and sixty acres for himself
and one hundred and sixty more for his wife. He employed great numbers of Indians and became their popular
patron. He built a large cabin of rough-hewn logs, containing a spacious room about twenty-five feet square, which
became the centre of the life of the settlement. It served
as a sort of commons,[2] a resort for the wood-choppers, a
place where King Seattle held his palavers, as town-hall,
jail, and church. Just as quickly as the trees were felled
on his land, Yesler laid out the ground in building-lots
and attracted settlers. A boom struck the place, Yesler
brought his family from Ohio, and permanent settlers
arrived in great numbers. Yesler grew very rich, and so
did those about him. A large saw-mill was soon located on
the opposite side of the Sound, and in spite of frequent
destructive fires the foundations were securely laid for
a great lumber and manufacturing centre. Yesler was the

[1] Yesler's was the first of the saw-mills put up with the design to establish
a trade with San Francisco. Cf. H. H. Bancroft, *Works*, vol. xxxi, *History of
Washington, Idaho, and Montana, 1845-1889*, p. 24.

[2] Yesler's "cook-house," as it was called, was for a number of years the
only place along the east shore of the Sound where comfortable entertainment could be had. There were many regrets when it was replaced by a
modern structure; it had served as town-hall, court-house, jail, military headquarters, storehouse, hotel, and church. Bancroft, *supra*, pp. 24-25.

mayor of Seattle, and a leading citizen for many years,
and during the Indian troubles in the sixties was instrumental in keeping the Indians of Washington Territory
at peace.[1]

California

A direct path to California was not known until Frémont's exploring party, returning from Oregon in the
winter of 1843, lost their way in the great desert between
the Sierra Nevada and the Rocky Mountains. Frémont
was forced to try the passes of the Sierra Nevada Mountains without guides, and in March, 1844, reached Sutter's
fort on the Sacramento River, in time to save his men.
Captain John A. Sutter[2] was one of the most adventurous
and resourceful characters in the history of the Far West,
and at one time he was the richest man in California.
Born in the Grand-Duchy of Baden in 1803, trained in a
Swiss military academy, his bold spirit brought him (in
1834) to the western part of the United States, where for
some years he carried on a caravan trade between St.
Louis and Santa Fé, New Mexico. He journeyed with
a party of trappers, in 1838, to Vancouver. After many
adventures, such as his trips to the Sandwich Islands, to
Alaska, and cruises along the Pacific coast, he was driven
into the Bay of San Francisco by storms. He had long
cherished the desire to penetrate California, concerning
which he had heard so much from the Indians during his
inland expeditions. He succeeded in reaching the neighborhood of the present Sacramento, and there founded
a settlement which he called New Helvetia. From Alva-

---

[1] Cf. A. E. Schade, "Denkschrift über H. L. Yesler," *Seventh Annual
Report of the Society for the History of the Germans in Maryland*, pp. 29–35.
(1892.)

[2] Cf. Körner, pp. 295–298 ; Eickhoff, pp. 388–389.

rado, the Mexican governor of Alta California, he received the right of citizenship and the title to his land, and was made a governor of the northern frontier territory of Mexico. Such he was when Frémont found him. In 1845 Sutter received in addition the magnificent gift of the Sobrante grant for services rendered in the Castro insurrection.

After California was made a part of the United States, Sutter was appointed alcalde or justice of his district, and Indian agent. His estate was now in a very prosperous condition; great areas of wheat were planted and numerous droves of cattle were pastured on his land. The prospects for himself and his colony were unparalleled, and he was accounted the richest man in the state. But fortune was all too generous; she had lavishly strewn gold upon his princely possessions. It was on the twentieth of January, 1848, when Jacob W. Marshall, employed by Sutter as overseer of a saw-mill, appeared with the startling news that he had discovered gold in the river sand. Chemical experts proved the truth of his statement. For Sutter this seemingly brilliant stroke of fortune proved the beginning of his ruin. In self-defense he tried to keep the secret from the public for a short time only, until he might gather in his crops and his cattle, but in vain. Gold-seekers, hordes of adventurers, and desperate characters, crowded upon his property. They trampled down his crops, devoured his cattle, and devastated his land. Even the titles to his estates were then disputed, and from the summit of his fortune Sutter was cast down to the humiliation of seeking redress for his wrongs. Although he appealed for justice to the Congress of the United States, he never regained possession of his property. The state of California voted him a pension of three thousand dollars annu-

ally during the years 1865 to 1872, in view of state taxes
which he had paid on the lands now no longer in his
hands. Honors of various kinds bestowed upon him, such
as his appointment as general of the militia of California,
showed nevertheless a general recognition of his prominent services. Sutter was, in reality, directly responsible
for the discovery of gold in California. It was he who
planned and built the saw-mill which occasioned Marshall's discovery. The discovery was made inevitable,
sooner or later, by the industries established by Sutter.
Although Marshall was the first to see the gold, a larger
amount of credit belongs to the man who prepared the
way, the pioneer who laid the foundation for the wealth
of thousands of people, and thereby became poor.

Besides furnishing a quota of gold-seekers, the German element contributed very largely toward promoting
the wine industry in California.[1] In the Sonoma Valley
most of the wine-ranches have German names. The pioneers, in 1858, were Gundlach and Dresel, who established the " Rhine Farm," now owned by the Gundlach-
Bundschu Wine Company of San Francisco. In Napa
County Charles Krug was the pioneer, also beginning
in 1858, at St. Helena. John Rock came to California in
1866 and founded the Rock Nurseries, and later the California Nurseries covering over five hundred acres, at
Niles, Alameda County. William Palmtag, of Hollister,
planted vineyards in San Benito County; the Eggers

[1] The German influence upon viniculture in California will be treated in
Volume II, Chapter II, of this work. The materials (unpublished) were
collected recently by Professor E. W. Hilgard (founder of the Experiment
Station, and for many years director of the College of Agriculture, University of California), and Mr. Charles Bundschu, of San Francisco, at the
request of the writer. Professor Hilgard and Mr. Bundschu are continuing
their investigations and expect to publish their researches in a special mono-
graph.

Vineyard Company (now sold to the Great Western Vineyards Company) had locations in both Fresno and Kern counties. In Fresno County Frederick Roeding established the Francher Creek Nurseries, continued by his son George C. Roeding, who has also contributed to the cultivation of the fig and other fruit trees. One of the finest plantations, growing the orange, lemon, and grape, near the Mission San Gabriel, belonged at one time to the German Rose.[1]

Los Angeles contains a large German population, as do the cities of San Bernardino, San Diego, and Santa Barbara. The town of Anaheim, twenty-eight miles from Los Angeles, was founded by Germans. Stockton, San Joachin County, the location of the Stockton Mining Company, was founded by Karl M. Weber.[2] San Francisco has always had a very large German population; in fact it owes a large part of its prosperity to such men as James Lick (born in Pennsylvania of German parents, whose family name was originally Lück), best known as the founder of the Lick Observatory; Adolph Sutro (born in Rhenish Prussia), the great mining engineer and philanthropist; and Claus Spreckels (born in Hannover), the sugar-king, founder of the Pacific steamship lines and of the trade with the Sandwich Islands.[3] To the prominent San Francisco Germans belong also Henry Miller (born in Würtemberg), the cattle-king, and his partner, Charles Lux (born in Baden). In 1857 they started a slaughterhouse in San Francisco, and soon gained control of the fresh-meat supply of the city. They acquired eight hundred thousand acres of land in California, besides other

[1] Cf. Eickhoff, *In der neuen Heimat*, p. 390.

[2] Cf. *Der deutsche Pionier*, vol. xiii, pp. 73–75.

[3] A more detailed account of the life-work of these men will be given in Volume II, Chapter III.

lands in Oregon and Nevada, and at one time owned eighty thousand head of cattle and one hundred thousand sheep. They were able to drive their herds from neighboring states to San Francisco practically on their own land, sheltering them overnight, or for convenient periods, in their own large ranch stations, and keeping up a perpetual chain of supply for the city and trade. When Charles Lux died, in 1887, a powerful syndicate was formed under the leadership of Henry Miller, who (though born in 1828) has ever kept up the keenest interest in the management of the details of his vast possessions. The Germans of San Francisco have always exhibited an inclination to keep up German traditions, as, for instance, in 1870, when they contributed two hundred and fifty thousand dollars to the Red Cross Fund collected in the United States for the benefit of German soldiers in the Franco-Prussian War.

By the summing-up of these numerous instances, the present chapter intended to show that Germans were conspicuous in the early settlement and the development of the resources of the Northwest, the Southwest, and the Far West. They followed the frontier line until it disappeared from the map, but settled most thickly in the district included in the North Central Division, particularly the states of Illinois, Michigan, Wisconsin, Minnesota, Iowa, and Missouri.

CHAPTER XVI

THE GERMAN ELEMENT IN THE WARS OF THE UNITED
STATES DURING THE NINETEENTH CENTURY

Germans in the War of 1812 : Walbach, Stricker, Armistead — Indian
wars : Heilman and Custer — War with Mexico : Kemper, Kautz, and
John A. Quitman (governor of Mississippi).
The Civil War — Statistics of the numbers of German volunteers compared
with those of other nationalities — 200,000 volunteers — German regi-
ments — The influence of the Germans in St. Louis and Missouri ; the
Turners, the Arsenal, Camp Jackson, Sigel's campaign, etc. — The
Eleventh Corps at Chancellorsville, Gettysburg, Lookout Mountain, etc.,
Missionary Ridge — German officers : Sigel, Hecker, Blenker, Willich,
Schurz, Steinwehr, Kautz, etc. — Engineers and artillerymen — German
West Point graduates — Germans on the Confederate side — Germany's
friendly attitude during the Civil War.
The Spanish War — German volunteers in army and navy — List of officers
— Distinguished service of Rear-Admirals Schley, Kautz, and Kempff.

IF in the wars of the eighteenth century the German element rendered conspicuous service, their share was more
than doubled in the wars of the United States during the
nineteenth century. Beginning with the War of 1812,
and ending with the Spanish War, the German element
was represented by large numbers in the rank and file
of the American armies, and quite as abundantly and
more gloriously in the lists of officers who excelled by
superior training. In the Mexican and the numerous Indian wars throughout the century, there was no campaign
without its quota of German participants. In the Civil
War the large element of brave and sturdy German soldiers in the Northern army constituted an invaluable and
indispensable instrument in turning the fortune of war
in favor of the Union. Soldiers by tens and hundreds of

thousands who performed their duties faithfully, even to the point of laying down their lives for the country of their adoption, must be passed by unnoticed in the following brief narrative. Only the most striking figures and noblest achievements of the men of German blood can be taken into account.

In the War of 1812, when the land forces of the United States almost invariably met with defeat and disgrace, a few brilliant feats were contributed by soldiers of German blood. Thus General Walbach is credited with saving the artillery at Chrystler's Field [1] (St. Lawrence River), in 1813. Walbach [2] had come to the United States after a distinguished career of service in the French, the Austrian, and the British (West Indian) service. He was born in Münster (Upper Rhine), Germany, in 1766. He came to America in 1798, and entered the American military service, being promoted after the battle of Chrystler's Field to the rank of colonel, and subsequently to that of brigadier-general, and commander of the Fourth Artillery, U. S. A.

When the British army, after their victory at Bladensburg and their burning of Washington, attempted to serve Baltimore in a similar way, they met with resistance. General John Stricker [3] was put in command of a brigade

[1] General Wilkinson, with the main body of the American army, there fought with a slightly superior force of the British. The battle lasted five hours, victory alternately favoring one and then the other. Night ended the conflict, with the British in possession of the field. The American loss was especially severe ; many of the bravest officers were killed or wounded. The total American loss was 339 ; the British, 187. *Encyclopædic Dictionary of American Reference*, vol. i, p. 146.

[2] He was the third son of Count Joseph de Barth and Marie Therese de Rohmer. Cf. Rosengarten, *The German Soldier in the Wars of the United States*, pp. 160–165. General Walbach's son was a graduate of West Point and a captain of ordnance. Another son died of fever in the United States Navy. A grandson served as a surgeon in the United States Army.

[3] General John Stricker was the son of Colonel George Stricker, of Revo-

which was sent forward to check the enemy's advance, and the battle of North Point followed, September 12, 1814. Although the British right put the American left to flight and caused the retreat of the American army, still the British forces had received a check keenly felt. When General Ross, the British commander, was killed by sharp-shooters on his advance toward Baltimore, the beginning was made for a British defeat. The repulse came before Fort McHenry, where Admiral Cochrane, with sixteen war-vessels, opened a bombardment of the fort. The guns of Fort McHenry failed to reach the fleet until some of the British vessels ran nearer. These were so fiercely received that they withdrew, suffering much damage. The American commander was Major Armistead, a German-Virginian, who held the fort with a garrison of one thousand men, and also defeated a British force of about the same number who landed to surprise the fort in the rear. The bombardment continued until midnight,[1] and next day the British withdrew. Baltimore, which so early in her history had been settled by Germans, was thus saved from the British by German-American commanders. Major George Armistead (also spelled Armistaedt or Armstädt) was born April 10, 1780, at New Market, Virginia, where

lutionary fame, and was born in Frederick, Maryland, in 1759. His mother's name was Springer (German). The son served as a cadet in Captain G. P. Keeport's company, in the German battalion, of which his father was lieutenant-colonel. The cadet was in the battles of Trenton, Princeton, Brandywine, Germantown, Monmouth, and others, and accompanied General Sullivan in his expedition against the Indians. In 1783 Captain Stricker came to Baltimore, associated himself in business with Commodore Barney, took a keen interest in the formation of the militia, and formed and trained one of the earliest commands in Baltimore. He was soon made brigadier-general and commander of the state troops. Cf. *Sixth Annual Report of the Society for the History of the Germans in Maryland*, pp. 47–48.

[1] It was during this night that Francis S. Key, while a prisoner on board a British ship, wrote the "Star Spangled Banner."

his ancestors had settled, coming originally from Hessen-Darmstadt. Five of his brothers served in the army during the War of 1812, three with the regulars and two with the militia. In 1813 George Armistead was promoted to the rank of major of the Third Artillery. He distinguished himself at the capture of Fort George (at the mouth of the Niagara River), and after his brilliant defense of Fort McHenry was raised to the rank of lieutenant-colonel.[1]

The Germans of Baltimore, in the War of 1812, put a full company of yägers into the field. The Pennsylvania Germans, as in the Revolution, again did their full share, several Pennsylvania-German families making distinguished war records. The Pennypacker war record is notable. During the Revolution this family had as its representatives in the Continental Army a captain, an ensign, a lieutenant, a corporal, and a private. In the War of 1812 it had two of its members in the field; in the Mexican War, three, one of whom, General Pennypacker, was a member of the staff of General Worth.[2] The an-

---

[1] One of his brothers, Walter Keith Armistead, born in 1785, was engineer and superintendent of the fortifications at Norfolk, Virginia, and was appointed director-general. The Armistead family is distinguished in Virginia history. The mother of President John Tyler was a daughter of Robert Armistead, whose grandfather had come from Hessen-Darmstadt. Schuricht, *History of the German Element in Virginia*, vol. ii, p. 22. From a letter of Mrs. Letitia Tyler Semple, addressed to the Honorable George G. Vest, U. S. Senator of Missouri, and dated Louisenheim, Washington, D. C., April 20, 1897, we learn the interesting fact that the Armstädts or Armisteads were relatives of four presidents of the United States. Mrs. Semple, the daughter of President Tyler, and during his term "first lady of the land," writes : "James Monroe, William Henry Harrison, John Tyler, and Benjamin Harrison are cousins, being related with the Armisteads and Tylers of Virginia."

[2] In the War of the Rebellion it furnished to the Northern army two major-generals, one adjutant, one colonel, one surgeon, one assistant surgeon, two captains, one lieutenant, five sergeants, eight corporals, one musician,

cestor of the family was Heinrich Pennypacker, who came to America from Germany before 1699 and settled on Skippack Creek. The Mühlenberg family, so distinguished through its founder and his sons, had no less than six representatives on the registers of the regular army during the nineteenth century. Frederick Hambright, a Pennsylvania German, was a major-general of militia in the War of 1812, and his brother George a colonel at the same time. The latter served also in the Mexican War and in the Rebellion. The same name occurs as that of an officer who was wounded in the battle of King's Mountain during the Revolutionary War. Colonel Hambright was in command of the North Carolina Germans, and though wounded in the battle continued fighting and helped to win the victory.

During the Indian wars of the nineteenth century German officers and enlisted men have always been numerous in the American armies. An authoritative statement[1] on this point is as follows: "From the beginning of our history it often proved difficult to get the best type of native American to go into the regular army save in time of war with a powerful enemy, for the low rate of pay was not attractive, while the disciplined subordination of the soldiers to their officers seemed irksome to people with an exaggerated idea of individual freedom and no proper conception of the value of obedience. Very many of the regular soldiers have always been of foreign birth; and in 1787, on the Ohio, the percentage of Irish and Germans in the ranks was probably fully as large as it was on the Great Plains a century later."

and sixty-five privates. It also furnished some officers and men to the Southern army. Cf. Rosengarten, p. 207.

[1] Roosevelt, *The Winning of the West*, vol. iii, pp. 282–283.

The presentation of lists of German names found upon the rolls of our Indian campaigns would be uninteresting. It will suffice to give two examples of officers who sacrificed their lives in the Indian wars for the cause of American civilization. Julius F. Heilman, one of the early graduates of West Point, fell in Florida, in 1836. He had risen to the rank of major of the Second Artillery, and was the son of a surgeon in Riedesel's Hessian Brigade, which was captured with the army of Burgoyne. Few would detect in the name Custer the German Küster, though it is a fact that the ancestor of General George A. Custer, the great Indian fighter, was a Hessian soldier paroled in 1778 after Burgoyne's surrender. He settled in Pennsylvania and changed his name Küster to Custer, which was easier for his English neighbors to pronounce. Perhaps also he attempted thereby to remove the stigma attaching to a Hessian, so offensive then to American sensibilities. The father of General Custer, born in Maryland in 1806, later removed to Ohio. The son, born in 1839, was sent to West Point, graduated in 1861, served with distinction in the Civil War as captain on the staff of General McClellan, and was appointed brigadier-general for his gallantry in the battle of Aldie, in Virginia. General George A. Custer was especially distinguished as a leader of cavalry. At the battle of Gettysburg he won fame as the commander of the Michigan Brigade, and likewise made a glorious record at Winchester, Fisher's Hill, Cedar Creek, Waynesboro, Five Forks, and Dinwiddie Court House. Subsequently, as lieutenant-colonel of the Seventh Cavalry, he served under General Hancock in a series of campaigns against the Indians. On June 26, 1876, Custer, with two hundred regulars, was sent in search of a band of Sioux Indians that had broken away from their Dakota reservation and were committing many depredations. Custer came suddenly upon the Indians, twenty-five hundred strong, commanded by their chief, Sitting Bull. It was in the Valley of the Little Big Horn. There was no chance to escape and a desperate battle ensued, in which Custer and his brave soldiers were massacred to the last man, making their enemies pay dearly, however, for their lives. A monument has been erected upon the site of the battle.[1]

The Mexican War

In the war with Mexico, 1846–47, the Germans were among the first volunteers. They submitted instantly to the authority of the government while the native element were still discussing the justice of the war. The German's innate respect for constituted authority allowed him to ask no questions, though he felt no sympathy for the slave party which would eventually become the gainer through the war. After the war was over, the Germans were again opponents of slavery. In St. Louis the first volunteers were Germans, and the German sections of Missouri, such as St. Charles and Hermann, sent a good percentage of their numbers. In Kentucky the first company for service was raised by a German. In New Orleans six hundred Germans volunteered. In Cincinnati the first regiment organized was German.[2] Many of the cavalry and artillery companies from Texas and Missouri were composed of German volunteers. Kentucky had a company of cavalry and a regiment of infantry that were German. The town of Belleville, Illinois, raised a German company under the command of J. C. Raith and Adolph

---

[1] *Encyclopædic Dictionary of American Reference*, vol. i, p. 198.
[2] Rosengarten, p. 266.

Engelmann. The German Virginian, James Lawson Kemper (governor of Virginia, 1873–78), was a captain of volunteers in the Mexican War. Louis A. Armistead (who later commanded a brigade in Pickett's Division at Gettysburg) distinguished himself in the Mexican War.

A number of Germans, trained abroad, served in the Mexican War, among them Captain Henry Koch, born in Bayreuth. In 1832 he arrived in America and established a colony of communists in Clayton County, Iowa. More noteworthy was General August V. Kautz, born in Baden in 1828. At the outbreak of the Mexican War, he enlisted in the First Iowa Regiment, and in reward for his services was appointed a lieutenant in the regular army. In the Civil War he was noted for his cavalry raids in southern Virginia, in 1864. Similarly Samuel P. Heintzelman (graduate of West Point) served as a captain in the Mexican War, which fitted him for greater achievements in the War of the Rebellion.[1]

The most dashing and imposing figure, however, among all the soldiers of German blood in the Mexican War was John A. Quitman. His brilliant career and commanding personality furnish a good example of how environment creates new types on the American soil. Few historians of American history have observed that General Quitman, subsequently governor of Mississippi, was the son of a Lutheran pastor, Dr. Quitman, who settled first in Schoharie and then for twenty-five years was the Lutheran minister at Rhinebeck-on-the-Hudson. There it was that his son John Anthony was born. The latter did not follow his father's profession, but became a teacher, then studied

---

[1] He held the rank of brigadier-general at Alexandria, Bull Run, Uniontown, Hamburg, and Fair Oaks, and in 1863 commanded the Northern Department. He was retired in 1864 with full rank of major-general, United States Army.

law, and thereupon migrated to Ohio. In 1821 he followed
the current of enterprise toward the Southwest, settling
down at Natchez, Mississippi. There he soon established
an excellent law practice, married the daughter of a
wealthy planter, and became a man of note. His personality harmonized with his surroundings. He was an eloquent speaker, an athlete of prodigious strength, and a
capital shot. In a trial of skill he defeated John Hawkins,
a crack marksman and owner of the famous rifle "Brown
Bess." Hawkins, a veteran frontiersman, was ready to
allow his opponent, Quitman, a handicap, but the latter
refused it, and defeated the would-be champion on three
separate trials. Hawkins was at first chagrined, but afterwards became a fast friend of Quitman.

The popular lawyer and planter entered politics and became president of the Mississippi state senate. In 1836,
when Santa Anna led an army into Texas, Quitman, having
organized a body of recruits, had a secret understanding
with General Houston. He quietly crossed the Sabine
River, but, on arriving at St. Augustine, found himself
face to face with many of the gamblers, murderers, and
the lawless element which, when commander of the state
militia, he had banished from Natchez. One of the de-
speradoes drew a dagger on him while he was lying on
his couch. But Quitman, who was only pretending to be
asleep, "got the drop on him" with his pistol and the
desperado withdrew, saying: "Captain, you are a brave
comrade; I will be your friend." With this comradeship
the trouble with the gamblers ceased. When Quitman's
contingent arrived at the camp of General Houston, the
battle of San Jacinto had just been fought, and the Mexican invasion was therewith ended. This expedition cost
Major Quitman a private outlay of more than ten thou-

JOHN A. QUITMAN

sand dollars. On his return he was active in finance and politics. When the Mexican War broke out he was made a brigadier-general. He was in command of a brigade at Monterey, and was one of the most daring of the fighting generals under Taylor. With General Worth he shared the honors of the attack on Monterey. He was sent with the forces that went to support General Scott, and led the assault on Vera Cruz. He commanded at Alvarado, and stormed Chapultepec. The storming of the latter fort, which was well defended, was decidedly his victory. The subsequent attack on the Belen Gate before Mexico he carried out successfully in person. The evacuation of the city occurred at night; next morning General Quitman was the first to enter the Grand Plaza of the City of Mexico. The entry of the American army was not a dress-parade. The American troops were exhausted, tattered, and soiled. Many were wounded and but half-clothed. Quitman himself is said to have worn but one shoe, having lost the other.

General Scott appointed Quitman governor of the City of Mexico. The dashing soldier was very much dissatisfied with the terms of peace that were proposed on the American side. His plan would have been a permanent occupation, and the annexation of Mexico. He returned to Washington especially to advocate such a policy, and to demonstrate the ease of its accomplishment. In the Democratic Convention of 1846, held in Baltimore, Quitman was proposed as a candidate for vice-president of the United States, and in 1849 he was elected governor of Mississippi by a great majority. He served as governor from 1850 to 1851, and was elected to the United States Congress as a Democrat, in 1855, and continued to 1858, the year of his death. He was an ardent secessionist and suggested the formation of a Southern Confederacy. His life, however, closed before he could witness the spreading of the flames that he had helped to kindle.[1]

The Civil War

That an important share was contributed by the German soldier in the great war which threatened to rupture the Union is commonly acknowledged, but the facts are not generally known. Exactly how large a part was taken by the men of German descent will never be ascertained, but an investigation made a few years after the war tells us, at least with some degree of accuracy, how large was the number of those born in Germany who enlisted as soldiers in the Civil War. The statistical work of B. A. Gould,[2] published for the United States Sanitary Commission in 1869, attempts the difficult problem of giving general summaries of the enlistments of soldiers according to their nativity. The results obtained, though not absolutely correct, are undoubtedly as near the truth as careful investigation can make them. The place of birth was not asked for in the early enlistments, being not put down until the organization of the provost-marshal-general's office. Out of the two and one half millions of men in the army, therefore, the nativity of only about one million, two hundred thousand could be ascertained by Dr. Gould from the records at the national and state capitals. About two hundred and ninety-three thousand more were obtained by written inquiries from regimental officers. The remaining numbers, whose nativity was not known, were

---

[1] Cf. Clayborne's *Life and Correspondence of General Quitman.* (New York, 1860.) Cf. also *Der deutsche Pionier*, vol. vi, pp. 321 ff.

[2] *Investigations in the Military and Anthropological Statistics of American Soldiers.* By Benjamin Apthorp Gould, actuary to the United States Sanitary Commission. (New York, 1869.)

allotted in the proportion of the known enlistments. A count was also taken of reënlistments, which were very frequent after the first period of three months, or the next period of three years. Employing this method Dr. Gould obtained the following results[1] for each state:—

Nativities of United States Volunteers

Place of enlistment	Native Americans	English	Irish	Germans	Total number of different white soldiers
Maine	48,135	779	1,971	244	54,800
New Hampshire	19,759	1,147	2,699	952	27,800
Vermont	22,037	325	1,289	86	26,800
Massachusetts	79,560	2,306	10,007	1,876	105,500
R. I. and Conn.	37,190	2,234	7,657	2,919	54,900
New York	203,622	14,024	51,206	36,680	337,800
New Jersey	35,496	2,491	8,880	7,337	59,300
Pennsylvania	222,641	3,503	17,418	17,208	271,500
Delaware	8,306	127	582	621	10,000
Maryland	22,435	403	1,400	3,107	27,900
Dist. of Columbia	9,967	152	698	746	12,000
West Virginia	21,111	248	550	869	23,300
Kentucky	38,988	117	1,303	1,943	43,100
Ohio	219,949	2,619	8,129	20,102	259,900
Indiana	141,454	1,248	3,472	7,190	156,400
Illinois	168,983	5,953	12,041	18,140	216,900
Michigan	54,830	1,310	3,278	3,534	72,000
Wisconsin	47,972	3,703	3,621	15,709	79,500
Minnesota	11,977	614	1,140	2,715	20,000
Iowa	48,686	1,015	1,436	2,850	56,600
Missouri	46,676	761	4,362	30,899	85,400
Kansas	13,493	429	1,082	1,090	16,800
Grand Total	1,523,267	45,508	144,221	176,817	2,018,200

From the above table it appears that 176,817 Germans, i. e., men born in Germany, volunteered in the Civil War. This is a conservative estimate, since a large number of German-born undoubtedly belong to the seventy-five thousand foreigners whose nativity was unknown. Large numbers were also taken out, in Gould's estimate, for

[1] Gould, p. 27. For convenience the columns " British Americans," "Other Foreigners," and " Foreigners not otherwise designated," have been omitted from the table.

reënlistment; in Missouri, for instance, as many as ten thousand. The statement which is often made, that over two hundred thousand Germans served in the Northern armies, is not at all exaggerated. Were we to consider the number of soldiers of German blood fighting for the Union cause, the numbers would swell to perhaps three times that figure.[1]

In order to test the relative amount of service contributed by each nationality, in proportion to its population in the United States, Dr. Gould constructs another interesting table.[2] He takes the census of 1860 as a basis, and having given 2,018,200 as the total number of white soldiers in the Union armies, he estimates what should be the contribution for each stock, if men of every nativity had enlisted in the exact proportion of their population. The result is as follows : —

	Enlistment called for in proportion to population	Actual enlistment
Native Americans	1,660,068	1,523,267
British Americans	22,695	53,532
English	38,250	45,508
Irish	139,052	144,221
Germans	118,402	176,817
Other foreigners	39,455	48,410
Foreigners not otherwise designated	278	26,445
Grand Total	2,018,200	2,018,200

[1] The ratio of " persons of German parentage " (including those born in Germany and their descendants of the first generation, born in the United States) to " Native Germans," in 1900 was as 2.9 : 1. The ratio was probably not as large in 1860, because the German immigration was very large after that time. The ratio 2½ : 1 would be a conservative one, and applied above, would give the German element five hundred thousand volunteers in the Northern armies. This number would not include the descendants of Germans who came to the United States in the eighteenth century or before.

[2] Page 28, Table IV, " Distribution of United States Volunteers according to the Nativities of the Population in 1860."

This shows that the native American stock fell short of its due proportion, but Gould points out that the military population of foreign birth had increased through immigration about two hundred and thirty thousand during the five years of the war, making the contribution of the foreigners so much larger. The foreigners in every case show an increase over the number which would naturally be expected of them. A very interesting comparison can be made between the German and Irish volunteers. The Irish population of foreign birth at that time was larger than the population of German birth, but the enlistment of the Germans was nevertheless larger than that of the Irish. According to the estimate of Gould, there were

| German Volunteers, | 176,817 |
| Irish Volunteers, | 144,221 |

The Germans, if they had volunteered in the proportion of the average, would have furnished only 118,402 men, while the Irish would have had 139,052 men. The Irish, therefore, sent 5169 men in excess of the general average, while the Germans sent 58,415 men in excess of the general average. The Germans therefore in their proportionate share surpassed both the native and the Irish elements, outstripping the latter also in actual numbers, by 32,596 volunteers, although they were not as numerous as the Irish in the population of the United States at that time (1860). This fact is exceedingly interesting when we remember that the Irish have so frequently been called the better and more numerous fighters in the history of the United States. The same impression has erroneously gained ground in regard to the Irish (or Scotch-Irish) element on the frontier [1] of the United States in the eighteenth

---

[1] Cf. Chapter x, pp. 267 ff., and Chapter xii, pp. 366 ff.

and nineteenth centuries. The whole question receives new illumination from the statistics of Mr. Gould; they furnish the only positive evidence there is available giving a basis for comparison of the various national stocks as soldiers. The same statistics show that the English element, though in actual numbers their contribution was small, furnished 7258 in excess of their ratio, which is even a larger proportionate share of their own numbers than in the case of the Germans. The Germanic element, therefore, in its foreign element shows superiority over the Celtic in the amount of its service in the Civil War.

The argument is made, in Gould's chapter on the "Nativity of the United States Volunteers," that the foreigners furnished more bounty-jumpers than the native population. " In general the manufacturing states — as, for instance, Massachusetts, Connecticut, Rhode Island, New York, and New Jersey — rank high in the column of desertion ; and this result is to be attributed not only to the fact that such states are dotted with towns and cities, but the secondary fact that these towns and cities are crowded with foreigners."[1] Europeans were attracted by the large bounties, and after desertion would enlist again for another bounty. But it is by no means proved that Europeans did so alone, — in fact a "green" immigrant would as a general thing not have half as good a chance as a native. He would not be acquainted with the methods, and as far as the Germans were concerned, he would be handicapped by insufficient acquaintance with the language. The localities named as the places where most desertions occurred were not those from which the Germans volunteered in greatest numbers ; in fact only one seventh of the German volunteers came from those East-

[1] Quoted by Gould from the words of General Fry, p. 29.

ern manufacturing states. Germans enlisted in greatest numbers in the Middle West, in the states of Missouri, Ohio, Wisconsin, Illinois, and Indiana.

Some of the regiments which might be called the German regiments of the United States Army were the following :[1]

New York Regiments:

Dickel's Mounted Rifles, Fourth New York Cavalry.

Blenker's Battery, Second Battery, Light Artillery, New York.

Steuben Regiment, Seventh New York Infantry.

First German Rifles, Eighth New York Infantry.

United Turner Rifles, Twentieth New York Infantry.

First Astor Regiment, Twenty-ninth New York Infantry.

Fifth German Rifles, Forty-fifth New York Infantry.

Frémont Regiment, Forty-sixth New York Infantry.

Sigel Rifles, or German Rangers, Fifty-second New York Infantry.

Barney Rifles, or Schwarzes-Yäger Regiment, Fifty-fourth New York Infantry.

Steuben Rangers, Eighty-sixth New York Infantry.

Pennsylvania Regiments:

First German Regiment, Seventy-fourth Pennsylvania Infantry.

Second German Regiment, Seventy-fifth Pennsylvania Infantry.

Ohio Regiments:

First German Regiment, Twenty-eighth Ohio Infantry.

Second German Regiment, Thirty-seventh Ohio Infantry (Colonel Siber).

Third German Regiment, Sixty-seventh Ohio Infantry (Colonel Bürsten-binder).

Indiana Regiment:

First German Regiment, Thirty-second Indiana, commanded successively by Willich, Von Trebra, and Erdelmeyer.

---

[1] Cf. Rosengarten, pp. 201–203.

Illinois Regiment:
Hecker's Yäger Regiment, Twenty-fourth Illinois.

Wisconsin Regiments:
First German Regiment, Ninth Wisconsin.
Second German Regiment, Twenty-sixth Wisconsin.

The German volunteers in Pennsylvania were numerous from the very start.[1] For the three months' service, the following regiments were full of Germans: —

Fourth, with Hartranft as its colonel;
Eighth, from Lehigh and Northampton;
Ninth, under Pennypacker;
Tenth, from Lancaster;
Eleventh, from Northumberland;
Fourteenth, from Berks;
Fifteenth, from Luzerne;
Sixteenth, from York;
Eighteenth, from Philadelphia, under Wilhelm;
Twenty-first, under Ballier.

The regiments for three years' service, formed afterwards in Pennsylvania and New York, containing a large German element, are too numerous to mention.[2] The record of some of them will be referred to in succeeding pages.

In the treatment of a subject of such wide scope within limited space, it will be necessary to make a selection from a mass of material. A few moments of the war will therefore be chosen to illustrate the work of the German soldier for the Union cause. Such an epoch came at the very beginning of the war, when one of the border states had

---

[1] Cf. Rosengarten, pp. 203 ff. Refers to Bates' *History of the Pennsylvania Regiments, etc., in the Rebellion* (five volumes).

[2] An account in detail can be found in Rosengarten, pp. 204 ff.

not yet clearly taken its stand. The one in question was the largest of the border states, viz., Missouri. The strong German population of Missouri was not embarrassed by inherited ideas of a dutiful allegiance to the state of their residence, in preference to loyalty to the national government. They made their influence felt, and under the leadership of Blair took the initiative in saving Missouri for the Union. "The story of Missouri for the next [first] four months," says Rhodes, "is of a contest between Blair and Jackson — a contest of political management, of martial proceeding, and of battle. Blair showed great political ability, and assisted by Lyon, who had military talent and whose forces constantly increased, made steady progress. St. Louis was soon gained and the Union sentiment in the state grew rapidly. July 30, the convention, sitting at Jefferson City, the capital, deposed Governor Jackson, appointed Gamble, a Union man, in his stead, and in other ways brought the machinery of the state government to the support of the Union cause. Though this did not end the fight for Missouri, yet she was henceforward officially, as well as in dominant sentiment, on the side of the North."[1] The bitterness of the struggle in St. Louis, which ended in the victory of Blair and the taking of Camp Jackson, does not appear in the quotation given from the historian of the Civil War. An

[1] J. F. Rhodes, *History of the United States from the Compromise of 1850*, vol. iii, pp. 393–394. Rhodes gives credit to the German population for their Union sentiments and for their "composing most of the regiments which were formed in defense of St. Louis." A detailed account of how great the service of the German recruits actually was is very rarely found in the histories of the Civil War. Rhodes refers to Carr's *Missouri;* to Snead, *The Fight for Missouri;* and Nicolay and Hay, *Abraham Lincoln*, vol. iv, chap. xi. The last of these references (p. 206) states : "This minority [anti-slavery, in the city of St. Louis] was made up principally of its German residents and voters, numbering fully one half the total population of the city, which in 1860 was 160,000."

excellent account of that stirring epoch is given, by the pen of a contemporary and participant, in the pages of "Der deutsche Pionier." [1] The following account is based upon his recollections : —

Missouri was for the most part loyal to the Union, but her governor, C. F. Jackson, was Southern in his sympathies, and to him was due the struggle in Missouri before the majority could gain full control. At first a large part of the native population attempted to remain neutral between North and South, a position which some of the other border states also tried at first to maintain. When neutrality became impossible, the state seemed about to be torn apart, the Southern sympathizers threatening war. On the seventh of January two German militia companies were, for reasons insignificant, disarmed by Brigadier-General Frost. On the next evening the Minute Men, as the secessionist militia called themselves, held a public meeting, in which secession speeches were made. Friedrich Münch, of Warren County, was threatened with violence if he published any more Union articles. In St. Louis, Olshausen, editor of the "Westliche Post," also Börnstein and Bernays of the "Anzeiger des Westens," courageously continued voicing Union sentiments. A few days later a German military company was organized called the "Schwarzes-Jäger Corps." Every German faithful to the Union and minded to join the company was invited to assemble in the "Jagdverein." The corps was nicknamed "Black Guards" (with a double meaning), by the Minute Men, who nevertheless stood in great awe of it.

The state election of April 1 gave the victory to the

---

[1] Vols. xi and xii, 1879–1880, " Der Ausbruch des Bürgerkrieges in Missouri," von Friedrich Schnake.

enemies of the Union. This was a sign either of bad organization on the part of the Union men or of a loss of self-confidence, and promised that St. Louis would be apathetic enough to throw itself into the arms of Governor Jackson. The Minute Men made a list of prominent adherents of the Union cause, "rebels against the state," whom they wished to render harmless. Their plans, however, could not be carried out because of the initiative taken by Lyon, Blair, and the Germans.

Within the borders of St. Louis there was located a United States arsenal. The possession of it meant a definite advantage to either side. Without it the Union forces of the Northwest would be in want of arms at the beginning of the struggle, and if the Southern forces got possession of it they could quickly overrun Missouri and Illinois. Expecting the arsenal to fall into the hands of the South, Floyd, Secretary of War, had the arsenal stocked to overflowing. It was guarded for weeks by only three men, the expectation being that the Southerners would take possession. But a mistake was made in putting Nathaniel Lyon, of the Second Infantry, in command, who, on arriving, immediately recognized the importance of the place. Through Congressman Blair, he at once communicated with prominent Union men for their assistance. A German surgeon, Dr. A. Hammer, lived in a house northwest from the arsenal on an eminence above it. On his orders, a brewery wagon, laden with beer barrels, entered the arsenal, and drove out again, without attracting attention. Under a cover spread over the barrels there was a box of muskets with necessary ammunition. It was the first gift of the commandant of the arsenal to his Union friends. Dr. Hammer at once put the students of the Humboldt Institution under arms, and day and night kept in his house a guard with which to fall upon the Minute Men if they attempted to attack the arsenal. But more important than that, Lyon communicated with the Black Guards, the Turner, and other German organizations, so as to be sure of their coöperation in case of necessity.[1] From the membership of the Turner societies there was organized the Union Guards, the section of riflemen (Schützen) being a very valuable factor. At the time of the election of Lincoln eighty-two native Americans left the Turners to join the Minute Men. The Turners recruited new members to fill the vacancies and then gave themselves effective military organization. On the sixth day of February a series of resolutions was passed by them, to the effect that they would never depart from their rights and duties as citizens of the United States, and that neither the legislative convention nor any other body, not even the majority of the people of the state of Missouri, had the right to wrest from them their citizen's rights, nor separate them from the Union. They resolved that, if the state of Missouri should secede, a provincial government should be erected for the county of St. Louis, which should remain faithful to the Union, and which should be defended by them with their property and their blood.

Three companies known as the Turner Battalion were put in readiness, and they were drilled by an officer of the United States Army, E. D. Larned, so that they might understand the American system of commands. The Turner Hall was put into a state of defense, the lower windows being nailed up and breastworks erected before the doors. Gollmer and Müller were in command at the Turnhalle. Both forces, the Turners and the Min-

---

[1] Cf. James Peckham, *General Nathaniel Lyon and Missouri, in 1861.*

ute Men, were apparently ready for combat. The latter, however, became inactive, in all probability owing to the strenuous preparations of the German forces.

Events on the outside soon brought about a clash. On Sunday, April 14, the day after the surrender of Fort Sumter, Lincoln issued a call for seventy-five thousand volunteers for three months' service. The quota of Missouri was to be four thousand men. Governor Jackson replied to the President: " Your requisition, in my judgment, is illegal, unconstitutional, and revolutionary in its object, inhuman and diabolical, and cannot be complied with." Congressman Blair gathered the members of the Committee of Safety more closely about him. He advised the officers of the state militia to resign and be available for the volunteer service of the United States. The first officer to act upon the suggestion was Major Friedrich Schäfer.[1] A large number of others immediately followed his example. Several of the United States officers in high places, such as General William A. Harney, through long residence in St. Louis, had many friends among the leaders of the Secessionists. Such men therefore looked upon the rebel preparations with complacency. General Harney's dilatory policy permitted the formation of Camp Jackson, and nearly resulted disastrously for the Unionists.

The great object at stake for the present was still the United States Arsenal. On the twentieth of April the news came that Liberty, Missouri, with all its supplies, had fallen into the hands of state troops, which were used by the governor in the interests of secession. The news gave the Minute Men courage, and they marched out

---

[1] He was subsequently colonel in Börnstein's Second Missouri Regiment, reorganized as the Second Regiment, for three years' service. He also served under General Frémont, and later under General Rosecrans.

apparently for an attack. But they lost courage when the people assumed a threatening attitude. Mayor Taylor, although of Southern sympathies, had much to do with the checking of the enthusiasm of the Minute Men. He explained to them how well prepared the Black Guards and the terrible Turners were for resistance ; that moreover they would not allow the arsenal to be taken without a desperate struggle. He himself was certain that such an undertaking would bring the horrors of bloodshed into the streets of St. Louis. The Minute Men, yielding, lost their last chance of overpowering the few defenders of the arsenal.

The Germans now clamored to be taken into the arsenal in order to defend it during this crisis, but Blair was not ready to take so bold a step. The Germans held a meeting, Finkelnburg presiding, which expressed its disapproval of the dilatory attitude of the men in power. The meeting was very stormy. Blair urged patience. Finkelnburg answered calmly but decisively that the refusal of the authorities to accept their offer to defend the arsenal would lead to the disorganization of the German Battalion. The meeting was adjourned until midnight, giving Blair a chance to consult Lyon at the arsenal. The Germans decided, in the mean time, to offer their services to the United States government, and to leave St. Louis at once in a body if their offer to defend the arsenal were not accepted. They did not wish to stand idly by while the government was being robbed, nor did they, unarmed, wish to be shot down in the streets without being able to defend themselves. About midnight Blair reëntered the Turnhalle, accompanied by Lieutenant Schofield of the United States Army. Blair said that he had brought the latter officer with him, so that the Turners might not be delayed if they felt they must offer their services to the United States; but that he could not open the arsenal; moreover that all telegraphic communication with Washington was interrupted. Friedrich Schnake called attention to the line of communication still open through Baltimore, and moved that a committee of three be appointed to offer the services of the organized German troops to the United States through the governor of Illinois, as volunteers of Missouri. This motion was unanimously adopted without debate. The die was cast; the committee was named and the assembly adjourned.

Blair and Schofield, knowing that the departure of the German Turners would leave the city and arsenal in Confederate hands, and now being convinced of the determination of the Germans, had a short interview with Lyon and decided to admit the Turners into the arsenal. At four o'clock in the morning of the twenty-second of April, the doors of the arsenal were opened and the volunteers of Missouri entered. Lieutenant Sexton, between two and three o'clock in the morning, had gone to the Turnhalle and affixed his signature to about three hundred slips of paper which served as passes into the arsenal. The third company was the first to enter. The others came in later by twos and threes.

The news of the garrisoning of the arsenal spread like wildfire, and the fear was entertained that, because the Germans had taken possession, the native element would start an insurrection, but nothing was done, not even to prevent the rest of the German troops from entering. A number of regiments were now regularly formed; F. P. Blair was in command of the First, Börnstein (editor of the " Anzeiger d. Westens ") of the Second, Franz Sigel of the Third, and Nicholas Schüttner of the Fourth regiment of volunteers. Since the number of applications increased, Lyon decided to organize a fifth regiment, which elected K. E. Salomon as its colonel.[1] The five regiments were called Home Guards, and were to serve especially in defense of the citizens and their property. It was now possible to send thirty thousand muskets to Governor Yates for the state of Illinois, likewise ten thousand pounds of powder, under the protection of the First Regiment. Thus the Illinois regiments were armed and enabled to occupy northern Missouri and parts of Illinois.

On the third of May, under the direction of the government, and under the command of Brigadier-General Frost, the Secessionists, or, as they were pleased to call themselves, "State's troops," were assembled at the west end of Olive Street, St. Louis, in Lindell Grove. This was called Camp Jackson in honor of the governor. Frost announced to Lyon that his purpose was to drill the troops in the service of the state. The real object, however, was to prepare for driving out the Germans and taking possession of the arsenal. Lyon answered that he would fire upon all that should come within range. He informed those in command at Camp Jackson that he would not tolerate the camp's existence. In order to reconnoitre the ground he drove to Camp Jackson in the disguise of a woman, wearing a veil over his face, and inspected the enemy's works. J. J. Witzig, who followed in a buggy, executed the order to bring the Committee of Safety together for a conference at the arsenal.

On the same evening there arrived in St. Louis a Ger-

---

[1] He was the brother of Edward Salomon, the War Governor of Wisconsin. Another brother, Friedrich Salomon, organized the Ninth Wisconsin (German) Regiment and for distinguished service in the Southwest, against Generals Kirby Smith and Price, was made brigadier-general and brevet major-general.

man artillery company under a captain whose name was Jackson.[1] They had been sent on a fool's errand to the borders of Kansas, to guard against fancied attacks, — in reality to be out of the way. This company did not know the nature of Camp Jackson, but had been ordered thither. Had they done what was there demanded of them, the victory of the Union regiments would have been in doubt. They recognized, however, that a treasonable demand was made of them, and when the decisive moment came these German gunners folded their arms and refused absolutely to act against their adopted country. Proudly they marched as prisoners of war to the arsenal, and having arrived there they instantly joined the Lyon organization. By their determined stand they contributed very largely to the final victory.

After declaring General Frost and his followers enemies of the United States, Lyon marched his division to Camp Jackson and laid siege to the camp. An honorable surrender was granted them, and no bloodshed followed except that for which the mob was responsible. Near the camp Captain Blandowsky, a German Pole, was shot with a revolver, after which a volley was fired into the mob by the troops, who acted in self-defense. The Secessionists fell back, leaving fifteen dead and several wounded on the open field north of the camp. Two men of the Third Regiment were killed and several wounded. The Minute Men and the mob were in a fury about the "treason" of Lyon and Blair, and their allowing Americans to be taken prisoners by "long-eared Dutchmen and mercenary Hessians." Violence was threatened, but nothing serious oc-

---

[1] His real name was Jacquin, and he was born in 1821 near Metz, in Lotharingia, within the present boundaries of the German Empire. His father was a Frenchman who had served as an officer under Napoleon I. His mother was a German.

curred, in the face of the disciplined troops. A bloody Sunday was predicted for the next day, and the mayor, D. G. Taylor, issued proclamations closing saloons and urging all citizens to be in their homes after dark. Only one fatal occurrence was recorded, though all day rumors were afloat of an attack on the Turnhalle, and also of revenge to be taken by the Germans who had suffered in the mob's attack. Large numbers of the wealthier class of St. Louis fled from the city.

Among the Union military authorities there was a divergence as to policy. Lyon and Blair, on the one hand, wished to see energetic measures taken against the Secessionists, while, on the other, Harney and McKinstry favored a conciliatory policy. Blair kept his brother, Montgomery Blair, Postmaster-General in Washington, well informed as to all that was going on in Missouri. The cabinet officer urged upon President Lincoln the dismissal of General Harney. A trustworthy man was desired from St. Louis to explain the condition of affairs in the state. The choice fell upon the editor of the "Anzeiger des Westens," K. L. Bernays. He very ably represented to the government what the prevailing conditions were in Missouri, and enabled the President to act intelligently thereafter. The immediate object of the mission, the removal of Harney, had already been accomplished, however, for on May 20, the appointment of Lyon as brigadier-general arrived, accompanied by another order removing General Harney.

A proclamation followed, by Governor Jackson, amounting to an open declaration of war, and the Secessionists within the state were organized. To counteract the movement General Lyon authorized "Home Guard" regiments to be formed throughout the state, to protect the United

States government's interests. J. A. Eppstein, a German, formed the first company at Boonville, recruited mostly of Germans. In St. Charles County, Arnold Krekel took a leading part in the establishment of Home Guards and was made colonel.[1] Other German names which were prominent in Missouri in this early period of organization were : Carl Dänzer, Theo. Olshausen, Heinrich Börnstein (the last two, editors of St. Louis papers), Friedrich Münch, Dr. A. Hammer, Daniel Hertle, Dr. Rudolph Döhn, Dr. Rösch, Franz Sigel, and on the other side of the Mississippi, at Belleville, Illinois, Friedrich Hecker and Gustav Körner. Two of the ablest orators[2] were Carl Schurz (then located in Wisconsin) and Friedrich Hassaurek. Seward once remarked in a stirring address that Missouri would have to be Germanized in order to be won for the Union.[3]

The fact that there were so many Germans on the Union side all the more enraged the Secessionists in the native population. Many deeds of violence were done, and foreign settlers in the rural districts were bullied and often driven from house and home. The first battle between the Secessionists and the Home Guards occurred at Cole Camp, in Benton County, where thousands of

[1] Arnold Krekel was born in 1815, in the district of Düsseldorf, Prussia. He settled in Missouri with his parents in 1832, in the neighborhood of the Duden settlement. He studied law and very early became prominent. He was a member of the state's convention, and as president of that body signed the emancipation order, January 11, 1865, whereby slavery was abolished in Missouri. He was appointed by Lincoln United States Judge of the Western District of Missouri and associate judge of the Circuit Court to which Missouri belonged.

[2] The Douglas Democratic party also had a German orator in Christian Kribben, who, however, had a very inconsiderable following among the Germans.

[3] For a literary picture of the period see Winston Churchill's historical novel *The Crisis*, e. g., book II, chap. x ("Richter's Scar").

German families lived. The so-called "state's troops" surprised Captain Brühl's Company F, in a barn. The Secessionists had used a Union flag and were allowed to pass by the guards. The company was found sleeping, and the assailants killed twenty-five men in cold blood before Captain Brühl's men were able to stir. This act of murder seems to have been committed not without the knowledge of the governor, who was not far distant. The Benton County Home Guards rallied after their loss and gave battle, forcing the "state's troops" to make a rapid retreat. The Southern forces soon withdrew to the southwestern corner of the state of Missouri, and there, joined by troops from Texas and Arkansas, they proposed to conquer Missouri. Their original plan of capturing Missouri for the Confederacy, unassisted, had been foiled mainly by the loyal German element.

After the battle of Cole Camp, on June 19, Lyon, being delayed until July 3 completing his organization, General Sigel was sent to the southwest to watch or engage the enemy. He arrived in the neighborhood of Carthage early in July, and finding the enemy in large numbers, he attempted to defeat them before they could unite their forces. The battle of Carthage resulted, July 3. According to Sigel's report he had no more than eleven hundred men (opposed to the enemy's five thousand). The victory has been claimed by both sides. Sigel was unacquainted with the extent of the loss he had inflicted on the enemy and therefore retreated to Springfield, fearing an attack of cavalry, wherein the enemy was superior.

General Frémont arrived in St. Louis July 25, to take command. He was welcomed by the German population, and many of their representatives were placed on his staff.[1]

[1] The German writers believe that the appointment of German officers in

The mistake was made by Frémont of sending all available soldiers to Northern Missouri, where there were a few "state's troops," who made a great stir with a definite purpose. They wished to conceal the more important action which the Southern Missouri division was planning to initiate. Lyon and Sigel were left to their own resources, though they clamored for reinforcements. They were by no means blind to what was happening about them. The enemy had gathered together superior forces and was about to attack Springfield. Knowing that the enemy's army was much larger than his own, Lyon sought salvation in a surprise. The battle of Wilson Creek followed. The plan was that Lyon should advance upon the Confederates, in the hope of surprising them, and Sigel at the same time was to make a flanking movement. The plan was well executed by both divisions. The disparity in numbers, however, was too great, probably five thousand against twelve thousand. Sigel's division consisted largely of men who had volunteered for three months, and whose terms of enlistment had already closed.[1] The Federal loss was over twelve hundred; the Confederates lost almost as many in killed and wounded. If McDowell had pursued the defeated Union army he might have

high places always aroused ill feeling among the graduates of West Point and also among the large "Knownothing" element.

[1] According to one of their officers, Friedrich Schnake, they had not been treated fairly by Lyon and Blair. The latter acted in a high-handed manner with them, not allowing them to return to their recruiting place in order to enlist in the three years' service, but trying to hold them unlawfully. Lyon did not wish to make the necessary concessions and privileges which were given in the three years' service. The soldiers declared they would not be treated like dogs. In order to coerce them, threats of withdrawing rations were made. Almost all of these soldiers later reënlisted, Schnake among them, in the Twenty-third Missouri Volunteers. The soldiers were not lacking in patriotism or bravery, but had been treated without tact, and perhaps without humanity.

captured their baggage-train and taken Springfield. As it was, the exhaustion of his own army and scant ammunition kept him from following up the victory. In the succeeding months the importance was felt of gaining the southern area of Missouri for the Union. Frémont was soon relieved by Hunter. General Pope took command next, and cleared Southern as well as Northern Missouri of open and secret rebels. The winning of Missouri for the Union gave a better opportunity for the opening of the Mississippi, and set up a bulwark against the Confederate states of the Southwest. The moral effect of the victory was strengthening and inspiring for the Union cause.

Bearing in mind the necessity of confining this chapter to moderate limits, it will be impossible to trace the history of the numerous German regiments in the Union service. The history of a single division will serve as an illustration for all, — a regiment which has been highly praised, and also more severely censured than any of the others. In the well-known Eleventh Corps there were several German regiments that probably saw as much service as any body of men in the Union forces. The Eleventh Corps was not entirely German,[1] but it contained two divisions, those of Steinwehr and Schurz, which were altogether German. Most of the officers were Germans who had experienced military service abroad. Steinwehr was descended from a family of soldiers.[2] He had taken part in the Mexican War in an Alabama volunteer regiment. At the outbreak of the Civil War he recruited a regiment of

[1] At the battle of Chancellorsville, the Eleventh Corps consisted of nearly thirteen thousand men and only forty-five hundred were Germans. Cf. Dodge, *The Campaign of Chancellorsville*, p. 100.

[2] He was born in 1822, at Blankenburg, Duchy of Brunswick.

Bruno Schmitz, Architect   Copyrighted by Bass and Woodworth

INDIANAPOLIS MONUMENT TO CIVIL WAR HEROES

volunteers in New York. His regiment of 872 men arrived in Washington June 27, 1861, and was made a part of the brigade of Blenker.[1] It consisted of the regiments of Stahel (Eighth New York), Von Steinwehr (Twenty-ninth New York), D'Utassy (Thirty-ninth New York), and Emstein (Twenty-seventh Pennsylvania). At the battle of Bull Run the German regiments alone held their ground at the stone bridge and slope west of Centerville. They shared with Richardson's brigade the honor of proving themselves capable soldiers, when others passed by them panic-stricken.[2]

Most of these regiments were found again in the Eleventh Corps, where they met most varied fortunes. At the battle of Chancellorsville, in 1863, the corps well-nigh lost its reputation. It was roundly blamed for the defeat of the Union army, and nativistic prejudices throughout the country gloated and secretly rejoiced over the ill fortune that befell the foreign regiment. The calmer judgment of later historians has placed the blame entirely upon the general in command, General Hooker, whose eccentric manœuvres and startling blunders brought defeat to his numerous army. He was pitted against the two greatest of the Southern generals in conjunction, Lee and Jackson. Instead of waiting in his secure position for an

---

[1] Ludwig Blenker was born in 1812 at Worms. In 1848 he was colonel of the militia of his native state, and in 1849 he was one of the leaders of the revolutionary party, and actively engaged in the campaigns of the revolution, in Hessen and Baden. After the suppression of the revolution he came to America. In April, 1861, he recruited the Eighth New York Volunteer Regiment and brought it to Washington. Their camp in front of Washington grew in numbers to a brigade, then to a division, and might have become a full army corps. It was through Blenker's demand to organize and lead it that McClellan was obliged to administer a reproof which led finally to Blenker's resignation from active service. Rosengarten, p. 192.

[2] Kettell, *Complete History of the Great American Rebellion*, vol. i, p. 172.

attack, Hooker advanced for a flanking movement around Lee's army. Lee and Jackson at the same time planned a flanking movement around Hooker's right. Jackson, with thirty thousand men, started on a march, which took him halfway around the Union army. His design was to attack and surprise the Eleventh Corps under General Howard. Jackson's column was seen by the Union forces, but its movement was misunderstood by Hooker and Howard, who thought that Jackson was retiring before the Union forces, superior in numbers. Even the capture of some rebels, who declared that Jackson was bent on fighting, not retreating, failed to convince the commanding general. Neither would Howard be convinced. Carl Schurz, who commanded a division in the Eleventh Corps, urged upon Howard that the facts pointed unmistakably to an attack from the west upon their right and rear. He advised a change of front in order to be prepared for it. But Howard would issue no such command, although Schurz on his own responsibility did change the position of two of his regiments, seeing the danger imminent. The Eleventh Corps had been further weakened by the detachment of a brigade, on an order from headquarters, for the support of Sickles.[1]

At three o'clock in the afternoon, after a march of fifteen miles, Jackson reached a point west of the Union army, directly opposite the position occupied by General Lee. His troops were quickly ready, and soon after five he gave the order to advance. The Eleventh Corps was not prepared; some of the men were getting their supper ready, others were resting, or amusing themselves with cards. The forest in front of them was just thick enough

[1] The above statements are taken from J. F. Rhodes, *History of the United States from the Compromise of 1850*, vol. iv, p. 261.

to screen the approaching enemy, but not to impede their progress. The warning came from the wild rush of deer and rabbits driven from their hiding-places by the quick step of the Confederates through the woods.

Twenty-six thousand of Jackson's men, "the best infantry in existence, as tough, hardy, and full of spirit as they are ill-fed, ill-clothed, and ill-looking," surprised less than half their number. The officers and men of the Eleventh Corps in the main did well. What can be expected of new troops taken by surprise and attacked in front, flank, and rear at once? [1]

Devens's division was one of the first to yield, and thereby confused Schurz's men. Some of Schurz's regiments stood firm, others fell back, but nowhere could a line stand long against the terrible onset. No organization was left in the Eleventh Corps, with the exception of one brigade of Steinwehr's division. [2]

Buschbeck has been speedily forming by a change of front before Devens and Schurz have left the field. Dilger's battery trains some of its guns down the road. The reserve artillery is already in position at the north of this line, and issues spherical case with rapidity. Howard and his staff are in the thickest of the fray, endeavoring to stem the tide. As well oppose resistance to an avalanche. Buschbeck's line stubbornly holds on. An occasional squad, still clinging to the colors of its regiment, joins itself to him, ashamed of falling thus disgracefully to the rear. Officers making frantic exertions to rally their men; useless effort. [3]

The conclusion which Colonel Dodge reaches, in regard to the service of the corps, is as follows: —

All reliable authorities put the time of the attack at six P. M. When the last gun was fired by the Buschbeck rifle-pits, it was

[1] Rhodes, vol. iv, pp. 261–262.
[2] T. A. Dodge, *The Campaign of Chancellorsville*, pp. 94 ff. (Boston, 1881.)
[3] Dodge, pp. 94–95.

dusk, at that season about quarter-past seven. It seems reasonably settled therefore that the corps retarded the Confederate advance for about a mile of ground for exceeding an hour. How much more can be expected of ten thousand raw troops telescoped by twenty-five thousand veterans? [1]

Carl Schurz has given a report of the attack on the Eleventh Corps which has been commonly praised for its frankness and accuracy, and which at the same time defends the German soldier against the injustice showered upon him by the partisan press of that day.

Even if the charge of panic and failure of spirit on this one occasion were justified, as it is not, the same corps gave abundant proof of its sterner fibre on succeeding battlefields. The most noteworthy instance of all occurred in the battle of Lookout Mountain. General Thomas remarked, in congratulating Hooker on his victory at Lookout Mountain, that "the bayonet charge of Howard's troops, made up the side of a steep and difficult hill over two hundred feet high, completely routing and driving the enemy from its barracks on its top, will rank with the most distinguished feats of arms of this war." [2]

The attack by Jackson's and Lee's forces at Chancellorsville was renewed next day and ended in the total defeat of Hooker's army. The Confederate loss, however, was greater than the defeat which the Union cause sustained, because of the death of Stonewall Jackson, probably the ablest lieutenant of the war. The victory at Chancellorsville meant a great deal to the Confederate army, and encouraged General Lee to carry the war into the enemy's country. The invasion of Pennsylvania fol-

[1] Dodge, p. 96.
[2] Dodge, p. 104. The author adds, " And it is asserted that this encomium was well earned and that no portion of it need be set down to encouragement."

lowed. Fate had in store for the Eleventh Corps another reverse against superior numbers, in which, however, their determined stand against the victorious enemy was of vital importance for the final outcome. It was on the first day of the great battle of Gettysburg, where in the end the seemingly invincible army of Lee was doomed to meet its first defeat.

The First and Eleventh corps came upon the van of General Lee's forces under A. P. Hill. General Reynolds, in command of the First Corps, attacked the Confederates fiercely, but the latter developed such numbers that Reynolds's men were repulsed and the brave general himself killed. General O. O. Howard became the senior officer on the field, and obeying General Reynolds's instructions, hastened his Eleventh Corps to the field of action. The Union troops were hard-pressed, and it is said the death of General Reynolds caused much confusion as to who was properly in command.[1] The two great points of achievement in the first day's battle on the Union side were, first, the holding back of the enemy long enough for the Federal forces to concentrate at Gettysburg, and secondly, the selection of advantageous ground for defense. The former duty fell to the lot of the First and Eleventh corps, which did as well as could be expected against superior numbers. After the death of Reynolds, the larger share fell to the Eleventh Corps, which was fresher, and then under the command of Carl Schurz. Upon the arrival of Ewell and after a severe engagement, the Federals were driven back through the town of Gettys-

[1] Buford's opinion was that " there seemed to be no directing person. All was confusion and looked like disaster when Hancock arrived on the field. On hearing that Reynolds was killed, Meade, with his excellent judgment of the right man for the place, sent Hancock to take the command." Rhodes, vol. iv, p. 283.

burg with heavy loss, but were not pursued, Hill and Ewell
waiting for Longstreet. The check to the enemy's advance
was well worth all the losses which the Eleventh Corps
sustained. Shattered, well-nigh annihilated, its purpose, of
giving the rest of the army time to concentrate, was served.
The famous fish-hook position was selected, formed by
Culp's Hill, Cemetery Ridge, and Round Top. The credit
for the choice has been variously assigned to Hancock and
Howard. Perhaps Reynolds gauged its value as he hurried
through the town to stem the approaching tide.[1] Hancock,
arriving on the battlefield in the afternoon, gave the command to fortify Culp's Hill, to the right of the position
taken by Steinwehr's brigade and what was left of the
Eleventh Corps. Howard claims to have selected the position of Cemetery Ridge himself, as a nucleus for the
Eleventh Corps, in case they were forced to retreat. In
his own words :[2]

I then rode slowly to the position Meizenburg and I had agreed
upon as a good one, near the cemetery gate, where very soon I
met General Carl Schurz in person, who had hastened on to see
me ; and I instructed him as soon as the troops should arrive to
place his reserve batteries and Steinwehr's division in support
on those heights and to send his other two divisions, Barlow's
and his own, now Schimmelpfennig's, to the right of Doubleday's
corps, as relief.

He refers to the position mainly on Cemetery Ridge occupied by Steinwehr. This does not affect the credit given
Hancock for developing the entire position for the Union
army, nor for his making a display of his forces on the
ridges, thereby deceiving Lee as to his strength and pre-

[1] Cf. T. A. Dodge, *A Bird's-Eye View of Our Civil War*, p. 137.
[2] O. O. Howard, *Campaign and Battle of Gettysburg*, *Atlantic Monthly*,
July, 1876, p. 54.

venting an attack that day. It has been claimed for General Steinwehr [1] that he called General Howard's attention to the high ground on Cemetery Ridge, and advised intrenching, instead of advancing against the enemy, as Reynolds had done.[2] General Howard says of Steinwehr's services : [3]

I must speak of General Steinwehr. He came upon the field with a hearty spirit, ready to do his part. During the retreat he kept his men steadily in position on Cemetery Ridge as a nucleus, on which the line of battle, probably the most important in the annals of our war, was formed.

It is claimed [4] for Steinwehr that his tenacious hold on his ground was executed in opposition to his superiors. At one time General Schurz's division was hard-pressed, and the latter implored aid of his superior, General Howard, who was ready to send the only brigade that was left, viz., that of Steinwehr. The latter, reasoning that his own brigade would meet the same fate as the rest of the corps, and that by remaining in his position he could save them from a rout, referred the matter to General

---

[1] General Adolph von Steinwehr was born in 1822, at Blankenburg, in the Duchy of Brunswick, Germany. He was of a family of soldiers. After coming to America he took part in the Mexican War in an Alabama volunteer regiment. At the outbreak of the Civil War he recruited a German regiment of volunteers in New York. He rendered distinguished service at the battles of Bull Run, Chancellorsville, Chattanooga, and elsewhere. He commanded the Second Division of the Eleventh Corps. In the Shenandoah Valley he adopted stringent methods against bushwhackers, taking hostages as security against them. The Confederate government declared that if captured he had lost the right to parole. After the war he prepared maps of the United States for *Stieler's Atlas* and the *Centennial Gazetteer of the United States*, in 1876. Yale College distinguished him with an honorary degree.

[2] Cf. *New York Herald :* " It was Steinwehr's *coup d'œil*, which first recognized the importance of this hill." The date, February 27, 1877, given for this quotation by *Der deutsche Pionier*, vol. ix, p. 99, the writer found to be incorrect. He has not yet been able to find the correct date.

[3] O. O. Howard, p. 60.   [4] Cf. *Der deutsche Pionier*, vol. ix, p. 103.

Hancock, who had just arrived on the field, and who then ordered Steinwehr to remain.

After the retreat of the forces of the First and Eleventh corps through the town of Gettysburg, they were formed as follows : —

> Wadsworth's division of the First Corps stayed and fortified Culp's Hill, where Hancock placed it. Ames's division of the Eleventh Corps carried on the line to the steep part of Cemetery Ridge, facing northwards. Then came Schurz's and Steinwehr's divisions behind the famous stone wall and the apple orchard near town. Doubleday's and Robinson's divisions, First Corps, were next, etc.[1]

There was a night engagement on the Cemetery Ridge, which General Howard describes as follows : —

> When we supposed we should have rest for the night, some troops in our front, said to be the " Louisiana Tigers," sprang from their cover on the steep hill on the north end of Cemetery Ridge, broke through Ames's division, and in three minutes were upon our batteries, Wiedrick's and others, almost without firing a shot. General Schurz by my order sent a portion of the brigade under Colonel Krizanowski [composed of Germans] to the battery's immediate relief ; the artillerymen left their guns, and used sponge-staffs, handspikes, or anything they could lay hold of, to beat back the enemy, and as soon as help came the batteries were cleared. Schurz also sent a brigade further to the right to help General Greene, who requested reinforcements — Generals Steinwehr and Newton immediately filled any gaps made on my left by sudden withdrawals.[2]

Thinking that he had secured a strong foothold on the Federal lines, General Lee on the third day ordered the famous attack on the centre of the Union forces, known as "Pickett's Charge." The Second Corps stood the brunt of that tremendous onslaught. General Hancock was in com-

---

[1] O. O. Howard, *supra*, pp. 61–62. [2] *Ibid.*, p. 65.

mand, "the best tactician of the Army of the Potomac," possessed of the same courage as Pickett, and an inspira-tion to his men.

In the last assault, Armistead, a brigade commander, pressed forward, leaped the stone wall, waved his sword with his hat on it, shouted, "Give them the cold steel, boys," and laid his hands upon a gun. A hundred of his men had followed. They planted the Confederate battle-flags on Cemetery Ridge among the cannon they had captured, and for the moment held. Armistead was shot down; Garnett and Kemper, Pickett's other brigadiers, fell. The wavering divisions of Hill's corps seemed appalled, broke their ranks, and fell back.[1]

The historian of the Civil War, J. F. Rhodes, exclaims after his description of the battle, "Decry war as we may and ought, 'breathes there the man with soul so dead' who would not thrill with emotion to claim for his countrymen the men who made that charge and the men who met it?"[2]

In the Second Corps, commanded by Hancock, there were a number of Pennsylvania regiments, in which the representation of Germans by descent, native in this country, was very large; e. g., the Sixty-ninth Pennsylvania, with Lieutenant-Colonel M. Tschudy (German Swiss name), who was killed in the battle; also the Seventy-first and Seventy-second Pennsylvania regiments, the latter with Lieutenant-Colonel Hesser (a German name). These regiments belonged to the Second Division, which, with the Third Division, bore the brunt of the attack. In the Third Division, First Brigade, there were several Ohio regiments which also contained many representatives

---

[1] "The Federals swarmed around Pickett," writes Longstreet, "attacked on all sides, involving and breaking up his command." Rhodes, p. 289.

[2] Rhodes, p. 290.

of Germans by descent. The Fourth Ohio, with Colonel L. W. Carpenter (perhaps the family Zimmermann, who hailed from Virginia); also the Eighth Ohio, and the Fourteenth Indiana, commanded by Colonel John Coons (a typical Pennsylvania-German name); also the Seventh West Virginia, commanded by Colonel Snyder (a Dutch name which appears frequently among the German settlers of West Virginia). The defense on Cemetery Ridge was carried on mainly by the divisions of Steinwehr and Schurz.

But as the historian Rhodes has pointed out, the glory of the defense was not one whit greater than that of the attack by the Confederate regiments, and it ought ever to fill the hearts of German-Americans with pride to know that two of the ablest of Pickett's generals were of German blood. They were the two mentioned in the quotation above as entering the lines on Cemetery Ridge, the one, General L. A. Armistead, losing his life, and the other, General Kemper, being severely wounded. Armistead had already proved his temper in the Mexican War, for at the storming of Chapultepec he was "the first to leap into the Great Ditch." His record in the Civil War had been extraordinary; at Seven Pines and at Malvern Hill he proved himself the bravest of the brave. He had also served in the Indian War in Florida, under his father, General W. K. Armistead.[1] General James L. Kemper was commander of the Third Brigade of Pickett's Division, was likewise a veteran of the Mexican War, and then served

---

[1] Brigadier-General Louis A. Armistead was born in Newbern, North Carolina, February 18, 1817. The family was distinguished for its military service, and was German. A member of the family, George Armistead, has already been named as the defender of Baltimore against the British fleet in 1814. Cf. Schuricht, *History of the German Element in Virginia*, vol. ii, p. 81, etc. The name was originally Armstädt.

with distinction in the Confederate army; notably at the battles of Manassas, South Mountain, Antietam, Fredericksburg, and Marye's Heights. He was carried off severely wounded after the great charge at Gettysburg, but recovered and was placed in command later of the forces at Richmond. He was governor of Virginia from 1873–1878.[1]

The deeds of the Eleventh Corps do not shine as brilliantly at Gettysburg as those of the Second Corps who resisted the great attack of the third day. Their usefulness, however, was quite as great. In the words of General Howard : —

The First and Eleventh corps and Buford's small division of cavalry did wonders ; held the vast army of Lee in check a day ; took up a strong position ; fought themselves into it, and kept it for the approaching Army of the Potomac to occupy with them, so as to meet the foe with better prospects of victory. General Lee saw our position, was deceived as to our numbers, and therefore waited for the remainder of his army before reattacking; but the battle cost them many valuable lives.[2]

The day was still to come when the Eleventh Corps was to be favored by fortune, when its fighting powers were also to receive the popular applause. The latter, indeed, was a fickle thing to reckon with, for not only were foreign soldiers and generals roundly abused in the newspapers, but everybody alike was exposed to similar impatient criticism during the war. The public in the South were at times as severe critics as in the North, and even General Lee did not escape censure. That notable commander, on taking leave of his veterans at Appomattox,

[1] General Kemper was descended from one of the oldest German settlers in Virginia, who settled at Germanna under the auspices of Governor Spotswood, in 1714. Cf. Schuricht, vol. i, p. 67 ; also the *Virginia Magazine*, vol. ix. Cf. also Chapter VII, above.

[2] O. O. Howard, *supra*, p. 60. It is frequently surmised that had Lee attacked on the first day, he could have carried the Union position, but he was not aware of the fact that the ridges were not strongly fortified.

said, "I have done the best I could do for you." It was often so with the regiments who tried their best, but were ill favored by fortune. If they fought long enough, as did the Eleventh Corps, their lucky day was bound to come.

Howard's corps, consisting of the two divisions of Schurz and Steinwehr, was joined to the Army of the Cumberland and destined to aid very materially in the glorious campaigns about Chattanooga. The Eleventh and Twelfth corps being joined together, now named the Twentieth, were placed under the command of the able General Thomas, and became one of the most notable sections of the Federal army. Lookout Mountain reëstablished the good name of General Hooker, who had once caused the disgrace of the Eleventh Corps. In the "Battle above the Clouds," as it is frequently called, Hooker's troops captured every one of the enemy's positions. It was the lucky day for the German soldiers. Probably the most conspicuous of the assaults was the bayonet charge of Howard's troops, consisting of Steinwehr's and Schurz's divisions. As above mentioned, it was made up the side of a steep and difficult hill, — according to the description of General Thomas, an ascent over two hundred feet high, — and the enemy were completely routed and driven from their barracks at the top.[1]

The most remarkable achievement in the campaign about Chattanooga, and one that stands out among all the glorious deeds of the war, was the storming of Missionary Ridge. General Grant had commanded the troops to move forward and drive the enemy from the rifle-pits at the base of the ridge, and there intrench before going further. On arriving there and dislodging the enemy,

---

[1] General Thomas says this will rank among the most distinguished feats of arms of the war. *Atlantic Monthly*, August, 1876, p. 210.

they encountered a terrible volley of grape and canister from nearly thirty pieces of artillery on the summit of the ridge. Spontaneously, and with a desire to balance up past defeats, and a certain jealousy for the glory, the Army of the Cumberland, as if by a sudden impulse, moved upward, following the defeated enemy and arriving at the second line almost as soon as the fleeing Confederates. On and on they continued to the crest of the hill, never wavering until the enemy was completely routed. General Grant observed the movement with admiration and amazement, as it was performed without orders. This gallant advance has been compared with Pickett's charge at Gettysburg, but the results were different for the attacking party. The latter numbered about thirty thousand effective men, in the divisions of Baird, T. J. Wood, Sheridan, and Johnson. Examining the roster of the divisions engaged, we find a number of German regiments among them; e. g., in Sheridan's division, General G. D. Wagner's brigade, consisting of Illinois, Indiana, Michigan, and Ohio regiments. In Wood's division there was the brigade of General Willich,[1] containing Illinois,

---

[1] General August Willich was of a Prussian family, born in the province of Posen, Prussia, in 1810. His father was a captain of hussars, and the son, though he departed from the traditions of the family in politics, did not in the choice of his profession. He joined the revolutionists in Baden in 1848, and was there with Hecker and Sigel. During the Civil War he first joined a German regiment in Cincinnati, later was made captain of the Thirty-second Indiana Regiment (also called the First German). He distinguished himself under General Buell in Kentucky ; also in the battle of Shiloh, where he was instrumental in the rescue of Grant's army. For his decisive bayonet attack he was made a brigadier-general. He served under Rosecrans, and in one of the aggressive movements was taken prisoner, but was exchanged after four months. He took prominent part in the battles of Liberty Gap (cf. *Records of the Rebellion*, vol. vii, Doc. p. 409) and Chickamauga, and after the taking of Missionary Ridge was sent to Texas. It is interesting to know that Willich in 1870 offered his services to the King of

Indiana, Kansas, Ohio, and Wisconsin regiments. A very large portion of his brigade was made up of German soldiers ; e. g., the Thirty-second Indiana, Forty-ninth Ohio,[1] and Fifteenth Wisconsin. General Willich and his brigade took active part in the storming of Missionary Ridge.

It is impossible to take account of any considerable number of the German regiments in the Civil War. They appeared in most of the army corps, and it is safe to say in every battle from 1861 to 1865. Just as much will it be impossible to give a complete record of the deeds of the German officers during the war. A very interesting group, which should not be omitted, were the refugees who had served as officers in the German revolution of 1848. Some of them have already been mentioned, such as Sigel, Hecker, Blenker, Engelmann, Willich, and last but not least, Carl Schurz. Of these, Sigel probably became most prominent as a commander in the Civil War. He and Hecker had been the two leading military figures in the South German uprising in 1848–49. Hecker had proclaimed the republic. Sigel, Blenker, and Hecker controlled the military movements until the revolutionists were scattered to the four winds, on the approach of the Prussian army. Their experience in actual campaigning stood them in good stead when the Civil War broke out. Sigel's services were invaluable in Missouri. Though he was less successful in the Shenandoah

Prussia, though he was once a "forty-eighter." His offer was appreciated, but declined with thanks. When sixty years of age he matriculated as a student of philosophy in the University of Berlin. Cf. *Der deutsche Pionier*, vol. ix, pp. 439 ff., 488 ff.

[1] The Ninth Ohio (the First German) also took part in this battle as well as in the entire campaign of the Army of the Cumberland, 1863–64. This regiment consisted very largely of German soldiers. Cf. *Die Neuner. Eine Schilderung der Kriegsjahre des 9ten Regiment Ohio Vol. Infanterie, 1861–1864. Mit einer Einleitung v. Oberst Gustav Tafel.* (Cincinnati, Ohio, 1897.)

Valley, still he did as well as any other general except Sheridan. Hecker, concerning whom General Howard says, "Colonel Hecker, whose name I never mention without a feeling of respect for his uniform loyalty and courage," might have stood out more brilliantly if he had not been severely wounded in the battle of Chancellorsville. Though wounded and not young (born in 1811), he continued as the commander of the Eighty-second Illinois Regiment during the campaign of Chattanooga under General Grant, after which he retired. He returned to his farm and remained an imposing figure, a fine type of soldier and country gentleman.

A. A. Engelmann, who came to America at the age of nine years, with his father, served in the Mexican War, and when the Revolution of 1848 broke out sailed for Germany to take part in the cause of liberty. He returned, after the failure of the revolutionary party, to Belleville, Illinois. In the Civil War he became the colonel of the Forty-third Illinois Regiment, after his predecessor, J. C. Raith, had fallen in the battle of Shiloh. The regiment had been organized by Gustav Körner, subsequently lieutenant-governor of Illinois, one of the most influential Germans in the state, and an ardent supporter of the Union cause.

Besides those already mentioned there were a very large number of other German officers in the Northern army during the Civil War, whose previous training in the German army was of great service to the Federal cause. Their experience and example were of particular importance in the early stages of the war, when it was necessary to create a disciplined army out of raw material, and prove to the native American volunteers the necessity of strict adherence to military routine. Some of the German officers were soldiers

of fortune ; most of them, however, had settled in this
country before the war, and entered the army merely from
patriotic motives. Such was August Moor, a veteran of
the Mexican War and colonel of the Twenty-eighth Ohio.
He was born in Leipsic in 1814, came to this country in
1843, and during the war rose to a brigadier-generalship [1]
as a reward for gallant service. Similarly the Missouri
officers, Osterhaus and Hassendeubel, entered the army
to help save the Union. Their initial step was to rescue
Missouri, with Sigel and others. Osterhaus, a native of
Coblenz, arrived in America in 1849. After distinguished
service in Missouri, Tennessee, and Georgia, he was made
a major-general and served under General Sherman in his
march to the sea. He was chief of staff to General Canby
at the surrender of the army of General Kirby Smith in
May, 1865.[2] Franz Hassendeubel, born in Rhenish Bavaria
in 1817, came to the United States in 1842. He served in
the Mexican War from beginning to end. He had gone
back to Germany, but when the Civil War broke out he returned to the United States, and became lieutenant-colonel
of Sigel's Third Missouri Regiment. He constructed the
plans for the defense of St. Louis, was mortally wounded
during the siege of Vicksburg, and died July 16, 1863.[3]

Every state with a German population had its quota of
German soldiers and officers in the war. There was Buschbeck, friend of Steinwehr, colonel of the Twenty-seventh
Pennsylvania, who stood like a wall at Chancellorsville,
when almost every one else was taking to flight, who was

[1] Cf. H. A. Rattermann, *August Moor*. (Reprint from *Der deutsche Pionier*.)

[2] In 1866 Osterhaus was appointed American consul in Lyons, France.
At the Republican Convention of 1904, held in Chicago, he received an ova-
tion as he appeared, a picturesque old warrior and one of the original members of the Republican party.

[3] Rosengarten, *The German Soldier in the Wars of the United States*, p. 244.

one of the ablest artillerymen in the service, and was warmly commended as such by Sherman in his Southern campaign. There was Von Schrader, colonel of the Seventy-fourth Ohio, Knobellsdorff and Küfner of Illinois regiments, Von Gilsa, Schimmelpfennig, and Von Amsberg, each commanding a New York regiment, doing valiant service at Gettysburg and elsewhere. Colonel Emile Frey was an officer of Hecker's Illinois regiments, the Twenty-fourth and Eighty-second. He was a Swiss by birth and, true to his blood, was a good shot and led a company of sharpshooters.[1] Numerous were the German soldiers and officers in the cavalry and artillery regiments. Thielemann's cavalry battalion, and Hotaling's company of the Second Illinois Cavalry, and Stolleman's and D'Osband's and Bumbart's artillery, were among the German organizations that frequently received honorable mention in the history of the Western campaigns.[2] Joseph Karge, once a Prussian officer, was lieutenant-colonel of the First, and colonel of the Second New Jersey Cavalry, and commanded the first brigade of Grierson's division of cavalry.[3]

But even more distinguished as cavalry leaders than those named, were Kautz, Custer, and Von Borcke. The name Kautz is one of distinction in the American army and navy. General August V. Kautz was born in Baden in 1828, and settled in Ohio when but a boy. At the outbreak of the Mexican War he joined the First Ohio Regiment and was rewarded with a lieutenancy in the regular army. He commanded the Sixth Cavalry under McClellan in the Peninsular Campaign in 1862, distinguished him-

[1] Rosengarten, pp. 234–235. Colonel Frey later became the diplomatic representative of his native country at Washington.
[2] Rosengarten, pp. 232–233.
[3] After the war he was a professor at Princeton University. Rosengarten, p. 251.

self at South Mountain, Petersburg, and Richmond. He
was appointed colonel of the Second Ohio Cavalry, chief
of cavalry of the Twenty-third Corps, and was brevetted
major-general in both the volunteer and regular service.
He was noted for his cavalry raids in Southern Virginia
during the year 1864.[1] General George A. Custer was
an even more popular figure, a fearless, dashing cavalry
leader, who loved the thickest of the fight. He distinguished himself as commander of his famous Michigan
brigade at Gettysburg. He also won fame in the Shenandoah Valley as Sheridan's right-hand man. An account
of the battles of Winchester, Fisher's Hill, Cedar Creek,
Waynesboro, Five Forks, and Dinwiddie Court House is
impossible without a narrative of his deeds of valor.[2] On
the Confederate side there was likewise a distinguished
cavalry leader in Von Borcke, a former Prussian officer
and chief of staff of General J. E. B. Stuart, commander
of the Confederate cavalry. Heros Von Borcke is described
as a jovial, impulsive, warm-hearted man, just such as
would win the hearts of the Southern soldiers. General
Stuart commends him frequently as a thorough soldier
and splendid officer.[3]

The artillery service needs special training, hence foreigners of experience were much sought after in this department of the service. Probably the most prominent of
the German artillery officers was Hugo Dilger, familiarly
known by the war correspondents as "Leather-breeches."
He commanded an independent Ohio battery, and there-

---

[1] Kautz is also the author of some excellent works on subjects of military
science. Cf. Rosengarten, p. 171.

[2] For Custer's birth, descent, and later career, compare above, pp. 517–
518.

[3] *War Department of the Confederacy Records.* Cf. Rosengarten, p. 179,
etc. Cf. also the book *Ein Reis vom alten Stamm.*

fore never obtained a higher rank than that of captain, but no foreign officer performed more brilliant service or was longer in the fight. His battery at Chancellorsville, in Buschbeck's brigade, impeded the victorious Stonewall Jackson for probably an hour.[1] Wherever the Eleventh Corps went, Dilger's guns played a prominent part.[2]

The name of Mordecai is intimately associated with the history of ordnance in this country. Alfred Mordecai was chief of ordnance, Army of the James, May to September, 1864, and subsequently in the Army of the Tennessee, and of the Cumberland, till July 4, 1865. He was a graduate of West Point in 1861, and was the son of Major A. Mordecai, of the class of 1823, who made a brilliant military record. Father and son both contributed to the science of ordnance by their investigations, their inventions, and publications.[3]

The first officer of the regular army killed in the war was Lieutenant John T. Greble, of the Second Artillery. He was a graduate of West Point, German by descent (his great-grandfather having been a native of Saxe-Gotha), born in Philadelphia, and he was killed in action at Big Bethel, Virginia, in June, 1861. His death resulted from his self-sacrifice for the lives of a company of soldiers imperiled by an overwhelming force.[4]

Foreign engineers were also much in demand in the

---

[1] Cf. Dodge, *The Campaign of Chancellorsville*, p. 94, etc.

[2] Captain Dilger had resigned a lieutenancy in the Baden Mounted Artillery, to take part in the Civil War. After its close he became a farmer in the Shenandoah Valley. Cf. Rosengarten, p. 284.

[3] Cf. Rosengarten, pp. 171–172. Major A. Mordecai was sent with General McClellan and General Delafield to the Crimea during the Russian War of 1854. His grandfather was a German.

[4] His son, Lieutenant E. S. Greble, graduated from West Point in the class of 1881, and served in the Second United States Artillery. Cf. Rosengarten, p. 174.

Federal service, and among them we meet large numbers of German names. There was William Heine, born in Dresden, in 1827, and a member of Perry's expedition to Japan. After the outbreak of the Civil War he entered the Union army as a captain of engineers and advanced to the rank of brigadier in March, 1865. General Godfrey Weitzel, a native of Germany, graduated at West Point in 1855. He planned the capture of New Orleans in 1862, commanded a division at Port Hudson and in the Lafourche campaign. He superintended the construction of defenses at Bermuda Hundred, James River, and Deep Bottom. He commanded a corps at Fort Harrison in 1864, and was second in command at Fort Fisher. He led a division under Grant in the final conquest of Richmond, and commanded all the forces north of the Potomac after March, 1865.[1] After the war he was frequently employed in his profession of engineer. Another example of an engineer of German descent was General Herman Haupt, born in Philadelphia, and graduated at West Point in 1835. During the war his services were of great value in the field and subsequently he was a pioneer in railroad building across the continent.[2] Count Zeppelin,[3] the German inventor of the dirigible air-ship, which promises to revolutionize modern methods of warfare and transportation, served as

[1] Cf. *Encyclopædic Dictionary of American Reference*, vol. ii, p. 360, and Rosengarten, p. 175. Rhodes, vol. v, p. 179, and ff., gives Weitzel credit for his good sense and tact when in control of Richmond ; when he permitted the churches to open on the following Sunday "on the general condition that no disloyal sentiments should be uttered," he was obeying Lincoln's verbal instructions "to let them" (the Richmond people) "down easy," but Stanton, Secretary of War, incapable of generosity to a prostrate foe, reprimanded Weitzel for following Lincoln's suggestion.

[2] Rosengarten, p. 166.

[3] Subsequently he served in the Prussian-Austrian War of 1866, and in the Franco-German War of 1870–71. Since 1873 he has worked steadily at his invention of the dirigible military balloon.

cavalry officer and engineer in the Civil War, beginning in 1863. He made his first experiments and his first ascent in a military balloon in this country.

Among the numerous West Point graduates of German descent who served with distinction in the Civil War the names of Heintzelman and Rosecrans stand out before most others. General S. P. Heintzelman was brevetted major for bravery in the Mexican War. He was commissioned colonel in the Civil War and then commanded as brigadier at Alexandria, Bull Run, Yorktown, Williamsburg, and Fair Oaks; in 1863 he commanded the Northern Department. He was retired in 1869 with full rank of major-general, U. S. A.[1] General William Starke Rosecrans, of Pennsylvania-German stock, graduated at West Point in 1842. Previous to the war he was a professor at the Academy, an engineer, and a financier. He served in West Virginia as colonel of Ohio volunteers in 1861, and won the battle of Rich Mountain. Succeeding McClellan in the Department of the Ohio, he gained the victory of Carnifex Ferry. As commander of the Army of the Mississippi, he was victorious at Iuka and at Corinth and succeeded Buell as commander of the Army of the Cumberland. He fought the great battle of Murfreesboro, proved himself a skillful strategist in the next months, but was compelled by peremptory orders from the War Department to advance before he was ready, with the result that he was defeated at Chickamauga.[2] Rosecrans was then succeeded, sent to the West and put

---

[1] Heintzelman's grandfather, a native of Augsburg, was the first white settler in Manheim, Pennsylvania. Rosengarten, p. 167.

[2] Cf. *Encyclopœdic Dictionary of American Reference*, vol. ii, pp. 180–181. He resigned in 1867; was Minister to Mexico, 1868–69; Democratic Congressman from California, 1881–85 ; and Registrar of the United States Treasury, 1885–93.

on waiting orders. Colonel Dodge[1] speaks of some of the Northern generals as unfortunate through early success. The victories in West Virginia, he says, "gave both McClellan and Rosecrans a reputation which did them eventually an injustice, inasmuch as it thrust them into prominent positions which no officer in the country was equal to without experience of many months and frequent failures. The nation was utterly uneducated in war — few of our officers had commanded even a regiment. Our only recent training had been in the Mexican War, a distinctly fine campaign, but of limited scope. The work now to be done required armies such as none since Napoleon had seen under his control. Unlucky they who were early placed in high command. The conditions of failure were strong in both themselves and the people for whom they fought."

It would make much too long a register of names and achievements to take account of the native soldiers of German descent in the Civil War. The Wister family of Pennsylvania sent representatives by the half-score. The names Pennypacker, Amen (Ohio), Hartranft, Hambright, and many good colonial names appear in great abundance in the lists of officers and men. In rare cases the families were divided between North and South. Francis Lieber, the prominent jurist and professor of law at Columbia College, New York, had a son with the Illinois troops, another in the Confederate service, and a third with a commission in the regular army of the United States. Lieber himself was a legal adviser to the United States government in matters of military and international law, and prepared a code of instructions for the government of armies of the United States in the field. He also main-

[1] *A Bird's-Eye View of Our Civil War*, pp. 13 ff.

F. W. Ruckstuhl, Sculp.

JOHN FREDERIC HARTRANFT

tained a correspondence with leading Germans, men like Bluntschli, Mohl, and Holtzendorff, securing in Germany sympathy for the cause which the North was battling to maintain.

The Germans in the South who had settled there early in the nineteenth, or whose ancestors had arrived in the eighteenth century, commonly adhered to the Confederacy. The more recent immigrants frequently turned their backs upon the South. An illustration of this is found in Texas, where Schleicher, mentioned above, belonging to an earlier immigration in the nineteenth century, became an adherent of the Secession cause, while Degener, of a more recent immigration, almost lost his life by his opposition to the current of Southern sympathy. It was quite natural for the Germans of Virginia to go with their state, as we saw in the case of Kemper, or Armistead, born in North Carolina, both of whom fought valiantly for the Southern cause. We find German-Virginian names, such as Helm, Hoke, Zollicoffer, adding glory to the military records of the Confederacy. Of those born in Germany few drew their swords for the slave states. But instances occurred, such as that of Von Zincken and some others.[1] Men born in Germany who had immigrated early in their lives, and had become associated for many years with all local interests of their Southern homes, would very naturally join hands with their fellow citizens. F. W. Wagener, a prominent citizen of Charleston, South Carolina, a representative of the best German element in that locality, became the captain of the first German regiment, of four hundred men, raised in Charleston. The regiment in question included three German companies of artillery which did good local service. In 1889 the survivors of the regiment erected a

[1] Scheibert, *Sieben Monate in den Rebellen Staaten.* (Stettin, 1868.) Cf. Rosengarten, p. 179.

monument to their fallen comrades. After the war General Wagener was elected mayor of Charleston by popular vote, and was one of Charleston's leading citizens.[1]

Viewing the German participation in the Civil War as a whole, we see that it weighed heavily on the Northern side, the aid given to the Southern armies being by no means of the same importance. For the Northern armies the German element furnished nearly two hundred thousand men, natives of Germany. The number furnished by men of German descent cannot be estimated, but would probably increase the number threefold. The contribution of German officers was of very great importance. They gave their experience and example, and taught the masses of impetuous and undisciplined volunteers the necessity of obedience and coöperation. Their soldierly bearing, encouraging words, and habitual discipline on the early battlefields created examples of imitation. The German soldier, as the German agriculturist, contributed also those qualities which are not heralded by fame, — patience, steadiness, and persistence. These essential staying qualities were exhibited not alone in battle, but as often in camp, on the march, or in the tedious waits incident to military life. To overcome discouragement in defeat, to encounter sickness and privation, were tests the German soldier endured as successfully as the dangers of actual combat. In fighting qualities all nations have given proof of heroism ; the excitement of battle, the inspiration of great leaders, can make lions out of sheep. That the Germans were superior to all others they never attempted to claim, but they can furnish abundant proofs of having fought as bravely and steadily on the great battlefields of the Civil War as any other national element.

[1] Cf. Rosengarten, p. 186.

An interesting phenomenon in connection with this subject is the attitude of Germany during the Civil War. The influence of such men as Lieber, already mentioned, and indeed the fact of a German immigration of a highly intellectual quality since 1848, were circumstances undoubtedly influential in establishing in the mother country sympathy for the Northern cause. Sentiment, based on an abhorrence of slavery, was also of moment in deciding Germany's position. It was not so everywhere in European countries. On his visit to Europe at the time, Andrew D. White found friends among all classes of Germans: " Germans everywhere recognized the real question at issue in the American struggle. Everywhere on German soil was a deep detestation of human bondage. Frankfort-on-the-Main became a most beneficial centre of financial influences, and from first to last Germany stood firmly by us." [1] The same author says of England, " In that time of our direst need, when among the leaders in England D'Israeli was indifferent, Palmerston jaunty, Earl Russell only too happy to let out the Confederate cruisers to annihilate our commerce, and when Mr. Gladstone was satisfied that Jefferson Davis had made a 'nation,' there was one whose heart recognized the wickedness of siding with the slave power, and whose mind recognized the folly of making the United States and Great Britain enemies for centuries, and that man, a German, the Prince Consort, Albert of Saxe-Coburg-Gotha." [2]

Germany gave not only her sympathy but her gold in defense of the Union, and the purchase of United States bonds in the German financial centres contributed very

[1] Speech of Andrew D. White, Ambassador to the German Empire, at a farewell banquet given by the German-Americans in New York on May 22, 1897.

[2] White, *supra*, p. 6.

largely toward sustaining the Union in the long struggle
which the government was forced to make against the
powerful Southern Confederacy.

The Spanish War

The subject of German volunteering in the recent
Spanish-American War was brought to public attention
by a peculiar incident. It was in the wake of the Spanish
War period, when several high ranking officers of our
navy and army were seeing on the horizon a war with
Germany, and were incidentally committing indiscretions
on convivial occasions. At Honolulu General McArthur
chose to say that a war with Germany was inevitable, and
that the Pan-Germanic sentiment had seized upon the
German-Americans to such an extent that a German name
in the regimental lists was a curiosity. Such a slap-in-the-
face was most startling. The general probably did not
know that he was committing an outrage upon the sensibilities of more than eighteen million American people,
German by birth or descent, who in all the wars of the
United States had furnished more than their proportionate
share of officers and volunteers. Civil War veterans of
German blood looked up in surprise, and wondered whether
their race had declined. The gauntlet cast down was
quickly taken up by the " Deutsch-Amerikanischer National Bund," on a motion of the United German Societies of Indianapolis,[1] who were conscious of a large
German quota sent by them to the Spanish-American
War.

---

[1] An organization representing forty-five societies and a membership of
about two thousand. Cf. *German-American Annals*, vol. ii, *Americana Germanica*, vol. vi, p. 173 (1904). For the " Deutsch-Amerikanischer National
Bund," cf. *German-American Annals*, vols. i, ii, etc., and of this work,
Volume II, Chapter IV.

The matter was investigated and the accusation was found to be totally false. It can be excused only on the basis of a lack of knowledge of German, which in these days of opportunity can hardly be pleaded in palliation. A good summary of the German representation in the American army and navy during the Spanish War was made by F. König, department commander, Spanish-American War Veterans.[1] He made lists of the German-Americans in the Pennsylvania regiments: First to Sixth, Eighth to Tenth, Twelfth to Sixteenth, the Eighteenth, and Batteries A, B, and C. It appeared that at least fifteen per cent of the entire number enlisted were Germans, and the enumeration did not pretend to be complete. A list of officers and men was also given, for the regiments named, numbering between four and five hundred; they are such as could not be mistaken for other than German names, and some of the persons they represent were personally known to the compiler. Mr. König also states that the ships fitted out in Philadelphia, the U. S. S. *St. Paul*, the U. S. S. *Peoria*, and the U. S. S. *Fishhawk*, were equipped with crews of which fully fifteen per cent were German-Americans. On the U. S. S. *Dorothea*, on which the compiler served, twenty per cent (twelve out of sixty) of the ship's crew were German-Americans. Naval officers serving in the United States Marine Corps during the Spanish War were the German-Americans: Majors Lauchheimer and Waller, Captains Meyers (b. in Germany) and Marix, and Lieutenant Schwalbe. Naval officers who were on the retired list for long and continued service, and who were placed upon the active list during the war with Spain, of German descent unless otherwise specified, were: Rear-Admiral Buehler, Commanders Chetky, Fickbohm

---

[1] *German-American Annals*, vol. ii, pp. 506–527.

(German), Hanus (German), Chief Gunner Sommers (German), Captains Kindelberger, Schenk, and Hoehling, Gunner Ritter, Lieutenants Ritter and Haggermann, Lieutenant-Commander Eckstein, and Lieutenants Kafer and Kaiser. Another long list of men that served on the war-vessels is given, most of them residents of Philadelphia, of German parentage.[1] Finally Mr. König gives a list of naval officers of German descent, including eleven boatswains, four ensigns, twenty-four lieutenants, twelve lieutenant-commanders, six commanders, four captains, and four rear-admirals. The list included also regular officers in the United States Navy. The captains were Reiter, Hunker, Reisinger, and Farenholt; the rear-admirals were Winfield Scott Schley, Louis Kempff, Norman von Heldreich Farghar, and Albert Kautz.

The record of the most distinguished of these, Rear-Admiral Schley, is still very familiar. Few if any of the naval officers of recent times have rendered such long and efficient service in the United States Navy. During the Civil War Schley served in the blockading squadron and in the engagement leading to the capture of Port Hudson, Louisiana. He suppressed the insurrection among the Chinese coolies on the Chin Chi Islands in 1864, and in the following year he landed one hundred men at San Salvador to protect the United States Consulate. He participated in the attack on the Salee River forts in Korea in 1871; after varied service on sea and land he took command in 1884 of the Greely Relief Expedition. He rescued Lieutenant Greely and six survivors at Cape Sabine, for which he was awarded a gold watch and the thanks of the legislature of his native state of Maryland. He commanded the cruiser *Baltimore* in 1891 and settled the trouble at Val-

[1] *German-American Annals*, vol. ii, p. 524.

paraiso, Chile, when several American sailors were stoned
by a mob. In February, 1898, he was promoted commodore,
and placed in command of the " Flying Squadron " on duty
in Cuban waters in the war with Spain. He was in immediate command at the destruction of Cervera's fleet off
Santiago, July 3, 1898, and thereupon promoted rear-admiral (August, 1898). During the Schley-Sampson controversy Rear-Admiral Schley comported himself in a most
dignified manner throughout. He was placed before a court
of inquiry, two members of which decided against him, the
third, however, Admiral Dewey, the only admiral in the
American Navy since Farragut, whose experience in naval
affairs gave weight to his judgment, discountenanced
every article of the findings against Schley. In command
of the cruiser *Brooklyn* at the battle of Santiago, Rear-
Admiral Schley was aboard the ship that received more
shots than all the rest of the American fleet put together,
and even his most severe detractors admit that Schley,
during the battle, behaved in a manner exemplary for an
American naval officer. The *Brooklyn*, which Schley
commanded, was the ship most instrumental in beaching
the *Colon*, the escape of which would, in the unequal
fight, have been equivalent to a Spanish victory.

Albert Kautz graduated from the Naval Academy
(1858) in time to serve in the Civil War. After a period
of capture and imprisonment he served as Farragut's flag
lieutenant on board the *Hartford*, at the capture of New
Orleans, April 1, 1862. He personally hauled down the
" lone-star " flag from the City Hall, which Mayor Monroe
refused to strike, and hoisted the stars and stripes on the
custom-house. He also served on the *Hartford* during
the engagement with the Vicksburg batteries in June
and July, 1862. He was made a rear-admiral in 1898,

and placed in command of the Pacific Station. In March and April, 1899, he was in command at Apia, Samoa, during the trouble with the native chiefs, and was commended for his conduct on that occasion.

Louis Kempff, born near Belleville, Illinois, was likewise a Civil War veteran. He left the Naval Academy in April, 1861, and served on the *Vandalia* in the blockade off Charleston. He captured and took to New York the schooner *Henry Middleton*, of Charleston, and then rejoined the *Vandalia* in the expedition against Port Royal Ferry, in 1862. He took part in the bombardment of Sewell's Point, Virginia, and in various other engagements. He was promoted rear-admiral in 1899 after good service on sea and land. He was on the Asiatic Station in 1900, and declined to join the foreign admirals in the attack on the Taku forts, but after the U. S. S. *Monocacy* was struck by a shot from Chinese forts he joined in with the forces at hand for the protection of life and property of the Americans. He commanded the Pacific Naval Station in 1903.

CHAPTER XVII

A SUMMARY VIEW OF THE GERMAN IMMIGRATIONS OF THE NINETEENTH CENTURY, THEIR LOCATION, DISTRIBUTION, AND GENERAL CHARACTER

Germans on the frontier — Diffusion of the German element over the territory of the United States ; equal distribution — The German Belt — The states in which the Germans are more numerous than any other foreign element — Table showing distribution of Germans — List of cities with largest German populations — Statistics of the German immigrations of the nineteenth century — Causes, in the United States and Germany, for the increase or decline of immigration — The general character of the nineteenth century immigrants from Germany — Friedrich Münch's three immigrations — Concluding remarks.

THE settlement of the German element within the territory of the United States has been sketched chronologically in the foregoing chapters. It was found that, before the Revolutionary War, the Germans, estimated at 225,000 in number,[1] had settled mainly on the frontier line, extending from the Mohawk in New York to the colony farthest south, Georgia. They had settled two vast physiographic areas, the Piedmont Plateau, lying at the base and east of the Appalachian ranges from New York to Georgia, and the Great Valley, lying between the Blue Ridge and Alleghany mountains, beginning in Pennsylvania, extending across Maryland and southwest through Virginia. " With their Scotch-Irish neighbors, they formed the outer edge of the tide of pioneers that was ready to flow through the passes of the mountains into the interior

---

[1] See Chapter x, and the accompanying map.

of the continent." [1] As shown in preceding chapters, the German immigrants were among the first to enter Kentucky and Tennessee from Virginia and the Carolinas; [2] they were the first settlers of the Ohio Valley. [3]

In the nineteenth century came another and greater " Völkerwanderung," reaching a total, for the hundred years, of 5,009,280 souls. New areas were settled by these hosts of peaceful invaders, who, no longer checked by a forbidding mountain range running from northeast to southwest, pushed on irresistibly over the limitless western plains, and, reinforced by new accessions from the coast, extended the frontier line ever farther to the westward until it reached the Pacific Ocean. [4] When the frontier ceased to be, an event announced in the Census Report of 1890, the Germans were diffused over the whole surface of the United States.

The last Census Report (1900) shows that the German population is not alone widespread, but is more equally distributed over the territory of the United States than any other foreign element. This can be seen by a comparison of the maps published by the Census Bureau, showing the "density of natives" of Germany, Ireland, Great Britain, Scandinavia, etc. [5] The other nationalities will be found massed in certain localities. For example, quoting from the Census Reports: [6] " The North Atlantic division contains more than three fourths of all French-Canadians. The same division also contains 73 per cent of all the natives of Hungary, 72.7 per cent of all the natives of Italy, and 70.7 per cent of all the natives of

---

[1] F. J. Turner, *German Immigration in the Colonial Period, Chicago Record-Herald*, August 28, 1901.

[2] Cf. Chapter xii. [3] Cf. Chapter xiii. [4] Cf. Chapter xv.

[5] *Statistical Atlas of the United States*, 1900, plates nos. 65–69.

[6] *Twelfth Census of the United States*, 1900, vol. i, p. clxxv.

Russian Poland. This same division contains also by far the largest proportion of all the natives of Austria, Ireland, and Russia, and more than half of all the natives of England, Scotland, and Wales. The North Central division contains very nearly 85 per cent of all the natives of Norway, a little more than 75 per cent of all the natives of Bohemia and Holland, very nearly 65 per cent of all the natives of Denmark and Sweden." The North Central division contains 54.9 per cent of all the natives of Germany, which is the ratio to which this division is entitled, considering its larger area, general fertility, and great cities. The North Atlantic division contains 33.2 per cent of all the native Germans, and with the North Central division forms the German belt which contains almost nine tenths of all native Germans.

In many other sections of the country, the Germans outnumber the other nationalities. The natives of Germany constitute a little more than one fourth of the entire foreign element in the United States, viz., 25.8 per cent. In the North Atlantic division, they number 18.6 per cent of the foreign element; in the North Central division, 35.1 per cent; in the South Atlantic division, 33.7 per cent; in the South Central division, 30.7 per cent, and in the Western division, 16 per cent of the entire foreign population. The native Germans are therefore slightly above their average of 25.8 per cent in the North Central and South Atlantic divisions, also in the South Central division, and below their average in the North Atlantic and Western divisions. They are outnumbered in the North Atlantic division by the Irish, but in the Western division, where their percentage is below their average (25.8), they nevertheless are more numerous than any other foreign element, the English being next with 12.1 per cent.

The natives of Russia are found mostly in cities, very nearly three fourths of them living in the large cities in 1900. So it is with the natives of Poland and Italy. The Irish inhabit the large cities also to the extent of 62 per cent of their number, very little less than the Italians, with 62.4 per cent. The Scandinavians, who are massed in the Northwest, principally Minnesota and the Dakotas, are not dwellers in cities, while the natives of Germany and England are about equally distributed in city and country.

The map following this page designates the states (with a cross-mark) in which the natives of Germany are more numerous than any other foreign element. It will be seen that all the states in the Union harbor a larger native German population than of any other foreign country, with the following exceptions : Maine and Michigan, which include a larger Canadian-English ; Vermont and New Hampshire, which contain a larger Canadian-French element; Massachusetts, Rhode Island, Connecticut, and Delaware, which hold a larger Irish population; Florida, a larger Cuban; Louisiana, a larger Italian ; Texas, New Mexico, and Arizona, a larger Mexican element. The Mormon states, Utah, Idaho, and Wyoming, contain a larger English, Montana and Washington a larger Canadian-English, element; Nevada includes more Irish and the Dakotas more Norwegians. All the remaining states — and it will be seen at a glance that they represent the great progressive area of the United States, together with the cream of the Pacific coast, California and Oregon — all of them contain a larger German than any other foreign population. Though the German immigration was not large between 1890 and 1900, the Germans did not lose ground in comparison with other national or racial elements. Louisiana, which was more largely inhabited by

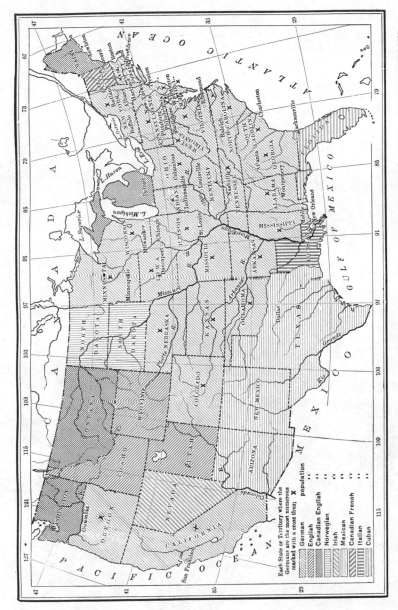

MAP SHOWING IN WHAT STATES THE GERMANS WERE MORE NUMEROUS IN 1900 THAN OTHER NATIONAL STOCKS

native Germans in 1890, now contains more Italians, but to compensate for that, California has now a larger German than Chinese population, and Pennsylvania and Virginia are now more largely inhabited by native Germans than by native Irishmen.

The following table, taken from the Census Report of 1900,[1] will show exactly where the Germans are located and compare them with the two next largest elements, the Irish and the English : —

German Population distributed over the United States

	Germans	Irish	English
The United States:	2,666,990	1,618,567	842,078
North Atlantic Division —	883,908	1,113,876	435,031
Maine	1,356	10,159	4,793
New Hampshire	2,006	13,547	5,100
Vermont	882	7,453	2,447
Massachusetts	31,395	249,916	82,346
Rhode Island	4,300	35,501	22,832
Connecticut	31,892	70,994	21,569
New York	480,026	425,553	135,685
New Jersey	119,598	94,844	45,428
Pennsylvania	212,453	205,909	114,831
South Atlantic Division —	72,705	36,606	20,274
Delaware	2,332	5.044	1,506
Maryland	44,990	13,874	5,299
District of Columbia	5,857	6,220	2,299
Virginia	4,504	3,534	3,425
West Virginia	6,537	3,342	2,622
North Carolina	1,191	371	904
South Carolina	2,075	1,131	474
Georgia	3,407	2,293	1,514
Florida	1,812	797	2,231

[1] *Twelfth Census of the United States*, 1900, vol. i (Population), part i, pp. clxxiii–clxxiv, table lxxxii.

North Central Division —	1,461,603	349,805	260,369
Ohio	204,160	55,018	44,745
Indiana	73,546	16,306	10,874
Illinois	332,169	114,563	64,390
Michigan	125,074	29,182	43,839
Wisconsin	242,777	23,544	17,995
Minnesota	117,007	22,428	12,022
Iowa	123,162	28,321	21,027
Missouri	109,282	31,832	15,666
North Dakota	11,546	2,670	2,909
South Dakota	17,873	3,298	3,862
Nebraska	65,506	11,127	9,757
Kansas	39,501	11,516	13,283
South Central Division —	109,743	31,640	22,183
Kentucky	27,555	9,874	3,256
Tennessee	4,569	3,372	2,207
Alabama	3,634	1,792	2,347
Mississippi	1,926	1,264	798
Louisiana	11,839	6,436	2,068
Texas	48,295	6,173	8,213
Indian Territory	842	397	779
Oklahoma	5.112	987	1,121
Arkansas	5,971	1,345	1,394
Western Division —	135,459	83,532	102,656
Montana	7,162	9,436	8,077
Wyoming	2,146	1,591	2,596
Colorado	14,606	10,132	13,575
New Mexico	1,360	692	968
Arizona	1,245	1,159	1,561
Utah	2,360	1,516	18,879
Nevada	1,179	1,425	1,167
Idaho	2,974	1,633	3,943
Washington	16,686	7,262	10,481
Oregon	13,292	4.210	5,663
California	72,449	44,476	35,746

Some of the principal cities of the United States contain very large German populations. Native Germans

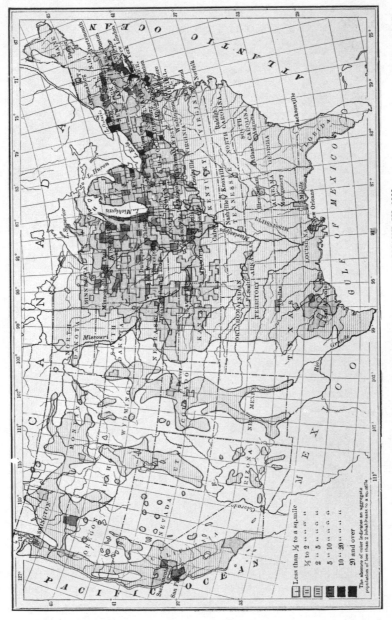

DISTRIBUTION OF NATIVES OF GERMANY IN 1900

Less than ½ to a sq. mile
½ to 2 " " " "
2 " 5 " " " "
5 " 10 " " " "
10 " 20 " " " "
20 and over

The absence of color indicates an aggregate
population of less than 2 inhabitants to a sq. mile

constitute very nearly two thirds of all the foreign-born in Cincinnati, substantially three fifths in Milwaukee, very nearly three fifths in Louisville, more than one half in St. Louis, and very nearly one half in Baltimore. These statistics become more interesting after comparison with others. The Irish number one third the total foreign population of Boston, Cambridge, Jersey City, New Haven, Philadelphia, and Providence; three tenths in Lowell, Washington, and Worcester; French-Canadians inhabit Fall River to the extent of 40.3 per cent of the total foreign population, 35.8 per cent in Lowell, 14 per cent in Worcester. The Swedes number very nearly one third of the foreign-born in Minneapolis, one fifth in St. Paul and Worcester. Italians are most numerous in New Orleans (19.3 per cent) and New Haven (17.1 per cent). Russians are most numerous in Baltimore, German Poles in Milwaukee, Norwegians in Minneapolis.

A list of cities of the United States is subjoined, in which the population born in Germany exceeds 5000. The total population of the city is placed in the first column, the foreign-born Germans in the second, and the number of persons of German parentage in the third. Under the last-named are included (1) all persons born in Germany, (2) all persons born in the United States with both parents born in Germany, (3) with one parent born in Germany and the other in some other foreign country, and (4) all persons born in the United States with one parent born in Germany and the other born in the United States.[1] The list is as given on the following page.

---

[1] Cf. *The Twelfth Census of the United States*, vol. i (Population), part i, pp. 878–881 (table 60) ; pp. 882–885 (table 61); pp. 890–893 (table 63).

City	Total Population	Born in Germany	Total of German Parentage
New York	3,437,202	322,343	761,795
Chicago	1,698,575	170,738	416,729
Philadelphia	1,293,697	71,319	190,144
St. Louis	575,238	58,781	199,182
Milwaukee	285,315	53,854	146,846
Cleveland	381,768	40,648	105.321
Cincinnati	325,902	38,219	136,087
Buffalo	352,387	36,720	113,102
San Francisco	342,782	35.194	58,935
Baltimore	508,957	33,208	107.506
Detroit	285,704	33,027	84,165
Newark	246,070	25,139	67,105
Pittsburg	321,616	21,222	64.204
Jersey City	206,433	17,375	44,247
Rochester	162,608	15,685	47,573
St. Paul	163,065	12,935	35,945
Louisville	204.731	12,383	47,514
Toledo	131,822	12,373	37,389
Allegheny	129,896	12,022	37,270
Hoboken	59,364	10,843	23,463
Boston	560,892	10,523	25,119
New Orleans	287,104	8,733	36,293
Indianapolis	169,164	8,632	29,163
Syracuse	108,374	7,865	21,753
Minneapolis	202,718	7,335	21,758
Dayton	85.333	6,820	22,861
Paterson	105,171	6,584	13,139
Columbus, Ohio	125,560	6,296	21,811
Davenport, Iowa	35,254	6,111	15,839
Albany	94.151	5.903	18.553
Washington	278,718	5,857	17,782
Omaha, Nebraska	102,555	5,522	13.826
Erie	52,733	5,226	16.841
Denver	133,859	5,114	14,780

Two significant facts are to be gathered from the statistics presented on the foregoing pages,— first, that of
the equal distribution of the German immigration in com-

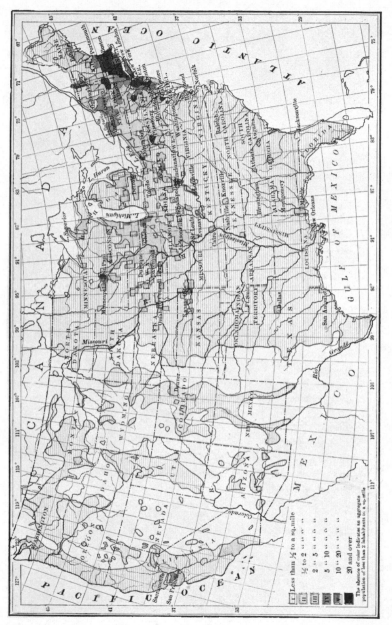

DISTRIBUTION OF NATIVES OF IRELAND IN 1900

Less than ½ to a sq. mile
½ to 2 " " "
2 " 5 " " "
5 " 10 " " "
10 " 20 " " "
20 and over

The absence of color indicates an aggregate
population of less than 2 inhabitants to a sq. mile

parison with other foreign elements, and secondly, the existence of a German belt, where the German element is most numerous and prosperous. Their equal distribution through town and country, and proportionately through all parts of the United States, recommends the German immigrants as a class desirable above others. In the eighteenth century they chose the lands best adapted for farming purposes and clung to them, and just so in the nineteenth they selected the area which at the present day corresponds to the most productive and progressive in the United States. The German belt lies between the northern boundaries of Massachusetts and of Maryland, spreads westward north of the Ohio River to the Great Lakes and onward into the neighboring two tiers of trans-Mississippi states. In this great general zone the lands of densest German settlement are along the coast, the Mohawk Valley, and in Eastern Pennsylvania; also along the shores of Lake Ontario, Lakes Erie and Michigan, along the Ohio River, and down the Mississippi from St. Paul to St. Louis.[1] The states which contain the most native Germans are, in order, New York, Illinois, Wisconsin, Pennsylvania, and Ohio.

The German immigration in the nineteenth century reaches a total considerably larger than that of any other foreign element. The following table gives their numbers in comparison with others : —

Germany	5,009,280
Ireland	3,871,253
Great Britain, including	
England, Scotland, and Wales	3,024,222
Norway, Sweden, and Denmark	1,439,060

[1] Cf. F. J. Turner, *The German Immigration to the United States*, II, *Chicago Record-Herald*, September 4, 1901.

Canada and Newfoundland	1,049,939
Italy	1,040,457
Austria Hungary	1,027,195
Russia and Poland	926,902
All other countries	1,726,913
Total	19,115,221

The enumeration of foreign immigrations was not begun before 1820. In the early period only the immigration going through the seaports was taken into account; the figures in the early period are therefore below the actual status; still they constitute the only information available. The German immigration by decades, taken from the Census Reports, is as follows: —

1821–30	6,761
1831–40	152,454
1841–50	434,626
1851–60	951,667
1861–70	787,468
1871–80	718,182
1881–90	1,452,970
1891–1900	505,152
Total	5,009,280

Up to 1850 the Irish immigration exceeded the German; from 1841 to 1850 the German immigration was about 24.2 per cent, the Irish 42.3 per cent of the total immigration. But in the decade 1851 to 1860 the German immigration surpassed the Irish and all others, and continued to do so until the last decade of the nineteenth century, when, although still exceeding the Irish and English, it fell far below the Slavic and Italian immigrations. The causes for the rise and fall in the wave of German immigration are very interesting, the increase commonly corresponding to a period of economic decline in certain

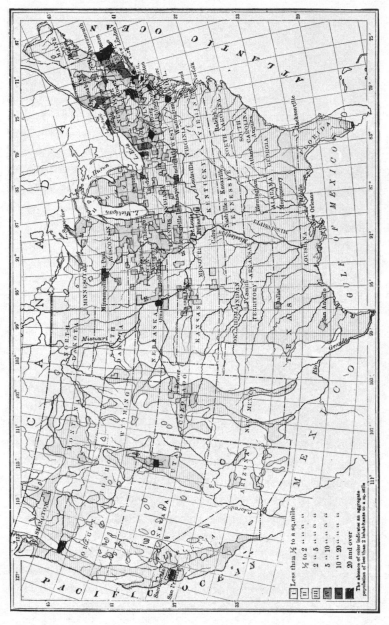

DISTRIBUTION OF NATIVES OF GREAT BRITAIN IN 1900

Less than ½ to a sq. mile
½ to 2 " " " "
2 " 5 " " " "
5 " 10 " " " "
10 " 20 " " " "
20 and over

The absence of color indicates an aggregate
population of less than 2 inhabitants to a sq. mile

parts of Germany and a contemporaneous era of prosperity or opportunity in the United States. A decrease in the German immigration occurred during all the periods of depression in the United States, especially if at the same time prosperity reigned in the mother country.

The impression is general that the immigration between 1790 and 1820 was very slight. There are no accurate statistics to controvert this impression. No good reason, however, has been urged why immigration should have practically ceased, and it is quite probable that between 1810 and 1820 there was considerable immigration to the United States, at least representing the upward slope toward the immigration between 1820 and 1830. There must have been quite a little immigration immediately before 1820, because it attracted attention onough to cause an official count to be instituted at the seaports. In 1820, for instance, there were nine hundred and sixty-eight Germans that arrived at American ports, and so large a number must have been preceded by at least hundreds, arriving annually in years just previous. After the close of the war with England it was less difficult to come to America, and when the reactionary governments assumed firm control in Europe there was considerable dissatisfaction in the German countries. Germans suffered much from the Napoleonic wars, especially Würtemberg, the country that had, in the previous century, supplied so many immigrants to the United States. The years 1817–18, the period of tyrannical persecution of the student societies, the "Burschenschaften," undoubtedly brought many refugees to the land of political liberty. The great increase, however, in German immigration did not come until the decade of 1831–40. In 1832, starting upward with over ten thousand, it reached more than twenty-nine thousand in 1840, and a total of over one hundred and fifty-two thousand for the decade.

There were various causes, such as over-population, over-production, over-crowding in the farming districts, and the ruin of the small hand industries in competition with the new factory system. Thousands of artisans who were brought up in the old master-system, in which each man made the whole article, were now left destitute because of the cheaper manufacture in factories.[1] Contemporary with this condition a period of prosperity and expansion existed in the United States.

It was an era of land speculation, town-building, and westward movement. A flood of settlers poured by way of the Erie Canal and steamboats into the land between the Ohio and the Great Lakes; the cotton culture spread population into the Gulf States, and Missouri received an important influx of settlers. These conditions were made known in Germany. Cheap lands, light taxes, the need of laborers, and the opportunity to gain a competence in a short time by toil, — these were conditions that attracted the Germans.[2]

At home impetuous German students and professors had vainly striven for reform against the misgovernment, taxation, and extravagance of the petty German rulers.

The triumph of Jacksonian Democracy here was contemporaneous with these German attempts to secure popular freedom, and it seemed to promise them the liberty they sought. This was the beginning of the influx of the so-called " Latin farmers " into Ohio, Indiana, and Missouri. German names dotted the map of the newly-settled areas of these regions. Letters and newspapers of these German pioneers were printed and circulated in the fatherland, particularly in the region of the Rhine,

[1] For a literary picture of such conditions, cf. the German novel *Meister Timpe*, by Max Kretzer.

[2] Turner, *Chicago Record-Herald*, September 4, 1901.

whence the old migrations to Pennsylvania had occurred, among the alert, enterprising people of these provinces. These reports were idealistic in the coloring they gave American life, and they left a deep impression, that America offered refuge from economic, social, and political evils of these lands. The influence of the cultivated German immigrants of the period was out of proportion to their number.[1]

The two decades, 1841–60, present an increase in the German immigration. The high wave came between 1846–54. Beginning with 57,500 German immigrants in one year the figures reached 215,009 for the year 1854. In the three years 1852–54 over five hundred thousand arrived, and during the nine years almost nine hundred thousand. Then the immigration decreased in volume until after the Civil War. The crest of the wave, from 1850–54, was contemporaneous with the revolutionary troubles in Germany of 1848, and following years, when many a son of liberty, like Hecker, Sigel, Blenker, and most famous of all, Carl Schurz, arrived on our shores. Economic conditions also contributed an important share, the failure of crops, the rise in the price of food-stuffs, the destruction of local industries through competition with machine products. These brought the rank and file. In 1850–53 there was a failure of the vintage in Würtemberg, — and earlier, in 1846–47, there had been failure of the potato crop in those southwestern portions of Germany which had always contributed largely to the American immigration. The local governments frequently found it necessary to encourage the exodus of their people. At the same period the American railroads were opening up the vast Western territories, and new states, such as Wisconsin, were making extraordinary efforts to attract German immigrants. The

[1] Turner, *Chicago Record-Herald*, September 4, 1901.

improvements in ocean travel made the journey shorter and cheaper, and better guarantees were now furnished for safe transportation.

Another high wave of German immigration came after the Civil War. From 1866, when the hundred thousand mark was passed again, the immigration continued to pour in until 1873, at the rate of about one hundred and thirty thousand annually. In Germany this period corresponds to the great wars of Prussia, and to the convulsions into which the German states were thrown before their being welded into one nation through the Franco-Prussian War of 1870. Military duty and hard pressure upon the population had much to do with increasing the immigration. The allurements on the other side were quite as strong an influence as hardships at home. A homestead being liberally offered to every worthy immigrant, the Germans, as in the century before, felt " keenly alive to the desirability of possessing land." The financial depression following the panic of 1873 showed its effect upon the German immigration, for in the following six years the immigration only once reached fifty thousand in one year, and that was in 1874.

A bound upward began in 1880, in which year the immigration was three times as large as that of 1879; in 1881 it nearly doubled again, almost reaching the two hundred and fifty thousand mark. In 1882 came the banner year with 250,630, a record which has never been surpassed. Large immigrations continued until 1885. Then the numbers went up and down, with another final rise in 1891–92, the immigration of the two years numbering 244,000. After that the number steadily declined, reaching the lowest point in 1898, namely, 17,111, and rising very little above that since (28,304 in 1902). The record of the immigration, year by year, is comparable to a pulse indicating the material prosperity of the two countries. Germany's great rise as an industrial nation, her development of colonies in Africa and elsewhere for her surplus population, her exemplary laws insuring the laboring class against accident, disability, etc., have made her population far less eager to emigrate to foreign parts. The disappearance of the frontier line and all areas of cheap land has rendered America far less attractive. In the laboɩ market came the competition of the Slavic and South Italian races, which the German, with a higher standard of living, finds difficult though by no means impossible to maintain. Nevertheless the field does not attract him.

In regard to the character of the German immigration of the nineteenth century, much applies to them that has already been said in regard to the immigration of the eighteenth century. Yet there were differences also. There was on the whole a much larger percentage of men of cul·ture in some of the immigrations of the nineteenth century. There were many refugees, not from religious persecution, as in the eighteenth century, but from political oppression and espionage. These were men who, if they had been tolerated, would have become influential in the public life of their native land. Coming to this country they spent their efforts in the development of political and social conditions in the United States, beginning with the improvement of their own people in their adopted country. Such were the refugees of the period from about 1817 to 1835, and of 1848 and the years immediately succeeding.

A representative of the earlier class of political refugees, Friedrich Münch, who has been described in a previous chapter as a successful "Latin farmer," typical of the class of permanent settlers, — Friedrich Münch, in a reminiscent mood, describes the German immigrations of the nineteenth century as follows:[1]

There were three periods. Immigration No. 1, attracted by such books as Duden's, turned to Missouri and other Western states, and devoted themselves to agriculture. Laborers and peasants, without any high standard of life and accustomed to hard work, found the situation to their satisfaction and gradually but steadily became prosperous. The better educated, sometimes even in spite of strenuous efforts, frequently died in the struggle. The adventurers of this group also met disappointment, and, although frequently useful as border fighters on the advance guard of civilization, did not achieve permanent success. There was also a group of refugees of 1817–18, and it was their office to elevate the tone of the other German immigrants. The Germans were commonly all Jeffersonian Democrats in their politics, as distinct from the aristocratic Whigs, and they were opposed to slavery. After the Mexican War and the discovery of gold in California, conditions in the West grew better and the German farmers became more prosperous.

The immigration No. 2 was heartily welcomed by the first immigration, but the former were not well satisfied with their countrymen in America. They did not like the backwoods condition of the earlier immigration, and only a few of them, as did Hecker, became farmers. Most of them went into the cities as merchants, manufacturers, or brain-workers of various kinds. A very frequent occupation for them was journalism, and in their newspapers they declared that we older men had not remained German enough, nor had we asserted our influence sufficiently. A war of words frequently occurred between the representatives of the two immigrations, the older receiving the nickname, "die Grauen," and the younger "die Grünen." The Grays had passed through an experience of twenty years of toil under primitive American frontier conditions, and had lost much of their youthful ardor for impracticable ideas. When

[1] Cf. *Der deutsche Pionier*, vol. i, pp. 243–250. The above is an abstract, not a literal quotation.

the younger element, the Greens, arrived, they set themselves
up as instructors or dictators, but the Grays were not disposed
to listen to them. A better understanding came about when the
new Republican party arose and the Lincoln campaign began.
Then the Germans united against slavery as one man, and the
old wounds which the Grays and the Greens had inflicted in
their newspaper campaigns were entirely forgotten. The Greens
were useful in quickening the minds of the older generation;
the latter, forming a conservative element, restrained the new
arrivals in their fantastic dreams. Without the first immigra
tion, the second would have had a much more difficult position.
It would not have gained influence and would have made many
a false step. Without the support of the first immigration, the
second might have been quickly absorbed without leaving a trace
behind. The second played an important part in American
history.

The third immigration came after the period of 1866. They
were mostly of the working class, with far better schooling than
the same class of thirty years before. In comparison with the
earlier immigrations they were overbearing, dissatisfied with
conditions as they found them in the new country, and too well
impressed with those they left at home. As a rule they would
not do the work of an inferior class, and as a result frequently
found all desirable positions occupied.

But in the end Münch subdues his resentment concerning even the last immigration.

Even these [he says] as a rule prosper well. Conditions are
so much better here than they were thirty or forty years ago,
and though the immigrants come in hundreds of thousands, they
will find a place after paying for their necessary experience. I
have no fear for the green or even the greenest [die Grünen
und Allergrünsten], is his conclusion.

This characterization of three types of German immigration in the nineteenth century, undertaken by the veteran "Latin farmer" Friedrich Münch, is by no means

a final word on the subject, yet it represents a sincere attempt at a judicial view. As shown in another chapter, Münch, when a younger man, was a leader in the camp of the first immigration (die Grauen). The important fact is that, when the period of slavery agitation arose, all petty differences were laid aside for the patriotic attempt to combine all the German forces against slavery and the disruption of the Union. It would be an invidious task to attempt narrow distinctions between the various German immigrations of the nineteenth century.[1] In the most general way it may be said that the first immigration resembled more closely the sturdy German folk of the eighteenth century; the second contained a larger number of refugees, whose influence was strongly felt in the political and cultural development of the United States; while the third immigration, coming after 1866 and also after the Franco-Prussian War, in culture and education more closely akin to the second immigration, contained a larger number of men seeking, with advantage to themselves, the advancement of the commerce and manufactures of the American nation; a large number also being destined to become prominent in the technical and professional branches. But the exceptions to these general rules are too numerous to encourage dogmatic statements. The question of such distinctions is not one of vital importance in a discussion of the influences of the

---

[1] Gustav Körner's book, *Das deutsche Element in den Vereinigten Staaten von Nordamerika, 1818–1848*, gives an excellent account of the Germans who came to the United States before the March Revolution of 1848, with an underlying purpose of showing that the earlier immigration achieved more than the later. A champion of the "forty-eighters" has never appeared, though materials are abundant for his arguments, and for a work of the dimensions of Körner's. Particularly in politics, journalism, and music the "forty-eighters" accomplished more than the earlier immigrations, as can be observed in the second volume of this work.

German element in the United States. In taking account of the latter, all immigrations of the nineteenth as well as of the preceding centuries are equally concerned; each is important in its time and place, and its influence is greatly determined by the conditions of period and location.

Having traced chronologically the settlements of the Germans from the earliest period to the present, having noted their location and distribution throughout the territory of the United States, and having sketched very briefly their activities in peace and war, we have received the necessary historical basis for approaching the subject of the influence of the German element in the United States. The latter is the theme of the second volume of this work.

END OF VOLUME I